Frommer's

Barcelona

2nd Edition

by Peter Stone

Here's what the critics say about Frommer's:

"Amazingly easy to use. Very portable, very complete."

—*Booklist*

"Detailed, accurate, and easy-to-read information for all price ranges."
—*Glamour Magazine*

"Hotel information is close to encyclopedic."

—*Des Moines Sunday Register*

"Frommer's Guides have a way of giving you a real feel for a place."
—*Knight Ridder Newspapers*

1807
WILEY
2007

Wiley Publishing, Inc.

Published by:

Wiley Publishing, Inc.

111 River St.

Hoboken, NJ 07030-5774

ISBN: 978-0-470-09692-5

Editor: Matthew Brown

Production Editor: M. Faunette Johnston

Cartographer: Guy Ruggiero

Photo Editor: Richard Fox

Anniversary Logo Design: Richard Pacifico

Production by Wiley Indianapolis Composition Services

Front cover photo: Barcelona: Church of Sagrada Família, man painting facade
Back cover photo: Barcelona, Museo Picasso: people admiring Picasso's "Las Meninas" series

For information on our other products and services or to obtain technical support, please contact our Customer Care Department within the U.S. at 800/762-2974, outside the U.S. at 317/572-3993 or fax 317/572-4002.

Wiley also publishes its books in a variety of electronic formats. Some content that appears in print may not be available in electronic formats.

Manufactured in the United States of America

5   4   3   2   1

Contents

List of Maps   vi

What's New in Barcelona   1

(1) The Best of Barcelona   3

1 The Most Unforgettable
Barcelona Experiences 4

2 The Best Splurge Hotels 5

3 The Best Moderately Priced Hotels 6

4 The Most Unforgettable Dining
Experiences .6

5 The Best Things to Do For Free 7

6 The Best Stuff to Bring Home 7

7 The Best Activities for Families 8

8 The Best Museums 9

(2) Planning Your Trip to Barcelona   10

1 Visitor Information 10

*Destination Barcelona:
Pre-Departure Checklist* 11

2 Entry Requirements & Customs 11

3 Money 15

*The Euro, the U.S. Dollar &
the British Pound* 16

What Things Cost in Barcelona 17

4 When to Go 19

Barcelona Calendar of Events 20

5 Travel Insurance 23

6 Health & Safety 24

ETA Strikes Again 27

7 Specialized Travel Resources 29

8 Planning Your Trip Online 33

*Frommers.com: The Complete
Travel Resource* 34

9 The 21st-Century Traveler 34

Online Traveler's Toolbox 36

10 Getting There 36

Getting Through the Airport 40

Flying with Film & Video 42

11 Packages for the Independent
Traveler 46

Ask Before You Go 46

12 Escorted General-Interest Tours 47

13 Special-Interest Trips 48

14 Recommended Books,
Films & Music 48

(3) Suggested Barcelona Itineraries   51

1 The Best of Barcelona in 1 Day 51

2 The Best of Barcelona in 2 Days 55

3 The Best of Barcelona in 3 Days 58

4 Getting to Know Barcelona   62

1 Essentials 62
The Barcelona Card 66
The Neighborhoods in Brief 67

2 Getting Around 72
Fast Facts: Barcelona 75

5 Where to Stay   82

1 The Best Hotel Bets 85
2 Ciutat Vella (Barri Gòtic,
El Raval & La Ribera) 87
3 L'Eixample 97
Family-Friendly Hotels 101
Barcelona's Self-Catering Boom . . .106
4 Sants, Paral.lel & Montjuïc 108

5 Barrio Alto & Gràcia 111
6 Barceloneta Vila Olímpica &
Poble Nou 112
Bright Lights, Spa City 113
7 On the Outskirts 115
8 Apartments & Aparthotels 118

6 Where to Dine   119

1 Food for Thought 119
Barcelona's Green Scene 121
2 The Best Restaurant Bets 121
3 Ciutat Vella: Barri Gòtic 123
Make It Snappy 127
4 Ciutat Vella: La Ribera 131
5 Ciutat Vella: El Raval 135
More Tapas 138

6 Poble Sec & Montjuïc 138
7 l'Eixample 139
Family-Friendly Restaurants 145
8 Gràcia 147
Eating Alfresco 150
9 Barceloneta & Vila Olímpica 151
10 Barrio Alto 157
11 Out of Town 158

7 What to See & Do   160

1 Ciutat Vella (Old City) 160
El Call: The Jewish Quarter 167
2 L'Eixample 174
Gaudí's Resting Place 176
Doing the Moderniste Walk 178
3 Gràcia 179
4 Montjuïc .181
The Magic Fountain 185

5 The Harborfront 187
6 Outer Barcelona 188
Mes Que un Club (More
Than a Club)! 191
Small but Good: Other
Barcelona Museums 192
7 Parks & Gardens 193
8 Outdoor & Sporting Pursuits 194

8 Strolling Around Barcelona   196

Walking Tour 1: Barri Gòtic (The
Gothic Quarter) 196

Walking Tour 2: La Ribera
(El Born & Sant Pere) 200

Walking Tour 3: El Raval 203

Walking Tour 4: Moderniste
Route (L'Eixample) 207

9 Shopping   211

1 The Shopping Scene 211

2 Shopping A to Z 213

The Zaravolución 218

La Boqueria: One of the World's
Finest Food Markets 220

To Market, to Market 223

Specialty Stores in
the Barri Gòtic 227

10 Barcelona After Dark   230

1 Best Bars & Pubs 232

2 The Performing Arts 232

3 Bars, Cafes, Pubs & Clubs 237

Dancing with the Green Fairy 240

Twisting by the Port 243

The Village People 244

11 Side Trips in Catalonia   250

1 Montserrat 250

Route of the Cistercian
Monasteries 253

2 Tarragona 254

Catalonia Remembers
Pablo Casals 256

The Beaches of the
Costa Daurada 259

3 Sitges 260

Where the Boys Are 262

Cava Country 265

4 Girona 266

El Call 269

Garden of Sea and Myrtle 272

5 Lloret de Mar 272

6 Tossa de Mar 275

7 Sant Feliu de Guíxols 278

8 Palafrugell & Its Beaches 279

A Room with a View 281

9 Figueres .281

The Mad, Mad World of
Salvador Dalí 282

10 Cadaqués 284

The Most Famous Chef
in the World 285

12 A Side Trip to Majorca   287

1 Palma de Majorca 290

2 Valldemossa & Deià (Deyá) 302

3 Port de Pollença & Formentor 305

Appendix A: Barcelona Past & Present   307

1 Barcelona Today 307   *Dateline* 308
2 History 101 308

Appendix B: The Catalan Culture   313

1 The Language of Catalonia 313   *Gaudí: The Saintly Architect* 316
2 Barcelona's Architecture 314   **4** A Taste of Catalonia 318
3 Art & Artists 315

Appendix C: Useful Terms & Phrases   323

1 Useful Words & Phrases 323   **2** Numbers 325

Index   326

General Index 326   Restaurant Index 337
Accommodations Index 336

List of Maps

Spain   12

The Best of Barcelona in 1 Day   52

The Best of Barcelona in 2 Days   57

The Best of Barcelona in 3 Days   59

Greater Barcelona   64

Barcelona Public Transportation   73

Ciutat Vella Accommodations   89

L'Eixample Accommodations   99

Sants, Paral.lel & Montjuïc
   Accommodations   109

Ciutat Vella Dining   125

L'Eixample Dining   141

Gràcia Dining   148

Barceloneta Dining   152

Vila Olímpica Dining   153

Barcelona Attractions   162

Walking Tour 1: Barri Gòtic (Gothic
   Quarter)   197

Walking Tour 2: La Ribera (El Born
   and Sant Pere)   201

Walking Tour 3: El Raval   205

Walking Tour 4: Moderniste Route
   (L'Eixample)   209

Catalonia   251

Tarragona   255

Sitges   261

Girona & the Costa Brava   267

Majorca   289

Palma de Majorca   291

An Invitation to the Reader

In researching this book, we discovered many wonderful places—hotels, restaurants, shops, and more. We're sure you'll find others. Please tell us about them, so we can share the information with your fellow travelers in upcoming editions. If you were disappointed with a recommendation, we'd love to know that, too. Please write to:

Frommer's Barcelona, 2nd Edition
Wiley Publishing, Inc. • 111 River St. • Hoboken, NJ 07030-5774

An Additional Note

Please be advised that travel information is subject to change at any time—and this is especially true of prices. We therefore suggest that you write or call ahead for confirmation when making your travel plans. The authors, editors, and publisher cannot be held responsible for the experiences of readers while traveling. Your safety is important to us, however, so we encourage you to stay alert and be aware of your surroundings. Keep a close eye on cameras, purses, and wallets, all favorite targets of thieves and pickpockets.

About the Author

Born in London, England, **Peter Stone** started his working life in the Foreign Office in Downing Street before moving on to translating and journalism. Over the last 27 years, he has resided in different regions of Spain, including Málaga, Barcelona, Alicante, Palma de Mallorca, and Las Palmas de Gran Canaria, and also lived in Greece and North Africa. A lifelong lover of Hispanic culture, history, and language, Peter made Madrid his home in 1998, and his publications on the Spanish capital include *Madrid Escapes* and *Frommer's Madrid.* He has also contributed to a wide variety of international magazines and guidebooks, including *Spain Gourmetour, Time Out, Insight,* and *Intelliguide.*

Other Great Guides for Your Trip:

Frommer's Spain
Frommer's Madrid
Frommer's Europe
Spain For Dummies

Frommer's Star Ratings, Icons & Abbreviations

Every hotel, restaurant, and attraction listing in this guide has been ranked for quality, value, service, amenities, and special features using a **star-rating system.** In country, state, and regional guides, we also rate towns and regions to help you narrow down your choices and budget your time accordingly. Hotels and restaurants are rated on a scale of zero (recommended) to three stars (exceptional). Attractions, shopping, nightlife, towns, and regions are rated according to the following scale: zero stars (recommended), one star (highly recommended), two stars (very highly recommended), and three stars (must-see).

In addition to the star-rating system, we also use **six feature icons** that point you to the great deals, in-the-know advice, and unique experiences that separate travelers from tourists. Throughout the book, look for:

Finds	Special finds—those places only insiders know about
Fun Fact	Fun facts—details that make travelers more informed and their trips more fun
Moments	Special moments—those experiences that memories are made of
Overrated	Places or experiences not worth your time or money
Tips	Insider tips—great ways to save time and money
Value	Great values—where to get the best deals

The following **abbreviations** are used for credit cards:

AE	American Express	DISC	Discover	V	Visa
DC	Diners Club	MC	MasterCard		

Frommers.com

Now that you have this guidebook to help you plan a great trip, visit our website at **www. frommers.com** for additional travel information on more than 3,500 destinations. We update features regularly to give you instant access to the most current trip-planning information available. At Frommers.com, you'll find scoops on the best airfares, lodging rates, and car rental bargains. You can even book your travel online through our reliable travel booking partners. Other popular features include:

- Online updates of our most popular guidebooks
- Vacation sweepstakes and contest giveaways
- Newsletters highlighting the hottest travel trends
- Online travel message boards with featured travel discussions

What's New in Barcelona

Ever inventive and dynamic, Barcelona continues to advance deeper and more creatively into the 21st century. One of the most impressive recent changes has sprung from a restructuring program called "Post Olympic," covering a 3.2km (2-mile) stretch of shoreline between the Port Olimpic section and the mouth of the Besòs River. Here, a 1.7 billion euro ($2.1 billion) development has added new parks, a restaurant-lined marina, and a bathing zone for swimming in unpolluted waters. Its impressive modern Forum is being further expanded at an additional cost of 4 million euros ($5 million) in readiness for the Euro Science Open Forum, scheduled for 2008; and an ambitious Housing Plan, which started in May 2006 and is due to be completed in 2008, involves rehabilitating 2,700 homes between San Adrià de los Besòs and Poble Sec.

PLANNING YOUR TRIP TO BARCELONA Expanded between 2004 and 2005 with the opening of a third runway and new southern terminal, the **El Prat de Llobregat Airport** now accommodates 25 million passengers a year, more than double its capacity at the time of the 1992 Olympic Games. There are further expansion plans for 2008 that will include a new loading area and an "industrial park" with a variety of amenities that will virtually change the airport into a small, self-contained town. Also of note for Barcelona visitors: A new ticket-sales company, **Clickair** (www.clickair.com), started business in October 2006, offering budget flights between Barcelona and many European cities with seats bookable only by Internet.

GETTING AROUND The Metro and city train lines continue to expand. October 2006 saw the inauguration of the T-5 Trambesòs line between Besòs and Glories, the latest of the ultra-modern Tren Ligero, or "Light Train," routes to join the T-1 to T-4 lines already operating in the city. In addition to the existing bus and suburban train network connecting El Prat Airport with the city center, two extended Metro lines—2 and 9—will run right into the heart of the airport, creating even easier access in 2007. Meanwhile, high at the back of the city, the 100-year-old Tibidabo funicular, updated at the end of 2006 at a cost of 4 million euros ($5 million), has now doubled the number of its daily journeys and passengers. On a wider front, the already busy **Sants Railway Station** is in the midst of a massive renovation and expansion program aimed at preparing for the high-speed trains to Madrid and France, due to be running in 2008. (The journey from Barcelona to Madrid will be shortened from 5½ to 3½ hr.) The transformed station will eventually incorporate new terminals, hallways, platforms, and underground parking areas.

ACCOMMODATIONS Barcelona's accommodations options continue to increase on all levels, from deluxe comfort to budget simplicity. Three hundred new hotels are due to open between 2006 and 2008, providing an additional 30,000 rooms. The overall trend is for hostelries with state-of-the-art facilities that include free Wi-Fi access, a standard feature now with innovative chains like **High Tech** and its sister company **Petit Palace,** whose latest hotel Petit Palace Opera Garden Ramblas opened in 2006 in the heart of the Barri Gòtic (p. 93). One of the newest hotels to burst on the scene (in Oct 2006) was the chic modern **Hotel Barcelona Catedral** (p. 95), located only a stone's throw from the city's great Gothic cathedral.

WHERE TO DINE   Barcelona's pioneering cuisine is now admired around the world. This doesn't necessarily involve denting the wallet at a high-end spot like Ferran Adrià's famed El Bulli, either. Among the most recent affordable new-style eclectic eateries to try is **Hisop** (p. 143). Vegetarian joints, too, are popping up more often, and the innovative **Juicy Jones,** in the Old Quarter, is one not to miss. (p. 128).

UP IN SMOKE   On January 1, 2006, a law took effect that officially banned smoking at all workplaces and throughout the entire Metro system. In bars, however, the decision was left to the discretion of the owner, and in 99% of cases smoking is still allowed (except in places larger than 100 sq. m./1,076 sq. ft., where a small smoke-free zone has to be installed). There is talk of stricter laws being imposed in 2007, though given the limited success of the few bars that have so far braved financial loss to keep their air clean, this remains at best a remote possibility.

ARCHITECTURE   Though Gaudí's incomparable **Sagrada Família** may hold the top spot for spiritually minded sightseers, it's the practical, 21st-century business buildings that are increasingly dominating the cityscape. In Barceloneta, the horseshoe-shaped Brullet-Pineda–designed **Biomedical Research Park,** between the Hospital del Mar and Arts

Hotel, is due for completion in 2007. It will feature a state-of-the-art range of laboratories, as well as an impressive auditorium and sports center. The **Fira of Barcelona,** just 3.2km (2 miles) from Montjuïc, is currently being developed to include an exhibition center, due to be finished in 2009. Currently the site hosts 80 trade fairs a year, and when finished it will be among the largest business centers in the world.

SHOPPING   The new face of market shopping in Barcelona is the **Mercat de Santa Caterina** (p. 200) in La Ribera, renovated in 2005 to a plan by local architect Enric Miralles, who also designed the Scottish parliament. In a cool functional setting topped by a colorful roof, you can browse through a wealth of well-stocked stalls whose offerings range from traditional produce to trendy balsamic vinegars and expensive *crianza* olive oils. Meanwhile, on the chic interior-design front, the big event in 2006 was the opening of **B & B Italia's** 167-sq.-m (1,800-sq.-ft.) showroom on Passeig de Gràcia. Its dazzling display of elegant furnishings shows just why this stylish company's shops have been a hit in no less than 54 countries.

PARKS   Opened in May 2006, Barcelona's newest park is the 11-hectare (27-acre), **Parc de la Pau (Park of Peace),** which lies on the city's eastern coastal outskirts. It adjoins a new beach (covered with imported sand), a marina, and a tree-lined promenade—amenities aimed at improving the quality of life in the Besòs area, which little more than a decade ago was one of the most run-down and depressed corners of the Catalan capital.

BARCELONA'S "BICI"-WORLD   In an effort to encourage more cyclists to get out and about and cut down on traffic and pollution, more bicycle routes are appearing yearly throughout the city. Some of the newest trails are in the above-mentioned Parc de la Pau.

The Best of Barcelona

Not since the 14th century, when the Catalan capital was the most powerful city in the Mediterranean, has Barcelona's future looked so promising. The catalysts for change have been many. The first—political—was in 1975, when General Francisco Franco, who had systematically and often brutally tried to eradicate the treasured Catalan language and culture, died. The city in turn started to live and breathe again independently. Today Barcelona is a proud, bilingual metropolis with street signs, newspapers, and television programs in both Catalan and Spanish. In 2006, a progressive statute granted an even greater degree of self-rule to the whole region.

The second—more cosmetic—catalyst came just before the 1992 Olympic Games, when feverish renovation work changed the city's image from that of a drab, gray burg to a new gleaming metropolis. The Barri Gòtic, many of whose central medieval buildings had for countless decades been coated with grime, could at last be seen in all its pristine glory, with newly sandblasted facades quietly glowing in the light of the quarter's atmospheric narrow alleys. The waterfront, once lined with large oily containers and sad-looking palm trees, was transformed into an open, sunlit area of promenades, marinas, and modern restaurants stretching several kilometers from beachside Barceloneta via the Vila Olímpica and the 2004 Forum site to Sant Adrià de Besòs

Suddenly Barcelona has become the weekender capital of Europe. Visitors jet in on low-cost flights for the fun lifestyle, superb Mediterranean climate, and an unrivalled location that offers easy access to the delectable coves of the Costa Brava, scenic mountain trails of the Pyrénées, historic cities of Gerona and Tarragona, and wealth of Gothic and Romanesque monuments that fill the countryside.

They also come to see Barcelona's many offerings in the world of art, architecture, and haute cuisine: the Picassos, Dalís, Tàpies, and Mirós; the *moderniste* extravaganzas of Gaudí and modern eccentricities of Gehry and Nouvel; and Ferran Adrià's "New Catalan Cuisine," lauded even by the French and spearheading a culinary revival that's resulted in half a dozen Michelin rated restaurants to date.

Yet for all its outward changes the city remains at heart what it's always been: practical, businesslike, proletarian, nonconformist, rebellious, artistic, and unabashedly hedonistic. It's a heady, complex blend that has survived many a dark time and whose freewheeling Mediterranean spirit is epitomized in the bustling Rambla avenue, which runs all the way down to the port from Plaza Cataluña along the source of a former riverbed. All this makes for a spirit as communal and sociable as the city's traditional Sardana dance, in which no one leads and no one follows and everyone moves together in unison.

1 The Most Unforgettable Barcelona Experiences

- **Strolling along La Rambla:** Barcelona's most famous promenade pulses with life. The array of street musicians, performers, hustlers, and eccentrics ensures that there is never a dull moment during your kilometer-long stroll. See p. 51.

- **Having a Drink at Sunset on the Beach:** The Catalan capital's 6.4km (4-mile) stretch of new city beaches, whose promenade, jetties, and marinas are lapped by inviting Mediterranean waters, have been transformed from a once-neglected area into a round-the-clock international playground. Their atmospheric *chiringuitos* (waterside bars and eating spots specializing in seafood dishes) are perfect spots either for lunch or a relaxing end-of-day drink, often accompanied by the music of an in-house DJ. See p. 242.

- **Exploring the El Born Neighborhood:** This compact medieval quarter, just inland from Barceloneta, was once one of its seediest corners. Now the "in" crowds converge on its narrow tangle of streets lined by renovated old mansions: by day to check out top museums like the Picasso and smart shops exhibiting the latest in cutting-edge fashion and design; at night to enjoy the many bars and restaurants offering the ultimate in New Catalan cuisine. See p. 69.

- **Attending a Concert at the Palau de la Música Catalana:** This masterpiece of *modernista* (Art Nouveau) architecture must be one of the most lavish concert halls in the world. All strains of classical and jazz are played, but even the most finicky music lover will be moved by the Palau's onslaught of decorative detail. See p. 233.

- **Eating Breakfast at the Boqueria:** There are about a dozen bars and restaurants in the city's main food market. Rub shoulders with Barcelona's top chefs and gourmands over a coffee and croissant and watch the day's deliveries coming in. See p. 220.

- **Bar-Hopping in the Barri Gòtic:** With its iconic, smoke-filled tapas bars, Irish pubs frequented by expats, and cocktail lounges filled with minimalist furniture and minimally clad patrons, Barcelona's Old City is a watering-hole mecca. One of the best locales is **Ginger,** a comfy, classy tapas and wine bar with the feel of a private club. See p. 239.

- **Spending a Sunday on Montjuïc:** The mountain of Montjuïc is the first sight that greets visitors arriving at the port. Behind its rocky seaside face are acres of pine-dotted parkland beloved by cyclists, joggers, and strollers on the weekend. Topped by a castle museum with stunning city views, it provides a tranquil alternative to the hustle of the city below and offers some welcome breathing space. See p. 181.

- **Going by Tram and Funicular to Tibidabo:** The summit of the city's distinctive inland backdrop is reached in two stages: first by a "blue tram" (Tramvia Blau), which winds past Sarrià district's elegant houses, and then by a creaky Art Deco funicular lift, which rattles its way up the mountainside to reveal increasingly breathtaking views of the city below. Both of these vintage forms of transport were built over a century ago to transport people to the church and amusement park on the mountain's peak. The exhilarating journey they provide is part of the fun. See p. 192.

- **Dining at Els Quatre Gats:** The original served as a fraternity house for late-18th-century dandies. It later became a preferred hangout for the young Picasso and his bohemian contemporaries. While most of the art adorning the walls is now reproductions, this classic Catalan restaurant is still alive with history. The resident pianist and general formality only add to the atmosphere. See p. 126.

- **Taking Your First Look at the Sagrada Família:** Nothing quite prepares you for the first glimpse of Gaudí's most famous work, which erupts from the center of a suburban city block like some retro-futurist grotto. Draw your eyes skyward from a facade rich in religious symbolism to the temple's four towers. Then step over the threshold to the (unfinished) interior. See p. 175.

- **People-Watching at the Museu d'Art Contemporani de Barcelona (MACBA):** The forecourt of the Museum of Contemporary Art is a snapshot of the new multicultural Barcelona. Spend some time at one of its outside bars watching Pakistani cricket players, local kids playing soccer, and Northern European skateboarders in a fascinating melting pot of recreational activity. See p. 172.

- **Staying Up until Dawn:** A long dinner, a few drinks at a bar, on to a club, and then before you know it the sun is rising over the Mediterranean's party capital, throwing a warm glow over the city's palm-filled plazas and streets. Nothing beats a slow walk home at this magical hour (preferably through the Old City). If you manage to catch up on your sleep during the day, chances are you will repeat the experience that night.

2 The Best Splurge Hotels

- **Hotel Ritz,** Gran Vía 668 (© **93-318-52-00**): Since it opened its doors in 1919, it has survived a civil war, a world war, an anarchist occupation, and the fall of a dictatorship—all while retaining an impeccable level of service and tradition. During all this, distinguished guests such as the Duke of Windsor, Ava Gardner, and Salvador Dalí have chosen to stay in its gilt and marble surroundings and to take refuge in the elegant tearoom and restaurant. See p. 100.

- **Hotel Casa Fuster,** Passeig de Gràcia 132 (© **93-225-30-00**): This *modernista* masterpiece was an emblematic building *before* it was recently converted into this luxury five-star. The rooms have been restored to turn-of-the-20th-century opulence, but now have all the modern conveniences. See p. 97.

- **Hotel Arts,** Marina 19–21 (© **93-221-10-00**): The preferred choice of top models and temperamental rock stars (P. Diddy reportedly partied up a storm when he came to Barcelona to host the 2002 MTV Awards), the Hotel Arts has remained a jet-set playground and symbol of "cool Barcelona" for over a decade. See p. 112.

- **Hotel España,** Sant Pau 11 (© **93-318-17-58**): This place combines comfort and luxury while evoking a bygone age. Designed by a contemporary of Gaudí, the street-level dining room, filled with florid motif and brass fixtures, will whisk you back to the early 1900s, when it was filled with chattering patrons taking supper after a trip to the opera house next door. See p. 96.

3 The Best Moderately Priced Hotels

- **Hotel Peninsular,** Sant Pau 34–36 (© **93-302-31-38**): Serenity and character abound in this nunnery-turned-hotel. Located on a colorful street just off Les Ramblas, the Peninsular's Art Nouveau elevator, long green and white hallways, and lush inner courtyard make it an oasis from the hustle and bustle outside. But book ahead. See p. 96.

- **Hostal D'Uxelles,** Gran Vía 688 and 667 (© **93-265-25-60**): This *hostal* looks as though it has stepped straight off the pages of one of those rustic-interiors magazines. Located

on the first floor of two adjacent buildings, each of the 14 rooms has a distinct character, but all include canopied beds, antique furniture, and Andalusian-style ceramic bathrooms. See p. 105.

- **Marina Folch,** Carrer del Mar 16, principal (© **93-310-37-09**): Family-run, this hotel is the only one in the beachside neighborhood of Barceloneta, with plenty of open-air bars and open spaces for the kids to run wild. Ask for a room at the front for a balcony with a view of the port. See p. 115.

4 The Most Unforgettable Dining Experiences

- **Having a Paella at the Beach:** One of the quintessential Barcelona experiences, and there is no place better to do it than **Can Majó,** Almirall Aixada 23 (© **93-221-54-55**). Right on the seafront, this restaurant prides itself on its paellas and *fideuàs* (which substitute noodles for rice) and is an established favorite among the city's well-heeled families. See p. 155.

- **Trying the Cuisine of Catalonia's Top Chef:** Carles Abellán has been hailed as the new wunderkind of nouvelle Catalan cuisine. His restaurant, **Comerç 24,** Comerç 24 (© **93-319-21-02**), was conceived as a playful take on all that's hot in the tapas world. Delights such as "kinder egg surprise" (a soft-boiled egg with truffle-infused yolk) and tuna sashimi pizza await the adventurous. See p. 132.

- **Having Barcelona's Best Sunday Lunch:** The lines say it all: **7 Portes,** Passeig Isabel II 14 (© **93-319-30-33**), one of the oldest restaurants

in Barcelona, is a Sunday institution. Extended families dine on their excellent meat and fish dishes in the turn-of-the-20th-century atmosphere. See p. 153.

- **Sampling the Finest Regional Dishes:** In spite of its Italian name, the **Via Veneto,** Ganduxer 10 (© **93-200-72-44**), is traditional to the core, serving up some of the finest Catalan cooking in the land. The restaurant exudes old-fashioned class, and one of the serving methods, the sterling silver duck press, seems to belong to another century (as do some of the clients). See p. 158.

- **Eating the Freshest Seafood in Barcelona:** You'll find it at **Els Pescadors,** Plaça Prim 1 (© **93-225-20-18**), in the atmospheric, working-class suburb of Poble Nou, is the place for you. People come here for the food, not the view; they serve whatever has been caught that day. Book ahead on weekends. See p. 152.

5 The Best Things to Do For Free

- **Enjoying the Freebie Cultural Treats:** Top visits here are the **Foment de les Arts Decoratives i del Disseny (FAD)** cultural center where you can view exhibitions and sometimes buy bargain paintings by promising young unknowns (p. 171) and **CaixaForum** art gallery, which has an ever-changing trio of stimulating exhibitions (p. 181). Around the city you'll find an impressive variety of open-air **public art** displays: Antoni Llena's bizarre metal **David i Goliat,** Frank Gehry's copper **Peix** (Fish) in the Olímpic Port, and Colombian sculptor Fernando Botero's rather chubby **Gat** (Cat) in El Raval. There's also Roy Lichtenstein's trademark comic-strip–style **Barcelona Head,** near the Columbus statue down by the harbor, and Joan Miró's **Dona i Ocell** (Woman and Bird) finished in 1981, just before his death and located in the park named after him in Sants.

- **Strolling in the Parks:** Despite its densely urban appearance, Barcelona is actually filled with parks where you can relax, stroll, and in many cases enjoy fun amenities. (Visit the website www.bcn.es/parcsijardins for the full list.) **Parc de la Ciutadella,** just to the east of the Old City, with its fountains and statues is a relaxing respite from the adjoining claustrophobic medieval labyrinth (p. 170), while **Parc Güell,** higher up in Gràcia district, delights visitors of all ages with its fairy-tale Gaudí structures (p. 180). In Montbau,

the **Parc de la Crueta del Coll** has a playground and public summer pool (which in winter reverts to being an artificial lake). To the west, rambling hilltop **Montjuïc**—with its marvelous harbor views, jogging paths, the **Fundació Joan Miró, Botanical Gardens,** and illuminated **Font Màgica** (magic fountain)—is an airy kaleidoscope of greenery and cultural and sporting attractions (p. 185). Less well known but more "countrified" is the **Parc d'en Castell de l'Oreneta,** just above the Pedralbes Monastery, where you get a chance to enjoy marvelous panoramic city and coastal views as you picnic and wander along signposted trails among meadows in the grounds of a long since disappeared castle.

- **Taking in the Ecclesiastical Gems:** The city is full of amazing historical and religious monuments. And many of them are free. For example, unlike in most of Spain's major cities, there is no charge for visiting the **Catedral** (p. 160). Other monumental treats are the **Capella de Sant Jordi** (p. 165), and churches of **La Mercè** (p. 164) and **Santa María del Pi** (p. 166), each of which makes its own unique contribution to the spiritual and architectural beauty of the city and shows you another aspect of its rich history. An additional marvel is **Santa María del Mar** in the Born section of La Ribera (p. 166).

6 The Best Stuff to Bring Home

- **Leather:** Leather has long been one of Spain's most highly valued products, and best buys range from stylish belts and handbags to handmade shoes and fine jackets. The top spot for such purchases in Barcelona is

Loewe, which mails its goods throughout the world. See p. 222.

- **Ceramics and Pottery:** Though this is not a Barcelona specialty, you'll find a wide selection of ceramic vases, dishes, and jugs from Valencia, some of which have the style and finesse of fine art. There's also plenty of choice from areas such as Toledo and Seville. **Artesana i Coses,** near the Picasso Museum, is a good place to browse. See p. 226.

- **Porcelain:** Most popular and widely available ornaments in this field are made by the Valencian company Lladró, similar in style to the Italian Capodimonte. Though considered rather affected by some, they're extremely popular with the majority of visitors. **Kastoria,** at Avinguda Catedral, is the place to check out statuettes and friezes. See p. 225.

- **Antiques:** If you're looking for some interesting traditional engravings, carvings, or just simple bric-a-brac to take home, you have an abundance of options. The best stocked (and most expensive) locale is the three-story **Sala d'Art Artur Ramón** in the Ciutat Vella. See p. 213.

- **Hats:** If you yearn to stroll around at home in a genuine wide-brimmed Spanish *sombrero* or a traditional low-key *campesino's* beret, the place to look is **Sombrería Obach** in the old Jewish quarter of El Call. See p. 221.

7 The Best Activities for Families

- **In the city:** Anything by Antoni Gaudí, the city's most famous architect, immediately appeals to young eyes and imaginations. His whimsical **Parc Güell** (p. 180) with its imagery from the animal kingdom and hidden grottoes is a particular favorite. Speaking of animals, the city's world-class **Aquarium** (p. 187) with its walk-through tunnels and superb collection of Mediterranean marine life is also a good bet. The somewhat older and less-funded **Parc Zoològic** (p. 170) has a fantastic primate collection and is located in the **Parc de la Ciutadella** (p. 170), which also boasts a lake with rowboats for hire, swings, and other assorted kiddie attractions. Museum-wise, a trip to the **Maritime Museum** (p. 188), with its 16th-century galley and early submarine, could be combined with a jaunt on **Las Golondrinas** (p. 195), quaint, double-decker pleasure boats that take you from the port to the breakwater. The **Museu de la Cera (Wax Museum;** p. 165), may not be up to the standard of its counterpart in London, but is interesting enough to make it worth a visit. Older children will also find the **Museu de la**

Xocolata (**Chocolate Museum;** p. 169) enticing and the newly opened **Science Museum** (p. 189) has excellent hands-on exhibits for all ages. Then, of course, there are the beaches—most with showers, toilets, bars, and hammocks for rent. **Happy Park** (p. 195) in L'Eixample, just off the Passeig de Gràcia, is a vast, indoor all-weather fun park where teenies can enjoy twister slides, ball pools, and other fun activities. There's also a day-care center for tots.

- **On the Outskirts:** An all-time favorite is the **Parc d'Atraccions Tibidabo** (p. 192). This veteran amusement park, perched on top of the city's highest peak, provides death-defying attractions and a few gentler ones from bygone days. The **Parc del Laberint d' Horta** (p. 194), meanwhile, is a neoclassical park complete with eponymous maze on the outskirts of the city; and up in the Zona Alta above Pedralbes, the **Parc del Castell de l'Oreneta** has miniature train rides, weekend pony canters, and playgrounds with games for kids aged 3 and up.

- **Farther Afield:** Montserrat (p. 250), Catalonia's "spiritual heart," offers plenty of walking trails amid its phantasmagoric terrain of huge

rocks, caves, and, of course, the monumental monastery itself.

8 The Best Museums

- **Museu Nacional d'Art de Catalunya (MNAC):** Located in the imposing Palau Nacional on the northern edge of Montjuïc, this museum overlooks the Font Màgica. Renovated a couple of years back, it's one of the greatest repositories of Romanesque religious works in the world. Many of the icons and frescoes have been moved here from tiny churches high up in the Pyrénées where replicas now fill the spaces they originally occupied. Gothic styles are also well represented and more recently there have been *moderniste* additions—many taken from the Manzana de la Discordia. See p. 184.

- **Fundació Joan Miró:** Found here is Spain's best collection of the famed Catalan contemporary artist's works (all donated by the great man himself). The museum is tucked away on Montjuïc in a location that enjoys marvelous vistas of port and city from its roof terrace, where there's an attractive garden filled with sculptures. Concerts take place here in summer. Highlights are the **Foundation Tapestry** and **Mercury Fountain,** by his American sculptor friend Alexander Calder. See p. 182.

- **Museu d'Art Contemporani de Barcelona (MACBA):** This is Catalonia's answer to Paris's Pompidou

Center, and it's right in the heart of the earthy yet partially gentrified Raval district. It has one of the best collections of modern art in Spain, featuring works by Tàpies and Barceló, and there's also a library, bookshop, and cafeteria. See p. 172.

- The **Picasso Museum:** One of the most visited cultural spots in the city, the museum is mainly dedicated to works by the younger Picasso, which have been collected and assembled by his friend Jaume Sabartés y Gual. It spreads through a quintet of medieval palaces in La Ribera's atmospheric Calle Montcada. The artist donated many of the works himself, and highlights include the famed *Las Meninas* and *The Harlequin.* See p. 169.

- **Museu Frederic Marès:** This charming old palace of secret patios and high ceilings houses one of the most richly varied collections of medieval sculptures in the world, all donated by Marès—a talented sculptor himself. Exhibits can be viewed on two floors—which open on alternate days—and range from polychromatic Roman crucifixes and Gothic statues to a "Ladies' Room" filled with Victorian knicknacks. See p. 165.

2

Planning Your Trip to Barcelona

This chapter is devoted to the where, when, and how of your trip—the advance planning required to get it together and take it on the road.

1 Visitor Information

TOURIST OFFICES You can begin your info search with Spain's tourist offices located in the following places:

In the United States For information before you go, contact the **Tourist Office of Spain,** 666 Fifth Ave., Fifth Floor, New York, NY 10103 (© **212/265-8822**). It can provide sightseeing information, events calendars, train and ferry schedules, and more. Elsewhere in the United States, branches of the Tourist Office of Spain are located at: 8383 Wilshire Blvd., Suite 956, Beverly Hills, CA 90211 (© **323/658-7188**); 845 N. Michigan Ave., Suite 915E, Chicago, IL 60611 (© **312/642-1992**); and 1221 Brickell Ave., Suite 1850, Miami, FL 33131 (© **305/358-1992**).

In Canada Contact the **Tourist Office of Spain,** 102 Bloor St. W., Suite 3402, Toronto, Ontario M5S 1M9, Canada (© **416/961-3131**).

In Great Britain Write to the **Spanish National Tourist Office,** 22–23 Manchester Sq., London W1M 5AP (© **020/7486-8077**).

WEBSITES You can find lots of great information at the following sites: **Tourist Office of Spain** (www.okspain.org), **All About Spain** (www.red2000.com), **Cybersp@in** (www.cyberspain.com).

Also check out **www.spaininfo.com**, which has loads of practical tips on driving, destinations, bringing in pets, and even learning Spanish. More Catalonia-specific information can be found on **www.barcelonaturisme.com**. The official site of city hall, **www.bcn.es**, is slow to load but useful for things such as opening times and upcoming events (in English). The *Barcelona Metropolitan,* the local magazine in English (www.barcelona-metropolitan.com), is mainly aimed at expats, but will appeal to the visitor who wants more of an insider's look at the city. For one-stop tour, hotel, and activity booking try **www.barcelona.com**. If you want to pre-book train tickets, **www.renfe.es** is the official site of Spain's rail network.

Just Plain Renting
There's a wealth of flats of all sizes to rent for long or short periods in Barcelona. See "Barcelona's Self-Catering Boom," in chapter 5, "Where to Stay."

Destination Barcelona: Pre-Departure Checklist

- If you're flying, are you carrying a current, government-issued ID? The citizens of E.U. countries can cross into Spain for as long as they wish, but citizens of other countries including the United States must have a passport.
- If you're driving, did you pack your driver's license and some detailed road maps?
- Did you check to see if any travel advisories have been issued by the U.S. State Department (http://travel.state.gov) regarding your destination?
- Do you have the address and phone number of your country's embassy or consulate with you?
- Did you find out your daily ATM withdrawal limit?
- Do you have your credit card PINs? If you have a five- or six-digit PIN, did you obtain a four-digit number from your bank? (Five- and six-digit numbers do not work in Spain.)
- To check in at a kiosk with an e-ticket, do you have the credit card you bought your ticket with or a frequent-flier card?
- If you purchased traveler's checks, have you recorded the check numbers, and stored the documentation separately from the checks?
- Did you bring your ID cards that could entitle you to discounts, such as AAA and AARP cards, student IDs, and so on?
- Did you leave a copy of your itinerary with someone at home?
- Do any theater, restaurant, or travel reservations need to be booked in advance?
- Did you make sure your favorite attraction is open? Call ahead for opening and closing times. (Bear in mind, for example, that most museums shut on Mon in Spain.)

2 Entry Requirements & Customs

ENTRY REQUIREMENTS
PASSPORTS

For information on how to get a passport, go to "Passports" in the "Fast Facts: Barcelona" section of chapter 4. For an up-to-date, country-by-country listing of passport requirements around the world, go to the "Foreign Entry Requirement" Web page of the U.S. State Department at **http://travel.state.gov**.

VISAS

No visas are required for U.S. visitors to Spain, providing your stay does not exceed 90 days. Australian visitors, however, need a visa. (See "Passports," under "Fast Facts: Barcelona" in chapter 4.)

MEDICAL REQUIREMENTS

For information on medical requirements and recommendations, see "Health & Safety," p. 24.

CUSTOMS
WHAT YOU CAN BRING INTO SPAIN

You can bring most personal effects and the following items duty-free: two still cameras and 10 rolls of film per camera; tobacco for personal use; 1 liter each of

Spain

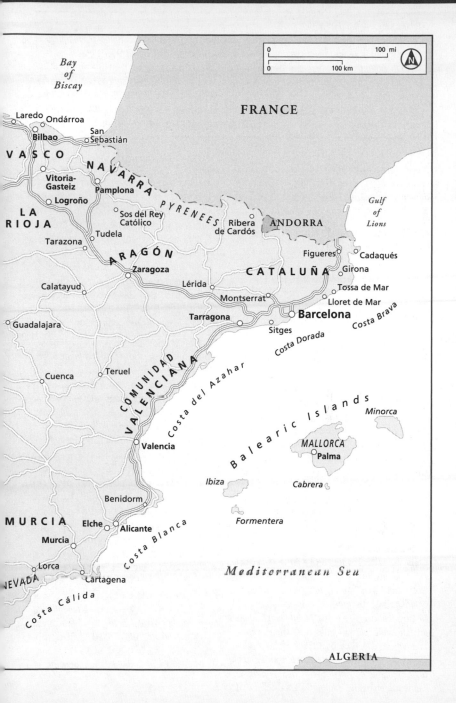

House-Swapping

House-swapping is becoming a more popular and viable means of travel; you stay in their place, they stay in yours, and you both get an authentic and personal view of the area, the opposite of the escapist retreat that many hotels offer. Try **HomeLink International** (Homelink.org), the largest and oldest home-swapping organization, founded in 1952, with over 11,000 listings worldwide ($75 for a yearly membership). **HomeExchange.org** ($49.95 for 6,000 listings) and **InterVac.com** ($68.88 for over 10,000 listings) are also reliable.

---

liquor and wine; a portable radio; a tape recorder; a typewriter; a bicycle; sports equipment; fishing gear; and two hunting weapons with 100 cartridges each.

WHAT YOU CAN TAKE HOME FROM SPAIN
U.S. Citizens

Returning **U.S. citizens** who have been away for 48 hours or more are allowed to bring back, once every 30 days, $400 worth of merchandise duty-free. You'll be charged a flat rate of 10% duty on the next $1,000 worth of purchases. Be sure to have your receipts handy. On gifts, the duty-free limit is $100.

For more specifics on what you can bring back and the corresponding fees, download the invaluable free pamphlet *Know Before You Go* online at **www.cbp. gov**. (Click on "Travel," and then click on "Know Before You Go! Online Brochure.") Or contact the **U.S. Customs & Border Protection (CBP),** 1300 Pennsylvania Ave., NW, Washington, DC 20229 (© **877/287-8667**) and request the pamphlet.

Canadian Citizens

Canada allows its citizens a C$750 exemption, and you are allowed to bring back duty-free 200 cigarettes, 2.2 pounds of tobacco, 40 imperial ounces (1.2 qt.) of liquor, and 50 cigars. In addition, you are allowed to mail gifts to Canada from abroad at the rate of C$60 a day, provided they are unsolicited and aren't alcohol or tobacco (write on the package: "Unsolicited gift, under $60 value"). All valuables should be declared on the Y-38 Form before departure from Canada, including serial numbers of, for example, expensive foreign cameras that you already own. *Note:* The C$750 exemption can be used only once a year and only after an absence of at least 7 days.

For a full summary of Canadian rules, write for the booklet *I Declare,* issued by the **Canada Border Services Agency** (© **800/461-9999** in Canada, or 204/983-3500; **www.cbsa-asfc.gc.ca**).

U.K. Citizens

If you're a citizen of the **United Kingdom,** you can buy wine, spirits, or cigarettes in an ordinary shop in any other European Union country and bring home *almost* as much as you like. (U.K. Customs and Excise does set theoretical limits.) But if you buy your goods in a duty-free shop, then the old rules still apply—you're allowed to bring home 200 cigarettes and 2 liters of table wine, plus 1 liter of spirits or 2 liters of fortified wine. If you're returning home from a non-E.U. country, the same allowances apply, and you must declare any goods in excess of these allowances. British Customs tends to be strict and complicated in its requirements.

For further details, get in touch with **HM Customs and Excise Office,** Passenger Enquiry Point, Wayfarer House, Great South West Road, Feltham, Middlesex, TW14 8NP (© **0845/010-9000;** from outside the U.K., 020/8929-0152), or consult their website at **www.hmce.gov.uk**.

Australian Citizens

The duty-free allowance in **Australia** is A$400 or, for those under 18, A$200. Australian citizens are allowed to mail gifts to Australia from abroad duty-free to a limit of A$200 per parcel. There are no other restrictions on unsolicited gifts; however, you could be subject to a customs investigation if you send multiple parcels of the same gift to the same address. Upon returning to Australia, citizens can bring in 250 cigarettes or 250 grams of loose tobacco, and 1,125 milliliters of alcohol. If you're returning with valuable goods you already own, such as foreign-made cameras, you should file form B263. A helpful brochure, available from Australian consulates or customs offices, is *Know Before You Go.* For more information, contact **Australian Customs Services,** GPO Box 8, Sydney NSW 2001 (© **02/9213-2000** or 1300/363-263.) Or log on to **www.customs.gov.au**.

New Zealand Citizens

The duty-free allowance for **New Zealand** is NZ$700. New Zealanders are allowed to mail gifts to New Zealand from abroad duty-free to a limit of NZ$70 per parcel. Beware of sending multiple parcels of the same gift to the same address; a Customs investigation could await your return home. Citizens over 17 years of age can bring in 200 cigarettes, or 50 cigars, or 250 grams of tobacco (or a mixture of all three if their combined weight doesn't exceed 250 grams); plus 4.5 liters of wine and beer, or 1.125 liters of liquor. New Zealand currency does not carry import or export restrictions. Fill out a certificate of export, listing the valuables you are taking out of the country; that way, you can bring them back without paying duty. Most questions are answered in a free pamphlet available at New Zealand consulates and Customs offices: *New Zealand Customs Guide for Travellers, Notice no. 4.* For more information, contact **New Zealand Customs,** The Customhouse, 17–21 Whitmore St., Box 2218, Wellington (© **04/473-6099** or 0800/428-786; **www.customs.govt.nz**).

3 Money

CURRENCY

The **euro** (€), the new single European currency, became the official currency in Spain and 11 other participating countries on January 1, 1999. After an overlapping period of just over 3 years, the old currency, the Spanish peseta, disappeared into history on March 1, 2002, and the euro became the sole currency in use. Exchange rates of participating countries were subsequently locked into a common currency fluctuating against the dollar. Unfortunately for U.S. visitors, in the last couple of years, the euro has gone from basically a one-to-one exchange rate with the dollar to a much stronger position. (For more details on the euro, check out **www.europa.eu.int/euro**.)

Much noise was made about the "rounding off" of prices upon the introduction of the euro, not just in Spain, but throughout Europe. Basically this meant that, if the normal price of a coffee in pesetas came out at say 81 eurocents, after January 1, 2002, it was hiked up to an "even" euro. This practice was especially widespread in the hospitality sector and anyone who has visited the country in the days of the peseta will notice a considerable difference in prices in bars and restaurants. If you're from an expensive city in the U.S., you will probably find a lot of the prices comparable, but if you're not used to large-city prices, you could have a bit of sticker shock.

The Euro, the U.S. Dollar & the British Pound

Euro €	US$	U.K.£	Euro €	US$	U.K.£
1.00	1.25	0.69	75.00	63.75	51.75
2.00	2.50	1.38	100.00	125.00	69.00
3.00	3.75	2.07	125.00	156.25	86.25
4.00	5.00	2.76	150.00	187.50	103.50
5.00	6.25	3.45	175.00	218.75	120.75
6.00	7.50	4.14	200.00	250.00	138.00
7.00	8.75	4.83	225.00	281.25	155.25
8.00	10.00	5.52	250.00	312.50	172.50
9.00	11.25	6.21	275.00	343.75	189.75
10.00	12.50	6.90	300.00	375.00	207.00
15.00	18.75	10.35	350.00	437.50	241.50
20.00	25.00	13.80	400.00	500.00	276.00
25.00	31.25	17.25	500.00	625.00	345.00
50.00	62.50	34.50	1,000.00	1,250.00	690.00

Spain is, therefore, no longer a budget destination and Barcelona itself is often quoted as being the most expensive city in the country (in studies based on everything from the cost of renting an apartment to the price of a loaf of bread). Everything is relative, however, and compared with other major European cities such as London or Paris, it can still be a bargain.

The old adage "You get what you pay for" is as true here as any other European city, up to a point. Reflecting a modern, cosmopolitan city that has to cater all budgets, you can choose to go either up- or downmarket in your choice of dining and accommodations. Often you will find that the most memorable experience is not wholly dependent on the price tag. Staying away from the tourist traps and seeking out family-run restaurants will generally make you more inclined to hand over your credit card with a smile when the check comes. In a climate of stiff competition (especially from the holiday apartment sector) hotels are usually

---

Tips Emergency Cash—The Fastest Way

If you need emergency cash over the weekend when all banks and American Express offices are closed, you can have money wired to you from **Western Union** (© **800/325-6000**; www.westernunion.com). You must present valid ID to pick up the cash at the Western Union office. However, in most countries, you can pick up a money transfer even if you don't have valid identification, as long as you can answer a test question provided by the sender. Be sure to let the sender know in advance that you don't have ID. If you need to use a test question instead of ID, the sender must take cash to his or her local Western Union office, rather than transferring the money over the phone or online.

clean and comfortable. Trains are very reasonably priced, fast, and on time, and most service personnel treat you with respect. And of course, once you move beyond Barcelona and into the rural areas you will find that the price of things (particularly hotels and restaurants) drops noticeably.

In Spain, many prices for children—generally defined as ages 6 to 17—are lower than for adults. Fees for children under 6 are generally waived.

For American Readers At the euro's inception, the U.S. dollar and the euro traded on par (that is, $1 approximately equaled 1€). But in recent years the euro has gained strength against the dollar and in converting prices to U.S. dollars, I used the current conversion rate of 1€=$1.25. For up-to-the minute exchange rates between the euro and the dollar, check the currency converter website **www.xe.com/ucc**.

For British Readers At this writing, £1 equals approximately US$1.85, and trades at 1.45 euros. These were the rates of exchange used to calculate the values in the table below.

Exchange rates are more favorable at the point of arrival. Nevertheless, it's often helpful to exchange at least some money before going abroad. Currency and traveler's checks (for which you'll receive a better rate than cash) can be changed at all principal airports, though standing in line at the *cambio* (exchange bureau) at Barcelona's airport could make you miss the next bus leaving for downtown.

Before leaving, therefore, check with any of your local American Express or Thomas Cook offices or major banks. Or order euros in advance from the following: **American Express** (© **800/221-7282;** www.americanexpress.com), **Thomas Cook** (© **800/223-7373;** www.thomas cook.com), or **Capital for Foreign Exchange** (© **888/842-0880**).

When you get to Barcelona, it's best to exchange currency or traveler's checks at a bank, not a *cambio,* hotel, or shop. Note the rates and ask about commission fees; it can sometimes pay to shop around and ask the right questions.

Many Barcelona hotels don't accept dollar- or pound-denominated checks; those that do will almost certainly charge for the conversion. In some cases, they'll accept countersigned traveler's checks or a credit card, but if you're prepaying a deposit on hotel reservations, it's cheaper and easier to pay with a check drawn on a Spanish bank.

This can be arranged by a large commercial bank or by a specialist such as **Ruesch International,** 700 11th St. NW, 4th Floor, Washington, DC 20001-4507 (© **800/424-2923;** www.ruesch.com), which performs a wide variety of conversion-related tasks, usually for only $5 to $15 per transaction.

If you need a check payable in euros, call Ruesch's toll-free number, describe what you need, and note the transaction number given to you. Mail your dollar-denominated personal check (payable to Ruesch International) to the address

What Things Cost in Barcelona	US$	UK£	Euro €
Cup of coffee	$1.50–$1.75	.8p–.93p	1.20€–1.40€
Glass of beer (half pint)	$2.50	£1.33	2.00€
Movie ticket	$7.75	£4.13	6.20€
Taxi from airport to center	$25–$31	£13–£17	20€–25€
Three-course meal for one with wine	$25–$31	£13–£17	20€–25€

above. Upon receiving this, the company will mail a check denominated in euros for the financial equivalent, minus the transaction fee. The company can also help you with many different kinds of wire transfers and conversions of VAT (value-added tax, known as IVA in Spain) refund checks, and also will mail brochures and information packets on request. Brits can contact **Ruesch International Ltd.,** Marble Arch Tower, 14 Floor, 55 Bryanston St., London W14 7AA, England (© **0207/563-3300**).

ATMS

The easiest and best way to get cash away from home is from an ATM (automated teller machine), sometimes referred to as a "cash machine," or a "cashpoint." In Spain only four-digit numbers are valid so be sure to change any five- or six-digit PINs you may have to a four-digit number before you go.

The **Cirrus** (© **800/424-7787;** www.mastercard.com) and **PLUS** (© **800/843-7587;** www.visa.com) networks span the globe; look at the back of your bank card to see which network you're on, then call or check online for ATM locations at your destination. Be sure you know your personal identification number (PIN) and daily withdrawal limit before you depart. *Note:* Remember that many banks impose a fee every time you use a card at another bank's ATM, and that fee can be higher for international transactions (up to $5 or more) than for domestic ones (where they're rarely more than

$2). In addition, the bank from which you withdraw cash may charge its own fee. For international withdrawal fees, ask your bank.

CREDIT CARDS

Credit cards are another safe way to carry money. They also provide a convenient record of all your expenses, and they generally offer relatively good exchange rates. You can withdraw cash advances from your credit cards at banks or ATMs, provided you know your PIN. Keep in mind that you'll pay interest from the moment of your withdrawal, even if you pay your monthly bills on time. Also, note that many banks now assess a 1% to 3% "transaction fee" on **all** charges you incur abroad (whether you're using the local currency or your native currency).

American Express, Visa, MasterCard, and Diners Club are all widely accepted in Spain.

TRAVELER'S CHECKS

Traveler's checks are accepted in Spain at banks, travel agencies, hotels, and some shops, and you can buy them at most banks before you leave.

They are offered in denominations of $20, $50, $100, $500, and sometimes $1,000. Generally, you'll pay a service charge ranging from 1% to 4%.

The most popular traveler's checks are offered by **American Express** (© **800/807-6233** or 800/221-7282 for card holders—this number accepts collect calls, offers service in several foreign languages,

---

Tips **Easy Money**

You'll avoid lines at airport ATMs by exchanging at least some money—just enough to cover airport incidentals and transportation to your hotel—before you leave home.

When you change money, ask for some small bills or loose change. Petty cash will come in handy for tipping and public transportation. Consider keeping the change separate from your larger bills, so that it's readily accessible and you'll be less of a target for theft.

and exempts Amex gold and platinum cardholders from the 1% fee); **Visa** (© 800/732-1322)—AAA members can obtain Visa checks for a $9.95 fee (for checks up to $1,500) at most AAA offices or by calling © **866/339-3378;** and **MasterCard** (© **800/223-9920**).

American Express, Thomas Cook, Visa, and **MasterCard** offer **foreign currency traveler's checks,** which are useful if you're traveling to one country, or to the euro zone; they're accepted at locations where dollar checks may not be.

If you carry traveler's checks, keep a record of their serial numbers separate from your checks in the event that they are stolen or lost. You'll get a refund faster if you know the numbers.

4 When to Go

CLIMATE

Barcelona is blessed with a benign, Mediterranean climate. Spring and fall are ideal times to visit, especially May to June and September to October. Even in the winter, days are crisp to cold (due to its proximity to the mountains) but often sunny. Snow is rare and never lasts more than a day or two. Most of the rainfall occurs in April but some quite spectacular storms, as is typical of the Mediterranean, can occur year-round. July and August are hot and humid, even at night, as the temperature often only drops minimally. The surrounding sea is warm enough to swim in from the end of June to early October. Inland the temperatures drop slightly, as does the humidity. North on the Costa Brava, a strong wind known as the *tramontana* often blows.

August is the major vacation month in Europe. The traffic from France, the Netherlands, and Germany to Spain becomes a veritable migration, and low-cost hotels along the coastal areas are virtually impossible to find unless booked well in advance. To compound the problem, many restaurants and shops also decide it's time for a vacation, thereby limiting the visitors' selections for both dining and shopping. That said, Barcelonese also head out of town for cooler climes, leaving tourists to enjoy the city for themselves. Barcelona is also a major international trade fair and conference destination. These happen throughout the year so if you plan to stay in a mid- to high-range hotel it should be booked well in advance. Barcelona is officially Spain's most popular destination, and tourism is now year-round. The only time you may not be rubbing shoulders with fellow travelers is Christmas!

Barcelona's Average Daytime Temperatures & Rainfall

	Jan	Feb	Mar	Apr	May	June	July	Aug	Sept	Oct	Nov	Dec
Temp. (°F)	48	49	52	55	61	68	73	73	70	63	55	50
Temp. (°C)	9	9	11	13	16	20	23	23	21	17	13	10
Rainfall (in.)	1.7	1.4	1.9	2	2.2	1.5	.9	1.6	3.1	3.7	2.9	2

CATALAN & NATIONAL HOLIDAYS

Holidays observed are January 1 (New Year's Day), January 6 (Feast of the Epiphany), March/April (Good Friday and Easter Monday), May 1 (May Day), May/June (Whit Monday), June 24 (Feast of St. John), August 15 (Feast of the Assumption), September 11 (National Day of Catalonia), September 24 (Feast of Our Lady of Mercy), October 12 (Spain's National Day), November 1 (All

Saints' Day), December 8 (Feast of the Immaculate Conception), December 25 (Christmas) and December 26 (Feast of St. Stephen).

If a holiday falls on a Thursday or Tuesday, many people also take off the weekday in between creating an extra-long weekend. While this only really affects those doing business in the city, you should book hotels well ahead of time on these popular *puentes* (bridges).

BARCELONA CALENDAR OF EVENTS

Barcelona—like Seville and Madrid—is a big *fiesta* city; whether it's a rip-roaring street car-nival or a culture fest, the year's calendar is sprinkled with events to keep in mind when planning your trip. Note that on official holidays (see above) shops, banks, and some restaurants and museums close for the day.

The dates for festivals and events given below may not be precise. Sometimes the exact days are not announced until 6 weeks before the actual festival. Also days allotted to cele-brate Easter, Carnaval, and some other religious days change each year. Check with the Barcelona Tourist Office (see "Visitor Informa-tion," earlier in this chapter) if you're planning to attend a specific event.

January

Día de los Reyes (Three Kings Day). Parades are held around the country on the eve of the Festival of the Epiphany, which is traditionally when Christmas gift-giving is done (the concept of "Santa Claus" has crept into the cul-ture in the past years, meaning that people now also exchange gifts on Christmas). In Barcelona, the three

"kings" arrive by boat at the port in the evening to dispense candy to all the incredibly excited children. January 5.

February

Carnaval. Compared to other parts of Spain, particularly Seville in the south, Carnaval in Barcelona is a low-key event. The most dressing up you are likely to see is done by groups of children or stall owners in the local markets who organize a competition among themselves for "best costume" (buying fresh fish off a woman dressed in full Louis VI regalia is one of those "only in Barcelona" experiences you will treasure) as well as the city's main Carnaval parade. Just south of the city, however, in the seaside town of Sitges, locals, especially the local gay commu-nity, go all out and many Barcelonese take the short train ride to celebrate along with them. Just before Lent.

March/April

Semana Santa (Holy Week). Catalo-nia has some Easter traditions not found in the rest of the country. The Mona is a whimsical chocolate and pastry creation given in the same way others give Easter eggs. On Palm Sun-day, palm leaves are blessed in Gaudí's Sagrada Família and the city's main cathedral has the curious L'ou com balla—a hollowed-out egg shell that is placed on top of a fountain in the city's cathedral's cloister to bob around and "dance." Out of town, the ominously named Dansa de la Mort (Dance of Death) sees men dressed as skeletons

---

Fun Fact St. George Conquers the World

In 1995, taking a cue from Catalonia, UNESCO declared April 23 "World Book Day" to encourage people to buy books, to think about books, and simply to read more. In the U.K., children receive a book token and online chat rooms are set up with well-known authors. The idea seems to be catching on with as many as 30 countries participating.

The Pooping Catalan

When you go to the Fira d' Santa Lucia, be on the lookout for one unique personage among the Magi, farm animals, and other *pessebre* figurines. The *caganer* is a small fellow, usually dressed in the garb of a peasant farmer (but also seen in anything from formal attire to the Barcelona Football Club attire). He is squatting, has his pants down, and a stream of excrement connects his bare buttocks to the earth. His origins are lost in folklore but it is generally believed that he sprang from the Catalan philosophy of "giving back to the earth what one takes from it." The artist Joan Miró placed him in *La Granja* (The Farm), one of his most famous works that is on display at Barcelona's Miró Foundation.

performing a "death" dance in the village of Verges, near Girona, and various Passion Plays are also performed, the most famous in the village of Esparraguera, 40km (25 miles) outside of Barcelona. 1 week before Easter.

La Diada de St. Jordi. Saint George (St. Jordi in Catalan) is the patron saint of Catalonia, and his name day coincides with the deaths of *Don Quixote* writer Miguel Cervantes and William Shakespeare. On this day men give a single red rose to the significant women in their lives (mother, girlfriend, sister, and so on), and women give a book in return (although, in the interest of gender equality, many men now give women a book). This is one of the most colorful days in Catalonia, as thousands of rose-sellers take to the streets and bookshops set up open-air stalls along the major thoroughfares. April 23.

May

May Day. Also known as Labor Day, this day sees a huge march by the city's trade-union members. Dozens of herbs, natural remedies, and wholesome goodies are sold along the Carrer de l'Hospital in the Fira de Sant Ponç. May 1.

Corpus Christi. During this festival, the streets of Sitges are carpeted in flowers. Can fall in May or June.

June

Verbena de Sant Juan. Catalonia celebrates the Twelfth Night with fiery

activities that can keep even grannies up until dawn. Families stock up on fireworks a week in advance before setting them off in streets and squares and even off balconies. Bonfires are lit along the beachfront, and the sky is ablaze with smoke and light. Lots of *cava* is consumed, and it is traditional to have the first dip in the sea of the year at dawn (officially the first day of summer). Madcap fun. June 23.

Sonar. This dance-music and multimedia festival has gained the reputation of being one of the best on the world circuit. Thousands from all over Europe descend on the city for the DJs, live concerts, and other related events. During the day, events are held at the Museum of Contemporary Art; at night, they move to the enormous trade-fair buildings. Purchase tickets to this wildly popular festival well in advance at www.sonar.es. Early to mid-June.

July

El Grec. International names in all genres of music and theater come to the city to perform in various open-air venues, including the mock-Greek theater, namesake of the city's main culture-fest. Beginning of July.

August

Festa Major de Gràcia. This charming weeklong fiesta is held in the villagelike neighborhood of Gràcia. All year long,

---

Tips **On Time in Spain**

In Spain, a time change occurs the first weekend of spring. Check your watch. Many unsuspecting visitors have arrived at the airport too late and missed their planes.

---

the residents of Gràcia work on elaborate decorations with themes such as marine life, the solar system, or even local politics to hang in the streets. By day, long trestle tables are set up for communal lunches and board games; at night, thousands invade the tiny streets for outdoor concerts, balls, and general revelry. Early to mid-August.

September

La Diada de Catalunya. This is the most politically and historically significant holiday in Catalonia. Although it celebrates the region's autonomy, the date actually marks the day the city was besieged by Spanish and French troops in 1714 during the War of Succession. Demonstrations calling for greater independence are everywhere, wreath-laying ceremonies take place at tombs of past *políticos,* and the *senyera,* the flag of Catalonia, is hung from balconies. Not your typical tourist fare, but interesting for anyone who wishes to understand Catalan nationalism. September 11.

La Mercè. This celebration honors Our Lady of Mercy (La Mercè), the city's patron saint. Legend has it she rid Barcelona of a plague of locusts, and the Barcelonese give thanks in rip-roaring style. Free concerts, from traditional to contemporary music, are held in the plazas (particularly Plaça de Catalunya and Plaça Sant Jaume), and folkloric figures such as the *gigants* (giants) and *cap grosses* (fat heads) take to the streets. People come out to perform the *sardana* (the traditional Catalan dance) and to watch the nail-biting

castellers (human towers). Firework displays light up the night, and the hair-raising *correfoc,* a parade of firework-brandishing "devils" and dragons is the grand finale. One of the best times to be in Barcelona, especially for children. September 24.

October

Día de la Hispanitat. Spain's national day (which commemorates Columbus's "discovery" of the New World) is met with mixed receptions in Catalonia, due to the region's overriding sense of independence. The only street events you are likely to see are demonstrations calling for exactly that, or low-key celebrations from groups of people from other regions of Spain. October 12.

November

All Saints' Day. This public holiday is reverently celebrated, as relatives and friends lay flowers on the graves (or *nichos*—in Spain, people are buried one on top of another in tiny compartments) of the dead. The night before, some of the bars in the city hold Halloween parties, another imported custom that seems to be catching on. November 1.

December

Nadal (Christmas). In mid-December stallholders set up Fira d' Santa Lucia, a huge open-air market held in the streets around the main cathedral. Thousands come to buy handicrafts, Christmas decorations, trees, and the figurines for their *pessebres* (nativity dioramas) that are hugely popular here. The Betlem Church on La Rambla holds an exhibition of them throughout the month and a life-size one is constructed outside the city hall in the Plaça Sant Jaume. December 25.

5 Travel Insurance

The cost of travel insurance varies widely, depending on the cost and length of your trip, your age and health, and the type of trip you're taking, but expect to pay between 5% and 8% of the vacation itself. You can get estimates from various providers through **InsureMyTrip.com**. Enter your trip cost and dates, your age, and other information, for prices from more than a dozen companies.

Check your existing insurance policies before you buy travel insurance to cover trip cancellation, lost luggage, medical expenses, or car rental insurance. You're likely to have partial or complete coverage. But if you need some, ask your travel agent about a comprehensive package. Insurance for extreme sports or adventure travel will cost more than coverage for a European cruise. Some insurers provide packages for specialty vacations, such as skiing or backpacking. More dangerous activities may be excluded from basic policies.

TRIP-CANCELLATION INSURANCE

Trip-cancellation insurance will help retrieve your money if you have to back out of a trip or depart early, or if your travel supplier goes bankrupt. Permissible reasons for trip cancellation can range from sickness to natural disasters to the State Department declaring a destination unsafe for travel.

For more information, contact one of the following recommended insurers: **Access America** (© 866/807-3982; www.accessamerica.com); **Travel Guard International** (© 800/826-4919; www.travelguard.com); **Travel Insured International** (© 800/243-3174; www.travelinsured.com); and **Travelex Insurance Services** (© 888/457-4602; www.travelexinsurance.com).

MEDICAL INSURANCE

For travel overseas, most U.S. health plans (including Medicare and Medicaid) do not provide coverage, and the ones that do often require you to pay for services upfront and reimburse you only after you return home. As a safety net, you may want to buy travel medical insurance, particularly if you're traveling to a remote or high-risk area where emergency evacuation might be necessary. If you require additional medical insurance, try **MEDEX Assistance** (© 410/453-6300; www.medexassist.com) or **Travel Assistance International** (© 800/821-2828; www.travelassistance.com; for general information on services, call the company's

---

Travel in the Age of Bankruptcy

Airlines go bankrupt, so protect yourself by **buying your tickets with a credit card.** The Fair Credit Billing Act guarantees that you can get your money back from the credit card company if a travel supplier goes under (and if you request the refund within 60 days of the bankruptcy). **Travel insurance** can also help, but make sure it covers against "carrier default" for your specific travel provider. And be aware that if a U.S. airline goes bust mid-trip, a 2001 federal law requires other carriers to take you to your destination (albeit on a space-available basis) for a fee of no more than $25, provided you rebook within 60 days of the cancellation.

Worldwide Assistance Services, Inc., at ℂ **800/777-8710**).

LOST-LUGGAGE INSURANCE

On flights within the U.S., checked baggage is covered up to $2,500 per ticketed passenger. On international flights (including U.S. portions of international trips), baggage coverage is limited to approximately $9.07 per pound, up to approximately $635 per checked bag. If you plan to check items more valuable than what's covered by the standard liability you may purchase "excess valuation" coverage from the airline, up to $5,000. See if your homeowner's policy covers your valuables, get baggage insurance as part of your comprehensive travel-insurance package, or buy Travel Guard's "BagTrak" product.

Before you leave home, compile an inventory of all packed items and a rough estimate of the total value to ensure you're properly compensated if your luggage is lost. You will only be reimbursed for what you lost, no more. Be sure to take any valuables or irreplaceable items with you in your carry-on luggage. If your main luggage is lost, immediately file a lost-luggage claim at the airport, giving full details of all contents, as most airlines enforce a 21-day deadline. Most airlines require that you report delayed, damaged, or lost baggage within 4 hours of arrival.

Once you've filed a complaint, persist in securing your reimbursement; there are no laws governing the length of time it takes for a carrier to reimburse you.

If you arrive at a destination without your bags, ask the airline to forward them to your hotel; they are required to deliver luggage, once found, directly to your house or destination free of charge and will usually comply. The airline may reimburse you for reasonable expenses, such as a toothbrush or a set of clothes, but the airline is under no legal obligation to do so.

Lost luggage may also be covered by your homeowner's or renter's policy. Many platinum and gold credit cards cover you as well. If you choose to purchase additional lost-luggage insurance, be sure not to buy more than you need. Buy in advance from the insurer or a trusted agent (prices will be much higher at the airport).

CAR-RENTAL INSURANCE

If you hold a private auto insurance policy, you probably are covered in the U.S., but not in Spain, for loss or damage to the car, and liability in case a passenger is injured. The credit card you used to rent the card also may provide some coverage.

Car-rental insurance probably does not cover liability if you caused the accident. Check your own auto insurance policy, the rental company policy, and your credit card coverage for the extent of coverage. Is your destination covered? Are other drivers covered? How much liability is covered if a passenger is injured? (If you rely on your credit card for coverage, you may want to bring a second credit card with you, as damages may be charged to your card, and you may find yourself stranded with no money.)

6 Health & Safety

STAYING HEALTHY

Spain does not pose any major health hazards. The rich cuisine—garlic, olive oil, and wine—may give some travelers mild diarrhea, so take along some anti-diarrhea medicine, moderate your eating habits, and even though the water is generally safe, drink mineral water only. Fish and shellfish from the polluted Mediterranean should only be eaten cooked, but though Barcelona is right beside the sea a lot of the fish and shellfish you see in markets and restaurants actually come from the cleaner Atlantic-washed northern provinces and

Avoiding "Economy Class Syndrome"

Deep vein thrombosis, or as it's know in the world of flying, "economy-class syndrome," is a blood clot that develops in a deep vein. It's a potentially deadly condition that can be caused by sitting in cramped conditions—such as an airplane cabin—for too long. During a flight (especially a long-haul flight), get up, walk around, and stretch your legs every 60 to 90 minutes to keep your blood flowing. Other preventative measures include frequent flexing of the legs while sitting, drinking lots of water, and avoiding alcohol and sleeping pills. If you have a history of deep vein thrombosis, heart disease, or another condition that puts you at high risk, some experts recommend wearing compression stockings or taking anticoagulants when you fly; always ask your physician about the best course for you. Symptoms of deep vein thrombosis include leg pain or swelling, or even shortness of breath.

you might risk the odd raw *percebe* (goose barnacle) if you can afford it.

If you are traveling around Spain (particularly southern Spain) over the summer, limit your exposure to the sun, especially during the first few days of your trip and, thereafter, from 11am to 2pm. Use a sunscreen with a high protection factor and apply it liberally. Remember that children need more protection than adults do.

The water is safe to drink throughout Spain; however, do not drink the water in mountain streams, regardless of how clear and pure it looks.

GENERAL AVAILABILITY OF HEALTHCARE

No shots of any sort are required before traveling to Spain. Once there, medicines for a wide variety of common ailments from colds to diarrhea can be obtained over-the-counter at local chemists or *farmacias.* Generic equivalents of common prescription drugs are also usually available in Spain. (However it does no harm to bring OTC medicines with you to be on the safe side.)

Contact the **International Association for Medical Assistance to Travelers (IAMAT;** © **716/754-4883** or, in Canada, 416/652-0137; **www.iamat.org)** for specific tips on travel and health concerns

in Spain and for lists of local, English-speaking doctors. The United States **Centers for Disease Control and Prevention** (© **800/311-3435;** www.cdc.gov) provides up-to-date information on health hazards by region or country and offers tips on food safety. The website **www.tripprep. com,** sponsored by a consortium of travel medicine practitioners, may also offer helpful advice on traveling abroad. You can find listings of reliable clinics overseas at the **International Society of Travel Medicine** (www.istm.org).

COMMON AILMENTS

CHANGE OF DIET   No need to go on a tempting cholesterol binge if you really don't want to. Vegetarians can follow their usual diet pattern in Barcelona, as there are an increasing number of vegetarian eating spots available as well as a multitude of *herbolarios,* or health-food shops.

SUN EXPOSURE   In the hot weather, do as the locals do and avoid the sun between noon and 4pm. Use a sunscreen with a high protection factor and apply it liberally. Remember that children need more protection than adults do.

SEA HAZARDS   Urban beaches in Barcelona have lifeguards on duty and are

Healthy Travels to You

The following government websites offer up-to-date health-related travel advice.

- **Australia:** www.dfat.gov.au/travel
- **Canada:** www.hc-sc.gc.ca/index_e.html
- **U.K.:** www.dh.gov.uk/PolicyAndGuidance/HealthAdviceForTravellers/fs/en
- **U.S.:** www.cdc.gov/travel

marked by flags; green is safe, yellow means you should take caution, and red means stay out. Where there are no guards on duty use your common sense and note that, particularly north of Barcelona along the Costa Brava, the seabed is rocky. Over the past years much has been done to improve the standard of Spain's beaches in terms of water pollution, leading to a consistently high rating in terms of cleanliness. At the onset of summer, jellyfish can be a problem. They are not poisonous but do have a nasty sting. If you do get bitten, seek assistance from the nearest *farmacia* (drugstore).

RESPIRATORY ILLNESSES Lodged between the mountains and the sea, Barcelona can often trap smog from its nearby industrial belt. While the quality of the air is monitored, local media do not publish "high risk" days. Although the problem is nowhere near the level of, say, Tokyo, common sense is required for people with respiratory illnesses.

WHAT TO DO IF YOU GET SICK AWAY FROM HOME

Spanish medical facilities are among the best in the world. If a medical emergency arises, your hotel staff can usually put you in touch with a reliable doctor. If not, contact the American embassy or a consulate; each one maintains a list of English-speaking doctors. Medical and hospital services aren't free, so be sure that you have appropriate insurance coverage before you travel.

Pack prescription medications in your carry-on luggage. Carry written prescriptions in generic, not brand-name form, and dispense all prescription medications from their original vials. Also bring along copies of your prescriptions in case you lose your pills or run out.

We list Barcelona **hospitals** and **emergency numbers** under "Fast Facts: Barcelona," in chapter 4, "Getting to Know Barcelona."

If you suffer from a chronic illness, consult your doctor before your departure. Pack **prescription medications** in your carry-on luggage, and carry them in their original containers, with pharmacy labels—otherwise they won't make it through airport security. Carry the generic name of prescription medicines, in case a local pharmacist is unfamiliar with the brand name.

For travel abroad, you may have to pay all medical costs upfront and be reimbursed later. See "Medical Insurance," under "Travel Insurance," above.

STAYING SAFE

TERRORISM The bomb attacks on three suburban trains in Madrid on March 11, 2004, resulted in the deaths of 200 people; since then, political and public attention throughout Spain has been strongly focused on the threat of terrorism.

A direct or indirect consequence of the massacre was that after a massive protest demonstration of two million people in the streets of the city, voters unexpectedly returned the Socialist party to power in the March 14, 2004, general elections. (The policy of the new president, Rodríguez Zapatero, had always been to oppose the war in Iraq, and one of his first acts was to

ETA Strikes Again

With the bombing of the huge multistory car park of Terminal 4 at Madrid's Barajas Airport on December 30, 2006, the outlawed Basque separatist-terrorist organization, ETA (Euskadi Ta Askatasuna, or Basque Homeland and Freedom), not only broke its 9-month truce with the government but also caused the first loss of life in 3½ years. (Two luckless Ecuadorians, who had been sleeping in their vehicles, did not hear the alarm bells and were killed.) The total repair work was estimated at 40 million euros ($50 million) but the psychological and political cost went far deeper. The governing socialist PSOE (Partido Socialista Obrero Español), led by President José Luis Rodriguez Zapatero, is convinced that patient attempts at negotiation are the only way for a resolution. Conversely, the opposition right-wing PP (Partido Popular), led by Mariano Rajoy, favors treating the terrorists as common criminals, and has become increasingly critical of what it regards as an unacceptably conciliatory attitude by the government.

Ironically, on the day prior to the airport attack, Zapatero had been particularly optimistic about the progress of negotiations with ETA. The unannounced bombing therefore was a shock. For its part, ETA claimed in an unapologetic official statement that secret "compromises" agreed to by the government in summer 2006 had not been honored, inferring that the bombing was intended to "jog the government's memory." (The group added—almost as an afterthought—that no loss of life had been intended.) The ruling PSOE declared all future talks with ETA "suspended" until the group renounced violence. The PP regarded this response as inadequate and demanded a total severance of all contact with the outlawed organization. ETA and its nonmilitant counterpart—the banned Herri Batasuna party—in turn pronounced the peace process "more alive than ever," but made no promise to totally reject violence. (Since 1968, when ETA began its campaign of violence, over 800 people have died.) The stalemate between the political parties remains unresolved at the time of this writing.

authorize the full withdrawal of Spanish troops from that country just over 3 months later.)

To date there is nothing to suggest that Islamic terrorism constitutes a more serious threat in Barcelona than in any other major world city. U.S. tourists traveling to Spain should, however, exercise caution and refer to the guidance offered in the Worldwide Caution Public Announcements issued in the wake of the September 11, 2001, terrorist attacks in the United States.

The more local threat comes from ETA, the Basque separatist-terrorist organization (see the "ETA Strikes Again" box above). A smaller Marxist group, GRAPO, which mounted several attacks since 1999 and killed three people, has in recent years been inactive.

Where all this leaves Barcelona is uncertain. Traditionally, ETA attacks have been aimed mainly at the seat of the central government in Madrid or at Basque cities like Bilbao and San Sebastián. Although Basque terrorist bombings in the Catalan capital have occurred in the past—the last and deadliest at a supermarket in the city center in

1987, which took 21 lives—the general feeling is that such actions are unlikely to occur here again. But given the almost pathological unpredictability of ETA, whose diminishing number of attacks are now possibly planned and carried out by a small team of radicals, the group's next move is anyone's guess.

CONVENTIONAL CRIME While most of Spain has a moderate level of conventional crime, and most of the estimated one million American tourists have trouble-free visits to Spain each year, the principal tourist areas have been experiencing an increase in violent crime. Barcelona has reported growing incidents of muggings and violent attacks, and older tourists and Asian-Americans seem to be particularly at risk. Criminals frequent tourist areas and major attractions such as museums, monuments, restaurants, hotels, beach resorts, trains, train stations, airports, subways, and ATMs.

Reported incidents have occurred in key tourist areas such as La Rambla and the narrow lanes of the Barri Gòtic. Travelers should exercise caution, carry limited cash and credit cards, and leave extra cash, credit cards, passports, and personal documents in a safe location. Crimes have occurred at all times of day and night, though visitors—and residents—are more vulnerable in the early hours of the morning.

Thieves often work in teams or pairs. In most cases, one person distracts a victim while the accomplice performs the robbery. For example, a stranger might wave a map in your face and ask for directions or "inadvertently" spill something on you. While your attention is diverted, an accomplice makes off with the valuables. Attacks can also be initiated from behind, with the victim being grabbed around the neck and choked by one assailant while others rifle through the belongings. A group of assailants may surround the victim, maybe in a crowded popular tourist area or on public transportation, and only after the group has departed does the person discover that he has been robbed. Some attacks have been so violent that victims have needed to seek medical attention afterward.

Theft from parked cars is also common. Small items like luggage, cameras, or briefcases are often stolen from parked cars. Travelers are advised not to leave valuables in parked cars and to keep doors locked, windows rolled up, and valuables out of sight when driving. "Good Samaritan" scams are unfortunately common. A passing car will attempt to divert the driver's attention by indicating there is a mechanical problem. If the driver stops to check the vehicle, accomplices steal from the car while the driver is looking elsewhere. Drivers should be cautious about accepting help from anyone other than a uniformed Spanish police officer or Civil Guard.

The loss or theft abroad of a U.S. passport should be reported immediately to the local police and the nearest U.S. embassy or consulate. U.S. citizens may refer to the Department of State's pamphlet, *A Safe Trip Abroad,* for ways to promote a more trouble-free journey. The pamphlet is available by mail from the Superintendent of Documents, U.S. Government Printing Office, Washington, D.C. 20402, via the Internet at www. gpoaccess.gov/index.html, or via the Bureau of Consular Affairs home page at http://travel.state.gov.

DEALING WITH DISCRIMINATION

As Barcelona's population slowly becomes more international, overt racial prejudice (never prevalent here, anyway) appears to be diminishing. Still, as in other places, there is a small fringe of hard-core racists.

Since the Madrid bombings of 2004, there has been a slight hardening of attitudes toward Arabs by certain members of the community; and some residents' attitudes toward Latin Americans have been soured by the appearance (in relatively small numbers) of young criminal gangs such as the "Latin Kings" and "Dominican Don't Play" in the outer areas of the city.

Barcelona is as liberal as any other city in its acceptance of gays and lesbians, including homosexual marriages. (See "Gay & Lesbian Travelers," below.)

Solo female travelers can expect to have a reasonably hassle-free trip. (See "Women Travelers," in "Specialized Travel Resources," p. 31.)

7 Specialized Travel Resources

TRAVELERS WITH DISABILITIES

Most disabilities shouldn't stop anyone from traveling. There are more options and resources out there than ever before.

Because of the endless flights of stairs in most buildings in Barcelona, visitors with disabilities may have difficulty getting around the city, but conditions are slowly improving: Newer hotels are more sensitive to the needs of persons with disabilities, and the more expensive restaurants are generally wheelchair-accessible. However, since most places have very limited, if any, facilities for people with disabilities, you might consider taking an organized tour specifically designed to accommodate such travelers.

For the names and addresses of such tour operators as well as other related information, contact the **Society for Accessible Travel & Hospitality,** 347 Fifth Ave., New York, NY 10016 (✆ 212/447-7284). Annual membership dues are $45, or $30 for seniors and students.

You can also obtain a free copy of *Air Transportation of Handicapped Persons,* published by the U.S. Department of Transportation. Write for Free Advisory Circular No. AC12032, Distribution Unit, U.S. Department of Transportation, Publications Division, M-4332, Washington, DC 20590.

For the blind or visually impaired, the best source is the **American Foundation for the Blind (AFB;** ✆ 800/232-5463; www.afb.org), 15 W. 16th St., New York, NY 10011 (✆ 800/232-5463 to order information kits and supplies, or 212/

502-7600). It offers information on travel and various requirements for the transport and border formalities for Seeing Eye dogs. It also issues identification cards to those who are legally blind.

Other organizations that offer assistance to disabled travelers include **Moss-Rehab** (www.mossresourcenet.org) and **SATH** (Society for Accessible Travel & Hospitality; ✆ 212/447-7284; www.sath.org). **AirAmbulanceCard.com** is now partnered with SATH and allows you to preselect top-notch hospitals in case of an emergency.

Many travel agencies offer customized tours and itineraries for travelers with disabilities. One of the best organizations serving the needs of persons with disabilities (wheelchairs and walkers) is **Flying Wheels Travel,** 143 W. Bridge, P.O. Box 382, Owatonna, MN 55060 (✆ 800/535-6790 or 507/451-5005; www.flying wheelstravel.com), which offers various escorted tours and cruises internationally. Others include **Access-Able Travel Source** (✆ 303/232-2979; www.accessable.com); and **Accessible Journeys** (✆ 800/846-4537 or 610/521-0339; www.disabilitytravel.com).

For a $35 annual fee, consider joining **Mobility International USA,** P.O. Box 10767, Eugene, OR 97440 (✆ 888/241-3366, or 541/343-1284 voice and TDD; www.miusa.org). It answers questions on various destinations and also offers discounts on videos, publications, and programs it sponsors.

If you're flying around Spain, the airline and ground staff will help you on and off planes and reserve seats for you with sufficient legroom, but it is essential to arrange for this assistance *in advance* by contacting your airline.

Avis Rent a Car has an "Avis Access" program that offers such services as a dedicated 24-hour toll-free number (© 888/879-4273) for customers with special travel needs; special car features such as swivel seats, spinner knobs, and hand controls; and accessible bus service.

The community website **iCan** (www.icanonline.net/channels/travel) has destination guides and several regular columns on accessible travel. Also check out the quarterly magazine *Emerging Horizons* (www.emerginghorizons.com), and *Open World* magazine, published by SATH.

For British Travelers with Disabilities The annual vacation guide *Holidays and Travel Abroad* costs £5 from **Royal Association for Disability and Rehabilitation (RADAR),** Unit 12, City Forum, 250 City Rd., London EC1V 8AF (© 020/7250-3222; www.radar.org.uk). RADAR also provides a number of information packets on such subjects as sports and outdoor vacations, insurance, financial arrangements for persons with disabilities, and accommodations in nursing care units for groups or for the elderly. Each of these fact sheets is available for £2. Both the fact sheets and the holiday guides can be mailed outside the United Kingdom for a nominal postage fee.

Another good service is the **Holiday Care,** 2nd Floor Imperial Buildings, Victoria Road, Horley, Surrey RH6 7PZ (© 01293/774-535; fax 01293/784-647; www.holidaycare.org.uk), a national charity that advises on accessible accommodations for elderly people or those with disabilities. Annual membership costs £15 (U.K. residents) and £30 (abroad). Once you're a member, you can receive a newsletter and access to a free reservations network for hotels throughout Britain and, to a lesser degree, Europe and the rest of the world.

GAY & LESBIAN TRAVELERS

In 1978, Spain legalized homosexuality among consenting adults. In April 1995, the parliament of Spain banned discrimination based on sexual orientation and marriage between same-sex couples became legal in 2005. Catalonia has helped pave the way in rights for gay couples, preempting national laws by granting same-sex couples the same official status and conjugal rights as heterosexual ones, and has given the green light for changes in the law that would facilitate same-sex couples adopting. Barcelona is one of the major centers of gay life in Spain, and two of the most popular resorts for gay travelers, Sitges (south of Barcelona) and the island of Ibiza, are within close proximity.

To learn about gay and lesbian travel in Spain, you can secure publications or join data-dispensing organizations before you go. Both lesbians and gay men might want to pick up a copy of *Gay Travel A to Z*, which provides general information as well as listings for bars, hotels, restaurants, and places of interest for gay travelers throughout the world.

The International Gay and Lesbian Travel Association (IGLTA; © 800/448-8550 or 954/776-2626; www.iglta.org) is the trade association for the gay and lesbian travel industry, and offers an online directory of gay- and lesbian-friendly travel businesses; go to their website and click on "Members."

Many agencies offer tours and travel itineraries specifically for gay and lesbian travelers. Among them are **Above and Beyond Tours** (© 800/397-2681; www.abovebeyondtours.com); **Now, Voyager** (© 800/255-6951; www.nowvoyager.com); and **Olivia Cruises & Resorts** (© 800/631-6277; www.olivia.com).

Gay.com Travel (© **800/929-2268** or 415/644-8044; www.gay.com/travel or www.outandabout.com), is an excellent online successor to the popular *Out & About* print magazine. It provides regularly updated information about gay-owned, gay-oriented, and gay-friendly lodging, dining, sightseeing, nightlife, and shopping establishments in every important destination worldwide.

The following travel guides are available at many bookstores, or you can order them from any online bookseller: *Frommer's Gay & Lesbian Europe* (www.frommers.com), an excellent travel resource to the top European cities and resorts; *Spartacus International Gay Guide* (Bruno Gmünder Verlag; www.spartacusworld.com/gay guide) and *Odysseus: The International Gay Travel Planner* (Odysseus Enterprises Ltd.); and the *Damron* guides (www.damron.com), with separate, annual books for gay men and lesbians.

FAMILY TRAVEL

Barcelona is a lively and very crowded city that also happens to be a very good destination for families with children. From the peaceful **Parc Güell** to the **Parque Zoologico,** as well as fun spots like **Happy Park Port Aventura** and **Cataluña en Miniatura,** there's plenty to choose from.

To locate accommodations, restaurants, and attractions that are particularly kid-friendly, refer to the "Kids" icon throughout this guide. Large family rooms are sometimes available, which saves considerably on having to pay for two doubles rooms.

To locate accommodations, restaurants, and attractions that are particularly kid-friendly, refer to the "Kids" icon throughout this guide.

Familyhostel (© **800/733-9753;** www.learn.unh.edu/familyhostel) takes the whole family, including kids ages 8 to 15, on moderately priced U.S. and international learning vacations. Lectures, field trips, and sightseeing are guided by a team of academics.

Recommended family travel websites include **Family Travel Forum** (www.familytravelforum.com); **Family Travel Network** (www.familytravelnetwork.com); **Traveling Internationally with Your Kids** (www.travelwithyourkids.com); and **Family Travel Files** (www.thefamilytravelfiles.com).

Also, be sure to check out our *Frommer's 500 Places to Take Your Kids Before They Grow Up.*

WOMEN TRAVELERS

In Barcelona women are as emancipated as in any other large European city. If a degree of machismo still exists it is minimal, and women are increasingly reaching high positions in all walks of life (though not as many as they would like). As for women exploring the city on their own, the degree of hassle experienced is scarcely different from that of Paris or London.

For general advice to female travelers check out the award-winning website **Journeywoman** (www.journeywoman.com), a "real life" women's travel-information network where you can sign up for a free e-mail newsletter and get advice on everything from etiquette and dress to safety; or the travel guide *Safety and Security for Women Who Travel* by Sheila Swan and Peter Laufer (Travelers' Tales, Inc.), offering common-sense tips on safe travel.

MULTICULTURAL TRAVELERS

As Barcelona becomes increasingly multicultural, visitors and residents of all nationalities are naturally accepted by what is in effect a fairly open-minded society. A person of a different race or skin color rarely draws more than a second glance, unlike a few decades back when a dark face was a rarity in a 99% *castizo* city.

That said, instances of racial conflict are not unknown, though these tend to be with African, Arabic, and Latin American locals rather than with foreign visitors. (See "Dealing with Discrimination," above.)

AFRICAN-AMERICAN TRAVELERS

Black Travel Online (www.blacktravel online.com) posts news on upcoming events and includes links to articles and travel-booking sites. **Soul of America** (www.soulofamerica.com) is a comprehensive website, with travel tips, event and family-reunion postings, and sections on historically black beach resorts and active vacations.

Agencies and organizations that provide resources for black travelers include **Rodgers Travel** (© 800/825-1775; www. rodgerstravel.com); the **African American Association of Innkeepers International** (© 877/422-5777; www.african americaninns.com); and **Henderson Travel & Tours** (© 800/327-2309 or 301/650-5700; www.hendersontravel. com), which has specialized in trips to Africa since 1957. For more information, check out the following collections and guides: *Go Girl: The Black Woman's Guide to Travel & Adventure* (Eighth Mountain Press), a compilation of travel essays by writers including Jill Nelson and Audre Lorde; *The African American Travel Guide* by Wayne Robinson (Hunter Publishing; www.hunter publishing.com); *Steppin' Out* by Carla Labat (Avalon); *Travel and Enjoy Magazine* (© 866/266-6211; www.traveland enjoy.com); and *Pathfinders Magazine* (© 877/977-PATH; www.pathfinders travel.com), which includes articles on everything from Rio de Janeiro to Ghana as well as information on upcoming ski, diving, golf, and tennis trips.

STUDENT TRAVEL

If you're traveling internationally, you'd be wise to arm yourself with an **International Student Identity Card (ISIC)**, which offers substantial savings on rail passes, plane tickets, and entrance fees. It also provides you with basic health and life insurance and a 24-hour help line. The card is available from **STA Travel** (© 800/781-4040 in North America; www.sta.com or www.statravel.com; or www.statravel.co. uk in the U.K.), the biggest student travel agency in the world. If you're no longer a student but are still under 26, you can get an **International Youth Travel Card (IYTC)** from the same people, which entitles you to some discounts (but not on museum admissions).

Travel CUTS (© 800/667-2887 or 416/614-2887; www.travelcuts.com) offers similar services for both Canadians and U.S. residents. Irish students may prefer to turn to **USIT** (© 01/602-1600; www.usit now.ie), an Ireland-based specialist in student, youth, and independent travel.

SINGLE TRAVELERS

Travel Buddies Singles Travel Club (© 800/998-9099; www.travelbuddies worldwide.com), based in Canada, runs small, intimate, single-friendly group trips and will match you with a roommate free of charge. **TravelChums** (© 212/787-2621; www.travelchums.com) is an Internet-only travel-companion matching service with elements of an online personals-type site, hosted by the respected New York–based Shaw Guides travel service. **The Single Gourmet Club** (www. singlegourmet.com/chapters.php) is an international social, dining, and travel club for singles of all ages, with club chapters in 21 cities in the U.S. and Canada. Many reputable tour companies offer singles-only trips. **Singles Travel International** (© 877/765-6874; www.singlestravel intl.com) offers singles-only trips to places like London, Fiji, and the Greek Islands. **Backroads** (© 800/462-2848; www.backroads.com) offers more than 160 active-travel trips to 30 destinations worldwide, including Bali, Morocco, and Costa Rica.

For more information, check out Eleanor Berman's latest edition of *Traveling Solo: Advice and Ideas for More Than 250 Great Vacations* (Globe Pequot), a guide with advice on traveling alone, either solo or as part of a group tour.

ECO-TOURISM

Barcelona is fortunate in being a fairly short distance from the marvelous coastline of the **Costa Brava** with its pine-fringed sandy coves and national parks of **Les Illes Medes** (underwater life) and **Aiguamoll de L' Alt Empordá** near Rosas (birdlife). As an added bonus there's the inland **Pyrenean** range with its countless mountain trails and parklands. If you don't want to rent a car to get to these areas you can easily make your way there by local train *(cercanías)* or bus. (For more details, see chapter 11, "Side Trips in Catalonia").

You can find eco-friendly travel tips, statistics, and touring companies and associations—listed by destination under "Travel Choice"—at the TIES website, www.ecotourism.org. **Ecotravel.com** is part online magazine and part eco-directory that lets you search for touring companies in several categories (water-based, land-based, spiritually oriented, and so on). Also check out **Conservation International** (www.conservation.org)—which, with *National Geographic Traveler,* annually presents **World Legacy Awards** (www.wlaward.org) to those tour operators, businesses, organizations, and places that have made a significant contribution to sustainable tourism.

8 Planning Your Trip Online

SURFING FOR AIRFARES

The most popular online travel agencies are **Travelocity** (**www.travelocity.com**, or www.travelocity.co.uk); **Expedia** (**www.expedia.com**, www.expedia.co.uk, or www.expedia.ca); and **Orbitz** (**www.orbitz.com**).

In addition, most airlines now offer online-only fares that even their phone agents know nothing about. For the websites of airlines that fly to and from your destination, go to "Getting There," p. 36.

Other helpful websites for booking airline tickets online include:

- www.biddingfortravel.com
- www.cheapflights.com
- www.hotwire.com
- www.kayak.com
- www.lastminutetravel.com
- www.opodo.co.uk
- www.priceline.com
- www.sidestep.com
- www.site59.com
- www.smartertravel.com

SURFING FOR HOTELS

In addition to **Travelocity, Expedia, Orbitz, Priceline,** and **Hotwire** (see above), the following websites will help you with booking hotel rooms online:

- www.hotels.com
- www.quickbook.com
- www.travelaxe.net
- www.travelweb.com
- www.tripadvisor.com

It's a good idea to **get a confirmation number** and **make a printout** of any online booking transaction.

Some Barcelona-based Internet hotel booking services include **Barcelona On Line** (www.barcelona-on-line.es) and **www.hotel-barcelona.com**. If you have a hotel in mind, search for their own website as discounts and special deals are often available for web bookers. Self-catering accommodations in Barcelona are done almost exclusively on the Net. Google "tourist apartment Barcelona" and you will be surprised how many hits come up.

Frommers.com: The Complete Travel Resource

For an excellent travel-planning resource, we highly recommend **Frommers. com** (www.frommers.com), voted Best Travel Site by *PC Magazine.* We're a little biased, of course, but we guarantee that you'll find the travel tips, reviews, monthly vacation giveaways, bookstore, and online-booking capabilities to be thoroughly indispensable. Special features include our popular **Destinations** section, where you can access expert travel tips, hotel and dining recommendations, and advice on the sights to see in more than 3,500 destinations around the globe; the **Frommers.com Newsletter,** with the latest deals, travel trends, and money-saving secrets; and our **Travel Talk** area featuring **Message Boards,** where Frommer's readers post queries and share advice, and where our authors sometimes show up to answer questions. Once you finish your research, the **Book a Trip** area can lead you to Frommer's preferred online partners' websites, where you can book your vacation at affordable prices.

SURFING FOR RENTAL CARS

For booking rental cars online, the best deals are usually found at rental-car company websites, although all the major online travel agencies also offer rental-car reservations services. Priceline and Hotwire work well for rental cars, too; the only "mystery" is which major rental company you get, and for most travelers the difference between Hertz, Avis, and Budget is negligible.

TRAVEL BLOGS & TRAVELOGUES

To read travel blogs about Barcelona, try **www.travelpost.com**. Other blogs include:

- www.gridskipper.com
- www.salon.com/wanderlust
- www.travelblog.com
- www.travelblog.org
- www.worldhum.com
- www.writtenroad.com

9 The 21st-Century Traveler

INTERNET ACCESS AWAY FROM HOME
WITHOUT YOUR OWN COMPUTER
To find cybercafes in your destination check **www.cybercaptive.com** and **www. cybercafe.com.**

Aside from formal cybercafes, most **youth hostels** and **public libraries** have Internet access. Avoid **hotel business centers** unless you're willing to pay exorbitant rates.

Most major airports now have **Internet kiosks** scattered throughout their gates.

These give you basic Web access for a per-minute fee that's usually higher than cybercafe prices.

WITH YOUR OWN COMPUTER
More and more hotels, cafes, and retailers are signing on as Wi-Fi (wireless fidelity) "hotspots." Mac owners have their own networking technology: Apple AirPort. **T-Mobile Hotspot** (www.t-mobile.com/hotspot) serves up wireless connections at more than 1,000 Starbucks coffee shops nationwide. **Boingo** (www.boingo.com) and **Wayport** (www.wayport.com) have

set up networks in airports and high-class hotel lobbies. IPass providers (see below) also give you access to a few hundred wireless hotel lobby setups. To locate other hotspots that provide **free wireless networks** in cities around the world, go to **www.personaltelco.net/index.cgi/ WirelessCommunities**.

For dial-up access, most business-class hotels throughout the world offer dataports for laptop modems, and a few thousand hotels in the U.S. and Europe now offer free high-speed Internet access. In addition, major Internet Service Providers (ISPs) have **local access numbers** around the world, allowing you to go online by placing a local call. The **iPass** network also has dial-up numbers around the world. You'll have to sign up with an iPass provider, who will then tell you how to set up your computer for your destination(s). For a list of iPass providers, go to www. ipass.com and click on "Individuals Buy Now." One solid provider is **i2roam** (www. i2roam.com; ℡ **866/811-6209** or 920/ 235-0475).

Wherever you go, bring a **connection kit** of the right power and phone adapters, a spare phone cord, and a spare Ethernet network cable—or find out whether your hotel supplies them to guests.

In Spain the electricity connection is 220 volts, though it may occasionally be 125 volts. A two-prong plug is needed to connect appliances into the mains. (For further details see "Electricity" section of "Fast Facts: Barcelona," in chapter 4.)

CELLPHONE USE

The three letters that define much of the world's wireless capabilities are GSM (Global System for Mobiles), a big, seamless network that makes for easy cross-border cellphone use throughout Europe and dozens of other countries worldwide. In the U.S., T-Mobile, AT&T Wireless, and Cingular use this quasi-universal system; in Canada, Microcell and some Rogers customers are GSM, and all Europeans and most Australians use GSM. If your cellphone is on a GSM system, and you have a world-capable multiband phone such as many Sony Ericsson, Motorola, or Samsung models, you can make and receive calls across civilized areas around much of the globe. Just call your wireless operator and ask for "international roaming" to be activated on your account. Unfortunately, per-minute charges can be high—usually $1 to $1.50 in western Europe and up to $5 in places like Russia and Indonesia.

For many, **renting** a phone is a good idea. (Even worldphone owners will have to rent new phones if they're traveling to non-GSM regions, such as Japan or Korea.) While you can rent a phone from any number of overseas sites, including kiosks at airports and at car-rental agencies, we suggest renting the phone before you leave home. North Americans can rent one before leaving home from **InTouch USA** (℡ 800/872-7626; www. intouchglobal.com) or **RoadPost** (℡ 888/ 290-1606 or 905/272-5665; www. roadpost.com). InTouch will also, for free, advise you on whether your existing phone will work overseas; simply call ℡ **703/222-7161** between 9am and 4pm EST, or go to **http://intouchglobal.com/ travel.htm**.

The French-owned store FNAC (main branch at Plaça Catalunya 4; metro: Catalunya; ℡ **93-344-18-00;** www.fnac. es) provides a pay-as-you-go mobile phone package, which actually works out to be cheaper than renting if you're staying a few weeks.

Buying a phone can be economically attractive, as many nations have cheap prepaid phone systems. Once you arrive at your destination, stop by a local cellphone shop and get the cheapest package; you'll probably pay less than $100 for a phone and a starter calling card. Local calls may be as low as 10¢ per minute, and in many countries incoming calls are free.

Online Traveler's Toolbox

Veteran travelers usually carry some essential items to make their trips easier. Following is a selection of handy online tools to bookmark and use.

- **Airplane Food** (www.airlinemeals.net)
- **Airplane Seating** (www.seatguru.com and www.airlinequality.com)
- **Foreign Languages for Travelers** (www.travlang.com)
- **Maps** (www.mapquest.com)
- **Subway Navigator** (www.subwaynavigator.com)
- **Time and Date** (www.timeanddate.com)
- **Travel Warnings** (http://travel.state.gov, www.fco.gov.uk/travel, www.voyage.gc.ca, or www.dfat.gov.au/consular/advice)
- **Universal Currency Converter** (www.xe.com/ucc)
- **Visa ATM Locator** (www.visa.com), **MasterCard ATM Locator** (www.mastercard.com)
- **Weather** (www.intellicast.com and www.weather.com)

Some Barcelona-specific sites include:

- *Barcelona Metropolitan* (www.barcelometropolitan.com) is a free monthly English-language magazine giving general coverage of what's what in the city.
- **Guia del Ocio** (www.guiadelocio.com), a comprehensive "what's on" in Barcelona (Spanish only).
- **Restaurants** www.spain.info has a good section on Barcelona attractions, especially eating spots.
- **Tourist information** (www.barcelonaturisme.com).
- **Weekly Events** are found at www.bcn.es (in English), issued by town hall.

Wilderness adventurers, or those heading to less-developed countries, might consider renting a **satellite phone ("satphone").** It's different from a cellphone in that it connects to satellites and works where there's no cellular signal or ground-based tower. You can rent satellite phones from RoadPost (see above). InTouch USA (see above) offers a wider range of satphones but at higher rates. Per-minute call charges can be even cheaper than roaming charges with a regular cellphone, but the phone itself is more expensive. As of this writing, satphones were outrageously expensive to buy, so don't even think about it.

10 Getting There

BY PLANE

Any information about fares or even flights in the highly volatile airline industry is not written in stone; even travel agencies with banks of computers have a hard time keeping abreast of last-minute discounts and schedule changes.

Below are included a list of major airlines that fly to Barcelona. For up-to-the-minute information, including a list of additional carriers that fly to the Spanish capital, check with a travel agent or the individual airlines.

FROM NORTH AMERICA Flights from the U.S. east coast to Spain take 6 to

7 hours. The national carrier of Spain, **Iberia Airlines** (✆ **800/772-4642;** www.iberia.com), has more routes into and within Spain than any other airline. It offers almost daily services from most major U.S. cities (New York, Washington, Chicago, Atlanta) either direct to Barcelona or via Madrid. Also available are attractive rates on fly/drive packages within Iberia and Europe; they can substantially reduce the cost of both the air ticket and the car rental.

A good money-saver to consider is **Iberia's SpainPass.** Available only to passengers who simultaneously arrange for transatlantic passage on Iberia, the SpainPass consists of coupons equivalent to a one-way/one-person ticket to destinations on mainland Spain and the Balearic Islands. Travelers must purchase a three-coupon minimum (228€/$285) and extra coupons can be bought at 60€ ($75) each. Their **EuroPass** services European destinations. Coupons (minimum of two) for destinations such as Rome, Geneva, Vienna, and Istanbul cost $139 each or $169 for Cairo or Tel Aviv. The EuroPass can only be purchased as a part of an Iberian Air itinerary from your home country.

Iberia's main Spain-based competitor is **Air Europa** (✆ **888/238-7672;** www. air-europa.com), which offers a daily service from Newark Airport using Continental Airlines to Madrid, with connecting flights to Barcelona. Fares are usually lower than Iberia's.

Delta (✆ **800/241-4141;** www.delta. com) runs daily nonstop service from Atlanta (its worldwide hub) and New York (JFK) to Barcelona. Delta's Dream Vacation department offers independent fly/drive packages, land packages, and escorted bus tours.

United Airlines (✆ **800/241-6522;** www.ual.com) does not fly into Spain directly. It does, however, offer airfares from the United States to Spain with United flying as far as Zurich, and then using another carrier to complete the journey. United also offers fly/drive packages and escorted motorcoach tours.

FROM THE U.K. British Airways (✆ **0845/773-3377;** www.britishairways. com), **Iberia** (✆ **020/7830-0011** in London), and **EasyJet** (www.easyjet.com) are the three major carriers flying between England and Spain. More than a dozen daily flights, on either BA or Iberia, depart from London's Heathrow and Gatwick airports. About the same number of EasyJet flights depart daily from Stansted, Luton, and Gatwick airports. EasyJet also has direct flights from Liverpool and Newcastle and another Internet service **MyTravelite** (www.mytravelite.com) offers a daily service from Birmingham. **Ryanair** (www.ryanair.com) which uses Girona (Gerona) airport, located about an hour outside of Barcelona, flies in from Bournemouth, Dublin and the East Midlands, as well as London. (There is a connecting bus service from Girona Airport to central Barcelona.) The best air deals on scheduled flights from England are those requiring a Saturday night stopover.

(*Tips* **Don't Stow It—Ship It**

Though pricey, it's sometimes worthwhile to travel luggage-free. Specialists in door-to-door luggage delivery include **Virtual Bellhop** (www.virtual bellhop.com), **SkyCap** International (wwww.skycapinternational.com), **Luggage Express** (www.usxpluggageexpress.com), and **Sports Express** (www. sportsexpress.com).

Budget airlines are giving the major carriers a run for their money and many have now had to slash their fares to compete. The efficiency of these services has been proven (both EasyJet and Ryanair have excellent "on time" records) and most travelers seem happy to forgo the frills and arrive in Barcelona with a few more euros in their pocket.

Charter flights to the regional Catalan airports of Reus and Girona leave from many British regional airports. Girona serves those heading to the Costa Brava north of Barcelona while Reus is mainly used by those holidaying on the resorts on the Costa Daurada in the south. **Trailfinders** (© **020/7937-5400** in London; www.trailfinder.com) operates charters to both destinations.

In London, there are many bucket shops around Victoria Station and Earls Court that offer cheap fares. Make sure the company you deal with is a member of the IATA, ABTA, or ATOL. These umbrella organizations will help you if anything goes wrong.

CEEFAX, the British television information service, runs details of package holidays and flights to Europe and beyond. Just switch to your CEEFAX channel and you'll find travel information.

FROM AUSTRALIA   From Australia, there are a number of options to fly to Spain. The most popular is **Qantas** (www. quantas.com)/**British Airways** (www. britishairways.com), which flies daily via Asia and London. Other popular and cheaper options are Qantas/**Lufthansa** (www.lufthansa.com) via Asia and Frankfurt, Qantas/**Air France** (www.airfrance. com) via Asia and Paris, and **Alitalia** (www.alitalia.com) via Bangkok and Rome. The most direct option is on **Singapore Airlines** (www.singaporeair.com), with just one stop in Singapore. Alternatively, there are flights on **Thai Airways** (www.thaiair.com) via Bangkok and Rome, but the connections are not always good.

GETTING INTO TOWN FROM THE AIRPORT

El Prat, Barcelona's airport, is 13km (8 miles) from the city center, and there are several options you can use to get into town. One is the **Aerobús,** which leaves just outside all three terminals every 15 minutes from 6am to midnight and stops at Plaça Espanya, Gran Vía Corts Catalanes, Plaça Universitat, and Plaça Catalunya (taking about 40 min. to reach the last stop). Another is by half-hourly **rail service** that departs between 6:15am and 11:15pm from the El Prat **train station** to Sants (25 min.), which has connections with the Metro or Subway. The third is by **taxi** from ranks outside all terminals. For further details including prices see chapter 4, "Getting to Know Barcelona."

If you've rented a car and are driving into the city, be sure to familiarize yourself

---

ⓘTips **EuroPass: A Cost-Cutting Technique**

A noteworthy cost-cutting option is Iberia's EuroPass. Available only to passengers who simultaneously arrange for transatlantic passage on Iberia and a minimum of two additional flights, it allows passage on any flight within Iberia's European or Mediterranean dominion for $250 for the first two flights and $133 for each additional flight. This is especially attractive for passengers wishing to combine trips to Spain with, for example, visits to such far-flung destinations as Cairo, Tel Aviv, Istanbul, Moscow, or Munich. For details, ask Iberia's phone representative.

Tips What You Can Carry On—and What You Can't

The Transportation Security Administration (TSA), the government agency that now handles all aspects of airport security, has devised new restrictions for carry-on baggage, not only to expedite the screening process but to prevent potential weapons from passing through airport security. Passengers are now limited to bringing just one carry-on bag and one personal item onto the aircraft (previous regulations allowed two carry-on bags and one personal item, like a briefcase or a purse). For more information, go to the TSA's website www.tsa.gov. The agency has released an updated list of items passengers are not allowed to carry onto an aircraft:

Not permitted: knives and box cutters, corkscrews, straight razors, metal scissors, golf clubs, baseball bats, pool cues, hockey sticks, ski poles, ice picks.

Permitted: nail clippers, nail files, tweezers, eyelash curlers, safety razors (including disposable razors), syringes (with documented proof of medical need), walking canes and umbrellas (must be inspected first).

The airline you fly may have **additional restrictions** on items you can and cannot carry on board. Call ahead to avoid problems.

---

with the road signs beforehand. These websites are a good place to start: www.asirt.org/roadwatch.htm and www.onemotoring.com.

FLYING FOR LESS: TIPS FOR GETTING THE BEST AIRFARE

- Passengers who can book their ticket either **long in advance or at the last minute,** or who **fly midweek** or **at less-trafficked hours** may pay a fraction of the full fare. If your schedule is flexible, say so, and ask if you can secure a cheaper fare by changing your flight plans.
- Search **the Internet** for cheap fares (see "Planning Your Trip Online," earlier in this chapter).
- Keep an eye on local newspapers for **promotional specials or fare wars,** when airlines lower prices on their most popular routes. You rarely see fare wars offered for peak travel times, but if you can travel in the off-months, you may snag a bargain.
- Try to book a ticket **in its country of origin.** If you're planning a one-way flight from Johannesburg to Bombay, a South Africa–based travel agent will probably have the lowest fares. For multi-leg trips, book in the country of the first leg; for example, book New York–London–Amsterdam–Rome–New York in the U.S. For Barcelona, check with local travel agents like **Viajes Iberia** (www.viajesiberia.com), not to be confused with Iberia Airlines, and **Viajes Marsans** (www.marsans.es) that have various branches throughout the city and can arrange inclusive hotel and flight deals with inland and coastal places of interest. **Solplan** (www.soltours.com), **JuliaTours** (www.juliatours.com), and **Politours** (www.politours.com) are other local agencies providing inclusive flight or train and hotel packages to various parts of Spain.
- **Consolidators,** also known as bucket shops, are great sources for international tickets, although they usually can't beat Internet fares within North America. Start by looking in Sunday newspaper travel sections; U.S. travelers should focus on the *New York*

Tips Getting Through the Airport

- Arrive at the airport 1 hour before a domestic flight and 2 hours before an international flight; if you show up late, tell an airline employee and he or she will probably whisk you to the front of the line.
- Beat the ticket-counter lines by using airport electronic kiosks or even online check-in from your home computer, from where you can print out boarding passes in advance. Curbside check-in is also a good way to avoid lines.
- Bring a current, government-issued photo ID such as a driver's license or passport. Children under 18 do not need government-issued photo IDs for flights within the U.S., but they do for international flights to most countries.
- Speed up security by removing your jacket and shoes before you're screened. In addition, remove metal objects such as big belt buckles. If you've got metallic body parts, a note from your doctor can prevent a long chat with the security screeners.
- Use a TSA-approved lock for your checked luggage. Look for Travel Sentry certified locks at luggage or travel shops and Brookstone stores (or online at www.brookstone.com).

Times, Los Angeles Times, and *Miami Herald.* U.K. travelers should search in the *Independent, The Guardian,* or *The Observer.* For less-developed destinations, small travel agents who cater to immigrant communities in large cities often have the best deals. *Beware:* Bucket shop tickets are usually nonrefundable or rigged with stiff cancellation penalties, often as high as 50% to 75% of the ticket price, and some put you on charter airlines, which may leave at inconvenient times and experience delays. **Vueling** (www.vueling.com) is the main Spanish specialist, with many bargain flights between European cities and Barcelona.

Several reliable consolidators are worldwide and available online. **STA Travel** has been the world's lead consolidator for students since purchasing Council Travel, but their fares are competitive for travelers of all ages. **ELTExpress (Flights.com;** © 800/ TRAV-800; www.eltexpress.com) has excellent fares worldwide, particularly to Europe. They also have "local" websites in 12 countries. **FlyCheap** (© 800/FLY-CHEAP; www.1800 flycheap.com), owned by package-holiday megalith MyTravel, has especially good fares to sunny destinations. **Air Tickets Direct** (© 800/ 778-3447; www.airticketsdirect.com) is based in Montreal and leverages the currently weak Canadian dollar for low fares; they also book trips to places that U.S. travel agents won't touch, such as Cuba.

- Join **frequent-flier clubs.** Frequent-flier membership doesn't cost a cent, but it does entitle you to better seats, faster response to phone inquiries, and prompter service if your luggage is stolen or your flight is canceled or delayed, or if you want to change your seat. And you don't have to fly to earn points; **frequent-flier credit** cards can earn you thousands of miles for doing your everyday shopping. With more than 70 mileage awards programs on the market, consumers have never had more options. Investigate the program details of your favorite airlines before you sink points into any one. Consider which airlines have hubs in the airport nearest you, and, of those carriers, which have the most advantageous alliances, given your most common routes. To play the frequent-flier game to your best advantage, consult Randy Petersen's **Inside Flyer** (www.inside flyer.com). Petersen and friends review all the programs in detail and post regular updates on changes in policies and trends.

LONG-HAUL FLIGHTS: HOW TO STAY COMFORTABLE

- Your choice of airline and airplane will definitely affect your leg room. Find more details about U.S. airlines at **www.seatguru.com**. For international airlines, the research firm Skytrax has posted a list of average seat pitches at **www.airlinequality.com**.

- Emergency exit seats and bulkhead seats typically have the most legroom. Emergency exit seats are usually left unassigned until the day of a flight (to ensure that someone able-bodied fills the seats); it's worth getting to the ticket counter early to snag one of these spots for a long flight. Many passengers find that bulkhead seating (the row facing the wall at the front of the cabin) offers more legroom, but keep in mind that bulkheads are where airlines often put baby bassinets, so you may be sitting next to an infant

- To have two seats for yourself in a three-seat row, try for an aisle seat in a center section toward the back of coach. If you're traveling with a companion, book an aisle and a window seat. Middle seats are usually booked last, so chances are good you'll end up with three seats to yourselves.

- Ask about entertainment options. Many airlines offer seatback video systems where you get to choose your movies or play video games—but only on some of their planes. (Boeing 777s are your best bet.)

Tips Coping with Jet Lag

Jet lag is a pitfall of traveling across time zones. If you're flying north–south and you feel sluggish when you touch down, your symptoms will be the result of dehydration and the general stress of air travel. When you travel east–west or vice versa, however, your body becomes thoroughly confused about what time it is, and everything from your digestive system to your brain is knocked for a loop. Traveling east, say from Chicago to Madrid, is more difficult on your internal clock than traveling west, say from London to Hawaii, because most peoples' bodies are more inclined to stay up late than fall asleep early.

Here are some tips for combating jet lag:

- **Reset your watch** to your destination time before you board the plane.
- **Drink lots of water** before, during, and after your flight. Avoid alcohol.
- **Exercise and sleep well** for a few days before your trip.
- If you have trouble sleeping on planes, **fly eastward on morning flights.**
- **Daylight** is the key to resetting your body clock. At the website for **Outside In** (www.bodyclock.com), you can get a customized plan of when to seek and avoid light.

Flying with Film & Video

Never pack film—exposed or unexposed—in checked bags, because the new, more powerful scanners in U.S. airports can fog film. The film you carry with you can be damaged by scanners as well. X-ray damage is cumulative; the faster the film, and the more times you put it through a scanner, the more likely the damage. Film under 800 ASA is usually safe for up to five scans. If you're taking your film through additional scans, U.S. regulations permit you to demand hand inspections. In international airports, you're at the mercy of airport officials. On international flights, store your film in transparent baggies, so you can remove it easily before you go through scanners. Keep in mind that airports are not the only places where your camera may be scanned: Highly trafficked attractions are X-raying visitors' bags with increasing frequency.

Most photo supply stores sell protective pouches designed to block damaging X-rays. The pouches fit both film and loaded cameras. They should protect your film in checked baggage, but they also may raise alarms and result in a hand inspection.

You'll have little to worry about if you are traveling with **digital cameras.** Unlike film, which is sensitive to light, the digital camera and storage cards are not affected by airport X-rays, according to Nikon.

Carry-on scanners will not damage **videotape** in video cameras, but the magnetic fields emitted by the walk-through security gateways and hand-held inspection wands will. Always place your loaded camcorder on the screening conveyor belt or have it hand-inspected. Be sure your batteries are charged, as you may be required to turn the device on to ensure that it's what it appears to be.

- To sleep, avoid the last row of any section or the row in front of an emergency exit, as these seats are the least likely to recline. Avoid seats near highly trafficked toilet areas. Avoid seats in the back of many jets—these can be narrower than those in the rest of coach. You also may want to reserve a window seat so you can rest your head and avoid being bumped in the aisle.

- Get up, walk around, and stretch every 60 to 90 minutes to keep your blood flowing. See the box "Avoiding 'Economy Class Syndrome,'" under "Healthy & Safety," p. 24.

- Drink water before, during, and after your flight to combat the lack of humidity in airplane cabins. Avoid alcohol, which will dehydrate you.

- If you're flying with kids, don't forget to carry on toys, books, pacifiers, and chewing gum to help them relieve ear pressure buildup during ascent and descent.

BY CAR

If you're touring the rest of Europe in a rented car, you might, for an added cost, be allowed to drop off your vehicle in Barcelona.

Highway approaches to Spain are across France on expressways. The most popular border crossing is near Biarritz, but there are 17 other border stations between Spain and France. If you plan to visit the north or west of Spain (Galicia), the Hendaye-Irún border is the most convenient frontier crossing. If you're going to Barcelona or Catalonia and along the Levante coast (Valencia), take the expressway in France to Toulouse, then the A-61 to Narbonne, and then the A-9 toward the border crossing at La Junquera. You can also take the RN-20, with a border station at Puigcerdà.

Barcelona is tucked away in the northeast corner of Spain, just below the Pyrénées. Main highways within Spain from the city run west and south and the best connections are with Madrid (NII) and Valencia (E15). To get to northern cities such as Pamplona, Burgos, and Bilbao take the A2 highway first to Zaragoza and look for the appropriate connection.

If you're driving from Britain, make sure you have a cross-Channel reservation, as traffic tends to be very heavy, especially in summer.

The major ferry crossings connect Dover and Folkestone with Dunkirk. Newhaven is connected with Dieppe, and the British city of Portsmouth with Roscoff. Taking a car on the ferry from Dover to Calais on **P & O Ferries** (© **800/677-8585** in North America or 08705/20-20-20; www.poferries.com) costs £99 ($188) and takes 1¼ hours. This cost includes the car and two passengers.

One of the fastest crossings is by hovercraft from Dover to Calais. It costs more than the ferry, but it takes only about half an hour. For reservations and information, call **Hoverspeed** (© **800/677-8585** for reservations in North America, or 0870/240 8070 in England; www.hoverspeed.com). The hovercraft takes 35 minutes and costs £138 to £215 ($262–$409) for the car and two passengers. The drive from Calais to the border would take about 15 hours.

You can take the Chunnel, the underwater Channel Tunnel linking Britain (Folkestone) and France (Calais) by road and rail. **Eurostar** tickets, for train service between London and Paris or Brussels, are available through Rail Europe (© **800/ EUROSTAR;** www.eurostar.com for information). In London, make reservations for Eurostar at © **0870/530-00-03.** The tunnel also accommodates passenger cars, charter buses, taxis, and motorcycles, transporting them under the English Channel from Folkestone, England, to Calais, France. It operates 24 hours a day, 365 days a year, running every 15 minutes during peak travel times, and at least once an hour at night. Tickets may be purchased at the tollbooth at the tunnel's entrance. With "Le Shuttle," gone are the days of weather-related delays, seasickness, and advance reservations.

Once you land, you'll have about a 18-hour drive to Barcelona.

If you plan to transport a rental car between England and France, check in advance with the rental company about license and insurance requirements and additional drop-off charges. And be aware that many car-rental companies, for insurance reasons, forbid transport of one of their vehicles over the water between England and France.

CAR RENTALS   Many of North America's biggest car-rental companies, including Avis, Budget, and Hertz, maintain offices throughout Spain. Although several Spanish car-rental companies exist, we've received lots of letters from readers of previous editions telling us they've had hard times resolving billing irregularities and insurance claims, so you might want to stick with the U.S.-based rental firms.

Note that tax on car rentals is a whopping 15%, so don't forget to factor that into your travel budget. Usually, prepaid rates do not include taxes, which will be collected at the rental kiosk itself. Be sure to ask explicitly what's included when you're quoted a rate.

Avis (© **800/331-1212;** www.avis. com) maintains about 100 branches throughout Spain. There are seven in Barcelona, located at El Prat airport (two); Carrers Corcega 293/295, Pallars 457, and Rita Bonat 5; Sants railway station; and at the World Trade Center in the harbor. If you reserve and pay for your rental by telephone at least 2 weeks before your departure from North America, you'll qualify for the company's best rate, with unlimited kilometers included.

You can usually get competitive rates from **Hertz** (© **800/654-3131;** www. hertz.com) and **Budget** (© **800/472-3325;** www.budget.com); it always pays to comparison shop. Budget doesn't have a drop-off charge if you pick up a car in one Spanish city and return it to another. All three companies require that drivers be at least 21 years of age and, in some cases, not older than 72. To be able to rent a car, you must have a passport and a valid driver's license; you must also have a valid credit card or a prepaid voucher. An international driver's license is not essential, but you might want to present it if you have one; it's available from any North American office of the American Automobile Association (AAA).

Two other agencies of note include **Kemwel Holiday Auto** (© **877/820-0668;** www.kemwel.com) and **Auto Europe** (© **800/223-5555;** www.auto europe.com).

Many packages include airfare, accommodations, and a rental car with unlimited mileage. Compare these prices with the cost of booking airline tickets and renting a car separately, in order to see if these offers are good deals. Internet resources can make comparison shopping easier. **Microsoft Expedia** (www.expedia. com) and **Travelocity** (www.travelocity. com) help you compare prices and locate car-rental bargains from various companies nationwide. They will even make your reservation for you once you've found the best deal. See "Planning Your Trip Online," earlier in this chapter, for tips.

Most cars rented in Spain are stick shift, not automatic. Most are air-conditioned and nearly all use unleaded gas.

Usual minimum-age limit for rentals 25 (or even older) while upper-age requirements reach 70 to 75 for certain vehicles

DRIVING RULES   Spaniards drive on the right side of the road. Drivers should pass on the left; local drivers sound their horns when passing another car and flash their lights at you if you're driving slowly (slowly for high-speed Spain) in the left lane. Autos coming from the right have the right of way.

Spain's express highways are known as *autopistas,* which charge a toll, and *autovías,* which don't. To exit in Spain, follow the SALIDA (exit) sign, except in Catalonia, where the exit sign says SORTIDA. On most express highways, the speed limit is 120kmph (75 mph). On other roads, speed limits range from 90kmph (56 mph) to 100kmph (62 mph). You will see many drivers far exceeding these limits.

The greatest number of accidents in Spain is recorded along the notorious Costa del Sol highway, Carretera de Cádiz.

If you must drive through Barcelona—or any other Spanish city—try to avoid morning and evening rush hours. Never park your car facing oncoming traffic, as that is against the law. If you are fined by the highway patrol *(Guardia Civil de Tráfico),* you must pay on the spot. Penalties for drinking and driving are very stiff (**Breathalysers** are now being far more strictly used than in the past).

MAPS   For one of the best overviews of the Iberian Peninsula (Spain and Portugal), get Michelin map no. 990 (folded version) or map no. 460 (spiral-bound version). For more detailed looks at

Spain, Michelin has a series of six maps (nos. 441–446) showing specific regions, complete with many minor roads.

For extensive touring, purchase *Mapas de Carreteras—España y Portugal,* published by Almax Editores and available at most leading bookstores in Spain. This cartographic compendium of Spain provides an overview of the country and includes road and street maps of some of its major cities.

The American Automobile Association (www.aaa.com) publishes a regional map of Spain that's available free to members at most AAA offices in the United States. Incidentally, the AAA is associated with the **Real Automóvil Club de España (RACE; ℂ 90-240-45-45;** www.race.es). This organization can supply helpful information about road conditions in Spain, including tourist and travel advice. It will also provide limited road service, in an emergency, if your car breaks down.

BREAKDOWNS   These can be a serious problem. If you're driving a Spanish-made vehicle that needs parts, you'll probably be able to find them. But if you are driving a foreign-made vehicle, you may be stranded. Have the car checked before setting out on a long trek through Spain. On a major motorway you'll find strategically placed emergency phone boxes. On secondary roads, call for help by asking the operator to locate the nearest Guardia Civil, which will put you in touch with a garage that can tow you to a repair shop.

As noted above, the Spanish affiliate of AAA can provide limited assistance in the event of a breakdown.

BY BUS

Bus travel to Spain is possible but not popular—it's quite slow. But coach services do operate regularly from major capitals of western Europe to Barcelona, from which bus connections can be made to Madrid. The busiest routes are from London and are run by **Eurolines Limited,** 52 Grosvenor Gardens, London SW1W 0AU (ℂ **0990/143-219** or 020/ 7730-8235). The journey from London's Victoria Station to Barcelona takes 27 hours and 15 minutes, departing from Victoria Station at 3.30pm and arriving at Barcelona Nord at 6:45pm the following day. There is a 30-minute wait in Lyon, France, en route.

If you're touring the rest of Europe in a rented car, you might, for an added cost, be allowed to drop off your vehicle in Barcelona.

BY TRAIN

If you're already in Europe, you may want to go to Spain by train, especially if you have a EurailPass. Even if you don't, the cost is moderate. Rail passengers who visit from Britain or France should make *couchette* (bunk beds in a sleeper car) and sleeper reservations as far in advance as possible, especially during the peak summer season.

Since Spain's rail tracks are of a wider gauge than those used for French trains (except for the TALGO and Trans-Europe-Express trains), you'll probably have to change trains at the border unless you're on an express train (see below). For long journeys on Spanish rails, seat and sleeper reservations are mandatory.

The most comfortable and the fastest trains in Spain are the AVE, ALTARIA, TER, TALGO, and Electrotren. However, you pay a supplement to ride on these fast trains. Both first- and second-class fares are sold on Spanish trains. Tickets can be purchased in either the United States or Canada at the nearest office of French Rail or from any reputable travel agent. Confirmation of your reservation will take about a week.

All trains in Catalonia are operated by **Spanish State Railways (RENFE).** At present, the only AVE (high-speed train) connection is Barcelona–Valencia, although rails are presently being laid for Barcelona–Madrid and Barcelona to the French border connections. RENFE's easy-to-navigate website (www.renfe.es) has information in English on timetables and train types.

If you want your car carried, you must travel Auto-Expreso in Spain. This type of auto transport can be booked only through travel agents or rail offices once you arrive in Europe.

To go from London to Barcelona by rail, you'll need to change not only the train but also the rail terminus in Paris. Trip time from London to Paris is about 6 hours; from Paris to Barcelona, about 12 hours, which includes 2 hours spent in Paris changing trains and stations. Many rail passes are available in the United Kingdom for travel in Europe.

If you plan to travel a great deal on the European railroads, it's worth buying a copy of the ***Thomas Cook Timetable of European Passenger Railroads.*** It's available exclusively in North America from **Forsyth Travel Library,** 44 S. Broadway, White Plains, NY 10601 (© **800/FORSYTH;** www.forsyth.com), at a cost of $28, plus $4.95 postage priority air mail in the United States plus $2 for shipments to Canada.

11 Packages for the Independent Traveler

Package tours are simply a way to buy the airfare, accommodations, and other elements of your trip (such as car rentals, airport transfers, and sometimes even activities) at the same time and often at discounted prices.

One good source of package deals is the airlines themselves. Among the airline packagers, **Iberia Airlines** (© **800/772-4642** or 902/400/500 in Spain; www.iberia.com) leads the way. Most major airlines offer air/land packages, including **American Airlines Vacations** (© 800/321-2121; www.aavacations.com), **Delta Vacations** (© 800/221-6666; www.deltavacations.com), **Continental Airlines Vacations** (© 800/301-3800; www.covacations.com), and **United Vacations** (© 888/854-3899; www.unitedvacations.com). Several big **online travel agencies**—Expedia, Travelocity, Orbitz, Site59, and

---

Tips **Ask Before You Go**

Before you invest in a package deal or an escorted tour:

- Always ask about the **cancellation policy.** Can you get your money back? Is there a deposit required?
- Ask about the **accommodations choices and prices** for each. Then look up the hotels' reviews in a Frommer's guide and check their rates online for your specific dates of travel. Also find out what types of rooms are offered.
- Request a complete **schedule.** (Escorted tours only)
- Ask about the **size** and demographics of the group. (Escorted tours only)
- Discuss what is included in the **price:** transportation, meals, tips, airport transfers, and so forth. (Escorted tours only)
- Finally, look for **hidden expenses.** Ask whether airport departure fees and taxes, for example, are included in the total cost—they rarely are.

Lastminute.com—also do a brisk business in packages.

Solar Tours (© 800/388-7652; www.solartours.com) is a wholesaler that offers a 7-day package tour to Barcelona that includes 3 days in Paris.

Spanish Heritage Tours (© 800/456-5050; www.shtours.com) is known for searching for low-cost airfare deals to Spain. The tour agent also features round-trip packages from the U.S. directly to Barcelona hotels (Tryp Apolo, Gallery, Hesperia Presidente, Melia, Avenida Palace, and Conde de Barcelona) for $1,299 to $1,549.

Discover Spain Vacations (© 800/227-5858; www.farandwide.com), the marketing arm of Iberia, is the most reliable tour operator and the agency used for air and land packages to Barcelona. Naturally, round-trip airfares on Iberia are included in the deal. Several fly/drive packages are also offered.

Travel packages are also listed in the travel section of your local Sunday newspaper. Or check ads in the national travel magazines such as *Arthur Frommer's Budget Travel Magazine, Travel + Leisure, National Geographic Traveler,* and *Condé Nast Traveler.*

12 Escorted General-Interest Tours

Escorted tours are structured group tours, with a group leader. The price usually includes everything from airfare to hotels, meals, tours, admission costs, and local transportation.

Despite the fact that escorted tours require big deposits and predetermine hotels, restaurants, and itineraries, many people derive security and peace of mind from the structure they offer. Escorted tours—whether they're navigated by bus, motorcoach, train, or boat—let travelers sit back and enjoy the trip without having to drive or worry about details. They take you to the maximum number of sights in the minimum amount of time with the least amount of hassle. They're particularly convenient for people with limited mobility and they can be a great way to make new friends.

On the downside, you'll have little opportunity for serendipitous interactions with locals. The tours can be jam-packed with activities, leaving little room for individual sightseeing, whim, or adventure—plus they often focus on the heavily touristed sites, so you miss out on many a lesser-known gem.

RECOMMENDED ESCORTED TOUR OPERATORS

There are many escorted tour companies to choose from, each offering transportation to and within Spain, prearranged hotel space, and such extras as bilingual tour guides and lectures. Many of these tours to Spain include excursions to Morocco or Portugal.

Some of the most expensive and luxurious tours are run by **Abercrombie & Kent International** (© 800/323-7308 or 630/954-2944; www.abercrombiekent.com), including deluxe 13- or 19-day tours of the Iberian Peninsula by train. Guests stay in fine hotels, ranging from a late medieval palace to the exquisite modern Hesperia on Avenida Castellana.

Trafalgar Tours (© 800/854-0103 or 212/689-8977; www.trafalgartours.com) offers a number of tours of Spain. One of the most popular offerings is an 18-day trip called "The Best of Spain" (this land-only package is $1,735; with land and air, it's $2,155–$2,565).

Insight Vacations "Highlights of Spain" is an 11-day tour that begins in Madrid, sweeps along the southern and eastern coasts, and concludes in Madrid. The company offers the tour for $1,370 to $1,785 including airfare, accommodations, and some meals. For information, contact your travel agent or Insight International (© **800/582-8380;** www. insightvacations.com).

Petrabax Tours (© **800/634-1188;** www.petrabax.com) attracts those who prefer to see Spain by bus, although fly/drive packages are also offered, featuring stays in *paradores* (high-standard,

state-run hotels—some modern, some in historic buildings). A number of city packages are also available, plus a 10-day trip that tries to capture Spain in a nutshell, with stops in places ranging from Madrid to Granada.

Recently, more and more special-interest tours to Madrid and Castile are being offered, including tours by **Archetours, Inc.** (© **800/770-3051;** www.archetours. com), which features tours devoted to Spanish architecture.

13 Special-Interest Trips

The **Barcelona Information Office** (www.barcelonaturisme.com) provides four detailed walks covering different architectural and artistic aspects of the city (Gòtic, Modernisme, Gourmet, and Picasso). They depart from the Plaça Catalunya, last between 1½ and 2 hours, and cost between 9.50€ and 14€ ($12–$18) per adult.

More personal—and expensive—walking trips are arranged by **My Favorite**

Things (© **637-265-405;** www.myft. net). These cover more off-beat and idiosyncratic aspects of Barcelona and cost up to 30€ ($38) per adult.

For food and wine lovers there's **Saboroso** (© **667-770-492;** www. saboroso.com), covering gastronomic gourmet tapas tours and visits to top Catalan vineyards such as Priorat and Penedés.

14 Recommended Books, Films & Music

FICTION & BIOGRAPHY
Denounced by some as superficial, James A. Michener's *Iberia* (Random House) remains the classic travelogue on Spain. The *Houston Post* claimed that this book "will make you fall in love with Spain."

The latest biography on one of the 20th century's most durable dictators is *Franco: A Concise Biography* (Thomas Dunne Books), which was released in the spring of 2002. Gabrielle Ashford Hodges documents with great flair the Orwellian repression and widespread corruption that marked the notorious regime of this "deeply flawed" politician.

The most famous Spanish novel is *Don Quixote* by Miguel de Cervantes. Readily available everywhere, it deals with the conflict between the ideal and the real in human nature. Despite the unparalleled

fame of Miguel de Cervantes within Spanish literature, very little is known about his life. One of the most searching biographies of the literary master is Jean Canavaggio's *Cervantes,* translated from the Spanish by J. R. Jones (Norton).

Although the work of Cervantes has attained an almost mystical significance in the minds of many Spaniards, in the words of Somerset Maugham, "It would be hard to find a work so great that has so many defects." Nicholas Wollaston's *Tilting at Don Quixote* (André Deutsch Publishers) punctures any illusions that the half-crazed Don is only a matter of good and rollicking fun.

Ernest Hemingway completed many works on Spain, none more notable than his novels of 1926 and 1940, respectively: *The Sun Also Rises* (Macmillan) and *For*

Tips Dial E for Easy

For quick directions on how to call Barcelona, see the "Telephones" listing in the "Fast Facts: Barcelona" section of chapter 4.

Whom the Bell Tolls (Macmillan), the latter based on his experiences in the Spanish Civil War. Don Ernesto's *Death in the Afternoon* (various editions) remains the English-language classic on bullfighting.

ECONOMIC, POLITICAL & SOCIAL HISTORY

For a firsthand account of the civil war and its devastating effects on Barcelona and Catalonia, George Orwell's *Homage to Catalonia* remains a classic. Irish writer Colm Tóibín takes a more light-hearted look at post-Orwell Barcelona, with plenty of anecdotes and colors through the eyes of a *güiri* (foreigner) in *Homage to Barcelona.* The city's most prolific writer, poet, and essayist is the late Manuel Vázquez Montalbán. His *Barcelonas* is more of an insider guidebook, which combines lively accounts of Catalan history, character, and culture with scathing wit and insight.

Barça: A People's Passion, by Jimmy Burns (Bloomsbury, 2000), is a dramatic history of the city's soccer team, the richest and possibly most politically charged soccer club in the world.

THE ARTS

Antoni Gaudí is the Catalan architect who most excites visitors' curiosity. The latest study is *Gaudi: A Biography,* by Gijs van Hensbergen (Perennial, 2003). The author claims Gaudí was "drunk on form," and that the architect still has not lost his power to astonish with his idiosyncratic and innovative designs.

Spain's most famous artist was the Malaga-born Pablo Picasso. Picasso spent his formative years in Barcelona, and the most controversial book about the late painter is *Picasso, Creator and Destroyer,* by Arianna Stassinopoulos Huffington (Simon & Schuster).

Catalonia's other headline-grabbing artist was Salvador Dalí. In *Salvador Dalí: A Biography* (Dutton), author Meryle Secrest asks: Was he a mad genius or a cunning manipulator?

Residents of Catalonia truthfully maintain that their unique language, culture, and history have been overshadowed (and squelched) by the richer and better-publicized accomplishments of Castile. Robert Hughes, a former art critic at *Time,* has written an elegant testament to the glories of the capital of this region: *Barcelona* (Knopf). This book offers a well-versed and witty articulation of the city's architectural and cultural legacy. According to the *New York Times,* the book is probably destined to become "a classic in the genre of urban history."

Andrés Segovia: An Autobiography of the Years 1893–1920 (Macmillan), with a translation by W. F. O'Brien, is worth seeking out if you want to know more about the great classical guitarist.

CUISINE

One of the best books out on the local gastronomy is written by an American. *Catalán Cuisine: Europe's Last Great Culinary Secret* (Grub Street, U.K.), by Colman Andrews, is a colorful exposé of food, wine, and culinary customs of Catalonia. Andrews's conversations with chefs, his descriptions of wild mushroom-picking and village food markets, and explanations of why the Catalans eat the way they do makes for terrific reading.

SPANISH CLASSICAL MUSIC

Three major **composers** stand out, two of whom were Catalans: Camprodón-born

Isaac Albeñiz—a child prodigy who played in piano concerts at the age of 4—with his *Iberia* suite and **Enrique Granados** from Lérida (now Lleida) with his lively *Goyescas*. **Manuel de Falla,** an ascetic from Andaluz (an unusual combination) was renowned for his *Three Cornered Hat* ballet.

The most talented Catalan **musician** of modern times was cellist **Pablo (Pau) Casals,** while one of today's leading opera singers (alongside Placido Domingo) is **Josep Carreras.** Barcelona's very own **Montserrat Caballé** is Spain's most loved soprano.

Suggested Barcelona Itineraries

You can cover quite a few of central Barcelona's monuments and architectural highlights in just a day. But the more time you have available, the more justice you can do to the wealth of sights in and near the city. Here are some recommendations on how to spend your time.

1 The Best of Barcelona in 1 Day

This is going to be a very full day so get an early start at the **Plaça Cataluña.** Spend the morning wandering down **La Rambla** to the statue and **Mirador de Colón,** beside the port. Return via the **Plaça Reial** and explore the neighboring **Barri Gòtic** with its central **Catedral.** In the afternoon visit Antoni Gaudí's unfinished masterpiece, **La Sagrada Família** and the **Parc Güell,** before returning to the **Raval** and **Poble Sec** districts on the western side of **La Rambla.** From there take the funicular to the top of **Montjuïc** for a fine view of Barcelona and its harbor. Explore the gardens and castle museum and if there's time pop into the Museu Nacional d'Art de Catalunya for a glimpse of the finest collection of Romanesque relics in Spain.

❶ Plaça de Cataluña
Located at the top of La Rambla and midway between the medieval Old City and wide-avenued, 19th-century L'Eixample, this circular plaza, with its fountains and sculptures, is the cultural hub of the city. Surrounded by large stores, open-air cafes, and hotels, it's a place to watch passersby, listen to the Latino buskers, feed the pigeons, and even try to join in and dance the *sardana* on festive occasions. As the afternoon proceeds it gets increasingly crowded and colorful. See p. 63.

❷ La Rambla ★★★
Also known as Les Ramblas, this mile-long avenue is divided into five distinct sections named successively Canaletes, Estudis, Sant Josep, Caputxins, and Santa Monica. It's a stage set of human statues, jugglers, singers, eccentrics, misfits, transvestites, caged animals, kiosks, cafes, and radiant flower stalls. Originally called *ramla* (riverbed) by the Arabs, it's the favorite strolling place for Barcelonese and visitors alike. For year-round atmosphere there's nowhere else like it in Spain. See p. 63.

❸ Mirador de Colón (Columbus Monument)
Situated at the port end of La Rambla, this ornate bronze statue in honor of the Genovese sailor who discovered you-know-where was built during Barcelona's 19th-century industrial boom. After 10pm you can get to the top by elevator and enjoy marvellous views of the harbor and Ciutat Vella. Notice, too, the deliberate mistake: He's pointing east across the Mediterranean to Majorca instead of west toward the Atlantic. See p. 164.

The Best of Barcelona in 1 Day

1. Plaça de Catalunya
2. La Rambla
3. Mirador de Colón
4. Café de l'Opera
5. Plaça Reial
6. Barri Gòtic
7. Catedral
8. Can Culleretes
9. Montjuïc
10. Montjuic Castle Café
11. Sagrada Famíilia
12. Parc Güell

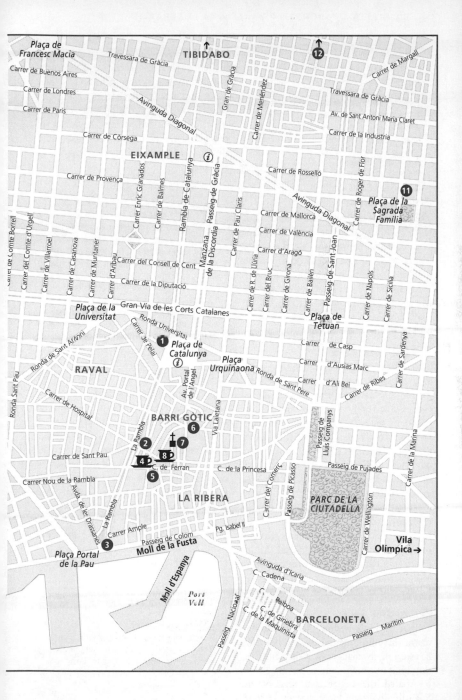

Plaça de
Francesc Macia

Travessara de Gràcia

TIBIDABO ↑

↑
12

Carrer de Buenos Aires

Carrer de Margall

Carrer de Londres

Avinguda Diagonal

Carrer de Gràcia

Carrer de Menéndez

Travessara de Gràcia

Carrer de Paris

Av. de Sant Antoni Maria Claret

Carrer de Còrsega

Carrer de la Industria

EIXAMPLE ⓘ

Carrer de Rosselló

Carrer de Roger de Flor

Carrer de Provença

Avinguda Diagonal

Plaça de la
Sagrada
Família

11

Carrer Enric Granados

Carrer de Balmes

Rambla de Catalunya

Passeig de Gràcia

Carrer de Pau Claris

Carrer de Mallorca

Carrer de Nàpols

Carrer de Sicilia

Carrer de València

Carrer del Comte Borrell

Carrer del Comte d'Urgell

Carrer de Villarroel

Carrer de Casanova

Carrer de Muntaner

Carrer d'Aribau

Carrer del Consell de Cent

Manzana
de la Discòrdia

Carrer de R. de Llúria

Carrer del Bruc

Carrer de Girona

Carrer de Bailèn

Passeig de Sant Joan

Carrer d'Aragó

Carrer de la Diputació

Plaça de la
Universitat

Gran Via de les Corts Catalanes

Ronda Universitat

Carrer de Pelai

Plaça de
Catalunya ⓘ

Plaça de
Tetuan

Carrer de Casp

Carrer d'Ausias Marc

Carrer de Sardenya

Ronda de Sant Antoni

RAVAL

Plaça
Urquinaona Ronda de Sant Pere

Carrer d'Ali Bei

Carrer de Ribes

Ronda Sant Pau

Carrer de Hospital

Av. Portal de l'Angel

BARRI GÒTIC

6

Via Laietana

Carrer de la Marina

La Rambla

2

7

Carrer de Sant Pau

4 8

C. de Ferran

C. de la Princesa

Passeig de Pujades

5

Carrer Nou de la Rambla

LA RIBERA

Carrer del Comerç

Passeig de Picasso

Passeig de Lluís Companys

PARC DE LA
CIUTADELLA

Carrer de Wellington

Avda. de les Drassanes

La Rambla

Carrer Ample

Passeig de Colom
Moll de la Fusta

Pg. Isabel II

Vila
Olímpica →

3

Plaça Portal
de la Pau

Avinguda d'Icària

C. Cadena

Moll d'Espanya

Port
Vell

C. Balboa

C. de Ginebra
C. de la Maquinista

BARCELONETA

Passeig Nacional

Passeig Marítim

53

> **◀TAKE A BREAK**
> Halfway down La Rambla, **Café de l'Opera,** La Rambla 74 (② **93-317-75-85**), is a 19th-century Parisian-style cafe. Its murals, iron columns, and wall mirrors with etchings evoke a more elegant age, when waiters with bow ties served you with delightful indifference. It's the ideal spot to sit back, enjoy a quality coffee, and watch the nonstop activity outside.

❺ Plaça Reial ✹

This is one of the city's great old squares, with neoclassical pillars and archways, 19th-century lampposts, slender aging palm trees, and enough semi-resident marginals—from drug addicts to transsexuals—to fill an Almodóvar movie. More ominous in the past, today it's virtually become a tourist attraction. Watch out for pickpockets, though.

❻ Barri Gòtic ✹✹✹

Said to be the largest inhabited (and probably most densely populated) medieval quarter in Europe, the narrow-alleyed Barri Gòtic really merits a minimum of a half-day's leisurely exploration. At night its illuminated streets and buildings give it a magical touch. If you're only here for a day, then the **Catedral** (see below; p. 160) is an absolute must. Also not to be missed are the central **Plaça del Rei** (p. 161) with its two key monuments, the **Museu d'Història de la Ciutat** (p. 161), built over a complete subterranean Roman township, and the **Palau Reial Major** (p. 161) in whose **Saló del Tinell** Columbus introduced American Indians to Spain's monarchs for the first time.

❼ Catedral ✹✹✹

Originally built within the old Roman town, this monumental place of worship has seen many changes over the centuries, though it was mercifully one of the few to be spared the destructive fury of the Spanish Civil War. Here the young Santa

Eulalia—cruelly martyred for protesting Dacian's treatment of Christians during his repressive rule—is buried. Don't miss the 14th-century choir stalls and chapter house and roof (extra charges payable); or the unexpectedly delightful cloister, which harbors tall palms, a cluster of orange trees, and a pond with geese amid the surrounding Gothic and Renaissance splendor.

> **◻TAKE A BREAK**
> For an atmospheric lunch you can't do better than Barcelona's oldest restaurant (est. 1786), **Can Culleretes,** Quintana 5 (② **93-317-64-85**). It's tucked away in a secretive lane in the heart of the Barri Gòtic. You won't be the only non-Catalan visitor—the place is in too many guidebooks—but the restaurant is a monument, the service and decor from another age, and the traditional food and wine pretty good. See p. 124.

❾ Montjuïc ✹✹

Topped by an imposing castle that is now a military museum, this distinctive hill on the city's west flank also offers some of the best vistas of the Catalan capital. After radical improvements prior to the 1992 Olympic Games (don't forget to take an quick peek at the stadium), it's now also the city's greatest green zone with a wealth of walkways, parklands, leisure areas, and cultural attractions to explore. Get there by the funicular from Poble Sec or by the more vertiginous *teleféric,* which carries you high above the harbor. See p. 181.

> **◻ TAKE A BREAK**
> Tucked away inside the castle with a patio section where you can sit outside in good weather, the **Montjuïc Castle Café** is a great spot for relaxing and savoring the old *"castell"* ambience.

⑪ Sagrada Família 👁👁

This is where you'll want to start your evening. Abandoned for decades, the still-unfinished cathedral finally saw restoration and expansion work carried out when its hermitlike architect, Antoni Gaudí (who was killed by a tram in 1926 and whose tomb can be viewed in the crypt), came back into fashion in the 1990s. The four original spires—designed by the master himself—are generally acknowledged to be far superior to the additional quartet. You can now take an elevator up to the top of one of the towers and enjoy the fine view. Loved and reviled in equal measure, the building remains unique. Current construction progresses slowly, however, and even the most optimistic forecaster doesn't believe the whole project will reach completion for at least another decade. See p. 175.

⑫ Parc Güell 👁👁

You can imagine gremlins living in this unique fairy-tale park located high up in the city and loved by children and adults alike. Look out for its mosaic serpent and Hansel and Gretel houses at the entrance (one of which is a tiny museum, the Centre d'Interpretació i Acollida, devoted to depicting creator Gaudí's building methods). At its center, up some steps, the Banc de Trencadís—a multicolored ceramic bench—curves around a spacious esplanade, while behind it footpaths climb into the pine woods of Vallcarca and Monte Carmel, offering scenic views through the trees of the city below. See p. 180.

2 The Best of Barcelona in 2 Days

On the first day, follow the itinerary described above. On the second day, stroll through the pond- and garden-filled **Parc de la Ciutadella** and, time permitting, visit the zoo. Then explore the narrow lanes of **La Ribera,** with its **Picasso Museum** and imposing **Santa María del Mar** church, and walk down to the old (but gentrified) maritime quarter and beachfront of **La Barceloneta,** with its modern adjoining Port Olímpic area. It's the ideal spot for an atmospheric seafood lunch. In the afternoon wander around **Port Vell** and explore the regenerated **El Raval** district.

❶ Parc de la Ciutadella 👁👁

Once the site of a fort (Ciutadella is Catalan for citadel), this verdant park is the most attractive and popular spot in lower Barcelona, complete with two lush but small botanical gardens, a Gaudí-designed fountain (La Cascada) with a huge statue of a primeval elephant, and a quiet lake where you can go rowing. Other attractions include the Castell dels Tres Dragons (Castle of the Three Dragons) and Parlement de Catalunya (Catalan Parliament), which you can visit free if you have time to make an appointment. The zoo's well worth a look, whatever your age, though its former main attraction Copito de Nieve (Snowflake),

the albino gorilla, has long since gone to the great forest in the sky.

❷ La Ribera 👁👁

The western part of La Ciutat Vella is really two districts, El Born and Sant Pere (referring to the area's oldest square and church, respectively). The name La Ribera actually means "the shore," as the sea once reached its southern edge. The central Carrer Montcada is lined with museums and the whole former medieval merchants' quarter is packed with traditional shops, tiny squares, and narrow streets named after various local trades that were carried out here—such as Carrer Carders (woolcombers), Carrer

Assaonadors (tanners), and Carrer Flassaders (blanketweavers). See p. 166.

❸ Museu Picasso ✵✵✵

By far the most popular art museum in town, the Picasso is tastefully spread throughout a quintet of fine old mansions in the heart of La Ribera. Be prepared for long lines but if you do manage to squeeze it into your time-challenged schedule, don't miss the Malagueño artist's version of Velázquez's *La Meninas*. The museum concentrates mainly on more conventional works and etchings by the adolescent Picasso, who arrived in town with his family in 1895 and wasted no time in opening his very first (and very modest) studio in Carrer de la Plata. See p. 169.

> **TAKE A BREAK**
> **Tèxtil Cafè,** Carrer Montcada 12 (✆ 93-268-25-98), is a charming spot nestled in the patio of the 14th-century mansion containing the Textile Museum, just a few steps away from the Picasso Museum. Enjoy your coffee and pastries in an elegant year-round setting. Even in winter—notwithstanding rare rainy days—you can still sit outside, under gas heaters.

❺ Santa María del Mar Church ✵

Once upon a time this magnificent church, with its soaring vaults and wonderful stained-glass windows, stood right on the shore of the Mediterranean (as the district's name, La Ribera, implies). It was the focal point of a then-vibrant seafaring and trading quarter which eventually receded, as did the sea. Today it's one of the best-preserved Gothic monuments in the city, and less crowded than some of the more renowned sights. See p. 166.

❻ La Barceloneta (& Port Olímpic) ✵

Built on the compact triangle of land (reclaimed from marshes) between the Port Vell and first of the city beaches

(Sant Sebastiá), this 18th-century working-class zone has today become more gentrified and sought after by visitors and residents alike. Its once-neglected beach is now well cared for and has a palm-lined promenade where folk walk their pooches. The original, much-loved *chiringuitos* (shacks) that bordered the shore and served delicious seafood dishes were demolished pre-1992 to make way for today's more acceptably salubrious establishments (still known as *chiringuitos*), which sell exactly the same food at higher prices. Moving with the times, it remains a great location (and a fun spot to stop and eat paella), as is the vibrant adjoining Port Olímpic with its long promenade, beaches, marinas, and even trendier eating spots and nightclubs.

> **TAKE A BREAK**
> You can't pass though Barceloneta without sampling one of its finest—and definitely oldest—seafood eating spots, **Can Costa,** Passeig de Joan de Borbón (✆ 93-221-59-03). It's located a block back from the waterfront, as all the genuine locales are. This is the real McCoy, with excellent *fideuà de paella* (made with noodles not rice) and baby calamares that are worth leaving home for. Can gets busy for lunch, so arrive early—and that's any time before 2pm in Spain. (p. 151).

❽ Marina Port Vell ✵

The main port is the most visibly changed part of Barcelona's waterfront, which for decades notoriously "turned its back on the sea." Today the once drab industrial zone, where piles of containers stood under sad looking palm trees, has been cleansed, revitalized, and transformed. At its northern end the large marina beside the older Moll de Barceloneta is lined with international vessels of all shapes and sizes. A promenade runs south around the harbor, past two large modern jetties: the Moll d'Espanya, whose exclusive Club

The Best of Barcelona in 2 Days

1. Parc de la Ciutadella
2. La Ribera
3. Museu Picasso
4. Tèxtil Cafè
5. Santa María del Mar
6. La Barceloneta
   (& Port Olímpic)
7. Can Costa
8. Marina Port Vell
9. Museu Marítim
10. El Raval
11. Bar Marsella

Maritim, aquarium, IMAX cinema, and Maremagnum zone of trendy shops and nightspots are all linked to the promenade by the curving Rambla de Mar footbridge; and the Moll de Barcelona, with its modern World Trade Center and Torre de Jaume 1 tower, opposite the 14th-century Reials Drassanes (Royal Shipyards) museum (p. 188 and see below.)

⑨ Museu Maritim

The Gothic arches inside the Royal Shipyards building loom impressively over what's probably the best nautical museum in the Mediterranean: a superb testament to Barcelona's great naval past. Check out the marvellous "Great Adventure of the Sea" collection with its full-scale replica of Don Juan of Austria's Royal Galley from the decisive 16th-century Battle of Lepanto when Spain defeated the Ottomans. There are smaller models of Magellan's world-navigating *Santa María,* and one of the earliest submarines, the *Ictíneo;* and just outside you can go on board the old *Santa Eulalia* sailing ship moored in Moll de la Fusta. See p. 188.

⑩ El Raval

Once largely a seedy, run-down district with red-light sections (some of which still exist) and dilapidated buildings, this is another rejuvenated corner of the city, more polyglot than most due to the large number of immigrant residents. In 2000, the center was bulldozed to provide much-needed breathing space in the form of a brand-new Rambla complete with trees, benches, and kids' play areas. It was all part of an ambitious "Raval obert al cel" (Raval open to the sky) project. Around it some of the city's most stimulating new art galleries sprang up, spearheaded by the MACBA (Museum of Contemporary Art of Barcelona). Still, there's the continuing proliferation of rough edges that, for some, enhances the barrio's appeal. And a few classic buildings like Gaudí's Palau Güell and the Romanesque Sant Pau del Camp evoke a real sense of history in this atmospheric western corner of the Ciutat Vella. (See p. 172 and 173.)

🍵 TAKE A BREAK

It's the end of your second day, so why not treat yourself to a well-earned snifter of cloudy anis-favored pastis at **Bar Marsella,** Carrer Sant Pau 65 (✆ **93-442-72-63**)? A Provençal-cum-Catalan landmark to hedonism, it's a 19th-century oasis of huge mirrors, heavy drapes, creaky rafters, and high chandeliers. The place has been run by the same family for five generations. Among its first customers was a young Jean Genet, reveling in the degeneracy of those early Raval days.

---

3 The Best of Barcelona in 3 Days

Spend the first 2 days as described in the above two itineraries. On Day 3, make a leisurely morning exploration of **L'Eixample,** the 19th-century district that expanded the city away from the congested Barri Gòtic and Ciutat Vella. This is where you'll find Barcelona's widest avenue, the **Passeig de Gràcia,** and the greatest concentration of *moderniste* (Art Nouveau) architecture, highlighted by the **Manzana de la Discordia,** where Gaudí's **Casa Batlló,** Puig i Cadalfach's **Casa Amatller,** and Domènech i Muntaner's **Casa Lleo Morera** are all very close to one another. Most famous of all is another Gaudí gem, **Casa Milà** (popularly known as **La Pedrera**), farther along the *paseo.* Pop into Vinçon, the city's famed design emporium and then continue up to the villagelike district of **Gràcia** at the northern edge of the Eixample. Return to the lower Eixample area to have lunch in **Casa Calvet,** a restaurant housed in one of Gaudí's early buildings. (This whole area is also covered by Walk 4 in Chapter 8, "Strolling Around Barcelona.")

The Best of Barcelona in 3 Days

Plaça de Francesc Macia

Carrer de Buenos Aires

Carrer de Londres

Carrer de Paris

Avinguda Diagonal

Travessara de Gràcia

Travessara de Gràcia

TIBIDABO

Gran de Gràcia

Carrer de la Industria

| 0 | 1/4 mi |
| 0 | 0.25 km |

✝ Church

☕ Take a Break

ⓘ Information

Carrer de Còrsega

EIXAMPLE

Carrer de Rosselló

Avinguda Diagonal

Carrer de Roger de Flor

Carrer de Comte Borrell

Carrer de Provença

Carrer Enric Granados

Carrer de Balmes

Rambla de Catalunya

Passeig de Gràcia

Manzana de la Discordia

Carrer de Pau Claris

Carrer de Mallorca

Carrer de R. de Lluria

Carrer de València

Carrer d'Aragó

Passeig de Sant Joan

Carrer de Napols

Carrer de Sicilia

Carrer del Comte d'Urgel

Carrer de Villarroel

Carrer de Casanova

Carrer de Muntaner

Carrer d'Aribau

Carrer del Consell de Cent

Carrer de la Diputació

Carrer del Bruc

Carrer de Girona

Carrer de Bailén

Plaça de la Universitat

Gran Via de les Corts Catalanes

Plaça de Tetuan

Ronda Sant Pau

Ronda de Sant Antoni

Carrer de Pelai

Ronda Universitat

Plaça de Catalunya

Plaça Urquinaona

Ronda de Sant Pere

Carrer de Casp

Carrer d'Ausias Marc

Carrer d'Ali Bei

Carrer de Ribes

RAVAL

Av. Portal de l'Angel

Carrer de Hospital

BARRI GÒTIC

Via Laietana

Carrer de Sant Pau

La Rambla

Carrer Nou de la Rambla

C. de Ferran

C. de la Princesa

Carrer del Comerç

Passeig de Picasso

Passeig de Lluis Companys

Passeig de Pujades

Carrer de Wellington

LA RIBERA

PARC DE LA CIUTADELLA

Avda. de les Drassanes

La Rambla

Carrer Ample

Passeig de Colom

Pg. Isabel II

Avinguda d'Icaria

Vila Olimpica →

Plaça Portal de la Pau

Moll de la Fusta

Moll d'Espanya

C. Cadena

C. Balbos

C. de Ginebra

C. de la Maquinista

Passeig Nacional

Port Vell

FRANCE

Barcelona

★ Madrid

PORTUGAL

SPAIN

1. Passeig de Gràcia
2. Manzana de la Discordia
3. Casa Alfonso
4. Casa Milà (La Pedrera)
5. Gràcia
6. Casa Calvet
7. Monestir de Pedralbes
8. Tibidabo
9. Merbeyé
10. Collserola Park

In the afternoon catch the Metro up to **Pedralbes** and visit its monastery and palace. Then continue up to up to **Tibidabo** by funicular for the best panoramic views of the city and coast stretching north toward the Costa Brava. In the evening, wander into the adjoining **Collserola Park.**

❶ Passeig de Gràcia

Compared with the color and life of La Rambla, this 60m-wide (197-ft.) avenue—with its traffic-filled center, two pedestrian mini-*paseos,* and four rows of trees—is both more urban and more cosmopolitan. Known locally as the "Queen of Paseos," and lined with elegant buildings, trendy shops, and wonderful eating spots, it rises gently from Plaza Cataluña through the heart of the 19th-century Eixample, ending at the villagelike district of Gràcia.

❷ Manzana de la Discordia

A short way up the *paseo* you'll find this remarkable block, with its trio of architectural standouts of the *moderniste* movement: the inimitable Gaudí's frilly and curvaceous **Casa Batlló,** Puig i Cadafalch's staid Flemish style **Casa Amatller,** and Domènech i Muntaner's decidedly eccentric **Casa Lleo Morera,** compared by some to a collapsed wedding cake. Manzana means both "block" and "apple" in Spanish, so the double-meaning could also refer to the mythical golden Apple of Discord, which was to be given to the winner of a beauty contest judged by Paris. Here you can decide for yourself which building comes out on top.

⓷ TAKE A BREAK
Casa Alfonso, Roger de Llúria 6 (ⓒ **93-301-97-83**), is a great tapas bar that serves a wide enough variety of mouthwatering snacks and *raciones* to satisfy anyone with an early-morning appetite. Their Jabugo ham from Huelva province is considered by many to be Spain's best. At this hour, though, you may simply prefer to settle for a *café con leche* and admire the aromatic rows of hanging pork. See p. 146.

❹ Casa Milà (La Pedrera)

You've not finished with *moderniste* architecture by a long shot. On its own, a bit farther up the avenue, is what many feel to be the most striking building of all: Casa Milà (by Gaudí again), also known as "La Pedrera" or the Rock quarry, since its twisted verandas and frivolous chimneys are all made of bizarrely sculptured limestone from Montjuïc. It's really a block of apartments, the most original in the entire city, and the high point of any visit comes when you get on to the roof and enjoy the Mary Poppins–like cityscape that's visible past those astonishing chimneys. See p. 174.

❺ Gràcia

This cosily intimate district at the northern end of the Passeig de Gràcia, just past the Avinguda Diagonal, started out as a small village built round an 18th-century convent; then, during Barcelona's Industrial Revolution, it became a working-class zone where a famed revolt over the re-introduction of military drafting is commemorated by a tall bell tower that stands in Plaça Ruis i Taulet. Today it's a sought-after and slightly gentrified corner of the city in which many traditional features, such as vintage *herbolarios* (homeopathic shops) and fortunetellers, have attractively lingered on amid the abundance of tiny squares and narrow lanes. Its mood is vaguely bohemian and many artists have chosen to establish their homes and workshops here. The August festival is a riot of street fun that lasts a week. Don't miss it if you're here then. See p. 179.

> **⑥ TAKE A BREAK**
> Head back down into the lower Eixample for an indulgent (but not too indulgent if you want to get through the afternoon) lunch at **Casa Calvet**, Carrer Casp 48 (℄ **93-412-40-12**). A Gaudí-designed ground-floor restaurant, its moderniste setting is complemented by a new-and-old blend of top Catalan cuisine. See p. 142.

⑦ Monestir de Pedralbes

Situated high up in one of the city's classiest suburbs alongside a Catalan Gothic church, this 14th-century gem founded by Queen Elisenda is one of Barcelona's oldest and most attractive religious buildings. Once inside, take a peek at its secluded garden and fountain, explore the beautiful three-floored cloister, and visit the pharmacy, kitchen, and high-vaulted refectory with restored artifacts of daily convent life. An attraction added in 1993 is the superb Thyssen-Bornemisza art collection of European masters highlighted by Fra Angelico's moving *Madonna of Humility* and Ferrer Bassa's murals in the tiny Sant Miquel chapel. See p. 190.

⑧ Tibidabo

You can arrive at this strange mixture of the ecclesiastic and the brassy either by Tramvia Blau ("Blue Tram"; weekends only in winter) and funicular lift, or—less dramatically—take a bus all the way up from Plaça Dr. Andreu. At the top, 488m (1,600 ft.) above the sea with sensational views of the city and coast, is one of the few places in the world you'll find a church next to a fun-fair. The church, named Sagrat Cor (or Holy Heart), is an unattractive, gray neo-Gothic, and its silhouette can be seen from so many miles away that it's become one of the city's most familiar landmarks. The fun-fair's been in operation for over 80 years and its truly vintage attractions include the wheezy Aeromàgic mountain ride and a 1928 flight simulator. The name is said to come from the Devil's words to Christ: "*ti dabo,*" meaning "I give to you," signifying Satan's offering to Jesus all he could see before him if he would follow the fallen angel. Tempting enough when you consider the panorama below.

> **⑨ TAKE A BREAK**
> **Merbeyé**, Plaça Doctor Andreu, Tibidabo (℄ **93-417-92-79**), is a showy and colorful cocktail bar–cum–cafe. It has a plush jazz-oriented lounge, with cool background music, plus a more tranquil open-air terrace where you can sit and unwind after the day's sightseeing over a daiquiri or *café con leche* and enjoy the great view.

⑩ Collserola Park

To the southwest of Tibidabo, on the same high massif, is this splendid 8,000-hectare (19,768-acre) area of wild countryside, where footpaths wind amid the oak forests and offer occasional spectacular vistas. Within the park are farmhouses, chapels, and springs, including the charming Font de la Budellera. Along the way you'll also see plaques with verses by the Catalan poet Jacint Verdaguer. (See the small museum dedicated to him inside the 18th-c. Villa Joana.) A far more recent eye-catcher is the 15-year-old Norman Foster–designed Torre de Collserola, shaped like a giant syringe, which is just 5 minutes' stroll away from Tibidabo (see above). There's an unbeatable view from the top, accessible by a vertigo-inducing elevator. At night you can see its lights flashing from way below.

4

Getting to Know Barcelona

Blessed with rich and fertile soil, an excellent harbor, and a hardworking population, Barcelona has always been prosperous. When Madrid was still a dusty Castilian backwater, Barcelona was a powerful, diverse capital, influenced by the empires that had their eye on this Mediterranean jewel. Rome, North African Muslims, the Visigoths, Charlemagne-era France, and Castile all overran Barcelona, and each left a unique and indelible mark on the region's identity.

The Catalans themselves are also marked by a distinct character. In their own words, they are a mixture of *seny* (common sense) and *rauxa* (which can best be translated as being predisposed to moments of madness). These two poles are evident in almost every aspect of Barcelonese life: a group of suited businesspeople singing in a local bar, an elegant street that features a bizarre piece of sculpture, or the entire city stopping to watch their beloved soccer team, Barça, compete against their archrivals, Madrid. They liken Barcelona to a

modern and vibrant European metropolis with an enormous respect for tradition and culture.

Landmark Gothic buildings and world-class museums fill the historic city of Barcelona, while the whimsical creations of the *moderniste* movement and cutting-edge contemporary architecture highlight the newer part of town. And an array of nightlife (Barcelona is a *big* party spot) and shopping possibilities, plus nearby wineries, ensures that you'll be entertained round-the-clock. It makes for some serious sightseeing; you'll need plenty of time not only to take everything in but to appreciate the city's unique, hidden charm.

The aim of this chapter is to introduce you to Barcelona's various multi-faceted *barris,* or districts, and to advise on how to get around by public transport (an excellent value) as well as on foot. Our "Fast Facts: Barcelona" section at the end briefly gets down to the nitty gritty and gives you practical information on everything from local taxes to tipping.

1 Essentials

VISITOR INFORMATION

Barcelona has two types of tourist offices. The autonomous government (the Generalitat) office deals with **Catalonia** in general. Its office is in the grandiose **Palau Robert,** Passeig de Gràcia 107 (© **93-238-40-00;** www.gencat.net/probert), where there are often exhibitions on aspects of Catalan culture. It's at the junction of Passeig de Gràcia and Diagonal and open daily from 10am to 7pm. The City Council *(Ajuntament)* runs **Turisme de Barcelona,** the source for information on the city itself. Its main office is located underground at the Plaça de Catalunya s/n (© **80-711-72-22** from inside Spain, or 93-368-37-30 from outside; www.barcelonaturisme.com). It has loads of information on the city, a hotel booking service, a gift shop, and a branch of

---

Tips Officer! Officer!

There are four police forces in Catalonia: the Guardia Urbana (whose main responsibility is traffic), the Policía Nacional (National Police), the Guardia Civil (Civil Guard), and the Mossos d'Escuadra (Catalonia's autonomous police force). Tourists are more likely to deal with the latter at the Turisme-Atenció station, Les Ramblas 43 (© **93-344-13-00**). It's open 24 hours, and there are officers who speak various languages. This is where you can report petty theft for insurance purposes. For more on health and safety, see p. 24.

---

the bank Caixa de Catalunya where you can change money. The office is open daily from 9am to 9pm.

The same organization has an office at the **Estació Central de Barcelona-Sants (Sants Railway Station),** Plaça dels Països Catalans (no phone; Metro: Sants-Estació). In summer, it's open daily from 8am to 8pm; in the off season, it is open Monday through Friday from 8am to 8pm, Saturday and Sunday from 8am to 2pm. Another branch is located on the Plaça Sant Jaume (Carrer Ciutat 2). It's open Monday through Friday 9am to 8pm, Saturday 10am to 8pm, and Sunday and holidays 10am to 2pm. There are also branches at the Barcelona airport at terminals A and B that are open 9am to 9pm daily. These offices are the places to pick up discount sightseeing cards such as the Barcelona Card (see below). In summer the Casaques Vermelles (Red Jackets) take to the streets. These are multilingual hosts ready to answer any queries tourists may have.

CITY LAYOUT

MAIN SQUARES, STREETS & ARTERIES Plaça de Catalunya (**Plaza de Cataluña** in Spanish) is the city's heart; the world-famous **La Rambla**—also known as Les Ramblas—its main artery. La Rambla begins at the Plaça Portal de la Pau, with its 49m-high (161-ft.) monument to Columbus, opposite the port, and stretches north to the Plaça de Catalunya. Along this wide promenade you'll find newsstands, stalls selling birds and flowers, portrait painters, and cafe tables and chairs, where you can sit and watch the passing parade. Moving northward along La Rambla, the area on your left is **El Raval,** the largest neighborhood in Barcelona, and to your right is the **Barri Gòtic (Gothic Quarter).** These two neighborhoods, plus the area of **La Ribera,** which lies farther to your right across another main artery—the Vía Laietana—make up the sizable **Ciutat Vella (Old City).** Within these three neighborhoods are two sub-regions. One is the infamous **Barri Xinès,** or **Barrio Chino** (literally, **Chinese Quarter,** though this is no Chinatown; see below), near the eastern end of El Raval bordering La Rambla. The other is El Born—prosperous in the Middle Ages and today Barcelona's bastion of cool—which is in the lower port-side pocket of La Ribera. Because this whole condensed, character-filled area is large—though not as large as the sprawling but amorphous Eixample (see below)—I have sub-divided all its attractions into El Raval, Barri Gòtic, and La Ribera.

Across the **Plaça de Catalunya** La Rambla becomes **Rambla Catalunya** with the elegant **Passeig de Gràcia** running parallel to the immediate right. These are the two main arteries of the **Eixample,** or the Extension. This is where most of the jewels of the *modernisme* period, including key works by Antoni Gaudí, dot the harsh grids of

Greater Barcelona

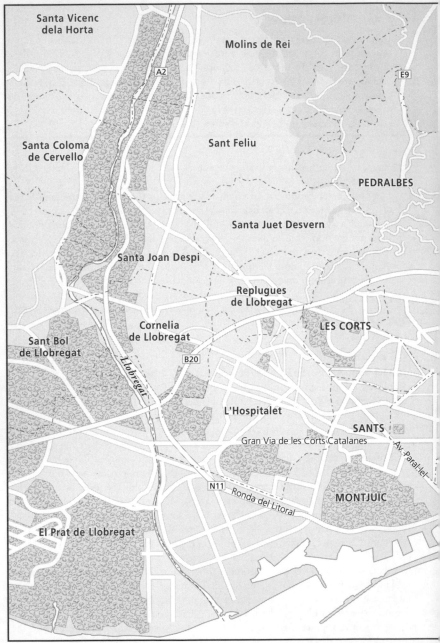

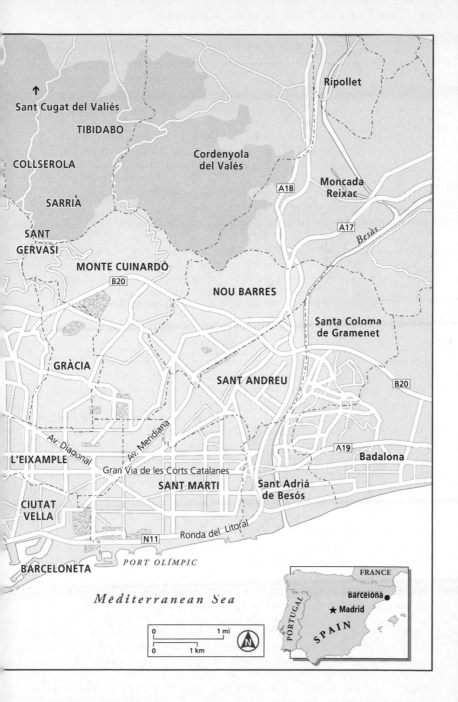

Sant Cugat del Valiés

TIBIDABO

Ripollet

COLLSEROLA

Cordenyola
del Valés

A18

Moncada
Reixac

SARRIÀ

A17

Besàs

SANT
GERVASI

MONTE CUINARDÓ

B20

NOU BARRES

Santa Coloma
de Gramenet

GRÀCIA

SANT ANDREU

B20

Av. Diagonal

Av. Meridiana

A19

Badalona

L'EIXAMPLE

Gran Via de les Corts Catalanes

SANT MARTI

Sant Adriá
de Besós

CIUTAT
VELLA

Ronda del Litoral

N11

BARCELONETA

PORT OLÍMPIC

Mediterranean Sea

FRANCE

Barcelona

★ Madrid

PORTUGAL

SPAIN

0   1 mi

0   1 km

N

Value **The Barcelona Card**

An ideal way to appreciate Barcelona better and save money at the same time is with the Barcelona Card, which is sold at tourist offices, El Prat airport, Sants railway station, the Estació Nord bus station, and various branches of the Corte Inglés. It's definitely a bargain if you stay in the city for more than an afternoon and do any sightseeing. For adults, it costs 23€ ($29) for 2 days, 28€ ($35) for 3 days, 31€ ($39) for 4 days, and 34€ ($43) for 5 days. For children 4 to 12 years old, the card costs 4€ ($5) less for each of the above options.

The 24-hour card covers unlimited travel on all public transport, and is valid for a free walking tour.

Culture vultures who hold the card can get discounts of 20% to 100% in all museums. Discounts on a host of theaters, shows, and attractions such as the aquarium and the Golondrinas pleasure boats are also on the menu, as are discounts in bars, restaurants, and some shops. The cards specify where they can be used. For those age 65 and above, the card is less of a bargain since seniors get discounts for museums and galleries anyway. Better just to get a transportation pass.

this graceful, middle-class neighborhood. Both end at the **Diagonal,** a major crosstown artery that also serves as the city's business and commercial hub. Northward across the Diagonal is the suburb of **Gràcia.** Once a separate village, it makes up for in sheer atmosphere what it lacks in notable monuments.

The other areas of interest for visitors are **Montjuïc,** the bluff to the southwest of the city, and the maritime area of **Barceloneta** and the beaches. The former is the largest green zone in the city, contains some its top museums, and was the setting for the principal events of the 1992 Summer Olympic Games. Barceloneta is a peninsula that has long been the city's populist playground, with dozens of fish restaurants, some facing the beaches that sprawl north along the coast. The other, higher mountain is **Tibidabo,** looming behind the city to the northwest; it has great views of both the city and the Mediterranean. It also has an amusement park and a kitsch pseudo-Gothic church that aspires to emulate Paris's Sacré Coeur.

FINDING AN ADDRESS/MAPS   Finding a Barcelona address doesn't generally pose too many problems. The Eixample district is built on a grid system, so by learning the cross street you can easily find the place you are looking for. Barcelona is hemmed in on one side by the sea *(mar)* and the mountain of Tibidabo *(montaña)* on the other, so often people just describe a place as being on the *mar* or *montaña* side of the street in L'Eixample. The Ciutat Vella, or Old City, is a little more confusing and you will need a good map (available in the news kiosks along La Rambla) to find specific places. The designation S/N *(sin número)* means that the building has no number, though this is mainly limited to large buildings and monuments. In built-up Barcelona, the symbol ° designates the floor (for example: the first floor is 1°). Street names are in Catalan. Some people still refer to them in Spanish but there is very little difference between the two and it shouldn't cause any confusion. The word for "street" (*carrer* in Catalan and *calle* in Spanish) is nearly always dropped; that is, Carrer Ferran is simply referred to as Ferran. *Passeig* (*paseo* in Spanish) and *avinguda* (*avenida* in Spanish), meaning "boulevard" and "avenue," are nearly always kept, as in Passeig de Gràcia and Avinguda de Tibidabo. *Rambla* means a long, pedestrian-only avenue while *plaça* (*plaza* in Spanish) indicates a square.

THE NEIGHBORHOODS IN BRIEF

I've briefly described the location of the major neighborhoods in "City Layout," above; here I take a look at what distinguishes each.

Ciutat Vella (Old Town)

Barri Gòtic Barcelona's golden age was between the 13th and 15th centuries, the Gothic period. The city expanded rapidly in medieval times, so much so that it could no longer be contained within the old Roman walls; new ones were built. They originally ran northward from the port along what was to become La Rambla, down the Ronda Sant Pere to Calle Rec Comtal, and back to the sea again. Except for a few remaining sections along the Vía Laietana, most of them have now been destroyed. But the ensemble of 13th- to 15th-century buildings that remain makes up the most complete Barri Gòtic (Gothic Quarter) on the Continent. These include government buildings, churches (including the main cathedral), and guild houses.

Guilds (*gremis*) were a forerunner to the trade unions and the backbone of Barcelona medieval life. Many of their shields can be seen on buildings dotted around the Barri Gòtic, which would have denoted the headquarters of each particular trade. Tiny workshops were also enclosed in the area and even now many street names bear the name of the activity that went on there for centuries—such as Escudellers (shield makers), Assaonadors (tanners), Carders (woolcombers), and Brocaters (brocade makers), to name a few. El Call, the original Jewish ghetto, is also located within the Barri Gòtic. A tiny area around the Carrer del Call and L'Arc de Sant Ramon del Call was the scene of the sacking of the Jews by Christian mobs in the late 1400s.

Apart from the big attractions such as the **Cathedral de la Seu,** the **Plaça Sant Jaume** (which contains the two organs of Catalan politics, the Ajuntament and the Generalitat), and the medieval palace of the **Plaça del Rei,** where Columbus was received after returning from the New World, the Barri Gòtic's charm lies in its details. Smaller squares, such as the **Plaça Felip Neri** with its central fountain, the oasis-like courtyard of the **Frederic Marès Museum,** gargoyles peering down from ancient towers and small chapels set into the sides of medieval buildings—these are what make the area so fascinating. Most of them can only be discovered on foot, ideally at sunset when the fading Mediterranean light lends the stone buildings a warm hue, and musicians, mainly of the classical nature, jostle for performance spaces around the Cathedral.

Some of the sites in the Barri Gòtic are not medieval at all (architecture and history purists argue that the name has remained simply for the sake of tourism) but of no less interest. The most famous of these is the so-called Bridge of Sighs (nothing like the Venetian original) in Carrer del Bisbe, built during the city's Gothic Revival in the 1920s. But even modern additions do nothing to diminish the character of the Barri Gòtic. There is an abundance of specialist shops, from old fan and espadrille makers to more cutting-edge clothes designers, not to mention dozens of outdoor cafes where you can enjoy a coffee or two as you look out onto an ancient edifice.

The sizable Barri Gòtic is hemmed in on one side by the ugly, ever-busy Vía Laietana and on the other by **La Rambla.**

The most famous promenade in Spain, ranking with Madrid's Paseo del Prado, was once a sewer. These days, street entertainers, flower vendors, newspaper vendors, cafe patrons, and strollers flow along its length. The gradual 1.5km (1-mile) descent toward the sea has often been called a metaphor for life because its bustling action combines cosmopolitanism and crude vitality.

La Rambla actually consists of five sections, each a particular *rambla*— Rambla de Canaletes, Rambla dels Estudis, Rambla de Sant Josep, Rambla dels Caputxins, and Rambla de Santa Mónica. The shaded pedestrian esplanade runs from the Plaça de Catalunya to the port—all the way to the Columbus Monument. Along the way you'll pass the **Gran Teatre del Liceu,** on Rambla dels Caputxins, one of the most magnificent opera houses in the world, restored to its former glory after a devastating fire in 1994. Watch out for the giant sidewalk mosaic by Miró halfway down at the Plaça de la Boqueria.

El Raval On the opposite side of La Rambla lies El Raval, Barcelona's largest inner-city neighborhood. This is where the ambitious plans for the post-Olympic "New Barcelona" are most evident: Entire blocks of dank apartment buildings were bulldozed to make way for modern edifices, squares, and boulevards. El Raval has been cited as the neighborhood with the greatest multicultural mix in Europe, a fact confirmed by a quick stroll around its maze of streets, where Pakistani fabric merchants and South American spice sellers stand side by side with traditional establishments selling dried cod and local wine. The *Adhan* (the Muslim call to prayer) wafts from mosques located in ground-floor locales located next to neo-hippie bars, yoga schools, and contemporary-art galleries. The largest of these is the **MACBA (Museum of Contemporary Art)**, a luminous white behemoth designed by the American architect Richard Meir. It fronts a huge concrete square that has, since its opening in 1995, become the neighborhood's most popular playground. At any time of day, the space is inundated by kids playing cricket and soccer, skateboarders cruising the ramps of the museum's forecourt, and housewives on their way to the nearby **Boqueria** market. Another favorite stamping ground is the Rambla del Raval; a wide, airy pedestrianized avenue dating from 2000 and lined with cafes and multi-national (mainly Asian) eating spots.

The signs of gentrification are everywhere, and while this still attracts its fair share of criticism, no one can deny the life-enhancing benefits of the above-mentioned developments for a neighborhood that has been historically deprived of light and breathing space. The neighborhood's former reputation as a seedy inner-city slum is gradually receding, though the area still has its rough edges.

Change is slower to come to the so-called **Barri Xinès,** or **Barrio Chino,** the lower half of El Raval between the waterfront and Carrer de l'Hospital. Despite the name, which means Chinese Quarter, this isn't Chinatown. In fact, most attribute its nickname to the writer Francisco Madrid, who in 1926 was influenced by a fellow journalist believing the area resembled New York's Chinatown. During the 1930s, the French writer Jean Genet wrote *A Thief's Journal* during a stint in one of the area's peseta-a-night whorehouses. In some pockets of the Chino, you would be forgiven for thinking that little has changed; while drug dealing has been largely shipped out to the outer suburbs, prostitution still openly exists, as does the general seediness of many of the streets. But, as with all of the Old City, the times they are a changin' and you may find yourself wandering down here at night to attend the opening of a new bar or club. Petty thieves, prostitutes, drug dealers, and purse-snatchers are just some of the neighborhood "characters," so exercise caution. Although Barri Xinès has a long way to go, an urban renewal program has led to the destruction of some of the rougher parts of the barrio.

La Ribera Another neighborhood that stagnated for years but is now well into a renaissance is La Ribera. Across the noisy artery Vía Laietana and south of Calle Princesa, this small neighborhood is bordered by the **Port Vell (Old Port)** and the **Parc de la Ciutadella.** Like the Barrio Chino (above), **El Born** is La Ribera's "neighborhood within a neighborhood." But far from being a rough diamond, El Born is a polished pastiche of the Old Town, where designer clothing and housewares showcases occupy medieval buildings and workshops. The centerpiece is the imposing **Santa María del Mar,** a stunningly complete Gothic basilica that was built with funds from the cashed-up merchants that once inhabited the area. Many of them lived in the mansions and palaces along the Carrer de Montcada, today home to a trio of top museums including the Museu Picasso. Most of the mansions in this area were built during one of Barcelona's major maritime expansions, principally in the 1200s and 1300s. During this time, El Born

was the city's principal trade area. The recently refurbished **La Llotja,** the city's first stock exchange, lies on its outer edge on the Plaça Palau; although the facade dates from 1802, the interior is pure Catalan Gothic. The central **Passeig del Born** got its name from the medieval jousts that used to occur here. At the northern end, the wrought-iron Mercat del Born was the city's principal wholesale market until the mid-1970s. Recent excavation work has revealed entire streets and homes dating back to the 18th century, sealing the edifice's fate as a new museum where these ruins can be viewed via glass flooring and walkways. Behind the Mercat del Born, the Parc de la Ciutadella is a tranquil oasis replete with a man-made lake, wide, leafy walkways, and yet more museums.

More Central Barcelona

Barceloneta, the Beaches & the Harbor Although Barcelona has a long seagoing tradition, its waterfront stood in decay for years. Today, the waterfront promenade, **Passeig del Moll de la Fusta,** bursts with activity. The best way to get a bird's-eye view of the area is to take an elevator to the top of the Columbus Monument in Plaça Portal de la Pau at the port end of La Rambla.

Near the monument are the **Reials Drassanes,** or royal shipyards, a booming place during the Middle Ages. Years before Columbus landed in the New World, ships sailed from here, flying the yellow-and-red flag of Catalonia. These days, the Reials Drassanes are home to the excellent Museu Marítim. On the other side of the road, the wooden swing bridge, known as the Rambla del Mar, takes you across the water to the Maremagnum entertainment and shopping complex.

To the east, the glitzy **Port Vell (Old Port)** was one of the main projects for the city's Olympic renewal scheme. Its chic yachting marina is similar to those of other great Mediterranean ports like Marseilles and Piraeus, and there are large expanses of open recreational areas where people get out and enjoy the sun. It is also home to the city's aquarium. On one side it is flanked by the **Passeig Joan de Borbón,** the main street of **La Barceloneta (Little Barceloneta).** Formerly a fishing district dating from the 18th century, the neighborhood is full of character and is still one of the best places to eat seafood in the city. The blocks here are long and narrow—architects planned them that way so that each room in every building fronted a street. The streets end at Barceloneta beach. This, like all the city's beaches, was neglected to the point of nonexistence pre-1992. The harborfront was clogged with industrial buildings—many of them abandoned—and shabby but well-patronized *chiringuitos* (beach bars) until the land was reclaimed, sand trawled in from offshore, and beach culture returned to Barcelona. Today these are some of the finest urban beaches in Europe. From Barceloneta, separated by breakwaters, no less than seven of them sprawl to the north. The **Port Olímpic,** dominated by a pair of landmark, sea-facing skyscrapers (one accommodating the five-star Hotel Arts and the city's casino) boasts yet another marina and a host of restaurants and bars. Take them all in at your leisure as you stroll along the Passeig Marítim (seafront promenade).

L'Eixample To the north of the Plaça de Catalunya is the large section of Barcelona (known as the Ensanche in Spanish) that grew beyond the old medieval walls. In the mid-1800s, Barcelona was simply bursting at the seams. The, dank, serpentine streets of the old walled city were not only breeding grounds for cholera and typhoid but for habitual mass rioting. Rather than leveling the Old Town, the city's authorities had a sloping sweep of land just outside the walls at their disposal and contracted the socialist engineer Idelfons Cerdà to offer a solution. His *Monograph on the Working Class of Barcelona,* done in 1865, became the first ever attempt to study the living, breathing landscape of a city: urbanization to you and me, a term Cerdà himself coined in the process.

Cerdà actually visited hundreds of Old City hovels before he drew up plans for Barcelona's New City. Needless to say, his fact-checking led him to the bowels of human suffering; he found out that life expectancy for the proletariat was half that of the bourgeoisie (this, while they paid double per square meter for their decaying hovels) and mortality rates were higher in the narrower streets. Above all, he concluded that air and sunshine were vital to basic well-being.

Today little remains of Cerdà's most radical plans for the Eixample, apart from the rigorous regularity of its 20m-wide (67-ft.) streets and famous chamfered pavements. The *modernistas* were the neighborhood's earliest architects, filling the blocks with their labored fantasies, such as Gaudí's La Sagrada Família, Casa Milà, and Casa Batlló. L'Eixample is a living, breathing museum piece with an abundance of Art Nouveau architecture and details not found anywhere else in Europe. See "Walking Tour 4: Moderniste Route (L'Eixample)," in chapter 8.

In accordance with Cerdà's basic plans, avenues form a grid of perpendicular streets, cut across by a majestic boulevard—**Passeig de Gràcia,** a posh shopping street ideal for leisurely promenades. L'Eixample's northern boundary is the **Avinguda Diagonal** (or simply the Diagonal) which links the expressway and the heart of the city and acts as Barcelona's business and banking hub.

Gràcia This charming neighborhood sprawls to the north of the intersection of the **Passeig de Gràcia** and **Diagonal.** Its contained, villagelike ambience stems from the fact that it was once a separate town, only connected to central Barcelona in 1897 with the construction of the Passeig de Gràcia. It has a strong industrial and artisan history and many street-level workshops can still be seen. Rather than in monuments or museums, Gràcia's charm lies in its low-level housing and series of squares—the Plaça del Sol and Plaça Ruis i Taulet, with its distinctive clock tower, being two of the prettiest. The residents themselves have a strong sense of neighborhood pride and a marked independent spirit, and their annual fiestas (p. 21) are some of the liveliest in the city. For the casual visitor, Gràcia is a place to wander through for a slice of authentic *barri* life.

Montjuïc & Tibidabo Locals call them "mountains" and while northerly Tibidabo does actually rise to over 488m (1,600 ft.), the port-side bluff of Montjuïc is somewhat lower. Both are great places to go for fine views and cleaner air. The most accessible, Montjuïc (named the "Hill of the Jews" after a Jewish necropolis that once stood there), gained prominence in 1929 as the site of the World's Fair and again in 1992 as the site of the Summer Olympic Games. Its major attractions are the Joan Miró museum, the Olympic installations, and the **Poble Espanyol (Spanish Village)**, a 2-hectare (5-acre) site constructed for the World's Fair. Examples of Spanish art and architecture are on display against the backdrop of a traditional Spanish village. Opposite the village lies the **CaixaForum,** one of the city's newer

contemporary-art showcases housed in a converted *moderniste* textile factory. In a recent push to raise Montjuïc's status even further, 8,000 sq. m (86,111 sq. ft.) of parkland have been added. At the base of Montjuïc is the working-class neighborhood of Poble Sec and the Ciutat del Teatre; location of the city's theatrical school and a conglomeration of performing-arts spaces. Tibidabo (503m/1,650 ft.) is where you should go for your final look at Barcelona. On a clear day you can see the mountains of Majorca, some 209km (130 miles) away. Reached by train, tram, and cable car, Tibidabo is a popular Sunday destination, with Barcelonese families heading to its Funfair.

Outer Barcelona

Pedralbes At the western edge of El Diagonal, next to the elite districts of Sant Gervasí and Putxet, is this equally posh residential area where wealthy Barcelonans live in either stylish blocks of apartment houses, 19th-century villas behind ornamental fences, or stunning *modernista* structures. Set in a park, the **Palau de Pedralbes,** Av. Diagonal 686, was constructed in the 1920s as a gift from the city to Alfonso XIII, the grandfather of King Juan Carlos. Today it has a new life, housing the Ceramic and Decorative Arts Museums. The Finca Güell is also part of the estate, the country home of Gaudí's main patron Eusebi Güell. Although not open to the public, the main gate and gatehouse, both designed by Gaudí, are visible from the street.

Pride of this zone is the 14th-century Gothic church-cum-convent of **Monestir de Pedralbes,** where you can not only view lovely cloisters and well-preserved kitchens but also take in a world-class art gallery with over 70 works donated by the Madrid-based Thyssen-Bornemizca museum (p. 190).

2 Getting Around

Barcelona's main airport is **El Prat,** 13km (8 miles) from the city center, and there are several options you can use to get into town. Travelers arriving from within the European Union on budget airlines such as Ryanair may land at **Girona** airport (103km/64miles northeast of Barcelona) or at **Reus** (110km/68 miles west of the city).

BY BUS   The **Aerobús** leaves just outside all three terminals at El Prat every 15 minutes from 6am to midnight. It takes about 20 to 25 minutes to get into the city (allow a few more minutes for the return journey), and costs 3.60€ ($4.50). The bus stops at Plaça Espanya, Plaça Universitat, and Plaça de Catalunya, all major hubs with Metro connections. Transport into Barcelona from **Girona** airport is by **Barcelona Bus** (✆ **902-361-550** or 902-130-014), which arrives in Barcelona at Passeig de Sant Joan 52. One-way tickets cost 12€ ($15); round-trip tickets (which must be purchased inside the terminal) are 21€ ($26). Journey time is 1 hour 10 minutes. Transport into Barcelona from **Reus** airport costs 11€ ($14) one-way and 18€ ($23) round-trip. Journey time is 1½ hours For information on buses between Reus and Barcelona call ✆ **93-804-44-51.**

BY TRAIN   El Prat also has its own train station. While this is convenient for those traveling farther afield by train (the journey finishes at Sants, the city's major terminal, which also has connections to the Metro), the station itself is a short walk from the airport terminal, making it inconvenient for those with lots of luggage. Trains leave every 30 minutes from 6:15am to 11:40pm, and the 25-minute journey costs 2.75€ ($3.45). From Girona and Reus it's clearly cheaper to take the train to Barcelona (average one-way ticket cost is 5€/$6.25), but it's a bit of a hassle having to catch a bus to either of the town's rail stations.

BY TAXI   There are taxi ranks outside all El Prat terminals, as well as at Girona and Reus (though you shouldn't take a taxi directly to Barcelon from Griona or Reus; the trip could cost as much 120€/$150). The 20-minute journey to the center from El Prat should cost about 25€ ($31), including the 2.10€ ($2.60) airport surcharge. Luggage that goes in the trunk is 1€ ($1.25) per piece. *Note:* There have been reports of unscrupulous Barcelona taxi drivers waiting for passengers disembarking from the above mentioned Aerobus. Make sure the meter is on when you hop in, and that you are not being taken a roundabout way to your destination.

GETTING AROUND IN BARCELONA

BY METRO (SUBWAY)   Barcelona has an excellent underground public transport system. The **Metro** goes pretty much any place in the city you will need to get to. It is run by the TMB (Transports Metropolitans de Barcelona), which also manages the bus network and the FGC (Ferrocarrils de la Generalitat), a pre-Metro, part underground, part over-ground system.

It is the efficient Metro system, however, that most visitors to the city are likely to use. There are five color-coded and numbered lines that fan out from the center of the city. Stations are recognizable by a red diamond-shaped sign with the letter M in the center. Maps are available from the stations themselves and from tourist information offices. The stations Catalunya, Sants, and Passeig de Gràcia connect with RENFE trains. When you purchase a ticket for another part of Spain or Catalonia (which you can do from RENFE offices at Sants and Passeig de Gràcia stations) make sure you ask which station it leaves from.

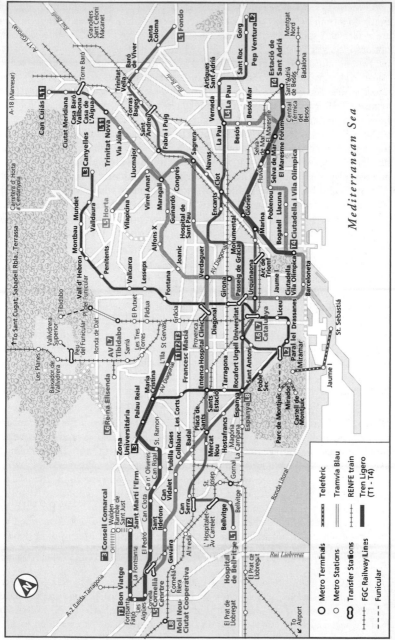

Mediterranean Sea

Legend:
- ○ Metro Terminals
- ○ Metro Stations
- 8 Transfer Stations
- ++++ FGC Railway Lines
- --- Funicular
- Telefèric
- Tramvia Blau
- +++ RENFE train
- Tren Ligero (T1- T4)

All Metro tickets can be bought on the day of journey or beforehand inside the station, either from the ticket office or a touch screen vending machine. Various options are available. A single (*senzill* or *sencillo*) ticket costs 1.20€ ($1.50). More economic options include a T-10 at 6.65€ ($8.30), which offers 10 journeys that can be shared by two or more people or a T-Día for unlimited 24-hour transport in central Barcelona for 5€ ($6.25). Travel Cards of 2 and 3 days (9.20€–13€/$12–$16) are also available. You can get reduced-price tickets for longer periods, but for most short visits the T-10 is your best bet with the T-Día in reserve for extra busy days. All these tickets are valid for the FGC and bus systems, as well as for the Metro.

Note that even with a *sencillo* ticket, once it is activated, it is valid for up to 75 minutes on a different form of transport if you need to do a combined Metro/bus journey. The Metro runs 5am to midnight Sunday to Thursday and 5am to 2am Friday and Saturday. TMB's easy to navigate website (**www.tmb.net**) has loads of information (in English) on the city's transport system, including which Metro stations and buses are equipped to take wheelchairs. Customer service centers (© **93-318-70-74**) are at Universitat, Sagrada Família, Sants, and Diagonal stations. While it's tempting to hop on and off the Metro when seeing the sights, remember that Metro stations are only often about a 5- to 10-minute walk apart; a good pair of shoes is the best way around central Barcelona!

BY BUS   Buses are plentiful, but less convenient than the Metro because they're at the mercy of the city's infamous traffic. Most bus routes stop at the Plaça de Catalunya, also the stop-off point for the Aerobús (see "Getting into Town from the Airport," in chapter 2) and the Bus Turístic (see below). Routes are clearly marked on each stop, as are timetables—but most buses stop running well before the Metro closes. One bus service that is particularly useful is the Nitbus, which runs from 11pm to 4am and is often the only alternative to the dearth of taxis from 2 to 3am. Nitbus is bright yellow, clearly marked with an N, and most leave from Plaça de Catalunya. Note that Travel Cards and other TMB passes are not valid on Nitbuses. Tickets (1.20€/$1.50 one-way) are bought directly from the driver.

BY TAXI   Taxis are plentiful and still reasonably priced. Most of the time you simply hail one in the street (a green light indicates their availability). Taxis have meters, but don't make the mistake of confusing the cheaper day rate (Tariff 2) and the more expensive, post-8pm night rate (Tariff 1). A list of prices and surcharges is (by law) on display on the back passenger window. There have been reports of some unscrupulous taxi drivers charging exorbitant fares for short distances, but this seems to be mainly be confined to the Ryanair bus drop-off point (see "Getting into Town from the Airport," in chapter 2). Nevertheless, make sure that the meter is turned on when you start your journey. If you wish to book a cab, call the **Institut Metropolità del Taxi** at © **93-223-51-51.** They can also give you information about booking wheelchair-accessible taxis.

BY BICYCLE   One growing form of transport in the city is the bicycle—there are a number of bicycle lanes in the center of Barcelona. You can rent bikes at **Un Coxte Menys,** Esparteria 3 (© **93-268-21-05**) or at **Biciclot,** Verneda 16 (© **93-307-74-75**). You are not required by law to wear a helmet (though you'd still be wise to do so).

OTHER FORMS OF TRANSPORTATION
At some point in your journey, you may want to visit the mountain of Tibidabo. A century-old tram called the **Tramvía Blau (Blue Streetcar)** goes from Plaça Kennedy

Tips All Aboard!

The most convenient way to see all of Barcelona, especially if your time is limited, is to hop on (and off) the **Bus Turístic** (© 93-318-70-74; www.tmb.net/en_US/turistes/busturistic/busturistic.jsp). This double-decker, open-top tourist bus travels to all the major areas and sights; you can either choose to disembark or stay on and continue your journey. There are two routes: the red, or Nord (North), route, which covers L'Eixample and Tibidabo, with Gaudí's main works (including the Sagrada Família) as the highlights; or the blue, or Sur (South), route, which allows you to see the Old Town and Montjuïc, both with multilingual commentary along the way. The main point of embarkation is Plaça de Catalunya, outside the El Corte Ingles department store. Cost is 17€ ($21) for the 1-day pass (10€/$13 children 4–12) and 21€ ($26) for the 2-day pass (13€/$16 children 4–12). Tickets can be purchased on board or at the Tourist Information Office at the Plaça de Catalunya. The service operates daily from 9am to 9:30pm. There is no service on Christmas or New Year's Day.

to the bottom of the funicular to Tibidabo. It operates daily from 10am to 8pm from mid-June to mid-September and 10am to 6pm on weekends the rest of the year.

At the end of the run, you can go the rest of the way by funicular to the top, at 503m (1,650 ft.), for a stunning panoramic view of Barcelona. The funicular operates only when the Funfair at Tibidabo is open. Opening times vary according to the time of year and the weather conditions. As a rule, the funicular starts operating 20 minutes before the Funfair opens, then every half-hour. During peak visiting hours, it runs every 15 minutes. The fare is 2.10€ ($2.60) one-way, 3.10€ ($3.90) round-trip.

The **Tibibus** goes from the Plaça de Catalunya, in the center of the city, to Tibidabo at limited times, again depending when the park opens and closes. The one-way fare is 2.10€ ($2.60). Call city hall's information hot line (© **010**) for times.

To reach Montjuïc, site of the 1992 Olympics, take the **Montjuïc funicular.** It links with subway line 3 at the Paral.lel Metro stop. The funicular operates daily from 9am to 8pm in winter, 9am to 10pm in summer. The round-trip fare is 2.10€ ($2.60).

Barcelona's newest form of public transportation is the sleek and comfortable Tramvía Baix, a modern cable car that mainly services the outer suburbs. It is handy for reaching the outer limits of the Diagonal and the Palau de Pedralbes (p. 71). Hop on at Plaça Francesc Macia.

FAST FACTS: Barcelona

American Express There are two American Express Offices in Barcelona: one at Passeig de Gràcia 101 (© **93-415-23-71**), and the other at **Les Ramblas 74** (© **93-301-11-66**).

Area Codes The area code for Barcelona is **93**.

ATM Networks Maestro, Cirrus, and Visa cards are readily accepted at all ATMs.

Business Hours Banks are open Monday through Friday from 8:30am to 2pm. Most offices are open Monday through Friday from 9am to 6 or 7pm. In July this changes from 8pm to 3pm for many businesses, especially those in the public sector. In August, businesses are on skeleton staff if they are not closed altogether. In restaurants, lunch is usually from 2 to 4pm and dinner from 9 to 11:30pm or midnight. There are no set rules for the opening of bars and taverns. Many open at 8am, others at noon and most stay open until midnight or later. Major stores are open Monday through Saturday from 9:30 or 10am to 8pm; staff at smaller establishments, however, often take a siesta, doing business from 9:30am to 2pm and 4:30pm to 8 or 8:30pm. Hours can vary from store to store.

Car Rentals See "Getting Around," above.

Currency See "Money," in chapter 2.

Driving Rules See "Getting Around," above.

Drugstores To find an open pharmacy outside normal business hours, check the list of stores posted on the door of any drugstore. The law requires drugstores to operate on a rotating system of hours so that there's always a drugstore open somewhere, even Sunday at midnight. Drugstores are called *farmacias* in Spanish and, when open, are identified by a neon green cross.

Electricity Most hotels have 220 volts AC (50 cycles). Some older places have 110 or 125 volts AC. Carry your adapter with you, and always check at your hotel desk before plugging in any electrical appliance. It's best to travel with battery-operated equipment.

Embassies & Consulates If you lose your passport, fall seriously ill, get into legal trouble, or have some other serious problem, your embassy or consulate can help. These are the Barcelona addresses and hours: The **United States Consulate,** Passeig de Reina Elisenda 23 (℗ **93-280-22-27;** FGC: Reina Elisenda), is open Monday through Friday from 9am to 1pm. The **Canadian Consulate,** Carrer de Elisenda Pinós 10 (℗ **93-204-27-00;** FGC: Reina Elisenda), is open Monday through Friday from 10am to 1pm. The **United Kingdom Consulate-General,** Diagonal 477 (℗ **93-366-62-00;** Metro: Hospital Clinic), is open Monday through Friday from 9:30am to 3pm. The **Republic of Ireland** has a small consulate at Gran Vía Carles III 94 (℗ **93-491-50-21;** Metro: María Cristina); it's open Monday through Friday from 10am to 1pm. In the adjacent building is the **Australian Consulate,** Gran Vía Carles III 98 (℗ **93-490-90-13;** Metro: María Cristina). It is open Monday though Friday from 10am to noon. Citizens of **New Zealand** have a consulate at Travesera de Gràcia 64 (℗ **93-209-03-99;** FGC: Gràcia); it's open Monday through Friday from 9am to 2pm and 4 to 7pm.

Emergencies For an ambulance dial ℗ **061;** or fire ℗ **080.**

Etiquette Contemporary Barcelona is the most relaxed and liberal of all Spanish cities. In Franco's day, many visitors would be arrested for the skimpy, revealing clothes worn around the city streets, but these days no one is going to bat an eyelid if you wear a pair of shorts and sandals down Les Ramblas, although in the interest of blending in with the locals consider reserving your resort wear for the beach. Church officials will not prevent you from visiting churches and cathedrals if you're scantily clad, but again, try and be as sympathetic as possible to local customs. Women can cover up when needed in the summer months by carrying around a light cardigan or shawl in their bag.

In spite of what you've heard in days of yore, when Spaniards showed up for appointments 2 or 3 hours late, most nationals now arrive on time as they do in the rest of the E.U. countries. It's always wise for men to wear a suit for business meetings. The familiar *tú* form is now widely used in Spain, a sign of the country's shaking off of their old-school image. But to be on the safe side, foreign Spanish speakers should address strangers, particularly older people, with the formal *usted.* Kissing on both cheeks is reserved for friends, or people your friends introduce you to. Handshakes are more the norm in business transactions.

Catalan nationalism is an extremely sensitive subject and often avoided even among the Catalans themselves. Unless you are an expert on the topic, stay away from it. If you are invited into a private home for dinner, you are not expected to bring a bottle of wine, although a small gift of chocolates or flowers will be appreciated. The Spanish and Catalans are openly affectionate. You should not be offended or feel uncomfortable when people touch you on the back, arms, and so on. I recommend reading *Culture Shock! Spain: a Guide to Customs and Etiquette* (Graphic Arts Centre Publishing).

Herbolistarias (herb shops) are also common, and many Spaniards use them for natural remedies for milder ailments such as colds and stomach upsets. As with *farmacias,* their staff is trained to diagnose and prescribe accordingly.

Holidays See "Barcelona Calendar of Events," in chapter 2.

Hospitals In Barcelona, the **Centre d'Urgències Perecamps,** located near Les Ramblas at Av. de las Drassanes 13–15, is a good bet.

Hot Lines Call the city hall information service at ⓒ **010** for opening and closing times of attractions, special events, and other hard-to-find info.

Information See "Visitor Information," earlier in this chapter.

Internet Access Internet access is plentiful, both in cybercafes and frequently in hotels.

Language There are two official languages in Catalonia: Castilian Spanish *(castellano)* and Catalan. After years of being outlawed during the Franco dictatorship, Catalan has returned to Barcelona and Catalonia with the language and its derivatives spoken throughout the *Països Catalans* (Catalan Countries), namely Catalonia, Valencia, the Balearic Islands (including Majorca, even though natives there will tell you they speak *mallorquín*), and pockets of Southern France and Aragon. Although street signs and media are in Catalan, no tourist is expected to speak it, although you will be met with delight if you can at least master a few phrases. Descriptions in museums are in both Catalan and Spanish with some also in English. Most restaurants have an English menu.

Laundromats There are a few self-service and serviced laundromats in the Old Town, including **Tigre,** Carrer de Rauric 20, and **Lavamax,** Junta de Comerç 14. Some dry cleaners *(tintorerías)* also do laundry.

Liquor Laws The legal drinking age is 18. Bars, taverns, and cafeterias usually open at 8am, and many serve alcohol until midnight or later. Generally, you can purchase alcoholic beverages in almost any market.

Lost & Found Be sure to tell all your credit card companies the minute you discover your wallet has been lost or stolen and file a report at the nearest police precinct. Your credit card company or insurer may require a police report number or record of the loss. Most credit card companies have an emergency toll-free number to call if your card is lost or stolen; they may be able to wire you a cash advance immediately or deliver an emergency credit card in a day or two. Visa's U.S. emergency number is ℂ **800/847-2911**, or 90-099-11-24 in Spain. American Express cardholders and traveler's check holders should call ℂ **800/221-7282** in the U.S., or 90-237-56-37 in Spain. MasterCard holders should call ℂ **800/307-7309** in the U.S., or 90-097-12-31 in Spain. For other credit cards, call the toll-free number directory at ℂ **800/555-1212**.

If you need emergency cash over the weekend when all banks and American Express offices are closed, you can have money wired to you via **Western Union** (ℂ **800/325-6000**; www.westernunion.com).

Identity theft and fraud are potential complications of losing your wallet, especially if you've lost your driver's license along with your cash and credit cards. Notify the major credit-reporting bureaus immediately; placing a fraud alert on your records may protect you against liability for criminal activity. The three major U.S. credit-reporting agencies are **Equifax** (ℂ **800/766-0008;** www. equifax.com), **Experian** (ℂ **888/397-3742;** www.experian.com), and **TransUnion** (ℂ **800/680-7289;** www.transunion.com). Finally, if you've lost all forms of photo ID, call your airline and explain the situation; they might allow you to board the plane if you have a copy of your passport or birth certificate and a copy of the police report you've filed.

Mail To send an Airmail letter to the United States costs .78€ (98¢). Airmail letters to Britain or other E.U. countries cost .57€ (71¢) up to 20 grams; letters within Spain cost .38€ (48¢). As well as at *oficinas de correos* (post offices), stamps can be bought at *estancos* (government-licensed tobacconists easily recognized by their brown-and-yellow logo). Postcards have the same rates as letters. Post your letters in the post office itself or in yellow post boxes called *buzones.* Allow about 8 days for delivery to North America, generally less to the United Kingdom; in some cases, letters take 2 weeks to reach North America. Rates change frequently, so check at your local hotel before mailing anything. As for surface mail to North America, forget it. Chances are you'll be home long before your letter arrives. For further information check Spanish Post office website: **www.correos.es.**

Newspapers & Magazines Foreign newspapers and magazines are available on the newsstands along Les Ramblas. *Catalonia Today* is a free newsletter in English published by the Catalan newspaper *El Punt. Barcelona Metropolitan* is a monthly magazine in English with loads of information on events as well as features on Barcelona living. You can pick it up in bars and pubs. The *Guía del Ocio* is the most comprehensive "What's On." There is a small section at the back in English.

Passports **For Residents of the United States:** Whether you're applying in person or by mail, you can download passport applications from the U.S. State Department website at **http://travel.state.gov/passport_services.html**. To find your regional passport office, either check the U.S. State Department website or call the **National Passport Information Center** toll-free number (ℂ **877/ 487-2778**) for automated information.

For Residents of Canada: Passport applications are available at travel agencies throughout Canada or from the central **Passport Office,** Department of Foreign Affairs and International Trade, Ottawa, ON K1A 0G3 (✆ **800/567-6868;** www.ppt.gc.ca).

For Residents of the United Kingdom: To pick up an application for a standard 10-year passport (5-year passport for children under 16), visit your nearest passport office, major post office, or travel agency or contact the **United Kingdom Passport Service** at ✆ **0870/521-0410** or search its website at www.ukpa.gov.uk.

For Residents of Ireland: You can apply for a 10-year passport at the **Passport Office,** Setanta Centre, Molesworth Street, Dublin 2 (✆ **01/671-1633;** www.irl gov.ie/iveagh). Those under age 18 or over 65 must apply for a 3-year passport. You can also apply at 1A South Mall, Cork (✆ **021/272-525**) or at most main post offices.

For Residents of Australia: You can pick up an application from your local post office or any branch of Passports Australia, but you must schedule an interview at the passport office to present your application materials. Call the **Australian Passport Information Service** at ✆ **131-232,** or visit the government website at www.passports.gov.au.

For Residents of New Zealand: You can pick up a passport application at any New Zealand Passports Office or download it from their website. Contact the **Passports Office** at ✆ **0800/225-050** in New Zealand, or 04/474-8100, or log on to www.passports.govt.nz.

Police The national police emergency number is ✆ **091,** although most tourist-related matters are dealt with by the local police force, the Guardia Urbana (✆ **092**).

Restrooms In Catalonia they're called *aseos, servicios,* or *lavabos,* and are labeled *caballeros* for men and *damas* or *señoras* for women.

Safety See "Health & Safety," in chapter 2.

Smoking Smoking is not allowed in airports, banks, post offices, and other "public" buildings. Nonsmoking sections in bars and restaurants are rare. Most good hotels have nonsmoking rooms.

Taxes The internal sales tax (known in Spain as *IVA*) ranges from 7% to 33%, depending on the commodity being sold. Food, wine, and basic necessities are taxed at 7%; most goods and services (including car rentals) at 13%; luxury items (jewelry, all tobacco, imported liquors) at 33%; and hotels at 7%.

If you are not a European Union resident and make purchases in Spain worth more than 90€ ($113), you can get a tax refund. To get this refund, you must complete three copies of a form that the store will give you, detailing the nature of your purchase and its value. Citizens of non-E.U. countries show the purchase and the form to the Spanish Customs Office. The shop is supposed to refund the amount owed to you. Inquire at the time of purchase how they will do so and discuss in what currency your refund will arrive.

Telephones If you don't speak Spanish, you'll find it easier to telephone from your hotel, but remember that this is often very expensive because hotels impose a surcharge on every operator-assisted call. In some cases it can be as high as 40% or more. On the street, phone booths (known as *cabinas*) have dialing instructions in English—very few actually take coins. Instead, purchase a *tarjeta telefónica* from a newsstand or tobacconist. If you need to make a lengthy overseas call, a *locutorio* (call center) is the best bet. Located throughout the Old Town, these call centers offer the best rates and booths are provided for privacy. *Locutorios* also sell phone cards supplied by private operators. You can purchase as much as 3 hours of call time to the U.S. for as little as 6€ ($7.50), although you will pay the connection fee (the cost of a local call) on top. These cards can be used from both fixed and mobile phones and must be used within a month of the first call.

When in Spain, the access number for an **AT&T** calling card is ☏ **800/CALL-ATT**. The access number for **Sprint** is ☏ **800/888-0013**.

More information is also available on the Telefónica website at www. telefonica.es.

For directory assistance: Dial ☏ **11818** for numbers within Spain, and **11825** for the rest of the world.

For operator assistance: If you need operator assistance in making an international call, dial ☏ **1008** for Europe and **1005** for the rest of the world.

Toll-free numbers: Numbers beginning with **900** in Spain are toll-free, but calling a 1-800 number in the States from Spain is not toll-free. In fact, it costs the same as an overseas call.

In Barcelona, most smaller establishments, especially bars, discos, and a few informal restaurants, don't have phones. Further, many summer-only bars and discos secure a phone for the season only, then get a new number the next season. Many attractions, such as small churches or even minor museums, have no staff to receive inquiries from the public.

In 1998 all telephone numbers in Spain changed to a nine-digit system instead of the six- or seven-digit method used previously. Each number is now preceded by its provincial code for local, national, and international calls. For example, everyone calling within and to Barcelona must dial 93, then the old seven-digit number. If you have a number that does not have a 93 in front of it, add it on and dial before you discount it as erroneous.

To call Spain: If you're calling Spain from the United States:

1. Dial the international access code: **011.**
2. Dial the country code for Spain: **34.**
3. Dial the city code for Spain and then the number. So the whole number you'd dial would be 011-34-93-000-0000.

To make international calls: To make international calls from Spain, first dial 00 and then the country code (U.S. and Canada 1, U.K. 44, Ireland 353, Australia 61, New Zealand 64). Next you dial the area code and number.

Time Spain is 6 hours ahead of Eastern Standard Time in the United States. Daylight saving time is in effect from the last Sunday in March to the last Sunday in October.

Tipping More expensive restaurants add a 7% tax to the bill and cheaper ones incorporate it into their prices. This is *not* a service charge, and a tip of 5% to

10% is expected in these establishments. For coffees and snacks most people just leave a few coins or round up to the nearest euro. Taxis do not expect tips.

Although tipping is not mandatory for hotel staff, you should be aware that wages in the hospitality industry are extremely low so any supplement will be more than welcome. Tip hotel porters and doorman between .80€ ($1) and 1€ ($1.25), and maids about the same amount per day.

Useful Phone Numbers **U.S. Department of State Travel Advisory,** 📞 202/647-5225 (manned 24 hr.); **U.S. Passport Agency,** 📞 202/647-0518; **U.S. Centers for Disease Control International Traveler's Hot Line,** 📞 404/332-4559.

Water Although the water in Barcelona is safe to drink, most people find the taste unpleasant and therefore buy bottled water.

Where to Stay

Barcelona may be one of the most expensive cities in Spain, but prices at its first-class and deluxe hotels can still be a bargain compared to those of other major European cities like Paris and London. This makes Barcelona a good place to splurge, especially with many hotels holding the line on raising their prices (or even pushing them down) because of stiff competition. Be sure to look online for weekend package deals and always ask about any special offers when you call to reserve.

Safety is an important factor when choosing accommodations and a former deterring factor with cheaper hotels was that they tended to be in less desirable parts of town. Today, however, those neighborhoods aren't quite what they used to be, and budget *hostales* are often found alongside high-standard hotels in *barris* once regarded as distinctly un-chic—such as El Raval.

A clear trend in hotels all over the city today, and one playing a major part in the general improvement in lodging quality, is the obligatory inclusion of "high tech" Internet facilities such as high-speed ADSL and Wi-Fi connections. Usually provided free, they are more or less standard in all levels of hostelries now appearing on the scene, as well as in some of the more established ones that realize they need to update to stay competitive. Check out the Petit Palace Opera Garden Ramblas (p. 93), in the heart of the Old City, for an example of 21st-century accommodations.

SAVING ON YOUR HOTEL ROOM

The **rack rate** is the maximum rate that a hotel charges for a room. The truth is, *hardly anybody pays rack rates* and, with the exception of smaller B&Bs, you can usually pay quite a bit less than the rates shown below. If you decide to come to Barcelona during the very hot months of July and August (in reality the "low season") you'll usually pick up some bargains in the higher priced hotels at lower rates than those we officially list here. Check hotel websites, or run through the database of the regularly updated website **www.venere.com**, which, by cutting out booking agents, is able to get some of the most competitive rates available. High-price times are Easter and Christmas, so avoid those periods if you can.

Here's how I've organized the price categories:

- **Very Expensive,** $350 and up
- **Expensive,** $250 to $349
- **Moderate,** $130 to $249
- **Inexpensive,** under $130

These are all high-season prices, with no discounts applied. But *always* peruse the category above your target price—you might just find the perfect match, especially if you follow the advice below. *Note to single travelers:* Rates for singles may be available in some of the accommodations listed in this chapter—call the hotel directly and inquire. To lower the cost of your room:

- **Ask about special rates or other discounts.** Always ask whether a room less expensive than the first one quoted is available, or whether any special rates apply to you. You may qualify for corporate, student, military, senior, or other discounts. Mention membership in AAA, AARP, frequent-flier programs, or trade unions, which may entitle you to special deals as well. Find out the hotel policy on children—do kids stay free in the room or is there a special rate?

- **Dial direct.** When booking a room in a chain hotel, you'll often get a better deal by calling the individual hotel's reservation desk rather than the chain's main number.

- **Book online.** Many hotels offer Internet-only discounts, or supply rooms to Priceline, Hotwire, or Expedia at rates much lower than the ones you can get through the hotel itself. Shop around. And if you have special needs—a quiet room, a room with a view—call the hotel directly and make your needs known after you've booked online.

- **Remember the law of supply and demand.** Resort hotels are most crowded and therefore most expensive on weekends, so discounts are usually available for midweek stays. Business hotels in downtown locations are busiest during the week, so you can expect big discounts over the weekend. Many hotels have high-season and low-season prices, and booking the day after "high season" ends can mean big discounts.

- **Look into group or long-stay discounts.** If you come as part of a large group, you should be able to negotiate a bargain rate, since the hotel can then guarantee occupancy in a number of rooms. Likewise, if you're planning a long stay (at least 5 days), you might qualify for a discount. As a general rule, expect 1 night free after a 7-night stay.

- **Avoid excess charges and hidden costs.** When you book a room, ask whether the hotel charges for parking. Use your own cellphone, pay phones, or prepaid phone cards instead of dialing direct from hotel phones, which usually have exorbitant rates. And don't be tempted by the room's minibar offerings: Most hotels charge through the nose for water, soda, and snacks. Finally, ask about local taxes and service charges, which can increase the cost of a room by 15% or more. If a hotel insists upon tacking on a surprise "energy surcharge" that wasn't mentioned at check-in or a "resort fee" for amenities you didn't use, you can often make a case for getting it removed.

- **Consider the pros and cons of all-inclusive resorts and hotels.** The term "all-inclusive" means different things at different hotels. Many all-inclusive hotels will include three meals daily, sports equipment, spa entry, and other amenities; others may include all or most drinks. In general, you'll save money going the "all-inclusive" way—as long as you use the facilities provided. The downside is that your choices are limited and you're stuck eating and playing in one place for the duration of your vacation.

- **Book an efficiency.** A room with a kitchenette allows you to shop for groceries and cook your own meals. This is a big money saver, especially for families on long stays.

WHICH QUARTER FOR FULL SATISFACTION?

The **Barri Gòtic (Gothic Quarter)** is good for *hostales* (not to be confused with hostels) and cheaper guesthouses, and you can live and eat less expensively here than in any other part of Barcelona, as well as save money on transport because most sights are within walking distance. Hold onto your belongings, however—bag snatching is rife here, in the gentrified El Born area, and in the still-edgy El Raval. While you're unlikely to suffer any bodily harm, be careful when returning to your hotel late at night.

More modern, but more expensive, accommodations can be found north of the Barri Gòtic in the **Eixample** district, centered on the Metro stops Plaça de Catalunya and Universitat. Many buildings here are in the *modernista* style, from the last decades of the 19th century. Be aware that sometimes the elevators and plumbing are of the same vintage. But the Eixample is a desirable and safe neighborhood, especially along its wide boulevards, and has plenty of good restaurants. Traffic noise is the only problem you might encounter.

The area around **Sants** and **Plaça Espanya** is the main hub of business hotels and convenient for conferences, meetings, and trade shows. It's also convenient for getting to or from the airport (just 20 min. away by taxi), and the hotels here tend to be quite good if family-size rooms are needed. But most leisure travelers will probably find it too far away from the city center.

Farther north, above the Avinguda Diagonal, you'll enter the **Gràcia** area, where you can enjoy distinctively Catalan neighborhood life. It has a village-y feel, low-rise buildings, and plenty of sunny plazas populated by students. The main attractions are a bit distant but easily reached by public transportation, still the neighborhood does have a uniquely eclectic feel that makes the barrio worth exploring. Above this, the neighborhoods of **Sarrià** and **Sant Gervasi** are mainly upper-class residential areas, with plenty of top-end bars and restaurants.

Barcelona's seafront has never been much of a hot spot for hotels, though after decades of practically ignoring its shoreline, the city has more recently transformed it into a bustling seaside promenade. The few hotels that do exist here tend to be four or five star, though the area of **Poble Nou** (regenerated by the cultural festival Forum2004) is becoming increasingly popular among new developers and is a good choice for anyone looking to get away from the tourist crowds while staying close to the beach.

Another option consider is **aparthotels** and short-term rented **apartments** (self-catering accommodations), which are becoming increasingly popular. They give you independence, a kitchen in which you cook for yourself, and the sensation of a home-away-from-home. Finally there is a new wave in **bed-and-breakfast** accommodations. Virtually unheard of until 2 or 3 years ago, these family-run guesthouses (often no more than two or three rooms) offer a highly personal and cheap alternative.

But whichever option you choose, you *must* book well ahead to secure something on your list of first choices. Don't even think of rolling into town without a reservation—if you do, you may find yourself sculling to the distant suburbs or out of Barcelona altogether. This is not true only during summer months, either: Tourism here is nonstop year-round.

Many of Barcelona's hotels were built before the invention of the automobile, and even the more modern ones rarely have garages. When parking is available at the hotel, I've indicated the price; otherwise, the hotel staff will direct you to a garage. Expect to pay upward of 14€ ($18) for 24 hours, and if you do have a car, you might as well park it and leave it there, because driving around the city can be excruciating. Indeed, if you don't plan to leave Barcelona, then you won't need to rent a car.

1 The Best Hotel Bets

- **Best for a Romantic Getaway:** Lovebirds have good reasons not to leave the confines of **Gran Hotel La Florida,** Carretera de Tibidabo s/n (© **93-259-30-00**), a fabulous historic hotel—and not all of those reasons are to be found in the bedrooms. The stainless-steel lap pool, spa, and gardens offering sweeping views of the city are enticement enough to keep you holed up for days. See p. 116.
- **Best for Art Lovers:** As stylish as anywhere in the city, the **Hotel Claris,** Pau Claris 150 (© **93-487-62-62**), has rooms and foyers dotted with early-Egyptian art and artifacts, 19th-century Turkish kilims, and even some Roman mosaics, a fruit of the owner's passion for collecting. See p. 98.
- **Best for Business Travelers:** In the heart of the business district, the **AC Diplomatic,** Pau Claris 122 (© **93-272-38-10**), exudes efficiency. The highly tasteful interior and amenities have just the right balance of detail and function, allowing those with a job to do to get on with it in comfort. See p. 102.
- **Best for Celebrity Spotting:** Preferred choice of top models and temperamental rock stars (P. Diddy reportedly partied up a storm here when he came to Barcelona to host the 2002 MTV Awards) the **Hotel Arts,** Marina 19–21 (© **93-221-10-00**), has remained a jet-set playground and symbol of "cool Barcelona" for over a decade. See p. 112.
- **Best for Service:** As well as being a highly regarded hotel, the **Prestige,** Passeig de Gràcia 62 (© **93-272-41-80**), offers a unique service to its clients. The role of the concierge is replaced with "Ask Me," specially trained information officers on call to find the answers to the most challenging queries: from how to score soccer tickets to where to find halal restaurants. See p. 100.
- **Best Grande Dame:** Since it opened its doors in 1919, the city's **Hotel Ritz,** Gran Vía 668 (© **93-318-52-00**), has survived a civil war, a world war, an anarchist occupation, and the fall of a dictatorship—all while retaining an impeccable level of service and tradition. During all this, distinguished guests such as the Duke of Windsor, Ava Gardner, and Salvador Dalí have chosen to stay in its gilt and marble surroundings and take refuge in the elegant tearoom and restaurant. See p. 100.
- **Best In-House Restaurant:** When celebrated chef Fermin Puig took over the food department of the highly regarded **Majestic,** Passeig de Gràcia 70 (© **93-488-17-17**), he not only revolutionized what clients receive on their breakfast tray but also created **Drolma,** one of the country's most celebrated haute-cuisine restaurants. Puig's take on traditional Catalan and Southern French cooking has impressed even the most demanding gourmand. See p. 98.
- **Best Historic Hotel:** The *modernista* masterpiece **Hotel Casa Fuster,** Passeig de Gràcia 132 (© **93-225-30-00**), was an emblematic building *before* it was converted into a luxury residence. The rooms have been restored to turn-of-the-20th-century opulence, but with all the modern conveniences expected by today's high society. See p. 97.
- **Best Modern Design:** Local talent joined forces to create the **Hotel Omm,** Rosselló 265 (© **93-445-40-00**), which was conceived as homage to the city's vibrant design culture. Daring concepts prevail, from the metal facade to the sleek

open-plan suites and private terraces. On the ground floor, the Omm's restaurant, Moo, is fast becoming the place to see and be seen among Barcelona's arts elite. See p. 100.

- **Best for Sheer Atmosphere:** If faded glory is your thing then look no further than the **Hotel España,** Sant Pau 11 (© **93-318-17-58**). Designed by a contemporary of Gaudí, the street-level dining room, with its florid motif and brass fixtures, will whisk you back to the early 1900s, when it was filled with chattering patrons taking supper after a trip to the opera house next door. See p. 96.

- **Best Location:** The **Colón,** Av. de la Catedral 7 (© **93-301-14-04**), is as enviably located as any hotel in the city. It stands directly in front of the cathedral's main entrance, overlooking an expansive square that buzzes day and night with color and activity. Ask for a front room with a balcony when you book here. See p. 87.

- **Best for Architecture Buffs:** Hailing from the early '50s, the **Park Hotel,** Av. Marquès de L'Argentera 11 (© **93-319-60-00**), was the first example of postwar *modernista* architecture in the city. The renovation carried out 4 decades later only enhances its singular style. Among its highlights is one of the most striking staircases in existence. See p. 93.

- **Best Boutique Hotel:** The boutique concept took its time coming to Barcelona. Forefront of the movement was **Banys Orientals,** Argenteria 37 (© **93-268-84-60**), and it remains the best. It's perfectly located in the middle of El Born district, Barcelona's bastion of urban chic. See p. 95.

- **Best Small Hotel: Hostal D'Uxelles,** Gran Vía 688 and 667 (© **93-265-25-60**), looks as if it has come straight from the pages of one of those rustic-interiors magazines. Located on the first floor of two adjacent buildings, the Hostal D'Uxelles has 30 rooms, each with a distinct character. All rooms, though, include canopied beds, antique furniture, and Andalusian-style ceramic bathrooms. See p. 105.

- **Best for Sea Views:** Imagine stepping off a luxury cruise liner and straight into a top-class hotel. That is possible at **Hotel Grand Marina,** World Trade Center, Moll de Barcelona (© **93-603-90-00**). It's housed in the western wing of the city's World Trade Center, on a wide jetty which is in effect a man-made island in the port. From its windows and terraces you can enjoy some splendid Mediterranean vistas. See p. 114.

- **Best Inexpensive Hotel:** Serenity and character abound in **Hotel Peninsular,** Sant Pau 34–36 (© **93-302-31-38**), a nunnery-turned-hotel. Located on a colorful street just off Les Ramblas, the hotel—with its Art Nouveau elevator, long hallways in tones of green and white, and inner-courtyard—is an oasis from the hustle and bustle outside. But book ahead. See p. 96.

- **Best for Families Who Don't Want to Break the Bank:** The family-run **Marina Folch,** Carrer del Mar 16 (© **93-310-37-09**), is located in Barceloneta, which has plenty of open-air bars and open spaces for the kids to run wild. Ask for a room at the front for a balcony with a view of the port. See p. 115.

- **Best *Hostal:*** Forget faded curtains and floral wallpaper. **Gat Raval,** Joaquín Costa 44 (© **93-481-66-70**), is a streamlined *hostal,* fitted out in acid green and black, which has been conceived for the modern budget traveler. On-demand Internet access and touches of abstract art add to its contemporary ambience and the foyer is always abuzz with travelers exchanging information. See p. 94.

2 Ciutat Vella (Barri Gòtic, El Raval & La Ribera)

The **Ciutat Vella (Old City)** forms the monumental center of Barcelona, taking in Les Ramblas, Plaça de Sant Jaume, Vía Laietana, Passeig Nacional, the Passeig de Colom, and the full-of-character Raval and La Ribera neighborhoods. It contains some of the city's best hotel bargains. Most of the glamorous, and more expensive, hotels are located in the Eixample and beyond.

VERY EXPENSIVE

Le Meridien Barcelona ✰✰✰   Originally built in 1956, this is the finest hotel in the Old Town, as the roster of famous guests (such as Michael Jackson) can attest. It's superior in comfort to its two closest rivals in the area, the Colón and the Rivoli Ramblas (and also more expensive). Guest rooms are spacious and comfortable, with extra-large beds and heated bathroom floors with tub/shower combos. All rooms have double-glazed windows, but that doesn't fully block out noise from Les Ramblas. The Renaissance Club, an executive floor popular with business people, provides extra luxuries. The hotel was refurbished at the end of 2006.

Les Ramblas 111, 08002 Barcelona. (C) **888/250-8577** in the U.S., or 93-318-62-00. Fax 93-301-77-76. www.meridien barcelona.com. 233 units. 400€–450€ ($500–$563) double; 500€–2,000€ ($625–$2,500) suite. AE, DC, MC, V. Parking 20€ ($25). Metro: Liceu or Plaça de Catalunya. **Amenities:** Restaurant; bar; health club; limited room service; babysitting; laundry service; dry cleaning. *In room:* A/C, TV, free Wi-Fi, minibar, hair dryer, safe.

EXPENSIVE

Duquesa de Cardona ✰✰✰ *(Moments)*   This small boutique hotel—popular with honeymooners—is across the road from the harbor of Port Vell, and the rooftop terrace and small plunge pool with Jacuzzi have splendid views of the pleasure and party boats that dock here year-round. Many of the Art Deco features of the 19th-century palace the hotel occupies have been preserved and mixed with elements of modern style to ensure maximum comfort. Communal areas include a stylish living room with deep, cream-colored sofas and a smart Mediterranean restaurant with original marble tiles. The bedrooms have an intimate, romantic feel and all have well-equipped bathrooms with tub/shower combos. If you're used to American-style bedrooms, however, they might seem a little cramped (especially those at the back). It's worth paying the extra money to get a front-facing room with views of the harbor.

Passeig Colom 12, Barri Gòtic, 08002 Barcelona. (C) **866/376-7831** in the U.S. and Canada, or 93-268-90-90. Fax 93-268-29-31. www.hduquesadecardona.com. 250€ ($313) double; 360€ ($450) junior suite; sea-view supplement 35€ ($44). 44 units. AE, DC, MC, V. Public parking nearby 20€ ($25). Metro: Jaume I or Drassanes. **Amenities:** Restaurant; 2 lounges; outdoor swimming pool; solarium; business center; 24-hr. room service; babysitting service; laundry service; dry cleaning; nonsmoking rooms. *In room:* A/C, TV, minibar, hair dryer, safe, Internet access.

Hotel Colón ✰✰ *(Kids)*   The Colón is in the heart of Barcelona's Ciutat Vella—a good choice if this is the part of town you've come to see—though it can seem a little old-fashioned, with traditional furniture and fittings and without any concessions to modernity. Situated opposite the main entrance to the cathedral (the best rooms on the sixth floor have small terraces with splendid views), this hotel sits behind a dignified neoclassical facade. Inside, you'll find conservative and slightly old-fashioned public rooms, a helpful staff, and good-size guest rooms filled with comfortable furniture. Despite recent renovations, the decor remains fairly old-fashioned with heavily patterned drapes and upholstery. All rooms have en-suite bathrooms containing a tub/shower combo. Not all rooms have views; however, those at the back of the building are quieter. Some of the lower rooms are rather dark. Upon request, families can often be given more spacious rooms and the hotel often has Christmas, New Year's, and summer-season deals.

Av. de la Catedral 7, 08002 Barcelona. ℂ 800/845-0636 in the U.S., or 93-301-14-04. Fax 93-317-29-15. www.hotel colon.es. 145 units. 250€ ($313) double; from 400€ ($500) suite. AE, DC, MC, V. Bus: 16, 17, 19, or 45. **Amenities:** Restaurant; bar; limited room service; babysitting; laundry service/dry cleaning. *In room:* A/C, TV, dataport, minibar, hair dryer, safe.

Hotel NH Calderón 🌊🌊   Efficiently maintained and well staffed with a multi-lingual corps of employees, this hotel delivers exactly what it promises: comfortable accommodations in a well-conceived, standardized format that's akin to many other modern hotels around the world. Originally built in the 1960s, this 10-story hotel wasn't particularly imaginative then, but was greatly improved in the early 1990s after its acquisition by the NH Hotel Group, with frequent renovations ever since. Accom-modations have comfortable, contemporary-looking furnishings with hints of high-tech design, good lighting, lots of varnished hardwood, and colorful fabrics. All units have bathrooms with tub/shower combos.

Rambla de Catalunya 26, 08007 Barcelona. ℂ 93-301-00-00. Fax 93-412-41-93. www.nh-hoteles.es. 253 units. Mon–Thurs 250€ ($313) double; Fri–Sun 180€ ($225) double. AE, DC, MC, V. Parking 15€ ($19). Metro: Passeig de Gràcia. **Amenities:** Restaurant; bar; indoor and outdoor pool; health club; sauna; business center; limited room serv-ice; laundry service; dry cleaning; nonsmoking rooms. *In room:* A/C, TV, minibar, hair dryer, safe, Internet access.

Rivoli Ramblas 🌊   Behind a dignified Art Deco town house on the upper section of La Rambla, a block south of the Plaça de Catalunya, this well-renovated hotel incorporates many fine examples of avant-garde Catalan design in its stylish interior. The communal areas have acres of polished marble and it's a popular choice for guests in town on business. One of the Rivoli's highlights is the handsome wood-decked roof terrace—a pleasant place to start the day. Guest rooms are carpeted, soundproof, and elegant, but rather cramped. All have neatly kept bathrooms with tub/shower combos.

La Rambla 128, 08002 Barcelona. ℂ 93-302-66-43. Fax 93-317-50-53. www.rivolihotels.com. 129 units. 250€ ($313) double; from 300€–725€ ($375–$906) suite. AE, DC, MC, V. Metro: Catalunya or Liceu. **Amenities:** Restaurant; bar; health spa; sauna; solarium; car rental; limited room service; babysitting; laundry service; dry cleaning; nonsmoking rooms. *In room:* A/C, TV, minibar, hair dryer, safe, Internet access (in some).

MODERATE

Catalonia Albioni 🌊🌊   An ideal choice for shopaholics, the Albioni is situated halfway up the Portal de l'Angel, where you'll find shoulder-to-shoulder Spanish fash-ion stores like Zara and Mango, as well as El Corte Inglés (Spain's major department store) at one end, and boutiques and trinket shops at the other. Housed in a former palace dating back to 1876, it was converted into a hotel in 1998. It remains on Barcelona's artistic-heritage list and many of the original romantic and baroque fea-tures have been beautifully preserved. Not least impressive is the elegant marble lobby and stately interior courtyard, where the bar and reception area are located. All 74 of the plush bedrooms have polished wood floors, comfortable beds and en-suite marble bathrooms with tub/shower combos. Breakfast (though overpriced) is served in a wedding-style tent.

Av. Portal de l'Angel 17, Barri Gòtic. 08002 Barcelona. ℂ 93-318-41-41. Fax 93-301-26-31. www.hoteles-catalonia.es. 74 units. 130€–180€ ($163–$225) double. AE, DC, MC, V. Public parking nearby 20€ ($25). Metro: Catalunya. **Amenities:** Cafeteria; car rental; limited room service; babysitting; laundry service; dry cleaning; comput-ers w/Internet. *In room:* A/C, TV, minibar, hair dryer, safe.

Ciutat Vella Accommodations

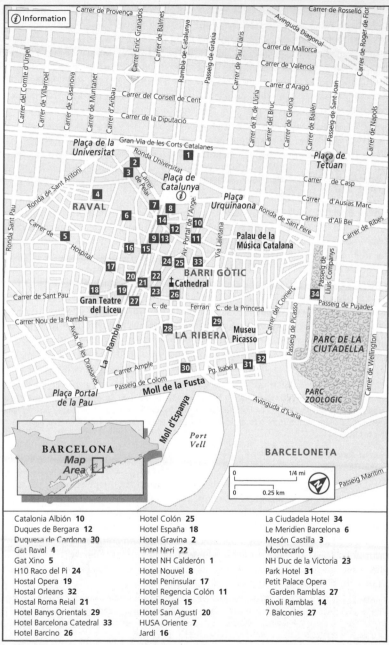

Catalonia Albión **10**
Duques de Bergara **12**
Duquesa de Cardona **30**
Gat Raval **4**
Gat Xino **5**
H10 Raco del Pi **24**
Hostal Opera **19**
Hostal Orleans **32**
Hostal Roma Reial **21**
Hotel Banys Orientals **29**
Hotel Barcelona Catedral **33**
Hotel Barcino **26**

Hotel Colón **25**
Hotel España **18**
Hotel Gravina **2**
Hotel Neri **22**
Hotel NH Calderón **1**
Hotel Nouvel **8**
Hotel Peninsular **17**
Hotel Regencia Colón **11**
Hotel Royal **15**
Hotel San Agustí **20**
HUSA Oriente **7**
Jardí **16**

La Ciudadela Hotel **34**
Le Meridien Barcelona **6**
Mesón Castilla **3**
Montecarlo **9**
NH Duc de la Victoria **23**
Park Hotel **31**
Petit Palace Opera
  Garden Ramblas **27**
Rivoli Ramblas **14**
7 Balconies **27**

Duques de Bergara 🏛️🏛️   This upscale hotel occupies an 1898 town house built for the Duke of Bergara by the architect Emilio Salas y Cortés (a protégé of Gaudí). Lots of elegant *modernista* touches remain, including the original wood-molded ceiling with a rose dome on the first floor, and a handful of original artworks from the era. In the reception area, look for stained-glass panels displaying the heraldic coat of arms of the building's original occupant and namesake, the Duke of Bergara. In 1998 the original five-story structure more than doubled in size with the addition of a new seven-story tower. Guest rooms throughout have the same conservative, traditional comforts. Each unit has large, comfortable beds with first-rate mattresses, elegant fabrics, and good lighting. The roomy marble bathrooms are equipped with tub/shower combos.

Bergara 11, 08002 Barcelona. 📞 93-301-51-51. Fax 93-317-34-42. www.hoteles-catalonia.es. 149 units. 180€–250€ ($225–$313) double; 225€–295€ ($281–$370) triple. AE, DC, MC, V. Public parking nearby 18€ ($23). Metro: Catalunya. **Amenities:** Restaurant; cafe/bar; outdoor pool; limited room service; laundry service; dry cleaning; Internet access. *In room:* A/C, TV, minibar, hair dryer, safe.

Hotel Barcino 🏛️ *Finds*   For reasons unknown, this smart four-star hotel, a stone's throw from the Plaza Jaume I—home to Barcelona's regional government and town hall—rarely gets a mention in the guidebooks. Nevertheless, it must be one of the best located, higher-end hotels in town. All main Barri Gòtic attractions are a short stroll away, including some of the best locales for tapas (**Taller de Tapas;** p. 134), contemporary Catalan fare (**Café de l'Academia;** p. 124), and cocktails (**Ginger;** p. 239). The staff is courteous and pleasant, while bedrooms are classically decorated and have en-suite bathrooms with tub/shower combos. The best rooms have whirlpool baths (big enough for sharing) and private terraces with views over the rooftops and the cathedral, perfect for a predinner drink. They offer a rather expensive buffet breakfast at 15€ ($19). However, there are numerous local cafes serving fresh coffee and pastries a stone's throw from the front door. All in all, this is a good choice if you want to be at the center of the action.

Jaume I no. 6, Barri Gòtic, 08002 Barcelona. 📞 93-302-20-12. Fax 93-301-42-42. www.hotelbarcino.com. 53 units. 225€ ($281) double. AE, DC, MC, V. Public parking nearby 15€ ($19). Metro: Jaume I or Catalunya. **Amenities:** Restaurant; cafe/bar; limited room service; babysitting; laundry service. *In room:* A/C, TV, minibar, hair dryer, safe, Internet access.

Hotel Gravina *Value*   Part of the reliable H10 chain, the Gravina is a three-star hotel on a quiet street close to the university. This means it's handy for public transport, sights, and shopping, but far enough removed from the main tourist drag to offer some breathing space from the bustle of the Ciutat Vella. The 19th-century facade promises great things inside, but don't get too excited. The interior has been built around the standard H10 model and therefore lacks any real atmosphere. That said, it's a good value with friendly, accommodating staff and comfortable, fully equipped bedrooms. It's worth specifying that you want a larger room. All have soundproof windows and en-suite bathrooms with tub/shower combos. This is an especially good choice for business travelers on a budget.

Gravina 12, 08001 Barcelona. 📞 93-301-68-68. Fax 93-317-28-38 www.hotel-gravina.com. 82 units. 140€–200€ ($175–$250) double; 210€–350€ ($263–$438) suite. AE, DC, MC, V. Public parking nearby 24€ ($30). Metro: Universitat or Catalunya. **Amenities:** Restaurant; cafe/bar; limited room service; laundry service; dry cleaning; non-smoking rooms; Internet access. *In room:* A/C, TV, minibar, hair dryer, safe.

Hotel Neri 🏛️🏛️🏛️   The Hotel Neri is a Gothic palace tucked neatly away on the delightful Plaça Felip Neri near the cathedral. With its velvet drapes and soft-lit, echoing hallways it's fast gaining a reputation as one of the most romantic places in the city. Bedrooms are plush with high-thread-count cotton sheets, shot-silk pillowcases, throws, and rugs. The minibar has all the usual tipples plus incense and candles. Some rooms have a tub as well as a shower. The Neri has just two suites (one of which was occupied by John Malkovich for a month while his play *Hysteria* was done at a local theater). Space, in fact, is of the essence in the cramped Barri Gòtic and the Neri has the added bonus of a terrace for coffee and cocktails on the plaza and a rooftop garden overgrown with jasmine plants and creepers. Pity they've felt the need to cram in sun loungers and it can feel a bit like a public pool when the place is busy. The somewhat overpriced gourmet "new Catalan cuisine" restaurant here is a further boon to followers of the super chef Ferran Adrià.

Sant Sever 5, Barri Gòtic, 08002 Barcelona. (C) **93-304-06-55.** Fax 93-304-03-37. www.hotelneri.com. 22 units. 180€–190€ ($225–$238) double; 200€–225€ ($250–$281) suite. AE, DC, MC, V. Public parking nearby 20€ ($25). Metro: Jaume I or Liceu. **Amenities:** Restaurant; cafe/bar; limited room service; babysitting service; laundry service; dry cleaning; nonsmoking rooms; book/CD library. *In room:* A/C, TV, minibar, hair dryer, safe, Internet access.

Hotel Nouvel *(Moments* A smart, atmospheric hotel with plenty of its original *modernista* flourishes, the Nouvel makes a charming retreat in the heart of the Old City. It's wonderful for lovers of the Art Deco style with many of the original carved wood panels, smoked-glass partitions, and elaborate floor tiles. The bedrooms offer a mix of newly renovated accommodations, though the rooms with the most character are the more old-fashioned kind with the original tiles. All have newly modernized bathrooms with tub/shower combos. The best have balconies and it's worth asking for a room at the rear if street noise bothers you.

Santa Ana 20, Barri Gòtic, 08002 Barcelona. (C) **93-301-82-74.** Fax 93-301-83-70. www.hotelnouvel.com. 54 units. 175€ ($219) double. Rate includes breakfast. MC, V. Public parking nearby 24€ ($30). Metro: Catalunya. **Amenities:** Restaurant (lunch daily, dinner Thurs–Sat); babysitting; laundry service; dry cleaning; nonsmoking rooms. *In room:* A/C, TV, minibar, safe in some rooms, Internet access.

Hotel Regencia Colón *(Value* This stately six-story stone building stands directly behind the pricier Hotel Colón and in the shadow of the cathedral. The Regencia Colón attracts tour groups because it's a good value for Barcelona. The formal lobby seems a bit dour, but the well-maintained rooms are comfortable and often roomy, albeit worn at the edges. Rooms are insulated against sound, and 40 have full bathrooms with tubs (the remainder have showers only). All have comfortable beds and piped-in music. The hotel's main draw is its location.

Sagristans 13–17, 08002 Barcelona. (C) **93-318-98-58.** Fax 93-317-28-22. www.hotelregenciacolon.com. 50 units. 160€ ($200) double; 185€ ($231) triple. AE, DC, MC, V. Public parking 18€ ($23). Metro: Catalunya or Urquinaona. **Amenities:** Restaurant; bar; car rental; babysitting; laundry service; dry cleaning. *In room:* A/C, TV, minibar, hair dryer, safe, Internet access.

Hotel Royal *(Value* The flat-packed front of this hotel with its glassed-in balconies looks rather like an office block in comparison with the more lavish architecture of the city—but don't let that put you off. Its tastefully stylish refurbishments mean it's better equipped than ever, offering spacious rooms with comfortable beds and furnishings and modern facilities. All rooms have en-suite bathrooms with tub/shower combos and the better bedrooms have balconies offering fabulous views over Barcelona's real-life street theater: La Rambla.

La Rambla 117, Barri Gòtic, 08002 Barcelona. (C) **93-304-12-12.** Fax 93-317-31-79. www.hroyal.com. 108 units. 150€–225€ ($188–$281) double. AE, DC, MC, V. Parking 14€ ($18). Metro: Catalunya. **Amenities:** Restaurant; cafe/bar; business center; room service (7am–midnight); babysitting service; laundry service; dry cleaning; nonsmoking rooms. *In room:* A/C, TV, minibar, hair dryer, safe.

Hotel San Agustí This is arguably the most upscale hotel in El Raval (though it may soon face strong competition as the neighborhood continues to gentrify). This tastefully renovated five-story hotel stands in the center of the Old City on a pretty square near the Boqueria market, overlooking the brick walls of an unfinished Romanesque church. The small guest rooms are comfortable and modern with tiled bathrooms with tub/shower combos. The outdoor cafe is a good place to chill out on a hot afternoon, and the immediate vicinity is full of the funky character that is making El Ravel the current Barcelona hot spot. Some units are equipped for travelers with disabilities.

Plaça de San Agustí 3, El Raval, 08001 Barcelona. ℂ **93-318-16-58.** Fax 93-317-29-28. 76 units. www.hotelsa.com. 100€–150€ ($125–$188) double; 165€–180€ ($206–$225) triple; 185€–195€ ($231–$244) quad; 225€–240€ ($281–$300) 2-bedroom family unit. Rates include breakfast. AE, DC, MC, V. Metro: Liceu. **Amenities:** Restaurant; lounge; room service (morning only); laundry service; free Internet. *In room:* A/C, TV, hair dryer, safe, Internet access.

H10 Raco Del Pi (★ Locations don't get much better than this one, right next to the Old City's prettiest plaza, which is bustling most days with cafes, weekend produce markets, buskers, and artists. The hotel itself has plenty of character, and is small and intimate with helpful staff that provides some nice touches like offering a glass of *cava* (sparkling wine) to guests on arrival. They also serve a good breakfast buffet offering a range of homemade products. The rooms tend to be compact and dark (one disadvantage of staying in the Barri Gòtic), but this seems a small price to pay for staying in such a cozy place and in such a desirable corner of the town center. All rooms have en-suite mosaic-tiled bathrooms with tub/shower combos.

Del Pi 7, Barri Gòtic, 08002 Barcelona. ℂ **93-342-61-90.** Fax 93-342-61-91. www.hotelracodelpi.com. 37 units. 175€ ($219) double. AE, DC, MC, V. Public parking nearby 20€ ($25). Metro: Liceu. **Amenities:** Restaurant; cafe/bar; car rental; business center; limited room service; laundry service; dry cleaning; nonsmoking rooms. *In room:* A/C, TV, minibar, hair dryer, safe, Internet access, scale.

HUSA Oriente Located on the site of a Franciscan monastery right beside the bustling Rambla, the Oriente was one of the original "grand hotels" of Barcelona, and dates back to 1842. Such was its prominence by the 1950s that it attracted the likes of Toscanini and Maria Callas. It became part of Hollywood legend when Errol Flynn once got so drunk that he passed out in the bar. The manager ordered two bartenders to carry him upstairs where they were instructed to strip the swashbuckling star. The manager then sent word to guests down below that they could see the star in the nude. People filed in for the viewing all night, and when Flynn woke the next morning, he was none the wiser. Renovations have improved the hotel's amenities, but it lacks the style and charisma of its former glory days, today attracting mainly frugal travelers. The arched ballroom of yesterday has been turned into an atmospheric lounge, and the dining room still has a certain grandeur. The simple but comfortable rooms all have tiled bathrooms with shower.

Rambles 45, 08002 Barcelona. ℂ **93-302-25-58.** Fax 93-412-38-19. www.husa.es. 142 units. 175€ ($219) double; 190€ ($238) triple. AE, DC, MC, V. Metro: Liceu. **Amenities:** Restaurant (summer only); bar; laundry service. *In room:* A/C, TV, safe.

Mesón Castilla (★ (*Value* This government-rated two-star hotel, a former apartment building now owned and operated by the Spanish hotel chain HUSA, has a Castilian facade with a wealth of Art Nouveau detailing on the interior. Filled with antiques and quirky trinkets, it's one of the most atmospheric spots to stay in town. It's also handily located close to the hip secondhand stores and record shops of the upper Raval, the MACBA, and the CCCB. The midsize rooms are comfortable—beds have ornate

Catalan-style headboards—and some open onto large terraces. The tiled bathrooms are equipped with tub/shower combos.

Valldoncella 5, 08001 Barcelona. ✆ 93-318-21-82. Fax 93-412-40-20. hmesoncastilla@teleline.es. 57 units. 130€ ($163) double; 175€ ($219) triple. Rates include breakfast. AE, DC, MC, V. Parking 20€ ($25). Metro: Catalunya or Universitat. **Amenities:** Breakfast room; lounge; room service; babysitting; laundry service; dry cleaning, safe. *In room:* A/C, TV, minibar, hair dryer.

Montecarlo ✮✮✮ The fabulously ornate facade of this La Rambla hotel dates back 200 years to the days when it was an opulent private home and the headquarters of the Royal Artistic Circle of Barcelona. Public areas include some of the building's original accessories, with carved doors, a baronial fireplace, and crystal chandeliers. In the 1930s, it was transformed into the comfortably unpretentious hotel you'll find today. It offers a level of comfort superior to that of most competitors. Each of the midsize guest rooms is smartly decorated, with extras that make all the difference, such as adjustable beds, large marble bathrooms with Jacuzzi tubs, bathrobes, and slippers. The service is exemplary and nothing is too much trouble, whether you want to book a winery excursion or simply park your car.

La Rambla 124, 08002 Barcelona. ✆ 93-412-04-04. Fax 93-318-73-23. www.montecarlobcn.com. 55 units. 160€–340€ ($200–$425) double; 395€ ($494) suite. AE, DC, MC, V. Parking 18€ ($23). Metro: Catalunya. **Amenities:** Lounge; bar; limited room service; babysitting; laundry service; dry cleaning; terrace solarium; free Internet. *In room:* A/C, TV, minibar, hair dryer, safe, Internet access.

NH Duc de la Victoria *Value* Part of the NH Hotel Chain, which aims to provide smooth, seamless comfort in mid-price accommodations, this smart hotel is well situated on a quiet street in the heart of the Barri Gòtic. Of a somewhat higher standard than most *hostales* in the area, it makes a great base for discerning visitors who want to have all central amenities right on their doorstep. Spotlessly clean throughout, it has few communal facilities aside from a breakfast room, but given its location, this hardly matters. The decent-size bedrooms have cool parquet floors, and all have compact bathrooms with tub/shower combos. Fifth-floor rooms with private balconies are the best.

Duc de la Victoria 15, Barri Gòtic, 08002 Barcelona. ✆ 93-270-34-10. Fax 93-412-77-47. www.nh-hotels-spain.com. 156 units. 180€ ($225) double; 250€ ($313) suite. AE, DC, MC, V. Public parking nearby 15€ ($19). Metro: Catalunya. **Amenities:** Restaurant; cafe/bar; limited room service; babysitting service; laundry service; dry cleaning; nonsmoking rooms. *In room:* A/C, TV, minibar, hair dryer, safe, Internet access.

Park Hotel ✮ A laid-back hotel near the Estació de Franca, the edifice is a unique example of mid-20th-century rationalist architecture. The interior is dominated by a stunning, spiral staircase, the foyer by a sleek, mosaic-tile bar. It also has one of the best restaurants in the city, **Abac** (p. 131). It's situated right on the edge of El Born, with numerous bars, restaurants, and boutique clothing stores just a stone's throw away. The Parc de la Ciutadella (central Barcelona's greenest area) is just across the road, and a 10-minute walk will take you to the beach in Barceloneta. Bedrooms are stylish (though slightly small), comfortably decorated in warm colors, and equipped with tastefully chosen furnishings. All have en-suite bathrooms with tub/shower combos.

Av. Marquès de l'Argentera 11, Born, 08003 Barcelona. ✆ 93-319-60-00. Fax 93-319-45-19. www.parkhotel barcelona.com. 91 units. 110€–190€ ($138–$238) double. AE, DC, MC, V. Parking 12€ ($15). Metro: Barceloneta or Jaume I. **Amenities:** Restaurant; lounge; limited room service; laundry service; dry cleaning; nonsmoking rooms. *In room:* A/C, TV, minibar, hair dryer, safe, Internet access.

Petit Palace Opera Garden Ramblas ✮ *Finds* Opened in September 2006, this well-appointed member of the Petit Palace high-tech hotel chain is magnificently located in the heart of La Rambla, close to two famous Barcelona landmarks: the Liceu Theater and huge Boqueria market. It's an ideal choice both for business travelers and vacationers who simply want to keep in touch with folks back home; the neatly furnished rooms all have laptop computers with free Wi-Fi connections. Accommodations cover everyone from single executives to families of four (with king-size beds) and all have hydro-massage showers (larger rooms also have saunas). General facilities include a business center in the main hall, and a bar/cafeteria and gourmet dining room.

Carrer La Boqueria 10, Ramblas 78, 8002 Barcelona. ⓒ 93-302-00-92. Fax 93-302-15-66. www.hthoteles.com. 70 units (27 high-tech, 31 executive, 22 family-size). 200€ ($250) single; 275€ ($344) high-tech room; 300€ ($375) double; 320€ ($400) 4-bed family size. AE, DC, MC, V. Metro: Liceu. **Amenities:** Restaurant; cafeteria; lounge; business center; meeting room; laundry service; nonsmoking areas and rooms. *In room:* A/C, TV, minibar, safe, Internet access.

INEXPENSIVE

Gat Raval *★★ Value*   From grim and grungy to green and groovy, the Gat Raval is the first in this extraordinary little chain's mini-empire and has been a pioneer in giving *hostal* accommodations a much-needed face-lift. The Gats (Catalan for "cats") are so feverishly cool, that even hipsters who would normally stay at places like the Omm and the Prestige are checking in, and saving themselves a few euros while they're at it. Decorated in bright acid greens with matte black trim, Internet connections in the lobby, and neat bedrooms decorated with original works from the local art school give it an upbeat Boho vibe. Only some of the bedrooms have en-suite bathrooms (stipulate when booking) and communal arrangements are so clean you could eat your dinner off the floor.

Joaquín Costa 44, 08001 Barcelona. ⓒ 93-481-66-70. Fax 93-342-66-97. www.gataccommodation.com. 24 units. 60€ ($75) double with washbasin; 75€ ($94) double with bathroom. MC, V. Metro: Universitat. **Amenities:** Safe; Internet service. *In room:* TV.

Gat Xino *★★ Finds*   Those wishing to experience the same Gat über-coolness with a dash more luxury should opt for the Gat Xino, opened in 2004 for a slightly more grown-up and affluent visitor. This hip spot has a sleek breakfast room, and there's a roof terrace for soaking up the rays. All the rooms have their own apple-green bathrooms with showers and a few added extras like flatscreen TVs and light boxes above the bedsteads giving abstract photographic views of the city. It's all terribly cool, not to mention affordable.

Hospital 149–155, 08001 Barcelona. ⓒ 93-324-88-33. Fax 93-324-88-34. www.gataccomodation.com. 35 units. 90€ ($113) double. Rate includes breakfast. MC, V. Metro: Liceu. **Amenities:** Safe (2€/$2.50 per day); Internet service. *In room:* A/C, TV.

Hostal Opera *Value*   Cheap and cheerful, this safe, well-maintained *hostal* is good for those traveling on a tight budget or alone. Make no mistake, this is basic, no-frills lodging: The walls are thin (light sleepers might do well to travel with earplugs) and there are no luxuries, but for all that, it's a pleasant little place with a young, upbeat personality. Some rooms are better than others, however, and if you arrive without a reservation, ask to look around first. Otherwise, opt for something at the back with a private bathroom (shower only) because the street outside can be noisy until the early hours.

Sant Pau 20, El Raval, 08001 Barcelona. ⓒ 93-318-82-01. www.hostalopera.com. 69 units. 60€ ($75) double. MC, V. Metro: Liceu. **Amenities:** Safe; Internet service. *In room:* A/C, phone to receive calls.

Hostal Orleans *(Value)*   Located just across the street from one of Barcelona's oldest and most imposing churches, Santa María del Mar, this modest hotel combines desirable location (El Born) with highly affordable rates. Some of the rooms have been redecorated in the not-too-distant past, and if this matters to you it's worth asking for a newer one. Otherwise, though spotlessly clean, the Hostal Orleans is filled with objects and color schemes that take you back to the 1970s. Bedrooms are for the most part small, but the beds are comfortable and all rooms have private bathrooms (also small) with just enough space for a half-size bath and shower. The best rooms have balconies overlooking the street, which is great for watching the world go by, though not so good for a peaceful night's sleep. The communal sitting room is a nice touch, well stocked with English-language magazines, and a good place to meet other guests. Other pluses are the friendly service and a genuinely Catalan vibe.

Av. Marquès de l'Argentera 13, 1st floor, El Born, 08003 Barcelona. © 93-319-73-82. Fax 93-319-22-19. www.hostal orleans.com. 27 units. 60€ ($75) double. MC, V. Metro: Barceloneta or Jaume I. **Amenities:** TV lounge. *In room:* 6€ ($7.50) supplement for A/C, TV.

Hostal Roma Reial   This is a good choice for those who want to be out bar-hopping and clubbing long into the night, and who don't mind a bit of background noise (the Plaza Reial is a magnet for budding songsters and partygoers unwilling to go home). If these things don't bother you, the Roma Reial is a bargain—friendly and cheap. Plus each of the large rooms has its own bathroom (unusual for a *hostal* of this ilk).

Plaza Reial 11, Barri Gòtic, 08002 Barcelona. © 93-302-03-66. Fax 93-301-18-39. hotelromareial@hotmail.com. 61 units. 70€ ($88) double. Rates include breakfast, depending on season. MC, V. Metro: Liceu. **Amenities:** Cafeteria; safe. *In room:* A/C, TV.

Hotel Banys Orientals *(Finds)*   There may not be a pool, gym, or minibar in sight, but that hasn't stopped the runaway success of this pioneer boutique hostelry. That's due to its location (El Born) and the fact that it's a few notches up the quality-and-comfort scale from competitors such as the Orleans (above). It's set in a 19th-century mansion and the spacious rooms have been relieved of their original adornments and given a soothing, sophisticated makeover that would not be out of place in a hotel four times as expensive. Also unusual is the fact that the edifice is shared with **Senyor Parellada,** a classic Barcelonese restaurant that now partly acts as the hotel's own. A buffet breakfast is served on its mezzanine and guests can run up a tab for lunch/evening meals as well. The downside of all this is that the sound of human revelry from the pedestrian street below reaches a crescendo during the summer months, although this can often be avoided by asking for a room at the back. Of course, those who want to be in the thick of it will love having the city's coolest shops and bars right on their doorstep and will possibly be partaking in the nocturnal street activity themselves. Most of the showers are spacious and walk-in; if you really want a bathtub, stipulate at time of booking.

Argenteria 37, 08003 (La Ribera) Barcelona. © 93-268-84-60. Fax 93-268-84-61. www.hotelbanysorientals.com. 43 units. 100€ ($125) double. AE, DC, MC, V. Public parking nearby 18€ ($23). Metro: Jaume I. **Amenities:** Restaurant; limited room service; laundry service; nonsmoking rooms; free minibar for refreshments. *In room:* A/C, TV, hair dryer, safe, Internet access.

Hotel Barcelona Catedral   One of Barcelona's newer hotels, opened in October 2006, the stylish but well-priced Barcelona Catedral aims at providing quality accommodations at affordable prices. It's ideally located on a narrow street close to the cathedral and all of Ciutat Vella's sights. On-site amenities range from a pool and "chill out" terrace area to full Internet access and rooms for guests with limited mobility. Special services include cooking lessons, wine tastings, and Sunday guided tours around the Barri Gòtic. All rooms have a private bathroom and shower.

Capellans 4, Ciutat Vella, 08002 Barcelona. (C) **93-304-22-55.** 80 units. 140€–160€ ($175–$200) double. AE, DC, MC, V. Parking 30€ ($38) per day. Metro: Jaume 1. **Amenities:** Restaurant; bar-terrace; gym; free high-speed Internet access; 24-hr. reception; VIP room service; business center; laundry; dry cleaning. *In room:* A/C, TV, radio, minibar, safe, ADSL Internet connection plus Wi-Fi.

Hotel España *(Value* Although the guest rooms at this cost-conscious hotel have none of the architectural *modernista* grandeur that characterizes the foyer and splendidly elegant dining room, they're well scrubbed, comfortably sized, and outfitted with functional furniture and neatly kept bathrooms containing tub/shower combos. The building itself is a relic of the city's turn-of-the-20th-century splendor, constructed in 1902 by fabled architect Doménech i Montaner, designer and architect of the Palau de la Música, and formerly patronized by the likes of Salvador Dalí. A somewhat aging elevator serves the building's four floors, and the hardworking staff is comfortable with non-Spanish-speaking visitors. The lower Rambla, near where this hotel sits, evokes either cultural fascination or indignation, depending on how urbanized you are. Anyway, overall the Hotel España is an acceptable, historically rich, and well-managed choice for a relatively reasonable price.

Carrer Sant Pau 11, El Raval, 08001 Barcelona. (C) **93-318-17-58.** Fax 93-317-11-34. www.hotelespanya.com. 60 units. 100€ ($125) double; 150€ ($188) triple. Rates include breakfast. AE, DC, MC, V. Metro: Liceu or Drassanes. **Amenities:** 3 restaurants. *In room:* A/C, TV, hair dryer, safe.

Hotel Peninsular *(Value* Just off La Rambla, this hotel in the Art Nouveau style is a welcoming haven for the budget traveler. Constructed within the shell of a monastery that used to have a passageway connection with Sant Agustí church, the hotel was thoroughly modernized in the early 1990s. Its use of wicker furnishings gives it a colonial air, and its inner courtyard, lined with plants, is its most charming feature. In the typical *modernista* style of its era, the Peninsular has long hallways and high doorways and ceilings. The bedrooms are basic but clean, and the better ones have en-suite bathrooms with shower.

Sant Pau 34–36, El Raval, 08001 Barcelona. (C) **93-302-31-38.** Fax 93-412-36-99. 70 units. 75€ ($94) double; 90€ ($113) triple. Rates include breakfast. MC, V. Metro: Liceu. **Amenities:** Breakfast bar; safe. *In room:* A/C.

Jardí *(Value* Having one of Barcelona's most desirable locations, in the heart of Ciutat Vella, this little hotel opens onto the tree-shaded Plaça Sant Josep Oriol, where cafes huddle around the Gothic medieval church of Santa María del Pi. The five-floor hotel has been upgraded and improved in recent years, with the installation of an elevator, though the over-bright general lighting dissipates the charm for some. Much of the original architectural charm remains, and though the guest rooms are somewhat austere, they are comfortable and equipped with bathrooms with tub/shower combinations. The quieter units are at the top and 5 of the accommodations have private terraces, while 26 have small balconies. Under separate management, **Bar del Pi,** on the ground floor, is a favorite of artists and students who live nearby.

Plaça Sant Josep Oriol 1, 08002 Barcelona. (C) **93-301-59-00.** Fax 93-342-57-33. hoteljardi@retemail.es. 40 units. 80€–100€ ($90–$125) double; 120€ ($150) triple. MC, V. Metro: Liceu. *In room:* A/C, TV, safe.

La Ciudadela Hotel *(R (Finds* Built in 2005, this small, homey, family-run hotel provides good-value accommodations in a quiet zone on the northern edge of the

Ciutatela Park. From here you can simply cross the road into the park or wander 5 minutes west into the popular La Ribera district. Besides the hotel's own restaurant (which preceded it by 30 years) there's a cafe terrace where you can relax in the sun in summer. The unpretentious but cozy rooms are all equipped with private bathroom and tub/shower combinations. For location and price this genial spot is remarkable value.

Paseo Lluis Companys 2 (esquina Pasje Pujols 5), 08018 Barcelona. 13 units. (C) 93-309-95-57. Fax 93-528-63-35. www.ciudadelaparc.com. 65€–75€ ($81–$94). MC, V. Public parking. Metro: Arc de Triomf. **Amenities:** Restaurant; cafe w/terrace. *In room:* A/C, TV, phone, safe, free Internet access.

7 Balconies 🏝 *(Finds* This charmingly old-fashioned, three-room guesthouse has been in the same family for over a century, and has a snug and inviting ambience that makes you feel instantly at home. Don't expect any modern conveniences; rather, this is a cozy, pristinely kept retreat filled with antique furniture, faded Art Deco tiling, black-and-white family photos, and crisp, cotton bed linens. The suite has two rooms (one of which has a sofa bed) and the other two share a bathroom. Few places beat it when it comes to atmosphere.

Cervantes 7, Barri Gòtic, 08002 Barcelona. (C) 65-423-81-61. Fax 93-302-07-52. www.7balconies.com. 3 units. 80€–120€ ($100–$150). MC, V for room deposit only. Room payment in cash only. Parking nearby 20€ ($25). Metro: Liceu or Jaume I. **Amenities:** Tearoom. *In room:* TV, fridge, safe.

3 L'Eixample

If *moderniste* architecture, designer shopping, and high-class restaurants are your bag, then the Eixample ("Extension" in Catalan) is the place to be. The area was built in the mid–19th century to cope with the overflow of the Ciutat Vella and has retained its middle-class, residential flavor.

VERY EXPENSIVE

Hotel Casa Fuster 🏝🏝🏝 *(Moments* Opened in 2004 for the first time as a hotel, Casa Fuster is one of the city's most emblematic *moderniste* buildings. In the early 20th century it served as private home for the Fuster family, before being bought by a state electricity company in 1960. Recently acquired by the Center Group, which invested 68 million euros ($78.2 million) in its ambitious face-lift, the Casa Fuster is now classified as a five-star deluxe hotel. The result is a combination of sheer luxury and state-of-the art amenities. The renovation has been meticulous in the foyer and downstairs Café Viennese, once a well-known meeting spot for the city's intelligentsia. A Belle Epoque color scheme in mauve, magenta, and taupe has been adopted in the rooms, many with balconies that look onto the elegant Passeig de Gràcia. In keeping with the period architecture, drapery, cushions, and padding are abundant, giving the hotel a slightly over-stuffed feel for some. But if it's total indulgence you are after, plus a chance to live like the turn-of-the-20th-century bourgeoisie, the Casa Fuster offers everything you could possibly want: from Loewe toiletries to hydro-massage showers and an extremely high staff-to-guest ratio. Unlike other luxury hotels such as the Arts (p. 112) or La Florida (p. 116), the Casa Fuster also has the added advantage of being located in the city center, with some of the best shopping and sightseeing on its doorstep. Check their website for special deals.

Passeig de Gràcia 132, 08008 Barcelona. (C) 90-220-23-45 for reservations, or 93-255-30-00. Fax 93-255-30-02. www.hotelcasafuster.com/?idioma=2. 105 units. 380€–475€ ($475–$594) double; 550€–1,950€ ($687–$2,312) suite. AE, DC, MC, V. Valet parking 25€ ($31). Metro: Diagonal. **Amenities:** Restaurant; bar; 11 lounges; pool; health center; Jacuzzi; sauna; solarium, business center; 24-hr. room service; babysitting service; laundry service; dry cleaning; nonsmoking rooms; free newspaper service; audiovisual equipment service. *In room:* A/C, TV, minibar, hair dryer, safe, Internet access.

Hotel Claris 🏆🏆🏆 This highly individual, postmodern lodging is one of the few genuine luxury properties in the city center. A landmark 19th-century building (the Verdruna Palace) with a historically important facade, it incorporates teak, marble, steel, and glass in its furnishings and decor. Many regard the Claris as the best hotel in town, though some feel the bathrooms are on the small side. Opened in 1992 (in time for the Olympics), it's a seven-story structure with a swimming pool and garden on its roof. There's a small museum of Egyptian antiquities from the owner's collection on the second floor. The blue-violet guest rooms contain state-of-the-art electronic accessories as well as unusual art objects—Turkish kilims, English antiques, Hindu sculptures, Egyptian stone carvings, and engravings. The spacious rooms are among the most opulent in town, with wood marquetry and paneling, custom furnishings, safes, and some of the city's most sumptuous beds. Bathrooms are roomy and filled with deluxe toiletries, and tub/shower combinations. If money is no object, book one of the 20 individually designed duplex units.

Pau Claris 150, 08009 Barcelona. ✆ **93-487-62-62.** Fax 93-215-79-70. www.derbyhotels.com. 120 units. 300€–395€ ($375–$494) double; 475€ ($594) suite. AE, DC, MC, V. Self/valet parking 20€ ($25). Metro: Passeig de Gràcia. **Amenities:** 2 restaurants; 2 bars; outdoor pool; fitness center; sauna; business center; limited room service; babysitting; laundry service; dry cleaning; nonsmoking rooms; private museum. *In room:* A/C, TV, minibar, hair dryer, safe, Internet access.

Hotel Condes de Barcelona 🏆 Located on the architecturally splendid Passeig de Gràcia, this former private villa (dating to 1895), is one of Barcelona's most glamorous quality hotels. Business was so good that it opened a 74-room extension across the street (**Carrer Majorca**), which regrettably lacks the flair of the original. It boasts a unique neomedieval facade that shows strong Gaudí influences, and modern attractions include having supper on the roof with a live jazz band. The comfortable midsize guest rooms all contain marble bathrooms, with tub/shower combos, reproductions of Spanish paintings, and soundproof windows. The Condes continues to be one of the most popular choices in the Eixample.

Passeig de Gràcia 73–75, 08008 Barcelona. ✆ **93-488-22-00.** Fax 93-467-47-81. www.condesdebarcelona.com. 183 units. 175€–350€ ($219–$438) double; 495€ ($619) suite. AE, DC, MC, V. Parking 16€ ($20). Metro: Passeig de Gràcia. **Amenities:** Restaurant; cafe; bar; outdoor pool; business center; limited room service; babysitting; laundry service; dry cleaning; nonsmoking rooms. *In room:* A/C, TV, minibar, hair dryer, safe, Internet access.

Hotel Majestic 🏆🏆 This hotel is one of Barcelona's most visible landmarks and has been since the 1920s, when it was built in this sought-after location that lies within a 10-minute walk from Plaça de Catalunya. In the early 1990s it was radically renovated and upgraded into deluxe status while retaining the dignified stateliness of the public areas, but with added color in the bedrooms. Today, each is outfitted in a different, mainly monochromatic color scheme, with carpets, artwork, and upholsteries. All units come equipped with bathrooms containing tub/shower combos. The staff is hardworking and conscientious, albeit sometimes swamped with tour buses containing dozens of clients arriving all at once. Its **Drolma** restaurant (p. 139) has a Michelin star.

Passeig de Gràcia 68, 08007 Barcelona. ✆ **93-488-17-17.** Fax 93-488-18-80. www.hotelmajestic.es. 303 units. 200€–375€ ($250–$469) double; 450€–625€ ($563–$781) suite. AE, DC, MC, V. Parking 16€ ($20). Metro: Passeig de Gràcia. **Amenities:** 2 restaurants; 2 bars; outdoor pool; fitness center; sauna; business center; limited room service; laundry service; dry cleaning; courtesy car for guests in suites and apts. *In room:* A/C, TV, minibar, hair dryer, safe, Internet access.

L'Eixample Accommodations

AC Diplomatic **12**
Avenida Palace **20**
Calderón **15**
Constanza **25**
Eurostars Gaudí **22**
Fashion House B&B **28**
Gallery Hotel **3**
Hostal d'Uxelles **26**
Hostal Girona **29**
Hostal Goya **27**

Hostal Residencia Oliva **14**
Hotel Actual **4**
Hotel Apsis Atrium Palace **23**
Hotel Astoria **1**
Hotel Axel **13**
Hotel Balmes **7**
Hotel Casa Fuster **2**
Hotel Claris **10**
Hotel Condes de Barcelona **8**
Hotel Inglaterra **17**

Hotel Jazz **16**
Hotel Majestic **9**
Hotel Omm **5**
Hotel Ritz **21**
Prestige **11**
Pulitzer **18**
Sagrada Família B&B **6**
Silken Gran Hotel Havana **24**
Silken Diagonal **30**

Hotel Omm ✰✰✰   This is the current darling of the Barcelona hotel scene. Since it opened in 2002, rock stars and architects, actors, and media types who find classic hotels such as the Ritz or the Majestic just a tad too passé have been staying here. It's the first hostelry project from the Tragaluz group, Barcelona's most famous restaurateurs, so naturally the in-house restaurant **Moo** (p. 143) is first-class and the foyer cocktail bar one of the hottest places around for a pre-dinner drink. Hype aside, the Omm is an outstanding example of intelligent, well-executed design. The striking "wafers of stone" facade has already become a landmark and the cream of the city's design talent was employed for the interior. In contrast to the dark, low-lit halls, the rooms are bathed in natural light and make the maximum use of their size. Bearing in mind that most of their guests would be heavy shoppers (and packers), the hotel has provided ample but non-intrusive cupboard and wardrobe space. Add to that a color-scheme of steel gray and blue, a flatscreen TV, DVD, stereo, and every other state-of-the-art convenience you can think of and you have a hotel that is hard to beat in terms of sheer, streamlined comfort. From the rooftop lap pool you can see Gaudí's La Pedrera, and the chic sun deck is a privileged spot where you can laze away languid Barcelonese evenings.

Rosselló 265, 08008 Barcelona. ✆ 93-445-40-00. Fax 93-445-40-04. www.hotelomm.es. 59 units. 320€–375€ ($400–$470) double; 500€ ($625) suite. AE, DC, MC, V. Parking 22€ ($28). Metro: Diagonal. **Amenities:** Restaurant; cocktail bar; health center; business center; room service; babysitting service; laundry service; dry cleaning; nonsmoking rooms. In room: A/C, TV, minibar, hair dryer, safe, Internet access.

Hotel Ritz ✰✰✰   Acknowledged by many to be the most prestigious and most architecturally distinguished hotel in Barcelona, the Art Deco Ritz dates from 1919. Richly remodeled during the late 1980s, it has welcomed more millionaires, famous people, and aristocrats (and their official and unofficial consorts) than any other hotel in northeastern Spain. One of its finest features is a cream-and-gilt neoclassical lobby, where afternoon tea is served to the strains of a string quartet. The sumptuous guest rooms are appropriately formal, high-ceilinged and richly furnished. Some have Regency furniture, bathrooms accented with mosaics, and showers with bathtubs inspired by those in ancient Rome. You get all the luxuries here: elegant fabrics, deluxe mattresses, and plush towels.

Gran Vía de les Corts Catalanes 668, 08010 Barcelona. ✆ 93-318-52-00. Fax 93-318-01-48. www.ritzbcn.com. 122 units. 400€ ($500) double; from 495€ ($619) suite. AE, DC, MC, V. Parking 21€ ($26). Metro: Passeig de Gràcia. **Amenities:** 3 restaurants; bar; fitness center; car rental; 24-hr. business center; limited room service; babysitting; laundry service; dry cleaning. In room: A/C, TV, minibar, hair dryer, safe, Internet access.

Prestige ✰✰✰   Opened in May 2002 in a blaze of glory not dissimilar to a well-received couture collection fresh off the catwalk, the Prestige is already well established on the scene of all that is hip and fab. It has some nice touches such as the **Zeroom** breakfast bar and library where you can enjoy laid-back mornings and the Oriental garden where you can also sip coffee amid the ivory sun loungers and bamboo planters. There's an "Ask Me" service ethic—staff vows to hunt down any sort of information on the city you need, whether it's the opening hours of a museum or the nearest kosher restaurant. The Japanese-inspired bedrooms are sleek and spacious with all the added extras one could possibly need for a good night's sleep. No doubt about it, this is one hotel that takes its name very seriously indeed. All that's missing is a fancy restaurant with a celebrity chef at the helm.

Passeig de Gràcia 62, 08007 Barcelona. ✆ 93-272-41-80. Fax 93-272-41-81. www.prestigepaseodegracia.com. 45 units. 195€–265€ ($244–$331) double; from 420€ ($525) suite. AE, DC, MC, V. Valet parking 2€ ($2.50)/hr. Metro: Diagonal. **Amenities:** Cafe/bar; lounge; health-and-beauty center; Jacuzzi; sauna; business center; 24-hr. room service;

babysitting service; laundry service; dry cleaning; nonsmoking rooms; shoeshine; free newspaper service; private garden; Barcelona and music library. *In room:* A/C, TV, minibar, hair dryer, safe, Internet access.

Pulitzer *&& (Finds*   Another newcomer to the Barcelona's designer scene, the super-trendy Pulitzer is a mere stone's throw from the Plaça Catalunya. Hotels in this quarter are usually more uniform and business-y. Not so this one, with its white leather sofas, black marble trim, and lounge area with floor-to-ceiling bookshelves lined with titles like *California Homes, Moroccan Interiors,* and *The World's Greatest Hotels.* There's also a chic cocktail bar—just the kind of place you might expect to find the *Sex and the City* ladies—a smart restaurant and a pleasant, candlelit roof terrace. Bedrooms follow the inky-black and charcoal gray color scheme (some are a little on the small side) and contain sumptuous fabrics: leather, silk, and down pillows. The showy bathrooms have tub/shower combos that are generous with the toiletries.

Bergara 8, Eixample Esquerra, 08002 Barcelona. © **93-481-67-67.** Fax 93-481-64-64. www.hotelpulitzer.es. 91 units. 150€–225€ ($188–$281) double. AE, DC, MC, V. Public parking nearby 24€ ($30). Metro: Catalunya. **Amenities:** Restaurant; cocktail bar; lounge; external health center; solarium; business center; 24-hr. room service; babysitting service; laundry service; dry cleaning; nonsmoking rooms; library. *In room:* A/C, TV, minibar, hair dryer, safe, Internet access.

Silken Gran Hotel Havana *&*   Situated opposite the Ritz, the Havana is a little less stuffy than its famous neighbor. It occupies a 19th-century building that was completely refurbished in 1991 and that retains an air of newness, which fits pleasingly with the *moderniste* architecture and design. In terms of service and quality of accommodations, it is pretty much as one would expect of a four-star hotel: spacious, well-equipped rooms; modern decor with vast, Italian marble bathrooms that have both walk-in shower and tub; and toiletries that are restocked on a daily basis. The best rooms are the executive suites on the sixth floor, which have private terraces with stunning views. Be wary of rooms that face the street; although theoretically soundproof, they can be a little noisy for light-sleepers. The rooftop pool and sun terrace are an added bonus.

Gran Vía de les Corts Catalanes 647, Eixample Dreta, 08010 Barcelona. © **93-412-11-15.** Fax 93-412-26-11. www.silken-granhavana.com. 145 units. 195€ ($244) double; 210€–360€ ($262–$450) suite. AE, DC, MC, V. Parking 18€ ($23). Metro: Passeig de Gràcia, Tetuan, or Girona. **Amenities:** Restaurant; bar; pool; business center; room service; babysitting service; laundry service; dry cleaning; nonsmoking rooms. *In room:* A/C, TV, minibar, hair dryer, safe, Internet access.

EXPENSIVE

Avenida Palace *&&*   This superb hotel stands behind a pair of mock-fortified towers in an enviable 19th-century neighborhood filled with elegant shops and apartment

---

Kids Family-Friendly Hotels

Hotel Colón (p. 87)   Families who ask usually can get spacious rooms at this hotel, opposite the cathedral in the Gothic Quarter.

Hotel Fira Palace (p. 110)   At the base of Montjuïc, one of the city's most expansive green zones. Areas where the kids can run wild are only a short distance away.

Citadines (p. 118)   An in-house kitchen and maid service take some of the hassle out of catering to little ones.

buildings. Despite its relative modernity (it dates from 1952), it evokes an old-world sense of charm, partly because of the attentive staff, and partly because of the flowers, antiques, and 1950s-era accessories that fill the public rooms. Celebrity guests have been coming for decades and the Beatles stayed here—in the master suite—after their summer concert in 1965. The more standard rooms are solidly traditional and quiet, with some set aside for nonsmokers. The soundproof rooms range from midsize to spacious, and have comfortable beds and mostly wood furnishings. Bathrooms are well equipped, with dual basins, tub/shower combos, and heat lamps.

Gran Vía de les Corts Catalanes 605 (at Passeig de Gràcia), 08007 Barcelona. © **93-301-96-00.** Fax 93-318-12-34. www.avenidapalace.com. 160 units. 225€–250€ ($281–$313) double; 325€ ($406) suite. AE, DC, MC, V. Parking 16€ ($20). Metro: Passeig de Gràcia. **Amenities:** 2 restaurants; bar; salon; room service (7am–11pm); babysitting; laundry service; dry cleaning; currency exchange. *In room:* A/C, TV, minibar, hair dryer, safe.

Calderón As business hotels go, the Calderón has two things in its favor, and is therefore a good value for the money: One, its location—it is situated right on the leafy promenade of Rambla de Catalunya with its pavement cafes and tapas bars, and is just minutes from the Barri Gòtic. Two, its size—it is huge, with plenty of amenities for those who need stay-at-home comforts with gargantuan, bright, airy bedrooms with plenty of modern conveniences and spacious en-suite bathrooms.

Rambla de Catalunya 26, 08007 Barcelona. © **93-301-00-00.** Fax 93-412-41-93. www.nh-hotels.com. 253 units. 235€ ($294) double; 550€ ($687) suite. AE, DC, MC, V. Parking 16€ ($20). Metro: Catalunya. **Amenities:** Restaurant; bar; cafeteria; lounge; indoor/outdoor pool sauna; health center; solarium; business center; room service; babysitting service; laundry service; dry cleaning; nonsmoking rooms. *In room:* A/C, TV, minibar, hair dryer, safe, Internet access.

MODERATE

AC Diplomatic ❧ This top-end, glass-fronted, four-star oozes style even though it's predominantly a business hotel. If you keep one eye on its pleasing Zen-like design focus and another on the small details that make a difference—such as 24-hour laundry service, free minibar, and nonsmoking rooms—you'll realize that these features alone make it a cut above most chain hotels. The restaurant, with its avant-garde aura, offers a *sanísimo* (low-fat) menu, instead of the usual steak and chips. Bedrooms are a good size and warmly decorated with wood paneling, parquet floors, and a small sitting area. All have en-suite bathrooms with shower and/or tub.

Pau Claris 122, 08009 Barcelona. © **93-272-38-10.** Fax 93-272-38-11 www.achoteldiplomatic.com. 211 units. 170€ ($213) double; 290€ ($363) suite. AE, DC, MC, V. Parking 20€ ($25). Metro: Passeig de Gràcia. **Amenities:** Restaurant; bar; lounge; outdoor pool; health center; sauna; limited room service; massage service; babysitting service; laundry service; dry cleaning; nonsmoking rooms; safe. *In room:* A/C, TV, minibar, hair dryer, Internet access.

Constanza A smart boutique hotel within easy walking distance of La Ribera's shopping, cultural, and culinary attractions, the recently renovated Constanza combines style and a young vibe with a fair amount of substance for its price range. True, it doesn't have a rooftop pool or city views, but it's smart and comfortable with an upbeat, trendy ambience. The lobby is filled with white boxy couches and red trim, and there's a minimalist breakfast room decorated flower prints. The first-floor bedrooms are bright and fresh with clean lines and leather-trimmed furniture, throw cushions a-plenty, and white cotton sheets. All have en-suite bathrooms with showers. Some are rather small, and those at the front can be noisy, but if you can book a room with its own private terrace the place is a bargain.

Bruc 33, 08010 Barcelona. © **93-270-19-10.** Fax 93-317-40-24. www.hotelconstanza.com. 20 units. 90€ ($113) double; 100€ ($125) suite; 120€ ($150) apt. AE, MC, V. Public parking nearby 20€ ($25). Metro: Urquinaona. **Amenities:** Health center; room service; laundry service; dry cleaning; safe. *In room:* A/C, TV, minibar, hair dryer, Internet access.

Eurostars Gaudí   Not to be confused with the Gaudí hotel in the lower Gothic Quarter, this recent member of the highly regarded Eurostars group, opened in June 2005, is located in the heart of the Eixample, just northwest of the city's Monumental main bullring. It's a contemporary hotel with a sense of space and a relaxing decor of rich color schemes. The staff is friendly and attentive, and the bright spacious dining room provides quality international cuisine and buffet breakfasts. Couples staying in the Romantic Double rooms receive a complimentary bottle of *cava* on arrival. From the rooftop sun terrace you get great city views that take in the nearby Sagrada Família. The stylish and comfortable rooms all have en-suite bathrooms with tub/shower combos.

Consell de Cent. 498–500, 08013 Barcelona. © **93-232-02-88.** Fax 93-232-02-87. www.eurostarsgaudihotel.com. 45 units. 150€–220€ ($188–$275) double. AE, DC, MC, V. Metro: Monumental. **Amenities:** Restaurant; bar; lounge; sun terrace w/panoramic view; facilities for visitors w/disabilities; laundry service; dry cleaning; 24-hr. reception. *In room:* A/C, flatscreen TV, Wi-Fi, minibar, hair dryer, safe, wheelchair access.

Gallery Hotel   Named after a nearby district of major art galleries, this stylishly decorated modern hotel lies between the Passeig de Gràcia and Rambla de Catalunya, just below the wide Diagonal avenue in the upper district of the Eixample. The Gallery was completely remodeled in 2002, and its guest rooms are mainly midsize and tastefully furnished with pleasing touches such as fresh flowers by the bed and crisp bed linens. All rooms have a small bathroom with tub and shower. The on-site restaurant is renowned for its savory Mediterranean cuisine.

Calle Rosello 249, 08008 Barcelona. © **93-415-99-11.** Fax 93-415-91-84. www.galleryhotel.com. 110 units. Mon–Thurs 200€ ($250) double, 330€ ($412) suite; Fri–Sun 130€ ($163) double, 155€ ($194) suite. AE, DC, MC, V. Parking 18€ ($23). Metro: Diagonal. **Amenities:** Restaurant; bar; fitness center; business center; sauna; solarium; 24-hr. room service; babysitting; laundry service/dry cleaning; nonsmoking rooms. *In room:* A/C, TV, minibar, hair dryer, safe, Internet access.

Hotel Actual *(Value*   Situated opposite the ultra-hip Omm Hotel (see above), it's no surprise that the Actual is somewhat overshadowed. You can, however, save yourself a few euros by staying at this stylish three-star place rather than across the road, and of course you can still make use of the Omm's wonderful bar and restaurant. Small but perfectly formed wood paneling and large windows give the hotel a light, airy feel with a designer edge. Bedrooms are simply but elegantly decorated with chocolate brown soft furnishings and plain white walls and bed linen, and all have compact bathrooms with tub/shower combos.

Rosselló 238, Eixample Esquerra, 08008 Barcelona. © **93-552-05-50.** Fax 93-552-05-55. www.hotelactual.com. 29 units. 200€ ($250) double. AE, DC, MC, V. Public parking 22€ ($28). Metro: Diagonal. **Amenities:** Cafeteria; lounge; outdoor pool; room service; babysitting service; laundry service; dry cleaning; nonsmoking rooms. *In room:* A/C, TV, minibar, hair dryer, safe, Internet access.

Hotel Apsis Atrium Palace 𝒦𝒦𝒦 *Finds*   This fabulously modern designer hotel with its sleek lines and oatmeal marble decor prides itself on its high-tech facilities. Wireless Internet is available throughout the building (they will even provide you with a Wi-Fi card), and the library-cum-business center, with its fat, squashy sofas and tea and coffee on tap, provides several flatscreen monitors for guests' use. Photocopy machines, printers, and a selection of international newspapers are also available in this brave new world of complimentary business facilities. The hotel's restaurant is softly lit with wave-rippled ceilings and the indoor swimming pool and Jacuzzi are surrounded by wood decking, which are very stylish and hugely welcome in winter months when even Barcelona gets chilly. Bedrooms are uncommonly spacious (28–32 sq. m/301–344 sq. ft. on average) with quilted throws and small sitting areas, and there are thoughtful little extras like a free daily quota of mineral water and fruit juice. Bathrooms are marble with tub/shower combos. The top-floor suites, however, go for maximum comfort: separate living room, two TVs, a private terrace with deck chairs, temperature-controlled hot tub, and views. It's superb value for money and the perfect place to combine business and pleasure.

Gran Vía de les Corts Catalanes 656, Eixample Esquerra, 08010 Barcelona. ✆ **93-342-80-00**. Fax 93-342-80-01. www.hotel-atriumpalace.com. 71 units. 120€–250€ ($150–$313) double; 275€–320€ ($344–$400) suite. AE, DC, MC, V. Parking 22€ ($28). Metro: Passeig de Gràcia or Catalunya. **Amenities:** Restaurant; bar; pool; health center; business center; limited room service; babysitting service; laundry service; dry cleaning; nonsmoking rooms; Barcelona library. *In room:* A/C, TV, minibar, hair dryer, safe, Internet access.

Hotel Axel 🏆🏆🏆   What began as a hotel targeting a metropolitan gay audience has become a hot spot for all style-savvy travelers where anything goes, providing it's hip. Though it remains unique for now, it probably won't be long before others try to emulate its success. There's a cool, scarlet-colored cocktail bar and restaurant in the lobby, and a rooftop pool and sun deck. Should you find yourself with nothing suitable to wear, check out the men's designer-clothing store next door (run, not coincidentally, by the Axel). A nice little extra touch is the provision of free bottled mineral water in refrigerators on every floor. All bedrooms are soundproof and have king-size beds strewn with squashy pillows. (There's definitely an emphasis on quality bed time here.) The art is erotic and the sleek en-suite bathrooms are designed for two with tub/shower combos. (Superior rooms have Jacuzzis.)

Aribau 33, Eixample Esquerra, 08011 Barcelona. ✆ **93-323-93-93**. Fax 93-323-93-94. www.hotelaxel.com. 66 units. 180€–225€ ($225–$281) double; from 300€ ($375) suite. AE, DC, MC, V. Parking 15€ ($19). Metro: Universitat. **Amenities:** Restaurant; bar; lounge; outdoor pool; solarium; health center; massage service; Jacuzzi; sauna; hammam (Arab-style bathhouse); limited room service; laundry service; dry cleaning; nonsmoking rooms; safe; library. *In room:* A/C, TV, minibar, hair dryer, Internet access.

Hotel Inglaterra *Value*   Despite the name, this sleekly elegant hotel has a quietly exotic Japanese-inspired decor. It was one of the first boutique hotels in town, and makes good use of communal space with comfortable living areas, a snazzy breakfast room and bar, and a well-equipped roof terrace for sunbathing and reading. The spacious minimalist rooms have private bathrooms with tub/shower combos All in all, this is a quality, laid-back hotel that is an excellent value for the money.

Pelayo 14, Eixample Esquerra, 08001 Barcelona. ✆ **93-505-11-00**. Fax 93-505-11-09. www.hotel-inglaterra.com. 55 units. 190€ ($238) double. AE, DC, MC, V. Public parking nearby 24€ ($30). Metro: Catalunya or Universitat. **Amenities:** Restaurant; lounge; room service; laundry service; dry cleaning; safe. *In room:* A/C, TV, minibar, hair dryer, Internet access.

Hotel Jazz   Just around the corner from Plaça Catalunya, the Jazz is located in an enclave of designer hotels. Quite low-key in spite of its name, it stands out as a modestly attractive, tempting alternative to those officially higher-rated competitors. The decor of bleached wood floors and oatmeal paintwork may be a little generic, but there's nothing offensive about it and the rooms are spacious enough, all en suite and all soundproof—a definite bonus on this busy stretch. The big plus comes on the roof, where you'll find a swimming pool and a wood-deck terrace, which is more than those pricier neighbors can boast.

Pelai 3, 08001 Barcelona. ✆ **93-552-96-96**, 0870-120-1521 (U.K.), or 207/580-2663 (U.S.). Fax 93-552-96-97. www.nnhotels.es. 180 units. 140€–195€ ($175–$244) double; 175€–220€ ($219–$275) suite. AE, DC, MC, V. Parking 20€ ($25) per day. Metro: Catalunya or Universitat. **Amenities:** Cafeteria; lounge; outdoor pool; solarium;

business center; room service; babysitting service; laundry service; dry cleaning; nonsmoking rooms. *In room:* A/C, TV, minibar, hair dryer, safe, Internet access.

Hotel Onix ⭐ *Value* Sleek and minimal, the Onix Rambla Catalunya opened in 2003 with all the facilities of a more expensive hotel including attractions such as a large sun terrace and rooftop plunge pool. Filled with discreet works of modern art, it's a good choice for anyone who wants to stay in a designer hotel without paying designer prices. There's a pleasant breakfast room and an on-site new-wave snack bar. Bedrooms are tastefully decorated with wood, leather, and tiles and all have en-suite bathrooms with tub/shower combos.

Rambla Catalunya 24, Eixample Esquerra, 08007 Barcelona. ℰ **93-342-79-80.** Fax 93-342-51-52. www.hotels onix.com. 40 units. 160€ ($200) double. AE, DC, MC, V. Metro: Passeig de Gràcia or Universitat. **Amenities:** Cafeteria; lounge; outdoor pool; health center; solarium; business center; room service; babysitting service; laundry service; dry cleaning; nonsmoking rooms. *In room:* A/C, TV, minibar, hair dryer, safe, Internet access.

Silken Diagonal Opened in December 2004, this addition to the prestigious Silken chain is located at the southeast end of the Eixample, next to the extraordinary Torre Agbar building. It was designed by local architect Juli Capella and features a striking black-and-white facade and a subtly tasteful interior that makes maximum use of natural light. Its spacious public areas include four lounges and wireless Internet access. There are facilities for non-smokers and guests with disabilities, and all rooms and suites have private bathrooms with tub/shower combos. The hotel's Piano restaurant specializes in designer cuisine, blending the best of Catalan and Basque specialties, and buffet breakfasts are served in the Tecla cafe. You get excellent city views from the (rather small) rooftop swimming pool and its surrounding wooden-floor solarium, where you can also enjoy snacks from the adjoining bar. Business and wedding receptions and cocktail parties are often held here.

Diagonal 205, 08018 Barcelona. ℰ **93-489-53-09.** Fax 93-489-53-09. www.hoteldiagonalbarcelona.com. 240 units. 200€–250€ ($250–$313) double. AE, DC, MC, V. Metro: Glòries. **Amenities:** Restaurant; cafeteria/bar; lounges; rooftop pool and solarium w/snack bar; nonsmoking areas; dry cleaning; laundry service. *In room:* A/C, TV, minibar, hair dryer, ironing board, safe, Internet access.

INEXPENSIVE

Fashion House B&B ⭐ *Finds* Bed-and-breakfast accommodations are still a relatively new concept in Barcelona, offering good-value and comfortable accommodations for those who prefer a more homey atmosphere. The Fashion House is located in an elegantly restored 19th-century town house decorated with stuccoes and friezes, adding an element of class to the overall feel of the place. Bedrooms share one bathroom for two rooms, and all are bright and nicely decorated with pastel colors. The best have verandas. La Suite doubles as a self-catering apartment, making it a good choice for families who need a little more space; it also has private access to the communal terrace, which is well supplied with shaded tables and chairs and plenty of greenery. Breakfast is served here in the summer.

Bruc 13 Principal, 08010 Barcelona. ℰ **63-790-40-44.** Fax 93-301-09-38. www.bcn-fashionhouse.com. 8 units. 70€ ($88) double; 85€ ($106) double with balcony; 80€ ($100) triple; 100€ ($125) triple with balcony; 120€ ($150) suite. Rates include breakfast. 10€ ($13) supplement in high season. MC, V. Metro: Urquinaona. **Amenities:** Breakfast room. *In room:* A/C, TV (suite only), kitchenette (suite only).

Hostal d'Uxelles ⭐ *Finds* This picture-postcard *hostal* had mixed reports in the past regarding the occasionally unhelpful attitude of the staff, though this now appears to be the exception rather than the rule. Pastel hues and lush drapes enhance the *hostal*'s rustic

Tips **Barcelona's Self-Catering Boom**

New hotels, particularly of the three- and four-star caliber, are opening in Barcelona at an astonishing rate, and a further 300 hotels are due to be built by 2008. However, many travelers still opt for quality self-catering accommodations, which allow visitors greater flexibility and independence than hotels.

If you've ever been curious about the cute-looking apartments in the Old City with their curved-beamed ceilings and balconies brimming with ferns, or the tiled-entrance apartments with Art Nouveau facades in L'Eixample, now's your chance to get up close and personal. Wander around the Barri Gòtic these days, and many of the residential apartments you see are available for rent at reasonable prices by the day (normally a 3-day minimum), week, or month, enabling visitors to get a taste of what its really like to live in the city: to shop in its markets, cook its food, and make merry over glasses of wine around the dinner table.

Google "self-catering accommodations Barcelona" and you'll come up with pages of options, with something to suit every whim and budget. The array of apartments on offer ranges from small, practical studios for couples, to luxury apartments and penthouses for families or groups of friends.

If you're looking for something cultural and unconventional, one of the most interesting options is **La Casa de les Lletres (House of Letters; ✆ 93-226-37-30;** www.cru2001.com), a thematic collection of apartments that pays homage to writers like George Orwell and the Catalan journalist and food writer Josep Pla, who had a special relationship with the city. Accommodations mix state-of-the-art facilities with an intellectual bohemian vibe. Poetry and prose are literally written on the walls. Situated in an elegant town house on the handsome Plaza Antonio López, the location couldn't be better, just minutes from Barceloneta and the Barri Gòtic.

---

charm, and all rooms are individually decorated with ornate Art Deco wood paneling and romantic flourishes, such as Cupid's bow drapes above the bed. Each room has its own bathroom complete with Andalusian tiling and tub/shower combo, and the best accommodations have private, plant-filled balconies big enough to hold a table and two chairs.

Gran Vía de les Corts Catalanes 667 (Hostal 2) and 668 (Hostal 1), Eixample Dreta, 08010 Barcelona. ✆ **93-265-25-60.** Fax 93-232-85-67. www.hotelduxelles.com. 30 units. 75€–90€ ($94–$113) double; 100€–115€ ($125–$144) triple; 140€–185€ ($175–$231) quadruple. AE, DC, MC, V. Parking nearby 18€ ($23). Metro: Tetuan or Girona. **Amenities:** TV lounge; room service; laundry service; safe. *In room:* TV.

Hostal Girona *(Kids) (Value)*   One of the most filled-with-character *hostales* in town, the Girona is decorated with wall hangings and rugs, gilded picture frames and tear-drop chandeliers, which offset the *moderniste* decor beautifully. The result is a place that feels like home, and, unsurprisingly, it's developed something of a loyal following. The Girona offers a variety of bedrooms, from singles without bathrooms to more plush doubles with en-suite bathrooms with tub/shower combos and balconies. All are comfortable and freshly painted with plain white linen bedspreads. A bargain.

Girona 24 1–1, Eixample Dreta, 08010 Barcelona. ✆ **93-265-02-59.** Fax 93-265-85-32. www.hostalgirona.com. 19 units. 60€–75€ ($75–$94) double. MC, V. Metro: Girona or Urquinaona. **Amenities:** Safe. *In room:* A/C, TV.

More basic accommodations can be found at **www.nivellmar.com**, which offers seaside apartments—or at least those that are no more than 200m (600 ft.) from the beach—all the way from Barceloneta to Poble Nou. The places they offer tend to go after function rather than form, but are reasonably decorated, clean, and fairly priced. They are ideal for young travelers, or those with young children, who just want to be close to the sea.

For apartments with character that won't break the bank, check out **www.visit-bcn.com**, which offers everything from Barri Gòtic town houses, such as the lovely Dos Amigos in the heart of the Old City to minimalist loft-style apartments.

If it's luxury you're after, try **www.friendlyrentals.com**; they offer chic properties at a surprisingly good value. Every place on their books is categorized for its artistic personality (for instance, Rembrandt, *modernista*, Impressionist, Romantic, or Art Deco), and is described and photographed in detail. Many have private terraces and/or swimming pools and are considerably cheaper than a hotel in the same class.

Most self-catering apartments, whether booked through an agency or directly through the owner, require a deposit of 1 night and possibly a security deposit, both of which are paid via credit card or PayPal. Things to be on the lookout for include "hidden" costs such as cleaning and extra-person charges. In general, compared to hotels, apartments are extremely cost-effective, especially for longer stays. Don't forget, though, that you are on your own—there is no concierge to help you find a drug store in the middle of the night, or direct you to the Picasso Museum.

Hostal Goya 🌟🌟 *Finds*   As *hostal* accommodations go, this is one of the best deals in the city: a smart, friendly place that's a cut above the others in terms of decor, cleanliness, and service (the newly renovated Principal wing is the quietest and has fresh, sleekly decorated rooms). Do remember, however, that it is a *hostal,* not a hotel, and therefore the clientele tend to be younger and sometimes noisy when coming in late at night. For most, this is no problem and the place itself is good enough to more than compensate for a fun-loving crowd. It offers a variety of different rooms. The best are doubles with large, sunny balconies; the worst are small, dark interior rooms (meaning no natural light) for single travelers, and some accommodations come without private bathrooms. Bonuses include a Scandinavian-look comfortable sitting room where free tea, coffee, and hot chocolate are available throughout the day. Given its central location and good-value prices, it's unsurprising that it gets booked up quickly, so make your reservations well in advance.

Pau Claris 74, Eixample Dreta, 08010 Barcelona. 📞 **93-302-25-65.** Fax 93-412-04-35. www.hostalgoya.com. 19 units. 60€ ($75) double without bathroom; 80€ ($100) double with bathroom; 95€ ($119) suite with bathroom and private terrace. MC, V. Metro: Urquinaona or Catalunya. **Amenities:** TV lounge. *In room:* A/C in some units.

Hostal Residencia Oliva *(Value)*   Most places in the Eixample are expensive. Not so the Oliva, which is one of the best values you'll find in the whole city. Don't expect any luxuries (only the finest rooms overlook Barcelona's shopping street and have their own bathrooms), but it's fine if you want to save your cash for other things and are simply looking for somewhere to lay your head at night. On the upside, its high ceilings and tiled floors have plenty of character, but it can be noisy (bring earplugs), and the dark interior rooms are rather grim.

Passeig de Gràcia 32, Eixample, 08007 Barcelona. *(2)* **93-488-01-62.** Fax 93-487-04-97. www.lasguias.com/hostaloliva/ homepageingles.htm. 16 units. 60€ ($75) double without bathroom; 75€ ($94) double with bathroom. No credit cards. Metro: Passeig de Gràcia. **Amenities:** Lounge. *In room:* TV.

Hotel Astoria *(Value)*   Another quality hotel in the Derby chain (they also own the Balmes and the Claris), this 1950s branch (renovated in the 1990s) is high up in the Eixample, close to where Carrer Enric Granados meets the Diagonal. The Art Deco facade makes it appear older than it is, and the high ceilings, geometric designs, and brass-studded detail in the public rooms are strongly influenced by Moorish and Andalusian styles. All guest rooms are comfortable, midsize, and soundproof, with slick louvered closets and gleaming white walls. Accommodations come equipped with private bathrooms containing showers. The more old-fashioned units have warm textures of exposed cedar and elegant, pristine modern accessories. Recent welcome additions are the rooftop pool and sauna. The Astoria is an exceptional value.

París 203, 08036 Barcelona. *(2)* **93-209-83-11.** Fax 93-202-30-08. www.derbyhotels.es. 115 units. 140€–195€ ($175–$244) double; 225€ ($281) suite. AE, DC, MC, V. Parking nearby 18€ ($23). Metro: Diagonal. **Amenities:** Bar; lounge; rooftop swimming pool and sauna; limited room service; laundry service; dry cleaning. *In room:* A/C, TV, minibar, hair dryer, safe.

Hotel Balmes   Set in a seven-story structure built in the late 1980s, this chain hotel successfully combines conservative decor with modern accessories and well-trained and friendly staff. Bedrooms have a warm color scheme of rich terra cottas and sunset yellows, which brighten an otherwise white interior. Marble-trimmed bathrooms come equipped with tub/shower combos, and all accommodations have enough space to allow residents, many of whom are in town on business, to live and work comfortably. If you're looking for a maximum of peace and quiet, rooms at the back of the hotel overlook a small garden and swimming pool and are calmer and more relaxing than those facing the busy street.

Majorca 216, 08008 Barcelona. *(2)* **93-451-19-14.** Fax 93-451-00-49. www.derbyhotels.es. 100 units. 150€–220€ ($188–$275) double; 195€–250€ ($244–$313) triple. AE, DC, MC, V. Parking 16€ ($20). Metro: Diagonal. **Amenities:** Restaurant; bar; outdoor pool; room service; laundry service; dry cleaning. *In room:* A/C, TV, minibar, hair dryer, safe.

Sagrada Família B&B *(Finds)*   This is a small, family-run bed-and-breakfast containing just three pleasantly decorated rooms with queen-size beds and their own balconies. This is a good choice for travelers looking for home-style comforts, and what really makes this place special is the large living room with open fireplace, perfect for snuggling up to on cold winter evenings.

Nápols 266, Eixample Dreta, 08025 Barcelona. *(2)* **65-189-14-13.** www.sagradafamilia-bedandbreakfast.com. 3 units. 60€–70€ ($75–$88) double. No credit cards. Metro: Diagonal. **Amenities:** Lounge; kitchen.

4 Sants, Paral.lel & Montjuïc

The place to be for business travelers, this is the hub of Barcelona's out-of-towner meeting district, with practical four-star accommodations galore, the Fira (exhibition

Sants, Paral.lel & Montjuïc Accommodations

BARCELONA
Map
Area

Barceló Hotel Sants **2**
Barcelona Universal Hotel **6**
B. Hotel Barcelona **4**
Catalonia Barcelona Plaza **3**
Gran Hotel Torre Catalunya **1**
Hotel Fira Palace **5**

centers of Plaça Espanya), and the World Trade Center at the bottom of Paral.lel. However, it's a bit of a tourist's dead zone, with little going on besides the art galleries and parks of Montjuïc.

EXPENSIVE

Catalonia Barcelona Plaza ☆ Located on a busy plaza overlooking a shopping mall converted from the former Arenas bullring, this large hotel caters mainly to business travelers attending the various conference and conventions held across the street. It's very convenient to the airport (about 20 min. by cab), and can host meetings of up to 700 people. That aside, it is a fairly standard business hotel: big, gleaming, and comfortable with all the necessary facilities, including in-house travel agency and bank. The rooms are blandly standardized and the lower ones get a certain amount of traffic noise, but they do provide a comfortable night's sleep, and all have en-suite bathrooms with tub/shower combos. The rooftop swimming pool (covered in winter) offers some unexpectedly fine panoramic views that take in Montjuïc and distant Tibidabo.

Plaça Espanya 6–8, 08014 Barcelona. ℂ **93-426-26-00.** Fax 93-426-04-00. www.hoteles-catalonia.com. 338 rooms. 175€–290€ ($219–$362) double; 310€–380€ ($387–$475) suite. AE, DC, MC, V. Parking 16€ ($20). Metro: Plaça Espanya. **Amenities:** Restaurant; lounge; bar; pool; solarium; health center; business center; room service; babysitting; laundry service; dry cleaning; nonsmoking rooms. *In room:* A/C, TV, minibar, hair dryer, safe, Internet access.

Gran Hotel Torre Catalunya ★★   A vast skyscraper-style hotel close to Sants railway station and the Plaça Espanya, this modern four-star is far and away the most deluxe in the area, offering American-esque facilities in terms of the size of the bedrooms (large), excellent service, and modern amenities. Added extras include turndown service, chocolates on the pillows, and huge marble bathrooms with walk-in showers and deep bathtubs. **Ciudad Condal,** the restaurant on the 23rd floor, has awesome views over the city and is worth the visit for these alone. The recent inclusion of spa facilities with massage cabins, Jacuzzi, Turkish bath, and indoor pool has enhanced the hotel's attraction.

Av. De Roma 2–4, Sants, 08014 Barcelona. ⓒ 93-325-81-00. Fax 93-325-51-78. www.expogrupo.com. 272 units. 110€–240€ ($138–$300) double; 170€–290€ ($212–$362) suite. AE, DC, MC, V. Free parking. Metro: Sants Estació. **Amenities:** Restaurant; bar; pool; gymnasium; health spa w/massage cabins, snow shower, and sauna; Turkish bath; business center w/7 conference rooms; limited room service; laundry service; dry cleaning; nonsmoking rooms; 24-hr. reception. *In room:* A/C, TV, CD player, ADSL Internet connection, minibar, hair dryer, safe.

Hotel Fira Palace ★★ *Kids*   Highly popular among business travelers because of its plush conference facilities and easy access to the exhibition centers of Plaça Espanya, this well-equipped hotel opened especially for the 1992 Olympics. The main disadvantage for leisure travelers is the hike to the city center and to the principal sights. That said, if you are traveling with kids, the Fira offers some of the best family-friendly accommodations around, including huge rooms with separate bathroom and shower facilities. It's also close to Montjuïc hill's gardens, parks, and rambling footpaths. The Fira has all the communal facilities one would expect from a hotel of this standard, including two pricey restaurants (it's more economical, though, to eat outside of the hotel), a selection of health and fitness facilities, and an indoor swimming pool (closed Sun).

Av. Ruis I Taulet 1–3, 08004 Barcelona. ⓒ 93-426-22-23. Fax 93-425-50-47. www.fira-palace.com. 276 units. 225€–290€ ($281–$362) double; 340€–390€ ($425–$487) suite. AE, DC, MC, V. Parking 16€ ($20). Metro: Plaça Espanya. **Amenities:** 2 restaurants; piano bar; indoor pool; sauna; health center; business center; limited room service; massage; babysitting service; laundry service; dry cleaning; nonsmoking rooms; patio garden. *In room:* A/C, TV, minibar, hair dryer, safe, Internet access.

Hotel Miramar ★   One of the most recent members of the prestigious SLH (Small Luxury Hotels of the World) group, the Miramar is attractively located right next to the Montjuïc i Llobera Botanical Gardens, overlooking both the city and the Mediterranean. Originally a 1920s palace, it was imaginatively restored and converted into a hotel in 2006, retaining the privacy, style, and charm of the original building while introducing bright avant-garde decor and state-of-the-art amenities that include well-equipped conference salons (one of which is integrated into the hotel's gardens). At mealtimes the Forestier restaurant, adjoining the former palace's secluded Patio de los Naranjos (Orange Tree Courtyard), provides a creative blend of Catalan and international dishes. The comfortable and tastefully furnished rooms all have en-suite bathrooms and terraces and enjoy garden or panoramic sea views. Some have wheelchair accessibility.

Plaça Carlos Ibáñez 3, 08068. ⓒ 93-281-16-00. Fax 93-281-66-01. www.slh.com/miramar. 75 units. 240€ ($300) single; 260€ ($325) double or twin; 750€ ($940) suite. Extra beds available for families: 140€ ($175). Cots free. AE, DC, MC, V. Nearby parking 20€ ($25). Metro: Paral.lel or Drassanes. **Amenities:** Restaurant; bar; lounge; indoor and outdoor swimming pools; conference rooms; hairdresser; 24-hr. room service. *In room:* TV, CD player, minibar.

MODERATE
B. Hotel Barcelona   Opened in April 2005 by the same innovative group that created the stylish Hotel Jazz, this modern, low-key spot is a comfortable and affordable

alternative to the high-price business hotels that tend to proliferate in the Sants area. Decor is modern-minimalist, and on-site facilities include a bar/cafeteria serving snacks and full buffet breakfasts. There's also an outdoor rooftop swimming pool and gym. Montjuïc hill, with its gardens and parks, is just a few minutes' walk away (convenient for families with children). Front rooms all have good views of the Plaça Espanya and all rooms have en-suite bathrooms with shower.

Gran Vía de les Cortes Catalanes 389, 08015 Barcelona. ⌀ **90-0214-15-15**. 84 units. 120€–175€ ($150–$219). AE, DC, MC, V. Metro: Plaça Espanya. **Amenities:** Bar/cafeteria; rooftop pool; conference rooms; solarium; gym; laundry service; dry cleaning; reception. *In room:* A/C, TV, minibar, safe, ADSL and Wi-Fi Internet connections.

Barceló Hotel Sants   The main reason to stay at this well-run, solidly equipped hotel? It's practical, located right on top of Estació de Sants—Barcelona's main train station—and couldn't be more convenient if you're arriving late at night or have an early-morning departure. Undeniably commercial, the Barceló Hotel Sants makes no attempt to dazzle guests with either history or culture, but instead honestly provides big, comfortable beds, well-equipped rooms, and clean and functional bathrooms with tub/shower combos.

Plaça dels Països Catalans s/n, 08014 Barcelona. ⌀ **93-503-53-00**. Fax 93-490-60-45. www.bchoteles.com. 377 units. 85€–190€ ($106–$238) double; 125€–240€ ($156–$300) suite. AE, DC, MC, V. Parking 13€ ($16). Metro: Sants Estació. **Amenities:** 2 restaurants; bar; pool; sauna; health center; business center; limited room service; massage; babysitting service; laundry service; dry cleaning; nonsmoking rooms. *In room:* A/C, TV, minibar, hair dryer, safe, Internet access.

Barcelona Universal Hotel   Predominantly catering to business travelers attending company meetings, the well-appointed Universal offers stylish, modern facilities within easy reach of the World Trade Center and the Exhibition sites at Plaza Espanya. Bonuses include a small rooftop terrace with raised wood decking and a sunken pool. Bedrooms are spacious and comfortable and all have en-suite bathrooms with tub/shower combos. Although guest rooms are theoretically soundproof, noise from the busy street can be a problem, so ask for something at the back, where you're less likely to be disturbed.

Av. Paral.lel 76–78, 08001 Barcelona. ⌀ **93-567-74-47**. Fax 93-567-74-40. www.hotelbarcelonauniversal.com. 167 units. 140€–190€ ($175–$237) double; 240€–300€ ($300–$375) suite. AE, DC, MC, V. Parking 20€ ($25). Metro: Paral.lel. **Amenities:** Restaurant; bar; pool; solarium; health center; business center; limited room service; babysitting; laundry service; dry cleaning; nonsmoking rooms. *In room:* A/C, TV, minibar, hair dryer, safe, Internet access.

5 Barrio Alto & Gràcia

The Alto represents the *pijo* (posh) part of town with swanky restaurants and cocktail bars, millionaires' mansions, and Mercedes; Gràcia, on the other hand, has a more eclectic, villagey atmosphere with its two-story houses, sunny plazas, and student/bohemian vibe.

EXPENSIVE

Hotel Meliá Barcelona Sarrià ⌀   One block from the junction of the Avinguda Sarrià and the Avinguda Diagonal in the heart of the business district, this hotel still lives up to its high-luxury government rating, granted when it opened back in 1976. Some rooms were renovated in the early to mid-1990s, but others look a bit worn. The Barcelona Sarrià offers comfortably upholstered, carpeted guest rooms done in neutral international-modern style. All have wide beds with firm mattresses and bathrooms with tub/shower combos. A member of the illustrious Meliá chain, the Barcelona Sarrià caters to both business travelers and vacationers.

Av. Sarrià 50, 08029 Barcelona. ℂ 800/336-3542 in the U.S., or 93-410-60-60. Fax 93-410-77-44. www.solmelia.com. 314 units. 210€–290€ ($262–$362) double; 350€–450€ ($437–$562) suite. AE, DC, MC, V. Parking 19€ ($24). Metro: Hospital Clinic. **Amenities:** 2 restaurants; bar; business center; limited room service; babysitting; laundry service; dry cleaning; nonsmoking rooms. *In room:* A/C, TV, minibar, hair dryer, safe, Internet access.

INEXPENSIVE

Acropolis Guest House 🛏   The Acropolis is nothing if not quirky, and more than a little chaotic, but it has a charm all its own, with its crumbling columns and peeling paintwork, and is well worth a stay for lovers of "new experience" hotels. If you plan to travel with your pet, this is also one of the few places in Barcelona that will welcome them. The overgrown garden and rustic kitchen are both communal, and the bedrooms are simply but comfortably decorated. Half of them have en-suite bathrooms but the place is spotlessly clean and sharing shouldn't be a problem. The best room has its own terrace with wonderful views.

Verdi 254, Gràcia, 08024 Barcelona. ℂ/fax **93-284-81-87.** acropolis@telefonica.net. 8 units. 60€ ($75) double with bathroom; 50€ ($63) double without bathroom. No credit cards. Metro: Lesseps. **Amenities:** TV lounge; safe.

Hostal Putxet   Last renovated in April 2006, this homely *hostal* has one of the most attractive locations in the city, high up in a peaceful residential zone near the entrance to Parc Güell—yet it's also within easy Metro access of the city center, just five stops away. (There's also a Bus Turístic stop about 100m from the hotel.) Service is helpful and friendly, and on-site amenities include reading rooms with information on the city. Bars and eating spots are within easy walking distance. Rooms are unpretentious but neat and all have their own private bathroom with tub/shower combos.

Ballester 11–13, 08023 Barcelona. ℂ **93-212-03-50.** www.hostalputxet.com. 24 units. 70€–100€ ($88–$125) double. AE, DC, MC, V. Metro: Lesseps. **Amenities:** Laundry service; reception. *In room:* A/C, satellite TV, safe, Internet services, CD player (on request).

6 Barceloneta, Vila Olímpica & Poble Nou

VERY EXPENSIVE

Hotel Arts 🛏🛏🛏   Managed by the Ritz-Carlton chain, this hotel occupies 33 floors of one of the tallest buildings in Spain, and one of Barcelona's landmark skyscrapers. It lies about 2.5km (1.6 miles) southwest of Barcelona's historic core, facing the sea and the Olympic Village. Planned as a key project of the 1992 Olympic Games (but not finished on time), the Arts wore *the* luxury hotel mantle and remained the shining example of "New Barcelona" for over a decade. All its rooms have recently been renovated and new amenities such as a luxury spa added (p. 113). Privileged clients flock here for the incredible skyline and the Mediterranean views, club rooms with their open bars and free snacks, state-of-the-art executive suites, Aqua de Parma toiletries, and a million other details that make this hotel top of its class. Its decor is contemporary and elegant. The spacious, well-equipped guest rooms have built-in furnishings, generous desk space, and large, sumptuous beds, flatscreen TVs, DVD players, and B&O sound systems. (Four units are equipped for guests with disabilities.) Clad in pink marble, the deluxe bathrooms have fluffy robes, Belgian towels, dual basins, and phones. The hotel features the city's only beachside pool—overlooking Frank Gehry's bronze *Peix* (fish) sculpture—and its new in-house bars and restaurants, such as **Arola** (p. 154), are jump-starting nightlife into the neglected Olympic Marina. The young staff is polite and hardworking, the product of Ritz-Carlton training.

Carrer de la Marina 19–21, 08005 Barcelona. ℂ **800/241-3333** in the U.S., or 93-221-10-00. Fax 93-221-10-70. www.ritzcarlton.com/hotels/barcelona. 482 units. 350€–800€ ($437–$1,000) double; 500€–2,000€ ($625–$2,500)

Bright Lights, Spa City

Barcelona has never been much of a spa town, though its meteoric rise as an international destination means that hotels are offering ever more luxurious amenities to seduce the city's visitors. First it was gourmet restaurants and movie-star cocktail bars, next came suites with clap-to-control features and rooftop swimming pools, but the latest thing to hit the Barcelona hotel circuit (and it's about time!) is spas.

It seems rather bizarre that spas should have been such a long time coming to cosmopolitan Barcelona, but somehow southern Europeans never seem to have embraced the whole spa-therapy thing as passionately as their American neighbors (and northern Europeans). The burgeoning market does, however, have some seriously stylish new outfits such as **Alquimia** (Pau Claris 104), **Aqua Urban Spa** (Gran de Grcaia 7), and **Pedralbes Wellness Center** (Eduardo Conde 2–6) that promise to do more than simply rest and rejuvenate travel-weary bodies. See www.esteticahidrotermal.net for a full list of spas.

The first on the spa scene was the **Royal Fitness Center** at the somewhat prim five-star Rey Juan Carlos I Hotel (p. 116), which recently upgraded its look with unfathomable 21st-century fitness technologies and a new line of aphrodisiacal massages in chocolate, honey, or volcanic stone. Who says romance is dead?

For sheer fabulousness, the Spa at the **Gran Hotel La Florida** (p. 116) offers a heavenly, high-class retreat in the clouds high above the hustle and bustle of the city below. Treatments here include beautiful mosaic-tiled Turkish steam rooms, a Finnish sauna, a bubbling hot tub, and a striking 37m-long (121-ft.) half-indoor/half-outdoor L shaped stainless steel infinity pool that elbows its way across the mountainside. The full range of Natura Bissé beauty treatments is on offer here, including body-remolding, mud, and algae therapies that promise to shave off the years and excess pounds. Serious spa lovers can check in for a 3-night "Relaxation and Beauty" package with prices starting at 900€ ($1,125). Non-guests can make use of La Florida's spa facilities for 100€ ($125) a day.

Hot on the heels of greatness, the Ritz-Carlton–owned **Hotel Arts** (p. 112) opened its rooftop sea-view spa on the 42nd floor in 2006, combining hip design with the latest in luxury treatments. They've teamed up with the award-winning Six Senses Spas to bring clients an exclusive range of holistic, all-natural beauty treatments in half-day, day, and weekend packages, including full-body wraps, facials, pedicures, and manicures, as well as a full range of massage therapies. Water facilities include an ice-shower, hammam, sauna, and plunge pool while the downstairs treatment rooms (eight in all) are havens of peace where infusions, fresh juices, and fruits are served in relaxation zones or on the deck. The intimate penthouse environment, with views over the sparkling Mediterranean, offers one of the most spectacular spots in Spain to pamper and preen. Treatments start from 95€ ($119) an hour.

Meanwhile, the **Hotel Omm** (p. 100) added spa facilities in 2006. Like the rest of the hotel, the spa features state-of-the-art design mixed with Mediterranean madness and all the comforts money can buy. Just say sp-*aah!*

suite. AE, DC, MC, V. Parking 20€ ($25). Metro: Ciutadella–Vila Olímpica. **Amenities:** 4 restaurants; cafe; 2 bars; outdoor pool; fitness center; business center; hairdresser; limited room service; babysitting; laundry service; dry cleaning; nonsmoking rooms. *In room:* A/C, TV, minibar, hair dryer, iron, safe, high-speed Internet access.

Hotel Front Marítim ⭐ *(Value)*   The renovated, white-facaded Front Marítim is the centerpiece of a major tourist development bordering the Nueva Mar Bella beach, a 10-minute walk away from Port Olímpic. The guest rooms are midsize and attractively and comfortably decorated, and each has its own tiled bathroom with shower or tub. The hotel offers a range of facilities including an lounge with large-screen TV, a la carte restaurant, and a well-equipped fitness center. All this for a very reasonable price.

Poble Nou, Diagonal Mar, 08019 Barcelona. © 93-303-44-40. 177 units. 100€–120€ ($125–$150) double; 150€ ($188 superior double. AE, DC, MC, V. Parking 12€ ($15). Metro: Selva de Mar. **Amenities:** Restaurant; bar; gym; sauna; large-screen TV; limited room service; laundry service/dry cleaning; nonsmoking rooms; rooms for those w/limited mobility. *In room:* A/C, TV, dataport, hair dryer.

Hotel Grand Marina ⭐⭐⭐   Staying here is like being on one of the luxury ocean-going liners you see docked across the port, minus the seasickness. It's located in the World Trade Center on the large jetty (Moll de Barcelona), opposite the Drassanes Maritim Museum. No other hotel in the city gets this close to the sea, and few can compare when it comes to design. Its architects were Henry Cobb and I. M. Pei—the man behind the pyramid at the Louvre—and it's crammed with artworks and sculpture offset by marble and glass architectural details that give it a distinctly 21st-century feel. A testament to minimalism, the overall look is bright and airy with an overriding feeling of space. The bedrooms, which all have en-suite bathrooms and Jacuzzis, are sleekly designed and plush without being claustrophobic. The Presidential Suite on the roof has magnificent views across the port to the city.

World Trade Center, Moll de Barcelona, 08039 Barcelona. © 93-603-90-00. Fax 93-603-90-90. www.grandmarina hotel.com. 278 units. 240€–350€ ($300–$438) double; 400€–800€ ($500–$1,000) suite. AE, DC, MC, V. Parking 16€ ($20). Metro: Drassanes. **Amenities:** Restaurant; lounge; piano bar; cafeteria; outdoor pool; health center; Jacuzzi; sauna; business center; room service; massage service; babysitting; laundry service; dry cleaning; nonsmoking rooms. *In room:* A/C, TV, minibar, hair dryer, safe, Internet access.

MODERATE

Vincci Marítimo Hotel ⭐⭐ *(Finds)*   This genuine 21st-century hotel with an emphasis on interior design—lots of glass panels, polished wood, and brushed steel—is not dissimilar to Glasgow's landmark Lighthouse building. But because it's tucked away in the nether reaches of the city, few people have discovered it. Its advantage, aside from being a design gem yet to be discovered, is its eastern seaboard location (great for hip city beaches like Bogatell and Mar Bella), which is an excellent location if your holiday aim is sunbathe by day, and "moon bathe" and listen to local DJ talent by night. If you want to explore the sights and soak up the atmosphere of old Barcelona, though, it's a 20-minute taxi ride—or slightly longer trip by Metro. Bedrooms are sleek and spacious, all with en-suite, light-filled bathrooms, and many have sea views. Communal facilities include a Japanese garden for relaxing breakfasts and early-evening cocktails, and a swanky, avant-garde restaurant. Check the website for deals. With rooms often going for less than 100€ ($125) a night, it's a real bargain.

Llull 340, Poble Nou, 08019 Barcelona. © 93-356-26-00. Fax 93-356-06-69. www.vinccihoteles.com. 144 units. 140€–190€ ($175–$237) double; 180€–225€ ($225–$281) suite. AE, DC, MC, V. Parking 14€ ($18). Metro: Poble Nou. **Amenities:** Restaurant; bar; room service; laundry service; dry cleaning; nonsmoking rooms; Internet service; garden. *In room:* A/C, TV, minibar, hair dryer, safe, Internet access.

Tips **A Pool with a View**

If you're looking for a hotel where you can take a swim, consider the following, whose pools also offer beautiful views:

- **Hotel Balmes** (p. 108), for a garden oasis in the middle of the Eixample.
- **Hotel Arts** (p. 112), the city's only beachside hotel.
- **Hotel Omm** (p. 100), for unbeatable views of Gaudí's rooftops.
- **Hotel Claris** (p. 98), for high-tech design, acres of steel, and wood decking.
- **Hotel Duquesa de Cardona** (p. 87), for rooftop views over the boats and gin palaces of the Port Vell.

INEXPENSIVE

Marina Folch *Finds*   This small, informal guesthouse is gradually earning itself a loyal following among visitors who want to be close to the sea without paying for the earth. Barceloneta (the old fishermen's district) is mysteriously lacking in reasonably priced places to stay, and the friendly Marina Folch is a gem. All 10 rooms have private bathrooms with shower while the bedrooms are simply decorated but fresh, clean, and comfortable. It's exactly what cheap, no-nonsense accommodations should be: a genuine retreat from the bustle of daily life minus the sometimes-tiring whistles and bells of more upscale accommodations. The only drawback is that it's located above a restaurant (same management), so mealtimes are noisy.

Mar 16, Barceloneta, 08003 Barcelona. *©* **93-310-37-09.** Fax 93-310-53-27. 10 units. 60€–65€ ($75–$81) double. AE, DC, MC, V. Parking 19€ ($24). Metro: Barceloneta. **Amenities:** Restaurant; room service; laundry service. *In room:* A/C, TV.

Marina View B&B   Just in front of the Port Vell (Old Port), and halfway between the Vía Laietana and Les Ramblas, this homey bed-and-breakfast is in a top spot for making the most of the city's prime sights as well as her beaches. Bedrooms are fairly small but pleasantly decorated, and all have private bathrooms with shower as well as some bonus extras like complimentary tea and coffee. Owner José María is the friendliest and most accommodating host one could hope for, and will even provide breakfast in bed for those who want it.

Passeig de Colom s/n, Barri Gòtic, 08002 Barcelona. *©* **60-920-64-93.** www.marinaviewbcn.com. 5 units. 100€–120€ ($125–$150) double; 150€ ($188) triple (includes breakfast). MC, V for down payment only. Public parking nearby 20€ ($25). Metro: Drassanes. **Amenities:** Lounge; laundry service. *In room:* A/C, TV, minibar, coffee/tea, Internet access.

---

7 On the Outskirts

VERY EXPENSIVE

Barcelona Hilton   This 11-floor, government-rated, five-star property, located on one of the city's main arteries, is part of a huge commercial complex with an adjoining office tower. The lobby as you enter is impressively sleek with lots of velvet chairs. Public-area furnishings are Hilton-standardized, but most of the large and well-equipped rooms feature thick carpets, rich wood decor, and some of the best combination bathrooms in the city with all the extras, including dual basins and robes. Some units are reserved exclusively for women.

Av. Diagonal 589–591, 08014 Barcelona. *©* **800/445-8667** in the U.S. and Canada, or 93-495-77-77. Fax 93-495-77-00. www.hilton.com. 287 units. 310€–375€ ($388–$469) double; 340€–445€ ($425–$556) suite. AE, DC, MC, V.

Parking 28€ ($35). Metro: María Cristina. **Amenities:** 3 restaurants; cafe; bar; health club; business center; room service; babysitting; laundry service; dry cleaning; nonsmoking rooms. *In room:* A/C, TV, minibar, hair dryer, iron, safe, Internet access.

Gran Hotel La Florida ★★★   If it were put to popular vote, Gran Hotel La Florida would probably win the title of Barcelona's finest hotel. And if it did win, it would be for the second time; when it first opened in the 1920s, it was the favorite choice for Spanish aristocracy, movie stars, and monarchy who came seeking out the fresher air at the top of Tibidabo mountain. It was subsequently used as a hospital during World War II, and didn't welcome guests again until 2003. After a complete overhaul by some of the world's most prolific artists and designers, it is now stuffed with art that would be the envy of many a high-profile gallery, and boasts several designer suites. The feeling of being somewhere special starts on arrival, when guests are offered glasses of rose-petal water before being shown to soothing, sand-colored rooms, which all have spacious marble bathrooms with separate tub and shower. (Most of them boast magnificent views as well.) It's a 20-minute taxi ride to the city center, but many visitors simply prefer to stay here and enjoy the marvelous setting and facilities. These include a world-class restaurant, **L'Orangerie** (p. 150), a spa and infinity pool, terraced gardens, and service that really does make you feel as if you've died and gone to heaven.

Carretera Vallvidrera (al Tibidabo) 83–93, 08035 Barcelona. (C) **93-259-30-00.** Fax 93-259-30-01. www.hotel laflorida.com. 74 units. 320€–610€ ($400–$762) double; 660€–890€ ($825–$1,112) suite. AE, DC, MC, V. Parking 18€ ($23) per day. 7km (4miles) from Barcelona. **Amenities:** Restaurant; private nightclub; indoor/outdoor pool; health club; Jacuzzi; sauna; solarium; Turkish bath; business center; room service; babysitting; laundry service; dry cleaning; nonsmoking rooms. *In room:* A/C, TV, minibar, hair dryer, iron, safe, Internet access.

Rey Juan Carlos I ★★★   Named after the Spanish king himself who attended its opening and has visited it several times since, this government-rated, five-star hotel competes effectively with other legendary spots such as the Ritz, Claris, and Hotel Arts. Opened just before the Olympics, it rises 17 stories at the northern end of the Diagonal in a wealthy neighborhood filled with corporate headquarters, banks, and upscale stores, a 15-minute Metro ride from Barcelona's top central attractions. Among its more striking design features is a soaring inner atrium with glass-sided elevators. The midsize-to-spacious guest rooms contain electronic extras, conservatively comfortable furnishings, and oversize beds. Many have views over Barcelona to the sea. Thoughtful touches include good lighting, adequate work space, spacious closets, and blackout draperies, plus marble bathrooms with tub/shower combos.

Av. Diagonal 671, 08028 Barcelona. (C) **800/445-8355** in the U.S., or 93-364-40-40. Fax 93-364-42-64. www.hrjuan carlos.com. 412 units. 375€ ($469) double; 505€–995€ ($631–$1,243) suite. AE, DC, MC, V. Parking 15€ ($19). Metro: Zona Universitària. **Amenities:** 2 restaurants; 2 bars; indoor pool; outdoor pool; fitness center; car rental; business center; salon; babysitting; room service; laundry/ironing service; dry cleaning; nonsmoking rooms. *In room:* A/C, TV, minibar, hair dryer, safe, Internet access.

EXPENSIVE

Relais d'Orsa ★★★   Those looking for a special place to stay need look no further than the Relais d'Orsa: a genuine, romantic hideaway in the tiny village of Vallvidrera, minutes away from the better-known Gran Hotel La Florida (see above). The sleepier and more secluded d'Orsa occupies a 19th-century mansion that has been renovated to create an intimate space, decorated with antiques and textiles collected from all over Europe by the French owner. Hidden away in a forest with sprawling, lovingly tended gardens filled with shade and flowers and a relaxing pool surrounded by teak decking, it is the perfect place for some quality rest and relaxation. And because it has just six bedrooms it has the feel of a private home. The black-and-white-tiled bedrooms, with antique beds and French Provençal furniture and linens, are sublime, with floor-to-ceiling windows ensuring plenty of light and fabulous views. Bathrooms, meanwhile, have tub/shower combos, fresh flowers, candles, and wonderful smelling L'Occitane products, also from Provence. A breakfast of local preserves, breads, and pastries is served in the dining room, or under a shady pagoda in summer.

Mont d'Orsa 35, 08017 Barcelona. © **93-406-94-11.** Fax 93-406-94-71. www.relaisdorsa.com. 6 units. 220€ ($275) double; 375€ ($469) suite. AE, DC, MC, V. Free parking. Closed Dec 24–Jan 6. From Barcelona take Av. Vallvidrera north of the city; from airport Exit 9 (Ronda de Dalt) and then Av. Vallvidrera. **Amenities:** Cafeteria; outdoor pool; room service; babysitting; laundry service; dry cleaning; private gardens. *In room:* A/C, TV, minibar, hair dryer, iron, safe, Internet access.

MODERATE

Abba Garden Hotel   Opened in 2002, this big, terra-cotta-red hilltop hotel is less than a mile from Barcelona's soccer stadium—Camp Nou—making the Abba a top choice for *fútbol* fans. Its distance from the city center (6km/3¾ miles) means that it enjoys plenty of space, with landscaped gardens, tennis courts, and a large outdoor swimming pool. It's also well located if you plan to spend your time ferrying to and from golf courses outside of Barcelona. The downside is that you might find yourself taking expensive taxi rides into town. If you're eating in, check out the reasonably good on-site restaurant and bar. Bedrooms are spacious and freshly decorated with flower-print fabrics, and all have en-suite bathrooms with tub/shower combos. Twenty-nine of the rooms are for nonsmokers.

Santa Rosa 33, Esplugues de Llobregat, 08950 Barcelona. © **93-503-54-54.** Fax 93-503-54-55. www.abbahotels.com. 138 units. 95€–160€ ($118–$200) double. AE, DC, MC, V. Parking 14€ ($18). Metro: Zona Universitària; RENFE: Reina Elisenda. From Barcelona take Av. Diagonal out of the center to the Pedralbes area and look out for signs to Hospital St. Jean de Deu next to hotel. **Amenities:** Restaurant; cafeteria; bar; health club; sauna; solarium; tennis courts; car rental; business center; room service; babysitting; laundry service; dry cleaning; nonsmoking rooms; private garden. *In room:* A/C, TV, minibar, hair dryer, safe, Internet access.

Hesperia Sarrià 🕸 *(Kids)*   This hotel on the northern edge of the city, a 10-minute taxi ride from the center, sits in one of Barcelona's most pleasant residential neighborhoods. Built in the late 1980s, the hotel was last renovated before the 1992 Olympics. You'll pass a Japanese rock formation to reach the stone-floored reception area with its adjacent bar. Sunlight floods the monochromatic guest rooms (which consist of singles, doubles—priced the same as singles—and suites). Although most rooms are medium-size, they have enough space for an extra bed, which makes this a good choice for families. Beds have quality mattresses and fine linen, and bathrooms have a generous assortment of good-size towels and tub/shower combos. The uniformed staff offers fine service.

Los Vergós 20, 08017 Barcelona. © **93-204-55-51.** Fax 93 204 43 92. www.hoteles-hesperia.es. 134 units. 145€–210€ ($181–$262) double; 180€–240€ ($225–$300) suite. AE, DC, MC, V. Parking 14€ ($18). Metro: Tres Torres. **Amenities:** Restaurant; bar; business center; room service; laundry service; dry cleaning; nonsmoking rooms. *In room:* A/C, TV, minibar, hair dryer, safe, Internet access.

Tryp Barcelona Aeropuerto   As the name suggests, the main reason for staying at this hotel is to be close to the airport. Tryp (part of the Sol Meliá group) is a reliable, four-star chain and excellent in terms of business facilities. This one is relatively new with completely modernized amenities. Comfortable, spacious bedrooms all have large, marble bathrooms and tub/shower combos. A buffet breakfast is included in the double-room price, and there's a free 24-hour airport shuttle bus.

Plaça del Pla De l'Estany 1–2, Polígono Mas Blau II, Prat de Llobregat, 08820 Barcelona. © 93-378-10-00. Fax 93-378-10-01. www.trypbarcelonaaeropuerto.solmelia.com. 205 units. 100€–135€ ($125–$169) double; 175€ ($219) suite. AE, DC, MC, V. Valet parking 16€ ($20). 1.5km (1 mile) from airport; 10km (6 miles) from Barcelona. **Amenities:** Restaurant; cafeteria; bar; health center; car rental; airport shuttle service; business center; limited room service; laundry service; dry cleaning; nonsmoking room; safe. *In room:* A/C, TV, minibar, hair dryer, Internet access.

8 Apartments & Aparthotels

Aparthotel Silver ★★ *Finds* Located in the heart of villagey Gràcia, the Silver apartments are a perfect base for those looking to remove themselves a little from the hustle and bustle of the city center. With its low-rise houses, cute sunny plazas, eclectic bars and restaurants, and bohemian vibe, Gràcia is one of Barcelona's least discovered barrios—and well worth getting to know. Silver's 49 studio apartments are smartly decorated with plenty of storage space, comfortable beds, and fresh linens. They come with a kitchenette with a small electric stove and a refrigerator, and all have private bathrooms with tub/shower combos. The building also has a private garden and lawn equipped with tables. This place is a bargain, especially for couples seeking a little independence.

Bretón de los Herreros 26, Gràcia, 08012 Barcelona. © 93-218-91-00. Fax 93-416-14-47. www.hotelsilver.com. 49 units. 70€–80€ ($88–$100) apt. AE, DC, MC, V. Metro: Fontana. Parking 10€ ($13). **Amenities:** Cafeteria; bar; room service; laundry service; Internet access; private garden. *In room:* A/C, TV, kitchenette w/refrigerator, safe.

Citadines *Kids* Modern, clean, and bright, this aparthotel is a good choice for those who want to be right on La Rambla with the option to cook for themselves (the wonderful fresh produce market La Boqueria is just up the street). Especially popular with groups and families with children, it provides fully equipped kitchens, optional maid service, and large, comfortable bedrooms with sofa beds in the living area. The bathrooms are clean and modern, too. One thing that gives the Citadines the edge over many similar self-catering places in town is the ninth-floor roof terrace offering 360-degree views over the whole city.

La Rambla 122, 08002 Barcelona. © 93-270-11-11. Fax 93-412-74-21. www.citadines.com. 115 studios; 16 apts. 150€–180€ ($187–$225) 2-person apt; 240€–260€ ($300–$325) 4-person apt. AE, DC, MC, V. Parking 20€ ($25). Metro: Plaça Catalunya. **Amenities:** Bar; solarium; laundry service; maid service; meeting rooms. *In room:* A/C; TV; kitchenette w/microwave, dishwasher, and fridge; hair dryer; safe; Internet access; stereo.

Hispanos Siete Suiza ★★★ Of all the aparthotels in Barcelona, the Suiza is far and away the most glamorous—a real home-away-from-home combined with the comforts of a luxury hotel. The wood-floored apartments all have two bedrooms, two bathrooms, a plush, cozy living room, and a kitchen. Continental breakfast is included in the price. It's worth knowing that **La Cupula** (the in-house restaurant) is overseen by Carles Gaig, a renowned Catalan chef. What makes Siete Suiza truly special is its unexpected history. A Catalan doctor, gynecologist Melchor Colet Torrabadella, originally owned the house. He was also a writer, poet, and philanthropist, and was hugely interested in the arts, as well as fine vintage cars (a collection of seven beautiful 1920s automobiles, from which the hotel gets its name, decorate the lobby). When his wife died of cancer, Colet set up a foundation in her memory, **Fundación Dr. Melchor Colet,** and part of the hotel's profits go to this cause.

Sicilia 255, Eixample Dreta, 08025 Barcelona. © 93-208-20-51. Fax 93-208-20-52. www.hispanos7suiza.com. 19 units. 140€–195€ ($175–$244) 2-bedroom apt for 2 with 40€ ($50) supplement for 3 or 4 guests. AE, DC, MC, V. Parking 14€ ($18). Metro: Sagrada Família. **Amenities:** Restaurant; cocktail bar; room service; laundry service; safe; shopping service; room for guests w/disabilities; DVD player/Playstation rental. *In room:* A/C, TV, kitchen w/washing machine and dryer, minibar, safe, Internet access.

6

Where to Dine

Whether it's a hearty nosh-up in an old-style tavern, a late supper in one of the new cutting-edge eateries, a tapa or two taken leaning against a bar, or an alfresco paella, Barcelona can accommodate you very nicely. Not only does it have a culinary tradition far different from that of the rest of Spain, but its new breed of chefs, led by Ferran Adrià of **El Bulli** fame (p. 285), has taken over the mantle from France as the Continent's new culinary hot spot. The turning point came in 2002, when that year's edition of *Le Guide des Gourmands,* the French foodie bible of where to buy and eat the best products, named Barcelona the "most gourmand" city in Europe—the first time a non-French city has been cited in its 15 years of publication. The criteria for the accolade are the availability of products; the quality of local wine, market produce,

and restaurants; and, in the spirit of the *bon vivant,* the sensibility of the local population as to what goes into their stomachs. Barcelona came up trumps in all areas.

The buzzwords in the metropolis's culinary world are "eclectic fusion," which mean roughly either blending a dish from one region (such as Navarra) with that of another (like Asturias) and adding a few extra herbs, spices, and *je ne sais quoi;* or unexpectedly mingling traditional local dishes like pigeon with, say, pears, or cherries with anis, or pigs' trotters with crab. The resultant hybrid *plato* is usually a delicious new taste experience. It's a feature you'll find in spots like **Gaig** (p. 142) and **Hisop** (p. 143) and light-years away from the hearty, no-frills *botifarras* (sausages) and *estofats* (stews) of yesteryear.

1 Food for Thought
WHAT MAKES IT CATALAN CUISINE?

Much of what these new chefs do is put an avant-garde twist on traditional Catalan cuisine. But what is that exactly? What Catalans eat is recognizably different from the cuisine in the rest of Spain, and it varies within the region from the Mediterranean coastline and islands to the inland villages and Pyrénées Mountains. Indeed, Catalan cuisine is more influenced by much of Europe (especially France) and the Mediterranean are rather than by Castile. Writer Colman Andrews in *Catalan Cuisine,* his definitive English-language book on the subject (Grub Street, 1997), calls it "Europe's Last Great Culinary Secret." Many of the techniques and basic recipes can be traced back to medieval times and, as any Catalan is only too willing to point out, the quality of the produce proceeding from the *Països Catalans* (Catalan countries) is some of the best available. The same goes for the locally produced wine. The D.O.s *(domaines ordinaires)* of the Penedès and Priorat regions are now as internationally renowned as La Rioja and the local *cava* (sparking, champagne-type wine) consumed at celebratory tables from Melbourne to Manchester.

If there is one food item that symbolizes Catalan cuisine, it is the *pa amb tomàquet.* Originally invented as a way of softening stale bread during the lean years of the civil war, there is barely a restaurant in Catalonia, from the most humble workman's canteen to a Michelin-starred palace that does not have it on the menu. In its simplest form, it consists of a slice of rustic white bread that has been rubbed with the pulp of a cut tomato and drizzled with olive oil. Sometimes, especially when the bread is toasted, you are given a tomato to do this yourself and a clove of garlic to add extra flavor. On these occasions, you top the bread with cheese, pâté, chorizo (or any other cured meat), or Iberian ham, producing what's known as a *torrada.*

Catalan cuisine is marked by combinations that at first seem at odds with one other: Red meat and fish are cooked in the same dish; nuts are pulped for sauces; poultry is cooked with fruit; pulse (bean) dishes are never vegetarian; and there is not one part of a pig that isn't consumed. Concoctions that you will see popping up on menus time and time again include *zarzuela* (a rich fish stew), *botifarra amb mongetes* (pork sausage with white beans), *faves a la catalana* (broad beans with Iberian ham), *samfaina* (a sauce of eggplant, peppers, and zucchini), *esqueixada* (a salted cod salad), *fideuà* (similar to a paella, but with noodles replacing the rice), and *miel i mato* (a soft cheese with honey). It's hearty fare, and far more elaborate than the food of Southern Spain. In its most traditional form, it doesn't suit light appetites, which is why many locals have only one main meal a day (normally at lunch), with perhaps a light supper of a *torrada* in the evenings. Breakfast is also a light affair: a milky coffee (*café con leche* in Spanish, *café amb llet* in Catalan) with a croissant or doughnut is what most people survive on until lunchtime. Many bars offer fresh orange juice.

WHEN YOU DINE IN BARCELONA

Catalans generally have lunch between 2 and 4pm and dinner after 9pm. Most kitchens stay open in the evenings until about 11pm. It is highly recommended that you make lunch your main meal and take advantage of the *menú del día* (lunch of the day) that is offered in the majority of eateries. It normally consists of three courses (wine and/or coffee and dessert included) and, at between 8€ and 12€ ($10–$15) per head, is an extremely cost-effective way of trying out some of the pricier establishments. Tipping always seems to confuse visitors, mainly because some restaurants list the 7% IVA (sales tax) separately on the bill. This is *not* a service charge; in fact, it is illegal for restaurants to charge for service. As a general rule, tips (in cash) of about 5% should be left in cheap to moderate restaurants and 10% in more expensive ones. In bars, just leave a few coins or round your bill up to the nearest euro. If you are really unhappy with the service or food and think that it warrants following up, you are entitled to ask for a *hoja de reclamación* (complaint form) from the management. These are then perused by independent inspectors.

In general, vegetarians don't fare well here. Vegetarian restaurants are more common than they were 10 or 15 years ago, but with some notable exceptions (such as **Organic;** p. 137) "creative cooking" coupled with "meat-free" isn't widely practiced in Barcelona. Contemporary places such as **Pla** (p. 127), **Anima** (p. 135), and **Juicy Jones** (p. 128) are a good bet, with always a couple of vegetarian options on offer. Apart from a tortilla, don't expect this in the traditional, old-style taverns and always double-check; the Catalan word *carn* (*carne* in Spanish) only refers to red meat. Asking for a dish "without" (*sens* in Catalan, *sin* in Spanish) does not guarantee it arrives fish- or chicken-free. Restaurants and bars of over 100 sq. m (1,076 sq. ft.) have nonsmoking areas, though

THE TRAVELOCITY GUARANTEE

...THAT SAYS EVERYTHING YOU BOOK WILL BE RIGHT, OR WE'LL WORK WITH OUR TRAVEL PARTNERS TO MAKE IT RIGHT, RIGHT AWAY.

*To drive home the point,
we're going to use the word "right" in every single sentence.*

Let's get right to it. Right to the meat! Only Travelocity guarantees everything about your booking will be right, or we'll work with our travel partners to make it right, right away. Right on!

Here's a picture taken smack dab right in the middle of Antigua, where the Guarantee also covers you.

The Guarantee covers all but one of the items pictured to the right.

For example, what if the ocean view you booked actually looks out at a downright ugly parking lot? You'd be right to call – we're there for you. And no one in their right mind would be pleased to learn the rental car place has closed and left them stranded. Call Travelocity and we'll help get you back on the right track.

Now, you may be thinking, "Yeah, right, I'm so sure." That's OK; you have the right to remain skeptical. That is until we mention help is always right around the corner. Call us right off the bat, knowing our customer service reps are there for you 24/7. Righting wrongs, left and right.

Now if you're guessing there are some things we can't control, like the weather, well you're right. But we can help you with most things – to get all the details in righting,* visit travelocity.com/guarantee.

*Sorry, spelling things right is one of the few things not covered under the Guarantee.

I'd give my right arm for a guarantee like this, although I'm glad I don't have to.

***travelocity**
You'll never roam alone.

Tips   Barcelona's Green Scene

Being a "veggie" no longer means being an outsider in the Catalan capital. In the past decade the traditional dominance of carnivore-oriented establishments has been challenged by a small but growing number of vegetarian restaurants. In this chapter you'll find some of the best.

You don't have to confine yourself to 100% green establishments to get the goods, though, as many standard Catalan eating spots offer a large choice of noncarnivorous *platos.*

Apart from the ubiquitous tortilla (made, *naturalmente,* with eggs Spanish-style and not from cornmeal Mexican-style), check out their menus for dishes like *escalivada* (grilled red and green pepper salad), *berengenas al horno* (eggplant baked in the oven), *calabaza guisada* (stewed pumpkin), *setas al jerez* (mushrooms cooked in sherry), and *pisto* (Spain's answer to ratatouille with tomatoes, peppers, eggplant courgettes, and onions all cooked in oil and garlic: Avoid the Manchego version, though, as this has bits of ham in it). *Jamón* (Mountain or cooked, Serrano or York), is scarcely regarded as "real" meat in Spain and can even appear in apparently innocuous dishes such as *caldo* (broth), so confirm with the waiter before you order.

Arabic, Indian, and Italian restaurants may also provide what you're looking for, with their inventive range of couscous, rice, and pasta-based dishes, and if fish is an acceptable option, there are of course, plenty of seafood restaurants to choose from, though these tend to be expensive.

in bars smoke often tends to drift across from the usually much larger smoking area. To be on the safe side, try one of the outside terraces for a relatively smoke-free (if not smog-free) meal or drink.

Below is only a small selection of the hundreds of Barcelonese restaurants, cafes, and bars. When deciding where to dine, be aware that Barcelona is a victim of its own popularity. The constant influx of tourists means that many places (especially on and around Les Ramblas) now think nothing of offering a microwaved paella or charging 10 times the average for a cup of coffee. But in the smaller streets of the Barri Gòtic, and along the blocks of the Eixample area (which has largely escaped the side effects of mass tourism) there are still plenty of value-for-money establishments that take enormous pride in introducing you to the delights of the local cuisine. And if you get tired of the local grub, you'll find cheap places to eat around El Raval, the city's most multicultural neighborhood, where dozens of restaurants are run by Pakistanis, Moroccans, and South Americans. *¡Bon profit!*

2 The Best Restaurant Bets

- **Hottest Chef:** Carles Abellán has been hailed as the new wunderkind of nouvelle Catalan cuisine. His restaurant, **Comerç 24,** was conceived as a playful take on all that's hot in the tapas world. Delights such as "kinder egg surprise" (a soft-boiled egg with truffle-infused yolk) and tuna sashimi pizza await the adventurous. See p. 132.

- **Best Newcomer:** Up in the Diagonal end of the Eixample a duo of highly professional young chefs thought it would be a good idea to launch a chic low-key locale in which they subtly produce stunningly flavored nouvelle Catalan dishes. Word soon got round and now **Hisop** is one of Barcelona's most "in" places to eat. See p. 143.

- **Best Spot for a Celebration:** You can make as much noise as you like at **Mesón David,** an old-school eatery with an interminable menu of dishes from all regions of Spain. Chances are you will be sitting next to a raucous group celebrating a birthday or engagement with waiters often joining in the revelry themselves. See p. 137.

- **Best Wine List:** You will be spoiled for choice at **La Vinya del Senyor,** a gorgeous wine bar opposite the towering Santa María del Mar church. Mull over the 300 varieties on offer while taking in its facade from the outside terrace, then order some of their delicious tapas to accompany your *vino.* See p. 157.

- **Best for Paella:** A paella-on-the-beach is one of the quintessential Barcelona experiences, and there is no place better to do it than **Can Majó.** Right on the seafront, this restaurant prides itself on its paellas and *fideuàs* (which replace noodles for rice) and is an established favorite among the city's most well-heeled families. See p. 155.

- **Best Modern Catalan Cuisine:** With over 10 restaurants, the legendary Tragaluz group has revolutionized Barcelona's gastronomic panorama. Its flagship eatery, **Tragaluz,** defines not only the city's contemporary design aesthetic but also its "market" cuisine. See p. 146.

- **Best Traditional Catalan Cuisine: Via Veneto** exudes old-fashioned class and serves up some of the finest Catalan cooking in the land. Some of the serving methods, such as the sterling silver duck press, seem to belong to another century (as do some of the clients). See p. 158.

- **Best for Kids:** Children are welcome almost everywhere in Spanish restaurants, but why not give them a real treat by heading for **La Paradeta?** As close as you can get to the Catalan version of a fish and chippery, it offers all kinds of seafood laid out on ice, which greets as you walk in. You pick what you want and a few minutes later, out it comes, hot and steaming in a cardboard box. See p. 133.

- **Best Fusion Cuisine:** Born in Catalonia but raised in Canada, chef Jordi Artal instinctively knows how to fuse Old and New World cuisines. The five-course tasting menu in his upscale **Cinc Sentits** is a memorable way to sample his expertise. See p. 142.

- **Best for Tapas: Taller de Tapas** was conceived to take the mystery out of tapas. Multilingual staff and menus ensure you don't get pigs' cheeks when you order green leeks, and the delectable dishes are a perfect initiation for the novice. See p. 134.

- **Best for People-Watching:** The food may not win any awards but that doesn't stop soccer stars, models, and other assorted semi-celebs from flocking to **CDLC,** which is right on the waterfront in the Olympic Village and decked out in fashionable faux-Thai chic. The real fun starts with the post-dinner disco, and you're not sure whether the breeze is rolling in off the Mediterranean or the rush of air kisses. See p. 155.

- **Best Outdoor Dining Area:** As well as being one of the best value restaurants in the city, the **Café de L'Academia** is blessed with one of the prettiest settings: a charming square in the Old Town flanked by Gothic buildings and an ancient water fountain. At night the warm glow of the table candles bounces off the stone walls, ensuring you linger long on after the last liquor. See p. 124.

- **Best View:** Dine on top of the world, or at least 75m (246 ft.) up in **Torre d'Alta Mar,** located in a cable-car tower. The vista couldn't be more mesmerizing, allowing you to take an almost-360-degree panorama of the city's skyline and the surrounding sea. See p. 154.
- **Best for Seafood:** Although good seafood is abundant in Barcelona, many swear that the best catches end up in **Cal Pep,** a tiny bar near the port. Mountains of *mariscos* are prepared in front of you by lightning-quick staff, and your dexterity is put to the test as you try not to elbow your neighbor while peeling your prawns. See p. 132.
- **Best Wine Bar:** Bathed in bordeaux red, with large arched windows looking out onto a tranquil square, **Vinissim** has a mind-boggling array of wines from all corners of the globe, plus a scrumptious array of tapas to soak them up. See p. 131.
- **Best for Sunday Lunch:** The lines say it all: **7 Portes,** one of the oldest restaurants in Barcelona, is a Sunday institution. Extended families dine on excellent meat and fish dishes in turn-of-the-20th-century surroundings. See p. 153.
- **Best Vegetarian Restaurant:** True vegetarian dining is still quite rare in Barcelona. Thank heavens for **Organic,** a barnlike place with communal wooden tables, an all-you-can-eat salad bar, and tempting rice, pasta, and tofu dishes. See p. 137.
- **Best for a Sweet Tooth:** Sweet but never sickly, **Espai Sucre** is perhaps the world's only restaurant that offers a menu made up entirely of desserts. Foodies rave about it and its reputation has spread far and wide as a once-in-a-lifetime gastronomic experience. Some savory dishes are available. See p. 132.
- **Best for Morning or Afternoon Tea:** The tiny street of Petritxol in the Old City is renowned for its *granjas,* cafes specializing in cakes, pastries, and hot chocolate. In addition to all this, **Xocoa** makes its own mouthwatering chocolates. See p. 215.
- **Best for Consistency: Pla** strikes that right balance between hip and highly creative without scaring you off. The menu focuses on local market produce with a touch of Asian and Arabic and the staff is unusually friendly and helpful. See p. 127.
- **Best Snack on the Go:** Before you embark on a visit to the Museum of Contemporary Art, fuel-up at **Foodball,** a new concept in fast food. Wholegrain rice balls filled with tofu, wild mushrooms, chickpeas, and the like, plus fresh juices and smoothies are served in a quirky setting where you can also eat in. See p. 130.

3 Ciutat Vella: Barri Gòtic

EXPENSIVE

Agut d'Avignon ✦ CATALAN One of my favorite restaurants in Barcelona is in a tiny alleyway near the Plaça Reial. The city's restaurant explosion has toppled Agut d'Avignon from its position as best in the city, but it's still going strong after more than 4 decades, and it has a dedicated following. It attracts politicians, writers, journalists, financiers, industrialists, and artists—and even the king and cabinet ministers, along with visiting dignitaries. Since 1983 Mercedes Giralt Salinas and her son Javier Falagán Giralt have run the restaurant. A small 19th-century vestibule leads to the multilevel dining area, which has two balconies and a main hall evoking a hunting lodge. You may need help translating the Catalan menu. The traditional specialties often include acorn-squash soup served in its shell, fishermen's soup with garlic toast, haddock stuffed with shellfish, sole with *nyoca* (a medley of nuts), large shrimp with aioli, duck with figs, and filet beefsteak in sherry sauce.

Trinitat 3, at Carrer d'Avinyó. © **93-302-60-34**. Reservations recommended. Main courses 15€–25€ ($19–$31); lunch menu 14€ ($18). AE, DC, MC, V. Daily 1–4:30pm and 9pm–12:30am. Metro: Jaume I or Liceu.

MODERATE

Agut *Finds* CATALAN   In a historic building in the Barri Gòtic, 3 blocks from the harborfront, Agut epitomizes the bohemian atmosphere surrounding this gritty area. For three-quarters of a century, this has been a family-run business, with María Agut García the current reigning empress. (Don't confuse Agut with the more famous Agut d'Avignon nearby.) The aura is evokes the 1940s and 1950s, with a cozy little bar to the right as you enter. Paintings on the walls are from well-known Catalan artists from the mid–20th century. Begin with *mil hojas de botifarra amb zets* (layers of pastry filled with Catalan sausage and mushrooms), or the *terrine de albergines amb fortmage de cabra* (terrine of eggplant with goat cheese gratinée). One of our favorite dishes is *soufle de rape amb gambes* (soufflé of monkfish with shrimp). For gastronomes only, try the *pie de cerdo relleno con foie amb truffles* (pork feet stuffed with duck liver and truffles). Or if you are ravenous, attempt the *chuletón de buey* (loin of ox) for two, which comes thick and juicy and accompanied by a mixture of fresh vegetables. For dessert, if you order *sortido,* you'll get a combination plate with an assortment of the small homemade cakes of the house.

Gignàs 16. © **93-315-17-09**. Reservations required. Main courses 9€–18€ ($11–$23); fixed-price lunch menu Tues–Fri 12€ ($15). AE, DC, MC, V. Tues–Sun 1:30–4pm; Tues–Sat 9pm–midnight. Closed Aug. Metro: Jaume I.

Café de L'Academia *Value* CATALAN/MEDITERRANEAN   In the center of Barri Gòtic a short walk from Plaça Sant Jaume, this 28-table restaurant looks expensive but is really one of the best and most affordable in the medieval city. The building dates from the 15th century, but the restaurant was founded only in the mid-1980s. Owner Jordi Casteldi offers an elegant atmosphere in a setting of brown-stone walls and ancient wooden columns. At a small bar you can peruse the varied menu and study the wines offered. Dishes of this quality usually cost three times as much in Barcelona. The chef is proud of his "kitchen of the market," suggesting that only the freshest ingredients from the day's shopping are featured. Try such delights as *bacallà gratinado i musselina de carofes* (salt cod gratinée with an artichoke mousse) or *terrina d'berengeras amb fortmage de cabra* (terrine of eggplant with goat cheese). A delectable specialty sometimes available is *codorniz rellena en cebollitas tiernas y foie de pato* (partridge stuffed with tender onions and duck liver). On warm evenings, go for one of the outside, candlelit tables on the atmospheric square dominated by a Gothic church.

Carrer Lledó 1, Plaça Sant Just. © **93-315-00-26**. Reservations required. Main courses 10€–16€ ($13–$20); fixed-price lunch menu 13€ ($16). AE, MC, V. Mon–Fri 9am–noon, 1:30–4pm, and 9–11:30pm. Closed 2–3 weeks in Aug. Metro: Jaume I.

Can Culleretes CATALAN   Founded in 1786 as a *pastelería* (pastry shop) in the Barri Gòtic, Barcelona's oldest restaurant retains many original architectural features. All three dining rooms are decorated with tile dadoes and wrought-iron chandeliers. The well-prepared food features authentic dishes of northeastern Spain, including sole Roman style, *zarzuela a la marinera* (shellfish medley), cannelloni, and paella and special game dishes, including *perdiz* (partridge). The service is old-fashioned, and sometimes it's

Abac **35**
Agut **38**
Anima **6**
The Bagel Shop **23**
Bar del Pi **22**
Bodega la Plata **33**
Café de l'Academia **30**
Cafe de la Opera **16**
Ca l'Estevet **41**
Cal Pep **42**
Can Culleretes **27**
Can L'isidre **2**
Casa Leopoldo **5**

Comerç 24 **43**
El Salón **34**
Els Quatre Gats **25**
Els Tres Tombs **1**
Espai Sucre **42**
Foodball **8**
Garduña **16**
Gente de Pasta **47**
Iposa **7**
Juicy Jones **20**
Kasparo **10**
La Cuineta **26**
La Dentellière **31**

La Paradeta **44**
La Rosca **24**
Las Campañas
  (Casa Marcos) **32**
Los Caracoles **19**
Lupino **7**
Mama Cafe **9**
Mesón David **3**
Murivecchi **46**
Organic **14**
Pla **29**
Pla de la Garsa **39**
Quo Vadis **12**

Restaurant Hoffmann **40**
Romesco **17**
Salsitas **18**
Sandwich & Friends **45**
Santa María **33**
Schilling **21**
Senyor Parellada **37**
Taller de Tapas **36**
Umita **13**
Vinissim **28**

filled more with tourists than with locals, but it retains enough authentic touches to make it feel like the real McCoy. Signed photographs of celebrities, flamenco artists, and bullfighters who have visited decorate the walls.

Quintana 5. © **93-317-64-85.** Reservations recommended. Main courses 8€–16€ ($10–$20); fixed-price menu Tues–Fri 15€ ($19). MC, V. Tues–Sun 1:30–4pm; Tues–Sat 9–11pm. Closed July. Metro: Liceu. Bus: 14 or 59.

El Salón *(Moments* MEDITERRANEAN/FUSION   Dominated by a huge gilt mirror and low lighting, El Salón has long been a favorite for couples looking for a romantic dinner spot. The menu, which changes daily, pushes the definition of eclectic with Asian, Italian, and especially French influences on local market produce. It's been around long enough to have a firm and faithful following, especially among the expat community, but the standard varies. When it's good, it's very, very good. But when it's an off night . . . well, you'll still go back for the sheer charm of the place.

L'Hostal d'en Sol 6–8. © **93-315-21-59.** Reservations recommended. Main courses 9€–18€ ($11–$23); fixed-price dinner 20€ ($25). AE, DC, MC, V. Daily 9pm–midnight. Metro: Jaume I.

Els Quatre Gats *(Moments* CATALAN   This has been a Barcelona legend since 1897. The "Four Cats" (Catalan slang for "just a few people") was a favorite of Picasso, Rusiñol, and other artists who once hung their works on its walls. (Reproductions still adorn them.) On a narrow cobblestone street in the Barri Gòtic, the *fin de siècle* cafe has been the setting for poetry readings by Joan Maragall, piano concerts by Isaac Albéniz and Ernie Granados, and murals by Ramón Casas. It was a base for members of the *modernista* movement and figured in the city's intellectual and bohemian life.

Today the restored cafe-restaurant is still a popular meeting place. Considering the restaurant's location, the fixed-price meal is one of the better bargains in town, and dinner dining is a good bet given the overall grandeur. The homespun Catalan cooking here is called *cucina de mercat* (based on whatever looked fresh at the market) but will always include such classics as *suquet de peix* (a fish and potato hot-pot) and *faves a la catalana* (baby broad beans with Serrano ham). The constantly changing menu reflects the seasons. For the best atmosphere come at lunch—in the evenings it sometimes gets a bit too touristy with musicians playing banal 1960s Spanish pop songs.

Montsió 3. © **93-302-41-40.** Reservations required. Main courses 14€–22€ ($18–$28); fixed-price lunch menu 12€ ($15). AE, DC, MC, V. Daily 1pm–1am. Cafe daily 8am–2am. Metro: Plaça de Catalunya.

Garduña CATALAN   This is the most famous restaurant in Barcelona's covered market, La Boqueria. Originally conceived as a hotel, it has concentrated on food since the 1970s. Battered, somewhat ramshackle, and a bit claustrophobic, it's fashionable with an artistic set that might have been designated as bohemian in an earlier era. It's near the back of the market, so you'll pass endless rows of fresh produce, cheese, and meats before you reach it. You can dine downstairs, near a crowded bar, or a bit more formally upstairs. Food is ultrafresh—the chefs certainly don't have to travel far for the ingredients. You might try "hors d'oeuvres of the sea," cannelloni Rossini, grilled hake with herbs, *rape* (monkfish) *marinera*, paella, brochettes of veal, filet steak with green peppercorns, seafood rice, or a *zarzuela* (stew) of fresh fish with spices.

Jerusalem 18. © **93-302-43-23.** Reservations recommended. Main courses 8€–28€ ($10–$35); fixed-price lunch 10€ ($13); fixed-price dinner 15€ ($19). DC, MC, V. Mon–Sat 1–4pm and 8pm–midnight. Metro: Liceu.

La Cuineta *(Value* CATALAN   This restaurant near the Catalan government offices is a culinary highlight of the Barri Gòtic. Decorated in typical regional style, it favors

Make It Snappy

It had to happen. Whether it's because of the tourist demand or a population that has less time to sit down and enjoy a midday meal, fast-food establishments are becoming increasingly common. McDonald's and Dunkin' Donuts now occupy prime retail real estate, but why not try some of the local takeout? All over the city, **Pans & Company** and **Bocata** dispense freshly made *bocatas* (crusty rolls) filled with tasty hot and cold combinations. Also everywhere are branches of **La Baguetina Catalana,** a fantastic, franchised fuelling-stop with mountains of carb-ridden cakes and pastries to go. A favorite with health-conscious backpackers, **Maoz** (mainly in the Old Town) churns out freshly made falafels, which you then top up yourself with as much salad as can possibly fit into the pita bread. Along the pedestrian boulevard the **Rambla del Raval** (and the streets to either side) there are dozens of places for enormous sharwamas: giant sandwiches filled with spit-roasted chicken or lamb and salad.

local cuisine. The fixed-price menu is a good value, or you can order a la carte. The most expensive appetizer is *bellota* (acorn-fed ham), but I suggest a market-fresh Catalan dish, such as *favas* (broad beans) stewed with *botifarra,* a tasty, spicy local sausage.

Pietat 12. © **93-315-01-11.** Reservations recommended. Main courses 16€–38€ ($20–$48); fixed-price menu 12€–26€ ($15–$33). AE, DC, MC, V. Daily 1–4pm and 8pm–midnight. Metro: Jaume I.

Los Caracoles *(Moments* CATALAN   This restaurant must be one of the easiest to find in Barcelona. As you walk down Escudellers, admittedly one of the city's less-salubrious streets, you are drawn on by the aroma of roasting chickens. This classic restaurant has them on an outside spit, over an open fire built into the side of the edifice. You enter through the main kitchen, where steaming pots surround hot-under-the-collar cooks. Inside it's a labyrinth; stairways lead to even more dining rooms, private one-table nooks are hidden under stairs, and there are colorful tiles, wooden beamed ceilings, and antique fittings everywhere. The place is long on atmosphere and the cuisine is Catalan comfort food: *arroz negre* (rice cooked in squid ink), grilled squid, and, of course, roast chicken. There's always a fair share of tourists and the food isn't always up to what it should be, but as an authentic slice of local culture it's definitely worth a visit.

Escudellers 14. © **93-302-31-85.** Reservations recommended. Main courses 8€–28€ ($10–$35). AE, DC, MC, V. Daily 1pm–midnight. Metro: Drassanes.

Pla *(Moments* MEDITERRANEAN   Pla is popular with locals and visitors alike for its consistently high standard of *carpaccios;* wide selection of market-fresh salads exposing tasty combinations such as spinach, mushrooms, and prawns; and main dishes with Asian and Arabic touches that nearly always include a Thai curry or a Moroccan couscous dish. The staff is amiable, bilingual, and informal, and will take the time to talk you through your selection.

Bellafila 5. © **93-412-65-52.** Reservations required. Main courses 7€–15€ ($8.75–$19). DC, MC, V. Sun–Thurs 9pm–midnight; Fri–Sat 9pm–1am. Closed Dec 25–27. Metro: Jaume I.

INEXPENSIVE

Iposa *Value* FRENCH/MEDITERRANEAN   Iposa is yet another cheap and cheerful Raval hangout with an outside leafy terrace that is coveted on sunny Saturday afternoons. The resident French chef ensures there is always something a little different on offer rather that the usual "Mediterranean Market" fare, but before you ask how they can serve up a main course, drink, and coffee at lunchtime for a measly 6€ ($7.50), be warned that the portions are small, so you my need to order an entree as well. The food changes daily and includes things like a vegetable couscous, fresh grilled fish, or a hot "hummus" soup.

Floirestes de La Rambla 14. © 93-318-60-86. Main courses 6€–10€ ($7.50–$13); fixed-price lunch 8€ ($10). V. Sept–July Mon–Sat 1:30–4pm and 9pm–midnight; Aug daily 9pm–midnight. Metro: Liceu.

Juicy Jones *Finds* VEGETARIAN   A brightly colored blend of strip cartoon and children's nursery decor greets you in this chummy Danish-run spot where the young international waiters are friendly but sometimes give the impression they're just passing through. Hardly conventional either in style or food, Juicy Jones offers a very reasonably priced couscous and rice-accompanied range of inventive dishes, ranging from bean sprouts and *escalivada* (grilled onion, aubergine, and red and green peppers) to tofu and ginger salads. The marvelous selection of fresh fruit juices includes pear, mango, and grapefruit in a large (4€/$5) or small (3€/$3.75) glass and there are also soya milkshakes, organic wines, and beer available. You can sit at the narrow counter near the entrance or down in the secluded sunken restaurant at the back.

Cardenal Casañas 7. © 93-302-43-30. Main courses 6€–9.50€ ($7.50–$12); lunch menu 8.50€ ($11) on weekdays. No credit cards. Noon–midnight daily. Metro: Liceu.

La Dentellière *Finds* FRENCH/INTERNATIONAL   Charming, and steeped in the French aesthetic, this bistro is imbued with a modern, elegant decor. Inside, you'll find a small corner of provincial France, thanks to the dedicated effort of Evelyne Ramelot, the French writer who owns the place. After an aperitif at the sophisticated cocktail bar, you can order from an imaginative menu that includes a lasagna made from strips of salt cod, peppers, and tomato sauce, and a delectable *carpaccio* of filet of beef with pistachios, lemon juice, vinaigrette, and Parmesan cheese. The wine list is particularly imaginative, with worthy vintages mostly from France and Spain.

Ample 26. © 93-218-74-79. Reservations recommended on weekend. Main courses 8€–14€ ($10–$18). MC, V. Tues–Sun 8:30pm–midnight. Metro: Drassanes.

La Rosca CATALAN/SPANISH   For more than half a century, owner Don Alberto Vellve has continued to welcome customers into this little Barri Gòtic eatery, close to Plaça de Catalunya. On a short street, the place is easy to miss, except to devotees who have been coming here for decades. Come here if you'd like to see the type of place where people dined inexpensively in the Franco era. A mixture of Catalan and modern Spanish cuisine is served in this house, which is small and in an old rustic style with high ceilings and white walls. The decor has nostalgic touches, such as old bullfighting posters and pictures of Barcelona in the mid–20th century. There are 60 unadorned tables, which diners fill quickly to take advantage of the cheap three-course luncheon menu. Dig into such hearty fare as veal stew or assorted fish and shellfish. Baby squid is cooked in its own ink, and one of the best dishes is white beans sautéed with ham and Catalan sausage. For a true treat, ask for the *rape a la plancha* (grilled monkfish).

Juliá Portet 6. © 93-302-51-73. Main courses 8€–14€ ($10–$18); fixed-price menu 9€–12€ ($11–$15). No credit cards. Sun–Fri 9am–9:30pm. Closed Aug 20–30. Metro: Urquinaona or Catalunya.

Romesco *(Value)* CATALAN/MEDITERRANEAN   Frequented by locals and travelers on a budget, Romesco is never going to win any Michelin stars, but it does offer up the sort of homemade food that is rapidly disappearing within the immediate vicinity of touristy La Rambla. The lighting is bright, the tables are laminated, and the waiters and food are no-nonsense and generously proportioned. At the top end, you have a hunk of freshly grilled tuna served with a simple salad, at the bottom *arroz a la cubana* (a hangover cure consisting of white rice, tomato sauce, a fried egg, and a fried banana—it's actually very good). Desserts include a creamy *crema catalana* (crème brûlée) or a rice pudding. Finishing it all off with a strong coffee certainly does the trick.

Sant Pau 28. ⓒ **93-318-93-81.** Main courses 6€–14€ ($7.50–$18). No credit cards. Mon–Fri 1pm–midnight; Sat 1–6pm and 8pm–midnight. Closed Aug. Metro: Liceu.

Salsitas MEDITERRANEAN   The pioneer *restaurclub* in Barcelona, Salsitas churns out some very good nosh before it morphs into a fun nightclub at 1am. Take a seat on one of the wrought-iron chairs among the plastic palm trees and you will be served a selection of "lite" cuisine (who wants to see a bulging stomach on the dance floor?), such as a pumpkin soup followed by grilled salmon. There's a DJ spinning dinner music in the background.

Nou de la Rambla 22. ⓒ **93-318-08-40.** Reservations recommended on weekend. Main courses 6€–18€ ($7.50–$23). AE, DC, MC, V. Tues–Sat 8:30pm–midnight. Metro: Liceu.

SNACKS, TAPAS & DRINKS

Bar del Pi TAPAS   One of the most famous bars in the Barri Gòtic, this establishment is midway between two medieval squares opening onto a Gothic church. Typical tapas, canapés, and rolls are available. Most visitors come to drink coffee, beer, or local wines, house-sangrias, and *cavas*. In summer you can refresh yourself with a tigernut milkshake (called an *horchata*) or a slushy ice drink. Sit inside at one of the cramped bentwood tables, or stand at the crowded bar. In warm weather, take a table beneath the single plane tree on the landmark square. The plaza usually draws an interesting group of young bohemian sorts, travelers, and musicians.

Plaça Sant Josep Oriol 1. ⓒ **93-302-21-23.** Tapas 2.50€–6€ ($3.10–$7.50). No credit cards. Mon–Fri 9am–11pm; Sat 9:30am–10:30pm; Sun 10am–1pm. Metro: Liceu.

Bodega la Plata TAPAS   Established in the 1920s, La Plata is one of a trio of famous bodegas on this narrow medieval street. This one occupies a corner building—whose two open sides allow aromatic cooking odors to permeate the neighborhood—and contains a marble-topped bar and overcrowded tables. The culinary specialty consists of *raciones* (small plates) of deep-fried sardines—head and all. You can make a meal with two servings coupled with the house's tomato, onion, and fresh anchovy salad. The highly quaffable Penedés house wine comes in three varieties, *tinto*, *blanco* and *rosado*, and is 80 centimos a glass.

Mercé 28. ⓒ **93-315-10-09.** Tapas/raciones 2€–4€ ($2.50–$5). No credit cards. Mon–Sat 9am–3:30pm and 6–11pm. Metro: Barceloneta.

Cafe de la Opera CAFE/TAPAS   This is one of the few emblematic cafes in the city that has managed to resist the ravages of modernization. The name comes from the Liceu Opera House, located directly across La Rambla, and once upon a time patrons would have gathered here for a pre-performance aperitif. Although it has been renovated over the years, the interior still retains Belle Epoque details. It's a great place to pull up with a book during its quieter daytime moments, and there is also a terrace if people-watching is more your thing. Tapas are limited, but the cakes are divine. Service is brusque, exuding a jaded formality in keeping with the surroundings.

Les Ramblas 74. ℂ 93-302-41-80. Tapas from 3€ ($3.75) Cakes from 4€ ($5). No credit cards. Mon–Fri 8:30am–2am; Sat–Sun 8:30am–3am. Metro: Liceu.

Foodball ℛ HEALTH FOOD   Foodball is the latest concept from the shoe company **Camper** (p. 226), aiming to transport their wholesome culture to the food industry. It's a cafe and takeout joint located near the MACBA museum, and its clientele reflects the neighborhood's neo-hippie vibe. The foodballs in question are wholegrain rice balls stuffed with either organic mushrooms, chickpeas, tofu and alga, or chicken. You can either take them out in recycled lunchboxes or choose to park yourself on the grandstand-style seating. The interior, with its abundance of organic colors and signage reminiscent of African barbershop imagery, is by the quirky Catalan Martí Guixé, who is also responsible for many of Camper's shoe shops. Besides the foodballs, the only other things available are fresh and dried fruit, juices, and purified water. If all this sounds just a bit too contrived don't be put off; healthy fast food is scarcer than hen's teeth in Barcelona, and the foodballs are actually very, very tasty. It's a brilliant concept.

Elisabets 9. ℂ 93-270-13-63. Foodballs 2€ ($2.50) each. Fixed-price menu 6€ ($7.50). Daily noon–11pm. Metro: Liceu.

Las Campañas (Casa Marcos) TAPAS   From the street (there's no sign), Las Campañas looks like a storehouse for cured hams and wine bottles. Patrons flock to the long, stand-up bar for chorizo pinioned between two pieces of bread. Sausages are usually eaten with beer or red wine. The place opened in 1952, and nothing has changed since. A tape recorder plays nostalgic favorites, from Edith Piaf to the Andrews Sisters.

Mercé 21. ℂ 93-315-06-09. Tapas 3€–12€ ($3.75–$15). No credit cards. Thurs–Tues 12:30–4pm and 7pm–2am. Metro: Jaume I.

Schilling CAFE   In a street where fast-food outlets and franchises are slowly encroaching, Schilling is a welcome exception. More Brussels than Barcelona, it's all comfy sofas, wooden tables, and newspaper reading during the day, making it a great place to rest your feet and enjoy a sandwich and coffee with some very good cakes. At night the volume goes up and Schilling welcomes crowds for a pre- or post-dinner drink.

Ferran 23. ℂ 93-317-67-87. Hot and cold sandwiches 4€–9€ ($5–$11). MC, V. Sept–July daily 10am–2:30am; Aug daily 5pm–2:30am. Metro: Liceu.

The Bagel Shop CAFE   If you are craving a bagel, head for this simple cafe just off the top end of La Rambla. All the staples are here: sesame, poppy seed, blueberry, plus a few European versions such as black olive. Fillings go from honey to salmon and cream cheese and they also have a yummy selection of cheesecakes. Takeout is available.

Canuda 25. ℂ 93-302-41-61. Bagels 1.75€–5.75€ ($2.20–$7.20). No credit cards. Mon–Sat 9:30am–9:30pm; Sun 11am–4pm. Metro: Liceu.

Venus Delicatessen CAFE   This pleasant cafe is on one of the inner city's alternative-fashion shopping streets. It's a good stopping point for tea and coffee as well as cakes and pastries. The "delicatessen" in the name is a bit misleading (there's not a deli counter in sight) but what it does do very well are light meals such as salads and quiches from midday to midnight. There are lots of international newspapers to thumb through and work by local artists on the wall to gaze at.

Avinyó 25. ☏ **93-301-15-85.** Main courses 6€–10€ ($7.50–$13); fixed-price lunch 10€ ($13). No credit cards. Mon–Sat noon–midnight. Metro: Jaume I.

Vinissim 🌟🌟 WINE/TAPAS   A warm burgundy and exposed-brick interior is the perfect backdrop for this cozy wine bar on a pretty square in the El Call pocket of the Barri Gòtic. It offers a selection of over 50 carefully selected wines—available by glass or bottle—from all regions of Spain and some of the city's most delectable tapas, which may include a plate of artisan goat's cheese, a medley of sun-dried tomatoes and caramelized onions, and a potato and cheese *raclette*. Try an excellent Finca Lobierira *albariño* from Galicia when you sample these dishes. Top desserts include a sticky date pudding—ideally splashed with fresh cream—and a superb white-chocolate cheese cake. You could accompany either of these with a 2001 Etim Moscatel whose sweetness comes from its grapes, which spend no less than 6 months under the Valencian sun. All in all, wine bars don't come much better than this.

Sant Domenec del Call 12. ☏ **93-301-45-75.** Tapas 3.50€–10€ ($4.35–$13); tasting menu 20€ ($25); fixed-price lunch 14€ ($18). AE, DC, MC, V. Mon–Sat noon–4pm and 8pm–midnight. Metro: Liceu.

4 Ciutat Vella: La Ribera

EXPENSIVE

Abac 🌟 *Finds* INTERNATIONAL   This is the showcase of a personality chef, Xavier Pellicer, who creates a self-termed *cuisine d'auteur*, meaning a menu of completely original dishes. Inside the 1948 Park Hotel, his minimalist restaurant has even attracted members of the Spanish royal family, eager to see what Pellicer is cooking on any given night. Some of his dishes may be too experimental for certain diners, but I've found his daring palate pleasing. He is a master in balancing flavors, and his dishes perk up the taste buds and even challenge them at times. He emphasizes color and texture, and his sauces are perfectly balanced. You never know on any given night where his culinary inspiration has led him. Perhaps a mushroom tartare will be resting on your plate, or else a velvety-smooth steamed foie gras. Roasted sea bass appears with sweet pimientos and oyster plant and Iberian suckling pig is cooked and flavored to perfection, as is his fennel ravioli with "fruits of the sea."

Carrer del Rec 79–89. ☏ **93-319-66-00.** Reservations required. Main courses 25€–35€ ($31–$44); tasting menu 85€ ($106). AE, DC, MC, V. Tues–Sat 1:30–3:30pm; Mon–Sat 8:30–10:30pm. Closed Aug. Metro: Jaume I or Barcelonesa.

Restaurant Hoffmann 🌟🌟 CATALAN/FRENCH/INTERNATIONAL   This restaurant is one of the most famous in Barcelona, partly because of its creative cuisine, partly because of its close association with a respected school that trains employees for Catalonia's hotel and restaurant industry. The culinary and entrepreneurial force behind it is German/Catalan Mey Hoffmann, whose restaurant overlooks the facade of one of Barcelona's most beloved Gothic churches, Santa María del Mar. In good weather, three courtyards hold tables. Menu items change every 2 months and often feature French ingredients. Examples include a superb *fine tarte* with deboned sardines, foie gras wrapped in puff pastry, baked John Dory with new potatoes and ratatouille, a ragout of crayfish with green risotto, succulent pigs' feet with eggplant, and rack of lamb with grilled baby vegetables. Especially flavorful, if you appreciate beef, is a filet steak cooked in Rioja and served with shallot confit and potato gratin. Fondant of chocolate makes a worthy dessert.

Carrer Argenteria 74–78. ⓒ 93-319-58-89. Reservations recommended. Main courses 16€–40€ ($20–$50); tasting menu 35€ ($44). AE, DC, MC, V. Mon–Fri 1:30–3:15pm and 9–11:15pm. Closed Aug and Christmas week. Metro: Jaume I.

MODERATE

Cal Pep 𝒢 *Finds* CATALAN   Cal Pep lies just north of the Plaça de Palau, nestled beside a tiny postage-stamp square. It's generally packed, and the food is some of the tastiest in La Ribera. There's actually a Pep himself, and he's a great host, going around to see that all diners are happy with their meals. In the rear is a small dining room (book if you intend to eat here), but most patrons like to occupy one of the counter seats up front. Try the fried artichokes or the mixed medley of seafood that includes small sardines. Tiny clams come swimming in a well-seasoned broth given extra spice by a sprinkling of hot peppers. A delectable tuna dish comes with a sesame sauce, and fresh salmon is flavored with such herbs as basil—sublime.

Plaça des les Olles 8. ⓒ 93-310-79-61. Reservations required. Main courses 14€–20€ ($18–$25). AE, DC, MC, V. Mon 8:30–11:30pm; Tues–Sat 1–4:30pm and 8:30–11:30pm. Closed Aug. Metro: Barceloneta or Jaume I.

Comerç 24 𝒢𝒢 *Finds* CATALAN/INTERNATIONAL   View a dining visit here as an opportunity to experience the culinary vision of a true artist. The chef is Carles Abellán, who worked with Ferran Adriá of El Bulli fame for a decade. He has given his imaginative, distinctive interpretation to all the longtime favorite dishes of Catalonia. With his avant-garde and minimalist design, he offers a soothing backdrop for his cuisine. The chef uses fresh seasonal ingredients, balanced sauces, and bold but never outrageous combinations, and he believes in split-second timing. Begin perhaps with his freshly diced tuna marinated in ginger and soy sauce, and Abellán will immediately win you over. Maybe you'll next sample his fresh salmon "perfumed" with vanilla and served with yogurt. His baked eggplant with Roquefort, pine nuts, and fresh mushrooms from the countryside is a vibrant and earthy feast. Only the great star Marlene Dietrich could make a better potato omelet than Abellán. Believe it or not, he serves that old-fashioned snack that Catalan children used to be offered when they came home from school, a combination of chocolate, salt, and bread flavored with olive oil. It's surprisingly good!

Carrer Comerç 24. ⓒ 93-319-21-02. Reservations required. Main courses 11€–25€ ($14–$31); tasting menu 48€ ($60). AE, DC, MC, V. Tues–Sat 1:30–3:30pm and 8:30pm–12:30am. Closed Christmas week and last 3 weeks in Aug. Metro: Jaume I.

Espai Sucre 𝒢𝒢 *Finds* DESSERTS   Espai Sucre (Sugar Space) is Barcelona's most unusual dining room, with a minimalist decor and seating for 30. For the dessert lover, it is like entering a heaven created by the sugar fairy himself. The place has a gimmick, and it works. The menu is devoted to desserts. There is a short list of so-called "salty" dishes for those who want to cool it with the sugar. Actually it's quite good and imaginatively prepared, including the likes of ginger couscous with pumpkin and grilled stingray or artichoke cream with a poached quail egg and *serrano* ham. The lentil stew with foie gras is first-rate, as are the spicy veal "cheeks" with green apples.

Forget all about those tearoom concoctions you'd find in a pastry cafe. The desserts here are original creations. Your "salad" is likely to be small cubes of spicy milk pudding resting on matchsticks of green apple with baby arugula leaves, peppery caramel, dabs of kaffir lime and lemon curd, and a straight line of toffee. Ever had a soup of litchi, celery, apple, and eucalyptus? If not, you can try them here. If some of the concoctions frighten your palate, you'll find comfort in the more familiar—vanilla cream with coffee sorbet and caramelized banana. Every dessert comes with a recommendation for the appropriate wine to accompany it.

Princesa 53. ☎ **93-268-16-30**. Reservations required. Main courses 9.50€–12€ ($12–$15); 3-dessert platter 28€ ($35); 5-dessert platter 35€ ($44). MC, V. Tues–Sat 9–11:30pm. Closed mid-Aug and Christmas week. Metro: Arc de Triomf.

Gente de Pasta ITALIAN   If you are having trouble finding a table at the trendy southern end of La Ribera, you could do worse than head for this gigantic restaurant that specializes (as the name suggests) in pasta dishes. Just don't expect gingham tablecloths and wicker wine baskets; the industrial, warehouse-like interior has nothing common with a typical trattoria. On busy nights, the bare walls and floor make the acoustics a nightmare for the aurally challenged, and the sheer size of the place means that waiters are not normally hovering when and where they should. That said, the pastas and other dishes are perfectly passable, with added attractions such as a *caprese* salad with anchovies and a fennel and prawns risotto.

Passeig de Picasso 10. ☎ **93-268-70-17**. Reservations recommended on weekends. Main courses 7€–18€ ($8.75–$23); fixed-price lunch 10€ ($13). AE, MC, V. Daily 1–4pm and 9pm–midnight. Metro: Jaume 1 or Barceloneta.

Re-Pla ★★ MEDITERRANEAN   Such was the popularity of the Pla restaurant in the Barri Gòtic (p. 127), that its owners opened this second branch in neighboring La Ribera, providing a similarly delicious blend of fresh produce and exotic Eastern and Arabic dishes on its colorful menu. Service is friendly and attentive and, unsurprisingly, it has proven just as hard to get a table here at as the Pla.

Montcada 2. ☎ **93-268-30-03**. Reservations required. Main courses 7€—15€ ($8.75—$19). DC, MC, V. Daily 1–4pm and 9pm–midnight. Closed Dec 25–27. Metro: Jaume I.

Senyor Parellada CATALAN/MEDITERRANEAN   The glossy contemporary-looking interior of this place is in distinct contrast to the facade of a building that's at least a century old. Inside, in a pair of lemon-yellow and blue dining rooms, you'll find menu items such as Italian-style cannelloni, stuffed cabbage, cod "as it was prepared by the monks of the Poblet monastery," baked monkfish with mustard and garlic sauce, roasted duck served with figs, and roasted rack of lamb with red-wine sauce. Patrons flock faithfully to this bistro, knowing they'll be served a traditional cuisine of northeast Spain with fine local produce. The chefs seem to know how to coax the most flavor out of the premium ingredients.

Carrer Argenteria 37. ☎ **93-310-50-94**. Reservations recommended. Main courses 8€–15€ ($10–$19). AE, DC, MC, V. Daily 1–4pm and 8:30pm–midnight. Metro: Jaume I.

INEXPENSIVE

La Paradeta (*Value* *Kids*) SEAFOOD   Most *marisco* (seafood) meals can set you back a ton in Barcelona. Not so at this busy restaurant that has more in common with a fish market than the trendy eateries of La Ribera's El Born district. (This could be because of the money they save on waitstaff.) The seafood—crabs, prawns, squid, and so on—is displayed in large plastic tubs. You pick out what you want at the counter, where it's weighed and then served up on a steaming platter. Wine offerings include some excellent *albariño* whites and other good, reliable local varietals. It's loads of fun, but order everything at once because you often have to wait in line for your dish and drink, especially on the weekends.

Comercial 7. (℃) **93-268-19-39**. Fish charged per kilo (varies). Average price with wine 18€–22€ ($23–$28). No credit cards. Tues–Thurs 8–11:30pm; Fri 8pm–midnight; Sat 1–4pm and 8pm–midnight; Sun 1–4pm. Closed Dec 22–Jan 22. Metro: Arc de Triomf.

Murivecchi *Kids* *Value* ITALIAN   If this family-run restaurant was just a few hundred meters farther in the thick of the El Born neighborhood, you would probably never get a table. The un-alarming decor doesn't do it any favors either, but the food is excellent and good value for money. There is a wood-fired oven for fans of real Neapolitan pizza and the pasta dishes are no less delectable: *tagliatelle al funghi porcini, spaghetti vongole*, and *linguini al pesto* are just a few examples. Add to this a list of *antipasti, risotti*, and *carpacci;* daily specials; and a sinful tiramisu—and you have some of the best Italian cuisine this side of Rome.

Princesa 59. (℃) **93-315-22-97**. Reservations recommended on weekend. Main courses 9€–14€ ($11–$18); fixed-price lunch Mon–Fri 10€ ($13). MC, V. Daily 1–4pm and 8pm–midnight. Metro: Arc de Triomf.

Pla de la Garsa *F* *Value* MEDITERRANEAN/CATALAN   Located on the eastern side of La Ribera, this historic building is fully renovated but still retains some 19th-century fittings, such as a cast-iron spiral staircase used to reach another dining area upstairs. The ground floor is more interesting. Here you'll encounter the owner, Ignacio Sulle, an antiques collector who has filled his establishment with an intriguing collection of objets d'art. He boasts one of the city's best wine lists, and features a daily array of favorite traditional Catalan and Mediterranean dishes. Begin with one of the pâtés, such as the goose, or a confit of duck thighs. You can also order meat and fish pâtés. One surprise is a terrine with black olives and anchovies. For a main course you can order a perfectly seasoned beef bourguignon or *fabetes fregides amb menta i pernil* (beans with meat and diced *serrano* ham). The cheese selection is one of the finest I've found in town, especially bountiful in Catalan goat cheese, including Serrat Gros from the Pyrénées.

Assaonadors 13. (℃) **93-315-24-13**. Reservations recommended on weekend. Main courses 6€–14€ ($7.50–$18). AE, DC, MC, V. Daily 8pm–1am. Metro: Jaume I.

SNACKS, TAPAS & DRINKS

Sandwich & Friends CAFE   Where else but in El Born would a sandwich be considered cool? On the main drag of the city's hippest quarter, Sandwich and Friends stands out from the rest thanks to its huge wall mural by local but internationally famous illustrator Jordi Labanda. His portrayal of a social gathering of bright young people mirrors the clientele itself, who come here to nibble on the cafe's awesome selection of over 50 sandwiches all named after "friends": *Marta* is a pork filet, tomato, and olive oil sandwich; *Daniel* is filled with frankfurter, bacon, and mustard. There is also a selection of salads if you are calorie counting.

Passeig del Born 27. (℃) **93-310-07-86**. Sandwiches and salads 3.75€–8€ ($4.70–$10). MC, V. Daily 9:30am–1am. Metro: Jaume I or Barceloneta.

Taller de Tapas *FF* TAPAS   For a foreigner, ordering tapas can be a daunting affair. Making yourself heard above the din is one thing, and then there is the lack of written menus. The Taller de Tapas (Tapas Workshop) has been conceived to take the trouble out of *tapeando*. Surrounded by a pleasant decor of exposed brick and beams (or on the outside terrace), patrons sit at a table and order from a trilingual menu. The tapas are prepared in an open kitchen where there is not a microwave in sight. The owners are always on the lookout for new ingredients that will work in tapas, which means that every week there is a board of specials. The regular menus consists of dozens of tapas delights from all over Spain; marinated anchovies from L'Escala on the Costa Brava, Palamós prawns with scrambled eggs, grilled duck foie, sizzling chorizo cooked in cider: It's all here. For those that like something substantial for breakfast, Taller de Tapas does a morning tortilla menu.

L'Argentaria 51. ℰ **93-268-85-59.** Tapas 3€–10€ ($3.75–$13). AE, DC, MC, V. Mon–Thurs 8:45am–midnight; Fri–Sat 8:45am–12:30am; Sun noon–midnight. Metro: Jaume I. There's another location at Plaça Sant Josep Oriol 9, Barri Gòtic (ℰ **93-301-80-20;** Metro: Liceu).

5 Ciutat Vella: El Raval

EXPENSIVE

Can L'Isidre ⓕ CATALAN   In spite of its seedy location (take a cab at night!), this is perhaps the most sophisticated Catalan bistro in Barcelona. Opened in 1970, it has served King Juan Carlos and Queen Sofía, Julio Iglesias, and the famous Catalan bandleader Xavier Cugat. Isidre Gironés, helped by his wife, Montserrat, is known for his fresh cuisine beautifully prepared and served. Try spider crabs and shrimp, a foie gras salad, sweetbreads with port and flap mushrooms, or carpaccio of veal, Harry's Bar–style. The selection of Spanish and Catalan wines is excellent.

Les Flors 12. ℰ **93-441-11-39.** Reservations required. Main courses 18€–45€ ($23–$56). AE, DC, MC, V. Mon–Sat 1:30–4pm and 8:30–11pm. Closed Sat–Sun June–July and all Aug. Metro: Paral.lel.

Casa Leopoldo ⓕⓕ *Finds* SEAFOOD   An excursion through the earthy streets of the Barri Xinès is part of the Casa Leopoldo experience. At night it's safer to come by taxi. Founded in 1939, this colorful restaurant with its attractive tiled walls and wooden beam ceilings serves some of the freshest seafood in town to a loyal clientele. There's a popular standup tapas bar in front and two dining rooms. Specialties include eel with shrimp, barnacles, cuttlefish, seafood soup with shellfish, and deep-fried inch-long eels.

Sant Rafael 24. ℰ **93-441-30-14.** Reservations recommended. Main courses 25€–40€ ($31–$50); tasting menu 45€ ($56). AE, DC, MC, V. Tues–Sun 1:30–4pm; Tues–Sat 9–11pm. Closed Aug and Easter week. Metro: Liceu.

Quo Vadis ⓕ SPANISH/CATALAN   Elegant and impeccable, this is one of the finest restaurants in Barcelona and a favorite with the opera crowd from the Liceu Opera House next door. In a century-old building near the open stalls of the Boqueria food market, it was established in 1967 and has done a discreet but thriving business ever since. The four paneled dining rooms exude conservative charm. Culinary creations include a ragout of seasonal mushrooms, fried gooseliver with prunes, filet of beef with wine sauce, and a variety of grilled or flambéed fish. There's a wide choice of desserts made with seasonal fruits imported from all over Spain.

Carme 7. ℰ **93-302-40-72.** Reservations recommended. Main courses 18€–26€ ($23–$33); fixed-price menu 30€ ($38). AE, DC, MC, V. Mon–Sat 1:15–4pm and 8:30–11.30pm. Closed Aug. Metro: Liceu.

MODERATE

Anima MEDITERRANEAN/FUSION   Located near the MACBA Museum of Modern Art, Anima is yet another of the new breed of Raval eateries. Inside it's all bright colors and minimalism, and a glance at the menu would lead you to think that the cuisine also skimps on the trimmings. But the food here is actually highly satisfying, especially when taken on their outdoor terrace in the summer. Under the plane trees, you may partake in mozzarella balls swimming in gazpacho, ostrich steak with caramelized cranberries, and crystallized chocolate truffles for dessert. If all this sounds a bit too risky, take a gamble with the great value lunch menu before you leap in.

Angels 6. ℂ **93-342-49-12.** Reservations recommended. Main courses 9€–16€ ($11–$20); fixed-price lunch 10€ ($13). AE, DC, MC, V. Mon–Sat 1–4pm and 9pm–midnight. Metro: Liceu.

Lupino MEDITERRANEAN FUSION Lupino was one of the first of the new wave of "cool" Barcelona restaurants. The waitstaff used to look like models dressed in black, there was a DJ, and the decor resembled a catwalk. Several years on, only the latter remains true. Lupino has softened around the edges and has been around long enough to learn that one cannot live by style alone. The food is a mélange of Mediterranean, French, Creole, and North African; grilled entrecote with couscous, cod with ratatouille and coconut emulsion, pork stuffed with goat's cheese with cassava chips on the side . . . you get the picture. It's very good and their lunchtime menu is one of the best deals around. A rear terrace overlooks the back of the Boqueria market (in reality a parking lot, but oversize parasols block out the unsightly bits), and the DJ now only makes an appearance Friday and Saturday nights for late-night cocktails.

Carme 33. ℂ **93-412-36-97.** Reservations recommended on weekend. Main courses 14€–20€ ($20–$25); fixed-price lunch Mon–Fri 9€ ($11), Sat–Sun 13€ ($16). AE, MC, V. Mon–Thurs 1–4pm and 9pm–midnight; Sat–Sun 1:30-4:30pm and 9pm–3am. Metro: Liceu.

Mama Cafe MEDITERRANEAN FUSION In the thick of El Raval's hub of funky eateries, this is one of the more reliable bets where style doesn't give way to substance. The boho crowd is greeted by an urban-savvy staff, who churn out the dishes from a frantic open kitchen. The quality of the hamburgers here is unusual in Barcelona (that is to say, they are very good), the salads (nearly always with a fruit or goat cheese) market fresh, and the pastas (such as salmon and capers) more than acceptable. Mama Cafe is one of the few inner-city restaurants open on Monday.

Doctor Dou 10. ℂ **93-301-29-40.** Reservations recommended on weekend. Main courses 9€–17€ ($11–$21); fixed-price lunch 12€ ($15). AE, MC, V. Daily 1–4pm and 9pm–midnight. Metro: Liceu.

Umita SUSHI Where else but Barcelona would you find designer sushi? Where else but the melting pot Raval would it be made not by natives from Japan but the very un-Nippon region of Peru? There is a reason for this—the thousands of Japanese émigrés to South America had a profound influence on local chefs. Purists will be tempted to pass this place by. But you shouldn't! Lovers of sushi will not be disappointed, as the standard of fresh fish available in Barcelona, plus the creativity of sushi-maestros, makes for a memorable meal. Seafood, vegetables, avocado, and other fruits in delicate combinations are part of the equation. The place is tiny, so book for a table. Better still, grab a stool at the bar to watch the masters at work.

Pintor Fortuny 15. ℂ **93-301-23-22.** Reservations recommended on weekend. Main courses 7€–18€ ($8.75–$23); fixed-price lunch 19€ ($24). AE, MC, V. Daily 1–4pm and 9pm–midnight. Metro: Catalunya.

INEXPENSIVE

Ca l'Estevet CATALAN/SPANISH This century-old eating spot is a veritable institution in El Raval, where the Estevat family has been welcoming a mixture of students, journalists, and intrepid tourists for decades. The warm homey ambience is matched by traditional Catalan dishes such as *caracoles* (snails), *exqueixada* (shredded salt cod salad), botifarra negre (black sausage), and *conill* (rabbit). Weekday lunches are the main thing here, though it can get very crowded so best to turn up a little earlier by Spanish standards. (that is at around 1:30pm).

Carrer de Valdonzella 46. © **93-302-41-86.** Main courses 8€–14€ ($10–$18); fixed-price lunch menu 12€ ($15). Mon–Sat 1:30–4pm and 9pm–midnight. Metro: Universitat.

Mesón David   SPANISH   Don't come here for a quiet evening. Mesón David is an absolute riot: Waiters scream at each other, tips are acknowledged by the ringing of a cowbell, crowds of diners sing and somehow you have to make yourself heard. But the effort is worth it. The food is fast, furious, and excellent, and the regional specialties range from Navarran trout stuffed with *serrano* ham and Galician-style broiled octopus to traditional Castilian roast suckling pork. Obviously, it isn't the place for a light meal. But it is an enormous amount of fun for a price that's unbelievably low for central Barcelona. On busy nights you may have to wait for a table at the bar—and be shown the door on your last gulp of coffee.

Carretes 63. © **93-441-59-34.** Reservations recommended. Main courses 6€–10€ ($7.50–$13); fixed-price lunch Mon–Fri 8€ ($10). AE, DC, MC, V. Thurs–Tues 1–4:30pm and 8pm–midnight. Metro: Paral.lel or Sant Antoni.

Organic   VEGETARIAN   Hip and hippie, Organic is one of the few vegetarian restaurants in Barcelona that doesn't feel like a convent when you walk in. At lunchtime, a happy waitstaff will show you to large communal tables and explain the system; the first course is a help-yourself soup and salad bar, all tasty and organically grown. The second (which you order from them) could be a vegetarian pizza, pasta, or perhaps a stir-fry. The self-serve desserts include apple cake, carob mousse, and fresh yogurt (smaller menus available). At night the menu is a la carte and on the weekends there is live Brazilian music. A small selection of health foods is also available, including their homemade bread, and a local masseuse is there to offer her services to the lunchtime crowd.

Junta de Comerç 11. © **93-301-09-02.** Main courses 6€–12€ ($7.50–$15); fixed-price lunch 6.50€–9€ ($8.10–$11). AE, DC, MC, V. Daily 12:30pm–midnight. Metro: Liceu.

SNACKS, TAPAS & DRINKS

Els Tres Tombs   CAFE/TAPAS   Els Tres Tombs is one of the most versatile bars around. It caters not only to housewives taking a break from shopping at the nearby Sant Antoni market but also to young people stopping off for breakfast after a night out clubbing. The facade is pure '70s, the waiters are distinctly old-school, and the placement of the terrace ensures it receives more direct sunlight that just about any bar in Barcelona. Inside there are breakfast pastries to choose from and mounds of tapas to satisfy any daytime hunger pangs. It's a city institution.

Ronda Sant Antoni 11. © **93-443-41-11.** Tapas 2.50€–11€ ($3.10–$14); fixed-price lunch 8€ ($10). No credit cards. Daily 6am–2am. Metro: Sant Antoni.

Kasparo   CAFE/TAPAS   This place has one of the all-time favorite terraces: a leafy, porticoed, and just a stone's throw from the MACBA (Museum of Modern Art). It's so popular, in fact, that you often see people nonchalantly milling around, waiting to pounce on the next free table. There is no real reason for this (other than the location), since the tapas are fairly basic, and the daily offerings such as a Greek salad or pasta dish are good but a tad overpriced. But if you can spring a table, you will probably find yourself lingering for a long time.

Plaça Vicenç Matorell 4. © **93-302-20-72.** Tapas 3.50€–6.50€ ($4.35–$8.10). No credit cards. Daily 9am–1pm (breakfast) and 1–11pm. Closed Dec 24–Jan 24. Metro: Catalunya.

More Tapas

Traditionally, Barcelonese don't go for a tapas crawl as often as their cousins in Madrid or Andalusia do. They prefer to sit down the old-fashioned way, over three courses, acres of linen, and a bucket of wine. But the trend for eating in small portions, and the influence of new chefs such as Carles Abellán at **Comerç 24** (p. 132), has sparked a heightened interest in this artful cuisine.

For classic Spanish tapas in the heart of the Old City, try **Taller de Tapas,** Calle de l'Argenteria 51 ((② 93-268-85-59). For a 50-strong list of snacks all freshly made on the spot **Cal Pep,** Plaça de les Olles 8 ((② 93-310-79-61), comes close to godliness when you're talking spanking fresh seafood (p. 132); or there's **Bar Celta,** Calle Mercè 16 ((② 93-315-00-06)—one of the oldest tapas joints in town—for purple octopus tentacles, pigs' lips and ears, and delightful green peppers known as *pimientos del padrón.* On the same street you can also down rustic farmhouse ciders, flaming chorizo, and dark, deeply satisfying slivers of *cecina* (cured beef) at the smattering of *sidrerías* (Asturian tapas bars) that still exist.

In La Ribera and the Born, **Mosquito,** Calle Carders 46 ((② 93-268-75-69), does a well-executed range of Indian, Thai, Malaysian, and Indonesian dishes along with gyoza dumplings and organic beers at unbeatable prices. More upmarket fare can be had from the ever inventive hands of Paco Guzmán at **Santa María,** Calle Comerç 17 ((② 93-315-12-27). Think Spanish-Asian fusion along the lines of local fruits stuffed with Thai spiced peanuts; raw sea bass with passion fruit, tomato, and lime vinaigrettes; and suckling pig with wasabi and soy.

If you're heading up town, avoid the monster barns on the Passeig de Gràcia and opt instead for **Ciudad Condal,** Rambla de Catalunya 18 ((② 93-318-19-97), arguably the city's most visited tapas bar for patatas bravas, fried fish, and anchovies. Then, push on up the road to **Cervecería Catalana,** Carrer Majorca 236 ((② 93-216-03-68), for juicy slices of filet beef skewered with peppers, and giant prawn brochettes. (*Note:* These tapas are chalked up on the blackboard, not in the cool chest.)

Finish off with a pudding course courtesy of Jordi Butrón at **Espai Sucre,** Calle Princesa 53 ((② 93-268-16-30; p. 132). For many years his was the only pudding restaurant in the world. Butrón can no longer claim that title, but this is still the ultimate end to a 21st-century tapas crawl.

6 Poble Sec & Montjuïc

INEXPENSIVE

La Bella Napoli ITALIAN   Like La Bodegueta (below), this Poble Sec eatery has also undergone a face-lift in recent years, but with more devastating results. Thankfully, there is plenty of character still left in the food, which is authentic Italian from the lasagna to the tiramisu. Most people, however, come for the thin-crust pizzas, which are hauled out of a wood-fired oven, perfectly crisp and ready to scarf down. Takeout is available.

Margarit 12. ✆ **93-442-50-56.** Reservations required. Main courses 10€–35€ ($13–$44). AE, DC, MC, V. Tues 8:30pm–midnight; Wed–Sun 1:30–4pm and 8:30pm–midnight. Closed Aug and Christmas week. Metro: Paral.lel or Poble Sec.

La Bodegueta TAPAS   This bodega is typical (or what was typical) of this working-class neighborhood and a longtime favorite. Even after its overhaul some years back, the period character remains, as does the original rose-petal-tiled floor. Owner Eva Amber is on hand to recommend her home cooking, which includes such favorites as lentils with chorizo and Catalan cannelloni. Meat *a al brasa* (grill flamed) and *torrades* (toasted bread with charcuterie) are also available.

Blai 47. ✆ **93-442-08-46.** Tapas 2.25€–12€ ($2.80–$15). MC, V. Mon–Fri noon–4pm and 7–10:30pm; Sat noon–4pm. Closed Aug. Metro: Poble Sec.

Quimet & Quimet ✿ TAPAS/CHEESE   This is a great tapas bar, especially for cheese, of which it offers the finest selection in Barcelona. Built at the turn of the 20th century, the tavern in the Poble Sec sector is still run by the fifth generation of Quimets. Their wine cellar is one of the best stocked of any tapas bar, and their cheese selection is varied. One night I sampled four on the same plate, including *nevat* (a tangy goat cheese), *cabrales* (an intense Spanish blue cheese), *zamorano* (a hardy, nutty sheep's milk cheese), and *torta del Casar* (a soft, creamy farm cheese). If I were a little more adventurous I could have gone for the *tou dels tillers*, a cheese stuffed with trout roe and truffles. Of course, you can also order other delights such as mussels with tomato confit and caviar, razor clams, and even sturgeon.

Poeta Cabanyes 25. ✆ **93-442-31-42.** Tapas 2.25€–12€ ($2.80–$15). MC, V. Mon–Fri noon–4pm and 7–10:30pm; Sat noon–4pm. Closed Aug. Metro: Paral.lel.

7 L'Eixample

VERY EXPENSIVE

Beltxenea ✿✿ BASQUE/INTERNATIONAL   In a building originally designed in the late 19th century to house apartments, this restaurant celebrates Basque cuisine. The Basques are noted as the finest chefs in Spain, and their cuisine is served here in one of the most elegantly and comfortably furnished restaurants in the city. Schedule a meal for a special night—it's worth the money. The menu might include hake fried with garlic or garnished with clams and served with fish broth. Roast lamb, grilled rabbit, and pheasant are well prepared and succulent, as are the desserts. There's dining outside in the formal garden during the summer.

Majorca 275. ✆ **93-215-30-24.** Reservations recommended. Main courses 18€–48€ ($23–$60); tasting menu 55€ ($69). AE, DC, MC, V. Mon–Fri 1:30–3:30pm; Mon–Sat 8:30–11:30pm. Closed Easter week, 3 weeks in Aug, and Christmas week. Metro: Passeig de Gràcia or Diagonal.

Drolma ✿✿✿ INTERNATIONAL   In business since 1999, this is one of Barcelona's best haute-cuisine restaurants. Fermin Puig is one of Spain's most celebrated chefs, his culinary showcase found in the Hotel Majestic. The restaurant's name is Sanskrit for Buddha's female side. I don't know what this has to do with anything. He might as well have called his restaurant "Majestic," as his food certainly is. Only the freshest ingredients go into his carefully balanced cookery based on the market's seasonal bounty. I especially like the personal spin he gives to seasonal dishes along with the luxurious foodstuffs presented nightly. What diner could not love the chef who presents pheasant-stuffed cannelloni in a velvety foie gras sauce, the dish delicately sprinkled with the rare black truffle? His wild turbot is enhanced with fresh mushrooms from the Catalan countryside, and his prawns with fresh asparagus tips in a virgin olive-oil sauce preserve the natural flavor of each ingredient. The lamb is aromatically grilled with fresh herbs, giving the meat a pungent and refreshing dimension. The baked goat with potatoes and mushrooms is bold yet delicate in flavor.

In the Hotel Majestic, Passeig de Gràcia 68. ℂ **93-496-77-10**. Reservations required. Main courses 35€–109€ ($44–$136). AE, DC, MC, V. Mon–Sat 1–3:30pm and 8:30–11pm. Closed Aug. Metro: Passeig de Gràcia.

Jaume de Provença ✦✦✦ CATALAN/FRENCH   This small, cozy restaurant with its rustic decor is just a few steps from the Estació Central de Barcelona-Sants railway station, at the western end of L'Eixample. Named after its owner and chef, Jaume Bargués, it features modern interpretations of traditional Catalan and southern French cuisine. Examples include gratin of clams with spinach, a salad of two different species of lobster, foie gras and truffles, and pigs' trotters with plums and truffles. Or you might order crabmeat lasagna, cod with saffron sauce, sole with mushrooms in port-wine sauce, or an artistic dessert specialty of orange mousse.

Provença 88. ℂ **93-430-00-29**. Reservations recommended. Main courses 11€–38€ ($14–$48). Fixed-price menu 45€ ($56); tasting menu 60€ ($75). AE, DC, MC, V. Tues–Sat 1–4pm and 9–11:15pm; Sun 1–4pm. Closed Easter week and Aug. Metro: Entença.

La Dama ✦✦✦ CATALAN/INTERNATIONAL   This is one of the few restaurants in Barcelona that deserves and gets a Michelin star. In one of the grand 19th-century buildings for which Barcelona is famous, this stylish and well-managed restaurant serves a clientele of local residents and civic dignitaries. You take an Art Nouveau elevator (or the sinuous stairs) up one flight to reach the dining room. Specialties include salmon steak served with vinegar derived from *cava* (sparkling wine) and onions, cream of potato soup flavored with caviar, a salad of crayfish with orange-flavored vinegar, an abundant platter of autumn mushrooms, and succulent preparations of lamb, fish, shellfish, beef, goat, and veal.

Diagonal 423. ℂ **93-202-06-86**. Reservations recommended. Main courses 15€–38€ ($19–$48); fixed-price menu 55€ ($69); tasting menu 75€ ($94). AE, DC, MC, V. Daily 1:30–3:30pm and 8:30–11:30pm. Metro: Provença.

EXPENSIVE
Alkimia ✦✦ MEDITERRANEAN   Alkimia is one of Barcelona's most individual and highly regarded restaurants. Owner Jordi Vilà—a chef's chef if ever there was one—is a proponent of New Catalan cuisine, the culinary wave started by Ferran Adrià (p. 285), which has been sweeping the city in recent years. The minimalist decor is not intended to distract you from the food, as you need to have your taste buds and wits fully about you when sampling these challenging dishes. Try, for starters, the deconstructed version of the simple but traditional *pa amb tomàquet* (white bread rubbed with tomato pulp and olive oil), in which Vilà filters the tomato, separates the juice—where all the flavor is—and then adds a little oil and some crumbs of toasted bread, serving it with some *lloganissa* salami. Other offbeat Vilà versions of traditional dishes include tuna belly instead of Iberian ham in *faves a la catalana* (Catalan style broad beans); truffle added to a plate of cabbage, potato, and sausage; and fried eggs and Majorcan sausage served with preserved quinces. Exceptional among his desserts is the imaginative combination of litchi soup, glacé celery, and eucalyptus ice cream.

Industria 79. ℂ **93-207-61-15**. Reservations required. Main courses 14€–28€ ($18–$35). Tasting menu 42€ ($53) and 56€ ($70). DC, MC, V. Mon–Fri 1:30–4pm; Sat 8am–noon. Closed Easter week and Aug 8–31. Metro: Sagrada Família.

L'Eixample Dining

Alkimia **14**	Cervecería Catalana **9**	Hisop **18**	Moo **13**
Bar Turò **1**	Cinc Sentits **8**	Il Giardinetto **4**	Neichel **1**
Beltxenea **15**	Ciudad Condal **19**	Jaume de Provença **7**	Reno **3**
Casa Alfonso **22**	Drolma **17**	La Bodegueta **11**	Rosalert **16**
Casa Calvet **21**	El Caballito Blanco **10**	La Dama **5**	Tragaluz **12**
Casa Tejada **2**	Gorría **20**	L'Olive **6**	

Casa Calvet ⭐⭐ MEDITERRANEAN   Probably the most intimate Gaudían experience you can have in Barcelona is eating at this sumptuous dining room. The Casa Calvet, one of the architect's first commissions, was built for the textile magnate Pere Calvet. Now private apartments, the building is off-limits to the public, but a restaurant occupies Calvet's former ground-floor offices. Replete with velvet drapery, florid stained glass, attractive tiles, Gaudí-designed furniture, and other memorabilia, the only thing that jolts you back to the 21st century is the contemporary twist on Miguel Alija's excellent Catalan cuisine, such as giant prawns with rosemary-infused oil or duck liver with oranges. And although the historic setting ensures a fair share of tourists, Casa Calvet is also very popular with locals. Thankfully, the staff treat everyone that walks over the carved wooden threshold with equal doses of measured hospitality.

Carrer Casp 48. ⓒ 93-412-40-12. Reservations recommended. Main courses 20€–32€ ($25–$40); tasting menu 50€ ($63). AE, DC, MC, V. Mon–Sat 1–3:30pm and 8:30–11pm. Metro: Passeig de Gràcia.

Cinc Sentits ⭐⭐ MEDITERRANEAN   Cinc Sentits is a relatively new kid on the block, but that hasn't stopped it from making waves in culinary circles. Chef Jordi Artal spent most of his life in Canada before coming back to his roots to open this cutting-edge eatery that aims to appease the *cinc sentits* (five senses). He recommends the "Gourmet" tasting menu this way: "When you sit down to eat and are presented with a big plate of food, the first bite is great, the second is good, but by the time you get to the fifth or sixth, your palate is bored and you have lost interest." You might eat a crème fraîche or caviar soup here. Artal's cuisine is a combination of Catalan culinary know-how and New World wit. An everyday white garlic soup is graced with pan-seared lobster, a monkfish sprinkled with bacon "dust," or a soft poached egg with tomato jam. Cinc Sentits is an example of what fusion food can be like with a combination of the finest ingredients and intelligence.

Aribau 58. ⓒ 93-323-94-90. Reservations required. Main courses 12€–26€ ($15–$33); tasting menu 40€ ($50) and 55€ ($69). AE, DC, MC, V. Mon 1:30–3:30pm; Tues–Sat 1:30–3:30pm and 8:30–11pm. Closed Easter week and Aug 8–31. Metro: Passeig de Gràcia.

Gaig ⭐⭐⭐ MODERN CATALAN   One of the shining culinary showcases of Barcelona, Gaig was founded some 130 years ago by the great grandmother of present owner Carlos Gaig. Back then it was an out-of-town *fonda,* or small inn for travelers. Now it's a new downtown locale with a sleek and luxurious interior. The restaurant is celebrated locally for the quality and freshness of its food. Eggs come from chickens seen wandering about the patio, where customers often dine alfresco in the summer months. The cuisine of Gaig centers on traditional Catalan recipes transformed and altered to suit lighter and more modern palates. Among the stellar dishes to order are *arroz del delta con pichón y zetas* (rice with partridge and mushrooms), *rape asado a la catalana* (grilled monkfish with local herbs), and *els petits filet de vedella amb prunes i pinyons* (small veal filets with prunes and pine nuts). One of the tastiest dishes is marinated roast pork thigh. Desserts include *crema de Sant Joseph* (a warm flan with wild strawberries on top), homemade chocolates, and a selection of tarts.

Aragó 214. ⓒ 93-429-10-17. Reservations recommended. Main courses 28€–40€ ($35–$50); tasting menu 75€ ($94). AE, DC, MC, V. Mon–Sat 1:30–3:30pm and 9–11pm; Sun 9–11pm. Closed 3 weeks in Aug and Easter week. Metro: Passeig de Gràcia.

Gorría ⭐ *Finds* BASQUE/NAVARRAN   If you're a devotee of the cookery of Navarre and of the coastal Basque country in northern Spain, make a date to head to Gorría.

This restaurant has been in business since the mid 1970s, standing only 200m (656 ft.) from La Sagrada Família and just 50m (164 ft.) from the Plaza de Toros Monumental (Barcelona's main bullring). Javier Gorría, who learned to cook from his more famous father, the chef Fermin Gorría, is in charge, and he's as good as his old man. In this residential setting in the heart of the Eixample, Gorría holds forth nightly, tempting your taste buds with his creations. He pampers his regular clientele, mainly homesick expats from Navarra and the Basque country. No dish is finer than the herb-flavored baby lamb baked in a wood-fired oven. The classic Basque dish, hake, comes in a garlic-laced green herbal sauce with fresh mussels and perfectly cooked asparagus on the side. His grilled turbot is fresh and straightforward, perfection itself with its flavoring of garlic, virgin olive oil, and a dash of vinegar. His braised pork also emerges from the wood-fired oven, and I could make a meal out of his *ponchas* (white beans). Another favorite is a platter of artichokes stuffed with shrimp and wild mushrooms.

Diputació 421. ℰ **93-245-11-64.** Reservations recommended. Main courses 18€–30€ ($23–$38). AE, DC, MC, V. Mon–Sat 1–3:30pm and 9–11:30pm. Closed Aug. Metro: Monumental.

Hisop ℱ MODERN CATALAN   In 2001, Guillem Pla and Oriol Ivem, two former chefs from the prestigious Neichel restaurant (see below), launched this adventurous eating spot in the upper Diagonal where the emphasis of its new Catalan cuisine is on small understated dishes with a complexity of flavors. In a coolly minimalist setting of high wooden ceilings, red and black decor, and white walls lined with thin vases—each containing a single red rose—you can enjoy such delicacies as stone bass *suquet* with *trompet,* scallops with figs and Jabugo ham, and mouthwatering desserts that include peach with ginger and fennel. There's also an excellent wine list favoring top vintages from the Rioja and local Penedés vineyards.

Passatge Marimón 9. ℰ **93-141-32-33.** www.hisop.com. Main courses 21€–29€ ($26–$36); tasting menu 48€ ($60). AE, DC, MC, V. Mon–Fri 1:30–4pm and 9pm–midnight; Sat 9pm–midnight. Closed Sun and last 2 weeks in Aug. Metro: Hospital Clinic.

Moo ℱℱℱ MODERN MEDITERRANEAN   The famed Roca brothers first launched their exquisite cuisine at the **El Cellar de Can Roca** (p. 143), a Michelin-starred eatery near Girona. Moo, their second restaurant, is located in Barcelona's applauded **Hotel Omm** (p. 100). Service by the mainly young staff is attentive and efficient, and all dishes, from the organic chicken with olives and mango or monkfish with wild mushrooms, are available in half-size portions, allowing you to create your own *menú de degustación.* You can try the set menu "Joan Roca"—five delightful dishes with wine from Moo's talented sommelier, Jordi Paronella. You might start with, say, a molded crescent of foie embedded with figs and covered with a gelatin of Pedro Ximénez sweet wine, followed first by a lobster, rose, and licorice curry, and then by a filet of wild sea bass on a bed of snow peas and pine nuts. The baby goat roasted in honey and rosemary on a bed of goat's milk foam is hard to resist. Accompany these dishes with excellent Penedés white wines. For dessert you might choose Bvlgari, a blend of Bergamot cream, lemon sorbet, and *pensamiento* flowers or a mouthwatering blend of chocolate cake, ginger, and 70% chocolate ice. Accompanied by a glass of San Emilio muscatel will provide a fitting end to your gourmet experience at this Roca brothers' haven.

Rosselló 265. ℰ **93-445-40-00.** Reservations recommended. Main courses 16€–25€ ($20–$31); Menu "Joan Roca" (with wine pairing) 85€ ($107); midday menu 45€ ($56). AE, DC, MC, V. Daily 1:30–4pm and 8:30–11pm. Metro: Diagonal.

Neichel ☆☆☆ FRENCH/MEDITERRANEAN   Alsatian-born owner Jean Louis Neichel is called "the most brilliant ambassador French cuisine has ever had within Spain." Neichel is almost obsessively concerned with gastronomy—the savory presentation of some of the most talked-about preparations of seafood, fowl, and sweets in Spain.

Your meal might include a "mosaic" of foie gras with vegetables, strips of salmon marinated in sesame and served with *escabeche* (vinaigrette) sauce, or slices of raw and smoked salmon stuffed with caviar. The prizewinning terrine of sea crab floats on a lavishly decorated bed of cold seafood sauce. Move on to *escalope* of turbot served with *coulis* (purée) of sea urchins, fricassee of Bresse chicken served with spiny lobsters, sea bass with a mousseline of truffles, Spanish milk-fed lamb served with the juice of Boletus mushrooms, or rack of lamb gratinéed in an herb-flavored pastry crust. The selection of European cheeses and the changing array of freshly made desserts are nothing short of spectacular.

Beltrán i Rózpide 1–5. ℂ **93-203-84-08.** Reservations required. Main courses 20€–40€ ($25–$50); fixed-price lunch 42€ ($53); tasting menu 55€ ($70). AE, DC, MC, V. Tues–Sat 1:30–3:30pm and 8:30–11pm. Closed Aug. Metro: Palau Reial or María Cristina.

Reno ☆ CATALAN/FRENCH   One of the finest and most enduring haute-cuisine restaurants in Barcelona, Reno sits behind sidewalk-to-ceiling windows hung with fine-mesh lace to shelter diners from prying eyes on the octagonal plaza outside. The impeccably mannered staff is formal but not intimidating. Seasonal specialties might include partridge simmered in wine or port sauce, a platter of assorted fish smoked on the premises, hake with anchovy sauce, or filet of sole stuffed with foie gras and truffles or grilled with anchovy sauce. An appetizing array of pastries gets wheeled from table to table on a cart. Dessert might also be crepes flambéed at your table.

Tuset 27. ℂ **93-200-91-29.** Reservations recommended. Main courses 15€–28€ ($19–$35); fixed-price lunch 32€ ($40); tasting menu 48€ ($50). AE, DC, MC, V. Mon–Fri 1–4pm and 9–11:30pm; Sat 9–11:30pm. Closed Aug. Metro: Diagonal.

MODERATE

Il Giardinetto ☆ *Moments* ITALIAN   This eatery, a perennial favorite of the uptown arts crowd, won a major design award when it was opened in 1973, and the "fantasy forest" surroundings haven't dated one iota. It's split into two levels, and the space is dominated by columns with painted branch motifs, the walls are covered with naive foliage cutouts, and the low ceilings sport swirls of pretty pale, green leaves. After taking it all in, curl into one of the teal-blue velvet banquettes and survey the menu of classic Italian dishes. You may wish to indulge in one of their heady black or white (when in season) truffle risottos or pastas, or a tuna *carpaccio* or tagliatelle with dainty vegetables and strips of Jabugo ham for something lighter. Salads of rocket and *radicchio* and mixed greens are as good as anything served in the *hosterías* of the Veneto and main courses are well executed and generous in size. There is a resident pianist in the evenings, and the service is old school without being stuffy.

La Granada del Penedès 22. ℂ **93-218-75-36.** Reservations recommended. Main courses 14€–20€ ($18–$25); fixed-price lunch 20€ ($25). AE, DC, MC, V. Mon–Fri 1:30–4:30pm and 8:30pm–1:30am; Sat 8:30pm–2am. Closed Aug. Metro: Diagonal.

L'Olive ☆ CATALAN/MEDITERRANEAN   You assume that this two-floor restaurant is named after the olive that figures so prominently into its cuisine, but actually it's named for the owner, Josep Olive. No Mediterranean restaurateur was more aptly named. The building is designed in a modern Catalan style with walls adorned with reproductions of famous Spanish painters, such as Miró, Dalí, or Picasso. The tables are topped in marble, the floors impeccably polished. There are sections on both floors where it's possible to have some privacy, and overall the feeling is one of elegance with a touch of intimacy. It's highly unlikely you'll be disappointed by anything on the menu—certainly not *bacallà a la llauna* (baked salt cod) or *filet de vedella al vi negre al forn* (veal filets cooked in the oven in a red-wine sauce), and the *salsa maigret* of duck with strawberry sauce. Monkfish flavored with roasted garlic is a palate pleaser, and you can finish with a *crema catalana* or one of the delicious Catalan pastries.

Calle Balmes 47. (C) **93-452-19-90.** Reservations recommended. Main courses 14€–22€ ($18–$28); *menú completo* 38€ ($48). AE, DC, MC, V. Mon–Sat 1–4pm and 8:30pm–midnight; Sun 1–4pm. Metro: Passeig de Gràcia.

Rosalert ⟨ CATALAN/SEAFOOD   Situated at the corner of Carrer Napols close to La Sagrada Família, this restaurant has been the domain of Jordi Alert for more than 4 decades. He specializes in *comida del mar a la plancha* (grilled seafood), and does so in a typical setting of hardwood floors and tile-covered walls. His seafood and crustaceans are grilled on a heated iron plate without any additives. There is no more awesome glass tank of live fish in Barcelona. You choose your fish, which is then extracted with a net and thrown on the grill. Of course, you find all the typical offerings, such as tiny octopus, succulent mussels, fat shrimp, squid, fresh oysters, and langoustines. If you're daring, you can order such unusual seafood as *dátiles,* a delicious shellfish whose shape resembles a date (hence the name). Begin with one of the freshly made tapas, such as salt cod in vinaigrette or fava beans laced with garlic and virgin olive oil. Your best bet might be the *parrillada* (assorted fish and shellfish from the grill). One of the best offerings is turbot cooked on the grill with potatoes and fresh mushrooms.

Diagonal 301. (C) **93-207-10-19.** Reservations recommended. Main courses 12€–25€ ($15–$31); fixed-price lunch 20€ ($25); tasting menu 48€ ($60). AE, DC, MC, V. Tues–Sun 9am–5pm and 8pm–2am. Closed Aug 10–30. Metro: Verdaguer/Sagrada Família.

⟨Kids⟩ Family-Friendly Restaurants

Dulcinea   This longtime favorite cafe/snack bar, at Petrixol 2 ((C) **93-302-68-24**), makes a great refueling stop any time of the day—guaranteed to satisfy any chocoholic. Lots of other sweet treats and drinks are on offer.

La Paradeta (p. 133)   Fish-and-chip fun: Fish-loving kids get to choose what they want and see it being cooked.

Mesón David (p. 137)   You don't have to worry about kids making too much noise here—the rest of the patrons and staff are just as ear bursting.

Murivecchi (p. 134)   Friendly, family-run Italian place with plenty of pasta dishes to suit the young ones.

Poble Espanyol (p. 186)   A good introduction to Spanish food. All the restaurants in the "Spanish Village" serve comparable food at comparable prices—let the kids choose what to eat.

Tragaluz ℛ MEDITERRANEAN   This is the flagship restaurant of the city's most respected group of restaurateurs. It offers three very contemporary-looking dining rooms on separate floors, scattered with eclectic pieces of art and very clever lighting. Menu items are derived from fresh ingredients that vary with the season. Depending on the month of your visit, you might find terrine of duck liver, Santurce-style hake (with garlic and herbs), filet of sole stuffed with red peppers, and beef tenderloin in a Rioja wine sauce. One of the best desserts is a semi-soft slice of deliberately under-baked chocolate cake. Diners seeking low-fat dishes will find solace here, as will vegetarians. The vegetables served are the best and freshest in the market that day. Downstairs you will find Tragarapíd, a faster, more casual version of what's upstairs, while across the road is an enormously popular Japanese restaurant that is directed by the same group. The Tragaluz chefs are adept at taking local products and turning them into flavorful, carefully prepared dishes.

Passatge de la Concepció 5. ✆ **93-487-06-21.** Reservations recommended. Main courses 16€–30€ ($20–$38); fixed-price lunch 23€ ($29); tasting menu 55€ ($69). AE, DC, MC, V. Sun–Wed 1:30–4pm and 8:30pm–midnight; Thurs–Sat 1:30–4pm and 8:30pm–1am. Metro: Diagonal.

INEXPENSIVE

El Caballito Blanco SEAFOOD/INTERNATIONAL   This Barcelona standby is famous for seafood and popular with the locals. The fluorescent-lit dining area does not offer much atmosphere, but the food is good, varied, and relatively inexpensive (unless you order lobster or other costly shellfish). The "Little White Horse," in the Passeig de Gràcia area, features a huge selection, including monkfish, mussels marinara, and shrimp with garlic. If you don't want fish, try the grilled lamb cutlets. Several different pâtés and salads are offered. There's a bar to the left of the dining area.

Mallorca 196. ✆ **93-453-10-33.** Main courses 9€–30€ ($11–$38). AE, DC, MC, V. Tues–Sat 1–3:45pm and 9–10:45pm; Sun 1–3:45pm. Closed Aug. Metro: Hospital Clinic and Diagonal.

SNACKS, TAPAS & DRINKS

Bar Turò TAPAS/CATALAN   Located in an affluent residential neighborhood north of Old Town, Bar Turò serves some of the best tapas in town. In summer you can sit outside or retreat to the narrow confines of the bar. You select from about 20 kinds of tapas, including Russian salad, fried squid, and *serrano* ham.

Tenor Viñas 1. ✆ **93-200-69-53.** Tapas 2.50€–12€ ($3.10–$15); main courses 6€–18€ ($7.50–$23). MC, V. Mon–Sat 8:30am–midnight; Sun 10am–4pm. Closed weekends in Aug. Metro: Hospital Clinic.

Casa Alfonso TAPAS   Spaniards love their mountain ham, which comes from many different regions. The best of the best is *jamón Jabugo,* the only one sold at this traditional establishment. Entire hams hang from steel braces. They're taken down, carved, and trimmed into paper-thin slices. This particular form of cured ham, generically called *jamón serrano,* comes from pigs that are fed acorns in Huelva, in deepest Andalusia. Devotees of all things porcine will ascend to piggy-flavored heaven. Also served are salads and grilled meat dishes.

Roger de Llúria 6. ✆ **93-301-97-83.** Tapas 4.50€–12€ ($5.60–$15); tasting menu 16€ ($20). AE, DC, MC, V. Mon–Tues 9am–midnight; Wed–Sat 9am–1am. Metro: Urquinaona.

Casa Tejada TAPAS   Covered with rough stucco and decorated with hanging hams, Casa Tejada (established in 1964) offers some of the best tapas. Arranged behind a glass display case, they include such dishes as marinated fresh tuna, German-style potato salad, ham salad, and five preparations of squid (including one that's stuffed). For variety, quantity, and quality, this place is hard to beat. There's outdoor dining in summer.

Tenor Viñas 3. ℭ **93-200-73-41.** Tapas 3€–17€ ($3.75–$21). MC, V. Daily 7am–1:30am. Closed Aug 8–21. Metro: Hospital Clinic.

La Bodegueta TAPAS   Founded in 1940, this old wine tavern is one of the more authentic options in this ritzy boulevard of franchised eateries. It specializes in Catalan sausage *(botifarra)*, salamis, and cheeses. Wash them all down with *vermut* or inexpensive Spanish wines from the barrel. It's loud, no-nonsense, and a favorite with students.

Rambla de Catalunya 100. ℭ **93-215-48-94.** Tapas from 1.95€–15€ ($2.45–$19). No credit cards. Mon–Sat 7am–1:30am; Sun 7pm–1am. Closed Aug 8–22. Metro: Diagonal.

8 Gràcia

EXPENSIVE

Botafumeiro ✸✸✸ SEAFOOD   Although the competition is strong, this classic *marisquería* consistently puts Barcelona's finest seafood on the table. Much of the allure comes from the attention of the white-jacketed staff. You can eat at the bar. Or, if you venture to the rear, you'll find a series of attractive dining rooms noted for the ease with which business deals seem to be arranged during the lunch hour. International businesspeople often rendezvous here, and the king of Spain is sometimes a patron.

Menu items include fresh seafood prepared in a glistening modern kitchen visible from parts of the dining room. The establishment prides itself on its fresh and saltwater fish, clams, mussels, lobster, crayfish, scallops, and several varieties of crustaceans—such as *percebes* (goose barnacles)—that you may have never seen before. Stored live in holding tanks or in enormous crates near the entrance, many of the creatures are flown in daily from Galicia, homeland of owner Moncho Neira. With the 100 or so fish plates, the menu lists only four or five meat dishes, including three kinds of steak, veal, and a traditional version of pork with turnips. The wine list offers a wide array of *cavas* from Catalonia and highly drinkable choices from Galicia, in particular the highly regarded *Albariño* white.

Gran de Gràcia 81. ℭ **93-218-42-30.** Reservations recommended for dining rooms. Main courses 24€–40€ ($30–$50). AE, DC, MC, V. Daily 1pm–1am. Metro: Fontana.

Jean Luc Figueras ✸✸✸ CATALAN   For a *Kama Sutra*–like dining experience, head for this hip Gràcia town house that was once the studio of Balenciaga. Even if food critics narrowed the list of Barcelona restaurants down to five, the chef and owner, Jean Luc Figueras, would likely appear on the list. The setting is modern and refined, the food both traditional and innovative, as Figueras stamps every dish with his personal touch. Highly dedicated to staying on top, Figueras is a seeker of the finest ingredients on the Barcelona market, and his menu is adjusted to take advantage of the best produce in any season. The emphasis is on fresh seafood, although his meat dishes are also sublime. His fried prawn and ginger-flecked pasta in a mango and mustard sauce would make the gods weep, and his sea bass with cod and blood sausage is no less brilliant. Your tastes buds will go into orbit if you're wise enough to select such nouvelle-inspired dishes as shrimp with a velvety smooth and golden pumpkin

Gràcia Dining

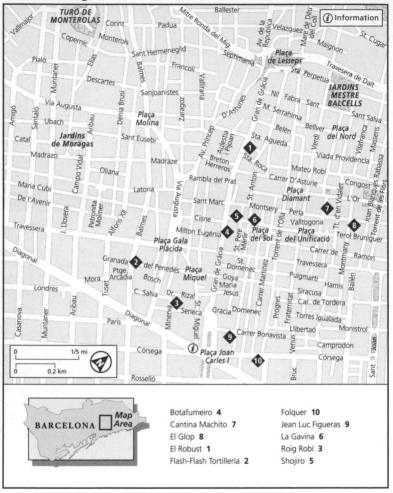

TURÓ DE MONTEROLAS

JARDINS MESTRE BALCELLS

JARDINS de Moragas

(i) Information

BARCELONA ☐ Map Area

Botafumeiro **4**	Folquer **10**
Cantina Machito **7**	Jean Luc Figueras **9**
El Glop **8**	La Gavina **6**
El Robust **1**	Roig Robí **3**
Flash-Flash Tortillería **2**	Shojiro **5**

cream sauce or the pork with a zesty goat cheese enlivened with peach honey. The desserts are homemade and inevitably sumptuous.

Santa Teresa 10. ✆ **93-415-28-77.** Reservations required. Main courses 23€–50€ ($28–$63); tasting menu 80€ ($100). AE, DC, MC, V. Mon–Sat 1:30–3:30pm and 8:30–11:30pm. Metro: Diagonal.

Roig Robí ⍟ INTERNATIONAL   This restaurant—in Catalan, the name means "ruby red" (the color of a perfectly aged Rioja)—serves excellent food from an imaginative kitchen with a warm welcome. Although I'm not as excited about this restaurant as I once was, it does remain one of the city's most dependable choices. Order an aperitif at the L-shaped oak bar, then head down a long corridor to a pair of flower-filled dining rooms. In warm weather, glass doors open onto a verdant walled courtyard. Menu items include fresh beans with pine-nut sauce, *hake al Roig Robí,* fresh mushroom salad with green beans and fresh tomatoes, and shellfish from the Costa Brava. Monkfish comes with clams and onion confit, ravioli stuffed with spring herbs, and chicken stuffed with foie gras. Cockscomb salad is available for those with adventuresome palates.

Séneca 20. ℂ **93-218-92-22.** Reservations required. Main courses 15€–40€ ($19–$50); tasting menu 65€ ($81); fixed-price menu 48€ ($60). AE, DC, MC, V. Mon–Fri 1:30–4pm; Mon–Sat 9–11:30pm. Closed Aug 8–21. Metro: Diagonal.

MODERATE

El Glop CATALAN   This place has been a Gràcia institution for decades, and offers affordable, local cuisine at great prices. It's located in a corner building with exposed beams and an interior patio. Many people pop in for some quick *torrades,* toasted rustic bread rubbed with tomato and topped with all manner of cheese, salamis, and hams. More substantial fare includes *botifarras* (Catalan sausages), chops, chicken, and other carnivore staples cooked over an open flame and served up with creamy aioli and snails. It's bright, informal, and always busy, and a good place to bring the kids.

Montmany 46. ℂ **93-213-70-58.** Reservations recommended. Main courses 6€–24€ ($7.50–$30); fixed-price menu 9€ ($11); tasting menu from 25€ ($31). MC, V. Daily 1–4pm and 8pm–1am. Metro: Joanic. Another branch is located at Caspe 21 (ℂ **93-318-75-75;** Metro: Catalunya).

Flash-Flash Tortillería *(Moments* OMELETS/HAMBURGERS   Hamburgers, steaks salads, and over 70 types of tortillas are served up in a pop-art setting of funky black-and-white murals and white leather banquettes. It's completely authentic; Flash-Flash opened in 1970 and the interior hasn't been altered since. The Twiggy-like model adorning the walls was the wife of Leopoldo Pomés, a well-known fashion photographer of the time and part owner. The food is very good; tortillas come out fresh and fluffy and the bunless burgers are some of the best in town. It's a favorite with uptown business types, some of whom have been coming here since the place opened.

Granada de Penedès 25. ℂ **93-237-09–90.** Reservations recommended. Main courses 9€–25€ ($11–$31). AE, DC, MC, V. Daily 1pm–1:30am. FGC: Gràcia.

Folquer *(Finds* CATALAN/SPANISH With its bright, sunny decor and animated—mainly Catalan—clientele, Folquer has an arty-bohemian feel. Rather discretely located at the southern end of Gràcia, it's a welcoming spot with inventive, tasty dishes, which make use of first-rate ingredients, and two particularly good-value lunchtime menus: the standard and the "Executive." Regional dishes dominate the a la carte list. Try their pungent *suquet de pop* (octopus stew).

Torrent de l'Olla 3. ℂ **93-217-43-95.** Main courses 15€–20€ ($19–$25). Set lunch 14€ ($18); Executive lunch 16€ ($20). AE, DC, MC, V. Mon–Fri 1–4pm, 9–11:30pm; Sat 9-11:30pm. Closed Sun and last 2 weeks of Aug. Metro: Diagonal or Verdaguer.

Shojiro ⊛ ASIAN FUSION   With Japanese restaurants now the norm in Barcelona, it was only a matter before Nippon cuisine was fused with the local one. This quirky restaurant, led by Shojiro Ochi, a native of Japan who arrived in Barcelona in 1979, does just that. Ochi presents his goodies to you in set-price four- and five-course menus. These delectable morsels include *bonito* (a type of A-grade tuna) preserved in a Catalan *escabeche,* tuna with a sherry reduction, or duck's breast with shitake mushrooms. Desserts include more unconventional delights such as a foie bon-bon and ostrich *tataki.*

Ros de Olano 11. ℂ **93-415-65-48.** Fixed-price lunch 18€ ($23); fixed-price dinner 32€–40€ ($40–$50). AE, DC, MC, V. Mon–Sat 1:30–3:30pm; Tues–Sat 9pm–12:30am. Metro: Fontana or Joanic.

Eating Alfresco

Finding a great terrace to sit out on in Barcelona is easier said than done. There are literally hundreds of sidewalk cafes where you can drink your cappuccino to the roar of passing traffic, and tourist-filled plazas lined by restaurants that serve the same old microwaved paellas. But a tucked-away garden, a tranquil terrace, or a hideaway by the sea—well, that's another matter altogether.

The **Café de L'Academia,** Calle Lledó 1 (© **93-319-82-53;** p. 124), is located on the one of the prettiest squares in Barcelona, Plaça Sant Just. Presided over by a church of the same name, it is reputedly Barcelona's oldest, and according to lore, if you believe your life to be in mortal danger you can still make a legally binding will at the altar with a friend as a witness. It was also on this square that the Romans executed the first Christians. Notwithstanding the ghosts of the past, today it is one of the most peaceful and unspoiled plaças in the Old City. In the Born, the **Tèxtil Cafè,** Calle Montcada 12 (© **93-268-25-98),** is an oasis of calm enclosed within the courtyard of an 18th-century palace. Providing you're not in a hurry (service is notoriously laid-back), it's an idyllic place in the to fuel up on tea, coffee, and hearty, wholesome lunches in the shade of large, white parasols or the warmth of outdoor gas fires in winter.

Barcelona's seafront has restaurant terraces a-plenty, but for something a little more hidden, continue along to the so-called Parc del Port Olímpic, which straddles two busy highways. Here, sunk from view and traffic noise, is the gorgeous **Anfiteatro,** Av. Litoral 36 (© **65-969-53-45;** p. 151)—a smart restaurant serving creative Mediterranean dishes with a spacious terrace that wraps around an ornamental pool. Another way to escape the crowds is to get up onto the rooftops at **La Miranda del Museu,** Museu d'Història de Catalunya, Plaça Pau Vila 3 (© **93-225-50-07),** which has fabulous views over the yachts in Port Vell. Frustratingly, the terrace is for drinks only, so go in time for an aperitif and linger over coffee.

Heading a little farther out and halfway up the hill to Montjuïc, **La Font del Gat,** Passeig Santa Madrona 28 (© **93-289-04-04),** is a secret garden and lunch spot chiseled out of the mountainside beneath the famed Joan Miró Foundation. The farther out you go, the prettier the surroundings, and if its real tranquillity you're seeking (not to mention exclusivity), the restaurants in the suburbs are what really shine. In Horta, **Can Travi Nou,** Jorge Manrique, Parc de la Vall d'Hebron (© **93-428-04-34),** is a converted 14th-century farmhouse with sprawling grounds, two or three ample terraces, and gardens for strolling. It's great for long Sunday lunches or evenings under the stars, and serves decent, if pricey, roast meats, fish dishes, and paella.

Finally, if you're looking to treat yourself (or somebody else) head for the Restaurant **L'Orangerie,** Gran Hotel La Florida, Carretera de Vallvidrera al Tibidabo 83–93 (© **93-259-30-00).** This fabulous eating spot is situated on the highest peak of the Collserola with stunning views over Barcelona, and its scented gardens and terraces make it one of the most spectacular dining destinations in the city.

INEXPENSIVE

Cantina Machito MEXICAN   This is generally considered to be the best Mexican restaurant in Barcelona. It's hard to get a table, especially when the cinema crowd from next door rolls in, but it's worth the wait. What they serve is far from the rudimentary Tex-Mex fare. The tacos and tortillas and a tangy guacamole are all present and, but so is a chicken mole and *sopa malpeña,* a warming soup of chickpeas, tomato, and chicken, plus an unusual lime and tequila mousse for dessert. The margaritas are renowned as are their parties on Mexican national days and *fiestas.*

Torrijos 47. ⓒ **93-217-34-14.** Reservations recommended. Main courses 7.50€–14€ ($9.35–$18). MC, V. Daily 1–4:30pm and 7pm–1:30am. Metro: Fontana or Joanic.

El Robust CATALAN   Locals wishing to escape the evening heat clamor for El Robust's pretty patio garden, replete with lemon and pine trees. The fare here is solid Catalan: organic meat *a la brasa* (flame grilled) and charcuterie from Vic, the inland town famed for its cured meats. Vegetarians will be appeased by a good selection of salads and other tidbits such as deep-fried Camembert.

Gran de Gràcia 196. ⓒ **93-237-90-46.** Main courses 8€–14€ ($10–$18). MC, V. Mon–Sat noon–4pm and 8:30pm–midnight. Closed Aug 8–31. Metro: Fontana.

La Gavina PIZZA   This place is hugely popular for pizzas, from your basic tomato and mozzarella type to a more lavish version with seafood and caviar. Well worth trying are the *payes,* paper-thin slices of potato, rosemary, and olive oil. The owner is obviously obsessed with heavenly bodies, as thousands of angels, virgins, and other religious deities are hung everywhere for a chic, junk-shop affect.

Ros de Olano 17. ⓒ **93-415-74-50.** Reservations recommended. Main courses 7.50€–12€ ($9.35–$15). No credit cards. Daily 1pm–1am; July–Sept daily 6pm–1am. Metro: Fontana.

9 Barceloneta & Vila Olímpica

EXPENSIVE

Anfiteatro ⓡ *Moments* MEDITERRANEAN   In spite of the fashionable pedigree, it's amazing how this restaurant manages to elude so many people—perhaps because it's tucked away on an underground level of a boulevard in the Olympic Village. Designed by the studio of Oriol Bohigas, one of the city's leading architects who is also responsible for the Olympic Village itself, it features rationalist lines that are softened by an abundance of mosaics, and a central pond surrounded by tables. In this unique setting of urban romanticism, you can try wild sea bass with grapes and a port sauce or cuttlefish and crab ravioli. If there is room for dessert, go for the mascarpone and vanilla ice cream with a mango purée.

Parc del Port Olímpic, Av. Litoral 37 (opposite Calle Rosa Sensat). ⓒ **65-969-53-45.** Reservations recommended on weekends. Main courses 16€–35€ ($20–$44); fixed-price lunch menu 32€ ($40); tasting menu 40€ ($50) and 55€ ($69). AE, MC, V. Tues–Sat 1–4pm and 8:30pm–midnight; Sun 1–4pm. Closed Easter week. Metro: Port Olímpic.

Can Costa ⓡ SEAFOOD   Established in the late 1930s, Can Costa is one of the oldest seafood restaurants in this seafaring town. It has two busy dining rooms, a practiced staff, and an outdoor terrace, although a warehouse blocks the view of the harbor. Fresh seafood prepared according to traditional recipes rules the menu, which includes the best baby squid in town—sautéed in a flash so that it has a nearly grilled flavor, almost never overcooked or rubbery. A long-standing chef's specialty is *fideuà*

Barceloneta Dining

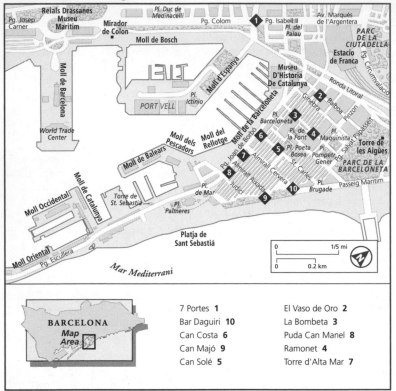

7 Portes **1**	El Vaso de Oro **2**
Bar Daguiri **10**	La Bombeta **3**
Can Costa **6**	Puda Can Manel **8**
Can Majó **9**	Ramonet **4**
Can Solé **5**	Torre d'Alta Mar **7**

de peix, a relative of the classic Valencian shellfish paella, with noodles instead of rice. Desserts are made fresh daily.

Passeig de Joan de Borbón 70. ℃ **93-221-59-03**. Reservations recommended. Main courses 16€–30€ ($20–$38). MC, V. Thurs–Tues 12:30–4pm and 8–11:30pm; Wed 12:30–4pm. Metro: Barceloneta.

Can Solé ⨕ CATALAN   Atmospherically located in Barceloneta's harbor area, Can Solé still honors the traditions of this former fishing village. Many of the seafood joints here are too touristy for my taste, but this one is authentic and delivers good value. The decor is rustic and a bit raffish, with wine barrels, lots of noise, and excellent food. Begin with the sweet tiny clams or the cod cakes, or perhaps some bouillabaisse. Little langoustines are an eternal but expensive favorite, and everything is perfumed with fresh garlic. You might also sample one of the seafood-rich dishes. Desserts are so good they're worth saving room for, especially the orange pudding or the praline ice cream.

Carrer Sant Carles 4. ℃ **93-221-50-12**. Reservations required. Main courses 10€–45€ ($13–$56). AE, DC, MC, V. Tues–Sat 1–4pm and 8:30–11pm; Sun 1–4pm. Metro: Barceloneta.

Els Pescadors ⨕⨕ SEAFOOD   This is generally acknowledged to be one of the best the fish restaurants in Barcelona. The fact that it's located slightly off the main

Agua **2**
Anfiteatro **6**
Arola **3**
Bestial **1**
CDLC (Carpe Diem) **5**
Els Pescadors **7**
Talaia Mar **4**

drag, in the working-class beachside suburb of Poble Nou, doesn't stop foodies from making the trip. The restaurant essentially has two *ambientes:* one is old school—with marble tabletops and wooden beams—while the other is modern Mediterranean. But no one has come to gawk at the surroundings. The only objective here (as it has been for many generations) is to enjoy the freshest seafood in Barcelona, cooked in classical ways with surprising touches. Local prawns are served with steaming chickpeas, or a baked fish, whatever has been trawled in that day, with clams and small white beans.
Plaça Prim 1. ⓒ **93-225-20-18.** Reservations recommended on weekend. Main courses 15€–35€ ($19–$44). AE, DC, MC, V. Daily 1–3:45pm and 8:30pm–midnight. Closed Easter week. Metro: Poble Nou.

7 Portes *Moments* CATALAN   Festive and elegant, 7 Portes been around since 1836, making it one of the oldest restaurants in Barcelona. Pretty much anybody who is anybody has dined here over the years. While these days it's more touristy than aristocratic, there is still enough authentic charm left in the decor (and patrons) to make it well worth the visit. The white-aproned staff members are constantly on the go, which in some ways makes it feel like an upmarket canteen. There is nothing slap-dash about the food, though: Regional dishes include fresh herring with onions and potatoes, a different paella daily (sometimes with shellfish, for example, or with rabbit), and a wide array of fresh fish, expertly deboned and skinned at the table. You might order succulent oysters or an herb-laden stew of black beans with pork or white beans with sausage. Portions are enormous. The restaurant's name means "Seven Doors," and it really does have seven doors underneath some charming porticoes that are typical to this portside pocket of Barcelona.

Passeig d'Isabel II 14. (C) **93-319-30-33**. Reservations required. Main courses 18€–35€ ($23–$44). AE, DC, MC, V. Daily 1pm–1am. Metro: Barceloneta.

Torre d'Alta Mar MEDITERRANEAN   Alta Mar is sort of a mile-high gastro club. Its unique setting is the 75m-high (246 ft.) Torre de Sant Sebastián, one of the three towers that serves the port-crossing, tourist carrying cable car (p. 186). But don't worry about rubbing shoulders with back-packers when you enter this exclusive eatery; patrons are whisked up in a private, high-tech glass elevator to be greeted by a simply breathtaking 360-degree view of the city and sea. Once your jaw finally stops dropping and you are settled in the plush decor, you can dine in style from a predominantly fish menu that includes such inventions as a hake, porcini, and artichoke stir-fry; stewed monkfish in *romesco* sauce; or salt-roasted bream.

Passeig de Joan de Borbón 88. (C) **93-221-00-07**. Reservations recommended. Main courses 22€–34€ ($28–$43). Daily 1–3:30pm and 8:45–11:30pm. Metro: Barceloneta.

MODERATE

Agua 𝒦 MEDITERRANEAN   It bustles, it's hip, and it serves well-prepared fish and shellfish in a hyper-modern setting overlooking the beach. A terrace beckons anyone who wants a close view of the sea, but if a chilly wind is blowing, you can retreat into the big-windowed blue-and-yellow dining room and, amid display cases showing the catch of the day, order heaping portions of meats and fish to be grilled over an open fire. Favorite choices include chicken, swordfish, prawns, and an especially succulent version of stuffed squid. Most of them are served with as little culinary fanfare, and as few sauces, as possible, allowing the freshness and flavor of the raw ingredients to shine through the chargrilled coatings. Risottos, some of them studded with fresh clams and herbs, are usually winners, with many versions suitable for vegetarians. The only problem here is its popularity; make sure you book on the weekends.

Passeig Marítim de la Barceloneta 30 (Vila Olímpica). (C) **93-225-12-72**. Reservations recommended. Main courses 8€–18€ ($10–$22). AE, DC, MC, V. Daily 1:30–4pm and 8:30pm–midnight (until 1am Fri–Sat). Metro: Ciutadella–Vila Olímpica.

Arola 𝒦 CATALAN/SPANISH   Blessed with two Michelin stars—not to mention handsome—Sergi Arola is one of the rising young stars of Spain's culinary world. He hails from Catalunya, but this is his first restaurant in Barcelona (his other, La Broche, is in Madrid) and the setting is no less than the luxury Hotel Arts in the Olympic Village. What Arola aims to do amid a quirky, pop-art decor in purple and lime green, is to give the *pica-pica* modern makeover. *Pica-pica* can be best translated as "nibbles," and could be bite-size pieces of Manchego cheese, Iberian ham, preserved shellfish, or high-end canned tuna. Thus your meal at Arola is likely to start with *patatas bravas* cut and arranged on a plate to look like dozens of tiny female breasts, tinned cockles that meticulously fan out from a dainty bowl of piquant dressing, and perfect asparagus spears that lay languidly on a bed of romesco sauce. Main courses include Mediterranean standards with a touch of Arola magic: steamed mussels with citrus juice and saffron, Gorgonzola cheese croquettes, grilled prawns with cold potato cream, and sea bass with an emulsion of watercress, to name just a few. The dessert of goat's cheese, macadamia nuts, tomato jam, and quince cream should convince you of Arola's talent.

Hotel Arts, Marina 19–21. ℂ **93-483-80-90.** Reservations required. Main courses 10€–32€ ($13–$40); tasting menu 48€ ($60). AE, DC, MC, V. Tues 8:30–11pm; Wed 1:30–3:30pm; Thurs–Fri 1:30–3:30pm and 8.30–11:30pm; Sat–Sun 2–4pm and 8:30–11pm. Closed Jan (month closed can vary each year). Metro: Ciutadella–Vila Olímpica.

Bestial MEDITERRANEAN/ITALIAN   One of the latest conquests of the Tragaluz group (p. 146) is the modern Mediterranean eatery Bestial. Mercifully unrecognizable from the location's previous tenant, Planet Hollywood, it brings some well-needed class to the gastronomically pedestrian Olympic Marina, and the menu has been designed as an Italian-influenced alternative to the dozens of packet-paella restaurants in the immediate vicinity. What sounds good on paper often doesn't transfer well to table. Seared tuna with black-olive risotto is good choice—nothing measly about the size of the fish chunks here. The outdoor setting, with its noise-absorbing wooden decking and oversize umbrellas, is highly stylish (and functional), but the inside dining room is like sitting in a sci-fi bus station.

Ramón Trias Fargas 30 (Vila Olímpica). ℂ **93-224-04-07.** Main courses 9€–20€ ($11–$25). AE, DC, MC, V. Mon–Fri 1:30–4pm and 8:30pm–midnight (until 1am on Fri); Sat 1:30–5pm and 8:30pm–1am; Sun 1:30–5pm and 8:30pm–midnight. Metro: Ciutadella–Vila Olímpica.

Can Majó *𝒜𝒜* SEAFOOD   Set close to the harbor, this is one of the finest seafood restaurants in Barcelona. In summer a terrace table here is as desirable a place to eat as anywhere in the port. The inviting interior is decorated in the rustic tavern style. Paintings line the walls, and the staff exudes a hospitable, friendly aura while they give excellent, if sometimes rushed, service. The food covers fairly familiar ground, but when it's good, it's good, and it can be very good indeed. The fish is fresh, bought each morning. Now open for some 4 decades, the restaurant still serves some of the best *sopa de pescado y marisco* (fish and shellfish soup) in the area. Its sautéed squid is a heavenly meal in itself, or in the words of one diner: "A day without *calamares* is a day in hell." *Bacalao* (dried cod) appears in a savory green sauce with little baby clams in their shells. Its paellas are as good as those served in the restaurants of Valencia, and their lobster bouillabaisse is extremely succulent.

Almirall Aixada 23. ℂ **93-221-54-55.** Reservations required. Main courses 14€–25€ ($18–$31). AE, DC, MC, V. Tues–Sat 1–4pm and 8:30–11:30pm; Sun 1–4pm. Metro: Barceloneta.

CDLC (Carpe Diem) MEDITERRANEAN FUSION   Before its nightly transformation into a club for *gente guapa* (beautiful people; p. 243), CDLC functions as a regular quality restaurant. Rather than the food or impeccable service, the attraction here is its sea-facing terrace. Not that the cuisine, with its strong Thai and Japanese influence, is in any way unacceptable, but true foodies may be suspicious of the fact that a plate of sushi can make it to your table in just under 30 seconds. It might be better to stick to the lunchtime fare, which includes very reasonably priced salads, sandwiches, and burgers. In true show-off style, the wine list includes some offerings priced to impress: You could, for example, treat your date to a 306€ ($383) bottle of Cristal champagne, and if that doesn't do the trick go for the 496€ ($620) Sant Emilion Cheval Blanc from 1996.

Passeig Marítim 32. ℂ **93-224-04-70.** Reservations required. Main courses 12€–25€ ($15–$31); fixed-price lunch 18€ ($22). AE, DC, MC, V. Daily noon–3am. Metro: Ciutadella–Vila Olímpica.

Puda Can Manel ✮ MEDITERRANEAN/SPANISH   One of the more annoying aspects of walking down Barceloneta's main boulevard is that waiters incessantly try to coax you into their often overpriced and ordinary outdoor restaurants. The reason none of this goes on at Puda Can Manel is that it's a considerable cut above the others along this touristy stretch. On Sunday afternoons you'll see locals waiting patiently for a table while its neighbors remain empty. They are lining up for succulent, tasty paellas and *fideuàs* (which replace rice for thin noodles), rich *arroz negre* (rice cooked in squid ink) and *calamares* fried to perfection, all at reasonable prices.

Passeig de Joan de Borbón 60 (Barceloneta). ℂ **93-221-50-13.** Reservations required. Main courses 9.50€–16€ ($12–$20). AE, DC, MC, V. Tues–Sun 1–4pm and 7–11pm. Metro: Ciutadella–Vila Olímpica.

Ramonet ✮ SEAFOOD   As far back 1763 this good but pricey restaurant was serving a large variety of fresh seafood in a Catalan-style villa near the seaport. The front room, with stand-up tables for seafood tapas, beer, and regional wine, is often crowded, and in the two dining rooms you can choose from a variety of marine dishes such as shrimp, hake, and monkfish. Other delights on offer include pungent anchovies, grilled mushrooms, black rice, braised artichokes, tortilla with spinach and beans, and mussels "from the beach."

Carrer Maquinista 17. ℂ **93-319-30-64.** Reservations recommended. Main courses 12€–26€ ($15–$33). DC, MC, V. Daily noon–midnight. Metro: Barceloneta.

Talaia Mar ✮✮ MEDITERRANEAN   This is the best restaurant at Olympic Port, and it has one of the most innovative menus in Catalonia. Javier Planes, the chef, devises unique menus and turns out food that is both amusing and savory. The presentations are often simple yet always elegant. To discover this chef's talent, sample his set menu, which he calls, quite appropriately, *festival gastronómico*. For a main course, sample his tuna tartare with guacamole and salmon eggs or his brochettes of lobster. The increasingly rare black truffle appears in some of his smooth and velvety risottos. He does a marvelous steamed hake in a balsamic reduction as well as a grilled sea bass with shrimp, which is flavored with asparagus juice among other delights. Fresh fish arrives from the market daily and is grilled to perfection, as is the aromatically roasted rack of lamb. I could return here night after night and always find some new dish to tempt the palate. Rising above the port, the restaurant is beside two towers, Hotel Arts and Torre Mapfre.

Marina 16. ℂ **93-221-90-90.** Reservations required. Main courses 18€–28€ ($22–$35); fixed-price menu 55€ ($69). AE, DC, MC, V. Tues–Sun 1–4pm and 8pm–midnight. Metro: Ciutadella–Vila Olímpica.

SNACKS, TAPAS & DRINKS

Bar Daguiri CAFE   This bar-cafe with a bohemian vibe is right on the beach, an enviable location for many a restaurateur. It serves up light meals such as salads, dips, and sandwiches, as well as coffee and drinks, and outside on the terrace there is always a street musician doing his or her thing. The service can be irritatingly inept, but it's all part of the laid-back beach culture in this neck of the woods. A plus is the free Internet access—bring your laptop and they will wire you up, and there is free music (mainly jazz and Latin) on Thursday evenings. The large selection of daily foreign newspapers is also a welcome touch.

Grau i Torras 59. ℂ **93-221-51-09.** Snacks 6€–9€ ($7.50–$11). MC, V. Daily 10am–midnight. Metro: Barceloneta.

El Vaso de Oro ✮ TAPAS   This is another very good Barceloneta tapas bar that also makes its own beer. The place is ridiculously narrow, making it a challenge not to elbow your neighbor as you raise your glass. Most people consider this part of the fun

---

Moments **A Wine Taster's Secret Address**

It doesn't get much better in Barcelona than an afternoon spent on the terrace of **La Vinya del Senyor**, Plaça Santa María 5 (© **93-310-33-79**), taking in the glorious Gothic facade of Santa María del Mar. You could even take a wine connoisseur like Mel Brooks (when he's not counting his take from *The Producers*), and I think even this hard-to-please man would be pleased. The wine list will inspire awe. Imagine, for example, 13 Priorats, 31 Riojas, and more than a dozen vintages of the legendary Vega Sicilia. In all, there are more than 300 wines and selected *cavas*, sherries, and *moscatells*, and the list is constantly rotated so you can always expect some new surprise on the *carte*. If you don't want a bottle, you'll find some two dozen wines offered by the glass, including a sublime 1994 Jané Ventura Cabernet Sauvignon. To go with your wine, tantalizing tapas are served, including walnut rolls drizzled in olive oil, cured Iberian ham, and French cheese. Tapas cost from 2.50€–6.50€ ($3.15–$8.15). American Express, Diners Club, MasterCard, and Visa are accepted. Hours are Tuesday through Saturday from noon to 1:30am and Sunday from noon to midnight. Metro: Jaume I or Barceloneta.

---

though as they tuck into the juiciest *solomillo* served with *pimientos del padrón* (miniature green peppers), the lightest croquettes, or a creamy Russian salad. If you are on a budget watch what you eat as the potions here are quite small, and the bill tends to add up unexpectedly.

Balboa 6 (Barceloneta). © **93-319-30-98**. Tapas 4.50€–15€ ($5.60–$19). MC, V. Daily 9am–midnight. Metro: Barceloneta.

La Bombeta *R* TAPAS This place is a real slice of local life and one of the best tapas bars in the city. It looks like a slightly modernized version of a *taverna*, and its house specialty is *bombas*, deep-fried balls of fluffy mashed potato served with a spicy *brava* sauce. Other tapas include succulent mussels, either steamed or with a marinara sauce, giant grilled prawns, plates of paper-thin *serrano* ham, and small chunks of deep fried calamari called *rabas*. Needless to say, when washed down with a jug of their excellent in-house sangria, this is a highly satisfying meal-in-itself.

Maquinista 3 (Barceloneta). © **93-319-94-45**. Tapas 4.50€–14€ ($5.60–$18). MC, V. Thurs–Tues 10am–midnight. Metro: Barceloneta.

10 Barrio Alto

MODERATE/EXPENSIVE

La Balsa INTERNATIONAL Situated on the uppermost level of a circular tower built as a cistern, La Balsa offers a fine view over most of the surrounding cityscape. To reach it you climb to the structure's original rooftop, where you're likely to be greeted by owner and founder Mercedes López. Food emerges from a cramped but well-organized kitchen several floors below. (The waiters are reputedly the most athletic in Barcelona, because they must run up the stairs carrying steaming platters.) The restaurant serves such dishes as a *judías verdes* (broad beans) with strips of salmon in lemon-flavored vinaigrette, stewed veal with wild mushrooms, a salad of warm lentils with anchovies, and pickled fresh salmon with chives. Undercooked maigret (breast) of duck is served with fresh, lightly poached foie gras, and baked hake (flown in from Galicia) is prepared in squid-ink sauce. The restaurant is 2km (1¼ miles) north of the city's heart—you'll need a taxi—in the Tibidabo district, close to the Science Museum (Museu de la Ciéncia). It's often booked several days in advance.

Infanta Isabel 4. ℂ 93-211-50-48. Reservations required. Main courses 12€–27€ ($15–$34). AE, DC, MC, V. Mon 9–11:30pm; Tues–Sat 2–3:30pm and 9–11:30pm. Aug buffet only 9–11:30pm. Closed Easter week.

El Mató de Pedralbes CATALAN   Mató is Catalan for cottage cheese—in this case prepared by the nuns at the Monastery of Pedralbes (p. 190), which is just round the corner from this homey eating spot. Located in an old house with various dining areas in this relaxing residential corner of the city, it's high above the fumes and the hubbub of traffic. Indeed, El Mató is ideal for a relaxing, traditional-style lunch. Sample Catalan dishes range form the reliable old standby *truite de patata i cebra* (Spanish omelet with potatoes and onions) to the more unique *escudella barejada* (broth with chunks of veal) and *escargols a la llauna* (snails in oil, thyme, and garlic sauce). An indoor terrace offers fine views. The service is friendly and attentive.

Bisbe Català 10. ℂ 93-204-79-62. Main courses 15€–30€ ($19–$38). AE, DC, MC, V. Mon–Sat 1–3:45pm and 8:30–11:45pm. Closed Sunday and 15 days in August. Metro: Reina Elisenda.

Via Veneto 𝒜𝒜𝒜 CATALAN   Given its consistently well-prepared cuisine and overall class, this uptown restaurant—which has been going strong for around 4 decades—mysteriously tends to fall under the radar. Not that this in any way worries the management, who are busy catering to regulars and visiting sports stars. The name, incidentally, alludes to the *glamoor* associated with the famous Roman boulevard in the mid-1960s (Fellini's notorious Dolce Vita era) and has nothing to do with the style of food, which has its roots firmly in Catalonia. It has a reputation for serving the finest *caza* (game) and fungi around. You might order a silky plate of *rovellons* and *ceps*, both wild mushrooms from the Catalan forests, cooked to perfection in olive oil and rock salt. There's also filet of hare stuffed with foie and served on a bed of baked apples, or Via Veneto's signature duck dish—a whole baby duck is slow roasted, brought to the table, and deboned. The bones are then put through an antique silver press, extracting the flavorsome juice, which accompanies the flesh in a culinary ceremony that seems to belong to another era. The wine list is legendary (and the size of an encyclopedia) so ask José, the amiable sommelier, to recommend one of their coveted Vega Sicilias (if money is no object!) or another of the 10,000 or so bottles they have in their underground bodega. Meals may be finished with a cheese platter or heady dessert combinations such as chocolate mouse spiced with mixed peppers and cinnamon ice cream.

Ganduxer 10. ℂ 93-200-72-44. Reservations required. Main courses 20€–45€ ($25–$56); tasting menu 65€ ($81). AE, DC, MC, V. Mon–Fri 1:15–4pm and 8:30–11:30pm; Sat 8:30–11:30pm. Closed Aug 1–20. Metro: FGC La Bonanova.

11 Out of Town

VERY EXPENSIVE

El Racó de Can Fabes 𝒜𝒜𝒜 MEDITERRANEAN   This is one of the great restaurants of Spain—some consider it the greatest. If you don't mind the 30-minute drive or the 45-minute train ride from Barcelona, a distance of 52km (32 miles), you will be transported to a gourmet citadel, housed in a 3-century-old building in the center of Sant Celoni, a Catalan village of 1,700 people. This Michelin three-star restaurant (its highest rating) is run with exquisite care and dedication. The restaurant is refined and elegant yet retains a rustic aura. One typical example of their inspired dishes is hot and cold mackerel with cream of caviar and tender pigeon with duck tartare. Another heavenly concoction is spicy foie gras with Sauterne and a *coulis* (purée) of sweet red and green peppers. Two different preparations of crayfish, each one a delight, come both raw and cooked. Roast pigeon is prepared in ways that correspond to the seasons and the "mood of the chef." For dessert, there's nothing finer than their "Festival de chocolate."

Sant Joan 6 (Sant Celoni). © 93-867-28-51. Reservations required. Main courses 30€–60€ ($38–$75); tasting menu 130€ ($163). AE, DC, MC, V. Tues–Sat 1:30–3:30pm and 8:30–10:30pm; Sun 1:30–3:30pm. Closed Jan 28–Feb 11 and June 24–July 8. Take any RENFE train from the Passeig de Gràcia station, heading for France, disembarking at Sant Celoni.

EXPENSIVE

Sant Pau 👍👍👍 CATALAN   If Picasso were around today, I'll bet he'd be hitting the culinary trail to the doorstep of Carme Ruscalleda, Spain's leading female chef, who owns this fashionable eating spot in the charming Maresme resort of Sant Pol de Mar, a 45-minute drive north of Barcelona. Even some of the top chefs of France are crossing the Spanish border to sample her cuisine. Michelin grants her two stars, but I feel she richly deserves three. Her virtuoso technique brings finesse to food and even a touch of fantasy to some of her dishes. She has the ability to take the freshest produce and add just the right spice or seasoning to maximize its flavor.

Carrer Nou 10 (Sant. Pol de Mar). © 93-760-06-62. Reservations required. Main courses 35€–55€ ($44–$69). AE, DC, MC, V. Tues–Sun 1:30–3:30pm; Tues–Sat 9–11pm. From Girona, take N-I about 55km (34 miles) south.

What to See & Do

Long a Mediterranean center of commerce, Barcelona is also one of the focal points of European tourism, a role sparked by the 1992 Olympic Games. Spain's second-largest city is also its most cosmopolitan and avant-garde.

Because of its rich history, Barcelona is filled with landmark buildings and world-class museums. These include Antoni Gaudí's famed Sagrada Família, the Museu Picasso, the Gothic cathedral, and La Rambla (also known as Les Ramblas), the multi-faceted tree-lined promenade cutting through the heart of Old Town.

You can also branch out from Barcelona to one of the sites of interest in its environs, including the beaches of Lloret and Tossa de Mar in the north and of Sitges in the south, the monastery at Montserrat, the Penedés vineyards, and the Pyrénées (see chapter 11).

To begin, however, you'll want to take in the artistic and intellectual aura of this unique seafaring city. Residents are justifiably proud of their Catalan heritage, and are eager to share it. Many of these sights can be covered on foot, and chapter 8 includes a walking tour of Old Town.

1 Ciutat Vella (Old City)

The Ciutat Vella (Old City) is where the top attractions are, and if you are short of precious time this is where you will want to spend most of it. The Gothic cathedral, the Roman foundations, the earthy Raval and funky Ribera districts are all located within this large chunk of the city's landscape that, owing to its abundance of one-way and pedestrianized streets, is best visited on foot. It seems a little daunting at first but striking landmarks such as the city's cathedral, the MACBA (Museum of Modern Art), and the Plaça del Rei will help you navigate your way around the maze. To make it easier, I have divided the attractions up into three sub-areas: the Barri Gòtic (east of La Rambla), El Raval (west of La Rambla), and La Ribera (west of Vía Laietana). For more information on these districts, see chapter 4.

BARRI GOTIC 𝄞𝄞𝄞

The old original Gothic Quarter is Barcelona's greatest urban attraction. Most of it has survived intact from the Middle Ages. Spend at least 2 or 3 hours exploring its narrow streets and squares, which form a vibrant, lively neighborhood. A nighttime stroll, when lanes and square are atmospherically lit, takes on added drama. The buildings are austere and sober for the most part, the cathedral being the crowning achievement. Roman ruins and the vestiges of 3rd-century walls add further interest. This area is intricately detailed and filled with many attractions that are easy to miss. (Follow Walking Tour 1, in Chapter 8, for a detailed rundown).

Catedral de Barcelona 𝄞𝄞𝄞   Barcelona's cathedral is a celebrated example of Catalan Gothic architecture. Its spires can be seen from almost all over the Barri Gòtic, and

---

Fun Fact How the Egg Dances

During the feast of Corpus Christi in June, a uniquely Catalan tradition can be seen in the cathedral's cloister. *L'ou com balla* (the egg that dances) consists of an empty egg shell that is placed on top of the fountain's gushes of water and left to "dance." The custom goes back to 1637, although its significance is disputed. Some say that the egg simply represents spring and beginning of a new life cycle, others that its form represents the Eucharist.

---

the large square upon which it resides, the Plaça de la Seu, is one of the neighborhood's main thoroughfares. The elevated site has always been Barcelona's center of worship: Before the present cathedral there was a Roman temple and later a mosque. Construction on the cathedral began at the end of the 13th century, under the reign of Jaume II. (On the exterior of its southern transept, on the Plaça de Sant Lu, there is a portal commemorating beginning of the work.) The bishops of the time ordered a wide, single nave, 28-side chapels, and an apse with an ambulatory behind a high altar. Work was finally completed in the mid–15th century (although the west facade dates from the 19th c.). The nave, cleaned and illuminated, has some splendid Gothic details. With its large bell towers, blending of medieval and Renaissance styles, high altar, handsomely sculptured choir, and Gothic arches, it ranks as one of the most impressive cathedrals in Spain. The most interesting chapel is the Cappella de Sant Benet, behind the altar with its magnificent 15th-century interpretation of the crucifixion by Bernat Martorell. It is the cloister, however, that enthralls most visitors. Consisting of vaulted galleries enhanced by iron grilles, it is filled with orange, medlar, and palm trees and features a mossy central pond and fountain, and is (inexplicably) home to a gaggle of white geese. Underneath the well-worn slabs of its stone floor, key members of the Barri Gòtic's ancient guilds are buried. The historian Cirici called this "the loveliest oasis in Barcelona." On its northern side, the cathedral's chapter house occupies the museum whose highlight is the 15th-century *La Pietat* of Bartolomé Bermejo. Another pocket of the cathedral that is worth seeking out is the alabaster sarcophagus of Santa Eulàlia, the co-patroness of the city. The martyr, allegedly a virgin daughter of a well-to-do Barcelona family, was burned at the stake by the Roman governor for refusing to renounce her Christian beliefs. You can take an elevator to the roof where you get a wonderful view of Gothic Barcelona, but only Monday through Saturday. At noon on Sunday, you can see the *sardana,* a Catalonian folk dance, performed in front of the cathedral.

Plaça de la Seu s/n. ℂ **93-315-15-54.** Free admission to cathedral; museum 1€ ($1.25). Elevator to roof: 10:30am–1:30pm and 5–6pm, 2€ ($2.50). Global ticket for 1–4:30pm guided visit to museum, choir, rooftop terraces, and towers 4€ ($5). Cathedral daily 9am 1pm and 5 7pm; cloister museum daily 10am–1pm and 4–6.30pm. Metro: Jaume I or Liceu.

Conjunt Monumental de la Plaça del Rei (Museu d'Història de la Ciutat and Palau Reial Major) ✸✸✸

These two museums are viewed as a double act, and both reside in Plaça del Rei, which is nestled underneath a remaining section of the old city walls. Visitors enter through the Casa Clariana Padellàs, a Gothic mansion that was originally located on the nearby Career Mercaders and was moved here when the construction of the Vía Laietana ripped though the Barri Gòtic in the early 1930s. The ground floor is dedicated to temporary exhibitions on Iberian and Mediterranean

Barcelona Attractions

CaixaForum **47**
Casa Amatller **12**
Casa Batlló **11**
Casa Lleó Morera **13**
Catedral de Barcelona **26**
Centre de Cultura
   Contemporània (CCCB) **15**
CosmoCaixa
   (Museu de la Ciència) **2**
Foment d'les Arts
   Decoratives (FAD) **17**
Fundació Antoni Tàpies **10**
Fundació Francisco Godia **9**
Fundació Joan Miró **45**
Galería Olímpica **42**
Gran Teatre del Liceu **39**
L'Aquarium de Barcelona **34**
La Hospital de la
   Santa Creu i San Pau **2**
La Mercè **35**
La Pedrera **7**
La Sagrada Família **5**
Mercat del Born **21**
Mirador de Colón **37**
Museu Barbier-Mueller
   Art Precolombí **30**
Museu d'Arqueologia
   de Catalunya **46**
Museu d'Art Contemporani
   de Barcelona (MACBA) **16**
Museu de Calçat **25**
Museu de Carrosses Fúnebres **14**
Museu de Ciències Naturals
   de la Ciutadella **22**
Museu de la Cera **36**
Museu de la Xocolata **23**
Museu de L'Esport
   Dr. Melcior Colet **3**
Museu d'Història de
   Catalunya **33**
Museu d'Història de
   la Ciutat **19**
Museu d'Textil i
   d' Indumentària **31**
Museu Egipci de Barcelona **8**
Museu Etnológic **44**
Museu FC Barcelona **1**
Museu Frederic Marès **24**
Museu Marítim **32**
Museu Militar de Montjuïc
   (Castell de Montjuïc) **43**
Museu Nacional d'Art de
   Catalunya (MNAC) **49**
Museu Picasso **29**
Museu Tauri **6**
Old Synagogue **28**
Palau de la Música Catalana **20**
Palau de la Virreina **18**
Palau Güell **38**
Palau Reial **19**
Parc Güell **4**
Plaça Sant Jaume **27**
Poble Espanyol **48**
Santa Maria del Pí **40**
Sant Pau del Camp **41**
Torre Agbar **6**

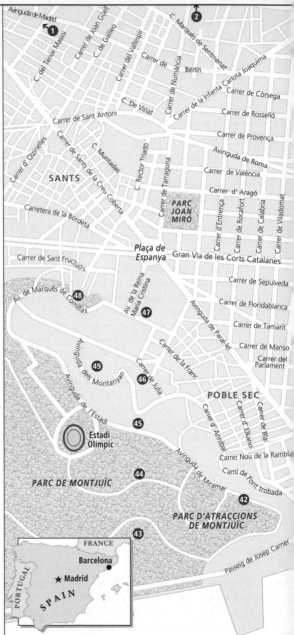

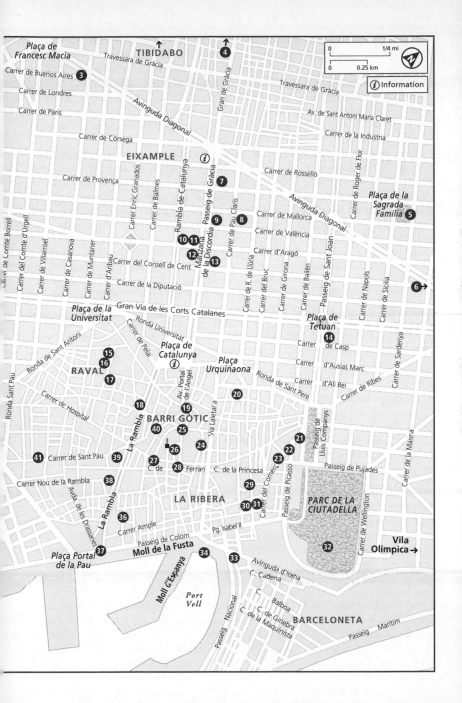

Plaça de
Francesc Macia

↑
TIBIDABO

Travessara de Gràcia

Carrer de Buenos Aires **3**

Carrer de Londres

Carrer de Paris

Avinguda Diagonal

Gran de Gràcia

4

Travessara de Gràcia

Av. de Sant Antoni Maria Claret

Carrer de la Industria

Carrer de Còrsega

EIXAMPLE *i*

Carrer de Rosselló

Carrer de Provença

Carrer Enric Granados

Carrer de Balmes

Rambla de Catalunya

Passeig de Gràcia

7

Avinguda Diagonal

Carrer de Roger de Flor

Plaça de la
Sagrada
Família **5**

Carrer de Pau Claris

9 **8**

Carrer de Mallorca

Carrer de València

Carrer d'Aragó

Carrer de Comte Borrell

Carrer del Comte d'Urgell

Carrer de Villarroel

Carrer de Casanova

Carrer de Muntaner

Carrer d'Aribau

10 11

Manzana de la Discòrdia

12

Carrer del Consell de Cent

13

Carrer de la Diputació

Carrer de R. de Llúria

Carrer del Bruc

Carrer de Girona

Carrer de Bailèn

Passeig de Sant Joan

Carrer de Nàpols

Carrer de Sicília

6 →

Plaça de la
Universitat

Gran Via de les Corts Catalanes

Ronda Universitat

Carrer de Pelai

Plaça de
Tetuan

14

Carrer   de Casp

Ronda de Sant Antoni

Plaça de
Catalunya
i

Plaça
Urquinaona

20

Carrer   d'Ausias Marc

Carrer   d'Ali Bei

Carrer de Sardenya

RAVAL

15
16

17

Carrer de Hospital

Av. Portal de l'Angel

Ronda de Sant Pere

Carrer de Ribes

Ronda de Sant Pau

18

BARRI GÒTIC

19

Via Laietana

Passeig de Lluís Companys

Carrer de la Marina

La Rambla

40   **25**

26

24

21

22

23

41 Carrer de Sant Pau **39**

27

28 Ferran

C. de la Princesa

Passeig de Pujades

Carrer Nou de la Rambla

38

C. de

29

PARC DE LA
CIUTADELLA

Avda. de les Drassanes

La Rambla

36

Carrer Ample

LA RIBERA

30 31

Passeig del Comerç

Passeig de Picasso

Vila
Olímpica →

Plaça Portal
de la Pau

37

Passeig de Colom
Moll de la Fusta

34

33

Pg. Isabel II

32

Carrer de Wellington

Moll d'Espanya

Port
Vell

Avinguda d'Icaria
C. Cadena

C.   Balboa

C. de Ginebra

C. de la Maquinista

BARCELONETA

Passeig   Maritim

Passeig   Nacional

culture with a permanent virtual-reality display on the history of the city. The highlight, however, lies underground, underneath the Plaça del Rei itself. Excavation work carried out for the relocation of the Casa Clariana Padellàs unearthed a large section of Barcino, the old Roman city. Workers unearthed a forum, streets, squares, family homes, shops, and even laundries and huge vats used for wine production. A clever network of walkways has been built over the relics, allowing you to fully appreciate the ebb and flow of daily life in old Barcino. Be on the lookout for a handful of beautiful mosaics, *in situ,* of what is left of family homes.

The visit continues aboveground in the medieval Royal Palace. The complex dates back to the 10th century, when it was the palace of the counts of Barcelona, then later became the residence of the kings of Aragón. The top step of its sweeping entrance is supposedly where King Ferdinand and Queen Isabella received Columbus after he returned from the New World. Immediately inside, the palace's chapel, the Capella de Santa Agüeda, is also used for temporary exhibitions. Adjacent to the chapel is the Saló del Tinell, a key work of the period featuring the largest stone arches to be found anywhere in Europe. Another palace highlight is the Mirador del Rei Martí (King Martin's Watchtower). Constructed in 1555, it is a later addition to the palace but in many ways one of its most interesting. King Martin was the last of the line of the city's count-kings, and this five-story tower was built to keep an eye on foreign invasions and peasant uprisings that often took place in the square below.

Plaça del Rei s/n. ✆ **93-315-11-11.** Admission 4€ ($5) adults, 2.50€ ($3.10) students, free for children under 16. June–Sept Tues–Sat 10am–8pm; Oct–May Tues–Sat 10am–2pm and 4–8pm; year-round Sun 10am–3pm. Metro: Liceu or Jaume I.

La Mercè The church of La Mercè is dear to the heart of the people of Barcelona. Our Lady of Mercy (La Mercè) is the city's patron saint; she earned the privilege after supposedly warding off a plague of locusts in 1637. Thus the city's main fiesta (Sept 24) is named in her honor and many Barcelona-born females are called Mercè (among males there is an abundance of Jordis—or George—Catalonia's patron saint).

The church itself is the only one in the city with a baroque facade. Perched on top is a statue of the lady La Mercè, a key feature of the city's skyline. The edifice resides on an elegant square with a central fountain of Neptune.

Plaça de la Mercè 1. ✆ **93-315-27-56.** Free admission. Daily 10am–1pm and 6–8pm. Metro: Drassanes.

Mirador de Colón This monument to Christopher Columbus was erected at the Barcelona harbor on the occasion of the Universal Exhibition of 1888. It consists of three parts, the first being a circular structure raised by four stairways (6m/20 ft. wide) and eight iron heraldic lions. On the plinth are eight bronze bas-reliefs depicting Columbus's principal feats. (These are copies; the originals were destroyed.) Next is the base of the column, consisting of an eight-sided polygon, four sides of which act as buttresses; each side contains sculptures. The third part is the 50m (164-ft.) column, which is Corinthian in style. It has representations of Europe, Asia, Africa, and America—all linked together. Finally, over a princely crown and a hemisphere recalling the newly discovered part of the globe, is a 7.5m-high (25-ft.) bronze statue of Columbus—pointing supposedly to the New World, but in reality toward the Balearic islands—by Rafael Ataché. Inside the iron column, a tiny elevator ascends to the *mirador.* From here, a panoramic view of Barcelona and its harbor unfolds.

Portal de la Pau s/n. ✆ **93-302-52-24.** Admission 2.40€ ($3) adults, 1.40€ ($1.75) children 4–12, free for children under 4. June–Sept 9am–8:30pm; Oct–May 10am–6:30pm. Metro: Drassanes.

Museu de la Cera *(Kids)* Madame Tussaud's it may not be, but Barcelona's Wax Museum still has plenty of appeal. Located in a 19th-century building that used to be a bank, the winding staircase and frescoes are a fitting setting for the array of Catalan and Spanish historical and cultural personages, plus Dracula, Frankenstein, and the usual suspects. Next door, the museum's cafe El Bosc de les Fades is fitted out "fairy forest" style with magic mirrors, bubbling brooks, and secret doors, further adding to the fantastical experience.

Passatge de la Banca 7. (€) **93-317-26-49.** Admission 6.65€ ($8.25) adults; 3.75€ ($4.70) children 5–11, students, and seniors. Oct–June Mon–Fri 10am–1:30pm and 4–7:30pm, Sat–Sun and holidays 11am–2pm and 4:30–8:30pm; July–Sept daily 10am–10pm. Metro: Drassanes.

Museu Frederic Marès *(RR)* One of the biggest repositories of medieval sculpture in the region is this interesting museum, situated just behind the cathedral. Marès was a sculptor and obsessive collector, and the fruit of this passion is housed in an ancient palace with beautiful interior courtyards, chiseled stone, and soaring ceilings. He amassed a simply mind-boggling collection of religious sculpture and imagery. Downstairs, the pieces date from the 3rd and 4th centuries, then travel through to the fixating poly-chromatic crucifixes and statues of the Virgin Mary from the Romanesque and Gothic periods. Upstairs, the collection continues into the baroque and Renaissance before becoming the so-called Museu Sentimental, a collection of everyday items and para-phernalia that illustrate life in Barcelona during the past 2 centuries. The Entertain-ment Room features toys and automatons, and the Women's Quarter has Victorian fans, combs, and other objects deemed for "feminine use only." Outside, the **Café d'Estiu** in the courtyard is an agreeable place to rest before moving on.

Plaça de Sant Iú 5–6. (€) **93-310-58-00.** www.museumares.bcn.es. Admission 3€ ($3.75) adults, free for children under 12. Tues–Sat 10am–7pm; Sun 10am–3pm. Free Wed 3–7pm. Metro: Jaume I.

Plaça Sant Jaume *(R)* The Plaça Sant Jaume is the political nerve center of Barcelona. Separated by a wide expanse of polished flagstones, the Casa de la Ciutat, home to the *ajuntament* (town hall), faces the Palau de la Generalitat, seat of Catalo-nia's autonomous government. The square itself frequently acts as a stage for protest gatherings, rowdy celebrations (such as when a local team wins a sporting event), and local traditions like the spectacular *castellers* (human towers).

The buildings are infrequently open to the public, but if you do happen to be here whey they're open, definitely check out the **Palau de la Generalitat** *(RR)*. Although the governing body of Catalonia has its origins in 1283, under the reign of Pere II, it wasn't until the 15th century that it was given a permanent home. The nucleus spreads out from the **Pati de Tarongers (Courtyard of Orange Trees),** an elegant interior patio with pink Renaissance columns topped with gargoyles of historical Catalan folk-loric figures.

Another highlight is the **Capella de Sant Jordi (Chapel of St. George),** which is resplendent with furnishings and objects depicting the legend of Catalonia's patron saint, whose image is a recurring theme throughout the Generalitat. The walls of the Gilded Hall are covered with 17th-century Flemish tapestries.

Across the square is the late-14th-century **Casa de la Ciutat** *(R)*, corridor of power of the *ajuntament.* Behind its neoclassical facade is a prime example of Gothic civil architecture in the Catalan Mediterranean style. The building has a splendid court-yard and staircase. Its major architectural highlights are the 15th-century Salón de Ciento (Room of the 100 Jurors) with gigantic arches supporting a beamed ceiling and the black marble Salón de las Crónicas (Room of the Chronicles). The murals here were painted in 1928 by Josep Maria Sert, the Catalan artist who went on to decorate the Rockefeller Center in New York.

Capella de Sant Jordi: Plaça de Sant Jaume s/n. ⓒ **93-402-46-17.** Free admission. 2nd and last Sun of each month, Apr 25, and Sept 24 10:30am–1:30pm. Casa de la Ciutat: Plaça de Sant Jaume s/n. ⓒ **93-402-70-00.** Free admission. Sun 11am–3:30pm. Metro: Jaume I or Liceu.

Santa Maria del Pi This church takes its name from the huge pine tree outside its main entrance. The church, built between the early 14th and late 16th centuries, resides on one of the most charming squares (of the same name) in the Barri Gòtic. There is always something happening on the square (which in effect merges into two other tiny plazas) whether it is an art market (Sun), a local cheese and artisan fair run by food hawkers (Thurs–Sat), street musicians strutting their stuff, or people milling around the plentiful outdoor cafes.

The church itself is a typical, if not the most complete, example of Catalan Gothic. Its wide, single nave spans nearly two-thirds of the building's length, lending the church its squat appearance. Above the main entrance is a gigantic rose window. Inside it's just as austere, although worth inspecting for the ingenious stone arch that has supported the structure's width for centuries.

Plaça del Pi 7. ⓒ **93-318-47-43.** Free admission. Daily 9am–1pm and 4–9pm. Metro: Liceu.

LA RIBERA

Smaller than the Barri Gòtic, La Ribera district boasts two major attractions: the Picasso Museum and the soaring Gothic church of Santa María del Mar. Additional smaller treasures abound in its atmospheric streets in the form of cafes, artisan workshops, and intimate boutiques. It's a wonderful place to stroll, window-shop, and grab a bite, and compact enough to cover in an afternoon. At night the bars and *coctelerías* open their doors and crowds roll in.

El Palau de la Música Catalana 𝄪𝄪𝄪 Not strictly within the borders of La Ribera but north of the Calle Princesa in the La Pere district, the Palau de la Música is, for many, the most outstanding contribution of the *modernista* movement. Declared a UNESCO World Heritage Site in 1997, it was designed by Lluis Domènech i Montaner—a contemporary of Gaudí—who was also responsible for the magnificent Hospital Sant Pau (p. 174).

In 1891 it was decided that the Orfeó Catalan (Catalan Coral Society) needed a permanent home. The Orfeó was a key player in La Renaixença, a heady political and cultural climate of renewed Catalan nationalism and artistic endeavor (with the two closely intertwined). The Orfeó, which still regularly performs at the Palau, had been touring Catalan rural areas, performing *catalanismo*-charged folk songs to much acclaim. The general opinion was that they deserved their own "Palace of Music." Domènech i Montaner obliged.

A riot of symbolism, the Palau de la Música Catalana, constructed between 1905 and 1908, is a feast for the senses. The facade features a rippling sculpture representing popular Catalan song and is crowned by an allegorical mosaic of the Orfeó underneath which reside busts of composers such as Bach, Beethoven, and the period's most popular composer, Wagner. The foyer is linked to the street by an arcade and features dazzling columns of mosaic. It is the first-floor auditorium, however, where the excesses of *modernisme* run wild. Using the finest craftsmen of the day, Domènech i Montaner ordered

El Call: The Jewish Quarter

Before the Catholic Monarchs Ferdinand and Isabella systematically set about persecuting all Jewish communities in Iberia in the late 15th century, Barcelona's Jews had lived harmoniously for centuries alongside Christians and enjoyed special status under the city's autonomous rule. Barcelona's Sephardic Jews flourished in the Middle Ages, reaching four million people in the 13th century—15% of the total population of the city. They were respected for their financial expertise, understanding of the law, and learned figures, including poet Ben Ruben Izahac and the astronomer Abraham Xija. The community resided in the city neighborhood El Call (pronounced "kye") reputedly from the Hebrew word *kahal,* which means "community" or "congregation." The area was bordered by the old walls to the west and east, and its entrance was through the Plaça Sant Jaume. Today this tiny, ancient neighborhood is marked by atmospheric, narrow streets with 14th- to 16th-century buildings, some with vestiges of its former residents. The largest and most complete is the main synagogue in Calle Marlet, no. 5. Consisting of two cellar-like rooms below street level, the space was virtually unknown, serving as a warehouse until 1995 when the building with its four floors added on top was put up for sale. It was acquired by the Asociación Call de Barcelona (see below), which embarked on a meticulous process of renovation.

On the same street, in the direction of the Arc de Sant Ramón, is a wall plaque dating from 1314 bearing the inscription (in Hebrew) "Holy Foundation of Rabbi Samuel Hassardi, whose life is never ending." The remains of the female Jewish public baths can be seen nearby in the basement of the pleasant Café Caleum at the intersection of the streets Banys Nous (which means "New Baths") and Palla. The men's baths are hidden in the rear of the furniture shop S'Olivier (Banys Nous 10), although you need to ask permission from the owner to take a peek.

Old Synagogue and Asociación Call de Barcelona: Marlet 5. ℭ **93-317-07-90.** Free admission. Hours are Tuesday through Sunday 11am to 2:30pm and 4 to 7:30pm. Metro: Jaume I or Liceu.

almost every surface to be embellished with the most extraordinary detail. The ceiling features a stained-glass inverted dome with the auditorium's main light source, surrounded by 40 female heads, representing a choir. On the stage's rear wall are the *Muses del Palau,* a series of dainty, instrument-bearing maidens in terra cotta and *trencadis* (broken mosaic collage). The *pièce de résistance* is the proscenium that frames the stages. Executed by Pau Gargallo, on the left it features the Orfeó's director, Josep Clavé, bursting forth from the "Flowers of May," a tree representing a popular Catalan folk song. On the opposite side, Beethoven peeks through a stampede of Wagner's Valkyries.

In 2003 local architect Oscar Tusquets completed his sensitive extension of El Palau, providing extra rehearsal space, a library, and another, underground auditorium. It is worth checking their program when in town; concerts range from international orchestras and soloists to jazz and sometimes world music. Tickets for local acts are often very reasonably priced. If not, there are daily tours of the building; see below. Advance purchase for these is recommended.

Career de Sant Francesc de Paula 2. ℭ **93-295-72-00** for information, or 902-442-882 to buy tickets. Tour 8€ ($10) adults, 7€ ($8.75) students. Tickets can be bought up to 1 week in advance from the gift shop adjacent to the building. Guided tours daily, every half-hour 10am–3:30pm. Metro: Urquinaona.

Mercat del Born   At the end of the Passeig del Born, the pretty promenade that is the heart of the neighborhood is the Mercat del Born, the city's steel-and-glass ode to the industrial age. Inspired by Les Halles in Paris, it acted as the city's wholesale market until 1973, and its closing marked the beginning of the neighborhood's decline before its current renaissance. Having lain abandoned for over 3 decades, a decision was made in 2003 to turn the edifice into a library and cultural center. When the renovation work started, the remains of entire streets and homes from Phillipe V's demolition orders (see Parc de la Ciutadella, below) were discovered underneath. Work still continues at the time of writing and includes plans to see these significant remains via glass flooring.

Carrer Comerç s/n. Interior closed to public.

Museu Barbier-Mueller Art Precolombí ℛ   Inaugurated in 1997, this museum is a smaller cousin to the museum of the same name in Geneva, which is one of the most important collections of pre-Columbian art in the world. In the restored Palacio Nadal, which was built during the Gothic period, the collection contains almost 6,000 pieces of tribal and ancient art. Josef Mueller (1887–1977) acquired the first pieces by 1908. The pre-Columbian cultures represented created religious, funerary, and ornamental objects of great stylistic variety with relatively simple means. Stone sculpture and ceramic objects are especially outstanding. For example, the Olmecs, who settled on the Gulf of Mexico at the beginning of the 1st millennium B.C., executed notable monumental sculpture in stone and magnificent figures in jade. Many exhibits focus on the Mayan culture, the most homogenous and widespread of its time, dating from 1000 B.C. Mayan artisans mastered painting, ceramics, and sculpture. Note the work by the pottery makers of the lower Amazon, particularly those from the island of Marajó, and the millennium-old gold adornments from northern Peru.

Carrer de Montcada 12–14. ℭ **93-310-45-16**. Admission 3€ ($3.75) adults, 1.50€ ($1.85) students, free for children under 16. Tues–Sat 10am–6pm; Sun 10am–3pm. Free on 1st Sun of the month. Metro: Jaume I.

Museu de Ciències Naturals de la Ciutadella (Geologia and Zoologia)
These two museums, which can be viewed with the same ticket, reside inside the elegant Parc de la Ciutadella (see below). The most crowd-pleasing is the **Museu de Zoologia** ℛ, which is housed in a whimsical building designed by the *moderniste* architect Lluis Domènech i Montaner. It was created (but not finished in time) as a cafe for the 1887-to-1888 World's Fair, which was largely centered around the park. Known at the time as the **Castell de Tres Dragons (Castle of the Three Dragons),** it is a daring example of medieval-inspired *modernisme* with fortress-like towers featuring ceramic heraldry, Mudéjar windows, and walls of exposed brick. Inside, although extremely altered, exhibits are displayed in Victorian-style wooden and glass cabinets. Specimens include Goliath frogs, giant crabs, and a section on Catalan flora. Located in a colonnaded neoclassical structure, the setting for the Geological Museum is slightly less inspiring. It was, however, the first building in the city to be constructed specifically for a museum, and it still holds the largest geology collection in the country. The left wing

displays various granites, quartzes, and naturally radioactive rocks. The more interesting right wing contains fossils with some nostalgic Jules Verne–type illustrations made in the 1950s, which depict prehistoric life.

Parc de la Ciutadella, Passeig Picasso 1. ⓒ **93-319-68-95** (Museu de Geologia) or ⓒ **93-319-69-12** (Museu de la Zoologia). Admission (for both) 3.50€ ($4.35) adults, free for children under 16. Tues–Sat 10am–7pm; Sun 10am–3pm. Metro: Barceloneta or Arc de Triomf.

Museu de la Xocolata ⚐ *Kids*   Opened in 2000 in a former convent, this museum is an initiative from the city's chocolate and pastry makers. More like a giant, hands-on textbook, the exhibition takes you through the discovery of the cocoa bean by New World explorers and its commercialization, and depicts chocolate as an art form. Every Easter, the museum is the venue for the annual *mona* competition. *Monas*, a Catalan invention, are elaborate chocolate sculptures, often of famous buildings, people, or cartoon characters. Chocolate makers display them in their windows during Easter week and try to outdo each other with sheer creativity and inventiveness. Once your appetite has been whetted, you can enjoy a cup of hot chocolate or pick up some bonbons at the museum's cafe.

Antic Convent de Sant Augustí, Comerç 36. ⓒ **93-268-78-78**. Admission 3.80€ ($4.75), free for children under 7. Mon–Sat 10am–7pm; Sun 10am–3pm. Metro: Jaume I or Arc de Triomf.

Museu d' Textil i d' Indumentària   Located in the stunning Palau dels Marquesos de Lló, a Gothic mansion adjacent to the Museu Barbier-Mueller Art Precolombí (see above), the city's textile museum is a slightly slapdash but overall interesting permanent display of fabric and lace-making techniques and costumes. The first floor covers periods from the Gothic through to Regency, the latter consisting of crinoline skirts with bone-crushing bodices plus a wonderful selection of fans and opera glasses. Upstairs you find the 20th-century exhibits, which include ensembles from the Basque-born creator Cristóbel Balenciaga, as well as Paco Rabanne and Barcelona's own Pedro Rodríguez. Temporary exhibitions have ranged from Catalan jewelry to the outfits of Australian *enfant terrible* performer Leigh Bowery. There are a great cafe in the courtyard and an above-average gift shop.

Montcada 12–14. ⓒ **93-319-76-03**. Admission 3.50€ ($4.40) adults, free for children under 16. Tues–Sat 10am–6pm; Sun 10am–3pm. Metro: Jaume I.

Museu Picasso ⚐⚐⚐   Five medieval mansions on this street contain this museum of the work of Pablo Picasso (1881–1973). The bulk of the art was donated by Jaume Sabartés y Gual, a lifelong friend of the artist. Although born in Malaga, Picasso moved to the Catalan capital in 1895 after his father was awarded a teaching job at the city's Fine Arts Academy in La Llotja. The family settled in the Calle Merce and when Picasso was a bit older, he moved to the Nou de Les Ramblas in the Barrio Chino. Although he left Spain for good at the outbreak of the Civil War—and refused to return while Franco was in power—he was particularly fond of Barcelona, where he spent his formative years painting its seedier side and hanging around with the city's bohemians. As a sign of his love for the city, and adding to Sabartés enormous bequest, Picasso donated some 2,500 of his paintings, engravings, and drawings to the museum in 1970. All of these were executed in his youth (in fact, some of the paintings were done when he was only 9), and the collection is particularly strong on his Blue and Rose Periods. Many works show the artist's debt to van Gogh, El Greco, and Rembrandt.

The highlight of the collection is undoubtedly *Las Meninas,* a series of 59 interpretations of Velázquez's masterpiece. Another key work is *The Harlequin,* a painting clearly influenced by the time the artist spent with the Ballet Russes in Paris. It was his first bequest to Barcelona. In addition to the key works here, many visitors are transfixed by his notebooks containing dozens of sketches of Barcelona street scenes and characters—proof of his extraordinary and often overlooked drawing talents. Because the works are arranged in rough chronological order, you can get a wonderful sense of Picasso's development and watch as he discovered a trend or had a new idea, mastered it, grew bored with it, and then was off to something new. You'll learn that Picasso was a master portraitist and did many traditional representational works before his flights of fancy took off. The exhibits in the final section ("The Last Years") were donated by his widow Jacqueline and include ceramic and little-known collage work.

Montcada 15–23. ⓒ **93-319-63-10.** Admission 5€ ($6.25) adults, 2.50€ ($3.10) students and those under 25, free for children under 16. Tues–Sat 10am–8pm; Sun 10am–3pm. Metro: Jaume I, Liceu, or Arc de Triomf.

Parc de la Ciutadella 𝕽𝕽

Barcelona's most formal park is also the one most steeped in history. The area was formerly a loathed citadel, built by Phillip V after he won the War of the Spanish Succession (Barcelona was on the losing side). He ordered that the "traitorous" residential suburb be leveled. Between 1715 and 1718, over 60 streets and residences were torn down to make way for the structure, without any compensation to the owners (although many were relocated to the neighborhood of Barceloneta). It never really functioned as a citadel, but was used as a political prison during subsequent uprisings and occupations. Once the decision to pull down the old city walls was made in 1858, the government decided that the citadel should go, too. Work on the park began in 1872, and in 1887 and 1888 the World's Fair was held on its grounds, with the nearby Arc de Triomf serving as the event's grandiose main entrance.

Today lakes, gardens, and promenades fill most of the park, which also holds a **zoo** (see below). Gaudí contributed to the monumental, Italianate fountain in the park when he was a student; the lampposts are also his. Other highlights include the Hivernacle, an elegant, English-style hothouse with an adjacent cafe and the unusual Umbracle, a glasshouse that contains no glass but whose facades are of bare brick with wooden louvers. Both these structures are on the Passeig de Picasso flank of the park. On the opposite side bordering Calle Wellington is the old arsenal, which now accommodates the parliament of Catalonia.

Entrances on the Passeig de Picasso and Passeig Pujades. Daily sunrise–sunset. Metro: Arc de Triomf.

Parc Zoològic 𝕽 𝓚𝓲𝓭𝓼

A large hunk of the Parc de la Ciutadella is taken up with the city's zoo. Until recently, the main attraction was Copito de Nieve (Snowflake), the only albino gorilla in captivity in the world. He died of skin cancer in 2003, but left behind a large family of children and grandchildren, none of whom fortunately (or unfortunately for the scientific world) inherited his condition. Despite the zoo's losing its star attraction, there are still plenty of other reasons for visiting, not least being the pleasant (at least for humans) leafy garden setting. Many of the enclosures are barless and the animals kept in place via a moat. This seems humane until you realize how little running space the creatures actually have at their disposal on their "islands." To be fair, Barcelona's zoo is probably a lot more progressive than many other zoos on the Continent, and unless you are of the firm belief that there is no such thing as a "good" zoo, you, and especially children, will delight at the mountain goats, llamas, lions, bears, hippos, huge primate community, and dozens of other species. There are also a dolphin show, sizable reptile enclosure, and an exhibition on the extinction of gorillas in Snowflake's memory, from the time he was captured in Equatorial Guinea in 1966 through his rise to celebrity status as the city's mascot.

Parc de la Ciutadella. (©) **93-225-67-80**. Admission 14€ ($18) adults, 8.50€ ($11) students and children 3–12. Summer daily 10am–7pm; off season daily 10am–6pm. Metro: Ciutadella or Arc de Triomf.

EL RAVAL

El Raval is a neighborhood of contrasts. Here, imaginative new buildings and urban projects are being created in the streets of the city's largest inner-city neighborhood. Historically working class, the district is clearly being gentrified in many areas, while other neglected corners are still markedly downtrodden. For many, El Raval symbolizes progressive 21st-century Barcelona with a new polyglot blend of Catalan, Arabic, Middle Eastern, and South American cultures evident at every turn.

Centre de Cultura Contemporània (CCCB)   Adjacent to the MACBA (see below), the CCCB is a temporary exhibition space located in what was a 19th-century poorhouse. The building has been ingeniously adapted to its current function. The extension is an impressive structure with sheer glass exterior walls supporting a large mirror that reflects the surrounding rooftops. You enter it via a pretty courtyard, and there is an exterior garden that has an outside cafeteria.

Exhibitions here tend to focus on writers and the world of literature or cultural/political movements such as situationism or Parisian surrealism. The setting is inundated in mid-June when **Sonar,** the annual dance music festival, stages its daytime events here, and other mini-festivals such as alternative film and the plastic arts are also part of its vibrant calendar.

Montalegre 5. (©) **93-306-41-00**. Admission 6.50€ ($8.10) adults, 4€ ($5) students, free for children under 14. Tues and Thurs–Fri 11am–2pm and 4–8pm; Wed and Sat 11am–8pm; Sun and holidays 11am–7pm. Metro: Catalunya or Universitat.

Foment de les Arts Decoratives i del Disseny (FAD)   FAD is the 100-year-old engine that drives the city's active design culture, in charge of dishing out design and architecture awards and grants and promoting its artists to Spain and the rest of the world. Its headquarters, easily identifiable by the huge steel letters spelling its name outside the main entrance, are in a converted Gothic convent opposite the MACBA, and continuous exhibitions are held in the exposed brick nave. These range from the winners of their various competitions to everyday, utilitarian objects from around the world. Fun stuff includes the Tallers Oberts, where artisans of the Raval throw open their workshops to the public, and *mercadillos* where young designers sell their wares at cut-rate prices.

Plaça dels Angels. (©) **93-443-75-20**. Free admission Mon–Sat 11am–8pm. Metro: Catalunya or Universitat.

Gran Teatre del Liceu   Barcelona's opera house, El Liceu, opened to great fanfare in 1847, and again in 2000 when a new and improved version was finished after a devastating fire destroyed the original 6 years before. During its first life, El Liceu had been a symbol of the city's bourgeoisie, often provoking the wrath of the proletariat. (A telling note is that in 1893, an anarchist threw two bombs from a first-floor balcony into the audience, killing 22 people.) It was the principal venue for the Wagnerian craze that swept the city in the late 19th century. During its second incarnation, El Liceu consolidated its reputation as one of the finest opera houses in the

world. The original design—based on La Scala in Milan—had a seating capacity of almost 4,000. The 1994 fire (started by sparks from the blowtorch of a stage worker) destroyed everything but the facade and members' room. The subsequent renovation saw the demolition of neighboring buildings for new rehearsal space and workrooms (much to the horror of neighborhood-action groups, provoking a further backlash), and the auditorium returned to its former gilt, red velvet, and marble glory. Tickets to the concerts, at least the evening performances, are quite expensive but, as with the Palau de la Música, tours of the edifice are available.

La Rambla 51–59. (② **93-485-99-00**. Guided tours depend on season. Information available at the Espai Liceu, the theater's bookshop and cafe in the foyer. Metro: Liceu.

Museu d'Art Contemporani de Barcelona (MACBA) 🌆🌆   A soaring white edifice in the once-shabby but rebounding Raval district, the Museum of Contemporary Art is to Barcelona what the Pompidou Center is to Paris. Designed by the American architect Richard Meier, the building is a work of art in itself, manipulating sunlight to offer brilliant, natural interior lighting. The permanent collection, which is expanding all the time, exhibits the work of modern international luminaries such as Broodthaers, Klee, Basquiat, and many others. Most of the museum, however, has been allotted to Catalan artistic movements, like the **Grup del Treball,** who were a bunch of reactionaries producing conceptual art criticizing Franco's dictatorship with enormous documents promoting independence for Catalonia. Photographs by Oriol Maspons and Leonardo Pómes illustrate Barcelona street life and the bohemians of the Gauche Divine (Divine Left) in the '70s. **Dau al Set,** a surrealist movement led by the brilliant "visual poet" Joan Brossa, meanwhile, provokes thought and reflection through the juxtaposition of everyday items. Catalonia's most famous contemporary artists, Tàpies and Barceló, are both represented. Temporary exhibitions highlight international artists or a monographic show on a particular city or political movement. The museum has a library, bookshop, and cafeteria. Outside, the enormous square has become a meeting place for locals and international skateboarders who make use of the MACBA's sleek ramp, presumably with the management's blessing.

Plaça dels Angels 1. (② **93-412-08-10**. Admission 8.50€ ($11) adults, 6€ ($7.50) students, free for children under 14. Wed only 3€ ($3.75). Mon and Wed–Fri 11am–7:30pm; Sat 10am–8pm; Sun 10am–3pm. Metro: Catalunya or Universitat.

Palau Güell 🌆🌆   This mansion is an important early work of Antoni Gaudí. Built between 1885 and 1889, it was the first major commission the architect received from Eusebi Güell, the wealthy industrialist who went onto become Gaudí's lifelong friend and patron.

A plot was chosen just off Les Ramblas in the lower Raval district, more for its close proximity to Güell's father's residence than anything else, and Gaudí was given carte blanche. Although much of the marble for the town house was supplied by Güell's own quarry, it is said that his accountants criticized the architect on more than one occasion for his heavy-handed spending. However, Sr. Güell himself, as much a lover of the arts as Gaudí was, wished to impress his family and Barcelona's high society with an extravagant showpiece. He got his wish. Sometimes heavy-handed in detail, the work's genius lies in its layout and inspired interconnected spaces.

The facade of the building is Venetian in style and marked by two huge arched entrances protected by intricate forged iron gates and a shield of Catalonia, lending it a fortress-like appearance. The interior of the Palau Güell can only be viewed by guided tour. First you'll see the basement stables, which feature the nature-obsessed architect's signature columns with mushroom capitals, then you ascend again to view the interconnected floors. The first, the anteroom, is in fact four salons. Most of the surfaces are dark, lending the rooms a heaviness, with Moorish-style detailing predominant throughout. Lightness comes in the form of an ingenious system that filters natural light via a constellation of perforated stars inlaid in a parabolic dome above the central hall. Also outstanding is the screened, street-facing gallery that sweeps the entire length of the facade, letting light into all salons except the "ladies room," where female visitors did their touchups before being received by Sr. Güell. The ceilings of the first floor, in oak and bulletwood, are beautifully decorated with foliage, starting off as buds in the first room and in full bloom by the fourth. The dining room and the private apartments contain some original furniture, a sumptuous marble staircase, and a magnificent fireplace designed by architect Camil Oliveras, a regular collaborator with Gaudí. But visitors are usually most impressed by the roof, with its army of centurion-like *trencadis*-covered chimneys. These chimneys, along with the rest of the building, were given an overhaul in the mid-1990s, and their tilework was restored; see if you can spot the one bearing a fragment of the Olympic mascot Cobi. *Note:* At the time of this writing, the building was closed for repairs scheduled to last until spring 2007.

Nou de la Rambla 3–5. ℂ 93-317-39-74. Admission 3€ ($3.75), free for children under 7. Mon–Sat 10am–6:15pm. Metro: Drassanes.

Palau de la Virreina
Built in the 1770s, this building was the former home of Manuel d'Amat, a wealthy viceroy who had made his fortune in the Americas. Set slightly back from the street, this grand structure is marked by typically Spanish top-heaviness. Inside there is a patio featuring columns and a staircase to the right leads to the interior, most of which is not open to the public. On the left, a large space is lent to rotating exhibitions, predominantly on some aspect of Barcelona. One of the most memorable recent exhibitions held here—from November 2006 to March 2007—was of Agustí Centelles's evocative Spanish Civil War photographs. An excellent gift shop and cultural information point can be found on the ground floor.

Les Ramblas 99. ℂ 93-316-10-00. Admission varies. Tues–Sat 11am–8:30pm; Sun 11am–3pm. Metro: Catalunya or Liceu.

Sant Pau del Camp
Architecture from the Romanesque period is rich in rural Catalonia, which only makes the presence of this church in an inner-city street even more surprising. Its name ("Saint Paul of the countryside") stems from the fact that the church was once surrounded by green fields outside the city walls and is the oldest church in Barcelona. Given its grand old age, Sant Pau is remarkably intact. Remains of the original 9th-century structure can be seen on the capitals and bases of the portal. The church was rebuilt in the 11th and 12th centuries and is shaped in the form of a Greek cross with three apses. The western exterior door features a Latin inscription referring to Christ, Saint Peter, and Saint Paul. In the 14th-century chapter house is the tomb of Guífre Borrell, count of Barcelona in the early 10th century. The small cloister, however, is the highlight, with its Moorish arches and central fountain.

Sant Pau 99. ℂ 93-441-00-01. Admission to cloister 2€. ($2.50). Mon–Fri noon–2pm and 5–8pm. Metro: Paral.lel.

2 L'Eixample

Barcelona's "new town," its extension beyond the old city walls, actually contains a glorious grid of 18th- and 19th-century buildings, including the most vibrant examples of the *moderniste* movement. The famous **Quadrat d'Or (Golden Triangle),** an area bordered by the streets Bruc, Aribau, Aragó, and the Diagonal, has been named the world's greatest living museum of turn-of-the-20th-century architecture. Most of the key buildings are within these hundred-odd city blocks, including Gaudí's **La Pedrera** and the ultimate *moderniste* calling card, the **Manzana de la Discordia** (see below). Many of these still serve their original use: luxury apartments for the city's 19th-century nouveau riche. Others are office buildings and even shops (the Passeig de Gràcia, the neighborhood's main boulevard, is the top shopping precinct). In case you were wondering, marine-colored, hexagonal tiles on the footpaths are reproductions of ones used by Gaudí for La Pedrera and the Casa Batlló.

L'EIXAMPLE DRETA

L'Hospital de la Santa Creu i San Pau ☆☆☆   The Avenida Gaudí, an elegant pedestrianized boulevard, stretches northward from the Sagrada Família; at the opposite end sits another key hallmark of the *moderniste* movement, almost equal in esteem to Gaudí's masterpiece. The Hospital San Pau (as it's more commonly known) is a remarkable work by the architect Domènech i Montaner. He is often referred to as the second most important *moderniste* architect (after Gaudí), and his magnificent Palau de la Música Catalana (p. 166) is one of the movement's most emblematic pieces.

The Hospital San Pau was commissioned by Pau Gil i Serra, a rich Catalan banker who wished to create a hospital based on the "garden city" model. While patients languished in turn-of-the-20th-century prisonlike edifices, Gil i Serra had the then-revolutionary idea of making their surroundings as agreeable as possible. He conceived a series of colored pavilions, each (like a hospital ward) serving a specific purpose, scattered among parkland. He only achieved half his vision. Although the first stone was laid in 1902, by 1911 funds had run out and only 8 of the 48 projected pavilions were completed. Domènech died in 1930. Work was later carried out by his son.

The Hospital San Pau is an inspiring place in which to wander. The interiors of the pavilions are off-limits, but their gorgeous Byzantine and Moorish-inspired facades and decoration, from gargoyles and angels to fauna and blossoming flora, greet you at every turn. The largest, the **Administrative Pavilion,** can be entered and explored. Its facade glows with mosaic murals telling the history of hospital care, and inside the building there are beautiful columns with floral capitals and a luxurious, dusty pink tiled ceiling.

Sant Antoni María Claret 167–171. ☎ **93-488-20-78.** www.santpau.es. Admission 5€ ($6.25) adults, 3€ ($3.75) students, free for children under 15. Free to walk around discreetly. Guided tours Sat–Sun 10am–2pm. Metro: Hospital San Pau.

La Pedrera (Casa Milà) ☆☆☆   Commonly known as La Pedrera (The Quarry), the real name for this spectacular work of Antoni Gaudí's is the Casa Milà. The nickname stems from its stony, fortress-like appearance, much ridiculed at the time, but which today stands as the superlative example of *modernista* architecture. The entire building was restored in 1996, the Espai Gaudí—a didactic museum—was installed in the attic, and one of the apartments was refurbished to look as it would have in the early 20th century.

The building was commissioned by Pere Mila i Camps, a rich developer who had just married an even richer widow. He wanted the most extravagant showpiece on the fashionable Passeig de Gràcia, so Gaudí, having just completed the Casa Batlló (see below), was the obvious choice.

La Pedrera occupies a corner block, and its sinuous, rippling facade stands in sharp contrast to its neoclassical neighbors. In fact, it is unlike any piece of architecture anywhere in the world. La Pedrera seems to have been molded rather than built. Its massive, wavelike curtain walls are of Montjuïc limestone and the balconies' iron balustrades look like masses of seaweed. Inside, as outside, there is not one straight wall or right angle, further adding to La Pedrera's cavelike appearance. (In a well-known anecdote, after French President Georges Clemenceau visited the building, he reported that in Barcelona they make caves for dragons.) The apartments (many of them still private homes) are centered on two courtyards whose walls are decorated with subtle, jewel-like murals. The highpoint of the visit (literally!) is the spectacular rooftop. It features clusters of centurion-like chimney stacks, artfully restored and residing on an undulating surface, mirroring the arches of the attic below, with outstanding views of the neighborhood, the Sagrada Família, and the port. In the summer months, jazz and flamenco concerts are held in this unique setting. The entire first floor has been handed over as an exhibition space (past shows have included artists of the caliber of Dalí and Chillida). Admission is included in the La Pedrera entry.

Provença 261–265 (on corner of Passeig de Gràcia). ☎ **93-484-59-80** or 93-484-59-00. Admission 8€ ($10) adults, 4.50€ ($5.60) students, free for children under 12. Daily 10am–7:30pm; English tours Mon–Fri 6pm. Metro: Diagonal.

La Sagrada Família ⭐⭐⭐ (Moments   Gaudí's incomplete masterpiece is one of the city's more idiosyncratic creations—if you have time to see only one Catalan landmark, you should make it this one. Begun in 1882 and incomplete at the architect's death in 1926, this incredible temple—the Church of the Holy Family—is a bizarre wonder. The languid, amorphous structure embodies the essence of Gaudí's style, which some have described as Art Nouveau run wild.

The Sagrada Família became Gaudí's all-encompassing obsession toward the last years of this intensely religious man's life. The commission came from the Josephines, a right-wing, highly pious faction of the Catholic Church. They were of the opinion that the decadent city needed an expiatory (atonement) temple where its inhabitants could go and do penance for their sins. Gaudí, whose view of Barcelona's supposed decadence largely mirrored that of the Josephines, by all accounts had a free hand; money was no object, nor was there a deadline. As Gaudí is known to have said, "My client [God] is in no hurry."

Literally dripping in symbolism, the Sagrada Família was conceived to be a "catechism in stone." The basic design followed that of a Gothic church, with transepts, aisles, and a central nave. Apart from the riot of stone carvings, the grandeur of the structure comes from the elongated towers: four above each of the three facades (representing the apostles) reaching 100m (329 ft.), with four more (the evangelists) shooting up from the central section at a lofty 170m (558 ft.). The words SANCTUS, SANCTUS, SANCTUS, HOSANNA IN EXCELSIUS (Holy, Holy, Holy, Glory to God in the Highest) are written on these, further embellished with colorful geometric tilework. The last tower, being built over the apse, will be higher still and dedicated to the Virgin Mary. It is the two completed facades, however, that are the biggest crowd pleasers. The oldest, and the only one to be completed while the architect was alive, is the **Nativity Facade** on

Moments   Gaudí's Resting Place

Before you leave the Sagrada Família, make sure you pay a visit to the crypt, Gaudí's resting place. The architect spent the last days of his life on the site, living a hermitlike existence in a workroom and dedicating all of his time to the project. Funds had finally dried up, and the *modernisme* movement had fallen out of fashion. In general, the Sagrada Família was starting to be viewed as a monumental white elephant.

In 1926, on his way to vespers, the old man did not see the no. 30 tram hurtling down the Gran Vía. He was struck and subsequently taken to a hospital for the poor (in his disheveled state no one recognized the great architect), where he lay in agony for 3 days before dying. Fittingly, he was laid to rest under a simple tombstone in the Sagrada Família's crypt.

In contrast to the rest of the Sagrada Família, the crypt is built in neo-Gothic style. The first part of the building to be completed, it is the work of Francesc de Villar, the architect who was originally commissioned for the project until Gaudí took over (Villar quit for unknown reasons). During the "Tragic Week" of 1936, when anarchists went on an anti-clerical rampage in the city, the crypt was ransacked. The only thing left intact was Gaudí's tomb.

the Carrer Marina. So rich in detail, upon first glance it seems like a wall of molten wax. As the name suggests, the work represents the birth of Jesus; its entire expanse is crammed with figurines of the Holy Family, flute-bearing angels, and an abundance of flora and fauna. Nature was Gaudí's passion; he spent hours studying its forms in the countryside of his native Reus, south of Barcelona, and much of his work is inspired by nature. On the Nativity facade, he added birds, mushrooms, even a tortoise to go along with the rest of the religious imagery. The central piece is the "Tree of Life," a Cyprus tree scattered with nesting white doves.

On the opposite side, the **Passion Facade** is a harsh counterpart to the fluidity of the Nativity Facade. It is the work of Josep M. Subirachs, a well-known Catalan sculptor who, like Gaudí, has set up a workshop inside the church to complete his work. His highly stylized, elongated figures are of Christ's passion and death, from Last Supper to the Crucifixion. The work, started in 1952, has been highly criticized. In the book *Barcelona,* art critic Robert Hughes called it "the most blatant mass of half-digested *moderniste* clichés to be plunked on a notable building within living memory."

Despite his and dozens of other voices of dissent, work moves forward. In 1936, anarchists attacked the church (as they did many others in the city), destroying the plans and models Gaudí had left behind. The present architects, aided by modern technology, are working from photographs of those models. The central nave is starting to take shape and the Glory Facade is limping along. It is estimated that the whole thing will be completed by 2026 (the centenary of Gaudí's death), funded entirely by visitors and private donations.

Admission includes a 12-minute video on Gaudí's religious and secular works as well as entrance to the museum, where fascinating reconstructions of Gaudí's original models are on show.

Mallorca 401. Ⓒ **93-207-30-31**. Admission 8€ ($10) adults, 5€ ($6.25) students, guide/audio guide 3€ ($3.75), elevator to the top (about 60m/197 ft.) 2€ ($2.50). Nov–Mar daily 9am–6pm; Apr–Sept daily 9am–8pm. Metro: Verdaguer or Sagrada Família.

L'EIXAMPLE ESQUERRA

Casa Amatller 𝕲𝕲   Constructed in a cubical design with a Dutch gable, this building was created by Puig i Cadafalch in 1900, and was the first building on the Manzana. It stands in sharp contrast to its neighbor, the Gaudí-designed Casa Batlló (see below). The architecture of the Casa Amatller, imposed on a pre-existing edifice, is a vision of ceramic, wrought iron, and sculptures. The structure combines grace notes of Flemish Gothic—especially on the finish of the facade—with elements of Catalan architecture. The gable outside is in the Flemish style. Look out for the sculptures of animals blowing glass and taking photos, both hobbies of the architect. They were executed by Eusebi Arnau, an artist much in demand by the *modernistas*.

Passeig de Gràcia 41. Ⓒ **93-216-01-75**. Ground floor open to public Mon–Sat 10am–7pm. Metro: Passeig de Gràcia.

Casa Batlló 𝕲𝕲𝕲   Next door to the Casa Amatller, Casa Batlló was designed by Gaudí in 1905, and is hands-down the superior of the three works in the Manzana. Using sensuous curves in iron and stone and glittering, luminous *trencadis* (collage of broken tiles and ceramic) on the facade, the Casa Batlló is widely thought to represent the legend of Saint George (the patron saint of Catalonia) and his dragon. The balconies are protected by imposing skull-like formations and supported by vertebrae-like columns representing the dragon's victims, while the spectacular roof is the dragon's humped and glossy scaled back. St. George can be seen in the turret, his lance crowned by a cross. The building was opened to the public in 2004, and although its admission price is steep compared to many other Gaudí attractions, the interior of the building is no less spectacular than the exterior, with sinuous staircases, flowing wood paneling, and a stained-glass gallery supported by yet more bonelike columns. Custom-made Gaudí-designed furniture is scattered throughout.

Passeig de Gràcia 43. Ⓒ **93-488-06-66**. Admission 17€ ($21) adults, 14€ ($18) children and students, free for children under 5. Daily 9am–8pm. Metro: Passeig de Gràcia.

Casa Lleó Morera 𝕲𝕲   The last building of the trio, on the corner of Carrer del Consell de Cent, is the Casa Lleó Morera. This florid work, completed by Doménech i Montaner in 1906, is perhaps the least challenging of the three, as it represents a more international style of Art Nouveau. One of its quirkier features is the tiered wedding cake–type turret and abundance of ornamentation. Comb the facade for a light bulb and telephone (both inventions of the period) and a lion and mulberry bush

---

La Manzana de la Discordia

The superlative showcase of the *moderniste* architecture is the so-called **Manzana de la Discordia (Illa de la Discordia)**. The "Block of Discord," which is on the Passeig de Gràcia between Consell de Cent and Aragó, consists of three works by the three master architects of the movement: Josep Puig i Cadafalch, Lluís Domènech i Montaner, and Antoni Gaudí. Although quite different from one another, they offer a coherent insight into the stylistic language of the period. The Casa Amatller houses the Centre del Modernisme an information point on the *modernistas* and the movement (see below).

(after the owner's name: in Catalan, lion is *lleó,* and mulberry is *morera*). Tragically, the ground floor has been mutilated by its tenant, who stripped the lower facade of its detail and installed plate glass. The shop's interior, which fared no better, is the only part of the building open to the public.

Passeig de Gràcia 35. Metro: Passeig de Gràcia.

Fundació Antoni Tàpies 𝕬   When it opened in 1990, this became the third Barcelona museum devoted to the work of a single, prolific artist (the others are museums for Miró and Picasso). In 1984 the Catalan artist Antoni Tàpies set up a foundation bearing his name, and the city of Barcelona donated an ideal site: the old Montaner i Simon publishing house. One of the city's landmark buildings, the brick-and-iron structure was built between 1881 and 1884 by that important exponent of Catalan *moderniste* architecture, Lluis Doménech i Montaner, also perpetrator of the Casa Lleó Morera around the corner (see above). The core of the museum is a collection of works by Tàpies (mostly contributed by the artist) covering stages of his career as it evolved into abstract expressionism. Here you can see the entire spectrum of media in which he worked: painting, assemblage, sculpture, drawing, and ceramics. His associations with Picasso and Miró are apparent. The largest of the works is on top of the building: a controversial gigantic sculpture, *Cloud and Chair,* made from 2,700m (8,858 ft.) of metal wiring and tubing. The lower floor is used for temporary exhibitions, nearly always on contemporary art and photography, and the upper floor has a library with an extremely impressive section on Oriental art, one of the artist's inspirations.

Aragó 255. ② **93-487-03-15.** Admission 4.20€ ($5.25) adults, 2.10€ ($2.60) students, free for children under 16. Tues–Sun 10am–8pm. Metro: Passeig de Gràcia.

Fundació Francisco Godia *(finds)*   Located in the heart of Barcelona, this intriguing museum showcases the famous art collection of Francisco Godia Sales, the Catalan art lover and entrepreneur. It's one of the greatest displays in the country. Godia (1921–90)

Tips **Doing the *Moderniste* Walk**

As most of Barcelona's *moderniste* legacy is in L'Eixample neighborhood, it makes sense to see it on foot. The **Centre del Modernisme** at the Casa Amatller, Passeig de Gràcia 41 (② **93-488-01-39;** Mon–Sat 10am–7pm, Sun 10am–2pm; Metro: Gràcia; there are also branches at the Hospital Sant Pau and the Finca Güell in Pedralbes), is a one-stop information point on the movement. They have devised the "modernism route," a tour of the city's 100 most emblematic Art Nouveau buildings. You can either pick up a free map or buy a well-produced, explanatory book (12€/$15), which includes a book of coupons offering discounts of between 15% and 50% on attractions that charge admission, such as Gaudí's Casa Batlló and La Pedrera.

If you wish to explore *modernisme* beyond the boundaries of Barcelona, the center can also supply you with information on towns such as Reus (Gaudí's' birthplace) and Terrassa, which has an important collection of *moderniste* industrial buildings. Tours are also offered. (See our own recommended Walking Tour 4, in chapter 8).

combined a desire for art with a head for business and a passion for motor racing. When he wasn't driving fast ("the most wonderful thing in the world"), he was amassing his collection. In gathering these treasures he showed exquisite taste and great sensitivity.

He collected a splendid array of medieval sculpture and ceramics but showed a keener instinct for purchasing great paintings. Godia acquired works by some of the most important artists of the 20th century, including Julio González, María Blanchard, Joan Ponç, Antoni Tàpies, and Manolo Hugué, the latter a great friend of Picasso. From its earliest stages, Godia realized the artistic importance of Catalan *modernisme* and collected works by sculptors like Josep Llimona and celebrated *moderniste* painters Santiago Rusiñol and Ramon Casas. Godia also dipped deeper into the past, acquiring works, for example, of two of the most important artists of the 17th century: Jacob van Ruysdael and Luca Giordano.

Carrer Valencia 284. ⓒ 93-272-31-80. Admission 4.50€ ($5.60) adults, 2.10€ ($2.60) students and seniors, free for children under 5. Wed–Mon 10am–8pm. Metro: Passeig de Gràcia.

Museu Egipci de Barcelona   Spain's only museum dedicated to Egyptology contains more than 250 pieces from the personal collection of founder Jordi Clos (owner of the Hotel Claris). On display are sarcophagi, jewelry, hieroglyphics, sculptures, and artwork. Exhibits focus on ancient Egyptians' everyday life, including education, social customs, religion, and food. The museum has its own lab for restorations. A library with more than 3,000 works is open to the public.

Valencia 284. ⓒ **93-488-01-88.** Admission 5.50€ ($6.85) adults, 4.50€ ($5.60) students and children. Mon–Sat 10am–8pm; Sun 10am–2pm. Guided tours Sat. Metro: Passeig de Gràcia.

3 Gràcia

Located above the Diagonal and l'Eixample Esquerra, Gràcia is a large neighborhood that has a distinct character, a product from when it was a separate town altogether. Although notable attractions here are not abundant, Gràcia is well worth visiting for a taste of authentic *barri* life. Shopping and cafe society are particularly good around the Calle Verdi and Plaça del Sol, and nocturnal activity here is lively. Gràcia boasts a unique mixture of proud locals, who have lived here all their lives, and young, progressive urbanites. This melting pot is reflected in its street life.

Casa Vicens ⓇⓇ   Although this early work of Gaudí can only be viewed from the exterior, the exuberance of its facade and form make the trip well worthwhile. The architect accepted the commission for a summer residence from the tile manufacturer Manuel Vicens i Montaner in 1883, making the Casa Vicens one of the first examples of Art Nouveau not only in Barcelona but in the whole of Europe.

Since the home was designed to be an exponent of Sr. Vicen's business, the entire facade is covered with florid, vividly colored tiles. At the time, Gaudí was deeply influenced by North African and Middle Eastern architecture, and this can be seen in the home's form. Its overall opulence and exoticism, with minarets and corbels, is reminiscent of the Indian Raj style. Inside, Ottoman, Koranic, and Andalusian influences can also be seen in eccentric touches such as the Turkish-style smoking room. The residence, on a narrow Graciàn street, is owned by descendants of Sr. Vicens and is still a private home (although they seem to have no objections to camera-flashing tourists). The interior, however, has been well photographed, and is always featured in books on Gaudí.

Carrer de les Carolines 18–24. Metro: Fontana.

Parc Güell 𝒢𝒢𝒢   After the abundant religious symbolism of the Sagrada Família and the heavy-handedness of the Palau Güell, Gaudí's whimsical Parc Güell often seems like light relief and is for many his favorite and most accessible work. Although it's now officially a public park, in 1900 the Parc Güell began as a real-estate venture for a friend, the well-known Catalan industrialist Count Eusebi Güell (see box, below), who planned to make this a model garden city community of 60 dwellings with its own market and church. It was never completed and the city took over the property in 1926.

Spread over several acres of woodland high above central Barcelona, with wonderful views at every turn, the Parc Güell is one of the most unusual man-made landscapes on the planet. It is abundant with the architect's unique vision and expertise at finding creative solutions posed by the demands of the project.

Arriving at the main entrance in the Carrer Olot, you are greeted by two gingerbread-style gatehouses. At the time they were built, Gaudí was working on some set designs for the opera *Hansel and Gretel* at the Liceu Opera House, so it is presumed that the inspiration for these whimsical structures came from that. Both shimmer with broken mosaic collage and are topped with chimneys in the shape of wild and toxic mushrooms. Much has been made of Parc Güell's symbolism, and it has even been suggested that these toadstool-chimneys reflect Gaudí's penchant for hallucinogenic substances. The fact is that mushroom-gathering is a national pastime and the work reflects a deep-rooted nationalism and respect for nature and Catalonia's history.

The main steps to the **Sala Hipóstila (marketplace)** feature a spectacular tiled lizard, the park's centerpiece. The covered would-be market supports a large platform above with 86 Doric columns connected by shallow vaults. This pagan-looking space is largely thought to be inspired by Barcelona's Roman foundations. The roof is embellished with four sun-shaped disks representing the seasons. Above, in the elevated square, a sinuous bench, said to be the longest in the world, snakes its way around the perimeter. The decoration on this elaborate piece was carried out by architect and craftsman Josep Marià Jujol. The story goes that all the workers on the park were ordered to bring Jujol all the shards of broken crockery and glass they could lay their hands on, which accounts for the work's extraordinary mixture of colors and textures. Palm trees and vistas of the skyline add to the effect.

Three kilometers (2 miles) of more rustic inspired paths and porticoes using material taken from the land itself weave through the rest of the park, which is filled with Mediterranean vegetation. In typical Gaudí style, sculptures and figurines pop up in the most surprising places. Worth hunting out is the **Closed Chapel,** at the highest point of the park, an archaic, six-lobed structure crowned by a cross that seems inspired by the ancient stone watchtowers or druid temples not uncommon in the Balearic Islands.

Only two homes were ever built in the colony, neither of them by Gaudí. One, designed by the architect Ramón Berenguer, became Gaudí's residence in the latter part of his life. It is now the **Casa-Museu Gaudí,** Carrer del Carmel 28 (© **93-219-38-11**), which contains furniture designed by the architect, drawings, and other personal effects, many of them arranged as they were when the architect lived his reclusive life there. Admission to the house is 4€ ($5); open daily from 10am to 6pm.

Carrer del Carmel 28. © **93-424-38-09.** Free admission. Daily 10am–sunset. Metro: Lesseps (then a 15-min. walk). Bus: 24.

> ### *Fun Fact* Gaudí's Patron
>
> **Eusebi Güell i Bacigalupi,** the man who launched Gaudí's career and went on to become a lifelong friend, was a product of the city's new, wealthy elite. He studied art, poetry, and theology in Paris and London, and upon returning to Barcelona put his acute business sense into practice in the shipping, banking, railroad, and textile sectors—all the industries that drove Catalonia's Industrial Revolution in the late 1800s.
>
> Enormously well respected, Güell was high-minded and took civic duty extremely seriously. He felt bound to improve the lives of his city's inhabitants (of all classes) through art and better working conditions. It seems Güell's first meeting with Gaudí was in a carpentry workshop that Gaudí had designed as a showcase for a Barcelona glove shop, and shortly afterward Güell saw the work displayed at the 1878 International Exhibition in Paris. The fruit of the relationship materialized in such marvels as the Parc Güell, the Palau Güell, and the church for the ambitious Colònia Güell, in outer Barcelona. Just before his death, in 1918, Güell was made a count by King Alfonso XIII.

4 Montjuïc

For many visitors, and certainly for those who arrive by sea, the mountain of Montjuïc is their first glimpse of Barcelona. Jutting out over the port on one side and facing the monumental Plaça Espanya on the other, Montjuïc is strategically placed as a pleasure ground, and a fortunate lack of a constant water source has deterred residential development. Instead, it became the focal point of two of the city's key international events: first the World Fair of 1929, of which many structures still remain, and second the 1992 Olympic Games.

The largest "green zone" in the city, Montjuïc's forests and parks have always been popular with joggers, cyclists, and strollers. In recent years, the city's council embarked on a project to spruce these up, install walkways and escalators, and reclaim some forgotten gems in the process. One of these is the **Font del Gat,** Passeig Santa Madrona 28 (© **93-289-04-04**), a once-fashionable cafe built by *moderniste* architect Josep Puig i Cadafalch that now acts as a Montjuïc information point and restaurant. Topflight hillside museums, such as the Miró Foundation and the MNAC, are additional good reasons to leave the bustle of city behind and take the rewarding climb up here.

CaixaForum 🏵🏵   This is one of the city's more exciting contemporary art spaces, both in terms of its setting and what's inside. Opened in 2002 in the Casaramona, an old *modernista* textile factory designed by Puig i Cadalfach that was used as police barracks in the '30s, the vibrant edifice features a red-brick facade and singular turret, to which the Japanese architect Arata Isozaki added a daring walkway, courtyard, and entrance. (Isozaki is the designer responsible for the Palau St. Jordi, a major music and meeting venue, farther up the hill of Montjuïc.) Inside, after passing the huge abstract mural by Sol Lewitt, the elevator whisks you up to three exhibition spaces, connected by exterior halls. These are changing constantly, meaning that three normally very diverse shows can be viewed at the same time. L'Art Nouveau exhibition, in 2006, showed 19th-century art dealer Siegfried Bing's collection, which ranged from Japanese and other Asian works to van Gogh and Toulouse-Lautrec. The foundation puts on a lively calendar of related events and performances, the latter focusing on world music and modern dance. There is an excellent bookshop in the foyer.

Av. Marquès de Comillas 6–8. ⓒ 93-476-86-00. Free admission. Tues–Sun 10am–8pm. Metro: Espanya. FGC: Espanya.

Fundació Joan Miró 𝒦𝒦𝒦   Born in 1893, Joan Miró was one of Spain's greatest artists, and along with Tàpies, the undisputed master of contemporary Catalan art. His work is known for its whimsical abstract forms, brilliant colors, and surrealism. Some 10,000 works, including paintings, graphics, and sculptures, are collected here. Constructed in the early 1970s, the building was designed by Catalan architect Josep Lluis Sert, a close friend of Miró (he also designed the artist's workroom in Majorca). Set in the parkland of Montjuïc, the museum consists of a series of white, rationalist-style galleries with terra-cotta floors. *Claraboias* (skylights) ensure that the space is bathed in natural light. Its hilltop setting affords some wonderful views of Barcelona, especially from the rooftop terrace that also serves as a sculpture garden.

The collection, donated by the artist himself, is so huge that only a portion of it can be shown at any one time. There is also a gallery put aside for temporary exhibitions, dedicated either to an aspect of Miró's work or to a contemporary artist or movement. Concerts are held in the gardens in the summer months.

The first gallery holds two of the collection's treasures: the magnificent 1979 **Foundation Tapestry,** which Miró executed especially for the space, and the extraordinary **Mercury Fountain,** a work by his friend the American sculptor Alexander Calder. In contrast to Miró's painting, which was nearly always carried out in a primary color palette, there is a huge collection of drawings from his days as student. It's obvious that, even as a young man, he had a deep sense of national identity and "Catalanism," which (logically) later led to an extreme horror at the Spanish Civil War. The key work representing this sentiment is the powerful *Man and Woman in Front of a Pile of Excrement* (1935), in the Pilar Juncosa Gallery, one of the so-called "Wild Paintings." Much of Miró's work, though, is dreamlike and uplifting, with the sun, moon, and other celestial bodies represented again and again. Note the poetic *The Gold of the Azure* (1967) in the same gallery: a transfixing blue cloud on a golden background with dots and strokes for the planets and stars.

Even if you are already familiar with Miró's work, the excellent commentary provided by the audio guide (available at the ticket office) will supply you with special insight into this fascinating artist.

Parc de Montjuïc s/n. ⓒ **93-443-94-70.** Admission 7.20€ ($9) adults, 3.90€ ($4.85) students, free for children under 14. July–Sept Tues–Wed and Fri–Sat 10am–8pm; Oct–June Tues–Wed and Fri–Sat 10am–7pm; year-round Thurs 10am–9:30pm and Sun 10am–2:30pm. Bus: 50 at Plaça d'Espanya or 55; Funicular de Montjuïc.

Galería Olímpica   An enthusiastic celebration of the 1992 Olympic Games, this is one of the few museums in Europe devoted to sports. Exhibits include photos, costumes, and memorabilia, with heavy emphasis on the events' pageantry, the number of visitors who attended, and the fame the events brought to Barcelona. Of interest to statisticians, civic planners, and sports buffs, the gallery contains audiovisual information about the building programs that prepared the city for the onslaught of visitors. There are conference facilities, an auditorium, video recordings of athletic events, and archives. In the cellar of the Olympic Stadium's southeastern perimeter, the museum is most easily reached by entering the stadium's southern gate (Porta Sud).

Passeig Olímpic s/n, Estadí Olímpic. ☎ 93-426-06-60. Admission 2.70€ ($3.35) adults, 1.50€ ($1.85) children and seniors. Apr–Sept Mon–Fri 10am–2pm and 4–7pm; Oct–Mar Tues–Sat 10am–1pm and 4–6pm. Metro: Espanya, then 15-min walk, or take bus no. 13 or 50 from Plaça Espanya.

Museu d'Arqueologia de Catalunya ⭑

The Museu d'Arqueologia occupies the former Palace of Graphic Arts, built for the 1929 World's Fair. It has been attractively restored, with some rooms retaining their Art Deco flavor. The artifacts, which are arranged chronologically, reflect the long history of this Mediterranean port city and surrounding province, beginning with prehistoric Iberian artifacts. The collection includes articles from the Greek, Roman, and Carthaginian periods. Some of the more interesting relics were excavated in the ancient Greco-Roman city of L'Empúries, in Northern Catalonia. The Greeks in particular developed a strategic trading post here with other Mediterranean peoples, and the vessels, urns, and other everyday implements they left behind make for fascinating viewing.

But undoubtedly the highlight of the collection is the Roman artifacts. The Roman Empire (using Empúries as an entry point) began its conquest of Iberia in 218 B.C., and the glassware, lamps, grooming aids, and utensils here are truly outstanding. The mosaics, many of them impressively intact, have been laid into the floor and visitors are invited to tread on them.

Passeig de Santa Madrona 39–41, Parc de Montjuïc. ☎ 93-424-65-77. Admission 2.40€ ($3) adults, 1.80€ ($2.25) students, free for children under 16. Tues–Sat 9:30am–7pm; Sun 10am–2:30pm. Metro: Espanya.

Museu Militar de Montjuïc ⭑

Although the collection at the city's museum is interesting enough, most people head up here for the views. Perched on the sea-facing side of Montjuïc, this fortress (Castell de Montjuïc) dates back to 1640 and was rebuilt and extended during the mid-1800s. Its gloomy cells served as a military prison during the Civil War, earning it an indifferent, if not hostile, reputation among the people of Barcelona. While there have been noises from the local government about changing the focus of the museum to a more peaceful and reflective tone, it remains pretty much the same as when it was opened, shortly after the army moved out in 1960.

The collection itself contains the usual assortment of paintings marking military events as well as dozens of rooms of armor, uniforms, weapons, and the instruments of war. One of the more entertaining exhibits (Room 8) contains thousands of miniatures forming a Spanish division, which first went on show during the 1929 World's Fair.

The terraces and highest points of the star-shaped fortress-castle, and the walkways that surround it, offer some breathtaking views of the Barcelona skyline and Mediterranean. The parkland around the castle is currently being dug up to make it more accessible and easier to walk around. If you don't mind an uphill stroll, note that the most spectacular way to get here is via the port-crossing cable car (see below). On the walk from the drop-off point, you will pass the famous statue of La Sardana, the traditional Catalan dance, which is featured on many postcards of the city. Otherwise, grab the funicular from Paral.lel Metro station, which drops you off pretty much at the door.

Parc de Montjuïc s/n. ☎ 93-329-86-13. Admission museum and castle 2.50€ ($3.10), castle and grounds 1€ ($1.25), free for children under 14. Nov to mid-Mar Tues–Sun 9:30am–5:30pm; mid-Mar to Oct Tues–Sun 9:30am–8pm. Transbordador Aeri (cable car; p. 186) from Barceloneta to Montjuïc, then uphill walk. Bus: PM (Parc Montjuïc); departs from Plaça Espanya 8am–9:20pm Sat–Sun and public holidays. Metro: Paral.lel, then funicular (tram) to top 9am–8pm (until 10pm July–Sept).

A Bicycle Built for Two

One of the star pieces of the MNAC's *moderniste* collection is a self-portrait of Ramón Casas and fellow painter Pere Romeu riding a tandem. This iconic work was originally done for **Els Quatre Gats** (p. 126), essentially a tavern that served as a fraternity house for *moderniste* movers and shakers, bohemians, intellectuals, and poets. A young Picasso designed the menu (and held his first exhibition there), and various other works donated to the owners still adorn the walls, although now most, such as Casas's peddling portrait, are reproductions of the originals. The colorful Casas, who had spent many years in the artistic circles of Montmartre, was a notable artist in his own right. His interpretations of *fin de siècle* Barcelona provide a valuable insight to this heady time.

Museu Nacional d'Art de Catalunya (MNAC) ✵✵✵ This museum, which recently underwent massive renovations and expansion, is the major depository of Catalan art. Although its mammoth collection also covers the Gothic period and 19th and 20th centuries, MNAC is perhaps the most important center for Romanesque art in the world. The majority of the sculptures, icons, and frescoes were taken from dilapidated churches in the Pyrénées, restored, and mounted as they would have appeared in the churches in expertly reproduced domes and apses. Larger works are shown with a photograph of the church and a map pointing out its location, drawing you further into this fascinating and largely underexposed 11th- to 13th-century movement. Simplistic yet mesmerizing, Romanesque art is marked by elongated forms, vivid colors, and expressiveness. Most outstanding is the **Apse of Santa María de Taüll** (in Ambit [Gallery] V) with a serene, doe-eyed Christ surrounded by the Apostles. Lapis lazuli was used to create the intense blue in the piece. Also look out for a series of ceiling paintings from an Aragonese chapter house. In a more subtle color scheme, they echo Tudor miniature painting (Ambit XI). The entire collection is in chronological order, giving the viewer a tour of Romanesque art from its beginnings to the more advanced late Romanesque and early Gothic eras.

The next section you visit deals with the Gothic period, made up of pieces from the 13th to 15th centuries. All styles that were adopted in Catalonia are represented: Italianate Gothic, Flemish Gothic, and a more linear, local Gothic style. Look out for *retablos* by Jaume Huguet (Room XIII). The primary artist in the Catalan School, Huguet mixed Flemish and Italian influences with local Romanesque conventions. The Gothic collection also holds some Barcelonese Gothic Quarter artifacts such as giant object-signs (made for an illiterate population) that used to hang outside workshops (shoes, scissors, and the like) and other decorative pieces. The Gothic section finishes with the Cambó collection. A bequest from a local businessman, the selection of 14th- to 19th-century paintings includes works by Rubens, El Greco, and Goya.

Thanks to the MNAC's most recent acquisitions—pieces of 19th- and 20th-century decorative art and painting, most stemming from the city's all-important *moderniste* movement—the collection now spans a millennium. While *moderniste* architecture in the city is abundant, most building interiors have been stripped bare of their mirrors, chandeliers, sculptures, and furnishings, many designed by architects such as Gaudí. Until mid-2004 they were on display at the Museu d'Art Modern in the Parc de la Ciutadella. At the MNAC they have a stunning new home.

Highlights of this collection, which spans the neoclassical, Art Nouveau (or *moderniste*), and subsequent *nou-centista* (or *fin de siècle*) movements are too numerous to mention. Look out for the marquetry pieces by Gaspar Homar (a master *moderniste* carpenter) and the Rodin-influenced sculptor Josep Clara. The superb private oratory by Joan Busquets will leave you breathless at the Art Nouveau movement's excesses and craftsmanship. There are also many pieces taken from the interiors of homes of the Manzana de la Discordia (earlier in this chapter).

Palau Nacional, Parc de Montjuïc. © **93-622-03-60.** www.mnac.es. Admission 4.80€ ($6) adults, 3.30€ ($4.10) students and youths 7–21, free for children under 7. Temporary exhibits: 4.20€ ($4.80). Tues–Sat 10am–7pm; Sun 10am–2:30pm. Metro: Espanya.

Pavelló Mies van der Rohe 𝒢𝒢   Directly across the road from the CaixaForum, this serene building stands in welcome contrast to the *moderniste* style of the Casaramona and the faux traditionalism of the Poble Espanyol. Designed by German architect Mies van der Rohe, it was originally built as the German Pavilion for the 1929 World's Fair and was the last of the architect's works before he emigrated to the United States. It is considered a key work of both his and the "International Style" movement for which van der Rohe and others, like Frank Lloyd Wright, became famous. The simple, horizontal structure contains his trademarks: precision, fluidity of space, and abundance of "pure" materials—in this case different kinds of marble and glass. The structure is built around a shallow pool featuring a statue by Georg Kolbe, the German sculptor known for his female nudes. Inside is the original **Barcelona Chair** designed by van der Rohe and seen (mainly in reproduction form) throughout the city in reception areas. Although the pavilion now stands on its original location, this wasn't always the case. After the World's Fair, it was banished to an outer suburb, only to be rescued and reconstructed in 1985 thanks to an initiative by a group of the city's prominent architects.

Av. Marquès de Comillas s/n. © **93-423-40-16.** Admission 3.50€ ($4.40) adults, free for children under 18. Daily 10am–8pm. Metro: Espanya. FGC: Espanya.

Moments   **The Magic Fountain**

Without a doubt, the most popular attraction for young and old alike in the Montjuïc area is the **Font Màgica (Magic Fountain).** During the day, the grandiose fountain at the base of the staircase to the MNAC seems like any other, but at night it takes on a different personality. At regular intervals, the fountain puts on a spectacular show. Music, ranging from pop ballads to pop classics, belts out from loudspeakers, and multifarious lights are beamed from inside the fountain itself. The gushes of water, controlled externally, "dance" to the mixture of light and sound. Supposedly the only one of its kind in the world, the fountain was designed by the visionary engineer Carles Buïgas for the 1929 World's Fair, pre-dating similar Vegas-type attractions by decades. It's free and never fails to enthrall. Grab a seat at one of the nearby outdoor cafes and enjoy. It's at Plaça Carles Buïgas 1. Metro: Espanya. The sound-and-light shows run from May to early October, Thursday through Sunday at 9:30, 10pm, 10:30, 11, and 11:30pm. The rest of the year, they are held on Friday and Saturday at 7, 7:30, 8, and 8:30pm.

Poble Espanyol ⭐⭐ *(Kids)*   This re-created Spanish village, built for the 1929 World's Fair, provokes mixed feelings: Purists see it as the height of kitsch, while others delight in its open spaces and Disneyland-type feel. But the question remains: Where else would you find over 100 styles of Spanish architecture crammed into one very pleasant spot? From the Levante to Galicia, from Castilian high Gothic to the humble whitewashed dwellings of the south and to colorful Basque homes—it's all here. At the entrance, for starters, stands a facsimile of the gateway to the grand walled city of Avila. This leads you to the center of the village with an outdoor cafe where you can sit and have drinks, and there are various other venues throughout, including the excellent flamenco *taberna,* the **Tablao de Carmen** (p. 235), and a couple of other trendy nightspots. The big names of July's El Grec festival also play here, in the main plaza just inside the gates. As was originally intended, numerous shops still sell provincial crafts and souvenir items, and in some of them you can see artists at work, printing fabric, making pottery, and blowing glass. If you are lucky, your visit may coincide with a wedding at the faux Sant Miquel monastery, one of the most popular places in the city to get married. A few years back, the Poble Espanyol added the **Fundació Fran Daural** (daily 10am–7pm), a collection of contemporary Catalan art with works by Dalí, Picasso, Barceló, and Tàpies. Many families delight in the faux-Spanish atmosphere, but the more discriminating find it a bit of a tourist trap.

Av. Marquès de Comillas s/n, Parc de Montjuïc. ℂ **93-508-63-00.** Admission 7.50€ ($9.40) adults, 5.50€ ($6.85) children 7–12, free for children under 7, 15€ ($19) family ticket, 2€ ($2.50) guided tours. Mon 9am–8pm; Tues–Thurs 9am–2am; Fri–Sat 9am–4am; Sun 9am–midnight. Metro: Espanya, then 10-min walk uphill, or take bus no. 13 or 50 from Plaça Espanya.

Jardí Botànic ⭐   Just behind the Castell de Montjuïc, the city's Botanical Garden opened in 1999 and has steadily gathered international praise for its cutting-edge landscaping. The foliage focuses on species of plants, flowers, and trees that flourish in a Mediterranean-type climate (all are clearly labeled in Latin, Catalan, Spanish, and English). The park is divided into sections representing each of these regions. The sci-fi telecommunications aerial you see a short distance away was designed by the Valencia-born architect Santiago Calatrava for the Olympic Games. This ingenious structure has a base decorated with broken tiles (a homage to Gaudí, one of the architect's main influences), and its position, leaning at the same angle as the hill's inclination, means that it also acts as a sundial.

Doctor Font i Quer s/n, Parque de Montjuïc. ℂ **93-426-49-35.** Admission 4€ ($5.25), free for children under 16. July–Sept Mon–Sat 10am–8pm; rest of year Mon–Sat 10am–5pm; Sun 10am–3pm. Transbordador Aeri (cable car; see below) from Barceloneta to Montjuïc, then an uphill walk. Bus: PM (Parc Montjuïc) departs from Plaça Espanya 8am–9:20pm Sat–Sun and public holidays. Metro: Paral.lel, then funicular (tram) to top 9am–8pm (until 10pm July–Sept).

Tips **Swinging over the Port**

Unless you suffer from vertigo, the most spectacular way to reach the Castell de Montjuïc, and the other attractions on the sea-face of the mountain of Montjuïc, is via a cable car that crosses the port. The **Transbordador Aeri** starts at Torre de Sant Sebastián at the very end of the Passeig de Joan de Borbó in Barceloneta (bus no. 17, 64, or 39), stops at the World Trade Center on the way, and finishes at the ascent to the peak of Montjuïc. The cable car runs every 15 minutes daily from 10:30am to 7pm. Cost is 6€ ($7.50) one-way, 7.20€ ($9) round-trip.

---

5 The Harborfront

For a city that for centuries "lived with its back to the sea," Barcelona now sports a spectacular harborfront, the busiest leisure port in the Mediterranean, and kilometers of urban beaches. The relocation of the commercial port and coastal freeway, and the demolition of industrial buildings that blocked the view of the sea, were pushed ahead for the 1992 Olympic Games. Without a doubt, the reclaiming of the city's coast has been the most life-enhancing change Barcelona has seen in the last century. Starting at the Columbus Monument, you can follow the city's coastal stretch via boardwalks and esplanades to the Olympic Village and beyond. Along the way you pass through the modern marina the Port Vell and the old fishermen's district of La Barceloneta, ending at Frank Gehry's famous fish sculpture at the Olympic Port.

L'Aquarium de Barcelona 𝕲𝕲 One of the most impressive testimonials to sea life anywhere opened in 1996, in Barcelona's Port Vell, a 10-minute walk from the bottom of La Rambla. The largest aquarium in Europe, it contains 21 glass tanks positioned along either side of a wide, curving corridor. Each tank depicts a different marine habitat, with emphasis on everything from multicolored fish and corals to seagoing worms to sharks. The highlight is a huge "oceanarium" representative of the Mediterranean as a self-sustaining ecosystem. You view it from the inside of a glass-roofed, glass-sided tunnel that runs along its entire length, making fish, eels, and sharks appear to swim around you. Kids can let off some steam in the **Explora** section, a collection of touchy-feely educational exhibits on Catalonia's Costa Brava and Ebro Delta.

Moll d'Espanya-Port Vell. ℭ **93-221-74-74.** Admission 15€ ($19) adults, 9.50€ ($12) children 4–12 and students, free for children under 4. July–Aug daily 9:30am–11pm; Sept–June Mon–Fri 9:30am–9pm, Sat–Sun 9:30am–9:30pm. Metro: Drassanes or Barceloneta.

Museu d'Història de Catalunya 𝕲 The Catalan History Museum is located in the Palau del Mar, a huge warehouse dating from the late 19th century. Many similar buildings stood alongside it before this flank of the port was re-developed for the 1992 Olympic Games, creating the marina and recreational area that now surrounds it.

The museum, divided into eight sections, aims to provide a stroll through history, and that pretty much sums up what it does. It's a sometimes exhausting, highly didactic tour of the country. **"Roots," "Birth of a Nation,"** and **"Our Sea"** look at Catalonia's ancient ancestors, the flourishing Romanesque period, and the Catalan-Aragonese sea trade. **"On the Periphery of an Empire," "Bases of the Revolution,"** and **"Steam and Nation"** study Catalonia's decline under the Habsburg rule and subsequent economic and cultural recovery in the industrial age. Finally, **"The Electric Years"** (which is by far one of the more entertaining parts of the exhibit) and **"Defeat and Recovery"** deal with the 20th century, the Spanish Civil War, Catalonia during Franco's dictatorship, and the first democratic elections after his death.

It's a lot of area to cover and the museum uses a mixture of multimedia, re-creations, models, and other interactive devices as their medium, most of the time with effective results. Because all the accompanying explanations are in Catalan, you are provided with a translation (in book form) at the entrance.

The temporary exhibitions on the ground floor are less weighty, and have included some excellent shows on the Mediterranean cultures, and the relationship between the famed poet Federico García Lorca and Salvador Dalí.

After all this you may need a break. The museum's **cafe** offers great food and an excellent view of the port; also on the port side is a handful of outdoor seafood restaurants.

Plaça de la Pau Vila 3. ℂ **93-225-47-00**. Admission 3€ ($3.75) adults, 2.10€ ($2.50) children 7–18 and students. Tues–Sat 10am–7pm (until 8pm Wed); Sun 10am–2:30pm. Metro: Barceloneta.

Museu Marítim ✮✮✮ *Kids*   Located in the former Royal Shipyards (Drassanes Reials), the city's Maritime Museum is the finest of its kind in Spain and possibly in the world. The seafaring cities of Venice, Genoa, and Valencia all had impressive arsenals, but only vestiges remain. In contrast, Barcelona's shipyards, with their majestic arches, columns, and gigantic vaults, are a preciously intact example of medieval civic architecture. This complex, which before the coastline receded sat right on the water's edge, was used to dry-dock, construct, and repair ships for the Catalan-Aragonese rulers. During the 18th century, the place went into decline, mainly due to the dissolution of naval construction. Right up until the Spanish Civil War, it served as an army barracks; it became a museum in the 1970s.

Its collection titled **"The Great Adventure of the Sea"** is homage to Catalonia's maritime history. The most outstanding exhibit occupies an entire bay. It is a reconstruction of La Galería Real of Don Juan of Austria, a lavish royal galley. In 1971, following extensive documentation, this model was built in celebration of the vessel's most glorious achievement 400 years earlier. The ship headed an alliance of Spanish, Venetian, Maltese, and Vatican vessels in a bloody battle against a Turkish squadron. The so-called "Holy League" won, effectively ending Ottoman rule in the Mediterranean. There is an excellent film re-creating the battle, which you watch onboard, and you can view the galley's elaborate hull, hold, and deck where each of its 59 oars were manned by the sailors.

Other exhibits chart the traditional fishing techniques and sailing as sport through neat little caravels and draggers, snipes, and sloops. The art of wooden shipbuilding, the charting of the oceans, and the launch into the steam age are also covered. Particularly fine is the collection of late-19th-century mastheads, navigational instruments, and models of the Compañía Trasmediterránea's fleet (this local company still operates the Barcelona–Balearic islands route). The collection also boasts a small model of *Ictíneo,* one of the world's first submarines designed by the Catalan visionary Narcís Monturiol.

Av. de les Drassanes s/n. ℂ **93-342-99-20**. Admission 6€ ($7.50) adults, 3€ ($3.75) children 7–16. Daily 10am–7pm. Metro: Drassanes.

6 Outer Barcelona

Barcelona's outer suburbs are largely residential. Once they were considered to be country areas, annexed over the years by the city's continuing sprawl. Thus there are a handful of notable buildings that once stood in a village or country estate. The *barri* of Sarrià, easily reached by the FGC station of the same name, has retained a particularly authentic villagey feel. Located at the foot of Tibidabo, it's a pleasant place to wander around and take in some clean air.

Colònia Güell ✮✮   For many, Gaudí's most prolific work lies not within Barcelona but outside. He designed the church for the Colònia Güell, an ambitious plan of Eusebi Güell's that lies 20 minutes by train inland from the city. Güell was a progressive man and wished to set up a colony for the workers of his textile mill, which was being transferred here from central Barcelona. The colony would contain a hospital, library, residences, a theater, and a church. Only the crypt was completed before Güell's death.

The haunting, grottolike structure stands on an elevated part of the *colònia* surrounded by a pine forest. Its cavernous dimensions and stone-forest interior are an ingenious method that the architect employed in the planning stages, one that is on display in the museums both the Sagrada Família and La Pedrera. Gaudí devised the models for his work using lengths of string attached to weights, with the weights taking the tension, photographed the pieces, then inverted the photos. What was concave became convex, as in an arch. Thus he was able to measure the angles, build the scaffolding and envision the forms, and pre-date three-dimensional computer drawing by a hundred years. The work is one of Gaudí's most organic: Walls bend and curve at impossible angles and windows open out like beetles' wings.

It's also worth taking a walk around the rest of the colony. The red-brick *moderniste* buildings were designed by architects Francesc Berenguer and Joan Rubió Bellver. Most of these are now private residences. Many of the other buildings, the factory, and warehouses have been abandoned, which gives the place a ghost town–like ambience.

Claudi Güell s/n, Santa Coloma de Cervelló. ℂ **93-630-58-07.** Admission 4€ ($5), free for children under 10. Mon–Sat 10am–2pm and 3–7pm; Sun 10am–3pm (Mass at 11am and 1pm). FGC: Colònia Güell. Lines S33, S34, S8, and S7 (all leave from Plaça Espanya).

CosmoCaixa (Museu de la Ciència) ⭐⭐⭐ *Kids*   This spectacular Science Museum

is an enlarged, much improved version of the 1980 original. Funded by a major bank (La Caixa) the Museu de la Ciència closed in 1998 and embarked on a 6-year overhaul. The result is the best, most high-tech, and certainly most hands-on, science museum in Europe.

Like the original, El Museu de la Ciència occupies a *moderniste* building (originally a poorhouse) at the foot of Tibidabo, but with a daring underground extension and renovation of the original edifice, effectively quadrupling its exhibition space to 3,700 sq. m (39,826 sq. ft.).

As well as the additional new bioresearch center, the permanent collection has been completely overhauled and through an imaginative combination of original material and multimedia takes the novice on a comprehensive tour of the scientific principles. The collection is divided into four categories: **"Inert Material"** deals with the Big Bang up to the first signs of life, **"Living Material"** to the birth of mankind, **"Intelligent Materials"** looks at the development of human intelligence, and **"Civilized Materials"** history and science from pioneers to the computer age.

The biggest crowd pleaser is **"The Flooded Forest,"** a living, breathing Amazonian rainforest *inside* the museum with over 100 species of animal and plant life. Kids come into close contact with animal life in the *"Toca Toca"* section, which has rats, frogs, spiders, and other fauna from diverse ecosystems, some which can be picked up and touched. There are a 3-D planetarium and the extraordinary "Geological Wall" that explains, through an interactive route, the history of the world from a geological perspective. All in all, the new Science Museum is a unique and highly entertaining window to the world of science.

Teodor Roviralta 55. ℂ **93-212-60-50.** Free admission. Planetarium 2€ ($2.50), "Toca Toca" (children come into contact with animals) 2€ ($2.50). Tues–Sun 10am–8pm. FGC: Avinguda Tibidabo (then 10-min. walk). Bus: 17, 22, 58, or 73.

Finca Güell 𝒦   The Finca Güell, or country estate of Eusebi Güell, features three works by Antoni Gaudí, the industrialist's favorite architect. Still on a private estate, they can only be viewed from the street but that doesn't detract from the impact they have upon the viewer. Eusebi Güell asked Gaudí to create an entrance gate, a gate-house, and stables. The first is probably one of the most stunning pieces of wrought-iron work in the world. Locally known as the Drac de Pedralbes (the Dragon of Pedralbes), a huge reptile literally jumps out at you, his tongue extended and ready to attack. The dwellings are no less powerful. Like the **Casa Vicens** (p. 179), they were designed early in Gaudí's career, when he was influenced by Islamic architecture, and feature turrets and white walls contrasted with brightly colored tiles. The pavilion on the right houses a library and Gaudían research center.

Gaudí took inspiration for the *finca* from the Greek myth of Hesperides. The ominous dragon is a metaphor for the beast that Hercules battled, and although they are a tad run down, the gardens behind the gate used to be lush and full of citrus trees—the legendary gardens of Hesperides themselves.

Av. Pedralbes 7. Metro: Palau Reial.

Monestir de Pedralbes 𝒦𝒦   The oldest building in Pedralbes (the city's wealthiest residential area) is this monastery founded in 1326 by Elisenda de Montcada, wife of Jaume II. It housed the nuns of the Order of Saint Clare (who are now taking up residence in a much smaller adjacent building), and after the king's death Queen Elisenda took up residence in the convent. She is buried in the Gothic church next door (where the nuns still sing their vespers) in a beautiful tomb surrounded by images of angels.

After passing over the threshold, you come to the serene cloister with a central fountain, well, herb gardens, and other greenery. There are nearly two dozen elegant arches on each side, rising three stories. Immediately to your right is a small chapel containing the chief treasure of the monastery, the incredibly intact Chapel of St. Michael. Inside, it is decorated with murals by Ferrer Bassa, a major artist of Catalonia in the 1300s, depicting the Passion of Christ.

The original nuns' residence houses an exhibition re-creating the monastic life of the 14th century: what they ate, how they dressed, the hours of prayer, and their general comings and goings. Some of the chambers contain original artifacts of the *monestir,* although the most evocative rooms are the kitchen and refectory and the communal dining room where the Mother Superior broke her vow of silence with mealtime Bible readings from the wooden pulpit.

In the renovated nuns' dormitory a treat lies in store for art lovers: 70 impressive paintings from the Thyssen-Bornemizca collection, which include works by Rubens, Titian, and Velázquez, as well as sculptures and Renaissance and baroque paintings.

Baixada del Monestir 9. ℭ **93-203-92-82.** Admission 5.50€ ($6.90) adults, 3.50€ ($4.35) students and seniors, free for children under 16. Tues–Sun 10am–2pm. FGC: Reina Elisenda.

Museu de les Arts Decoratives/Museu de Ceràmica 𝒦   The city's museums of decorative arts and ceramics occupy the Palau de Pedralbes and can be seen together. The palace is set in an elegant garden that once belonged to the Finca Güell, the country estate of Gaudí's patron and friend Eusebi Güell.

The neoclassical residence was taken over by King Alfonso XIII (who hardly ever used it) in 1920, then 10 years later he handed it over to the local government, which turned it into an exhibition space for the decorative arts. During the dictatorship,

Mes Que un Club (More Than a Club)!

Next to the Picasso, the most visited museum in the city is the **Museu FC Barcelona,** or the museum of the city's beloved football team Barça. It's inside their home ground Camp Nou, the largest stadium in Europe, with a capacity of 120,000. Despite its size, tickets to matches are scarce as hen's teeth. Most of the seats are taken by *socis* (members) of the richest soccer club in the world. As their slogan goes, Barça is *"Mes que un club"* (More than a club). Membership, which is often handed down through the generations, is a mark of *catalanismo* (Catalan identity). During the dictatorship, the war was played out on the football field with the capital's team seen as representative of the loathed central government. Madrid is still Barça's arch enemy (old grudges die hard in soccer) and when the two meet at Camp Nou, the whole city stops.

Along with the museum, you can choose to see the (empty) stadium, the chapel where players say a prayer before a big match, the club and press-rooms, and the tunnel through which players enter the field. The collection consists of photos, trophies, documents, kits, and other paraphernalia telling the dramatic history of the club, from its beginnings in 1899 to the present. It's fun, makes for some light relief from other heady, cultural offerings, and is not just for die-hard soccer fans.

Camp Nou stadium, access doors 7 and 9. Arístides Maillol s/n. ℂ **93-496-36-09.** Admission museum and stadium: Guided Tour: 9.50€ ($12) adults, 6.50€ ($8.10) children under 13. Museum only: 6.50€ ($8.10) adults, 3.70€ ($4.60) children under 13. Monday through Saturday 10am to 6:30pm; Sunday 10am to 2pm. Metro: Collblanc.

General Franco made it his Barcelona abode, before it finally regained its status as a museum again in 1960.

Inside, the lavish halls with their gilt, marble, and frescoes make a picturesque backdrop for both these collections. By far the superior of the two is the Ceramic Museum, whose collection, arranged regionally, spans from the 11th century to the present day. Particularly striking are the Mudéjar and metallic inlay work from the South and the baroque and Renaissance pieces from Castile. One extraordinary exhibit from Catalonia is an enormous plaque from the 18th century depicting a chocolate feast in the countryside.

Compared with the collection of decorative arts at the MNAC (p. 184), the small exhibition here is a slight letdown. The name is somewhat deceiving, as the focus here, at least in the latter part of the collection, is really on design, as opposed to decorative objects that may or may not be functional. That said, Catalonia's design heritage is an important one, and there are many pieces here from the city's design boom of the '80s and early '90s featuring top names such as Javier Mariscal and Oscar Tusquets. In the future, this collection may form part of the projected Design Museum, a project that is currently on the drawing board.

Av. Diagonal 686. ℂ **93-280-16-21.** Admission (for both) 3.50€ ($4.40) adults, 2€ ($2.50) students, free for children under 16. Tues–Sat 10am–6pm; Sun 10am–3pm. Metro: Palau Reial.

Tips **Small but Good: Other Barcelona Museums**

There are dozens of small private museums in Barcelona, some the fruit of a collector's obsessive passion, others that display an ancient guild's craft. Many are free; others charge a minimal entrance fee or ask for a donation. The charming **Museu de Calçat,** Plaça Sant Felip Neri 5 (© 93-301-45-33; 2.50€ ($3.10) Tues–Sun 11am–2pm; Metro: Liceu), is housed in the ancient head-quarters of the city's shoemaker guild. The collection spans from Roman san-dals to the boots of the famous Catalan cellist Pau Casals. The **Museu de Carrosses Fúnebres (Museum of Funeral Carriages),** Sancho d' Avilla 2 (© 93-484-17-00; Mon–Fri 10am–1pm and 4–6pm, Sat–Sun 10am–1pm; Metro: Marina), also has an unusual location: the basement of the city's morgue.

Although bullfighting is not popular in Catalonia except among a hand-ful of die-hard *aficionados,* La Monumental, Barcelona's bullring, is an exotic structure that also houses the **Museu Tauri,** Gran Vía 749 (© 93-310-45-16; Apr–Sept Tues–Sat 10:30am–2pm and 4–7pm, Sun 10am–1pm; Metro: Monumental), a small museum of memorabilia, costumes, and other related items. The taboo and the most sacred of cultures around the world are explored in the **Museu Etnológic,** Passeig de Santa Madrona s/n (© 93-424-64-02; Tues–Sun 10am–2pm; Metro: Espanya). In a similar vein, ethnographic pieces collected by Capuchin nuns in the Amazon region can be viewed in their convent at the **Museu Etnogràfic Andino-Amazónic,** Cardenal Vives i Tutó 2–16 (© 93-204-34-58; by appointment only; Metro: María Cristina). In 1982 the prominent Barcelonese doctor Melcior Colet donated his home, a *moderniste* dwelling designed by Puig i Cadafalch, and amassed sporting memorabilia for the city. The result, the **Museu de L'Esport Dr. Melcior Colet,** Buenos Aires 56–58 (© 93-419-22-32; Mon–Fri 10am–2pm and 4–8pm; bus: 7, 15, 33, 34, or 59), is a collection of objects relating to Catalan sporting achievements.

In an outer Barcelona park, an extraordinary collection of period carriages, adornments, and uniforms worn by coachmen is at the **Museu de Carruatges,** Plaça Josep Pallach 8 (© 93-427-58-13; Mon–Fri 10am–1pm; Metro: Mundet). One of the prettiest of all the city's private museums is at the rear of a per-fume shop. **The Museu del Perfum,** Passeig de Gràcia 39 (© 93-216-01-21; Mon–Fri 10:30am–1pm and 5–8pm, Sat 11am–1:30pm; Metro: Passeig de Gràcia), holds over 5,000 examples of perfume bottles, vials, and parapherna-lia from Egyptian times to the present day. Watch out for the Dalí-designed Le Roi de Soleil.

Parc d'Atraccions Tibidabo 🐸🐸 *Kids*   The mountain of Tibidabo has been a pop-ular retreat for Barcelonese since 1868, when a road was built connecting it to the city. You arrive there on the creaky old funicular—or less dramatically by bus—to find yourself confronted by an amusement park that combines tradition with modernity. In summer, the place takes on a carnival-like atmosphere, and most of the credit for this can go to a wealthy pill manufacturer by the name of Dr. Andreu who believed (quite sensibly) that fresh, mountain air was good for your health. He created the Sociedad Anónima de Tibidabo, which promoted the slopes as a public garden and was instrumental in installing both the blue tram and aforementioned funicular which get you there (p. 74). Some of the attractions in the park date back from Andreu's time. **L'Avio,** for example, is a quaint replica of the first plane that served the Barcelona-Madrid route. In the Tibidabo version, you are treated to a whisk over the summit in a toy-like craft suspended from a central axis. Another dated attraction designed to scare you out of your wits is **Aeromàgic,** an exhilarating mountain ride which is greatly enhanced by the elevated position of the park itself. On a more relaxed level you can also visit a charming museum of period automatons.

The church next to the amusement park is **Temple de Sagrat Cor,** an ugly and highly kitschy building dating from 1902 that was meant to provide Barcelona with its own Sacré Coeur. Its distinctive mountaintop silhouette can be seen from all over the city.

Plaça Tibidabo 3. ⓒ **93-211-79-42.** 22€ ($28) for unlimited rides, 11€ ($14) for 6 rides, 9€ ($11) children under 1.2m (4 ft.), free for children under 3. Summer daily noon–10pm; off season Sat–Sun noon–7pm. Bus: 58 to Avinguda Tibidabo Metro, then take the Tramvía Blau, which drops you at the funicular. Round-trip 3.10€ ($3.60).

7 Parks & Gardens

Museums aren't Barcelona's only attractions, and contrary to first impressions, it is not solely a city of concrete squares and stone streets. In a fine Mediterranean climate, life takes place outside, in unique parks and gardens, many of which were designed by the city's top architects for the Olympic renewal frenzy. The most popular ones are the leafy and formal **Parc de la Ciutadella** (p. 170), Gaudí's visionary **Parc Güell** (p. 180), and the mountain of **Montjuïc** (p. 181). But there are plenty more parks, gardens, wide-open spaces, and leafy hideaways for a bit of solitude or one-on-one with nature. Most parks are open 9am to sunset.

Not strictly a park but a large open square, one of the city's most famous "hard plazas," the **Parc de Joan Miró,** Aragó 1 (Metro: Espanya), occupies an entire L'Eixample block, once the city's slaughterhouse. Its main features are an esplanade and a pond from which a towering sculpture by Miró, *Woman and Bird,* rises. Palm, pine, and eucalyptus trees, as well as playgrounds and pergolas, complete the picture. Nearby, the enormous Parc de l'Espanya Industrial, next to the Sants train station (access Plaça dels Països Catalans), is a surrealist landscape of amphitheater-type seating, watchtowers, and postmodern sculpture juxtaposed with more vegetated parkland at the rear. On the opposite side of L'Eixample, the **Parc de L' Estació del Nord,** Nápoles 70 (Metro: Arc de Triomf or Marina), is a whimsical piece of landscape gardening featuring sculptures and land art by the U.S. artist Beverly Pepper.

Another daring urban space is the **Parc de la Creuta del Coll,** near the Parc Güell, Castellterçol 24 (Metro: Penitents). Located in a former quarry, this urban playground features a man-made pool and an enormous oxidized metal sculpture, the *Elogia del Agua* by Basque sculptor Eduardo Chillida. Looking somewhat like a huge claw, it is theatrically suspended from a cliff face. Even farther north is **Collserola,** a natural parkland of nearly 1,800 hectares (4,446 acres). Urbanites come up here in droves on the weekend to cycle, stroll, or have a picnic. The best way to get here is to take the FGC from Catalunya to either Baixador de Vallvidrera (which has an information office on the park) or Les Planes.

For those who like their parks more traditional, the romantic **Parc del Laberint** (Passeig de Castanyers s/n; Metro: Mundet) in the outer suburb of Horta is the oldest, and therefore most established, in the city. As the name suggests, there is a central maze of Cyprus trees and the rest of the site is laid out over terraces with Italianate-style statues and balustrades.

8 Outdoor & Sporting Pursuits

GOLF

One of the city's best courses, **Club de Golf Vallromanes,** Afueras s/n, Vallromanes, Barcelona (© **93-572-90-64**), is 20 minutes north of the center by car. Nonmembers who reserve tee times in advance are welcome to play. The greens fees are 75€ ($94) on weekdays, 125€ ($156) on weekends. The club is open Wednesday through Monday from 9am to 9pm. Established in 1972, it is the site of Spain's most important golf tournament.

Reial Club de Golf El Prat, El Prat de Llobregat (© **93-379-02-78**), is a prestigious club that allows nonmembers to play under two conditions: They must have a handicap issued by the governing golf body in their home country; and they must prove membership in a golf club at home. The club has two 18-hole par-72 courses. Greens fees are 60€ ($75) Monday through Friday. Weekends are for members only. From Barcelona, follow Avinguda Once de Septiembre past the airport to Barrio de San Cosme. From there follow the signs along Carrer Prat to the golf course.

SWIMMING

Swim where some Olympic events took place, at **Piscina Bernardo Picornell,** Av. de Estadí 30–40, on Montjuïc (© **93-423-40-41**). Adjacent to the Olympic Stadium, it incorporates two of the best swimming pools in Spain (one indoors, one outdoors). Custom-built for the Olympics, they're open to the public Monday through Friday from 7am to midnight, Saturday from 7am to 9pm, and Sunday from 7am to 4pm. Entrance costs 8.50€ ($11) for adults and 4€ ($5) for children and allows full-day use of the pool as well as the gymnasium, the sauna, and the whirlpools. Bus no. 61 makes frequent runs from the Plaça d'Espanya.

TENNIS

The **Centre Municipal de Tennis,** Passeig Vall d'Hebron 178 (© **93-427-65-00;** Metro: Montbau), has been the training ground for some of the country's top players. It has 17 clay and 7 grass courts set over beautiful grounds, but you will need to supply your own racket and balls.

Tips **Act Like an Olympian**

One of the city's most prestigious fitness centers, **Piscina Bernardo Picornell** (see "Swimming," above), is adjacent to the Olympic Stadium in an indoor/outdoor complex whose main attractions are its two beautifully designed swimming pools. Built for the 1992 Summer Olympics, the facility contains a health club and gym, and it's open to the public (see below).

Kids Happy, Happy, Joy, Joy!

Happy Park is the perfect solution for kids who need to let off a little steam. It's a huge covered labyrinth-type setup full of bouncy, touchy, feely, jumpy, rubbery contraptions for the little darlings to romp around on. Monitors are on hand and there is a special enclosed area for tiny tots. There are two in Barcelona: one at Comtes de Bell-lloc 74–78 (*C* 93-490-08-35; Metro: Sants) and the other at Pau Claris 97 (*C* 93-317-86-60; Metro: Urquinaona). Both are open Monday to Friday 5 to 9pm and weekends 11am to 9pm. Cost is 4€ ($5) per hour for children, free for adults.

HORSEBACK RIDING

Located high above the city on the mountain of Montjuïc, this is a top setting for a riding school. The **Escola Municipa d' Hípica,** Av. Muntayans 14–16 (*C* **93-426-10-66;** Metro: Espanya), imparts classes to all ages from 15€ ($19) per hour.

SURFING & WINDSURFING

When the wind blows, Barcelona's beaches offer good conditions for wind and kite surfing and regular surfing, and the latter has really taken off. **Wind 220°,** on the corner of Passeig Marítim and Pontevedra (*C* **93-221-47-02;** Metro: Barceloneta), right on the beach at Barceloneta, has all the equipment you need for rent, plus storage facilities, a cafe, information, and courses.

THE SWALLOW BOATS

Las Golondrinas (Swallow Boats; *C* **93-442-31-06)** are pretty little double-deckers that take you on a leisurely cruise of the city's port, or port and northern coast combined. Boats depart from the port side of the Plaça Portal de la Pau, directly in front of the Columbus statue. The port-only tour leaves every hour (weekends only) between 11:45am and 6pm, and the port and coast excursion departs daily at 11am and 12:20, 1:15, and 3:30pm. Prices for adults are 3.80€ ($4.75) for port-only and 9.20€ ($12) for port and coast; children 4 to 14 pay 1.90€ ($2.40).

Strolling Around Barcelona

Like many of the world's great cities, Barcelona is far more rewarding for travelers who see it on foot. Ideally located beside the sea and bordered on two sides by hills, it boasts a rich variety of neighborhoods, from a narrow-laned medieval center and wide-avenued 19th-century residential district to a rejuvenated beach- and marina-lined waterfront. Explore these areas at your leisure using our quartet of comprehensive do-it-yourself walking tours.

WALKING TOUR 1	BARRI GOTIC (THE GOTHIC QUARTER)

Start:	Plaça Nova (Metro: Jaume I).
Finish:	Same point at Plaça Nova or the Vía Laietana opposite Port Vell (Metro: Barceloneta).
Time:	2 to 3 hours.
Best Times:	Any sunny day or early evening.

Begin at the:

❶ Plaça Nova

Set within the shadow of the cathedral, this is the largest open-air space in the Gothic Quarter. Behind you, the facade of the **Collegi de Architects,** the city's architecture school, features a frieze designed (but not executed) by Picasso. From Plaça Nova, climb the incline of the narrow asphalt-covered street (Carrer del Bisbe).

At the approach of the first street on the right, the Carrer de Montjuïc del Bisbe de Santa Llúcia, turn right and follow this winding street to the:

❷ Plaça de Sant Felip Neri

This small square is often cited as the most charming in the Barri Gòtic. Although none of the buildings are in fact Gothic (and some have been moved from other parts of the city), the central fountain, majestic trees, and overall tranquillity more than qualify it for the status of "urban oasis." The holes you see in the stonework of the lower facade of the 17th-century church (which unfortunately lost many of its baroque features in the late 18th c.) were caused by a bomb dropped by Fascist troops that killed 20 children from the adjoining school. On the opposite side, the oldest building is Renaissance in style and serves as the headquarters of the shoemakers guild with a Shoe Museum inside.

Walk back to the Carrer del Bisbe. Backtrack left, then take the immediate right, Carrer de Santa Llúcia. This will lead you to:

❸ Casa de L'Ardiaca (Archdeacon's House)

Constructed in the 15th century as a residence for Archdeacon Despla, the Gothic building has sculptural reliefs with Renaissance and early-20th-century

Walking Tour 1: Barri Gotic (Gothic Quarter)

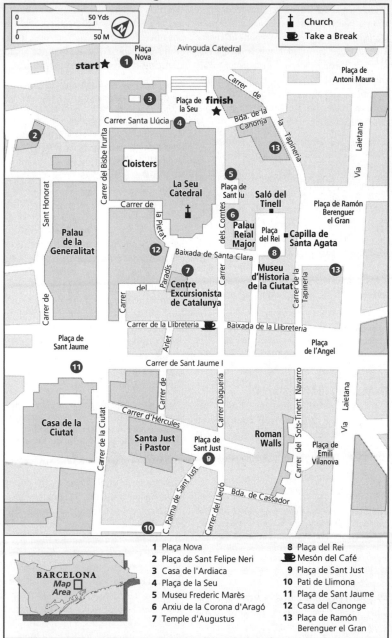

Church
Take a Break

0   50 Yds
0   50 M

Plaça Nova
Avinguda Catedral

start ★ ①

Plaça de
Antoni Maura

③

Plaça de
la Seu   **finish** ★

Carrer de
Bda. de la
Canonja

Carrer Santa Llúcia ④

⑬

Carrer del Bisbe Irurita

la Tapineria

Via Laietana

Cloisters

Plaça de
Sant Iu ⑤

Saló del
Tinell

Plaça de Ramón
Berenguer
el Gran

**La Seu
Catedral**

Carrer de

la Pietat

⑥

**Palau
Reial
Major**

Plaça
del Rei

**Capilla de
Santa Agata**

**Palau
de la
Generalitat**

Sant Honorat

⑫

Baixada de Santa Clara

⑧

Paradís

⑦

**Centre
Excursionista
de Catalunya**

del

Carrer

Carrer dels Comtes

**Museu
d'Historia
de la Ciutat**

Carrer de la Tapineria

⑬

Carrer

Carrer de la Llibreteria ☕ Baixada de la Llibreteria

Arlet

Plaça
de l'Angel

Plaça de
Sant Jaume

Carrer de Sant Jaume I

⑪

Carrer de la Ciutat

Carrer de

Carrer d'Hércules

Carrer Dagueria

Carrer del Sots-Tinent Navarro

Via Laietana

**Casa de la
Ciutat**

**Santa Just
i Pastor**

Plaça de
Sant Just

**Roman
Walls**

Plaça de
Emili
Vilanova

⑨

C. Palma de Sant Just

Carrer del Lledó

Bda. de Cassador

⑩

BARCELONA
Map
Area

1 Plaça Nova
2 Plaça de Sant Felipe Neri
3 Casa de l'Ardiaca
4 Plaça de la Seu
5 Museu Frederic Marès
6 Arxiu de la Corona d'Aragó
7 Temple d'Augustus

8 Plaça del Rei
☕ Mesón del Café
9 Plaça de Sant Just
10 Pati de Llimona
11 Plaça de Sant Jaume
12 Casa del Canonge
13 Plaça de Ramón
   Berenguer el Gran

motifs. In its cloister-like courtyard are a fountain and a palm tree. Notice the mail slot, designed by the *modernista* architect Domènech i Montaner, where five swallows and a turtle carved into stone await the arrival of important messages. This beautiful setting now holds the city's archives, but you are free to inspect the courtyard and exterior.

As you exit the Archdeacon's House, continue in the same direction several steps until you reach the:

❹ Plaça de la Seu

This square is in front of the main entrance to the **Catedral de Barcelona** (p. 160). If you are here in the first couple of weeks of December, you will be lucky to coincide with the lively Mercat de Santa Llúcia, an outdoor market selling Christmas trees, decorations, and figurines such as the pooping Catalan, the *caganer* (p. 21).

After touring the cathedral, exit from the door you entered and turn right onto Carrer dels Comtes, admiring the gargoyles along the way. After about 100 paces on the left, you'll approach the:

❺ Museu Frederic Marès

This wonderful museum holds an extraordinary collection of Romanesque and Gothic religious artifacts (p. 165). Even if you don't go in, the courtyard of this 13th-century former Bishop's palace is worth taking in. The outdoor cafe is a soothing spot to take a break.

Exit through the same door you entered and continue your promenade in the same direction. You'll pass the portal of the cathedral's right side, where the heads of two rather abstract angels flank the throne of a seated female saint. A few paces farther, on the left, notice the stone facade of the:

❻ Arxiu de la Corona d'Aragó

This is the former archives building of the crown of Aragon and Catalunya. Formerly called **Palau del Lloctinent**

(Deputy's Palace), this Gothic building was the work of Antonio Carbonell. It is not open to the public but you can get a glimpse of its patios and upper arcades, admiring the century-old grapevines.

As you exit from the courtyard, you'll find yourself back on Carrer dels Comtes. Take the street in front of you, the Carrer de la Pietat, which follows the rear facade of the cathedral and then the first street on your left, the Carrer del Paradis. At no. 10 is one of the Barri Gòtic's best kept secrets, the:

❼ Temple d'Augustus

Inside the courtyard of this medieval building, these four majestic Corinthian columns are all that remain of Roman Barcelona's main temple. Most historians believe that it was dedicated to the emperor Caesar Augustus, hence its name. What is certain is that on the highest point of the city, it was once the prominent feature of the Roman Forum. June through September, the temple is open Tuesday to Saturday from 10am to 8pm, Sunday from 10am to 2pm; the rest of the year, it's open Tuesday to Saturday from 10am to 2pm and 4 to 8pm, Sunday from 10am to 2pm.

Retrace your steps back along the Carrer de la Pietat to the Palau del Lloctinent. Continue in the same direction on the same street and it will bring you to one of the most famous squares of the Gothic Quarter:

❽ Plaça del Rei

The Great Royal Palace, an enlarged building of what was originally the residence of the counts of Barcelona, dominates this square. Here you can visit both the **Palau Reial** and the **Museu d'Història de la Ciutat** (p. 161). On the right side of the square stands the **Palatine Chapel of Santa Agata,** a 14th-century Gothic temple that is part of the Palau Reial. In this chapel is preserved the altarpiece of the Lord High Constable, a 15th-century work by Jaume Huguet.

TAKE A BREAK
Mesón del Café, Llibrería 16 (🕾 93-315-07-54), founded in 1909, specializes in coffee and cappuccino. It is one of the oldest coffeehouses in the neighborhood, sometimes crowding 50 people into its tiny precincts. Some regulars perch on stools at the bar and order breakfast. Coffee costs 1.20€ ($1.50), and a cappuccino goes for 2.20€ ($2.75). The cafe is open Monday to Saturday from 7am to 9:30pm.

Exit the Plaça de Rei on its southern side. Turn left into the steep Baixada de Llibretería. At no. 7 you will see the beautiful candle shop the Cereria Subira, the oldest continuous retail establishment in Barcelona. A few paces on turn left, crossing over the busy Carrer Ferran. Continue along the Carrer de la Dagueria. This will lead you to:

⑨ Plaça de Sant Just

The square is dominated by the entrance to the **Església dels Sants Just i Pastor.** Above the entrance portal, an enthroned Virgin is flanked by a pair of protective angels. The Latin inscription hails her as VIRGO NIGRA ET PULCHRA, NOSTRA PATRONA PIA (Black and Beautiful Virgin, Our Holy Patroness). This church dates from the 14th century, although work continued into the 16th century. Some authorities claim that the church, in an earlier, 4th-century manifestation of the present structure, is the oldest in Barcelona. You'll find that its doors are usually closed except during Sunday Mass.

Opposite the church, at Plaça de Sant Just 4, is the 18th-century **Palau Moixó,** an aristocratic town house covered with faded but still elegant frescoes of angels cavorting among garlands. At its base is a public well, the oldest water source in the city.

Continue walking in the same direction down the Carrer de la Dagueria, which changes its name to the Carrer de Lledó. If you like, take a detour to the street parallel to you on your left,

the Carrer del Sorts-Tinent Navarro; here you will see the remains of the old Roman walls. Otherwise, take the second street on your right, the Carrer Cometa (so named for a sighting of comet here in 1834). Turn right again into the Career del Regomir. At no. 3 is the:

⑩ Pati de Llimona

This lively community center, named after its interior patio and lemon tree, has a beautiful 15th-century gallery and vestiges of the old Roman sewerage system displayed underneath glass in the floor. Next door, the tiny 16th-century open **chapel of St. Christopher** is protected from the street by an iron gate. It's worth checking out what exhibitions are on in the center, normally by local artists and photographers.

Continue walking up the Carrer Regomir (which changes its name to the Carrer de la Ciutat) until you reach the:

⑪ Plaça de Sant Jaume

In many ways, this plaza is the political heart of Catalan culture. Across this square, constructed at what was once a major junction for two Roman streets, go politicians and Catalonian government bureaucrats. On Sunday evenings you can see the *sardana,* the national dance of Catalonia. Many bars and restaurants stand on side streets leading from this square.

Standing in the square, with your back to the street you just left (Carrer de la Ciutat), you'll see immediately on your right the Doric portico of the **Palau de la Generalitat,** the parliament of Catalonia. Construction of this exquisite work, with its large courtyard and open-air stairway, along with twin arched galleries in the Catalonian Gothic style, began in the era of Jaume I. A special feature of the building is the Chapel of St. George, constructed in Flamboyant Gothic style between 1432 and 1435 and enlarged in 1620 with the addition of vaulting and a cupola with hanging capitals. The back of the building encloses an orange-tree courtyard, begun in 1532. In the Gilded Hall, the Proclamation of the Republic was signed. Across the square are the Ionic columns of the **Casa de la Ciutat/Ayuntamiento,** the Town Hall of Barcelona. Both these buildings are only periodically open to the public (p. 165).

With your back to the Casa de la Ciutat, cross the square to the right and turn left, once again into the Carrer del Bisbe. On your immediate right is the:

⑫ Casa del Canonge (House of the Canon)

This series of buildings, once a group of canon's houses, dates from the 14th century and was restored in 1925; escutcheons from the 15th and 16th centuries remain. Notice the heraldic symbols of medieval Barcelona on the building's stone plaques— twin towers supported by winged goats with lion's feet. On the same facade, also notice the depiction of twin angels. The building today is used as the town residence of the President of the Generalitat.

Connecting it to the Palau de la Generalitat across the road is a charming **bridge**

carved into lacy patterns of stonework also dating from the 1920s.

Continue walking along Carrer del Bisbe until you reach your starting place, the Plaça Nova. If you wish to continue your walk, cross the square to the right to the busy Vía Laietana. Here you will see:

⑬ Plaça de Ramón Berenguer el Gran

An equestrian statue dedicated to this hero (1096–1131) is ringed with the gravel of a semicircular park, whose backdrop is formed by the walls of the ancient Roman fort and, nearby, a Gothic tower. Keep walking down the Vía Laietana toward the port and you will see more of these. Known as Las Murallas in Spanish, they were constructed between A.D. 270 and 310. The walls followed a rectangular course, and were built so that their fortified sections would face the sea. By the 11th and 12th centuries, Barcelona had long outgrown their confines. Jaume I ordered the opening of the Roman Walls, and the city expansion that ensued virtually destroyed them, except for the foundations you see today.

WALKING TOUR 2   LA RIBERA (EL BORN & SANT PERE)

Start: Plaça de l'Angel (Metro: Jaume I).
Finish: Arc de Triomf at northern end of Parc de la Ciutadella (metro Arc de Triomf).
Time: 2 to 3 hours.
Best Times: Any day or early evening.

Begin at the:
① Plaça de l'Angel
Known in medieval times as the Plaça del Blat (Square of Wheat), since all grain sales were made here, this small square stands at the busy junction of Jaume 1 and Laietana, on the eastern edge of the Barri Gòtic.

From the Plaça de l'Angel take Carrer Boria east, then turn north into Carrer Mercaderes and immediately east again to Plaça Santa Caterina and the:

② Mercat de Santa Caterina
This is the oldest working market in the area. It occupies the original site where the medieval convent of Santa Caterina once stood and provides the usual rich cornucopia of Mediterranean produce. In 2005, after a protracted period of renovation, the market was reopened. It has a stunning new *moderniste* design, by the late Enric Miralles, whose colorful waved roof owes more than a little to Gaudí.

Walking Tour 2: La Ribera (El Born and Sant Pere)

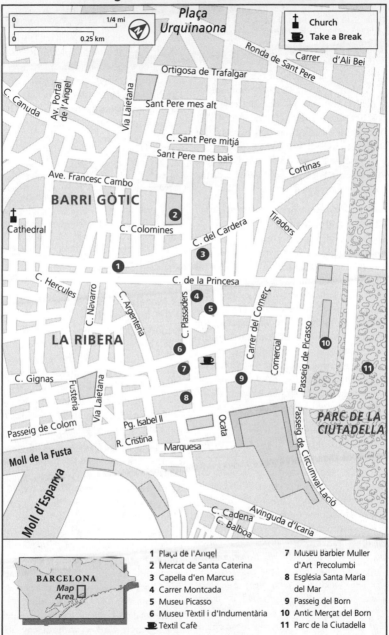

0   1/4 mi
0   0.25 km

† Church
☕ Take a Break

Plaça Urquinaona

Ronda de Sant Pere

Carrer d'Ali Bei

Ortigosa de Trafalgar

C. Canuda

Av. Portal de l'Angel

Via Laietana

Sant Pere mes alt

C. Sant Pere mitjá

Sant Pere mes bais

Cortinas

Ave. Francesc Cambo

BARRI GÒTIC

† Cathedral

C. Colomines

2

C. del Cardera

Tiradors

3

1

C. Hercules

C. Navarro

C. Argenteria

C. de la Princesa

C. Plassaders

4

5

Carrer del Comerç

Comercial

Passeig de Picasso

10

LA RIBERA

6

7

☕

11

C. Gignas

Fusteria

Via Laietana

8

9

PARC DE LA CIUTADELLA

Passeig de Colom

Pg. Isabel II

R. Cristina

Marquesa

Ocata

Passeig de Circumval·lació

Moll de la Fusta

Moll d'Espanya

C. Cadena

C. Balboa

Avinguda d'Icaria

BARCELONA
Map Area

1 Plaça de l'Angel
2 Mercat de Santa Caterina
3 Capella d'en Marcus
4 Carrer Montcada
5 Museu Picasso
6 Museu Tèxtil i d'Indumentària
   ☕ Tèxtil Cafè
7 Museu Barbier Muller d'Art Precolumbi
8 Església Santa María del Mar
9 Passeig del Born
10 Antic Mercat del Born
11 Parc de la Ciutadella

From the south-facing side of the market take Carrer Sant Jacint, turn east into Carrer Corders, and then south into the Placeta d'en Marcus.

❸ Capella d'en Marcus

Well worth a peep is this diminutive 12th-century chapel nestling in the tiny Placeta d'en Marcus square, near the junction of Calle Montcada and Calle Carders (Woolcomber's Street). Originally conceived by one Bernat Marcus as a sanctuary for luckless travelers who reached the city after the gates had been closed, it's also said to have been the headquarters of the country's first postal service.

Continue south across Carrer Princesa to reach:

❹ Carrer Montcada

Named after the powerful merchant Guillem de Montcada, who in 1153 built a long-since-disappeared palace here, this charming medieval street would be interesting enough to stroll along even if it didn't contain three of the city's most interesting museums (to which, alas, you won't be able to do justice if you're to finish this walk in a single day). The elegant buildings lining the street are reminders of the time it was a wealthy trading center, where huge fortunes were made by adroit and ambitious merchants.

❺ Museu Picasso

Located in no less than five former palaces in Carrer Montcada, the Picasso is generally rated the most popular museum in town. In essence it covers "The Artist as a Young Man," and even the older works on display were created when the *malagueño* was a mere 20-something. Exhibits range from notes and rough sketches to lithographs, ceramics, and oil canvases. Highlights are *Las Meninas* (Picasso's take on Velázquez) and *The Harlequin,* and though time will be short, keep an eye open for *La Ciencia y la Caridad* (*Science and Charity*), a masterpiece created when the artist was still at school.

❻ Museu Tèxtil i d'Indumentària

Over a thousand years of fashion fill the salons of this extraordinary museum, which spreads thoughout the Palau dels Marquesos de Llio, which features its original medieval ceilings. The oldest exhibits date from early Egypt but it's the flamboyant baroque, Regency, and 20th-century styles that really catch the eye.

> **TAKE A BREAK**
> **Tèxtil Cafè,** Carrer Montcada (✆ **93-268-25-98**), is a convenient spot for a break between museums. This chic little cafe is tucked away in a secluded cobbled courtyard on grounds of the Museu Textil itself. An ideal spot in which to relax over a *café llet (café con leche)* and Danish pastry.

❼ Museu Barbier Muller d'Art Precolumbi

Atmospherically housed in the 15-century Palau Nadal, close to the above two museums, this branch of the great Geneva museum offers one of the world's best displays of pre-Columbian art and has been drawing in the crowds since it opened in 1997. Among its highlights is a dazzling selection of gold, jewelery, and masks.

Continue down Carrer Montcada to the Passeig del Born. Turn west (right) into Carrer de Santa María.

❽ Església de Santa María del Mar

Built in the 14th century during a period of just over 50 years (quick for the time), this grandiose high-vaulted basilica, honoring the patron saint of sailors, used to stand on the city's shore when the sea reached farther inland. As the welfare of sailors mainly depended on the clemency and protection of "Our Lady of the Sea," in those days large numbers of impecunious people worked without pay on its construction. Bronze figures of two porters on the door commemorate this while the west portal is flanked by statues of Peter and Paul.

Today it's one of Barcelona's most imposing Gothic structures, noted for its soaring columns and uncluttered aura of space. Look out for the superb stained-glass windows, particularly the 15th-century rose-shaped windows above the main entrance. (A belated 1997 addition is, in contrast, jarringly unimpressive). Incidentally, you'll want to return here for an evening concert—particularly a performance of Handel. In such a timeless setting it's an unforgettable experience.

Go back east again to the:

❾ Passeig del Born

This short, wide *passeig,* or avenue, was once a center for tournaments and jousting events. (The name "Born" in Catalan means, among other things, the point of a jousting lance). In medieval times, when Catalonia was a major naval power, the *passeig's* fame was such that the saying *"Roda el món i torna al Born"* ("Go round the world and return to the Born") became widespread. It was the spiritual heart of the city from the 13th century through the 18th century, when La Rambla took over that spot. Today the Born's revelry assumes a more modern nocturnal form, centered mainly around the countless bars and cafes that fill the bustling side streets.

At the end of the avenue is the:

❿ Antic Merçat del Born

This massive building, with its wrought-iron roof, was once among the city's biggest wholesale market. Closed since the 1970s, it's scheduled to reopen as a museum and cultural center—it stands above a zone of 18th-century excavations, which can be viewed through glass flooring.

Cross the Passeig de Picasso just past the eastern end of the market and you enter:

⓫ Parc de la Ciutadella

Built on the site of a much-hated 18th-century Bourbon citadel, which was destroyed by General Prim in 1878 (see his statue), this 30-hectare (75-acre) oasis of greenery was introduced in the late 1890s, just after serving as the site for the Universal Exhibition. Its many highlights include statues, fountains (one designed by a young Gaudí), a boating lake, a waterfall (La Cascada) with a giant hairy mammoth sculpture, the Domènech i Muntaner–designed Castell dels Tres Dragons (Castle of Three Dragons), which houses the zoological museum, two arboretums, and a small botanical garden. There's also a Science Museum and—last but not least—the Catalan parliament, which is located in the former citadel's arsenal and can be visited by appointment. Stroll to the northern end of the park to view the *moderniste*-cum-neo-Mudéjar–style Arc de Triomf, which served as the entrance to the Universal Exhibition.

WALKING TOUR 3 | EL RAVAL

Start:	Mirador de Colón (Metro: Drassanes).
Finish:	Universidat (Metro: Universitat).
Time:	2 to 3 hours.
Best Times:	Any sunny day or early evening.

Walk north La Rambla and then turn left into the Carrer Nou de la Rambla. Almost immediately on your left is:

❶ Palau Güell

Gaudí's first architectural creation—in reality an extension of his parents' old house, which has since been turned into a hotel—was this citadel-like *moderniste* building, located just a stone's throw from La Rambla. Current renovation work is due to be complete by early 2007, and in the meantime, from the street you can admire its Venetian facade, entrance archways, and rooftop array of bizarre chimneys.

Continue along Carrer Nou de la Rambla. When you reach the wide, busy Avinguda del Paral.lel turn right into Carrer de l'Abat Safont and then right again into Carrer de Sant Pau. On your immediate right is the:

❷ Església de Sant Pau de Camp

This rare urban example of Romanesque architecture (officially declared a national monument) is in fact Barcelona's grandaddy of all churches, filled with fascinating small sculptures and grotesque figures. When it was originally built by monks in the 9th century, the surrounding area consisted of fields and woodlands (hence its name "Saint Paul of the Countryside"). Today's rather squat building is a delightfully intact blend of 11th- to 14th-century styles, including some Visigothic decor, all of which is highlighted by a beautiful tiny cloister with Moorish archways and a stone fountain.

Continue along Carrer de San Pau to the:

❸ Rambla de Raval

This is one of the city's newest *paseos,* created in 2000 when a large quadrangle of congested alleyways and unsalubrious tenements were removed as part of a commendable and necessary "Raval open to the heavens" plan. Today it's a sunny pedestrianized area where children play and locals can relax under the slightly uneasy-looking palm trees. Surrounded by a new blend of eating spots, including various kabob locales opened by Pakistani immigrants, it now exudes an international flavor, though some of the earlier grittiness remains. More changes are planned as the area becomes increasingly gentrified and cosmopolitan. Look for the huge black cat statue at the southern end.

At the northern end of the Rambla de Raval turn right into Carere de l'Hospital. After 200 yards on your left is the:

❹ Antic Hospital de Santa Cruz

The name is misleading because the famed former hospital—one of Spain's biggest in the Middle Ages—ceased to cater to the sick and needy over 80 years ago, when one of its last patients was the dying Gaudí. Today, instead, it provides sustenance for the mind. Its blend of Gothic, baroque, and neoclassical styles is spread throughout several buildings, which were converted in 2001, after substantial renovation work, into a variety of cultural institutions including the main Catalan library located in the Massana Arts School.

On the right of the Antic Hospital is the:

❺ Carrer d'en Robador

This narrow winding sunless street in the heart of the old Barrio Chino (or Barri Xino as its known today) was once the notorious stamping grounds not of robbers *(robadors)* but of posturing frieze-like prostitutes of all shapes and sizes who filled every doorway and lined every corner. Today it's more low-key, though not entirely tart-free, a mildly risqué corner of unadorned medieval Barcelona.

At the end of Carrer d'en Robador turn right into San Pau and continue to the end where you'll come to La Rambla and the:

❻ Gran Teatre del Liceu

Tragically destroyed over a decade ago by fire, this magnificent, traditional opera house, overlooking La Rambla, has risen phoenix-like from the ashes and today once more hosts some of the best classical performances in the world. Its new facade belies the opulent interior of rich, dark colors and intricate carvings where a 19th-century setting has been revived alongside various modern accouterments.

Carry on left up La Rambla to the:

❼ Mercat de Boqueria

In a class all its own, this ever-colorful, ever-dynamic food market is among the

Walking Tour 3: El Raval

0   1/4 mi
0   0.25 km

- ✝ Church
- ☕ Take a Break
- ⓘ Information

Gran Vía de les Corts Catalanes

Plaça de la Universitat

Ronda Universitat

Torres Amat

Plaça de Catalunya
ⓘ

de Floridablanca

Ronda de Sant Antoni

C. Tigre

Carrer Valldonzella

Carrer de Pelai

Carrer dels Tallers

11

Carrer de Ferlandia

C. Riera Alta

10 **9**

RAVAL

Peu de la Creu Pintor Fortuny

C. Canuda

Av. Portal de l'Angel

C. de la Cera

C. de Carmen

C. de Hospital

La Rambla

C. Portaferrisa Boters

BARRI GÒTIC

C. de C arretes

C. de Riereta

C. Robador

4

8

7

3

5

6

C. Boqueria

✝ Cathedral

C. de la Ciutat

C.Sots Tinent Navarro

C. de Sant Pau

M. de Barberá C. l Inió

C. de Ferran

2

de la Rambla

1

Carrer Nou

Teatre C. dels

LA RIBERA

C. Arc del Teatre

Avda. de les Drassanes

Sera

Carabassa

Via Laietana

Paral·lel

Carrer Ample

Passeig de Colom

Moll de la Fusta

BARCELONA
Map
Area

1 Palau Güell
2 Església de Sant Pau de Camp
3 Rambla de Raval
4 Antic Hospital de Santa Cruz
5 Carrer d'en Robador
6 Gran Teatre del Liceu
7 Mercat de Boqueria
☕ Bar/Cafe en el Mercat de Boqueria

8 Palau de la Virreina
9 MACBA (Museu d'Art Contemporani de Barcelona)
10 FAD (Foment de Les Arts i Dissenys)
11 CCCB (Centre de Cultura Contemporània de Barcelona)

biggest and best in Europe. Under its high wrought-iron ceilings, countless stalls sell a kaleidoscopic mix of Atlantic and Mediterranean seafood, Castilian meat, Valencian fruit, and local vegetables. The picture-postcard stalls at the front tend to be more expensive, so take an admiring look and then head farther back for the better-value stuff.

TAKE A BREAK
Inside the market you'll find several good-value **bars and cafes** where locals come for early breakfasts or a snifter, or where chefs from top restaurants pause for a *café solo* between making their purchases. The bars may not look like much but they serve some of the best coffee in the city.

Almost adjoining the Boqueria is the:

⑧ Palau de la Virreina

Built in 1770, this classical baroque palace is named after the widow of a viceroy who returned to Barcelona a wealthy man after a successful period of duty in Peru. Today it's a cultural-events center, mainly private but with occasional public exhibitions dedicated to Barcelona history and traditions. The downstairs photographic displays are usually worth a look. You can also buy souvenirs here and consult the information desk for up-to-date cultural events.

Turn west away from La Rambla along Carrer Carmé and take the fourth left onto Carrer del Angel to arrive at the Plaça dels Angels (not to be confused with Plaça de l'Angel, in the La Ribera walk). Here you'll see the following trio of avant-garde arts centers. Straight in front of you across the square is the:

⑨ MACBA (Museu d'Art Contemporani de Barcelona)

Opened in 1995 with a rather tentative display, this American-designed glass-walled emporium—with its bright white walls, intricately planned ramps, and triple atrium—illuminates its now more adventurous collection of modern art masterpieces with natural light. Alongside international favorites, there's a strong presence of Catalan artists reflecting various reactionary movements both in paintings and photography. Displays are constantly changing and temporary exhibitions feature new creative works.

To your left is the:

⑩ FAD (Foment de les Arts i Dissenys)

Located in the old Convent dels Angels, just opposite the MACBA, this essentially administrative body promotes talented artists and awards grants to promising newcomers, while organizing many exhibitions of its own. Workshops and "art markets" also give burgeoning artists a chance to sell their work.

Behind the MACBA, reached by Carrer Montealegre, is the:

⑪ CCCB (Centre de Cultura Contemporània de Barcelona)

Built on the site of a spacious former Casa de Caritat (Alms House), this is Spain's biggest cultural center. Its design—by Viaplana and Piñón, who also created the Maremagnum commercial center by the port—is mainly a modern conglomeration of steel and glass, though the patio and facade of the former building remain. It offers an eclectic blend of movie and video shows, art exhibitions, conferences and courses, music and dance performances, and even organized walks around offbeat areas of the city. There's also a well-stocked bookshop and a bar/restaurant.

Then turn right into Carrer Valldoncella and then left along Carrer dels Tallers, past Plaça de Castella, for University Square and metro stop.

Start: Plaça Urquinaona (Metro: Urquinaona).
Finish: Plaça Catalunya (Metro: Cataluña).
Time: 2–3 hours.
Best Times: Any sunny day or early evening.

Start at Plaça Urquinaona and head down to Carrer Sant Francesc de Paula to the:

❶ Palau de la Musica Catalana

This haven for Barcelona music lovers, designed by Domènech i Mantaner and tucked away just above La Ribera, is well worth a slight detour before you begin your meander up into L'Eixample. Ornately extravagant, its highlights include busts of Palestrina, Bach, and Beethoven; multicolored mosaics and columns; and a large, allegorical frieze of the *Orfeu Català* by Lluis Bru. The thing to do, of course, is to come back one evening to enjoy an concert in the even more magnificent interior.

Return to Urquinaona and walk east along Carrer Ausias March to no. 31, where you'll find:

❷ Farmacia Nordbeck

Built in 1905, this is one of the best examples of a pharmacy built in a complete *moderniste* style, with stained-glass windows and dark mellow wood. Throughout L'Eixample you'll notice similarly exotic chemists—such as the Argelaguet in Carrer Roger de Llúria—emphasing the link between curing the body and satisfying the soul.

And three buildings down the street (on the same side), you'll see:

❸ Cases Tomàs Roger

This duo of houses at numbers 37 and 39, designed by Enric Sagnier at the end of the 19th century, is noted for its fine archways and well-restored *sgraffito*.

Return to Plaça Urquinaona and head north up Carrer Roger de Llúria. At no. 85 you'll find:

❹ Queviures Murrià

Run by the same family for more than 1½ centuries, this marvelous grocery store is

also an impressive work of art. The array of goodies inside are complemented by this lavish exterior by the *moderniste* painter Ramón Casas.

> ☕ **TAKE A BREAK**
> Café Baume, Roger de Llúria 124 (𝄐 93-459-05-66), is a traditional cafe in which to put your feet up in one of old-fashioned, well-worn leather chairs. Enjoy a morning coffee or tea between the exhausting business of checking out the area's artistic attractions. On Sundays, the place is particularly popular with locals who come to relax and read about the latest scandals and spats with Madrid in *La Vanguardia*.

Continue up Roger de Llúria to Carrer de Mallorca. Turn right and proceed to no. 291 to find:

❺ Bd. Ediciones de Diseño

One of the classiest interior-design shops you'll find anywhere, this stylish building—known as Casa Tomas—was designed not by one but by several key *moderniste* architects including the great Domènech i Mantaner. Browse through the (highly expensive) selection of chic reproductions and furnishings by the likes of Dalí and Gaudí.

Continue farther up Roger de Llúria and then turn right into the wide Avinguda Diagonal. On the opposite (north) side of the road at nos. 416–420 is the:

❻ Casa de les Punxes (Casa Terrados)

Known locally as the "House of Spikes" because of its sharply pointed turrets, this neo-Gothic castlelike eccentricity built by Puig i Cadafalch in 1905 has four towers and a trio of separate entrances (one for each of the family's daughters). Its ceramic panels have patriotic motifs. Controversial in the past (a then-prominent politician, Alejandro Lerroux, called it "a crime against the nation"), it's regarded today as one of *modernisme*'s great landmarks.

Farther along the Avinguda Diagonal at no. 442 is:

❼ Casa Comalat

Designed by the Gaudí-influenced architect Salvador Valeri i Popurull, this unusual house has two distinct facades, formal at the front, more playful at the back. The former has a dozen curvy stone balconies with wrought-iron railing; the latter, which opens onto Carrer Corséga, features polychrome, ceramic work, and wooden galleries. Though not open to the public, it's well worth a look from the outside.

Now walk west along the avenue to:

❽ Palau de Baró de Cuadras

Built in 1904 to a design by the ubiquitous Puig i Cadafalch, this mansion features a unique double facade that combines Plateresque and Gothic styles on the Diagonal-facing side; the more staid rear facade reflects the fact that the building was essentially a mere block of apartments overlooking Carrer Rosselló. Inside, the decor is predominantly Arabic with a wealth of mosaics, sgraffito, and polychrome woodwork. It houses the **Casa Asia** exhibition (www.casaasia.es; free admission), which aims to foster both cultural and economic relations between Asia and Europe.

Return west along Diagonal to Plaça Joan Carles 1 and turn left into Passeig de Gràcia. Head south down this avenue to the junction with Carrer Provença, where you'll find:

❾ Manzana de la Discordia

This small zone of the Eixample is the highlight of any *moderniste* enthusiast's visit. Here you have, almost on top of

each other, works by not just one great architect but three. (*Manzana,* incidentally, means both "plot of land" and "apple" in Spanish, so its double meaning intriguingly hints at the Greek myth in which Paris has to choose which beauty will win the coveted Apple of Discord.)

If there is a single victor here it's generally acknowledged to be Gaudí's exotically curvaceous **Casa Battló** (at no. 43), which has only been allowing the public in since 2002. Permanently illuminated at night, it's known affectionately by Catalans as the *casa dels ossos* (house of bones)—and sometimes alternatively the *casa del drach* (house of the dragon)—and it features an irregular blend of mauve, green, and blue fragmented tiles topped by an equally bizarre azure chimney-filled roof, which in 2004 was also opened to a grateful public.

Next comes Puig i Cadalfach's cubical-style **Casa Amettler** (no. 41), with its gleaming ceramic facade, Flemish Gothic pediments, and small bizarre Eusebio Arnau–sculpted statues of precociously talented animals (one of them blowing glass). Finally, Doménech i Mantaner's **Casa Lleo Morera** (no. 35) whose dominant turret resembles a melting (pale blue) wedding cake atop a sea of esoteric ornamentation that includes models of a lion *(lleo)* and mulberry bush *(morera)*.

Continue up a few blocks to:

❿ La Pedrera (Casa Milà)

Created between 1905 and 1910, this building is, after La Sagrada Família, Gaudí's most extraordinary work. **Casa Milà**—the building's original name—may baldly be a block of apartments, but it's like no other on earth. The highly sculpted, undulating limestone facade earned the place its nickname, **La Pedrera** (stone quarry), while its stunning wrought-iron balconies, parabolic arches, and gnarled fairy-tale chimneys evokes the fantastic. The rooftop itself is

Walking Tour 4: Moderniste Route (L'Eixample)

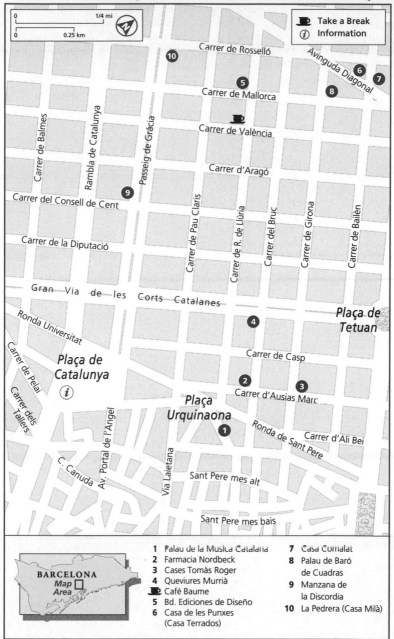

Take a Break

(i) **Information**

Carrer de Rosselló

Avinguda Diagonal

Carrer de Mallorca

Carrer de València

Carrer d'Aragó

Carrer de Balmes

Rambla de Catalunya

Passeig de Gràcia

Carrer del Consell de Cent

Carrer de la Diputació

Carrer de Pau Claris

Carrer de R. de Llúria

Carrer del Bruc

Carrer de Girona

Carrer de Bailèn

Gran Via de les Corts Catalanes

Ronda Universitat

Plaça de Tetuan

Carrer de Pelai

Carrer dels Tallers

Plaça de Catalunya

Carrer de Casp

Plaça Urquinaona

Carrer d'Ausias Marc

Ronda de Sant Pere

Carrer d'Ali Bei

C. Canuda

Av. Portal de l'Angel

Via Laietana

Sant Pere mes alt

Sant Pere mes bais

BARCELONA
Map Area

1 Palau de la Musica Catalana
2 Farmacia Nordbeck
3 Cases Tomàs Roger
4 Queviures Murrià
Café Baume
5 Bd. Ediciones de Diseño
6 Casa de les Punxes
(Casa Terrados)

7 Casa Comalat
8 Palau de Baró
de Cuadras
9 Manzana de
la Discordia
10 La Pedrera (Casa Milà)

209

spellbinding, even more so than the views it affords, and concerts are held here on summer weekends.

The fourth-floor comprises an entire *moderniste* apartment, the Pis de Pedrera—*pis* means apartment in Catalan—whose rooms are laden with wondrous knick-nacks and antiques. In the attic you can see the **Espai Gaudí (Gaudí Space),** which comprehensively summarizes Gaudí's style of working.

Shopping

The shopping possibilities in Barcelona are enough to satisfy the most demanding consumer. Its shops are on par with those in the world's major cities, and *fashionistas* here tend to look outward for inspiration (to other parts of Europe), rather than toward the rest of Spain.

Yet in spite of the increasing publicity the city receives, many visitors still arrive with a mental picture of a few dusty old establishments and department stores. Thus, the glittering avenues of top-name boutiques, polished and well-kept specialty stores, cutting-edge designer showcases, fascinating markets, and modern malls come as a pleasant surprise. Some of the leading global fashion names (Zara

and Camper, to name a couple) are in fact Spanish, and stock a larger range of their offerings—at more competitive prices—in Barcelona.

Travelers not *au fait* with Barcelona's scene tend to max out their credit cards in London or Paris and then kick themselves for not waiting to arrive in the city where, in addition to the world-class shopping now available to them, the euro goes a lot further. So if you have been sensible enough to set aside some reserve funds, you could well find yourself spending more time shopping than gallery-hopping—not of course that there's any reason to feel guilty about that!

1 The Shopping Scene

The elegant Passeig de Gràcia contains some of the most expensive retail space in Spain. Along its wide octagon-tiled footpaths, the big guns of fashion have set up shop in gorgeous 19th- and 20th-century buildings; Chanel, Max Mara, and Loewe jostle for your attention alongside Benetton, Zara, and Diesel. All along the avenue there are dozens of outdoor cafes in which to relax, enjoy a tapa or two, and examine your booty. The Rambla de Catalunya, which runs parallel to the Passeig de Gràcia, has lesser internationally known—but equally glitzy—establishments with more focus on housewares, books, and beauty. Don't bypass the cross streets that run between the two, as they are also scattered with some of the city's top shopping, particularly Valencia, Provença, and Consell de Cent, the latter of which is renowned for its expensive antiques shops and art galleries. The top end of the Passeig de Gràcia intersects El Diagonal, one of the city's main arteries. Here you will find the housewares giant Habitat, the megamall L'Illa, and various other boutiques in between. The Metro does not service this part of town and the shops are spread out, but don't despair: The *tombus* is a comfortable minibus that does the "shopping line" along the Diagonal; hop on at any regular bus stop.

The throngs hit the Portal d'Angel and Portaferrisa at the top end of the Barri Gòtic on Friday evenings and Saturdays, seeking out new arrivals in fashion from the top High Street names such as H&M, Levi's, Benetton, and other global fashion labels.

With the major department store El Corte Inglés in the immediate vicinity, these two streets (which intersect) make up the city's most central, convenient, and popular shopping hub.

Farther into the Old Quarter (El Raval, El Born, and the Barri Gòtic) is where you will find more one-of-a-kind retailers. One promising new hub is around the MACBA, the city's museum of contemporary art in El Raval. Smaller galleries come (and go) here at various intervals, and there are fashion and design shops springing up all the time. In the direction of the port, shops on the streets running off La Rambla (particularly Carme and Hospital) reflect the melting-pot nature of the neighborhood: Wine shops sit side by side with *halal* butchers and traditional Catalan bakers; other shops seem to have survived for centuries selling scissors. This is where you see the dusty, old-school emporiums of yesteryear, ones that have sadly disappeared from cities like London and New York. While not enough is done here to protect their heritage, many are still surviving the onslaught of the mall. At least for the moment.

Catalonia has largely resisted the lure of Sunday trading, mainly at the insistence of the trade unions. The good news is that most shops in the center (Passeig de Gràcia, Portal d'Angel, and Portaferrisa) stay open through the lunch hour and generally don't close until 9pm, even on Saturdays, with department stores extending this to 10pm. As a general rule of thumb, smaller shops are open Monday through Saturday 9:30 or 10am to 1:30 or 2pm then open again in the afternoon at 4 or 4:30pm to 8:30pm. You will always find exceptions to this, especially as the tourist trade fans out over the city. You may come across some that frustratingly take Monday morning off, or decide to take a 3-hour afternoon break, but even that adds to the unique experience of Barcelona's being a modern city that has retained its quaint retro feel.

Credit cards are accepted nearly everywhere, even for smallish purchases. Note, however, that you (along with everyone else) must show a form of photo ID (passport or driver's license) when making a purchase with your credit card. Don't be offended when the assistant asks for this; it is an effective guard against fraudulent credit card use.

Sales tax is called IVA; for food items it is generally charged at 7%, rising to 16% for most other goods. Cash-register receipts will show this as a separate charge (if they don't, ask). If you see a *"Compra Libre de Tasas"* (Tax-Free Shopping) sticker displayed in a shop, and are a non-E.U. resident, you can request a tax-free check on purchases of over 90€ ($113). Present this to the Cash Refund counter at the airport (Terminal A) when you depart the E.U. and you will be issued a cash refund. Refunds can also be made to your credit card or by check. For more information see www.globalrefund.com.

Sales (*rebajas* or *rebaixes*) start early July and early January. Discounts are extraordinary, often starting at 50%, but surprisingly you never see mad rushes. On the whole, shopping in Barcelona is a genteel affair; small business and trading have historically been a major backbone of its economy and many establishments here, in terms of both service and presentation, still feel like a piece of living history.

WHAT TO BUY

Stylish clothing and shoes and leatherwear are the items to go for in Barcelona. Leather shoes, belts, jackets, and coats are particularly good buys; whether you want a high-end brand such as Loewe or succumb to the leather hawkers on La Rambla, the quality and value of leather goods is superb. Barcelona has always been renowned for its expertise in design and has a vibrant design culture supported by the local government. Decorative objects and housewares here are original and well made and can be found in the shops around the MACBA and Picasso Museums. Artisan pieces, such as ceramic tiles and earthenware bowls and plates are cheap and plentiful. Cookware, crockery, wineglasses, and utensils in general are a great buy; a poke around a humble hardware store can unearth some great finds, too.

What follows is only a limited selection of some of the hundreds of shops in Barcelona.

2 Shopping A to Z

ANTIQUES

Serious collectors should check out the maze of streets around the Calle Palla near the Plaça de Pi in the Barri Gòtic; while there are few bargains to be had you will find everything from bric-a-brac to old posters and lace. Consell de Cent in the Eixample houses a range of shops selling fine antiques and antiquities. Every Thursday, many of these traders set up stalls outside the cathedral, transferring to Port Vell (the port end of La Rambla) at the weekend.

Angel Batlle *(Finds)*   This shop has an unbeatable collection of old posters, from travel to advertising and music to sport, postcards, engravings, maps, prayer cards—really anything that's printed. Some of them make a wonderful souvenir or memento; perhaps you'd prefer to take home a 1950s sherry poster instead of a Picasso or Miró print. Palla 23. © **93-301-58-84.** Metro: Liceu.

El Bulevard des Antiquaris   This 70-unit indoor market off one of the town's most aristocratic avenues has a huge collection of art, antiques, bric-a-brac, and just plain junk assembled in a series of stands and small shops. It's great for browsing, although the erratic opening hours (stall owners set their own hours) may drive you mad. Passeig de Gràcia 55. No phone. Metro: Passeig de Gràcia.

L' Arca de l'Aviva *(Moments)*   This gorgeous shop sells lace and linen bedspreads and curtains, petticoats and handkerchiefs, and other assorted textiles from the 18th to early 20th centuries. Some of the sequined numbers worn by Kate Winslet in the film *Titanic* were snapped up here from their exquisite collection of period clothing. Prices aren't cheap but the quality of their collection is unsurpassable. Banys Nous 20. © **93-302-15-98.** Metro: Liceu.

Sala d'Art Artur Ramón   One of the finest antiques and art dealers in Barcelona can be found at this three-level emporium. Set on a narrow flagstone-covered street near Plaça del Pi (the center of the antiques district), it stands opposite a tiny square, the Placeta al Carrer de la Palla. The store, which has been operated by four generations of men named Artur Ramón, also operates branches nearby and is known for its 19th- and 20th-century painting and sculpture, 19th- and 20th-century drawings and engravings, and 18th- and 19th-century decorative arts and objets d'art; additionally, there are rare ceramics, porcelain, and glassware. Prices are high, as you'd expect, but the items are of high quality and lasting value. Palla 23. © **93-302-59-70.** Metro: Jaume I.

Urbana *(Finds)*   Urbana sells an array of architectural remnants (usually from torn-down mansions), antique furniture, and reproductions of brass hardware. There are antique and reproduction marble mantelpieces, wrought-iron gates, and garden seats, even carved wood fireplaces with the *modernisme* look. It's an impressive, albeit costly, array of merchandise. Còrsega 258. © **93-218-70-36.** Metro: Hospital Sant Pau.

BOOKS

Altaïr   This excellent, up-to-date shop has its main branch here and another in the Palau Robert (p. 62). Staff are friendly and helpful and the wide selection of books—mainly in Spanish but also some in English—covers nature, anthropology, history, and global travel. There's a good choice of material on Barcelona, of course, as well as kids' books, comics, CDs, and DVDs. Gran Vía de las Cortes Catalanes 616. © **93-342-71-71.** www.altair.es. Metro: Universitat.

BCN Books   Though the main content of this English-language bookshop is language-learning material that includes basic grammar and phrase books and a wide range of dictionaries, there's also a good selection of travel books, contemporary fiction, and classical novels. (You can visit another branch at Carrer Rosselló 24, also in the Eixample.) Roger de Llúria 118. © **93-457-76-92.** Metro: Passeig de Gràcia.

Buffet y Ambigú *Finds*   In among the deli stalls at the back of the Boqueria market is this unique book outlet. The stall sells cookbooks catering to most tastes, from the best tapas recipes to manuals for chefs and special editions such as El Bulli's encyclopedia explaining techniques of the Catalan super-chef Ferran Adriá. Many of the books are in English. Mercat de la Boqueria, Parada 435. No phone. Metro: Liceu.

Casa del Llibre *Value*   This huge book barn covers all the genres from novels to self-help, travel to technical. There are sections of foreign-language books, including English, and prices here tend to be the same as you would pay back home. Passeig de Gràcia 62. © **93-272-34-80.** Metro: Passeig de Gràcia.

Cooperativa d'Arquitectes Jordi Capell   For books on Spain's architects and interior designers, head to the basement of the city's architecture school. This bookshop has a huge range of technical books for architects as well as monographs and photographic books of the work of leading architects, from Gaudí to Gehry. Plaça Nova 5. © **93-481-35-62.** Metro: Liceu.

FNAC *Value*   The Plaça Catalunya branch of this music and entertainment megastore has a solid section of English-language books. Most of the novels are bestsellers (or recent bestsellers), and a large range of the current travel guides to Barcelona and the rest of Spain are available. There is also a bilingual dictionary and language textbook section. El Triangle, Plaça Catalunya. © **93-344-18-00.** Metro: Catalunya.

Hibernian Books   Already in its second Gràcia location after opening in the villagey *barri* in 2004, this friendly, secondhand English-language bookshop is a favorite with residents and visitors alike. The books cover topics ranging from health to hobbies, and exchanges and generous discounts are available. The shop also gives you the lowdown on Anglo-Irish social and theatrical goings on in the city. A kids' corner and tea and coffee service add to the homey atmosphere, and there are armchairs where you can sit and browse before you buy. Carrer Montseny. © **93-217-46-96.** www.hibernian-books.com. Metro: Fontana.

LAIE *Value Value*   A good selection of English-language books, including contemporary literature, travel maps, and guides, is at LAIE. The bookshop has an upstairs cafe with international newspapers and a terrace. It serves breakfast, lunch (salad bar), and dinner. The cafe is open Monday through Saturday from 9am to 1am. The shop also schedules cultural events, including art exhibits and literary presentations. Pau Claris 85. © **93-318-17-39.** Metro: Catalunya or Urquinaona.

CHOCOLATES & CAKES

Cacao Sampaka ✶✶   If there were such a thing as *haute chocolat*, this establishment would be the Christian Dior. Using only the finest cacao available, a mind-boggling selection of sweetmeats is categorized into "collections": "flowers and herbs," "liquors and digestives," "gastronomic innovations," and "spices of the Americas" to name just a few. The sleek packaging turns them into true objects of desire, and there is a bar/cafe where you can enjoy a cup of creamy hot chocolate, pastries, and high-cholesterol sandwiches, all made of the highest quality ingredients at prices not dissimilar to those found in more pedestrian places. Consell de Cent 292. ✆ **93-272-08-33.** Metro: Passeig de Gràcia.

Escribà ✶ *Finds*   You may have already seen the glittering facade of this beautiful Art Nouveau shop on postcards. But far from a curious relic, it sells the goods of one of the city's finest families of chocolate and cake makers. You can pop in for a coffee and croissant (there are outside tables in the summer) or pick up a box of bonbons or a bottle of dessert wine to take home. At Easter, the windows display *monas,* elaborate chocolate sculptures decorated with jewels and feathers. La Rambla 83. ✆ **93-301-60-27.** Metro: Liceu.

Xocoa ✶   Brothers Marc and Miguel Escurell have managed to thoroughly modernize their century-old family business by employing top graphic artists to design their packaging and unveiling some novel ideas such as chocolate candles, incense, even a CD for chocolate lovers. Try the house specialty, the *Ventall,* a scrumptious cake of almond pastry and chocolate truffle. Petritxol 11. ✆ **93-301-11-97.** Metro: Liceu. There's also a branch at Roger de Llúria 87 (no phone; Metro: Girona).

DEPARTMENT STORES

El Corte Inglés   The main Barcelona branch of Spain's largest department store chain—which now has few serious competitors—sells a wide variety of merchandise, ranging from traditional handicrafts to high-fashion items, and from Spanish records to food. The store has a restaurant and cafe and offers consumer-related services, such as a travel agent. It also has a department that will mail your purchase. Not only that, but you can have shoes repaired, hair and beauty treatments, and food and drink in the rooftop cafe. The basement supermarket (Plaça Catalunya branch only) is the best place to pick up wines and other foodstuffs to take back home. Open Monday through Saturday from 10am to 10pm. Plaça de Catalunya 14. ✆ **93-306-38-00.** www.elcorteingles.es. Metro: Catalunya. Other Barcelona locations are at Av. Diagonal 617–619 (✆ **93-366-71-00;** Metro: María Cristina) and Av. Diagonal 471 (✆ **93-493-48-00;** Metro: Hospital Clinic).

DESIGNER HOMEWARES

BD Ediciones de Diseño ✶✶✶   Started by a group of prominent Catalan architects, this gorgeous gallery-shop, housed in a sumptuous *moderniste* edifice, offers only the best contemporary pieces alongside reproductions by the likes of Gaudí, Dalí, and Mackintosh. Items by Oscar Tusquets, one of the shop's founders and a leading Catalan designer, should also be sought out. Goodies range from furniture, fittings, and rugs, to smaller easily packed items such as kitchenware and decorative objects. Sleek and serious, BD is Barcelona's bastion of design culture. Casa Tomás, Mallorca 291. ✆ **93-458-69-09.** Metro: Passeig de Gràcia.

Dom   The pop aesthetic truly lives on in this housewares/objects store. Beaded curtains, bubble furniture, plastic stools, chrome lamps, and kitchenware in bold colors, plus an informed selection of international-design magazines and knickknacks ensure that there is something on offer for all budgets. The result is either extremely hip or horribly kitschy, depending on your taste and age. The shop is open Monday to Saturday from 10:30am to 9pm. Provença 249–251. ℂ **93-487-11-81.** Metro: Passeig de Gràcia. There's another branch at Avinyó 7 (ℂ **93-342-55-91;** Metro: Jaume I).

Gotham *Finds*   Although the fad for retro design pieces has been established in Spain, this shop was a pioneer. Furniture from the '50s through '60s is here, as are ceramics, crockery, vases, lights, and other items hailing from the same epoch. Prices aren't cheap, but most objects have either been restored or are in faultless condition. Cervantes 7. ℂ **93-412-46-47.** Metro: Jaume I.

Ici Et Là ⪆   Craftsmanship and quirky design characterize the pieces on display in this corner shop in the heart of the El Born shopping strip. Most pieces are limited editions by local artists, but they also receive regular shipments of, say, Nepalese chairs, African baskets, or Indian textiles. Glass is also featured strongly, from candleholders to delicately embossed wine glasses. Nearly everything in this shop could be described as a "conversation piece." Plaça Sant Maria 2. ℂ **93-268-11-67.** Metro: Jaume I or Barceloneta.

Vinçón ⪆⪆   Fernando Amat's Vinçón is the best design emporium in the city, with 10,000 products—everything from household items to the best in Spanish contemporary furnishings. Its mission is to purvey good design, period. Housed in the former home of artist Ramón Casas—a contemporary of Picasso during his Barcelona stint—the showroom is filled with the best Spain has. The always-creative window displays alone are worth the trek: Expect *anything*. Passeig de Gràcia 96. ℂ **93-215-60-50.** Metro: Diagonal.

Vitra ⪆⪆   The famed Swiss contemporary-design company has a formidable, two-story showcase in Barcelona, featuring unique pieces by Charles and Ray Eames, Phillipe Starck, Alväro Siza, and Frank Gehry to name but a few. The prices may be restrictive, and the size of most of their items mean they will not fit into your luggage, but it's okay to dream isn't it? Plaça Comercial 5. ℂ **93-268-72-19.** Metro: Jaume I or Arc de Triomf.

FABRICS, TEXTILES & TRIMMINGS

Antiga Pasamaneria J. Soler *Finds*   If fringes, ribbons, braids, tassels, and cords are your thing, then look no further. This place has been selling them since 1898, and has a wall-to-wall display of everything from dainty French grosgrain ribbons to thick tapestry braids and borders. Plaça del Pi 2. ℂ **93-318-64-93.** Metro: Liceu.

Coses de Casa ⪆   Appealing fabrics and weavings are displayed in this 19th-century store, called simply "Household Items." Many are hand-woven in Majorca, their boldly geometric patterns inspired by Arab motifs of centuries ago. The fabric, for the most part, is 50% cotton, 50% linen; much of it would make excellent upholstery material. Cushions, spreads, and throws can be made to order. Plaça de Sant Josep Oriol 5. ℂ **93-302-73-28.** Metro: Jaume I or Liceu.

Gastón y Daniella ⪆⪆   This century-old company originally hails from Bilbao, although these days its name is synonymous with fine fabrics for upholstery and drapery all over Spain. Every one of their damasks, polished cottons, brocades, and tapestries is extremely lush, more suited to a time when children's fingerprints and cat hair was not an issue. It's great to browse in, even if it's just for an end-piece for a new cushion cover. Pau Claris 171. ℂ **93-215-32-17.** Metro: Diagonal.

FASHION

Adolfo Domínguez 🎗 This shop, one of many outlets across Spain and Europe, displays fashion that has earned for the store the appellation of "The Spanish Armani." There's one big difference: Domínguez's suits for both women and men, unlike Armani's, are designed for those with hips and limited budgets. And they cover all ages at their stores, including the youth market. As one fashion critic said of their offerings, "They are austere but not strict, forgivingly cut in urbane earth tones." Passeig de Gràcia 32. ℭ **93-487-41-70.** Metro: Passeig de Gràcia.

Antonio Miró 🎗 This shop is devoted exclusively to the clothing design of Miró, but without the Groc label. It carries fashionable men's and women's clothing. Before buying anything at Groc, survey the wares at this store, which seems even more stylish. Consell de Cent 349. ℭ **93-487-06-70.** Metro: Passeig de Gràcia.

Comité *(finds)* This store is typical of the fashion startups in the streets around the MACBA. Inside is a charming decor of pastel colors and meters of white curtains, and much of the clothing is made of recycled items: An embroidered sheet or tablecloth is transformed into a wrap skirt or dress, or a striped men's shirt is retouched and tucked into a blouse. Notariat 8. ℭ **93-317-68-83.** Metro: Catalunya or Liceu.

Commercial Woman 🎗 This French-owned boutique stocks beautifully detailed and highly feminine clothing for day and evening by the likes of Cacharel, Paul&Joe, Comme des Garçon, and Spain's own Jocomomola. There is also a selection of artisan Parisian perfumes and accessories by the bijoux jewelry brand Scooter. A menswear outlet is located across the street. Calle Rec 52. ℭ **93-319-34-63.** Metro: Jaume I or Barceloneta.

Custo-Barcelona 🎗 First it was Hollywood, with the likes of Julia Roberts and Drew Barrymore seen sporting Custo T-shirts. Now they have taken over the world, with stores from Chicago to Perugia to Shanghai. As the name suggests, however, these tops and shirts, skirts, and pants in mad mixes of fabrics and emblazoned with '60s retro motifs are a homegrown product and have become a symbol of "Cool Barcelona." Plaça de les Olles 6. ℭ **93-268-78-93.** Metro: Jaume I or Liceu. There's another location at Calle Ferran 36 (ℭ **93-342-66-98**; Metro: Jaume I or Barceloneta).

El Mercadillo This is Barcelona's temple to alternative culture, with in-house DJs, piercing salons, and dozens of stalls selling urban and club wear, leather and suede jackets, records and secondhand clothes. The kids love it but you may have a hard time of it if you have a post-30 or post-teenage body size. Portaferrisa 17. ℭ **93-301-89-13.** Metro: Liceu.

Giménez & Zuazo 🎗 Quirky, colorful, and very Barcelonese, Giménez & Zuazo's creations are characterized by daring prints and unusual fabrics. Their skirts may have the silhouette of a svelte female splashed across the front, or a shirt collar may be bordered in contrasting cross-stitch. Their Boba T-shirts, with hand-painted imagery, have become something of a cult item. Elisabets 20. ℭ **93-412-33-81.** Metro: Catalunya or Liceu. There's another location at Rec 42 (ℭ **93-310-67-43**; Metro: Jaume I or Barceloneta).

Jean-Pierre Bua 🎗🎗 Another pioneer, this boutique was the first to import big-name Parisian fashion to Barcelona. There is a large stock of Gaultier (the French *enfant terrible* and Bua are personal friends); Comme des Garçon; Spain's most international designer, Sybilla; and Brussels is represented with Dries van Noten. Despite the price tags, the staff are laid-back and no one seems to mind if you spend time simply looking. Diagonal 469. ℭ **93-439-71-00.** Bus: 5, 7, 15, 33, or 34.

The Zaravolución

Many visitors to Spain are already familiar with the **Zara** clothing label. Now with over 800 (2,100, counting the Zara offshoot brands) outlets in 50 countries, including megastores in the fashion capitals of Milan, Paris, London, and New York, Zara is hard to ignore. But many are not aware, and probably surprised to know, that Zara is Spanish-owned.

Zara was started back in the early '70s by an industrious young Galician, Amancio Ortega, now the richest man in Spain. He saw a necessity for stylish housecoats for the women in his rural village and out of that an empire grew. Today Zara is one of the few fashion empires in the world that vertically controls the entire process, from textile manufacture to design to retail. Using a global network of buyers and trend-spotters, they interpret (many within the industry use the word "plagiarize") hot-off-the-catwalk pieces for men, women, and children at astoundingly affordable prices. They appeal to the full, cross-generational, demographic, from urban tribes to executives. Zara's calendar doesn't just consist of four seasons; they produce and distribute clothing year-round in their behemoth headquarters in Ortegas's native Galicia and in Zaragoza. New, never-to-be-repeated models arrive every day, meaning converts return again and again and again . . .

A revolution needs a charismatic leader and Ortega is no exception. Until he took the company public in 2001, the press possessed only one photo of a man estimated to be worth $10.3 billion. He imposes a strict "no-press" policy on his staff, and never gives interviews. He never accepts any of the dozens of accolades awarded to him in person. What he has done, in less than a generation, is democratized fashion and made it possible to dress like a film star for a song. *¡Viva la revolución!*

Located at Pelayo 58 (✆ **93-301-09-78;** Metro: Catalunya), Passeig de Gràcia 16 (✆ **93-318-76-75;** Metro: Passeig de Gràcia), as well as other places throughout the city.

Josep Font ✿✿   With a masterful eye for fabrics and attention to detail that recalls vintage St. Laurent, Catalan designer Josep Font is in class of his own. His sumptuous shop has retained many of its original Art Nouveau features customized with Font's inherent quirkiness. Bold yet feminine, with only a slight nod to the current trends, his designs remain timeless. Provença 30. ✆ **93-487-21-10.** Metro: Passeig de Gràcia.

La Boutique del Hotel   In the lobby of Hotel Axel, Barcelona's "Gay Hotel" (p. 104), the Boutique stocks (as one would perhaps expect) the best and brightest names in menswear: John Richmond, Helmut Lang, and Rykiel Homme to name just a few. In a city that is somewhat lacking in cutting-edge menswear stores, this one is frequented by homo-, hetero- and metrosexuals alike. Aribau 33. ✆ **93-323-93-98.** Metro: Passeig de Gràcia.

Loft Avignon   This emporium was largely responsible for converting this shabby Barri Gòtic street into the fashion hub that it is today. The clothes for men and women feature labels such as Vivienne Westwood, Gaultier, and Bikkembergs. Be warned, however, that the staff members are merciless, and you may find yourself handing over your credit card for a micromini you never intended to purchase. Avinyó 22. ⓒ **93-301-24-20.** Metro: Jaume I or Liceu.

Mango *(Value)*   Apart from Zara (see above), Spain's other main fashion export is Mango, which in foreign countries often goes under the name MNG. Young, trendy, and mid-priced is the deal here, and although the range isn't quite as extensive as their main competitor's (nor do they do men's or children's wear), it's a sad day in Retailand when you can't find something here to pop on for that special evening out. If your visit coincides with the winter season, their suede and leather coats and jackets are definitely worth considering. Portal de l'Angel 7. ⓒ **93-317-69-85.** Metro: Catalunya. There are other branches all over Barcelona, including the one at Passeig de Gràcia 65 (ⓒ **93-215-75-30;** Metro: Passeig de Gràcia).

On Land *(Value)*   Although On Land is surrounded by hyper-trendy boutiques, the men's and women's clothing here is highly wearable; it's cross-generational without forfeiting a cutting edge. Their own label produces some well-cut trousers and jackets, and when complemented by one of Monte Ibáñez's hand-painted T-shirts you have a distinctive outfit. Prices are good and sizes (mercifully) generous. Princesa 25. ⓒ **93-310-02-11.** Metro: Jaume I.

Textil i d'Indumentaria   Operated as a showcase for Catalonian design and ingenuity by Barcelona's Museum of Textile and Fashion, and set on a medieval street across from the Picasso Museum, this shop proudly displays and sells clothing and accessories for men, women, and children, all of which is either designed or at least manufactured within the region. Inventories include shoes, men's and women's sportswear and formal wear, jewelry, teddy bears, suitcases and handbags, umbrellas, and towels, each shaped and cut by up-and-coming Catalans. Two of the most famous designers include menswear specialist Antonio Miró (no relation to the 1950s and 1960s artist Joan Miró) and women's clothing designer Lydia Delgado. Montcada 12. ⓒ **93-310-74-04.** Metro: Jaume I.

FINE FOOD & WINE

Caelum *(Finds)*   Everything in this shop has been produced in monasteries and nunneries throughout Spain: jams and preserved fruit, quality cakes and biscuits, marzipan and liquors. The ornate, ecclesial packaging makes them great gifts, and there is a cafe downstairs where you can sample before you buy. Palla 8. ⓒ **93-302-69-93.** Metro: Liceu.

E & A Gispert   If you have trouble finding this shop behind the Santa María del Mar church, simply follow your nose. Coffee and nuts are roasted here daily (go for the almonds straight out of the oven) and sold alongside dried and candied fruit of all descriptions: Turkish figs, apricots, currants and raisins, and even French *marron glacé.* Sometimes the lines spill out onto the street, such is the quality of everything this century old shop sells. Sombrerers 23 ⓒ **93-319-75-35.** Metro: Jaume I.

La Botifarreria de Santa María *(Finds)*   If you haven't already noticed that when offered a rib-eye filet and a *botifarra* (sausage), Catalans will opt for the latter, then visit the shop opposite the Gothic Santa María del Mar church. As well as making their own *botifarras* (reputed to be the finest in the land) on the premises, they sell the richest *jamón Jabugo* (acorn-fed ham), rare cheeses, sweet *fuet* (a thin salami) from central Catalonia, and other meaty delicacies. They will vacuum pack your edibles for traveling (check if you can bring it back to your home country), or take some of their produce to the nearby Parc de Ciutadella for a picnic. Santa María 4. ⓒ **93-319-91-23.** Metro: Jaume I or Barceloneta.

La Boqueria: One of the World's Finest Food Markets

The **Boqueria market,** La Rambla 91–101 (© **93-318-25-84;** Mon–Sat 8am–8pm; Metro: Liceu), is the largest market in Europe (and probably the greatest in the world) and a must-see in the Catalan capital. It's located right in the middle of any visitor's top destination: the famous boulevard La Rambla. While many markets have little to offer a visitor in terms of practical shopping, the Boqueria boasts some of the best bars and cafes in the city, and a chance to rub shoulders with the people who are helping put the city at the forefront of Mediterranean cuisine.

Its central location is linked to a historical twist of fate: In the mid-1800's, the demolition of the city's medieval walls began. *Pageses* (Catalan peasants) had been selling their bounty roughly on the spot of the present market (originally one of the city's gates) and around the perimeter of the neighboring Convent de Sant Josep for centuries, and the authorities saw no reason to move them as the work began. When the convent burned to the ground in 1835, the market expanded, and 30 years later the engineer Miquel de Bergue finished his plans for a grandiose, wrought-iron market of five wings supported by metal columns, a project that wasn't finished until 1914. The official name of the market is Mercat de Sant Josep (a reference to the Capuchin nuns' old dwelling), although the term *boquería* (meaning *abattoir,* or butcher shop, in Catalan) has stuck since the 13th century, when the site was a slaughterhouse.

The Boqueria's 330 stalls are a testament to the fertility of the peninsula (Spain has the widest variety of farm produce in all Europe) and its surrounding seas. What lies inside is a gastronomic cornucopia that changes from season to season. Early autumn sees the hues of burnt yellow, orange, and brown in the cluster of stalls selling the dozens of varieties of *bolets,* wild mushrooms from the hills and forests of Catalonia. In spring, the candy colors of fresh strawberries and plump peaches and in early summer the greens of a dozen different lettuces, from curly bunches of escarole to pert little heads of endives and *cogollos* (lettuce hearts), make an appearance. The fish and seafood section takes prime place in a central roundabout known as the Isla del Pescado (Island of Fish), a pretty marble and shiny steel affair that was given priority in the Boqueria's recent overhaul. The variety here is awesome—from giant carcasses of tuna that send Japanese tourists into a camera-flashing frenzy, to the ugly but tasty scorpionfish, prawns the size of bananas, live crayfish, octopi, bug-eyed grouper, and countless other species. Other stalls range from game and delicatessens to bewildering businesses that survive by specializing in one product, whether it is lettuces, potatoes, or smoked salmon.

The best time to visit the Boqueria is early morning, as it comes to life. Able-bodied men drag cartloads of produce to the stalls, while women arrange it into patterns and combinations that border on food art. Have breakfast at Pinotxo on the immediate right of the main entrance. Here you will rub shoulders with the city's main chefs before they embark on their daily sourcing spree. If you wish to do a bit of shopping yourself, avoid the stalls at the front unless you want to pay "tourist" prices.

Lavinia ⚘⚘   Sort of like a wine megastore, Lavinia makes selection easy because all their products are displayed according to country of origin: from Germany to Uruguay, Australia to California. As expected, the Spanish section is the most extensive, bulging with Riojas, Priorats, *cavas*, albariños, and sherries. There is a pack-and-send service, which is handy as most bottles come cheaper by the dozen (check your country's laws about what/how much you can send back). Diagonal 605. ℂ **93-363-44-45.** Metro: María Cristina.

Origins 99.9% ⚘   Purveyors of fine, exclusively Catalan foodstuffs (.1% being the margin of error, presumably), this shop sells olive oils from Lleida, *mató* (a fresh, ricotta-like cheese) from the mountains, and wines from the Penedès and Priorat regions. There is a cafe next door where you can try before you buy. This a good place to pick up presents for foodies back home. (Check regulations on what you can legally bring back to your country!) Vidrería 6–8. ℂ **93-310-75-31.** Metro: Jaume I or Barceloneta.

Vina Viniteca ⚘⚘   This awesome wine shop in the heart of the El Born neighborhood supplies most of the restaurants in the area. The selection here can be frightening for the non-vinicultured among us, but those in the know rave about it. There are 4,500 different wines, sherries, *cavas,* liquors, and spirits from all over Spain, many of which are exclusive to the shop. Check out the bargain basket at the counter, where the last in the crates are sold for a song. Agullers 7–9. ℂ **93-310-19-56.** Metro: Jaume I or Barceloneta.

GALLERIES

Despite showing the work of some of the world's great artists, small galleries have a notoriously hard time surviving in Barcelona. This could be due to the fickleness of the scene. At the moment, gallery hubs include the streets around the Picasso Museum, the MACBA museum, and Calle Petritxol in the Barri Gòtic.

Art Picasso   Here you can get good lithographic reproductions of works by Picasso, Miró, and Dalí, as well as T-shirts emblazoned with the masters' designs. Tiles often carry their provocatively painted scenes. Tapinería 10. ℂ **93-310-49-57.** Metro: Jaume I.

Iguapop *Finds*   The Iguapop company is one of the leading promoters of contemporary music in Barcelona. Hardly surprising, then, that the emphasis is firmly on youth culture in their first gallery. Graffiti and video artists, magazine design, and contemporary photography by young people from both Spain and abroad can be seen in their airy, white space located near the Ciutadella Park. There is an adjoining shop that sells cult streetwear and accessories. Comerç 15. ℂ **93-310-07-35.** Metro: Jaume I.

Sala Parés ⚘⚘   Established in 1840, this is a Barcelona institution. The Maragall family recognizes and promotes the work of Spanish and Catalan painters and sculptors, many of whom have gone on to acclaim. Paintings are displayed in a two-story amphitheater, with high-tech steel balconies supported by a quartet of steel columns evocative of Gaudí. Exhibitions of the most avant-garde art in Barcelona change about every 3 weeks. Petritxol 5. ℂ **93-318-70-20.** Metro: Plaça de Catalunya.

HATS

Sombrería Obach *Finds*   This reassuringly old-fashioned shop in the Call district (old Jewish quarter) stocks the largest color-range of berets on earth, as well as panamas, Kangol flat caps, straw sun hats, and a host of other headgear for men and women. Check out the classic Spanish sombrero: wide-brimmed, black, and very stylish. Carrer del Call 2. ℂ **93-318-40-94.** Metro: Jaume I or Liceu.

HERBS & HEALTH FOODS

Comme-Bio   Comme-Bio is one-stop shopping for organic fruit and vegetables, health foods, tofu and other meat substitutes, and natural cosmetics. Don't get a shock from the prices; demand here for health foods is just starting to take off, so expect to pay more than in the U.K. or U.S. Next to the supermarket is a juice bar and restaurant open for lunch and dinner, although the food here is a bit pedestrian. Vía Laietana 28. ℂ **93-319-89-68.** Metro: Jaume I.

Mantantial de Salud   This period shop sells dried medicinal herbs, aromatic pills and potions, and its own range of natural beauty products all displayed in pretty pale and green glass cabinets or large ceramic urns. Many locals pop in here for a natural cure to what ails them. The staff are extremely knowledgeable and used to dealing with foreigners, although you should look up a few key words in your dictionary beforehand. Xucla 23. ℂ **93-301-14-44.** Metro: Liceu.

JEWELRY

Forvm Ferlandina *ⓕⓕ*   Contemporary jewelry and accessories from over 50 designers are on show here in tiny cubist cases that give the shop the feel of a contemporary gallery. Silversmithing, enamel work, beading, and most of the disciplines are featured. Particularly lovely are felt-flower bouquet brooches, rings, and hair ornaments that are produced in the rear workroom. Ferlandia 31. ℂ **93-441-80-18.** Metro: Liceu or Catalunya.

Platamundi *Value*   The string of Platamundi stores offers highly affordable, high-quality pieces of silver, both imported and by local designers such as Ricardo Domingo, head of the jewelry wing of FAD, the city's design council. Seek out the pieces that combine silver with enamel work in Mediterranean shades. Hospital 37. ℂ **93-317-13-89.** Metro: Liceu. There are other branches at Montcada 11 (Metro: Jaume I), Plaça Santa María 7 (Metro: Jaume I), and Portaferrisa 22 (Metro: Liceu).

Tous   Depending on your point of view, the jewelry and objects made by this Catalan family are either must-haves or too overrated to contemplate. Tous's leifmotif is the teddy bear, and the little fellow features in everything from earrings to key rings to belts and bracelets. They are adored by the city's VIP set and their popularity has grown to such an extent that you now see pirated versions. Everything in Tous is produced to a very high standard in precious metals and semi-precious stones. Passeig de Gràcia 75. ℂ **93-488-15-58.** Metro: Passeig de Gràcia.

LEATHER

Acosta *ⓕ*   Started in the '50s, this chain of stylish, Spanish leather belts and bags now has 37 shops all over Spain and one in both Lisbon and Brussels. It's still family-run, which is perhaps why everything sold has the air of being lovingly and meticulously produced. Prices are excellent, given the overall quality. Diagonal 602. ℂ **93-414-32-78.** Bus: 5, 7, 15, 33, or 34.

Loewe *ⓕⓕⓕ*   Barcelona's biggest branch of this prestigious Spanish leather-goods chain is in one of the best-known *modernista* buildings in the city. Everything is top-notch, from the elegant showroom to the expensive merchandise to the helpful salespeople. The company exports its goods to branches throughout Asia, Europe, and North America. With designer José Enrique Ona Selfa now at the helm, their clothing line is looking better than ever. Passeig de Gràcia 35. ℂ **93-216-04-00.** Metro: Passeig de Gràcia.

Lupo 🏵🏵   The current name in luxe leather goods is Lupo. Trading from a minimalist silver-and-white shop in L'Eixample, their bags and belts stretch the limits of the craft by molding and folding leather into incredible shapes and using new dyeing techniques to create the most vivid colors. The world has taken notice, and the company now exports to the U.S., the rest of Europe, and Japan. Majorca 257, bajos. ✆ **93-487-80-50.** Metro: Passeig de Gràcia.

LINEN & TOWELS

El Indio *Finds*   Established in 1870 and easily recognizable from the florid facade and arched windows, this emporium sells all sorts of textile goods, from sheets to tea towels to tablecloths. The service and wood-lined surroundings are charmingly old school and the range of offerings mind-boggling: from cheap polyester sheets to the finest linen napkins. If they don't have it, it probably doesn't exist. Carme 24. ✆ **93-317-54-42.** Metro: Liceu.

Ràfols 🏵   This store has beautiful made to order and hand-embroidered bed linen, towels, tablecloths, and other items for your trousseau. The nimble-fingered staff will whip up any design you like, and the pure cottons and linens used are pure heaven. Bori i Fontestà 4. ✆ **93-200-93-52.** Metro: Diagonal.

To Market, to Market . . .

There are various outdoor markets on the streets of Barcelona. Practice your bartering skills before heading for **El Encants flea market,** held every Monday, Wednesday, Friday, and Saturday in Plaça de les Glòries Catalanes (Metro: Glòries). Go anytime during the day to survey the selection of new and used clothing, period furniture, and out-and-out junk (although the traders will try to convince you otherwise). **Coins** and **postage stamps** are traded and sold in Plaça Reial on Sunday from 10am to 8pm. It's off the southern flank of La Rambla (Metro: Drassanes). A **book** (mainly Spanish-language) and **coin market** is held at the Ronda Sant Antoni every Sunday from 10am to 2pm (Metro: Universitat) with a brisk trade in pirated software and DVDs taking place around the periphery. All types of fine quality **antiquarian** items can be found at the Mercat Gòtic every Thursday 9am to 8pm, on the Plaça Nova outside the city's main cathedral (Metro: Liceu), although don't expect any bargains. More like a large **car-boot sale** is the Encants del Gòtic, Plaça George Orwell; Saturdays 11am to 4pm (Metro: Drassanes). The wide promenade the Rambla del Raval (Metro: San Antoni) is taken over by hippie-type traders all day, every Saturday hawking **handmade clothing, jewelry,** and other objects. Nearby, the **vintage and retro clothing traders** of the Riera Baixa (Metro: San Antoni) drag their goods out to the street (some real bargains are to be found here). Over 50 painters set up shop every weekend in the pretty Plaça del Pi (Metro: Liceu) in a **Mostra d' Art** that is of a surprisingly high standard. If food is more your thing, over a dozen purveyors of artisan cheese, honey, biscuits, olives, chocolate, and other **Catalan delicacies** can also be found in the Plaça del Pi, on the first and third weekend of every month from 10am to 10pm.

LINGERIE

Le Boudoir *(Finds)*   This may look like an upmarket sex shop (and in many ways it is), but in reality the scarlet red walls house a gorgeous collection of silk and lace lingerie and racy bedroom accessories: from furry handcuffs to music CDs designed to "get you in the mood" and other objects for intimate moments. In summer, they bring in an exclusive range of swimwear. Naughty but very, very nice. Canuda 21. © **93-302-52-81.** Metro: Catalunya.

Women'sSecret *(Value)*   This chain of lingerie, underwear, and sleepwear stores will make you wish you had one in your hometown. The prints are hip and colorful, the designs funky, and the prices highly palatable. From their basics range of pure cotton bras and nighties to striped PJs and panty sets with matching slippers and toiletry bags, this is concept retailing at its cleverest. There are several shops in the city center; the biggest are at Portaferrisa 7–9 (© **93-318-92-42;** Metro: Liceu), Puerta de l'Angel 38 (© **93-301-07-00;** Metro: Catalunya), Diagonal 399 (© **93-237-86-14;** Metro: Diagonal), and Fontanella 16 (© **93-317-93-69;** Metro: Urquinaona).

MAPS

Llibreria Quera *(Finds)*   This establishment was started in 1916 by the legendary adventurer Josep Quera, who pretty much covered every square inch of Catalonia and Andorra in his lifetime. Whether you are going hiking in the Pyrénées, motoring along the coast, or rock-climbing in the interior, you can plan your trip here with their selection of specialized books and maps. Petritxol 2. © **93-318-07-43.** Metro: Liceu.

MUSIC

Casa Beethoven *(Finds)*   Established in 1920, this store carries the most complete collection of sheet music in town. The collection naturally focuses on the works of Spanish and Catalan composers. Music lovers might make some rare discoveries. La Rambla 97. © **93-301-48-26.** Metro: Liceu.

Discos Castelló   With six shops over Barcelona, Castelló pretty much has the CD market sewn up. Half of them are located in the Calle Tallers, a street of door-to-door music and vinyl shops. Opened in 1934, their flagship store at no. 7 is mainly pop rock. Next door, "Overstocks" has more of the same plus sections on jazz, world, Spanish, and country music. Classical music is sold at no. 3. Calle Tallers. © **93-318-20-41.** Metro: Catalunya.

FNAC *(Value)*   If you don't want anything too out of the mainstream, the best place to pick up music is the FNAC megastore in central Barcelona. The second floor has CDs of all kinds—rock, pop, jazz, classical, and a tempting selection that consists of mostly not-quite-current releases of current artists at rock-bottom prices. You can ask to listen before buying, which is handy for making purchases of Spanish music and flamenco. It's open 10am to 10pm Monday through Saturday. Plaça de Catalunya 4. © **93-344-18-00.** Metro: Catalunya.

OUTLETS & SECONDS

Contribución y Moda *(Finds)*   This large split-level store sells men's and women's designer clothing from last season and beyond. It's the sort of place where you may pick up a pair of Vivienne Westwood woolen trousers for as little as 100€ ($125), or wonder if that Gaultier skirt was really worth 250€ ($312) at full price. That said, you can normally find at least one item to your taste and budget (especially at the beginning of the season), although the different size ranges can make you want to scream. Riera de Sant Miquel 30. (*C* **93-218-71-40**. Metro: Diagonal.

La Roca Village   Only true bargain hunters will be bothered to make the trip to this outer Barcelona "outlet village." But those who do will be rewarded with up to 60% off over 50 brands, from high-fashion labels such as Roberto Verino, Versace, and Carolina Herrera; shoes from Camper; luxury leatherware from Loewe and Mandarina Duck; and even sportswear from the likes of Billabong and Timberland. The setting is actually quite pleasant with a playground for the kids, cafes, and the like, and the savings here are legendary. Open daily from 11am to 9pm. La Roca del Vallès. (*C* **93-842-39-00**. By car: Take the AP-7 to Exit 12, head to Cardedeu and then to the Centre Comercial. By train: Take the train from Sants Station to Granollers Center (trains leave every half-hour; trip time: 35 min.). From the station, a bus leaves for La Roca Village every hour at 23 min. past; a taxi will cost you 10€ ($13). By bus: Sagalés ((*C* **93-870-78-60**) runs buses directly to La Roca Village from the Fabra i Puig Bus Terminal (Passeig Fabra i Puig, next to the Metro entrance). Buses (4€/$5 round-trip) leave Mon–Fri at 9am, noon, and 4 and 8pm (trip time: 50 min.).

MNG Outlet *(Value)*   MNG is Mango, one of the biggest chains in Spain for young fashion. Their outlet store has items with *taras* (faults—of varying dimensions) and last season's stock at the silliest of prices. It's not unusual to pick up a pair of jeans here for 10€ ($13) or a T-shirt for as low as 5€ ($6.25). There is also a good selection of shoes and bags at rock-bottom prices. It gets frustratingly busy on Saturdays. A few other outlet stores are located in the immediate vicinity. Girona 37. No phone. Metro: Tetuan or Urquinaona.

112   People with a foot fetish will love this Barrio Alto shop selling last year's shoes, boots, and bags at 50% off. Marc Jacobs, Givenchy, Emma Hope, Emilio Pucci, Robert Clegerie, and Rossi are just some of the names. Laforja 105. (*C* **93-414-55-13**. FGC: Gràcia.

PERFUME & COSMETICS

La Galería de Santa María Novella *(Finds)*   This is the Barcelona outlet of the famed Officina Profumo-Farmaceutica di Santa Maria Novella in Florence, the oldest and possibly most luxurious apothecary in the world. The perfumes and colognes are unadulterated scents of flowers, spices, and fruits; the soaps handmade; and the packaging seemingly unchanged since the 18th century. Prices are high. Espasería 4–8. (*C* **93-268-02-37**. Metro: Jaume I or Barceloneta.

Regia *(R)*   This high-end perfume and cosmetics shop has a secret: Wander through the racks stacked with Dior and Chanel and you reach a small door that leads to a unique museum (free admission). There are over 5,000 examples of perfume bottles and flasks from Grecian times to the present day. The star of the collection is the dramatic "Le Rei Soleil" by Salvador Dalí. Passeig de Gràcia 39. (*C* **93-216-01-21**. Metro: Passeig de Gràcia.

Sephora   Cosmetics addicts may be forgiven for thinking they have died and gone to heaven when they enter this beauty megastore. All the desired brands are here: Clarins, Dior, Arden, Chanel, and the like—plus hard-to-finds such as Urban Decay and Phytomer. The house brand's range of makeup is a great value and Sephora claims not to be knowingly undersold. El Triangle, Pelayo 13–37. (*C* **93-306-39-00**. Metro: Catalunya.

PORCELAIN

Kastoria   This large store near the cathedral is an authorized Lladró dealer, and stocks a big selection of the famous porcelain. It also carries many kinds of leather goods, including purses, suitcases, coats, and jackets. Av. Catedral 6–8. © 93-310-04-11. Metro: Plaça de Catalunya.

POTTERY

Artesana i Coses   If you are in the vicinity of the Picasso Museum, pop into this jumble of a shop selling pottery and porcelain from every major region of Spain. Most of the pieces are heavy and thick-sided, and you can pick up a coffee mug for a little as a couple of euros. Placeta de Montcada 2. © 93-319-54-13. Metro: Jaume I.

Art Escudellers   This is one-stop shopping, unashamedly aimed at the tourist market but in reality it contains a great range of pottery and ceramics from all over Spain. You'll see the more colorful, hand-painted pieces of the south to the earthy, brown and green earthenware of the north, everyday utilitarian objects, and spectacular conversation pieces. It has a shipping service and hundreds of Spanish wines to taste and buy. Escudellers 23–25. © 93-412-68-01. Metro: Drassanes.

Baraka   Baraka's owner regularly raids the *souks* of Morocco and brings back the booty to this small shop in the trendy Born area. There is a lovely range of brightly colored and patterned pottery and ceramics, plus traditional *dhurries* (woven rugs), *bubucha* slippers, earthenware *tagines,* lamps, and other North African paraphernalia. Canvis Vells 2. © 93-268-42-20. Metro: Jaume I.

Itaca *(Finds*   Here you'll find a wide array of handmade pottery from Catalonia and other parts of Spain, as well as from Portugal, Mexico, and Morocco. The merchandise has been selected for its basic purity, integrity, and simplicity. There is a wide range of Gaudí-esque objects, inspired by trademark *trencadis* (broken tile) work. Ferran 26. © 93-301-30-44. Metro: Liceu.

SCARVES, SHAWLS & ACCESSORIES

Rafa Teja Atelier 🏵🏵   This shop has a sublime collection of wool, cotton, and silk scarves and shawls from India, Asia, and Spain, all neatly hung on wooden rails or folded into glorious, multicolored stacks. Whether it's a pashmina wrap, a mohair collar, or an extravagant shawl to match an evening dress, you are bound to unearth it here. They also do their own limited range of clothing, such as evening coats in Chinese brocades or sarong-style skirts in Indonesian batiks. Passeig del Born 18. © 93-310-27-85. Metro: Jaume I or Barceloneta.

SHOES

Camper 🏵🏵   Made on the island of Majorca, Camper shoes have now truly conquered the world. Their distinctive molded shapes in unusual colors are seen treading the streets of New York and Sydney. But Barcelona has the biggest range at better prices. The shop interiors, often done by the quirky Catalan designer Martí Guixe, reflect the brand's wholesome yet hip culture. There are several locations throughout the city. Valencia 249. © 93-215-63-90. Metro: Passeig de Gràcia.

Casas 🏵🏵   If you are serious about footwear, then this is the only name you need to know. With three shops in central Barcelona, Casas is a one-stop shoe shop for the most prominent Spanish brands (Camper, Vialis, Dorotea, and so on) and coveted imports from Clergerie, Rodolfo Zengari, and Mare, plus sports and walking shoes. Three locations: La Rambla 125 ((© 93-302-75-52), Portaferrisa 25 ((© 93-302-11-32), and Portal de l'Angel 40 ((© 93-302-11-12). Metro: Catalunya or Liceu.

Specialty Stores in the Barri Gòtic

The streets around the Barri Gòtic are packed with traditional establishments specializing in everything from dried cod to dancing shoes, some of them remnants from when mercantile activity and trading was Barcelona's lifeblood. If you see a shop window that entices, don't be shy; most of the shopkeepers welcome curious tourists, and a brief exchange with one of them just may be one of those fleeting traveler's experiences you cherish long after its over.

Dating from 1761, the **Cereria Subira,** Baixada de Llibreteria 7 (© **93-315-26-06**), has the distinction of being the oldest continuous shop in Barcelona. It specializes in candles, from long and elegant white ones used at Mass to more fanciful creations. It's worth popping in to see the two torch-bearing Maure figures alone. Magicians and illusionists love the **Rei de la Magia,** Princesa 11 (© **93-319-39-20**), a joke and magic shop dating from 1881. Behind the ornate Art Nouveau facade of **Alonso,** Santa Ana 27 (© **93-317-60-85**), lie dozens of gloves, from dainty calfskin to more rugged driving gloves plus pretty fans and lace *mantillas* (Spanish shawls). More traditional Spanish garb is to be found at **Flora Albaicín,** which specializes in flamenco dancing shoes and spotty, swirly skirts and dresses. The **Herbolisteria del Rei,** del Vidre 1 (© **93-318-05-12**), is another shop seeped in history; it has been supplying herbs, natural remedies, and cosmetics and teas since 1823. **Casa Colmina,** Portaferrisa 8 (© **93-412-25-11**), makes its own *turrones,* slabs of nougat and marzipan that are a traditional Christmas treat. Nimble fingers will love the **Antiga Casa Sala,** Call 8 (© **93-381-45-87**), which has an enormous range of beads and trinkets just begging to be turned into an original accessory. In the old Born food hub, **Angel Jobal,** Princesa 38 (© **93-319-78-02**), is the city's most famed spice merchant, from Spanish saffron to Indian pepper and oregano from Chile. **Ganiveteria Roca,** Plaça del Pi 3 (© **93-302-12-41**), has an enormous range of knives, blades, scissors, and all sorts of special-task cutting instruments. **Xancó Camiseria,** La Rambla 78–80 (© **93-318-09-89**), is one of the few period shops remaining on La Rambla: They have been making classic men's shirts in cottons, wools, and linens since 1820. If you get caught in the rain, head to **Paraguas Rambla de Las Flores,** La Rambla 104 (© **93-412-72-58**), which stocks all manner of umbrellas and walking sticks. And finally, you never know when you may need a chicken feather; the **Casa Morelli,** Banys Nous 13 (© **93-302-59-34**), has sacks of them, for simple stuffing or decorating a party outfit.

Czar   If sports shoes and trainers are your thing then look no further than Czar. They have everything from the Converse, Le Coq Sportif, and Adidas classics to more bizarre creations by Diesel, W&LT, Asics, and other cult labels. Passeig del Born 20. © 93-310-72-22. Metro: Jaume I or Barceloneta.

La Manual Alpargatera *Finds*   The good people at this Old Town shop have been making espadrilles on the premises for nearly a century. As well as the classic, slip-on variety, you will find the Catalan *espadenya,* which has ribbon ankle-ties, wedge-heeled versions in fashion colors, toasty lambs-wool slippers, and other "natural" footwear. Clients have included Michael Douglas and the pope. Avinyó 7. ℂ **93-301-01-72.** Metro: Jaume I or Liceu.

Lotusse   These Majorcan cobblers are revered for extraordinary quality of their work. The brogues, loafers, T-bars, and other classic styles for men and women actually look and feel handmade. They won't make you stand out in a crowd, but are liable to last you a lifetime. Lotusse also sells bags, wallets, and belts. Rambla de Catalunya 103. ℂ **93-215-89-11.** Metro: Passeig de Gràcia.

Muxart 🅐🅐   Hermenegildo Muxart knows how to make heels that appeal, offering sexy, cutting-edge shoes and handbags from his L'Eixample shop. A pair of black stilettos may feature a red disc on the toe, for example, or metallic silver and electric blue leather plaited together with straw to form an intricate tapestry. While this may sound a bit faddy, Muxart knows when to draw in the reins, making a pair of his shoes an investment buy rather than an expensive whim. Rosselló 230. ℂ **93-488-10-64.** Metro: Diagonal. There's another location at Rambla de Catalunya 47 (ℂ **93-467-74-23;** Metro: Passeig de Gràcia).

SHOPPING CENTERS & MALLS
Shopping malls are a bit of a contentious topic in Catalonia. Many small traders feel malls are squeezing them out of the market. The local government has reacted by limiting their construction, especially in central Barcelona. But there are still enough in existence to appease any mall fan.

Centre Comercial Glòries   Built in 1995, part of a huge project to rejuvenate a downtrodden part of town, this is a three-story emporium based on the California model. It has more than 230 shops, some posh and others far from it. Most people head here for the Carrefour department stores, the cheaper cousin of El Corte Inglés that mainly sells electrical and home goods. Although there's a typical shopping-mall anonymity to some aspects of this place, it's great for kids, with lots of open spaces and bouncy things to jump on. Open Monday through Saturday from 10am to 10pm. Av. Diagonal 208. ℂ **93-486-04-04.** Metro: Glòries.

Diagonal Mar   This is the newest of the malls, part of a huge urban project that is breathing residential and commercial life on the city's northern coastline. Reflecting the surrounding property prices, shops here tend to be mid- to high-end. All the fashion staples are here, plus a branch of the music and entertainment megastore FNAC, and even a cinema. Open Monday to Saturday from 10am to 10pm. Av. Diagonal s/n. ℂ **90-253-03-00.** Metro: Maresme/Forum, Selva de Mar, or Besós-Mar.

L'Illa Diagonal   Located in an expensive part of town, shopping here is mainly high-end. Thus, this two-story mall has stores primarily devoted to fashion and luxury products: Benetton, Mandarina Duck, Zara, Diesel, Miss Sixty, as well as a scattering of home, gift, and toy boutiques. The first level has a huge supermarket and food hall selling everything from handmade chocolates to dried cod. Open Monday through Saturday 10am to 9:30pm. Av. Diagonal 557. ℂ **93-444-00-00.** Metro: María Cristina.

Pedralbes Centre   This two-story arcade focuses mainly on fashion. Check out the street and club wear from E4G and ZasTwo, froufrou party frocks by Puente Aereo, and the brightly colored quirky cloths of Agata Ruiz de la Prada. Diagonal 609–615. ℂ **93-410-68-21.** Metro: María Cristina.

SPORTING GOODS

Decathlon *(Value* If you plan to do some physical activity in Barcelona beyond a stroll down the La Rambla, Decathlon is really the only name you need to know. Every single sport is covered in this French-owned megastore, from soccer and tennis to *ja-kai* (Basque handball) and Ping-Pong. There is swimwear, clothing for jogging, aerobics, cycling hats (and cycles), ski gear, hiking boots, and wet suits. Their prices are pretty much unbeatable, especially on their house items. Canuda 20. ℂ **93-342-61-61.** Metro: Catalunya or L'Illa. There's another location at Diagonal 557 ((ℂ **93-444-01-65;** Metro: María Cristina).

10

Barcelona After Dark

Barcelona is a great nighttime city, and the array of after-dark diversions is staggering. There is something to interest almost everyone and to fit most pocketbooks. Fashionable **bars** and **clubs** operate in nearly every major district of the city, and where one closes, another will open within weeks.

Locals sometimes opt for an evening in the *tascas* **(taverns),** or they settle in for a bottle of wine at a cafe, an easy and inexpensive way to spend an evening people-watching. The legal drinking age drinking is 18, though it's rarely enforced with much vigor.

With the passing of a new law on January 1, 2006, all bars of over 100 sq. m (1,076 sq. ft.) must have a nonsmoking area. The reality, however, is that though these zones do now exist there's not much you can do about the smoke wafting into the nonsmoking section from the far larger smokers' zone. So, as before, you usually have to air out your clothes when you get back from a night out.

If the weather is good (which is most of the time) the city's outdoor squares are at least half-filled with as many tables and chairs as they can reasonably fit. Beware where two tables are squeezed next to each other: The occupants of each will be fiercely protective of its chairs and won't like it if you drag a chair from one place to make an extra seat at the table of another. Alfresco drinking has become so popular that the local government has been forced by complaining neighbors to restrict its hours in some areas—around midnight, it's usual to be asked to finish your drinks or to go inside. Particularly good places to sit and see the world go by are **Plaça del Sol** in Gràcia and **Passeig del Born, Plaça del Pi,** and **Plaça Reial** in the Old Town. The squares are also popular drinking haunts for groups of teenagers, but their tipple tends to be more of the supermarket-bought variety. The old Spanish tradition of the *botellón,* whereby groups of young people sit around on the cement swilling beer or wine, is treated as a nuisance by the local government and noise-sensitive neighbors. Despite cracking down on the practice, it persists, especially in the summer.

People-watching of a more flesh-exposed nature can be done down at the beach in the summer. Between May and October, a line of *chiringuitos* (beach bars) opens for nighttime frivolity in the sands along Barcelona's urban beaches (Barceloneta to Poble Nou). Each one has its own flavor—some play chill-out music, others have live DJs/bands. Owners, names, and styles change from year to year, but generally they open at lunchtime (or late breakfast) and stay open until 2 or 3am.

Also down near the sands are plenty of bars and restaurants around the Olympic marina and port. This, as well as Maremagnum, the entertainment and leisure complex, and the port end of La Rambla offer more foreigner-focused spots for those looking for strong drinks and fellow English speakers.

Other areas filled with bars include the **Carrer Avinyó** in the Barri Gòtic, the **Rambla del Raval** in El Raval, and the streets of **El Born** in La Ribera—just to discover; you just follow the crowd for walk around and see where the noise is a while. coming from. There are plenty of streets

JOINING IN BARCELONA NIGHTLIFE

Nightlife will begin for many Barcelonese with a **promenade** *(paseo)* from about 8 to 9pm. Then things quiet down a bit until a second surge of energy brings out the post-dinner crowds from 11pm to midnight. Serious drinking in the city's pubs and bars usually begins by midnight. For the most fashionable places, Barcelonese will delay their entrances until at least 1am—meeting friends for the first drink of the evening after midnight certainly takes some getting used to. If you want to go on to a club, you should be prepared to delay things even longer—most clubs don't open until around 2am, and then they're mostly empty for the first half-hour or so, until the bars close at 3am. Many clubs stay open to as late as 6am. Most of them offer free entrance or discount flyers available in bars or on the streets; these will save you between 5€ and 10€ ($6.25–$13), which is the normal club entrance price, if there is one. Cover charges largely depend on the night of the week, the DJ, and what the doorman thinks you look like. The price of a mixed drink (such as a *cuba libre*—a rum and coke) hovers between 5€ and 10€ ($6.25–$13). This may seem pricey but drinks here are *strong*. If you are charged an admission, ask if its *amb consumició* (drink included). If so, take your ticket to the bar to get the first drink free.

Barcelona is a trendy town and the clubbing scene is notoriously fickle. New things come up and others disappear. Although I've recommended places that have been around for a while, don't be too surprised if names and styles of the places have changed from what is printed here when you roll up.

A lot of famous international names, from the Rolling Stones to Anastasia, include Barcelona in their tours. The biggest concerts take place at the **Palau Sant Jordi** on Montjuïc, a flexible and cavernous space that's also used to house the city's basketball games. In a city where the cult of the DJ reigns, Barcelona is short of small and mid-size exclusively live music venues (although some clubs do both, with a concert taking place before the club kids roll in).

One of the best places to see people playing instruments (as opposed to spinning records) is on the street. In the summer you'll see plenty of free entertainment—everything from opera to Romanian Gypsy music—by walking around the Barri Gòtic. Festivals such as **El Grec** (July–Aug) and **La Mercè** (late Sept) are when the biggest musical offering tends to take place.

If you want to find out what's going on in the city, the best source of local information is a little magazine called *Guía del Ocio,* which previews "La Semana de Barcelona" (This Week in Barcelona). It's in Spanish, but most of its listings will be comprehensible. Every news kiosk along La Rambla carries it. If you have Internet access, *Le Cool* magazine (www.lecool.com) also carries an English summary of some of the more alternative options each week.

If you've been scared off by press reports about La Rambla between the Plaça de Catalunya and the Columbus Monument, know that the area's been cleaned up in the past decade. Still, you will feel safer along the Rambla de Catalunya, in the Eixample, north of the Plaça de Catalunya. This street and its offshoots are lively at night, with many cafes and bars.

The main area where things feel a little uneasy is in El Raval, or the Barrio Chino (that is, the lower half of the right-hand side of La Rambla as you go toward the port), an area still known for occasional nighttime muggings. But despite (or because of?) this, a lot of the new trendy bars have opened there (such as Bar Pastis; see p. 242). Indeed, there are some great bars and in El Raval, but do use caution if you go there, especially when withdrawing money from a cash machine (although more and more of these are locked at night anyway).

1 Best Bars & Pubs

- **Best Champagne Bar:** Sparkling wine in Spain is called *cava,* and often there is very little difference between the local version and what you get north of the border in France. **El Xampanyet,** Montcada 22 (© **93-319-70-03**), a tiny, ceramic-lined *cava* bar opposite the Picasso Museum, has been serving up its house variety for generations and is one of the more atmospheric places to down a bottle or two. See p. 248.
- **Best Bar View:** The trek up to the peak of Tibidabo is worth it for **Mirablau,** Plaça Doctor Andreu 2 (© **93-418-58-79**), a chic bar that provides an unparalleled, panoramic view of the city from its floor-to-ceiling glass windows. See p. 247.
- **Best Bar for Predinner Drinks:** Strategically located just off the top end of La Rambla, **Boadas,** Tallers 1 (© **93-318-95-92**), is another historic watering hole, with its roots in Havana, Cuba. Predictably, *mojitos* and daiquiris are a specialty, and it's relaxed enough to wander in casually dressed. See p. 238.
- **Best Irish Pub:** While Barcelona abounds with good Celtic-style pubs, their wood-lined interiors and leather seating are not altogether congenial on a summer night. **The Fastnet,** Passeig Juan de Borbón 22 (© **93-295-30-05**), has an outdoor terrace that looks out onto the port, and is a favorite hangout of visiting yachties and beach-loving expats. See p. 243.

2 The Performing Arts

Long a city of the arts, Barcelona experienced a cultural decline during the Franco years, but now it is filled once again with the best opera, symphonic, and choral music. At the venues listed here, unless otherwise specified, ticket prices depend on the event. Tickets can be bought at the venues, but it's often more convenient and easier to use one of the special ticket services. The bank Caixa Catalunya sells *entradas* for many events and it also has the wondrous **Servicaixa**—an automated machine that dispenses theater and cinema tickets—in many of its branches. *Tel-entrada* (© **90-233-22-11**) lets you buy over the phone with your credit card.

CLASSICAL MUSIC

Gran Teatre del Liceu ✿✿✿   This monument to Belle Epoque extravagance, a 2,700-seat opera house, is one of the grandest theaters in the world—and it's very easy to find, halfway down La Rambla. It was designed by the Catalan architect Josep Oriol Mestves. On January 31, 1994, a huge fire gutted the opera house, shocking Catalans, many of whom regarded this place as the very citadel of their culture. The government immediately vowed to rebuild and was helped by the proceeds of a spectacular open-air concert in the burned-out shell of the old building. The new Liceu was reopened in 1999, well before the millennium deadline set by the cultural czars. Included in the rebuilding were a quiet cafe and an extensive shop in the basement, open during the day. Each show offers a couple of reduced-rate performances, where ticket prices are half-price (or close to it). Guided tours of the theater (lasting about an hour) are also available daily 10am to 6pm. Rambla dels Caputxins 51–59. ℂ **93-485-99-13.** Metro: Liceu.

La Casa dels Músics   Pianist Luis de Arquer has established a small chamber company in his 19th-century Gràcia home. They now call it the smallest opera house in the world, and they're probably not wrong since the singers are almost sitting on your lap as they perform small-scale productions of *opera buffa* and *bel canto*. Shows usually begin at 9pm, but you must call to confirm if presentations will go on and to make reservations. For the true music lover, this could be your most charming evening in Barcelona. Encarnació 25. ℂ **93-284-99-20.** Tickets 22€ ($28). Metro: Fontana.

L'Auditori ☆☆   This is the newest of the city's classical music bastions, designed as a permanent home for the Orfeó Catala choral society and the OBC (Barcelona's Symphony Orchestra), although top-flight international names perform here as well. The building was designed by the award-winning Spanish architect Rafael Moneo, and its acoustics are said to be state-of-the-art. Lepant 150. ℂ **93-247-93-00.** Metro: Glòries.

Palau de la Música Catalana ☆☆☆   In a city chock-full of architectural highlights, this one stands out. In 1908 Lluis Domènech i Montaner, a Catalan architect, designed this structure as a home for the choral society the Orfeó Catala, using stained glass, ceramics, statuary, and ornate lamps, among other elements. It stands today as the most lush example of *modernisme*. Concerts (mainly classical but also jazz, folk, and other genres) and leading recitals take place here, as do daily guided tours of the buildings (p. 166). But they say you only really appreciate it when enjoying a concert. A new extension called Petit Palau, including a luxury restaurant, recently opened. Open daily from 10am to 3:30pm; box office open Monday through Saturday from 10am to 9pm. Sant Francesc de Paula 2. ℂ **93-295-72-00.** Metro: Urquinaona.

CINEMA

In Barcelona there's a good choice of cinemas showing original language *(versió original)* movies—mostly in English—with Spanish subtitles. Some offer Monday and Wednesday discounts. Weekends are very popular (and crowded) with most movie houses also featuring late-night shows that start at 1am. Check the *Guía del Ocio* and local papers such as *El País* and *La Vanguardia* for information on showings and times.

Casablanca   This modern multiplex shows a variety of up-to-date mainstream and art releases. Some find its minimalist-style seats distractingly hard, especially if the film you're watching doesn't keep you hooked. Passeig de Gràcia 115 (L'Eixample). ℂ **93-218-43-45.** Tickets: 6.20€ ($7.75). 4 showings a day. Metro: Diagonal.

Filmoteca   Funded by the Catalan government, this *cineaste*'s haven shows classics and lesser-known works. It offers special seasons devoted to famous and not-so-famous directors, and you can buy booklets of 20 or more tickets, which bring the already low entry price down even further. Occasional children's shows are an additional attraction. All in all a bargain. Cinema Aquitania, Av. Sarria 31–33. ℂ **93-410-75-90.** www.cultura.gencat.net/filmo. Tickets: 3€ ($3.75). Metro: Hospital Clinic.

Icária Yelmo Cineplex   Located in a large mall down in the Port Olimpic area, this large 15-screen multiplex features popular mainstream releases as well as the occasional offbeat European movie. Seats are numbered at the weekend, when crowds flock in, so it's a safer bet to book your seat on their website. Salvador Espriu 61 (Vila

Olimpica). ✆ **93-221-75-85**. www.yelmocineplex.es. Tickets 6.20€ ($7.75) Tues–Sun, 5€ ($6.25) Mon. Late shows Fri and Sat.

Méliès Cinemes   Two screens here provide a blend of art-house and standard commercial releases. Anything from classics to contemporary works is shown, sometimes with special seasons focusing on particular directors or stars. The program is constantly changing, so it's well worth keeping an eye on this place if you're in town for a while. Carrer de Villaroel 10 (L'Eixample). ✆ **93-451-0051**. www.cinessmelies.blogspot.com. Tickets 5€ ($6.25) Tues–Sun, 3€ ($3.75) Mon. No credit cards. 8 programs a week. Metro: Urgell.

Renoir-Floridablanca   One of the city's most centrally located cinemas, the Renoir Floridablanca features conventional—but totally up-to-date—releases on a quartet of small screens. Usually there's a choice of eight different films on any given day. Its sister movie house, the Renoir Les Corts, offers a similar program. Floridablanca: Floridablanca 135 (L'Eixample). ✆ **93-228-93-93**. www.cinesrenoir.com. Les Corts: Eugenie d'Ors 12 (Les Corts). ✆ **93-490-55-10**. For both: tickets 6.20€ ($7.75) Tues–Sun, 4.50€ (5.60) Mon. Metro: Sant Antoni. Late shows Fri and Sat.

Verdi   Cozily situated in the heart of Gràcia, this five-screen moviehouse—the first in town to feature original-version movies—is a recognized institution in Barcelona. Films shown tend to be more adventurous and radical than the norm, and its popularity is demonstrated by long weekend lines. Get there early then, or book before. Its four-screen annex, Verdi Park, is close by. Verdi: Verdi 32 and Verdi Park Torrijos 49 (Gràcia). ✆ **93-238-79-90**. Tickets: 6€ (7.50). Late shows Fri and Sat. Metro: Fontana.

THEATER

The majority of theater in Barcelona is presented in the Catalan language by Spanish production companies. Avant-garde theater and comedy are particularly strong. La Fura dels Baus is an internationally renowned troupe, El Comedients and La Cubana draw on local folklore and popular culture to make theatergoers laugh, and El Tricicle is a well-loved trio of comedians whose medium is mime. The Catalan director Calixto Bieito is one of the world's leading directors, renowned for his contemporary and often violent versions of Shakespeare's work.

Institut del Teatre 🎭🎭🎭   This grand complex is where the city's theater and dance schools are located. There are three auditoriums of varying capacities, and performances range from student showcases, to cutting-edge international companies such as New York's Wooster Group, to 24-hour circus "marathons." Plaça Margarida Xirgú s/n. ✆ **93-227-30-00**. Metro: Espanya.

L'Antic Teatre *Finds*   This is a true avant-garde small theater near the Palau Musica Catalana, which hosts both touring companies and locals. It's only been open for a couple of years, when an old venue was "rediscovered," after being left to ruin for decades. You never know what to expect, so it's worth reading through the schedules on the door, if you can understand them—one night it's Belgian mime, the next South American circus skills, the next a Jamaican documentary. Tickets are always an excellent value, whatever you end up seeing. Verdaguer i Callis 12. ✆ **93-315-23-54**. Tickets around 6.50€ ($8.10). Metro: Urquinaona.

Mercat de Los Flors 🎭🎭   Housed in a building constructed for the 1929 International Exhibition at Montjuïc, this is the other major Catalan theater. Peter Brook first used it as a theater for a 1983 presentation of *Carmen*. The theater focuses on innovators in drama, dance, and music, as well as European modern dance companies. It

---

(Moments I Could Have Danced All Day

Although the city caters to music lovers of most tastes, the really big thing here is electronic dance music. DJs are the new rock heroes, and the Woodstock of this generation is called **Sonar** (www.sonar.es). The festival began more than 10 years ago in a small, outside venue as a way of showcasing some of the more unusual experimental music coming out of different parts of Europe. Now it takes over a significant part of the city for a long weekend in mid-June, drawing people from far and wide. It's now really two festivals, in two separate locations. During the day, it's held at a number of stages around the MACBA and CCCB museums in El Raval. At night, it moves to a huge congress and trade-fair hall outside the center, with a special bus shuttling people between locations. For the day and night gigs, tickets are sold separately, although you can buy a pass to the whole thing. Recent Sonar nighttime headliners have included Massive Attack and Björk, but the daytime music is much more open and eclectic, often accompanied by strange visuals. Of course, this being Barcelona, there's also a string of unofficial festivals running at the same time, all of which are much cheaper (or sometimes free) and can be read about on walls and from flyers in bars. This, claim the purists, is where you find the true experimental music, Sonar having sold out to the big sponsors years ago. The best thing is probably to enjoy both—but if you want to go to the official Sonar festival, you should buy your tickets (and book your accommodations) well beforehand.

---

also often features avant-garde art festivals. The 999-seat house has a restaurant overlooking the city rooftops. Lleida 59. ℂ **93-426-18-75.** Metro: Espanya.

Teatre Nacional de Catalunya   Josep Maria Flotats heads this major company in a modern, mock-Roman building a little out of the center near L'Auditori (see above). The actor-director trained in the tradition of theater repertory, working in Paris at Théâtre de la Villa and the Comédie Française. His company presents both classic and contemporary plays. Plaça de les Arts 1. ℂ **93-306-57-06.** Metro: Plaza de las Glorias.

Teatre Victoria   Situated in the west of the city, this unpretentious, large-capacity theater hosts big-scale productions, usually musical spectaculars or comedies. A couple of years ago it even hosted *Hysteria,* a comedy production in Spanish that was directed (with the help of a translator) by John Malkovich. Paral.lel 65. ℂ **93-329-91-89.** Metro: Paral.lel.

FLAMENCO

Flamenco isn't the rage here that it is in Seville and Madrid, but it still has its devotees. It's not a Catalan tradition, though Barcelona has an active Andalusian population and dancers with as much verve and color as any you'd find farther south.

El Tablao de Carmen 𝔾𝔾𝔾   This club presents a highly rated flamenco cabaret in the re-created imitation "typical Spanish artisan village" of Poble Espanyol on Montjuïc. You can go early and explore the village, and even have dinner there as the sun sets. This place has long been a tourist favorite. The club is open Tuesday through Sunday from 8pm to past midnight—around 1am on weeknights, often until 2 or 3am on weekends, depending on business. The first show is always at 9:30pm; the second show is at 11:30pm on Tuesday, Wednesday, Thursday, and Sunday, and midnight on Friday and Saturday. Reservations recommended. Poble Espanyol de Montjuïc. ✆ 93-325-68-95. Dinner and show 55€–80€ ($69–$100); drink and show 30€ ($38). Metro: Espanya.

Los Tarantos 😿😿 Established in 1963, this is the oldest flamenco club in Barcelona, with a rigid allegiance to the tenets of Andalusian flamenco. Its roster of artists changes regularly. Performers often come from Seville or Córdoba, stamping out their well-rehearsed passions in ways that make the audience appreciate the arcane nuances of Spain's most intensely controlled dance idiom; other nights it's a lesser-known local artist or a percussion show. No food is served. The place resembles a cabaret theater, where up to 120 people at a time can drink, talk quietly, and savor the nuances of a dance that combines elements from medieval Christian and Muslim traditions. Shows are sporadic, so check before you come. Plaça Reial 17. ✆ 93-318-30-67. Cover (includes 1 drink) normally around 20€ ($25). Metro: Liceu.

Tablao Flamenco Cordobés 😿 At the southern end of La Rambla, a short walk from the harborfront, you'll hear the strum of the guitar, the sound of hands clapping rhythmically, and the haunting sound of the flamenco, a tradition here since 1968. Head upstairs to an Andalusian-style room where performances take place with the traditional *cuadro flamenco*—singers, dancers, and guitarist. Cordobés is said to be the city's best flamenco showcase. Three shows are offered nightly with dinner, at 7, 8:30, and 10pm. Reservations are required. La Rambla 35. ✆ 93-317-57-11. Dinner and show 50€–60€ ($63–$75); 1 drink and show 30€–35€ ($38–$44). Metro: Drassanes.

Tirititran A flamenco restaurant run by genuine *gitanos*, the background music, the pictures on the wall, and the menu all sing of the same passionate musical tradition. In the basement they have a small stage, music, and, late on weekends, groups of Andalusians often come by to strum a guitar and drink some hard liquor. The atmosphere is friendly and, although you won't see many beautifully dressed dancers or roses between the teeth, they know their flamenco here. Buenos Aires 28. ✆ 93-363-05-91. Metro: Urgell.

CABARET, JAZZ & MORE

Espai Barroc 😿😿😿 One of Barcelona's most culture-conscious (and slightly pretentious) nightspots occupies some of the showplace rooms of the Palau Dalmases, a stately Gothic mansion in La Ribera. In a room lined with grand art objects, flowers, and large platters of fruit, you can listen to recorded opera arias and sip glasses of beer or wine. The most appealing night is Thursday—beginning at 11pm, 10 singers perform a roster of arias from assorted operas, one of which is invariably *Carmen*. Since its establishment in 1996, the place has thrived. Almost everyone around the bar apparently has at least heard of the world's greatest operas, and some can even discuss them in-depth. Montcada 20. ✆ 93-310-06-73. Metro: Jaume I.

Harlem Jazz Club 😿😿 Although its recent, rather soulless makeover would suggest otherwise, this is one of Barcelona's oldest and finest jazz clubs. It's also one of the smallest, with just a handful of tables that get cleared away when the set ends so that people can dance. No matter how many times you've heard "Black Orpheus" or "The Girl from Ipanema," they always sound new again here. Music is viewed with a certain reverence; no one talks when the performers are on. Live jazz, blues, tango, Brazilian funk, Romanian Gypsy music, African rhythms—the sounds are always fresh. Most gigs start around 10pm, slightly later on the weekends. Comtessa de Sobradiel 8. ✆ 93-310-07-55. Free admission Mon–Thurs. 6€ ($7.50) Fri–Sat. 1-drink minimum. Closed first 2 weeks in Aug. Metro: Jaume I.

Jamboree ⭐⭐ Among the boisterous revelry of the Plaça Reial just off Les Ramblas, this has long been one of the city's premier locations for good blues and jazz, although it doesn't feature jazz every night. Sometimes a world-class performer will appear here, but most likely it'll be a younger group. The crowd knows its stuff and demands only the best talent. The varied program is constantly changing and you could be entertained by a Chicago blues group or Latin American dance band when you drop in. As it gets late, the music changes totally and the place opens up as a nightclub for a young crowd, with hip-hop downstairs and world music upstairs. Most shows begin between 10pm and midnight. Plaça Reial 17. ⓒ **93-301-75-64.** Admission (includes 1 drink) 8€($10); shows 8€–12€ ($10–$15). Metro: Liceu.

Luz de Gas ⭐⭐ This theater is renowned for Latino jazz. The place itself is a turn-of-the-20th-century delight, with colored-glass lamps, red drapery, and other details, but it's also a world-class live music venue. It was once a theater, and its original seating has been turned into different areas each with its own bar. The lower two levels open onto the dance floor and stage. If you'd like to talk, head for the top tier, which has a glass enclosure. Call to see what the lineup is on any given night: jazz, pop, soul, rhythm and blues, salsa, bolero, whatever. Be warned that the management can be somewhat snooty, so go with attitude. Montaner 246. ⓒ **93-209-77-11.** Cover (includes 1 drink) usually 20€–22€ ($25–$28). Bus: 6, 27, 32, or 34.

3 Bars, Cafes, Pubs & Clubs

CIUTAT VELLA
BARS, CAFES & PUBS

Almirall ⭐ Quiet and dimly lit, this bar might help you imagine Barcelona as a late-19th-century bohemian artists' hangout. A huge Art Nouveau mirror behind the bar completes the picture. The crowd is still bohemian and it's a good place to pop in for a pre-club drink. Joaquín Costa 33 (El Raval). No phone. Metro: Sant Antoni.

Barcelona Rouge (Finds) Hidden in deeply unfashionable Poble Sec, this scarlet-red bar serves unique cocktails (including some with absinthe) and has an overstuffed collection of furniture to cozy up in, making the overall look one of a turn-of-the-20th-century bordello. There are sporadic performances (of the legal nature) of anything from Argentine tango to acrobats. The music is more of the old-school variety and regulars tend to shimmy up and ask you to dance. Poeta Cabanas 21 (Poble Sec). ⓒ **93-442-49-85.** Metro: Poble Sec.

The Black Horse This is where many of the neighborhood expats hang out. It has a traditional old-pub feel and offers classic British beers on draft. It also shows all the major soccer games and even has a bilingual pub quiz on Sundays. It's good place to hear what the situation in the city is from those who've been living here for years. Allada Vermell 16 (La Ribera). ⓒ **93-268-33-38.** Metro: Jaume I.

Borneo The name is a pun on the area it's in, known as El Born, but the only concession to the historical theme is a slideshow straight from the pages of *National Geographic.* Otherwise what you have is a spacious, relaxed bar with an upstairs area for those who want to escape for a while. Rec 49 (La Ribera). ⓒ **93-268-23-89.** Metro: Jaume I.

Café Bar Padam One of the new breed of chic bars in a down-at-the-heel part of town, the clientele and decor here are modern and hip. The only color in the black-and-white rooms comes from fresh flowers and modern paintings. French music is sometimes featured as well as art expositions. Rauric 9 (El Raval). ⓒ **93-302-50-62.** Metro: Liceu.

Is It a Bar, Cafe, Pub, or Club?

In Barcelona, it's not unusual for places to have several personalities. During the day, that peaceful cafe is the perfect place to sit and read a book or enjoy a fresh croissant. Then, as night falls, the staff changes, the music is turned up, and suddenly you might look up from your book and find yourself in a cool bar surrounded by a loud group of trendy young things. If you wait longer, you might find yourself moved from your table as the furniture is stored away so that the DJ can turn it up and people can dance.

Café Zurich   At the top of La Rambla overlooking Plaça Catalunya, this is a traditional meeting point in Barcelona, and it's also great for the passing parade around Catalonia's most fabled boulevard. If the weather is fair, opt for an outdoor table and a cold beer, and enjoy the gaiety, which often includes live music. Launched in the early 1920s, the cafe was moved out as they built the Triangle shopping center, and then swiftly moved back in. Despite the high-ish prices, grumpy waiters, and rudimentary tapas, it's been going strong ever since. Location says it all. Plaça de Catalunya 1. ℂ 93-317-91-53. Metro: Catalunya.

Cocktail Bar Boadas 🞰   This intimate, conservative bar is usually filled with regulars. Established in 1933, it is the city's oldest cocktail bar. It's located at the top end of La Rambla, and many visitors stop in for a pre-dinner drink and snack before wandering to one of the area's many restaurants. It stocks a wide array of Caribbean rums, Russian vodkas, and English gins, and the skilled bartenders know how to mix them all. You won't regret trying a daiquiri. Tallers 1 (El Raval). ℂ 93-318-95-92. Metro: Catalunya.

Eat, Drink, Life   This bar combines the best of all the atmospheres a homesick tourist could want. Comfortable seats, low lighting, friendly English-speaking staff, and TVs showing English-language news and sports. They do good food, although in small portions, all day, while at night things get more lively. A great place to go with friends if you want a place that mixes local with English in the best way. Princesa 23. ℂ 93-268-86-19. Metro: Jaume I.

El Born   Facing a rustic-looking square, this former fish store has been cleverly converted. There are a few tables near the front, but my preferred spot is the inner room decorated with rattan furniture and modern paintings. The music might be anything from Louis Armstrong to classic rock 'n' roll. The upstairs buffet serves dinner. The room is somewhat cramped, but you'll find a simple, tasty collection of fish, meat, and vegetable dishes, all carefully laid out. Passeig del Born 26 (La Ribera). ℂ 93-319-53-33. Metro: Jaume I or Barceloneta.

El Bosc de las Fades *Finds*   This is the most bizarre bar-cafe in Barcelona, evoking a fairy-tale forest—or at least trying to. It's brought to you by the same people who created Museu de la Cera (Wax Museum; p. 165), which is next door. Expect "unreal trees" and the whispering sound of waterfalls, plus a "gnome" or two—and a magic mirror that merits 30 seconds' closer inspection. At night the place attracts essentially a young crowd who enjoy the faux woodland dell, the loud background music, and the drinks. Pasaje de la Banca 7 (Barri Gòtic). ℂ 93-317-26-49. Metro: Drassanes.

El Café Que Pone Muebles Narvarro *Finds*   A strange little bar that likes to feel trendy. The name means "The bar where they put Narvarro Furniture." It's an old furniture storeroom and it does sort of feel as if you're drinking alcohol while sitting in an old-fashioned IKEA. Good music, though. Riera Alta 4–6 (El Raval). © **60-718-80-96.** Metro: San Antoni.

Fonfone   A great example of a bar that fits as many in as it can when the music gets them dancing. The colorful, lighting-based decor is particularly original and the dance music is always of high quality for those who like modern, accessible electronica. This isn't a place to stand and talk, but rather a good place to fill in those awkward hours when you're ready to go out but it's still too early to hit the clubs. The location is perfect for finding your way anywhere in the Old Town later on. Escudellers 24 (Barri Gòtic). © **93-317-14-24.** Metro: Drassanes.

Ginger 🕸🕸   A stylish, split-level cocktail, wine, and tapas bar on a pretty Barri Gòtic square. The well-mixed cocktails (including a rarity—a traditional Pimms) makes it worth hunting out, as do the tasty snacks, which include imaginative morsels such as sausages flamed-cooked in *orujo* and grilled foie. It's the sort of place you pop in for one and stay for three. Lledó 2 (Barri Gòtic). © **93-310-53-09.** Metro: Jaume I.

Hivernacle *(Finds*   This is an airy bar-cafe luring a young, hip crowd to a setting of towering palms in a 19th-century greenhouse. The location is just inside the gates of the city's most centrally located park, but it stays open after the park is closed (the entrance is down one side, on Passeig Picasso). A fashionable crowd likes to come here to "graze" upon the tapas. A restaurant adjoins and there is live music during the summer months. Parc de la Ciutadella s/n (La Ribera). © **93-295-40-17.** Metro: Arc de Triomf.

La Concha *(Finds*   There aren't many bars that have that Moroccan gay kitsch feeling, but this place does, and it's also great fun to go there and hang out while staring at the walls filled with color-treated photos of Spain's starlet from the 1960s, Sara Montiel. One part of the bar becomes a tiny dance floor on weekends. This bar is a Barrio Chino institution and it's still a bit hairy, but perfect to experience an authentic slice of bohemia. Guàrdia 14 (El Raval). © **93-302-41-18.** Metro: Drassanes.

La Fianna   With its Moroccan feel, this is a perfect spot to lie back and relax if it's raining or when you don't want a night that's too wild. The place is international and is a real find. It houses a restaurant at the back and some normal tables and barstools, but the best thing is to get there early and secure one of the cushion-filled platforms—the coziest places to curl up with a few drinks and a friend or three. They also do big American-style Sunday brunches. Banys Vells 15 (La Ribera). © **93-315-18-10.** Metro: Jaume I.

La Oveja Negra *(Value*   An Old City classic, "the black sheep" is like a hidden beer hall. The crowd is young—it's a student favorite—and the drinks are a great value. Noisy, friendly, with a beer-stained pool table and a remarkable cavelike setting, this is a fun place for young people to order some jugs of cheap sangria and meet some people. There will almost certainly be a line at the foosball table, so that's not a bad place to start. Sitges 5 (El Raval). No phone. Metro: Catalunya.

L'Ascensor 🕸   "The Elevator" has an entrance just like you'd expect: You pass through (rather than go up or down in) an old European sliding-door-style elevator to get into this very local bar so well known for its *mojitos* (Cuban rum cocktails) that it has a line of mint-and-sugared glasses waiting to be filled. Bellafila 3 (Barri Gòtic). © **93-318-53-47.** Metro: Jaume I.

Margarita Blue 🕸   They may try to cram in a few too many tables in the Mexican restaurant part, but if you can find a corner to stand in then the bar is well worth

Dancing with the Green Fairy

If you're feeling adventurous, there's good reason to go to **Bar Marsella,** Sant Pau 65 (no phone; Metro: Liceu), and that's its specialty: absinthe *(absenta)*. Picasso and Dalí are reputed to have been regulars here and it looks as though they haven't dusted the bottles since. The bar's been here more than 150 years serving the homemade drink that gives it its fame. Absinthe is an impossibly strong aniseed-tasting drink made, in part, with the herb wormwood. Some countries still ban it for its alleged hallucinogenic qualities, which led to it being called "the green fairy." Here they serve it the traditional way: with a fork, a small bottle of water, and a sugar cube. You place the sugar on the fork prongs and balance it over the rim of your glass. Then slowly drip a little of the water (not too much!) over the sugar so that it slowly dissolves into the drink. Wait for it to sink in, and then keep adding drips of water so that the sugar has nearly all dripped into your glass. Then mix the last of the sugar into your glass with the fork, and then drink. One glass won't do you much harm, but you can see those around the bar who've had at least a few by their glassy expressions and loose jaws.

visiting. The music's good, the crowd lively, and the cocktails very good, especially the namesake Blue Margarita. Josep Anselm Clavé 6 (Barri Gòtic). © **93-317-71-76.** Metro: Drassanes. They also have a sister club called Rita Blue, Plaça Sant Agustí 3 (Barri Gòtic). © **93-342-40-86.** Metro: Liceu.

Molly's Fair City   The hangout of expats, plus visiting Brits and Irishmen, and like all of Barcelona's beer halls it is incredibly popular. The sound of English voices is heard throughout the pub, growing louder as the evening wears on, and that can be very late. Expect blaring music, loud voices, and beer flowing like a river. Plus, if there's a major soccer game, you'll hear a lot of friendly shouting. Ferran 7 (Barri Gòtic). © **93-342-40-26.** Metro: Liceu.

Nao Colón ⑯   Though really a designer restaurant, on Thursday to Sunday it becomes a club playing funk, soul, and house. If you dine here on a Thursday, you'll get live jazz from 10pm with the meal. It sounds more pretentious than it actually is. Marquès de l'Argentera 19 (La Ribera). © **93-268-76-33.** Metro: Barceloneta.

Pitin Bar   Easy to spot thanks to the lit-up stars over the door, this is a great place to sit with friends. The bar downstairs may not look like anything special, and the patio, though nice, is fairly standard . . . but if you can brave the small spiral staircase, upstairs is a cozy, beamed room with some funky little decorations. It's a great place to sit and talk while watching people through the windows—but tall people may have trouble with the low roof. Passeig del Born 34 (La Ribera). © **93-319-50-87.** Metro: Jaume I.

So_Da ⑯   If just the thought of shopping makes you thirsty, this bar has the perfect concept. At the back of a trendy clothes store is a cute little bar where you can have a drink and look enviously at the outfits. If you're not careful, you might find yourself agreeing to return the next day, when the shop section is open, to try some of them on. Music is of the electronic variety. Avinyó 24 (Barri Gòtic). © **93-342-45-29.** Metro: Jaume I.

Travel Bar   The place for the solo backpacker to start, built entirely to help introduce the city to those who are passing through. It's a convenient bar to get a sandwich or a beer, to find out what you need to know—or to hook up with others for a night of exploring. If you need some guidance on where to go, the bar also runs its own nightly pub crawls around local haunts. Boqueria 27 (Barri Gòtic). ✆ **93-342-52-52.** Metro: Liceu.

CLUBS

Apolo 🎭🎭   A genuine multifaceted venue located in a turn-of-the-20th-century ballroom—Tuesdays it's an alternative cinema, Thursdays it's a funk club, sometimes they have rock concerts, Sundays they have a hugely popular gay night, and on Fridays and Saturdays it's a dance club called Nitsa. Check out listings to find out what's going on when you're in town. Nou de la Rambla 113 (Poble Sec). ✆ **93-318-99-17.** Metro: Poble Sec.

Café Royale 🎭🎭   Right next to Plaça Real, this trendy bar is a place for beautiful people—grungy students may have problems getting past the bouncer. But if you can, it's worth it for the subtle gold lighting, the in-house DJs, and the comfortable seating all around the small dance floor. A classic central location for local trendies and models. Nou de Zurbano 3 (Barri Gòtic). ✆ **93-412-14-33.** Metro: Drassanes.

Club 13 🎭🎭   This new addition to Barcelona's night scene has made itself a favorite of the trendy set. The meeting point for those who like to see and be seen in the heart of Plaça Reial, it gets few tourists, so the majority of those striking a pose are local. Don't be fooled by how small it looks upstairs—all the real action, and the very loud music, happens in the basement where two rooms—one small, one large—house the dancing masses and the cool cats until late. The music is usually electronic dance. Plaça Reial 13 (Barri Gòtic). ✆ **93-317-23-52.** Metro: Drassanes.

Dot   Anyone who's both a hard-core dance music fan and a Star Trek geek will love this small bar/club. The music is loud and rhythmical but by far the best thing about the place is the transporter-style doorway between bar and dance floor. Beam me up. Nou de Sant Francesc 7 (Barri Gòtic). ✆ **93-302-70-26.** Metro: Drassanes.

La Luz de Luna 🎭   For lovers of music a little more Latin, La Luz de Luna ("the light of the moon") is a friendly place that specializes in salsa. Don't worry about making a

---

Old-Time Dancing

Plenty of nightclubs claim to be "classics" but none can beat **La Paloma**, Tigre 27 (✆ **93-301-68-97;** Metro: Universitat)—more than 103 years young and still going strong. The name means "the pigeon" and it opened as a ballroom in 1903, with its famous murals and chandelier added in 1919. It's a part of Barcelona's history—Pablo Picasso met one of his long-term girlfriends here, and Dalí used to sit in a box by the long balcony and sketch the people who came in. During the religiously strict time of Franco, someone called "El Moral" was employed to make sure that couples didn't get too close to each other. But there's none of that now. During the early evening, it opens as before for lovers of the fox-trot, tango, bolero, and so forth, accompanied by live orchestras. But from Thursday to Sunday, the place undergoes a transformation and becomes a hip and happening nightclub from 2:30 to 5am. From its incredible decor to the mimes that stand outside trying to keep people quiet, this place is a true original. Admission is 8€ ($10)—more on special nights.

fool of yourself on the dance floor if you don't know the moves—but if you do, you'll find no shortage of partners who also really know where to put their feet and at what point to twirl you around. Comerç 21 (La Ribera). ℂ **93-272-09-10.** Admission after 2am 5€ ($6.25). Metro: Jaume I.

Magic   Make devil horns with your hands and rock your sweaty mullet at this hard rock/metal club. It's all harmless fun, though, and tourists are more than welcome, as long as they can mosh with the best of them. Passeig Picasso 40 (La Ribera). ℂ **93-310-72-67.** Metro: Barceloneta.

Moog ℛ   The place where lovers of techno music and hard pumping beats gather to crash heads. The music is heavy but the people are friendly. Upstairs is a much smaller space where, strangely, 1980s disco (including a wide selection of Abba) is played and the DJ himself is part of the experience. Arc del Teatre 3 (El Raval). ℂ **93-301-72-82.** Metro: Drassanes.

New York   Talk about late-, late-night life in Barcelona. The gang of 20-something patrons who like this club don't show up until 3am. It's a former strip joint, and the red lights and black walls still evoke its heyday when the women bared all. Recorded music—mainly hip-hop and soul/funk—is heard in the background. Carrer Escudellers 5 (Barri Gòtic). ℂ **93-318-87-30.** Cover after 2am (includes 1 drink) 10€ ($13). Metro: Drassanes.

Sidecar   Upstairs is an international restaurant and bar, but when it gets late, they open downstairs—a lively and fun dance club with an indie feel in a brick-lined sizeable basement. Sometimes there's live music, too. Plaça Reial 7 (Barri Gòtic). ℂ **93-302-15-86.** Admission 6€ ($7.50). Metro: Drassanes.

BEACH CLUBS, PORT CLUBS & BEACH BARS
Baja Beach Club   If you want to dance to classic disco tracks, there's no place quite like Baja. It can feel like a bit of a meat market and it's as far from the sophisticated trendy club or upmarket cocktail bar as you can possibly go, but if you don't mind topless waiters and bikini-clad waitresses, and you're looking for a night of dancing to

---

⌒Moments Piaf, Drag Queens & a Walk on the Wild Side

Do you long to check out the seedy part of Barcelona that writers such as Jean Genet brought so vividly to life in their books? Much of it is gone forever, but *la Vida* nostalgically lives on in pockets like the **Bar Pastis,** Carrer Santa Mónica 4 (ℂ **93-318-79-80;** Metro: Drassanes).

Valencianos Carme Pericás and Quime Ballester opened this tiny bar just off the southern end of Les Ramblas in 1947. They made it a shrine to Edith Piaf, and her songs still play on an old phonograph in back of the bar. The decor consists mostly of paintings by Ballester, who had a dark, rather morbid vision of the world. The house special, naturally, is the French aniseed-flavored drink pastis (to be drunk straight or with a mixer) and you can order four kinds of pastis in this dimly lit so-called "corner of Montmartre"—the district of Paris that contains the famous Sacre Coeur church.

Outside the window, check out the view—often a parade of transvestite prostitutes. The bar crowd is likely to include almost anyone, especially people who used to be called bohemians. The bar also features live music of the French, tango, and folk variety, squeezed into one corner.

Twisting by the Port

At the bottom end of La Rambla, and over the wooden swing bridge known as the Rambla del Mar, lies the entertainment/shopping mall **Maremagnum.** Touted as a one-stop drink-and-dance venue when it opened in 1988, the Barcelona City Council hoped that it would attract millions (especially tourists) for its privileged surrounded-by-water position and swinging selection of restaurants, bars, and clubs. It did, and was perhaps a little unprepared (and under-trained) for its popularity. Over the next couple of years Maremagnum hit the headlines for the wrong reasons, namely the aggressiveness of its security staff toward ethnic minorities. This left a sour taste in the mouth of many, and clients started to stay away in droves. Since new management took over a few years back there has been more emphasis on shops than nightlife, and chic outlets like Calvin Klein, Mango, and Lollipops (specializing in Parisian gear) are now prime spots for shoppers. Xocoa is an "in" spot for buying chocolate. Maremagnum's bars and nightspots are still handy for a post-dinner bop if you're near La Rambla. A couple of the better venues here include **Irish Winds** (Local 202), which often has live music of the rock/pop variety, and **Mojito** (Local 58), which serves up some mean Brazilian cocktails to a bossa nova beat.

cheesy songs you can sing along to from the '80s and '90s, then this is probably where to head. You probably won't find many other places at which the entrance is a giant beach ball and the DJ is standing in a speedboat on the dance floor! It's located right on the beach and also serves reasonably priced food during the day. Paseo Marítimo 34. (✆) **93-225-91-00.** Metro: Vila Olímpica/Ciutadella.

Carpe Diem Lounge Club ⭑ People on a budget should avoid the dress-code conscious CDLC. Prices are high and so is the snob factor at this achingly cool bar on the edge of the beach. The VIP section is a favorite of famous soccer players but if you want to join them on the comfortable-looking white chill-out beds, you'll have to buy a 120€ ($150) bottle of spirits. It has a fairly large outside terrace for passersby to gawk at the beautiful people. The trendy night is Sunday, when chill-out music plays early (around 11pm) for those cool enough to not have to wake up first thing on Monday. Paseo Marítimo 32. (✆) **93-224-04-70.** Metro: Vila Olímpica/Ciutadella.

The Fastnet Bar ⭑⭑ Out of the dozens of Irish pubs and bars in the city, this is the only one that seems to have realized that it is situated in Mediterranean climes and not wet and windy Dublin. Located on a boulevard overlooking the marina, the bar has an ample outside terrace, which fills up on soccer and rugby days, when the large-screen TV is turned out onto the street. The rest of the time it is frequented by Anglo-Saxon yachters, who pop in for a Guinness and hearty bacon-and-egg breakfast. Passeig Juan de Borbón 22. (✆) **93-295-30-05.** Metro: Barceloneta.

Le Kashba ⭑ Situated next to the Olympic port in the old Palau del Mar building now occupied by the Museu de Catalunya, this cool little bar/dance floor plays projections on the wall, has cushions on the benches, and offers good dance music both

The Village People

During the day it's dedicated to small artisan shops, market stalls, and street theater (see chapter 7), but at night **Poble Espanyol**, Av. Marquès de Comillas s/n (© **93-508-63-30**; Metro: Espanya), turns into a party town. Built as a "typical Spanish village" for the World's Fair in 1929, it may look old but the whole place—right down to the huge fortified towers that dominate the entrance—is fake. At night, that makes it the perfect location to party, as no one actually lives inside and the gates can be strictly guarded. You have a couple of options: One is to buy a 3€ ($3.75) ticket and enter the village to pass the night in three or four small bars that offer drinks, Spanish pop music, and outside tables. The other, more expensive option is to pay for a ticket (20€–24€/$25–$30) *outside* to one of the clubs that lie *inside* the walls (entrance to the village is included in your ticket price). There are two main venues: **Discotheque**, a self-consciously trendy location for dance music fans, and the venue of choice for many of the big-name visiting DJs and, during the summer, **La Terrazza**, an outdoor-only club that's open from May to October—again, trendy dance music and a great place to dance the night away until the sun comes up (but not so much when it's raining). Due to a falling-out between the owners of the two, the ticket lines and entrances to the two clubs are separate, so check which is which before you start to line up. If you stay for the duration (until 6am on a weekend), look for flyers about, and sometimes even buses to, "after parties," situated a little out of town and open until noon.

inside and outside on the terrace. Great place to head to on a hot evening. Plaça Pau Vila 1. © **62-656-13-09**. Metro: Barceloneta.

Shoko 𝄐   A relatively new addition to the bars by the beach, this Asian restaurant-cum-club has an annoying faux spiritual decor that doesn't sit well with its high drink prices and fashionable clientele, many of whom spill over from the neighboring über-trendy nightspot CDLC (see above). That said, it's a nice place to boogie among the bright young things, and the VIP lounge is open to anyone willing to splash out on champagne. Passeig Marítim 36. © **93-225-92-03**. Metro: Vila Olímpica/Ciutadella.

L'EIXAMPLE

The bars and clubs of the L'Eixample tend to attract a slightly more mixed-age group than those of the Old City. They are also more spread out, so you may find yourself hopping in and out of cabs if you plan to bar hop.

Antilla Latin Club 𝄐𝄐𝄐   Catering to Barcelona's sizable Latin American and Caribbean community, this is the city's biggest salsa club. Some of the biggest names in salsa, merengue, mambo rumba, son, and all their derivatives have passed through, and when there's not live music the recorded variety is just as stomping. If you are unsure how to shake your booty, check out the club's dance school on Monday and Wednesday though Friday between 9 and 11:30pm (cost 60€–120€/$75–$150 per week); on Tuesday, classes are free when you've paid your entrance fee. Open late at weekends. Aragó 141. © **93-451-21-51**. Cover (include 1 drink) 10€ ($13). Metro: Urgell.

City Hall ⍟   This dark, busy club has a small, cool VIP room upstairs and a reasonably sized dance floor downstairs. The music is usually the standard electronic dance music fare, but there's also has a small, urban chill-out garden with a bar outside at the back. If you get one of the comfortable seats out there, it can be difficult to get up. The other big advantage of this place is that it's situated very close to Plaça Catalunya—very convenient for taxis and many hotels. Discount flyers can be found in many bars. Rambla Catalunya 2–4. ✆ **93-317-22-77.** Cover (includes 1 drink) 10€ ($13). Metro: Catalunya.

Costa Breve ⍟   Sitting uptown, this is a decent disco playing a mixture of Spanish and European commercial music, with the odd surprise thrown in such as a stripper or live gig. Hugely popular with office workers in the area, and young *picos* (yuppies), the vibe is different from that of the Old Town clubs, but its tourist-free clientele makes for a nice change. Aribau 230. ✆ **93-441-427-78.** Cover 10€ ($13). FGC: Gràcia.

Nick Havanna ⍟⍟   Started in 1987, this was one of the first of the city's "designer bars"—postmodern drinking palaces that spent more on decor than practicalities (such as plumbing). It's still very stylish, although in a more retro sort of way with a dome over the dance floor, uncomfortable metal seating, and some of the most highly designed toilets in the city. Rosselló 208. ✆ **93-215-65-91.** Metro: Diagonal.

Toscano Anticuo ⍟   A noisy Italian cocktail bar that's a million miles away from the slickness you might expect. They serve all the cocktails in the same style of glass, the music is loud, and the decor very rough-and-ready. But the drinks are excellent and they even offer free Italian food on the bar before 10:30pm. The place is all staffed and owned by Italians (the name means "Old Tuscany") and is so Italian that it even has its own ice-cream shop a few blocks down (and that stays open until 1am on summer weekends). For directions, ask at the bar for the *cremería.* Aribau 167. ✆ **93-532-15-89.** Metro: Diagonal.

GRACIA

Though the area is filled with small squares and hidden corners, the center of the Gràcia world is Plaça del Sol. In the summer, it's the best place to head to meet young Catalans and to watch people on their way to party. Just as many bring their own cans of beer as buy from the bars around the square—the atmosphere is noisy and fun and drives the neighbors mad.

Alfa   A great club if you like indie and rock music. The walls are filled with framed covers of classic albums from bands like U2 and the Smiths, which gives you a good idea of the music. It's as local as you can get (its location in a quiet, shop-filled street means there aren't many tourists), and the enormous candles dripping wax onto the bar just add to the atmosphere. It's not a big place, nor a particularly clean one, but it does what it does just fine. Mayor de Gràcia 36. ✆ **93-415-18-24.** Metro: Fontana.

Café del Sol   The center of the young Catalan scene, this bar is filled with bohemians, pro-independence Catalan youths, and just people who go to enjoy the tapas and the view over the plaza from the large collection of outside tables. Plaça del Sol 16. ✆ **93-415-56-63.** Metro: Fontana.

Cibeles ⍟⍟   Similar to La Paloma (see above), although not quite as spectacular, Cibeles morphs every Friday from a dance hall for tango and *pasodoble* lovers into **The Mond Club**—the dance music venue of choice in this part of town. Around the corner, **The Mond Bar,** Plaça del Sol 21 (✆ **93-457-38-77**) has the same music without the dance floor. Còrsega 363. ✆ **93-457-38-77.** Cover 10€ ($13). Metro: Diagonal.

> ### ⌐Tips Finding Munchies!
>
> After a long night out, the one thing you need is food—and the greasier the better. If you're out of the city's center, you might come across a traveling *churros* stand selling fresh potato chips, long strips of greasy fried donut dough, and sometimes cups of hot chocolate to dip them in to. Some tapas bars are open late or very early, such as **El Reloj** (Vía Laietana 47). If it's any early morning but Sunday, the markets usually have bars open too—the local favorite is **Bar Pinotxo** in the Boqueria Market on La Rambla. Also open very early is the real local secret: the **croissant factory** hidden on the small Carrer Lancaster on the Raval side of La Rambla near the corner of Nou de la Rambla. It opens about 5am and, for 2.50€ ($3.15), you can buy a box of greasy, chocolate cream-filled doughy croissants that you'll be hard-pressed to finish.

KGB   If the dance music is getting you down, KGB is the place where independent pop acts (metal, reggae, hip-hop) come to find people of their own kind. Gigs are normally Thursday through Saturday. The rest of the time, it's a more standard club. Alegre de Dalt 55. ✆ **93-210-59-06.** Cover 10€ ($13). Metro: Lesseps.

BARRIO ALTO

Barrio Alto is sometimes seen as a world of its own. Here is where all the rich families live, in houses no less (something unheard of down in the city), and many of them never leave the Alto enclave. The same applies to going out—rich kids aplenty, alongside some more normal types, throughout the area. The main bars and clubs are concentrated around a street called Marie Cubí, near the FGC Gràcia stop. They're all very quiet during the week, though. *Note:* The Metro system doesn't serve this part of town.

Bikini 𝕂𝕂𝕂   A classic of the Barcelona nightlife scene, this place opened first as an outdoor bar and minigolf place in the 1950s, then reopened in the mid-1990s. It is now a venue both for live music and for lively dancing. One room plays Latin rhythms, another disco/punk/rock/or whatever's hot, plus there's a chill-out cocktail bar tucked away. It's also one of the better places to hear live music; when the gig's over, the walls roll back and disco rules. Deu i Mata 105. ✆ **93-322-00-05.** Cover (if no concert) 15€ ($19) including 1 drink.

Gimlet 𝕂𝕂𝕂   This is a stylish uptown cocktail bar with a smaller sister bar downtown. The lights are low, the music is jazz, and the drinks are generous. Sit at the tables or head for the bar at the back and chat with the waitstaff as they shake and mix the libations, pour them into retro glasses, and place them on the cute little coasters. There's nothing they can't whip up, and everything is done with admirable style. Santaló 46 (La Ribera). ✆ **93-201-53-06.** (The other branch is at Rec 24)

Otto Zutz 𝕂𝕂𝕂   If you're anyone who's anyone in Barcelona, you'll have one of the gold VIP cards to Otto Zutz, which allows you access to the bar/small dance floor on the top floor, where you can watch all the trendy wannabes down below strutting their stuff and, if the whim strikes you, go down and invite one of them up to join you at the balcony. The dance floor is a good size and the small stage often features club dancers who pose and pout almost as much as those upstairs. There's no shortage of discount cards in bars all over town, but its location means that it can be hard to get back home afterward, if you're staying in the Old Town. Lincoln 15. ℰ **93-238-07-22.** Cover 10€ ($13). Train: FGC Gràcia.

Up and Down ⍣ The chic atmosphere here attracts elite Barcelonans of all ages. The more mature patrons, specifically the black-tie, post-theater crowd, head upstairs, leaving the downstairs section to loud music and flaming youth. Up and Down is the most cosmopolitan disco in Barcelona, with impeccable service, sassy waiters, and a welcoming atmosphere. Technically, this is a private club—you can be turned away at the door. Numància 179. ℰ **93-205-51-94.** Cover (includes 1 drink) 12€–18€ ($15–$23). Metro: María Cristina.

Universal Uptown fun for the rich set, Universal's name is apt: It's the place where two generations of nighttime revelers go—while the 20-somethings bop around downstairs, those of a more mature age can be found upstairs with the jazz DJ. Marià Cubí 182. ℰ **93-201-35-96.** Train: FGC Muntaner.

OUTER BARCELONA

Danzatoria Dress up reasonably smart for Danzatoria, for this is far from the grungy student scene. The setting is a mansion house on the hillside and it's a great place to go, especially in the summer when the three-tier garden with three bars is open. Inside, from the bottom up, there's a chill-out room with a sofa suspended from the roof, a small dance floor bathed in ultraviolet light, a grand bar in the entrance hall, and an upstairs restaurant open until around midnight, when it turns into a bar playing modern music. There isn't a view of the city; the place is hidden away in the trees, but it's a great ambience. The only way to get here is by taxi. If you're relying on a taxi home, though, you should leave at least a half-hour before it closes (which is at 3am) and walk down the hill to find one. Drinks are pricey. Av. Tibidabo 61. ℰ **93-268-74-30.** Train: nearest stop (10 min. walk away) FGC Avda Tibidabo.

Mirablau It's all about the location at Mirablau. Although there are worse disco/bars in the city, there are certainly better ones, too. But you don't go for the music, the bar prices, or the crowd—you go for the view. Mirablau is situated right next to the funicular near the top of Tibidabo hill and has a huge window overlooking the twinkling lights of the entire city, from the hill to the sea. It's open during the day for coffee, but the view at night is something else entirely. If it's pretty enough to help tune out the music, all the better. Plaça Doctor Andreu 2. ℰ **93-418-58-79.** Train: FGC Tibidabo, then Tramvía Blau.

Razzmatazz Five clubs in one, each with its own style of music, this venue is an enormous multi-leveled warehouse. It's not unusual to have a big-name, chill-out DJ playing the main stage while upstairs, oblivious, a group of goths and rock chicks mosh themselves into a frenzy. If you can't find music you like here, you probably don't like music very much. The crowd can be dominated by students, but it depends very much on the night. One ticket gets you entry to all the clubs, so intrepid dancers can spend the night trying them all. Almogàvers 122. ℰ **93-320-82-00.** Cover (except for special concerts) 12€ ($15). Metro: Bogatell.

CHAMPAGNE BARS

The Catalans call their own version of sparkling wine *cava* and it comes from the nearby Penedès region (p. 265). In Catalan, champagne bars are called *xampanyerias*. With more than 50 Catalan companies producing *cava,* and each bottling up to a dozen grades of wine, the best way to learn about Catalan "champagne" is to sample the products at a *xampanyeria*.

Champagne bars usually open at 7pm and stay open until midnight or later. They serve a small range of tapas, from caviar to smoked fish to frozen chocolate truffles. The traditional local time to go is late morning on a Sunday, when entire families will have a pre-lunch sip. Most establishments sell only a limited array of house *cavas* by the glass, and more esoteric varieties by the bottle. You'll be offered a choice of *brut* (slightly sweeter), *brut nature*, or *rosat* (rosé or pink champagne).

Can Paixano *Value*   If you want to sample the cheapest *cava* in town alongside a bewildering selection of sandwiches, this is the best place to go. It's a rowdy *cava* bar where the most expensive Can Paixano bottle is a little over 5€ ($6.25). There are no seats, though. If you go at lunchtime, you'll be able to find some space to enjoy your drink—but if you go at night, expect the place to be crammed full. It's a good way to get tipsy early, but don't say I didn't warn you about the evenings—anytime after 7pm will start to get very, very full. It's compulsory to order two mini sandwiches with the first bottle you buy. Open 10:30am to 10pm. Reina Cristina 7. No phone. Metro: Barceloneta.

El Xampanyet ✶✶✶   This little champagne bar, our favorite in Barcelona, has been operated by the same family since the 1930s. When the Picasso Museum opened nearby, its popularity was assured. Set on this ancient street, the tavern is adorned with colored tiles, antique curios, marble tables, and barrels. With your sparkling wine, you can order fresh anchovies in vinegar, impressively fat green olives, or other tapas. If you don't want the *cava*, you can order fresh cider at the old-fashioned zinc bar. Closed in August. Montcada 22. ✆ 93-319-70-03. Metro: Jaume I.

Xampanyeria Casablanca   Someone had to fashion a champagne bar after the Bogart-Bergman film, and this is it. It serves four kinds of house *cava* by the glass, plus a good selection of tapas, especially pâtés. Bonavista 6. ✆ 93-237-63-99. Metro: Passeig de Gràcia.

Xampú Xampany   At the corner of the Plaça de Tetuan, this *xampanyeria* offers a variety of hors d'oeuvres in addition to wine. Abstract paintings, touches of high tech, and bouquets of flowers break up the pastel color scheme. Gran Vía de les Corts Catalanes 702. ✆ 93-265-04-83. Metro: Girona.

GAY & LESBIAN BARS

The city has a vibrant, active gay nightlife, with bars and clubs to suit all tastes. The best thing to do is walk around the area known locally as "Gayxample"—a part of the lower Eixample area, more or less between Carrer Sepulveda and Carrer Aragon, and Carrer Casanova and Plaça Urquinaona. By no means every bar there is gay, but many are—and all of the trendy-looking ones almost certainly will be. Most bars welcome people of any persuasion—but hetero couples should be prepared to be discreet.

Aire—Sala Diana   Lesbians aren't generally well served by the city, but this is the classic club of note for everyone from fashionable young things to older women. It's a large venue with a big dance floor and a buzzing bar. Carrer Valencia 236. ✆ 93-487-83-42. Metro: Passeig de Gràcia.

Café Dietrich   As if you didn't already know by its namesake, this cafe stages the best drag strip shows in town, a combination of local and foreign divas "falling in love again" like the great Marlene herself. It remains Barcelona's most popular gay haunt. The scantily clad bartenders are hot, and the overly posh decor lives up to its reputation as a "divinely glam musical bar/disco." Many of the drag queens like to fraternize with the handsomest of the patrons, to whom they offer deep kisses on the mouth. Consell de Cent 255. ✆ 93-451-77-07. Metro: Gràcia or Universitat.

Caligula   This kitschy bar is fun for people of all persuasions. Though the decor is attractive, the most stunning feature is the occasional nightly floor show, where a series of transsexuals mime to international diva hits. No nudity, nothing seedy—just great entertainment with its tongue firmly in its cheek. Consell de Cent 257. No phone. Metro: Universitat.

Medusa   This minimalist-decorated bar draws a trendy young crowd, mainly of cute boys. "The cuter you are, the better your chances of getting in if we get crowded as the night wears on," I was assured by one of the staff members. A super-trendy place, Medusa draws the fashionistas. I prefer its DJs to all others in town. The place gets very cruisy after 1am. Casanova 75. ✆ 93-454-53-63. Metro: Urgell.

Metro   One of the most popular gay discos in Barcelona, Metro attracts a diverse crowd—from young fashion victims to more rough-and-ready macho types. One dance floor plays contemporary house and dance music, and the other traditional Spanish music mixed with Spanish pop. This is a good opportunity to watch men of all ages dance the *sevillanas* in pairs with a surprising degree of grace. The gay press in Barcelona quite accurately dubs the backroom here as a "notorious, lascivious labyrinth of lust." One interesting feature appears in the bathrooms, where videos have been installed in quite unexpected places. Sepulveda 185. ✆ 93-323-52-27. Cover 10€ ($13). Metro: Universitat.

New Chaps   Gay Barcelonese refer to this saloon-style watering hole as Catalonia's premier leather-and-denim bar. In fact, the dress code usually is leather of a different stripe: more boots and jeans than leather and chains. Behind a pair of swinging doors evocative of the old American West, Chaps contains two different bar areas. Some of Barcelona's horniest guys flock to the downstairs darkroom in the wee hours. Diagonal 365. ✆ 93-215-53-65. Metro: Diagonal.

Punto BCN   Barcelona's largest gay bar attracts a mixed crowd of young "hotties" and foreigners. Always crowded, it's a good base to start out your evening. There is a very popular happy hour on Wednesday from 6 to 9pm. Montaner 63–65. ✆ 93-453-61-23. Metro: Eixample.

Salvation   This leading gay dance club has been going strong since 1999. It's still the flashiest dive on the see-and-be-seen circuit, and a good place to wear your see-through clothing, especially as the hour grows late. There are two rooms devoted to different types of music, the first with house music and DJs, the other with more commercial and "soapy" themes. A habitué told me, "I come here because of the sensual waiters," and indeed they are the handsomest and most muscular in town. Look your most gorgeous if you want to get past the notoriously selective doorman. Ronda de Sant Pere 19–21. ✆ 93-318-06-86. Metro: Urquinaona.

11

Side Trips in Catalonia

About six million people live in Catalonia, and twice that many visit every year, flocking to the beaches along the Catalan *costas* (coasts), the area of Spain that practically invented package tourism. Though some areas—such as Lloret de Mar—have become over-developed, there are many unspoiled little seaside spots still to be found.

Three of the most attractive resorts are on the **Costa Brava (Rocky Coast),** 100km (62 miles) north of Barcelona: the southerly town of **Tossa de Mar,** with its walled Ciutat Vella, the idyllic coastal village of **Calella de Palafrugell,** and the northerly whitewashed fishing village of **Cadaqués,** up near the French border.

Inland from the latter lies the laid-back capital of the Alt Empordà, **Figueres,** birthplace of the father of surrealism, Salvador Dalí, and home to his eccentric museum, which enthralls everyone from art lovers to the downright curious. The capital of this whole region is **Girona,** an ancient town steeped in history with a magnificent Old Quarter and cathedral.

South of Barcelona, along the **Costa Daurada (Golden Coast)** the beaches are wider and sandier. **Sitges,** a fine resort town that has a huge gay following and **Tarragona,** the UNESCO World Heritage City, are the two destinations to visit here, the latter for its concentration of Roman ruins and architecture.

Away from the coast, amid attractive wooded hills and fertile valleys at the meeting point of Tarragona and Lleida provinces, is a fine trio of smaller but not-to-be-missed Cistercian monasteries—**Poblet, Santes Creus,** and **Vallbona de les Monges**—all dating from the 12th century.

These are eclipsed, however, by the greatest monastery of them all: **Montserrat,** a hugely popular day excursion to the northwest of Barcelona. The serrated outline made by the sierra's steep cliffs led the Catalonians to call it *montserrat* (sawtoothed mountain). Today this Benedictine sanctuary remains the religious center of Catalonia, and thousands of pilgrims annually visit the monastery complex to see its Black Virgin.

Due northeast of Barcelona, the atmospheric Romanesque towns of **Vich, Ripoll,** and **Camprodón** are well worth an off-the-beaten-track tour.

1 Montserrat ★★

56km (34 miles) NW of Barcelona, 592km (368 miles) E of Madrid

The monastery at **Montserrat,** which sits atop a 1,200m-high (3,937-ft.) mountain, 11km long (7 miles) and 5.5km wide (3½ miles), is one of the most important pilgrimage spots in Spain. It ranks with Zaragoza and Santiago de Compostela in Galicia, at the end of the pilgrimage route of Saint James. Thousands travel here every year to see and touch the medieval statue of La Moreneta (The Black Virgin), the most important religious icon in Catalonia. Many newly married couples flock here for her blessing.

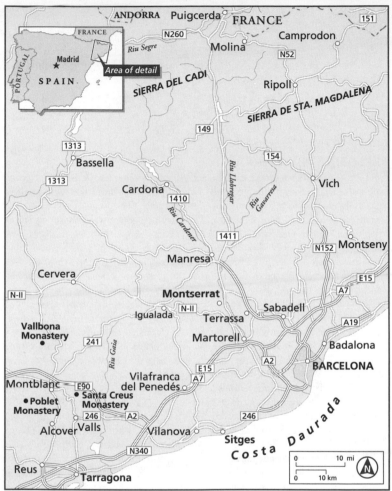

Avoid visiting on Sunday, especially if the weather is nice, because thousands of locals pour in. At all times, remember to take along warm sweaters or jackets, since it can get cold.

ESSENTIALS

GETTING THERE   The best and most exciting way to go is via the Catalan railway. **Ferrocarrils de la Generalitat de Catalunya** to Montserrat-Aeri leaves every hour from the Plaça d'Espanya in Barcelona. The train connects with a high-tech funicular (Aeri de Montserrat), which leaves every 15 minutes.

The train, with its funicular tie-in, has taken over as the preferred and cheapest means of transport. However, long-distance **bus** service is also provided by **Autocar Julià** in Barcelona. Daily service from Barcelona to Montserrat is generally available, with departures near the Estació de Sants on the Plaça de Països Catalans. Buses leave at 9:15am, returning at 5pm and at 6pm in July and August; the round-trip ticket costs 10€ ($13) on weekdays and 12€ ($15) on weekends. Contact the Julià company (© **93-490-40-00**).

To drive here, exit via the Avinguda Diagonal, then take the A-2 (exit Matorell). The signposts and exit to Montserrat will be on your right. From the main road, it's 15km (9 miles) up to the monastery through eerie rock formations and dramatic scenery.

VISITOR INFORMATION   The **tourist office** is at the Plaça de la Creu (© **93-877-77-77**), open daily from 8:50am to 7:30pm. This office can provide you with various maps for walks around the mountain.

EXPLORING MONTSERRAT

Among the monastery's noted attractions is the 50-member **Escolanía** 𝕲𝕲, one of the oldest and most renowned boys' choirs in Europe, dating from the 13th century. At 1pm daily (noon on Sun) you can hear them singing "Salve Regina" and the "Virolai" (hymn of Montserrat) in the basilica. The basilica is open Monday to Friday from 7:30am to 7:30pm and Saturday to Sunday from 7:30pm to 8:30pm. Admission is free. To view the Black Virgin, said to have been carved by St. Luke around A.D. 50, enter the church through a side door to the right. She was found in one of the mountain caves (see below) in the 12th century and is said to be have been carved by the hands of Saint Luke himself.

At the Plaça de Santa María you can also visit the **Museu de Montserrat** (© **93-877-77-77**), known for its collection of ecclesiastical paintings, including works by Caravaggio and El Greco. Modern Spanish and Catalan artists are also represented (see Picasso's early *El Viejo Pescador*, 1895). Works by Dalí and such French Impressionists as Monet, Sisley, and Degas are shown. The collection of ancient artifacts is quite interesting. Be sure to look for the crocodile mummy, which is at least 2,000 years old. The museum is open Monday through Friday from 10am to 6pm, and Saturday and Sunday from 9:30am to 6:30pm, charging 4.50€ ($5.65) adults and 3€ ($3.75) for children and students.

The 9-minute **funicular ride** (Aeri de Montserrat; www.aeridemontserrat.com) to the 1,236m-high (4,005-ft.) peak, Sant Joan, makes for a panoramic trip. The funicular operates about every 20 minutes daily from 9:25am to 1:45pm and 2:20 to 6:45pm March through October; November to February it runs 10:10am to 1:45pm and 2:20 to 5:45pm (6:45pm on public holidays). Cost is 7€ ($8.75) round-trip, 4.50€ ($5.65) one-way. From the top on a clear day you'll see not only most of Catalonia but also the Pyrénées and—if you're very lucky—the islands of Majorca and Ibiza.

You can also make an excursion to **Santa Cova (Holy Grotto),** the alleged site of the discovery of the Black Virgin. The grotto dates from the 17th century and was built in the shape of a cross. You go halfway by funicular but must complete the trip on foot. The grotto is open year-round daily from 10am to 1pm and 2pm to 5:45pm. The funicular operates every 20 minutes daily from 11am to 6pm at a round-trip cost of 2.60€ ($3.65) adults, 1.35€ ($1.70) children. For more information, visit www.cremallerademontserrat.com.

WHERE TO STAY & DINE

Few people spend the night here, but most visitors will eat at least one meal during their visit. There is only one restaurant on Montserrat and it is expensive (see below). Consider bringing a picnic lunch from Barcelona instead.

Route of the Cistercian Monasteries

Near the medieval town of **Montblanc**, 113km (70 miles) west of Barcelona in the heart of Tarragona province, is a lesser-known trio of smaller but exquisite monasteries, all founded in the 12th century, by Benedictine monks, with the purpose of returning to a simple life of austerity detached from material concerns.

The oldest and largest of them, **Santa María de Poblet** (Oficina Comarcal de Turismo, Monasterio de Poblet; ℂ **977-87-12-47**; Mon–Fri 10am–12:30pm and 3–6pm. Closes at 5:30pm in winter; 4.50€/$5.60), nestles on the wooded slopes of the Prades mountains. (Its name derives from the Latin *populetum,* meaning white poplars). Founded in 1151, yet continuously expanded and reconstructed over the centuries, its styles range from Romanesque (13th-c. St. Catherine's chapel) to the Gothic (15th-c. St. George's chapel), and baroque. In its great high vaulted chapterhouse the kings of Cataluña and Aragón are laid to rest in (restored) tombs. The present active community of monks originates from 1945 when the Poblet Brotherhood was created.

The nearby smaller **Monasteri de Santes Creuses** (ℂ **977-63-83-29**; March 15–Sept 15 10am–1:30pm and 3–7pm; Sept 16–Jan 15 10am–1:30pm and 3–5:30pm; Jan 16–Mar 15 10am–1:30pm and 3–6pm; 4€/$5) is set in a secluded wooded valley beside the River Gaia. Founded 7 years later than Poblet, it also underwent transitional work as recently as the 18th century. Among its highlights are the ancient Trinitat chapel and 14th-century Gothic cloister with its striking Romanesque octagonal pavilion.

The convent of **Vallbona de les Monges** (ℂ **973-33-02-66**; Tues–Sat 10am–1:30pm and 4:30–6:45pm; weekends and holidays: noon–1:30pm and 4:30–6:45pm; 2€/$2.50) lies just inside neighboring Lleida province in a fertile valley noted for its excellent olive oil. Founded by the Cister's feminine branch in the 12th century, it originally housed daughters of noble families from the House of Aragón. Today it still has a resident community of some 30 nuns as well as an active cultural and spiritual center. Romanesque styles predominate, especially in the north transept doors, south and east wings of the superb cloister, and the 14th-century bell tower.

Montblanc itself is atmospheric enough to warrant an overnight stay. It was once center of a thriving Jewish community, as the scenic Carrer Jeues (Street of Jews) testifies. Two-thirds of the surrounding 13th-century walls are still intact and the Royal Palace (Palau Reial) is a standout. Book a room at the two-star Fonda Cal Blasi, which is located in a converted 19th century house in the town center at Carrer Alenyá 11 (ℂ **977-86-13-36**); a double goes for 70€ to 80€ ($88–$100).

Abat Cisneros   This modern hotel on the main square of Montserrat offers few pretensions and a history of family management from 1958. The small rooms are simple and clean, each with a comfortable bed, and the bathrooms come with tub/shower combos. Rudimentary regional dishes are served in the in-house restaurant. The hotel's name is derived from a title given to the head of any Benedictine monastery during the Middle Ages.

Plaça de Montserrat s/n, 08199 Montserrat. (C) **93-877-77-00.** Fax 93-877-77-24. interhotel.com/spain/es/ hoteles/1829.html. 56 units. 50€–95€ ($63–$119) double. Rates include breakfast. AE, DC, MC, V. Parking 6€ ($7.50). Bus: Autobuses Julià from Plaça Espanya in Barcelona. Train: Montserrat line from Estació Sants and then Ferrocarril. **Amenities:** Restaurant; bar; lounge; laundry service. *In room:* TV, safe.

2 Tarragona ★★

97km (60 miles) S of Barcelona, 554km (344 miles) E of Madrid

The ancient Roman port city of **Tarragona,** on a rocky bluff above the Mediterranean, is one of the grandest but most unfairly neglected sightseeing centers in Spain. Honoring its abundance of Roman and medieval remains, UNESCO named Tarragona a World Heritage City in 2000.

The Romans captured Tarragona *(Tarraco)* in 218 B.C., and during their rule the city sheltered one million people behind 64km-long (40-mile) city walls. One of the four capitals of Catalonia when it was an ancient principality, and once the home of Julius Caesar, Tarragona today consists of an Old Quarter filled with interesting buildings, particularly the houses with connecting balconies. The upper walled town is mainly medieval; the town below is newer.

In the new town, walk along the **Rambla Nova,** a fashionable wide boulevard that's the city's main artery. Running parallel with Rambla Nova to the east is the **Rambla Vella,** which marks the beginning of the Old Town. The city has a bullring, good hotels, and even some beaches, particularly the Platjes del Miracle and del Cossis.

After seeing the attractions listed below, cap off your day with a stroll along the **Balcó del Mediterráni (Balcony of the Mediterranean),** where the vistas are especially beautiful at sunset.

ESSENTIALS

GETTING THERE   Daily, there are **trains** every 15 to 45 minutes making the 1-hour trip to and from the Barcelona-Sants station. In Tarragona, the RENFE office is in the train station, the Plaza Pedrera s/n ((C) **90-224-02-02**).

From Barcelona, there are eight **buses** per day from Monday to Saturday and two on Sunday and bank holidays to Tarragona (1½ hr.) run by the company Plana ((C) **97-721-44-75**). Another company, Hispania, also operates a service that continues to Reus. All buses leave from outside the María Cristina Metro station and cost 8. 95€ ($11) one-way.

To **drive,** take the A-2 southwest from Barcelona to the A-7, via Vilafranca. The route to Tarragona is well marked.

VISITOR INFORMATION   The **tourist office** is at Carrer Major 39 ((C) **97-725-07-95;** www.costadorada.org). It's open July to the end of September Monday through Friday from 9am to 9pm, Saturday 9am to 2pm and 4 to 9pm, and Sunday 10am to 2pm. The rest of the year, it's open Monday to Saturday 10am to 2pm and 4 to 7pm, and Sunday 10am to 2pm.

EXPLORING THE TOWN

Amfiteatre Romà ★   At the foot of Miracle Park and dramatically carved from a cliff that rises from the beach, this Roman amphitheater recalls the days in the 2nd century when thousands gathered here to be entertained by games and gladiator fights.

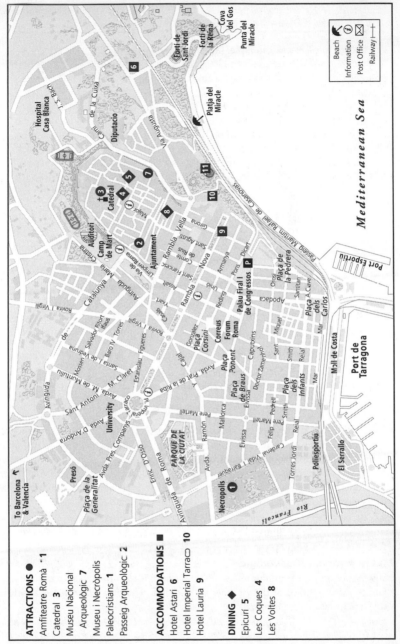

Beach
Information
Post Office
Railway

Mediterranean Sea

Cova del Gos
Punta del Miracle
Forti de la Reina
Forti de Sant Jordi
Platja del Miracle

Hospital Casa Blanca
Diputacio

Catedral

Auditori
Camp de Mart
Ajuntament

Rambla Vella
Sant Agustí

Girona

Port Esportiu

Port de Tarragona

Palau Fira i de Congressos

Plaça de la Pedrera

Plaça A. Clavé dels Carlos

Forum Romà
Correus
Plaça Corsini

Plaça Ponent
Plaça de Braus
Plaça dels Infants

Rambla Nova

University
Presó
Plaça de la Generalitat

PARQUE DE LA CIUTAT

Moll de Costa

Poliesportiu
El Serrallo

Rio Francolí

Necropolis

To Barcelona & València

ATTRACTIONS ●
Amfiteatre Romà 1
Catedral 3
Museu Nacional Arqueològic 7
Museu i Necròpolis Paleocristians 1
Passeig Arqueològic 2

ACCOMMODATIONS ■
Hotel Astari 6
Hotel Imperial Tarraco 10
Hotel Lauria 9

DINING ◆
Epicuri 5
Les Coques 4
Les Voltes 8

Catalonia Remembers Pablo Casals

Fleeing from Franco and the fascist regime, the world's greatest cellist, Pablo Casals, left his homeland in 1939. Today his body has been returned to El Vendrell, 72km (45 miles) south of Barcelona, where he is remembered with a museum in his honor. The museum is installed in the renovated house where he lived until he went into self-imposed exile.

Seventeen rooms are filled with Casals memorabilia, including his first cello, photographs and films of his performances, the Peace Medal awarded by the United Nations in 1971, and photographs of the artist with such famous men as John F. Kennedy, who awarded him the Medal of Freedom.

Casals died in Puerto Rico in 1973 at the age of 96, and he was finally returned to his beloved Catalonia in 1979, where he is buried at the El Vendrell graveyard.

Casa Pau Casals is at Av. Palfuriana 59–61, in Sant Salvador-El Vendrell (© **97-768-42-76**). From September 16 to June 14 it is open Tuesday through Friday from 10am to 2pm and 4 to 6pm, Saturday from 10am to 2pm and 4 to 7pm, and Sunday from 10am to 2pm. From June 15 to September 15 it's open Tuesday through Saturday from 10am to 2pm and 5 to 9pm, and Sunday from 10am to 2pm. Admission is 5€ ($6.25) for adults, 3€ ($3.75) for children, students, and seniors, and free for children under 8. Allow 1 hour.

To reach El Vendrell from Barcelona, head south along C-32 until you come to the El Vendrell exit just past Calafell.

Parc del Milagro s/n. © **97-724-25-79**. Admission 2.10€ ($2.60) adults, 1€ ($1.25) students and seniors. Mar–Sept Tues–Sat 9am–9pm, Sun 9am–3pm; Oct–Feb Tues–Sat 9am–5pm, Sun 10am–3pm. Closed Dec 25, Jan 1, and Jan 6. Bus: 2.

Catedral 𝕲𝕲   At the highest point of Tarragona is this 12th-century cathedral, whose architecture represents the transition from Romanesque to Gothic. It has an enormous vaulted entrance, fine stained-glass windows, Romanesque cloisters, and an open choir. In the main apse, observe the altarpiece of Santa Tecla, the patron of Tarragona, carved by Pere Joan in 1430. Two flamboyant doors open into the chevet. The east gallery is the **Museu Diocesà**, with a collection of Catalan art.

Plaça de la Seu s/n. © **97-723-72-69**. Admission to cathedral and museum 2.40€ ($3) adults, 1.50€ ($1.85) students and seniors, free for children under 16. Mar–May daily 10am–1pm and 4–7pm; June–Sept daily 10am–7pm; Oct–Feb daily 10am–2pm. Bus: 1.

Museu Nacional Arqueològic 𝕲   Overlooking the sea, the Archaeology Museum houses a collection of Roman relics—mosaics, ceramics, coins, silver, sculpture, and more. The outstanding attraction here is the mosaic **Head of Medusa** 𝕲𝕲, with its penetrating stare.

Plaça del Rei 5. © **97-723-62-09**. Admission for museum and Museu i Necròpolis Paleocristians 2.40€ ($3) adults, 1.20€ ($1.50) students, free for seniors and children under 18. June–Sept Tues–Sat 10am–8pm, Sun 10am–2pm; Oct–MayTues–Sat 10am–1:30pm and 4–7pm, Sun 10am–2pm. Bus: 8.

Museu i Necròpolis Paleocristians 𝕲   This is one of the most important burial grounds in Spain, used by the Christians from the 3rd to the 5th century. It stands outside town next to a tobacco factory whose construction led to its discovery in 1923. While on the grounds, visit the **Museu Paleocristià,** which contains a number of sarcophagi and other objects discovered during the excavations.

Av. de Ramón y Cajal 80. ✆ **97-723-62-09.** Admission to museum, necropolis, and Museu Arqueològic 2.40€ ($3) adults, 1.20€ ($1.50) students, free for seniors and children under 18. June–Sept Tues–Sat 10am–1:30pm and 4–7pm, Sun and holidays 10am–2pm; Oct–May Tues–Sat 10am–1:30pm and 3–5:30pm, Sun and holidays 10am–2pm. Bus: 4.

Passeig Arqueològic 𝕽𝕽   At the far end of the Plaça del Pallol, an archway leads to this .8km (½-mile) walkway along the ancient ramparts, built by the Romans on top of gigantic boulders. The ramparts have been much altered over the years, especially in medieval times and in the 1600s. There are scenic views from many points along the way.

El Portal del Roser s/n. ✆ **97-724-57-96.** Admission 2.10€ ($2.60) adults, 1€ ($1.25) students and seniors, free for children under 16. Oct–Mar Tues–Sat 9am–7pm, Sun and holidays 10am–3pm; Apr–Sept Tues–Sat 9am–9pm, Sun and holidays 9am–3pm. Bus: 2.

THEME PARK THRILLS

A 10-minute ride from the heart of Barcelona, the **Port Aventura Amusement Park,** Port Aventura (✆ **97-777-90-90**), is Spain's biggest theme park. Universal Studios has acquired a prime stake in it and has plans to make it even larger. On a vast 809 hectares (1,998 acres), it'll be expanded to become Europe's largest entertainment center. Since its acquisition in 2004 by La Caixa, it's become the largest Universal Studios entertainment center in Europe, covering over 809 hectares (2,000 acres) and hosting 3.5 million guests annually.

The park is a microcosm of five distinct worlds, with full-scale re-creations of classic villages ranging from Polynesia to Mexico, from China to the old American West. It also offers a thrilling variety of roller-coaster and white-water rides, all centered on a lake you can travel to via the deck of a Chinese junk.

The park is open daily March 23 to November 4; Saturdays and Sundays from November 10 to December to January 5. It's closed January 6 to March 22. A 1-day pass costs 37€ ($46) adults, 24€ ($30) children; a 2-day pass costs 53€ ($66) adults, 36€ ($45) children. Nighttime admission, available only in summer months, is 25€ ($31) adults, 20€ ($25) children. The fee includes all shows and rides.

WHERE TO STAY
EXPENSIVE
Hotel Imperial Tarraco 𝕽𝕽   About .4km (¼ mile) south of the cathedral, atop an oceanfront cliff whose panoramas include a sweeping view of both the sea and the Roman ruins, this hotel is the finest in town. It was designed in the form of a crescent and has guest rooms that may angle out to sea and almost always include small balconies. The accommodations, all with bathrooms containing tub/shower combos, contain uncomplicated plain modern furniture. The public rooms display lots of polished white marble, Oriental carpets, and leather furniture. The staff responds well to the demands of both traveling businesspeople and art lovers on sightseeing excursions.

Paseo Palmeras s/n, 43003 Tarragona. ✆ **97-723-30-40.** Fax 97-721-65-66. www.fut.es/~imperial. 170 units. 110€–150€ ($138–$188) double; 170€–210€ ($213–$263) suite. AE, DC, MC, V. Free parking on street; Mon–Fri parking lot 14€ ($18) per day. Bus: 1. **Amenities:** Snack bar; outdoor pool; tennis court; limited room service; babysitting; laundry service; dry cleaning. *In room:* A/C, TV, minibar, hair dryer, safe.

MODERATE/INEXPENSIVE

Hotel Astari *Value*   Travelers in search of peace and quiet on the Mediterranean come to the Astari, which opened in 1959. This resort hotel on the Barcelona road offers fresh and airy, though rather plain, accommodations. Most rooms are small, but each comes with a good bed and a bathroom with a tub/shower combo. The Astari has long balconies and terraces, one favorite spot being the outer flagstone terrace with its umbrella-shaded tables set among willows, orange trees, and geranium bushes. This is the only hotel in Tarragona with garage space for each guest's car.

Vía Augusta 95, 43003 Tarragona. © **97-723-69-00.** Fax 97-723-69-11. www.gsmhoteles.es. 81 units. 70€ ($88) double; 85€ ($106) business suite. AE, DC, MC, V. Parking 8€ ($10). Bus: 9. **Amenities:** Restaurant; bar; pool; room service; laundry service; dry cleaning. *In room:* A/C, TV, minibar, hair dryer, safe.

Hotel Lauria *F*   Less than half a block north of the town's popular seaside prome-nade (Passeig de les Palmeres), beside the tree-lined Rambla, this government-rated three-star hotel offers unpretentious clean rooms, each of which has been recently modernized. Room sizes range from small to medium, and each bathroom is equipped with a tub/shower combo. Long considered the leading hotel in town until the arrival of some newcomers, it still draws loyal repeat visitors. The rooms in back open onto a view of the sea.

Rambla Nova 20, 43004 Tarragona. © **97-723-67-12.** Fax 97-723-67-00. www.hlauria.es. 72 units. 60€–70€ ($75–$88) double. AE, DC, MC, V. Parking 10€ ($13). Bus: 1. **Amenities:** Bar; outdoor pool; business center; limited room service; laundry service; dry cleaning. *In room:* A/C, TV, hair dryer, safe.

WHERE TO DINE

Epicurí *FF* *Value* CATALAN/CONTINENTAL   In 2002 this long-established restaurant was bought by chef Javier Andrieu, who poured years of experience into a site in the heart of town, a very short walk from the archaeological treasures of medieval Tarragona. Within a cozy dining room whose decor falls midway between the organic *modernisme* of Gaudí and the Art Nouveau opulence of turn-of-the-20th-century Paris, this restaurant gives diners a choice of two set menus, one at 20€ ($25) that includes three courses; and a much more lavish one, priced at 42€ ($53), that features an aperitif plus six courses. Cuisine is based on securing the best market-fresh ingredients in town. The most intriguing dishes include half-cooked foie gras served with grapes, a succulent entrecôte of veal with artichokes, steamed veal cutlets with lemon or Madeira sauce, maigret of duckling with tiny Catalan mushrooms known as *moixernons,* and a heaven-sent filet of turbot with an almond-flavored saffron sauce. If the ingredients are available in the market, you might find other such dishes as a ragout of squid cooked in black beer.

Mare de Deú de la Mercè s/n. © **97-724-44-04.** Reservations required. Main courses 8€–16€ ($10–$20); set din-ner menu 24€–36€ ($30–$45). AE, DC, MC, V. Mon–Sat 8–12:30am. Closed Dec 25–Jan 2.

Les Coques *F* *Finds* MEDITERRANEAN   This is a real discovery in the historic core of Tarragona. Sophisticated Les Coques specializes in fare from both land and sea and does so exceedingly well. For example, they prepare the best grilled octopus (the miniature variety) in town. They also offer marvelously tender and succulent lamb chops flavored with rich burgundy sauce. The specialties depend on the season. Their selection of wild mushrooms *(seta)* can be prepared in almost any style without losing their marvelously woodsy taste.

Sant Lorenzo 15. © **97-722-83-00.** Reservations required. Main courses 18€–24€ ($23–$30). AE, DC, MC, V. Mon–Sat 1–3:45pm and 9–10:45pm. Closed 1 week in Feb and July 24–Aug 14.

The Beaches of the Costa Daurada

Running along the entire coastline of the province of Tarragona, for some 211km (131 miles) from Cunit as far as Les Cases d'Alcanar, is a series of excellent beaches and impressive cliffs, along with beautiful pine-covered headlands. In the city of Tarragona itself is **El Milagre** beach, and a little farther north are the beaches of **L'Arrabassade, Savinosa, dels Capellans,** and the **Llarga.** At the end of the latter stands **La Punta de la Mora,** which has a 16th-century watchtower. The small towns of **Altafulla** and **Torredembarra,** both complete with castles, stand next to these beaches and are the location of many hotels and urban developments.

Farther north still are the two magnificent beaches of **Comarruga** and **Sant Salvador.** The first is particularly cosmopolitan, the second more secluded. Last come the beaches of **Calafell, Segur,** and **Cunit,** all with modern tourist complexes. You'll also find the small towns of **Creixell, Sant Vicenç de Calders,** and **Clarà,** which have wooded hills in the background.

South of Tarragona, the coastline forms a wide arc that stretches for miles and includes **La Piñeda** beach. **El Recó** beach fronts the Cape of Salou where, in among its coves, hills, and hidden-away corners, many hotels and residential centers are located. The natural port of **Salou** is nowadays a center for international, family-oriented package tourism but is pleasant enough if you don't mind the crowds and noisy night scene.

Continuing south toward Valencia, you next come to **Cambrils,** a maritime town with an excellent beach and an important fishing port. In the background stand the impressive Colldejou and Llaberia mountains. Farther south are the beaches of **Montroig** and **L'Hospitalet,** as well as the small town of **L'Ametlla de Mar** with its small fishing port.

After passing the Balaguer massif, you eventually reach the delta of the River Ebro, a wide lowland area covering more than 483km (300 miles), opening like a fan into the sea. This is an area of rice fields crisscrossed by branches of the Ebro and by an enormous number of irrigation channels. There are also some lagoons that because of their immense size are ideal as hunting and fishing grounds. Moreover, there are some beaches over several miles in length and others in small hidden estuaries. Two important towns in the region are **Amposta,** on the Ebro itself, and **Sant Carles de la Ràpita,** a 19th-century port town favored by King Carlos III.

The Costa Daurada extends to its most southwesterly point at the plain of **Alcanar,** a large area given over to the cultivation of oranges and other similar crops. Its beaches, along with the small hamlet of **Les Cases d'Alcanar,** mark the end of the Tarragona section of the Costa Daurada.

Les Voltes ⓡ *(finds* MEDITERRANEAN   This excellent restaurant lies within the vaults of the Roman Circus Maximus. Chiseled stone from 2,300 years ago abides harmoniously with thick plate glass and polished steel surfaces. A large 250-seat restaurant, Les Voltes offers a kitchen of skilled chefs turning out a flavorful and well-seasoned Mediterranean cuisine. The menu features time-tested favorites such as a succulent baked lamb from the neighboring hills. *Rape,* or monkfish, deserves special billing, served with roasted garlic in a cockle-and-mussel sauce. Showing surehanded spicing, the loin of veal is peppery and served with broiled eggplant.

Carrer Trinquet Vell 12. ℭ **97-723-06-51.** Reservations recommended. Main courses 7.50€–20€ ($9.40–$25). DC, MC, V. Tues–Sun 1–4pm; Tues–Sat 8:30–11:30pm. Closed Dec 25–Jan 2.

3 Sitges ★★

40km (25 miles) S of Barcelona, 596km (370 miles) E of Madrid

Sitges is one of the most popular resorts of southern Europe and the brightest spot on the Costa Daurada. It's especially crowded in summer, mostly with affluent young northern Europeans, many of them gay. Throughout the 19th century, the resort largely drew prosperous middle-class industrialists and traders (known as *indios* since they made their fortunes in the Americas) and many of their stately homes still stand along the sea-facing promenade, the Passeig Marítim. Today, Sitges easily accommodates a mixed crowd of affluent residents, vacationing families and couples, and swarms of day-trippers from Barcelona.

Sitges has long been known as a city of culture, thanks in part to resident artist, playwright, and bohemian dandy Santiago Rusiñol. The 19th-century *modernisme* movement was nurtured in Sitges, and the town remained the scene of artistic encounters and demonstrations long after the movement waned. Sitges continued as a resort of artists, attracting such giants as Salvador Dalí and poet Federico García Lorca. The Spanish Civil War (1936–39) erased what has come to be called the "golden age" of Sitges. Although other artists and writers arrived in the decades to follow, none had the impact of those who had gone before.

ESSENTIALS

GETTING THERE   RENFE runs **trains** from Barcelona-Sants and Passeig de Gràcia to Sitges, a 30- to 40-minute trip. Call ℭ **90-224-02-02** in Barcelona for information about schedules. If you plan to stay late, check what time the last train leaves once in Sitges as they vary.

Sitges is a 45-minute **drive** from Barcelona along the C-246, a coastal road. There is also an express highway, the A-7, which passes through the Garraf Tunnels. The coastal road is more scenic, but it can be extremely slow on weekends because of the heavy traffic, as all of Barcelona seemingly heads for the beaches.

VISITOR INFORMATION   The **tourist office** is at Carrer Sínea Morera 1 (ℭ **93-894-42-51;** www.sitges.org). From June to September 15, it's open daily from 9am to 9pm; from September 16 to May, hours are Monday through Friday from 9am to 2pm and 4 to 6:30pm, and Saturday from 10am to 1pm.

SPECIAL EVENTS Carnaval at Sitges is one of the outstanding events on the Catalan calendar and frankly makes all other Carnaval celebrations in the region look lame. For more than a century, the town has celebrated the days before the beginning of Lent. Fancy dress, floats, feathered outfits, and sequins all make this an exciting event. The party begins on the Thursday before Lent with the arrival of the king of the Carnestoltes and ends with the Burial of a Sardine on Ash Wednesday. Activities reach their flamboyant best on Sant Bonaventura, where gay people hold their own celebrations. During the week of Corpus Christi in June blankets of flowers are laid in the streets of the Old Town, and on the night of June 23, the feast of Sant Joan, the beach lights up with fireworks and bonfires.

Sitges

Beach
Campground
Information
Parking
Post Office
Railway

To Vilafranca del Penedès
To Barcelona & Tarragona

0   1/10 Mi
0   .2 Km

POBLE SEC

SINIA MORERA

SANT CRISPI

PARC FACUNDO BACARÍ MASSÓ

Plaça de E. Maristany   Train Station

Plaça d'Espanya

Platja del Bassa Rodona

Platja del Ribera

Platja del Fragata

Plaça del Baluard

Platja del St. Sebastià

Mediterranean Sea

SPAIN   Sitges
★
Madrid
PORTUGAL

ATTRACTIONS ●
Museu Cau Ferrat **8**
Museu Maricel **9**
Museu Romàntic **4**

ACCOMMODATIONS ■
Hotel El Cid **2**
Hotel Noucentista **1**
Hotel Romàntic de Sitges **5**
Meliá Gran Sitges **7**
Terramar **13**

DINING/CLUBS ◆
El Fresco **6**
El Velero **11**
Fragata **10**
Mare Nostrum **12**
Mediterráneo **3**

FUN ON & OFF THE BEACH

The old part of Sitges used to be a fortified medieval enclosure. The castle is now the seat of the town government. The local parish church, called **La Punta (The Point)** and built next to the sea on top of a promontory, presides over an extensive maritime esplanade, where people parade in the early evening. Behind the side of the church are the Museu Cau Ferrat and the Museu Maricel (see "Museums," below).

Most people are here to hit the beach. The beaches have showers, bathing cabins, and stalls; kiosks rent motorboats, watersports equipment, beach umbrellas, and sun-beds. Beaches on the eastern end and those inside the town center are the most peaceful—for example, **Aiguadolç** and **Els Balomins. Playa San Sebastián, Fragata Beach,** and the **"Beach of the Boats"** (below the church and next to the yacht club) are the area's family beaches. A young, happening crowd heads for the **Playa de la Ribera** to the west.

Where the Boys Are

Along with Ibiza, Key West, and Mikonos, Sitges has established itself firmly on the A-list of gay resorts. It's a perfect destination for those who want a ready-made combination of beach and bars, all within a few minutes' walk of each other. It works well as a temporary, calmer alternative to Barcelona, which is about 30 minutes away by train, and so is great for a day trip or a few days out of the city. In the off season, it's pretty quiet on the gay front apart from Carnaval in February, when hordes of gays and lesbians descend from Barcelona and the party really begins.

Summer, however, is pure hedonistic playtime, and the town draws males in from all over Europe. Sitges is never going to tax the intellect, but it might well exhaust the body. There's a gay beach crammed with the usual overload of muscles and summer accessories in the middle of the town in front of the Passeig Marítim. The other beach is nudist and farther out of town, between Sitges and Vilanova. The best directions are to go as far as the L'Atlántida disco and then follow the train track to the farther of the two beaches. The woods next to it are unsurprisingly packed with playful wildlife sporting short hair and deep tans.

All along the coast, women can and certainly do go topless. Farther west are the most solitary beaches, where the scene grows racier, especially along the **Playas del Muerto,** where two tiny nude beaches lie between Sitges and Vilanova i la Geltrú. A shuttle bus runs between the church and the Hotel Terramar. From here, go along the road to the club L'Atlántida, then walk along the railway. The first beach draws nudists of every sexual persuasion, and the second is almost solely gay. Be advised that lots of action takes place in the woods in back of these beaches.

MUSEUMS

Beaches aside, Sitges has some choice museums, which really shouldn't be missed.

Museu Cau Ferrat 𝒢𝒢 *Moments*   The Catalan artist Santiago Rusiñol combined two charming 16th-century cottages to make this house, where he lived and worked; upon his death in 1931 he willed it to Sitges along with his art collection. More than anyone else, Rusiñol made Sitges a popular resort. The museum's immense and cluttered collection includes two paintings by El Greco and several small Picassos, including *The Bullfight*. A number of Rusiñol's works are on display, along with his prolific collection of wrought-iron objects and a dazzling display of Mediterranean tilework. The edifice, with its dramatic sea views from tiny windows, is worth the visit alone.

Carrer Fonollar s/n. © **93-894-03-64.** Admission 3.50€ ($4.35) adults, 1.75€ ($2.20) students, free for children under 12; combination ticket for the 3 museums listed in this section is 6.40€ ($8) adults, 3.50€ ($4.35) students. June 15–Sept Tues–Sun 10am–2pm and 5–9pm; Oct–June 14 Tues–Fri 10am–1:30pm and 3–6:30pm, Sat 10am–7pm, Sun 10am–3pm.

Museu Maricel 𝒢   Opened by the king and queen of Spain, the Museu Maricel contains art donated by Dr. Jesús Pérez Rosales. The palace, owned by American Charles Deering when it was built right after World War I, is made up of two parts connected by a small bridge. The museum has a good collection of Gothic and

Romantic paintings and sculptures, as well as many fine Catalan ceramics. There are three noteworthy works by Santiago Rebull and an allegorical painting of World War I by José María Sert.

Carrer del Fonollar s/n. (*) **93-894-03-64.** Admission 3.50€ ($4.35) adults, 1.75€ ($2.20) students, free for children under 12; admission included in combination ticket (see Museu Cau Ferrat, above). Same hours as Museu Cau Ferrat.

Museu Romàntic ("Can Llopis")   This museum re-creates the daily life of a Sitges land-owning family in the 18th and 19th centuries. The family rooms, furniture, and household objects are most interesting. Upstairs, you'll find wine cellars and an important collection of antique dolls.

Sant Gaudenci 1. (*) **93-894-29-69.** Admission (including guided tour) 3.50€ ($4.35) adults, 1.75€ ($2.20) students, free for children under 12; admission included in combination ticket (see Museu Cau Ferrat, above). All museums have the same hours and dates.

WHERE TO STAY

In spite of a building spree, Sitges just can't handle the large numbers of tourists who flock here in July and August. By mid-October just about everything—including hotels, restaurants, and bars—slows down considerably or closes altogether.

EXPENSIVE

Hotel Romàntic de Sitges ✦ *Finds*   Made up of three beautifully restored 19th-century villas, this hotel is only a short walk from the beach and the train station. The romantic bar is an international rendezvous, and the public rooms are filled with artwork. You can have breakfast in the dining room or in a garden filled with mulberry trees. The rooms, reached by stairs, range from small-to-medium-size and are well maintained, with good beds and bathrooms with shower stalls. Overflow guests are housed in a nearby annex, the Hotel de la Renaixença.

Sant Isidre 33, 08870 Sitges. (*) **93-894-83-75.** Fax 93-894-81-67. www.hotelromantic.com. 60 units. 80€–95€ ($100–$119) double without bathroom; 90€–110€ ($113–$138) double with shower/bathroom. Rates include breakfast. AE, MC, V. Closed Nov–Mar 15. **Amenities:** Bar; babysitting. *In room:* Hair dryer, safe.

Meliá Gran Sitges ✦   Designed with steeply sloping sides reminiscent of a pair of interconnected Aztec pyramids, this hotel dates from 1992, when it housed spectators and participants in the Barcelona Olympics. The hotel has a marble lobby with what feels like the largest window in Spain, overlooking a view of the mountains. Each mid-size room comes with a large furnished veranda for sunbathing, and each bathroom has a tub/shower combo. Many guests are here to participate in the conferences and conventions held frequently in the battery of high-tech convention facilities. It's about a 15-minute walk east of the center of Sitges, near the access roads leading to Barcelona.

Joan Salvat Papasseit 38, Puerto de Aiguadolç, 08870 Sitges. (*) **800/336-3542** in the U.S., or 93-811-08-11 (hotel) or 90-214-44-44 (reservations) Fax 93-894-90-34. www.solmelia.com. 307 units. 90€–225€ ($111–$281) double; 260€ ($325) suite. Some rates include breakfast. AE, DC, MC, V. Parking 9€ ($11). **Amenities:** Restaurant; bar; indoor pool; outdoor pool; health club; sauna; business center; limited room service; babysitting; laundry service; dry cleaning. *In room:* A/C, TV, minibar, hair dryer, safe.

Terramar ✦✦ *Finds*   Facing the beach in a residential area of Sitges, about half a mile from the center, this resort hotel, one of the first "grand hotels" along this coast, is a Sitges landmark. Its balconied front evokes a multi-decked yacht and the interior, renovated in the 1970s, is a near-perfect example of retro design. The foyer has a quirky marine theme, the floors and wall panels are lined with different marbles, and the ladies' restroom is hot pink. The spacious and comfortable guest rooms contain the same sort of eccentric detailing.

Passeig Marítim 80, 08870 Sitges. 📞 **93-894-00-50.** Fax 93-894-56-04. www.hotelterramar.com. 209 units. 110€–165€ ($138–$206) double; 150€–170€ ($188–$213) suite. Rates include breakfast buffet. AE, DC, MC, V. Closed Nov–Mar. **Amenities:** 2 restaurants; 2 bars; outdoor pool; 2 outdoor tennis courts; children's center; business center; limited room service; babysitting; laundry service; dry cleaning. *In room:* A/C, TV, minibar, hair dryer, safe.

MODERATE

Hotel Noucentista 🔗 *Value*   Owned by the same family that owns the popular Hotel El Xalet across the street, this is a winning choice. After undergoing 3 years of renovation, it is now better than ever. The name, Noucentista, means 1900, the year of the building's original construction. The interior is quite stunning, a statement of *modernisme* with much use of antiques. The small-to-midsize bedrooms are stylishly and comfortably furnished with ample closet space and bathrooms, each with a shower. Some of the accommodations open onto small private balconies. The inn is a 10-minute walk from the beach. The hotel is also graced with a small courtyard garden, and guests have access to Xalet's swimming pool and restaurant.

Isla de Cuba 21, 08870 Sitges. 📞 **93-811-00-70.** Fax 93-894-55-79. www.elxalet.com. 12 units. 65€–100€ ($81–$125) double; 115€ ($138) suite. AE, DC, MC, V. *In room:* A/C, TV, minibar, hair dryer, safe.

INEXPENSIVE

Hotel El Cid 🔗   El Cid's exterior evokes Castile, and inside, appropriately enough, you'll find beamed ceilings, natural stone walls, heavy wrought-iron chandeliers, and leather chairs. The same theme is carried out in the rear dining room and in the pleasantly furnished rooms, which, though small, are still quite comfortable, with fine beds and bathrooms containing shower stalls. Breakfast is the only meal served. El Cid is off the Passeig de Vilanova in the center of town.

San José 39 bis, 08870 Sitges. 📞 **93-894-18-42.** Fax 93-894-63-35. 77 units. 45€–70€ ($56–$88) double. Rates include continental breakfast. MC, V. Closed Oct–Apr. **Amenities:** Bar; outdoor pool; babysitting. *In room:* No phone.

WHERE TO DINE
EXPENSIVE

El Velero 🔗 SEAFOOD   This is one of Sitges's leading restaurants, positioned along the beachside promenade. The most desirable tables are found on the glass greenhouse terrace, opening onto the esplanade, though there's a more glamorous restaurant inside. Try a soup, such as clam and truffle or whitefish, followed by a main dish such as paella marinara (with seafood) or suprême of salmon in pine-nut sauce.

Passeig de la Ribera 38. 📞 93-894-20-51. Reservations required. Main courses 18€–38€ ($23–$48); tasting menu 38€ ($48); gastronomic menu 50€ ($63). AE, DC, MC, V. Tues–Sun 1:30–4pm and 8:30–11:30pm. Closed Dec 22–Jan 6.

MODERATE

El Fresco 🔗🔗 *Finds* FUSION   Many people, especially in the gay community, reckon this is the best bet in Sitges, which perhaps has to do with the fact that it is more like an eatery you would encounter in Sydney. Owned by an Australian couple, the restaurant's eclectic menu draws heavily on Asian influences. Upstairs there is a cheaper cafe, an enormously popular breakfast spot; here, you can feed your hangover on such un-Spanish fare as blueberry pancakes, fresh muesli, and muffins, or choose from a selection of salads such as Thai beef or Caesar for lunch.

Pau Barrabeitg 4. 📞 93-894-06-00. Reservations recommended. Main courses 9€–24€ ($11–$30). MC, V. May–Sept Tues–Sun 8:30am–midnight; Oct–Apr Wed–Sun 8:30am–midnight. Closed Dec 20–Jan 20.

Fragata 🔗 SEAFOOD   Though its simple interior offers little more than well-scrubbed floors, tables with crisp linens, and air-conditioning, some of the most

Cava Country

The Penedès region is Catalonia's wine country, the place where the crisp whites, hearty reds, and sparkling *cava* that you've tried in Barcelona's restaurants are produced. After years of being thought of solely as an agrarian region, wine tourism is starting to take off in the villages and rolling vineyards of this delightful destination.

The capital is Vilafranca del Penedés, a bustling provincial town that has a fine outdoor market on Saturday mornings and is famous for its local *castellers* (human towers) team. The **Museu del Vi,** Plaça Jaume I 1 (© **93-817-00-36),** has a collection of viniculture equipment and memorabilia considered to be the best of its kind in Europe. If you are curious to know more, the Museu de Vilafranca, located next door, has a collection of works by artists on wine-related themes and a gorgeous collection of Spanish and Catalan ceramic work from the 15th century onward. If you have time, check out the Basílica de Santa María (also located in the Plaça Sant Jaume), a Gothic church dating from the 15th century. Ascend the 52m (171 ft.) bell tower for a panoramic view of the town and surrounding area.

Nothing, however, beats the hands on-experience of seeing the process of winemaking from start to finish. A handful of bodegas (wineries) are open to the public, the best being the estate of **Codorníu** (© **93-818-32-32)** the top *cava* maker in Catalonia. Their magnificent winery is located 10km (6 miles) from Vilafranca in the village of Sant Sadorni d'Anoia. Designed at the end of the 19th century by Josep María Puig i Cadafalch (a master architect of the *modernisme* movement), his beautiful project reflects the luxurious product made within; the complex is replete with Art Nouveau touches and details and 15km (9 miles) of sinuous underground tunnels where the product is aged. Another highlight is a museum containing gorgeous past advertising posters of the product, many by renowned artists of the period. Codorníu is open to the public Monday through Friday 9am to 5pm and Saturday 9am to 1pm. A minitrain whisks you around the estate, including the vineyards, and a *cava* tasting nicely rounds off your visit.

Another sumptuous *moderniste* wine palace is **Freixenet,** Av. Casetas Mir s/n (© **93-891-70-25),** Codorníu's main competition. Freixenet's landmark bodega, located right beside the train station of Sant Sadorni d'Anoia, also gives tours of its headquarters (by previous appointment) on Saturday from 10am to 1pm. Its colorful, florid facade is one of the area's landmarks.

The tourist office in Vilafranca del Penedès is located at Carrer de la Cort 14 (© **93-892-03-58;** www.turismevilafranca.com). It's open Tuesday to Friday from 9am to 1pm and 4:30 to 7pm, and Saturday 10am to 1pm. **RENFE** (© **90-224-02-02;** www.renfe.es) runs dozens of trains a day (trip time: 55 min.) from Barcelona to Vilafranca del Penedès and Sant Sadorni d'Anoia, leaving from Catalunya station. If you're driving, head west out of the city via the A-7. Follow the signs to Sant Sadorni d' Anoia and then stay on the same highway to Vilafranca.

delectable seafood specialties in town are served here, and hundreds of loyal customers come to appreciate the authentic cuisine. Specialties include seafood soup, a mixed grill of fresh fish, cod salad, mussels marinara, several preparations of squid and octopus, plus some flavorful meat dishes, such as grilled lamb cutlets.

Passeig de la Ribera 1. ℂ **93-894-10-86.** Reservations recommended. Main dishes 12€–24€ ($15–$30). AE, DC, MC, V. Daily 1–4:30pm and 8:30–11:30pm.

Mare Nostrum 𝕽𝕽 SEAFOOD   This landmark dates from 1950, when it opened in what had been a private home in the 1890s. The dining room has a waterfront view, and in warm weather tables are placed outside. The menu includes a full range of seafood dishes, among them grilled-fish specialties and steamed hake with champagne. The fish soup is particularly delectable. Next door, the restaurant's cafe serves ice cream, milkshakes, sandwiches, tapas, and three varieties of sangria, including one with champagne and fruit.

Passeig de la Ribera 60. ℂ **93-894-33-93.** Reservations required. Main courses 10€–23€ ($13–$28). AE, DC, MC, V. Thurs–Tues 1–4pm and 8–11pm. Closed Dec 15–Feb 1.

SITGES AFTER DARK

One of the best ways to pass an evening in Sitges is to walk the waterfront esplanade, have a leisurely dinner, then retire at about 11pm to one of the dozens of open-air cafes for a nightcap and some serious people-watching.

If you're straight, you may have to hunt to find a late-night bar that isn't predominantly gay in the center of town. For the locations of Sitges's gay bars, look for a pocket-size map that's distributed in most of the gay bars—you can pick it up in the Parrot's Pub (in the Plaza de la Industria) or it can be downloaded on **www. gaymap.info**. Nine of these bars are concentrated on **Carrer Sant Bonaventura,** a 5-minute walk from the beach (near the Museu Romàntic). If you grow bored with the action in one place, you just have to walk down the street to find another. Drink prices run about the same in all the clubs.

Mediterráneo, Sant Bonaventura 6 (no phone), is the largest gay disco/bar. It sports a formal Iberian garden and sleek modern styling. And upstairs in this restored 1690s house just east of the Plaça d'Espanya are pool tables and a covered terrace. On summer nights, the place is filled to overflowing.

4 Girona 𝕽𝕽

97km (60 miles) NE of Barcelona, 90km (56 miles) S of the French city of Perpignan

Founded by the Romans, **Girona** is one of the top-10 important historical sites in Spain. Later, it became a Moorish stronghold and later still, it reputedly withstood three invasions by Napoleon's troops in the early 1800s. For that and other past aggressions, Girona is often called the "City of a Thousand Sieges." These days, residents go about their daily business smug in the knowledge that their city is consistently rated the best in the country in terms of quality of life.

Split by the Onyar River, this bustling, provincial city often only gets a nod from the crowds of tourists who use its airport as a springboard for the resorts and beaches of the nearby Costa Brava. When you arrive, make your way to the narrow lanes and hidden staircases of the Old City and the Call, the remains of the sizable Jewish community, via the ancient stone footbridge across the Onyar. From here, you'll have the finest view of ocher-colored town houses flanking each side, instantly recalling Venice. Bring good walking shoes, as you will want to circumnavigate the old city walls to

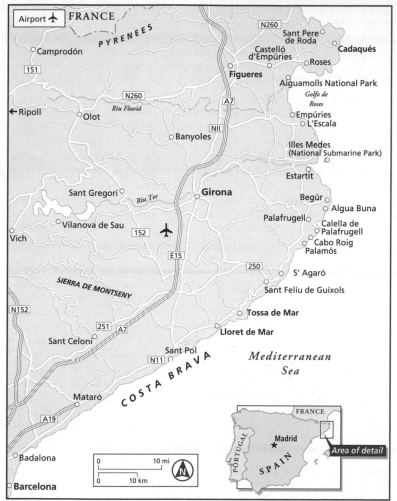

fully take in the splendid stone edifices and lush countryside of their surroundings. Much of Girona can be appreciated from outside the walls, but there are some important attractions you'll want to see on the inside, too.

ESSENTIALS

GETTING THERE   More than 26 **trains** per day run between Girona and Barcelona-Sants or Passeig de Gràcia stations. Trip time is 1 to 1½ hours, depending on the train. Trains arrive in Girona at the Plaça Espanya (© **97-220-70-93** for information).

By **car** from Barcelona, take the A-7 at Ronda Litoral and head north via the A-7.

VISITOR INFORMATION   The **tourist office** at Rambla de la Libertat 1 (© **97-222-65-75**; www.ajuntament.gi) is open Monday through Friday from 8am to 8pm, Saturday from 8am to 2pm and 4 to 8pm, and Sunday from 9am to 2pm.

EXPLORING THE MEDIEVAL CITY

Banys Arabs 🏛   These 12th-century Arab baths, an example of Romanesque civic architecture, are in the Old Quarter of the city. Visit the **caldarium (hot bath),** with its paved floor, and the **frigidarium (cold bath),** with its central octagonal pool surrounded by pillars that support a prism-like structure in the overhead window. Although the Moorish baths were heavily restored in 1929, they'll give you an idea of what the ancient ones were like.

Carrer Ferran el Catolic s/n. ⓒ **97-221-32-62.** Admission 2€ ($2.50) adults, 1€ ($1.25) students, free for seniors and children under 16. Apr–Sept Mon–Sat 10am–7pm, Sun 10am–2pm; Oct–Mar Tues–Sun 10am–2pm. Closed Jan 1, Jan 6, Easter, and Dec 25–26.

Catedral 🏛🏛🏛   Girona's major attraction is its magnificent cathedral, reached by climbing a 17th-century baroque staircase of 90 steep steps. The 14th-century cathedral represents many architectural styles, including Gothic and Romanesque, but it's most notably Catalan baroque. The facade you see as you climb those long stairs dates from the 17th and 18th centuries; from a cornice on top rises a bell tower crowned by a dome with a bronze angel weather vane. Enter the main door of the cathedral and go into the nave, which, at 23m (75 ft.), is the broadest example of Gothic architecture in the world.

The cathedral contains many works of art, displayed for the most part in its museum. Its prize exhibit is a **tapestry of the Creation,** a unique piece of 11th- or 12th-century Romanesque embroidery depicting humans and animals in the Garden of Eden. The other major work displayed is one of the world's rarest manuscripts—the 10th-century *Códex del Beatus,* which contains an illustrated commentary on the Revelation. From the cathedral's **Chapel of Hope,** a door leads to a **Romanesque cloister** from the 12th and 13th centuries, with an unusual trapezoidal layout. The cloister gallery, with a double colonnade, has a series of biblical scenes that are the prize jewel of Catalan Romanesque art. From the cloister you can view the 12th-century **Torre de Carlemany (Charlemagne's Tower).**

Plaça de la Catedral s/n. ⓒ **97-221-44-26.** Free admission to cathedral; nave, cloister, and museum 4€ ($5), students and seniors 3€ ($3.75). All free on Sundays. Cathedral daily 9am–1pm and during cloister and museum visiting hours. Cloister and museum: July–Sept Tues–Sat 10am–8pm, Sun 10am–2pm; Oct–Feb Tues–Sat 10am–2pm and 4–6pm, Sun 10am–2pm; Mar–June Tues–Sat 10am–2pm and 4–7pm, Sun 10am–2pm.

Església de Sant Feliu 🏛   This 14th- to 17th-century church was built over what may have been the tomb of Feliu of Africa, martyred during Diocletian's persecution at the beginning of the 4th century. Important in the architectural history of Catalonia, the church has pillars and arches in the Romanesque style and a Gothic central nave. The **bell tower**—one of the Girona skyline's most characteristic features—has eight pinnacles and one central tower, each supported on a solid octagonal base. The main facade of the church is baroque. The interior contains some exceptional works, including a 16th-century **altarpiece** and a 14th-century alabaster *Reclining Christo.* Notice the eight pagan and Christian **sarcophagi** set in the walls of the presbytery, the two oldest of which are from the 2nd century A.D. One shows Pluto carrying Persephone off to the depths of the earth.

Pujada de Sant Feliu s/n. ⓒ **97-220-14-07.** Free admission. Daily 8am–7:45pm.

Museu Arqueològic 🏛   Housed in a Romanesque church and cloister from the 11th and 12th centuries, this museum illustrates the history of the region from the Paleolithic to the Visigothic periods, using artifacts discovered in nearby excavations.

The monastery itself ranks as one of the best examples of Catalan Romanesque architecture. In the cloister, note some Hebrew inscriptions from gravestones of the old Jewish cemetery.

Sant Pere de Galligants, Santa Llúcia 1. © **97-220-26-32.** Admission 2€ ($2.50) adults, 1.50€ ($1.90) students, free for seniors and children under 16. Oct–May Tues–Sat 10am–2pm and 4–6pm, Sun 10am–2pm; June–SeptTues–Sat 10am–1:30pm and 4–7pm, Sun 10am–2pm.

Museu d'Art *In a former Romanesque and Gothic Episcopal palace (Palau Episcopal) next to the cathedral, this museum displays artworks spanning 10 centuries (once housed in the old Diocesan Museum and the Provincial Museum). Stop in the throne room to view the **altarpiece of Sant Pere of Púbol** by Bernat Martorell and the **altarpiece of Sant Miguel de Crüilles** by Luis Borrassa. Both of these works, from the 15th century, are exemplary pieces of Catalan Gothic painting. The museum is also proud of its **altar stone** of Sant Pere de Roda, from the 10th and 11th centuries; this work in wood and stone, depicting figures and legends, was once covered in embossed silver. The 12th-century *Crüilles Timber* is a unique piece of Romanesque polychrome wood. *Our Lady of Besalù,* from the 15th century, is one of the most accomplished depictions of the Virgin carved in alabaster.

Pujada de la Catedral 12. © **97-220-38-34.** Admission 2€ ($2.50) adults, 1.50€ ($1.90) students, free for seniors and children. Mar–Sept Tues–Sat 10am–7pm, Sun 10am–2pm; Oct–Feb Tues–Sat 10am–6pm, Sun 10am–2pm. Closed Jan 1, Jan 6, Easter, and Dec 25–26.

Museu de Cinema *Film buffs flock to this film museum, the only one of its kind in Spain. It houses the Tomàs Mallol collection of some 25,000 cinema artifacts, going all the way up to films shot as late as 1970. Many objects are from the "pre-cinema" era, plus other exhibits from the early days of film. The museum even owns the original camera of the pioneering Lumière brothers. Fixed images such as photographs, posters, engravings, drawings, and paintings are exhibited along with some 800 films of various styles and periods. There's even a library with film-related publications.

El Call

The Jewish diaspora made an indelible mark on the city of Girona. A sizable chunk of the Old Town is taken up with the remains of **El Call,** once Spain's most sizable Jewish ghetto. From 20-odd families who arrived at the end of the 9th century, the community grew to nearly 2,000, with three synagogues, butchers, bakers, and other mercantile activity taking place in the neighborhood's cobbled streets. In 1492, along with other Jewish communities on the peninsula (including Barcelona and Majorca), they were blamed for the spread of the plague and unceremoniously ousted by Catholic powers. The **Centre Bonastruc Ca Porta,** Calle La Força 8 (© **97-221-67-61**), in the heart of El Call, contains exhibitions on medieval Jewish life and customs, with an emphasis on the cohabiting of Jews and Christians, as well as exhibitions by contemporary Jewish artists. It also conducts special-interest tours of the area and courses on Jewish culture and history. It's open Monday to Saturday 10am to 8pm, Sunday 10am to 3pm.

Sèquia 1. ⓒ **97-241-27-77.** Admission 3€ ($3.45) adults, 1.50€ ($1.70) students and seniors, free for children under 16. May–Sept Tues–Sun 10am–8pm; Oct–Apr Tues–Fri 10am–6pm, Sat 10am–8pm, Sun 11am–3pm. Closed Dec 25–26, Jan 1, and Jan 6.

WHERE TO STAY
MODERATE

Hotel Carlemany 𝒻   In a commercial area only 10 minutes from the historic core, this 1995 hotel is often cited as the best in town. A favorite of business travelers, its facilities are top class. Overall, it's contemporary with a modern (though slightly lacking in character) design. That said, the midsize-to-spacious rooms are soundproof and airy, and the bathrooms contain tub/shower combos.

Plaça Miquel Santaló s/n, 17002 Girona. ⓒ **97-221-12-12.** Fax 97-221-49-94. www.carlemany.es. 90 units. 120€ ($150) double; 160€ ($200) suite. AE, DC, MC, V. Parking 12€ ($15). **Amenities:** Restaurant; 2 bars; limited room service; laundry service; nonsmoking rooms. *In room:* A/C, TV, hair dryer, safe.

Hotel Ciutat de Girona 𝒻   This hip and high-tech four-star hotel is located right in the town center, and is a good choice for people who prefer modern conveniences to rustic charm. Opened in 2003, all the classy rooms are decked out in *diseño catalán* style in tones of taupe and cream with dramatic swathes of red, and all have Internet connections (you can even get your own PC upon request). The classy cocktail bar in the foyer clinches the stylish deal.

Nord 2, 17001 Girona. ⓒ **97-248-30-38.** Fax 97-248-30-26. www.hotel-ciutatdegirona.com. 44 units. 125€–140€ ($156–$175) double; 160€ ($200) triple. AE, DC, MC, V. Parking 14€ ($18). **Amenities:** Restaurant; bar; limited room service; laundry service. *In room:* A/C, TV, free minibar, dataport, hair dryer.

Hotel Ultonia   Restored in 1993 and now better than ever, this small hotel lies a short walk from the Plaça de la Independencia. Since the late 1950s it has been a favorite with business travelers, but today it attracts more visitors because it's close to the historical district. The rooms are compact and furnished in a modern style, with comfortable beds and bathrooms, most of which have tub/shower combos. Double-glazed windows keep out the noise. Some of the rooms opening onto the avenue have tiny balconies. In just 8 to 12 minutes, you can cross the Onyar into the medieval quarter. Guests can enjoy a breakfast buffet (not included in the rates quoted below), but no other meals are served.

Av. Jaume I no. 22, 17001 Girona. ⓒ **97-220-38-50.** Fax 97-220-33-34. 45 units. 80€–100€ ($100–$125) double. AE, DC, MC, V. Parking 10€ ($13) nearby. **Amenities:** Laundry service. *In room:* A/C, TV, minibar.

INEXPENSIVE

Bellmirall 𝒻𝒻 *Moments*   Across the Onyar River, this little discovery lies in the heart of the old Jewish ghetto. It's one of the best values in the Old Town. The building itself, much restored and altered over the years, dates originally from the 14th century. Christina Vach took control of the venerated building and proceeded to restore it, converting it to a hotel. She has succeeded admirably in her task. Bedrooms are small to midsize and are decorated in part with antiques set against brick walls. Some of these walls are adorned with paintings, others come with carefully selected ceramics. Each room comes with a small bathroom with shower. In summer, it's possible to order breakfast outside in the courtyard.

Carrer Bellmirall 3, 17004 Girona. ⓒ **97-220-40-09.** 7 units. 60€ ($75) double; 80€ ($100) triple. Rates include breakfast. No credit cards. Free parking (hotel provides permit). Closed Jan–Feb. *In room:* No phone.

Hotel Peninsular 𝒻   Devoid of any significant architectural character, this modest hotel provides clean but uncontroversial accommodations near the cathedral and the river. The small rooms, which benefited from a 1990 renovation, are scattered over five floors. All units contain neatly kept bathrooms with showers. The hotel is better for short-term stopovers than for prolonged stays. Breakfast is the only meal served (and is not included in the rates quoted below).

Nou 3, 17001 Girona. (✆ **97-220-38-00.** Fax 97-221-04-92. www.novarahotels.com. 47 units. 60€–65€ ($75–$81) double. AE, DC, MC, V. Parking 8€ ($10) nearby. **Amenities:** Breakfast bar; laundry service. *In room:* TV, hair dryer, safe.

WHERE TO DINE

Bronsoms ⊛ CATALAN   In the heart of the Old Town, within an 1890s building that was once a private home, this restaurant is one of the most consistently reliable in Girona. Praised by newspapers as far away as Madrid, it has been under its present management since 1982. It's perfected the art of serving a Catalan-based *cocina del mercado*—that is, cooking with whatever market-fresh ingredients are available. The house specialties include fish paella, *arroz negro* (black rice, tinted with squid ink and studded with shellfish), white beans, and several preparations of Iberian ham.

Sant Francesc 7. (✆ **97-221-24-93.** Reservations recommended. Main courses 8€–16€ ($10–$20); fixed-price menu 9€ ($11). AE, MC, V. Mon–Sat 1–4pm and 8–11:30pm; Sun 1–4pm.

Cal Ros CATALAN   In the oldest part of Girona, near the Plaza de Cataluña, this restaurant thrives as a culinary staple and has done so since the 1920s. It was named after a long-ago light-haired owner, although exactly who that was no one today seems to remember. You'll be seated in one of four rustic dining rooms, each with heavy ceiling beams, exposed stone and plaster, and a sense of old Catalonia. Menu items include savory *escudilla,* made with veal, pork, and local herbs and vegetables; at least four kinds of local fish, usually braised with potatoes and tomatoes; tender fried filets of veal with mushrooms; and flaky homemade pastries, some of them flavored with anise-flavored cream. Kosher and halal dishes are also prepared.

Cort Reial 9. (✆ **97-221-73-79.** Reservations recommended. Main courses 6€–28€ ($7.50–$35). AE, DC, MC, V. Nov–Mar Tues–Sun 1–4pm, Tues–Sat 8–11pm; Apr–Oct Sun–Mon 1–4pm and 8–11pm.

El Cellar de Can Roca ⊛⊛⊛ CATALAN   Just 2km (1¼ miles) from the center of Girona, El Cellar de Can Roca is the best of the new spate of Catalonian restaurants and represents the success of the campaign to transform Girona into one of the more fashionable cities in Spain. Run by three young brothers (one of whom now heads the achingly fashionable Moo Restaurant in Barcelona), the restaurant is intimate, with only 12 tables. The cuisine is an interesting combination of traditional Catalan dishes creatively transformed into contemporary Mediterranean fare. Start with an avocado purée, and for dessert you can't pass up the mandarin orange sorbet with pumpkin compote.

Taiala 40. (✆ **97-222-21-57.** Reservations recommended. Main courses 17€–38€ ($21–$48); fixed-price menus 60€ ($75). AE, DC, MC, V. Tues–Sat 1–4pm and 9–11pm. Closed Dec 22–Jan 6 and June 23–July 14. Bus: 5.

SHOPPING

There are some interesting shops to be found around El Call and the Old Town. Look out for little specialty shops selling local wares such as beige and yellow-colored ceramic cookware and more upmarket designer joints. The famous Barcelonese design and furniture emporium BD has a branch here at Calle La Força 20 ((✆ **97-222-43-39**) one of a handful of design and object stores on the same medieval street in El Call. There are also a couple of open-air, artisan markets on Saturdays, one at the Pont de Pedra (stone bridge) and another in the Plaça Miquel Santaló and Plaça de les Castanyes.

Garden of Sea and Myrtle

The **Jardí Botànic Marimurtra,** with its meandering paths and white cliff-top pergolas, towers beside the fishing town of Blanes (30km/20 miles from Girona), at the southern extremity of the Costa Brava. You'll be hard-pressed to find a more lovely evocation of nature in the whole Mediterranean than this 16-hectare (40-acre) Garden of Eden with its 200,000 species of plants and shrubs from the five continents. Declared an Area of National Cultural interest, it was founded by biologist Karl Faust at the beginning of the 20th century as a research center for universal flora. Allow an hour for a full stroll, longer if you feel like soaking up the atmosphere and meditating in some quiet corner like the tiny Plaça de Goethe. Jardí Botànic Marimurtra is at Passeig de Carles Faust 9, Blanes (© **97-233-08-26;** www.jbotanicmarimurtra.org). Admission is 4€ ($5.25), and hours are daily 9am to 6pm (Apr–Oct; till 8pm in mid-summer), 10am to 5pm (Nov–Mar). Weekends and fiestas 10am to 2pm.

GIRONA AFTER DARK

Central Girona has a good number of tapas bars and cafes. Many of them are scattered along **Les Ramblas,** around the edges of the keynote **Plaça de Independencia,** and within the antique boundaries of the **Plaça Ferran el Catòlic.** Moving at a leisurely pace from one to another is considered something of an art form. Some animated tapas bars in the city center are **Bar de Tapes,** Carrer Barcelona 13 (© **97-241-01-64**), near the rail station, and **Tapa't,** Plaça de l'Oli s/n (no phone), which is noteworthy for its old-fashioned charm. Also appealing for its crowded conviviality and its impressive roster of shellfish and seafood tapas is **Bar Boira,** Plaça de Independencia 17 (© **97-220-30-96**). In a street that is the hub of Girona's bar culture, **Zanpanzar,** Cort Real 10–12 (© **97-221-28-43**), pulls in the crowds for its mouthwatering Basque-style *pintxos.* **La Sala del Cel,** Pedret 118 (© **97-221-46-64**), Girona's "palace of techno," is located in an old convent with outdoor gardens. The DJs, both local and international, are top class. Be prepared for lines and a *very* late night out. Slightly more subdued is the **Sala de Ball,** Carretera de la Deversa 21 (© **97–220-14-39**), an elegant, old-style dance hall that aims to please most tastes from hip-hop to house and salsa, depending on the night.

5 Lloret de Mar

100km (62 miles) S of the French border, 68km (42 miles) N of Barcelona

Although it has a good half moon–shaped sandy beach, **Lloret de Mar** is neither chic nor sophisticated, and most people who come here are Europeans on inexpensive package tours. The competition for cheap rooms is fierce.

Lloret de Mar has grown at a phenomenal rate from a small fishing village with just few accommodations to a bustling resort with more hotels than anyone can count. And more keep opening, though there never seem to be enough in July and August. The accommodations are typical of those in other Costa Brava towns, running the gamut from impersonal, modern box-type structures to vintage flowerpot-adorned whitewashed buildings on the narrow streets of the Old Town. There are even a few pockets of posh, including the Hostal Roger de Flor (see below). The area has rich vegetation, attractive scenery, and a mild climate.

ESSENTIALS

GETTING THERE   From Barcelona, take a **train** to Blanes, then take a **bus** 8km (5 miles) to Lloret. If you **drive,** head north from Barcelona along the A-19.

VISITOR INFORMATION   The **tourist office** at Plaça de la Vila 1 (© **97-236-47-35;** www.lloret.org) is open Monday to Friday 9am to 1pm and 4 to 7pm, Saturday 10am to 1pm.

WHERE TO STAY

Many of the hotels—particularly the government-rated three-star places—are booked solid by tour groups. Here are some possibilities if you reserve in advance.

EXPENSIVE

Gran Hotel Monterrey ⊀⊀   Ranked just beneath the Roger de Flor (see below), this government-rated four-star hotel is similar to a deluxe country club in a large park. It's a short walk from the casino, town center, and beaches. The hotel opened in the 1940s and has been partly renovated almost every year since. It's well known as a retreat for those who want to recharge their batteries. The interior areas have big windows with expansive views. The guest rooms are spacious and luxuriously decorated; most have balconies or lounge areas. Bathrooms contain tub/shower combinations.

Carretera de Tossa, 17310 Lloret de Mar. © **97-236-40-50.** Fax 97-236-35-12. www.ghmonterrey.com. 225 units. 120€–175€ ($150–$219) double; 130€–185€ ($163–$231) suite. AE, DC, MC, V. Free parking. Closed Oct–Mar. **Amenities:** Restaurant; 2 bars; 2 pools (1 indoor); 3 tennis courts; health club; beauty spa; whirlpool; sauna; children's play area; limited room service; massage; babysitting; laundry service/dry cleaning. *In room:* A/C, TV, hair dryer, safe.

Hostal Roger de Flor ⊀⊀⊀   This much-enlarged older hotel, some of which is reminiscent of a private villa, is a pleasant diversion from the aging slabs of concrete filling other sections of the resort. Set at the eastern edge of town, it offers the most pleasant and panoramic views of any hotel. Potted geraniums, climbing bougainvillea, and evenly spaced rows of palms add elegance to the combination of new and old architecture. The midsize rooms are high ceilinged, modern, and excellently furnished. Well-maintained bathrooms have tub/shower combos. The public rooms contain plenty of exposed wood and open onto a partially covered terrace.

Turó de l'Estelat s/n, 17310 Lloret de Mar. © **97-236-48-00.** Fax 97-237-16-37. www.rogerdeflor.com. 100 units. 110€–190€ ($138–$238) double; 150€–250€ ($188–$313) suite. Rates include breakfast. AE, DC, MC, V. Free parking. **Amenities:** Restaurant; 2 bars; saltwater pool; 2 tennis courts; fitness center; Ping-Pong table; car rental; limited room service; babysitting; laundry service/dry cleaning. *In room:* TV, minibar, hair dryer, safe.

Hotel Santa Marta ⊀⊀ *Finds*   This tranquil hotel, a short walk above a crescent-shaped bay favored by swimmers, is nestled in a sun-flooded grove of pines. Both public and guest rooms are attractively paneled and traditionally furnished. The spacious guest rooms offer private balconies overlooking the sea or a pleasant garden, and all contain bathrooms with tub/shower combos. The neighborhood is quiet but desirable, about 2km (1½ miles) west of the commercial center of town.

Playa de Santa Cristina, 17310 Lloret de Mar. © **97-236-49-04.** Fax 97-236-92-80. www.hstamarta.com. 78 units. 150€–250€ ($187–$313) double; 240€–390€ ($300–$488) suite. AE, DC, MC, V. Free parking. Closed Dec 23–Jan 31. **Amenities:** 2 restaurants; 2 bars; outdoor pool; sauna; solarium; car rental; limited room service; babysitting; laundry service/dry cleaning; room for those w/limited mobility. *In room:* A/C, TV, minibar, hair dryer, safe.

MODERATE

Hotel Vila del Mar   This century-old hotel is a short walk from the beach, close to the heart of town near the bus station. The mundane but well-maintained interior has a nautical feel. The soundproof guest rooms are pleasantly decorated and well equipped, and the bathrooms come with hydromassage and tub/shower combos.

Calle de La Vila 55, 17310 Lloret de Mar. ℭ **97-236-50-08.** Fax 97-237-11-68. www.hotelviladelmar.com. 36 units. 75€–150€ ($94–$187) double. AE, DC, MC, V. Parking 12€ ($15). **Amenities:** Restaurant; bar; outdoor pool; health club; sauna; babysitting; laundry service/dry cleaning; nonsmoking rooms; room for those w/limited mobility. *In room:* A/C, TV, dataport, minibar, hair dryer, safe.

INEXPENSIVE

Hotel Excelsior   This hotel attracts a beach-oriented clientele from Spain and northern Europe. The Excelsior sits almost directly on the beach, rising six floors above the esplanade. All but a handful of the rooms offer either frontal or lateral views of the sea. The furniture is modern but uninspiring. Most of the bathrooms contain tub/shower combos. During midsummer, half-board is obligatory. Even though the hotel is modest, one of the Costa Brava's greatest restaurants, Les Petxines, is located here (see below).

Passeig Mossèn Jacinto Verdaguer 16, 17310 Lloret de Mar. ℭ **97-236-61-76.** Fax 97-237-16-54. www.gna.es/lloret. 45 units. July–Sept 60€ ($75) per person double; Oct–June (including breakfast) 35€–45€ ($44–$56) per person double. AE, DC, V. Parking 10€ ($13). Closed Nov 1–Mar 21. **Amenities:** 2 restaurants; bar; babysitting; laundry service. *In room:* A/C, TV, safe.

WHERE TO DINE

El Trull SEAFOOD   This restaurant attracts hordes of Spaniards who appreciate the beautiful scenery of the 3km (2-mile) trek north of Lloret into the hills. Set in the modern suburb of Urbanización Playa Canyelles and known for its enduring popularity, El Trull positions its tables within view of a well-kept garden and a (sometimes crowded) pool. The food is some of the best in the neighborhood. Menu items focus on seafood and include fish soup; fish stew heavily laced with lobster; many variations of hake, monkfish, and clams; and an omelet "surprise." (The waiter will tell you the ingredients if you ask.)

Cala Canyelles s/n. ℭ **97-236-49-28.** Main courses 40€–80€ ($50–$100); fixed-price menus 12€ ($15), 38€ ($48), and 60€ ($75). AE, DC, MC, V. Daily 1–4pm and 8–11pm.

Les Petxines ✦✦✦ MEDITERRANEAN   The resort's most carefully orchestrated food is served within the Franco-era (ca. 1954) dining room of the Hotel Excelsior, a simple 45-room seafront hotel. Thirty people at a time sit in relative intimacy within a big-windowed dining room. The cuisine varies with the season, the inspiration of the chef, and the availability of ingredients in local markets, but you can always expect superlatively fresh fish and shellfish (*petxines* in Catalán, hence the restaurant's name). The best examples include several versions of fish soup, some of them with a confit of lemons and shrimp-stuffed ravioli, and an extremely succulent ragout of fish and shellfish. Meat-eaters can occasionally order flavorful versions of pigeon, one of them stuffed with foie gras.

In the Hotel Excelsior, Passeig Mossèn J. Verdaguer 16. ℭ **97-236-41-37.** Reservations required. Main courses 20€–30€ ($25–$38); fixed-price menu 30€ ($38); 6-course "surprise menu" 60€ ($75). AE, DC, MC, V. Tues–Sun 1:15–3:35pm; Tues–Sat 8:30–11pm. Open Sun nights July–Aug.

Restaurante Santa Marta ✦ INTERNATIONAL/CATALAN   Set in the 40-year-old hotel of the same name (see "Where to Stay," above), the Santa Marta is about 2km (1½ miles) west of the commercial center of town. This pleasantly sunny enclave offers well-prepared food and a sweeping view of the beaches and the sea. Menu specialties vary with the seasons but might include pâté of wild mushrooms in a special sauce, smoked salmon with hollandaise on toast, medallions of monkfish with a mousseline of garlic, ragout of giant shrimp with broad beans, filet of beef stroganoff, and a regionally inspired cassoulet of chicken prepared with cloves.

In the Hotel Santa Marta, Playa de Santa Cristina. © **97-236-49-04.** Reservations recommended. Main courses 20€–40€ ($25–$50); fixed-price menu 44€ ($55). AE, DC, MC, V. Daily 1:30–3:30pm and 8:30–10:30pm. Closed Dec 15–Jan 31.

LLORET DE MAR AFTER DARK

At the **Casino Lloret de Mar,** Carrer Esports 1 (© **97-236-61-16**), games of chance include French and American roulette, blackjack, and chemin de fer. There's a restaurant, buffet dining room, bar-boîte, and dance club, along with a pool. The casino is southwest of Lloret de Mar, beside the coastal road leading to Blanes and Barcelona. Drive or take a taxi at night and bring your passport for entry. Hours are Sunday through Thursday from 5pm to 3am, Friday and Saturday from 5pm to 4am. (The casino closes 30 min. later in summer.) Admission is 4.50€ ($5.65).

The dance club **Hollywood,** Carretera de Tossa (© **97-236-74-63**), at the edge of town, is the place to see and be seen. Look for it on the corner of Carrer Girona. It's open nightly 10pm to 5am.

6 Tossa de Mar ★★

90km (56 miles) N of Barcelona, 12km (7½ miles) NE of Lloret de Mar

The gleaming white town of Tossa de Mar, with its 12th-century walls, labyrinthine Old Quarter, fishing boats, and fairly good sand beaches, is perhaps the most attractive base for a Costa Brava vacation. Its character and *joie de vivre* come midway between the devil-may-care excesses of Lloret and the laid-back aplomb of Sant Feliu de Guíxols, just up the coast (see below). The battlements and towers of Tossa were featured in the 1951 Ava Gardner and James Mason movie *Pandora and the Flying Dutchman,* sometimes still seen on TV. A life-size bronze statue of the screen goddess herself in evening dress, built in 1998 and facing a stone inscription of an Omar Khayam quote from the movie, overlooks the bay from a high vantage point in the Vila Vella.

In the 18th and 19th centuries, Tossa survived as a port center, growing rich on the cork industry. But that declined in the 20th century, and many of its citizens immigrated to America. In the 1950s, tourists began to discover the charms of Tossa, and a new industry was born. To experience these charms, walk through the 12th-century walled town, known as **Vila Vella,** built on the site of a Roman villa from the 1st century A.D. Enter through the Torre de les Hores.

Tossa was once a secret haunt for artists and writers—Marc Chagall called it a "blue paradise." It has two main beaches, **Mar Gran** and **La Bauma.** The coast near Tossa, north and south, offers even more possibilities.

As one of the few resorts that has withstood exploitation and retained most of its allure, Tossa enjoys a broad base of international visitors—so many, in fact, that it can no longer shelter them all. In spring and fall, finding a room may be a snap, but in summer it's next to impossible unless reservations are made far in advance.

ESSENTIALS

GETTING THERE   Direct **bus** service is offered from Blanes and Lloret. Tossa de Mar is also on the main Barcelona-Palafruggel route. Service from Barcelona is daily from 8:15am to 8:15pm, taking 1½ hours. For information, call © **90-226-06-06** or 93-265-65-08. **Drive** north from Barcelona along the A-19.

VISITOR INFORMATION   The **tourist office** is at Av. El Pelegrí 25 ((© **97-234-01-08;** www.infotossa.com). April, May, and October, it's open Monday to Saturday 10am to 2pm and 4 to 8pm, Sunday 10:30am to 1:30pm; November to March it's open Monday to Saturday 10am to 1pm and 4 to 7pm; June to September it's open Monday to Saturday 9am to 9pm, Sunday 10am to 2pm and 5 to 8pm.

WHERE TO STAY

VERY EXPENSIVE

Grand Hotel Reymar ⋆   A triumph of engineering a 10-minute walk southeast of the historic walls—the hotel occupies a position on a jagged rock above the sea edge—this graceful building was constructed in the 1960s and renovated in the early 1990s. The Reymar has several levels of expansive terraces ideal for sunbathing away from the crowds below. Each good-size room has a mix of modern wood-grained and painted furniture, a bathroom with a tub/shower combo, a balcony, and a sea view.

Platja de Mar Menuda, 17320 Tossa de Mar. © **97-234-03-12.** Fax 97-234-15-04. www.bestwesternghreymar.com. 148 units. 130€–290€ ($163–$362) double; 330€–375€ ($412–$469) suite. Rates include breakfast. AE, DC, MC, V. Parking 8€ ($10). Closed Nov–Apr 17. **Amenities:** 4 restaurants; 3 bars; disco; outdoor pool; health club; whirlpool; sauna; solarium; car rental; room service; babysitting; laundry service/dry cleaning. *In room:* A/C, TV, minibar, hair dryer, safe.

MODERATE

Best Western Mar Menuda ⋆⋆ *Finds*   This hotel is a gem, a real Costa Brava hideaway surviving amid tawdry tourist traps and fast-food joints. Its terrace is the area's most panoramic, overlooking the sea and the architectural highlights of the town. The guest rooms range from midsize to spacious, each tastefully furnished and containing a good-size bathroom with tub/shower. The staff are helpful in arranging many watersports, such as scuba diving, windsurfing, and sailing, and the cuisine served here is first-class.

Platja de Mar Menuda, 17320 Tossa de Mar. © **800/528-1234** in the U.S., or 97-234-10-00. Fax 97-234-00-87. www.bestwestern.com. 50 units. 140€–150€ ($175–$188) double with breakfast; 180€ ($225) suite. AE, DC, MC, V. Free parking. Closed Nov–Dec. **Amenities:** Restaurant; bar; tennis courts; children's playground; limited room service; babysitting; laundry service/dry cleaning; nonsmoking rooms. *In room:* A/C, TV, hair dryer, safe.

INEXPENSIVE

Canaima *Kids*   Lacking the charm of Hotel Diana, this little inn is the resort's bargain. It lies in a tranquil zone in a residential area 150m (492 ft.) from the beach. The palm trees in this sector of Tossa evoke a real Mediterranean setting. Built in 1963, the hotel bounced back with a series of restorations that lasted from 1997 to 2001. Most of the midsize guest rooms, each with a tiled bathroom with shower and tub, have a balcony opening onto a view. Since some of the rooms have three beds, the Canaima is also a family favorite. The hotel doesn't, however, have a lot of amenities.

Av. La Palma 24, 17320 Tossa de Mar. © **97-234-09-95.** Fax 97-234-26-26. www.hotelcanaima.com. 17 units. 60€–70€ ($75–$88) double. Rates include continental breakfast. AE, MC, V. Parking 5€ ($6.25). **Amenities:** Terrace bar. *In room:* Safe, no phone.

Hotel Cap d'Or *Finds* Perched on the waterfront on a quiet edge of town, this 1790s building nestles against the stone walls and towers of the village castle. Built of rugged stone itself, the Cap d'Or is a combination of old country inn and seaside hotel. The guest rooms come in different shapes and sizes but are decently maintained, each with a good bed and a small bathroom with a shower stall. Although the hotel is a bed-and-breakfast, it does have a terrace on the promenade offering a quick meal.

Passeig de Vila Vella 1, 17320 Tossa de Mar. ℂ/fax **97-234-00-81**. hcapdor@terra.es. 11 units. 75€–85€ ($94–$106) double. Rates include breakfast. MC, V. Closed Nov–Mar. **Amenities:** Restaurant; bar; laundry service/dry cleaning. *In room:* TV.

Hotel Diana Set back from the esplanade, this government-rated two-star hotel is a former villa designed in part by students of Gaudí. It boasts the most elegant fireplace on the Costa Brava. An inner patio—with towering palms, vines, flowers, and fountains—is almost as popular with guests as the sandy front-yard beach. The spacious rooms contain fine traditional furnishings and bathrooms with shower stalls; many open onto private balconies.

Plaça de Espanya 6, 17320 Tossa de Mar. ℂ **97-234-18-86** or 97-234-02-50. Fax 97-234-18-86. 21 units. 75€–145€ ($94–$181) double; 140€–175€ ($175–$219) suite. Rates include breakfast. AE, DC, MC, V. Closed Nov–Apr. **Amenities:** Restaurant; bar; room service (breakfast). *In room:* A/C, TV, minibar, hair dryer.

Hotel Neptuno The popular Neptuno sits on a quiet residential hillside northwest of Vila Vella, somewhat removed from the seaside promenade and the bustle of Tossa de Mar's inner core. Built in the 1960s, the hotel was renovated and enlarged in the late 1980s. Inside, antiques are mixed with modern furniture. The beamed-ceiling dining room is charming. The guest rooms are tastefully lighthearted and modern, each with a good bed and a small bathroom with shower. This place is a longtime favorite with northern Europeans, who often book it solid during July and August.

La Guardia 52, 17320 Tossa de Mar. ℂ **97-234-01-43**. Fax 97-234-19-33. www.ghthotels.com. 124 units. June–Sept 60€–120€ ($75–$150) per person double; off season 50€ ($63) per person double. Rates include breakfast. AE, DC, MC, V. Free parking. Closed Nov–Mar. **Amenities:** Restaurant; bar; outdoor pool; laundry service/dry cleaning. *In room:* A/C, TV, hair dryer, safe.

Hotel Tonet Opened in the early 1960s, in the earliest days of the region's tourist boom, this simple family-run pension is one of the resort's oldest. Renovated since then, it's on a central plaza surrounded by narrow streets and maintains the ambience of a country inn, with upper-floor terraces where you can relax amid potted vines and other plants. The small guest rooms are rustic, with wooden headboards, simple furniture, and bathrooms equipped with shower stalls. The Tonet maintains its own brand of Iberian charm.

Plaça de l'Esglesia 1, 17320 Tossa de Mar. ℂ **97-234-02-37**. Fax 97-234-30-96. www.tossa.com/hoteltonet. 36 units. 60€ ($75) double. Rates include breakfast. AE, DC, MC, V. Parking 10€ ($13) nearby. **Amenities:** Bar. *In room:* TV.

WHERE TO DINE

Bahía CATALAN Adjacent to the sea, Bahía is well known for a much-awarded chef and a history of feeding hungry vacationers since 1953. Menu favorites are for the most part based on time-honored Catalán traditions and include *simitomba* (a grilled platter of fish), *brandade* of cod, baked monkfish, and an array of grilled fish—including *salmonete* (red mullet), *dorada* (gilthead sea bream), and *calamares* (squid)—depending on what's available.

Passeig del Mar 29. ℂ **97-234-03-22**. Reservations recommended. Main courses 12€–35€ ($15–$44); *menú del día* 16€–30€ ($20–$38). AE, DC, MC, V. Daily 1–4:30pm and 7:30–11:30pm.

La Cuina de Can Simon ✦✦✦ CATALAN   Some of the most sought-after dining tables in Tossa de Mar are within this charming, cozy, and intimate establishment containing only 18 seats. The antique, elegantly rustic stone-sided dining room was originally built in 1741. Its small size allows the hardworking staff to prepare some extremely esoteric courses. During the colder months, a fire might be burning in the stately looking fireplace. Most diners select the *menu gastronómico,* consisting of six small courses that together make a memorable meal. Expect seductive, modern dishes that display unerring technique and imaginative flavors. Courses might include oven-roasted duckling with a sweet-and-sour sauce; crayfish-stuffed ravioli with Beluga caviar and truffle oil; or a monkfish suprême with scalloped potatoes and golden-fried sweet onions.

Portal 24. © 97-234-12-69. Reservations required. Main courses 18€–48€ ($23–$60); fixed-price menus 50€–65€ ($63–$81). AE, DC, MC, V. Wed–Mon 1–4pm and 8–11pm.

TOSSA DE MAR AFTER DARK

In Tossa de Mar's fast-changing nightlife, there's little stability or reliability. However, one place that's been in business for a while is the **Ely Club,** Carrer Bernat 2 (© 97-234-00-09). Fans from all over the Costa Brava come here to dance to up-to-date music. Daily hours are from 10pm to 5am between April 1 and October 15 only. In July and August, there's a one-drink minimum. The Ely Club is in the center of town between the two local cinemas.

7 Sant Feliu de Guíxols

110km (68 miles) N of Barcelona, 35km (22 miles) SE of Girona

Sant Feliu de Guíxols has a quiet dignity apropos of its role as the official capital of the Costa Brava. Trade with Italy in past centuries may have given it what the late Catalan scribe Josep Pla (see "Palafrugell & Its Beaches," below) described as an Italianate look, though as he pointed out it lacks the brighter colors of its Ligurian coastal counterparts. The once lucrative local industries of sardine fishing and cork production (with the natural product taken straight from the cork trees of the inland Gavarres forests) have waned, but the town still gives the rare (for this area) impression that it exists for more than just tourists. High-rise buildings have been kept to a minimum and the elegant wide Passeig Maritim facing the enclosed sandy bay is lined with a blend of stylish cafes and impressive *moderniste* buildings. Three kilometers (2 miles) to the north, the crescent sandy beach of Sant Pol adjoins the exclusive hotel resort area of S'Agaró with the legendary five-star Hostal de la Gavina (see below) and marvellous coastal path (Cami de Ronda) that leads past Sa Conca (another gem of a beach) to over-developed Platja d'Aro and then on as far as the sprawling port-resort of Palamós.

ESSENTIALS

GETTING THERE   The **bus** company SARFA runs services from Plaza Urquinaona and the Estación Nort in Barcelona starting at 8am. Travel time is 1½ hours. From June to September, coastal *cruceros* **(pleasure cruisers)** take the scenic sea route here from Blanes, Lloret, and Tossa. If you're renting a **car** and fancy an adrenalin-charging drive, try the cliff-top coastal route from Tossa: It's 20km (12 miles) of twists and turns through pine-wooded headlands and past dozens of tiny coves. Movie buffs should check out *Pandora and the Flying Dutchman* (see "Tossa de Mar," above) and a lesser known black-and-white 1950s thriller, *Chase a Crooked Shadow,* starring Ann Baxter and Richard Todd, for an idea of the thrill and spills involved.

VISITOR INFORMATION   The **Tourist Office** is in the Plaça del Merçat 28 (© **972-82-00-51**). It's open Monday through Saturday 10am to 1pm and 4 to 7pm, Sunday 10am to 2pm.

WHAT TO SEE   The historic highlight is the 10th-century **Benedictine Monastery** (reconstructed in 1723) at the southern end of the town, whose **Porta Ferrada** has three archways. The **Cultural Center** and **History Museum** exhibitions recall Sant Feliu's prosperous 19th-century cork and sardine days. Outside town, just off the Tossa road, the charming 19th-century **Chapel of Sant Elm** offers splendid panoramic coastal views.

WHERE TO STAY

Curhotel Hipócrates ⭐   Located halfway between Sant Feliu and S'Agaró, with easy access to coastal walks, this large hotel prides itself on its selection of superb facilities, which range from steam baths to a well-equipped "aquagym." With over 2 decades of experience in health treatments and therapies, it's an ideal place to relax and get in shape. Service is friendly and attentive and the comfortable rooms, each with en-suite bathroom with tub and shower, all have sea or mountain views.

Carretera San Pol 229, Sant Feliu de Guíxols (Girona). © **97-232-06-62**. www.hipocratescurhotel.com. 92 units (88 doubles plus 4 suites). 130€–200€ ($163–$250) double; 200€–400€ ($250–$500) suite. AE, DC, MC, V. Free parking. **Amenities:** Restaurant; health food bar; outdoor pool; heated indoor pool; solarium; gym; fitness program; personalized therapies; room service; gardens; laundry service. *In room:* A/C, TV, safe, phone.

Hostal de la Gavina ⭐⭐⭐   This very chic Costa Brava *hostal* is the grandest address in the northeast corridor of Spain. Since it opened in the early 1980s, the Hostal de la Gavina has attracted the rich and glamorous including King Juan Carlos, Elizabeth Taylor, and a host of celebrities from northern Europe. It's on a peninsula jutting seaward from the center of S'Agaró, within a thick-walled Iberian villa built as the home of the Ansesa family (the hotel's owners) in 1932. Most of the accommodations are in the resort's main building, which has been enlarged and modified. The spacious guest rooms are the most sumptuous in the area, with elegant appointments and deluxe fabrics. Bathrooms contain plush towels, toiletries, and tub/shower combos.

Plaça de la Rosaleda, 17248 S'Agaro (Girona). © **97-232-11-00**. Fax 97-232-15-73. www.lagavina.com. 74 units. 250€–350€ ($312–$438) double with balcony; 300€–820€ ($375–$1,025) suite. AE, DC, MC, V. Free parking outside, garage 20€ ($25). Closed Nov–Apr. **Amenities:** 2 restaurants; 2 bars; pool; tennis courts; health club; whirlpool; sauna; room service; massage; babysitting; laundry service/dry cleaning. *In room:* A/C, TV, minibar, hair dryer, safe.

WHERE TO DINE

Casa Buxó *(Finds)*   Open to a grateful public since 1931, this welcoming family-run establishment in the center of San Feliu is now under its third generation of ownership. The kitchen is famed for its traditional Catalan starters such as *torrada amb escalivada i anxovies* (anchovy and pepper salad on toast) and first-rate main course paella and *bacallà* (cod) dishes, all best accompanied by the house white Penedés wine.

Carrer Mayor 18, Sant Feliu de Guíxols (Girona). © **97-232-01-87**. Main courses 10€–20€. ($13–$25).

8 Palafrugell & Its Beaches

124km (77 miles) N of Barcelona, 36km (23 miles) E of Girona

The prosperous but laid-back junction town of **Palafrugell** is noted for two things. First, it's the birthplace of Catalonia's most famous 20th-century regional chronicler, Josep Pla. Second, and of more interest to most hedonistically minded visitors, it's just a few kilometers away from three of the coast's most exquisite beach resorts, where the clear waters are a paradise for snorkelers. **Calella de Palfrugell** (not to be confused with the characterless popular resort of Calella de la Costa, farther south on the road between Blanes and Barcelona) is a white former fishing town with many attractive summer villas located just north of the charming **Cap Roig** gardens. From beneath the 19th-century archways of its diminutive Ses Voltes paseo you look out past a series of sandy inlets and jutting rocks to the tiny offshore **Illes Formigues.** A 15-minute coastal walk north around the headland brings you to the sister resort of **Llafranch** with its single beach and yachting marina nestling below the cliff-top lighthouse of San Sebastian. A couple of kilometers farther north, isolated from these twin resorts, is one of Pla's favorite spots, **Tamariu,** a small sandy cove backed by delectable seafood restaurants.

ESSENTIALS

GETTING THERE   The **bus** company SARFA (℃ **902-30-20-25**) runs service from Plaza Urquinaona and the Estación Nort in Barcelona starting at 8:15am. Travel time is 2 hours 15 minutes; the cost is 14€ ($18). From Palafrugell bus station, there are half a dozen daily buses to Calella and Llafranch. A separate service runs three times a day to Tamariu. Each costs 1.20€ ($1.50) one-way and takes 10 to 15 minutes.

VISITOR INFORMATION   There's an tourism information office at Carrilet 2 (℃ **97-230-02-28**). It's open daily 10am to 1pm and 4 to 7pm.

WHAT TO SEE   In Palafrugell the Sunday open **market** is one of the best on the coast, and if you want to check out the rather esoteric Josep Pla literary route, visit the Fundación Josep Pla, Carrer Nou 49–51 (℃ **97-230-55-77**).

WHERE TO STAY

El Far de Sant Sebastià ⚅   This highly unique little hotel stands next to a restored medieval watchtower and an 18th-century hermitage on a promontory overlooking both Calella de Palfrugell and Llafranc. Named after the lighthouse that towers amid the wooded hills on the cliff edge above it, the hotel is an ideal spot for relaxing and enjoying the best of Costa Brava coastal scenery. It's open year-round and has a fine restaurant where you can sample typical Empordà cuisine ranging from fresh seafood to hearty stews.

Platja de Llafranc, s/n Llafranc (Girona). ℃ **97-230-43-28.** 10 units (9 doubles and 1 suite). 160€–190€ ($200–$238) double; 250€ ($313) suite. AE, DC, MC, V. **Amenities:** Restaurant; lounge; gardens; terrace overlooking sea. *In room:* A/C, TV, minibar, work desk, hair dryer, safe.

Mas de Torrent ⚅⚅⚅   Just a few minutes' drive inland from **Palafrugell,** this member of Relais & Châteaux was elegantly created from a 1751 farmstead *(masía).* Mas de Torrent is one of the most artful and best hotels in Spain. Try for 1 of the 10 rooms in the original farmhouse, with its massive beams and spacious bathrooms with deep tubs and power showers. The rooms in the more modern, bungalow-style annex are just as comfortable but lack the mellow atmosphere. From the rooms' stone balconies, visitors can enjoy vistas of the countryside, with Catalonian vineyards in the distance. In the restaurant, the chef focuses mainly on the classic dishes of Catalonia, including monkfish in saffron or fine noodles simmered in fish consommé and served with fresh shellfish.

Afueras de Torrent, Torrent 17123 Girona. ℃ **97-230-32-92.** Fax 97-230-32-93. www.mastorrent.com. 39 units. 295€–350€ ($369–$438) double; 475€–550€ ($594–$688) suite. Rates include breakfast. AE, DC, MC, V. Free parking.

A Room with a View

Radiating out around the hilltop town of **Bagur,** just 6km (4 miles) to the north of Palafrugell, is a series of idyllic sandy coves that epitomize the very best the Costa Brava has to offer: pines, rocks, secluded inlets with hidden caves that can only be reached by boat, and tiny resorts with evocative names like **Sa Tuna, Aigua Xelida,** and **Aigua Blava** that vie with the Palafrugell resorts for the title of most beautiful spot on the coast. Access is difficult unless you have a car, with only occasional buses running from Bagur. Should you decide to overnight here, don't miss the chance to stay at one of the most dramatically located hotels in Spain: the cliff-top **Parador de Aiguablava** (*Ⓒ* **972-62-21-62;** www.parapromotions-spain.com/parador/spain/aiguablava.html), where a double will cost from 185€ ($231) and the Mediterranean vistas through the surrounding pines are out of this world. Book well ahead.

37km (23 miles) east of Girona. **Amenities:** 2 restaurants; 2 bars; pool; tennis court; 24-hr. room service; babysitting; laundry; room for those w/limited mobility. *In room:* A/C, TV, minibar, hair dryer, safe.

WHERE TO DINE

La Casona CATALAN   This well-regarded restaurant is situated right in the heart of the town and is a favorite with visitors and locals alike. The setting is homey, the service first-rate, and main dishes include regional specialties like *suquet de peix* (seafood stew) and *pollastre pagès amb sepia i escarlamans* (country-style chicken with squid and langoustines).

Paraje de La Seulada 4, Palafrugell (Girona). *Ⓒ* **97-230-36-61.** Main courses 22€–30€ ($28–$38). Lunch only on Sun. Closed Mon.

9 Figueres

The sleepy, laid-back capital of the northerly Alt Empordá region of Catalonia, **Figueres** once played a significant role in Spanish history. Philip V wed María Luisa of Savoy here in 1701 in the church of San Pedro, thereby paving the way for the War of the Spanish Succession. But that historical fact is nearly forgotten today: The town is better known as the birthplace of surrealist artist Salvador Dalí in 1904. In view of the lack of other worthy sights in the here most people stay only a day in Figueres using Girona, Cadaqués, or any of the other towns along the Costa Brava as a base.

ESSENTIALS

GETTING THERE   RENFE, the national railway of Spain, has hourly **train** service between Barcelona and Figueres, stopping off at Girona along the way. All trains between Barcelona and France stop here as well.

Figueres is a 1½- to 2-hour **drive** from Barcelona. Take the excellent north–south A-7 and exit at the major turnoff to Figueres.

VISITOR INFORMATION   The **tourist office** is at the Plaça del Sol s/n (*Ⓒ* **97-250-31-55;** www.figueresciutat.com). From November until Easter, hours are Monday through Friday from 8:30am to 3pm. From Easter to the end of June and October, the

The Mad, Mad World of Salvador Dalí

Salvador Dalí (1904–89) became one of the leading exponents of surrealism, depicting irrational imagery of dreams and delirium in a unique, meticulously detailed style. Famous for his eccentricity, he was called "outrageous, talented, relentlessly self-promoting, and unfailingly quotable." At his death at age 84, he was the last survivor of the three famous *enfants terribles* of Spain (the poet García Lorca and the filmmaker Luis Buñuel were the other two).

For all his international renown, Dalí was born in Figueres and died in Figueres. Most of his works are in the eponymous Theater-Museum there, built by the artist himself around the former theater where his first exhibition was held. Dalí was also buried in the Theater-Museum, next door to the church that witnessed both his christening and his funeral—the first and last acts of a perfectly planned scenario.

Salvador Felipe Jacinto Dalí i Domènech, the son of a highly respected notary, was born on May 11, 1904, in a house on Carrer Monturiol in Figueres. In 1922 he registered at the School of Fine Arts in Madrid and went to live at the prestigious Residencia de Estudiantes. There, his friendship with García Lorca and Buñuel had a more enduring effect on his artistic future than his studies at the school. As a result of his undisciplined behavior and the attitude of his father, who clashed with the Primo de Rivera dictatorship over a matter related to elections, the young Dalí spent a month in prison.

In the summer of 1929, the artist René Magritte, along with the poet Paul Eluard and his wife, Gala, came to stay at Cadaqués, and their visit caused sweeping changes in Dalí's life. The young painter became enamored of Eluard's wife; Dalí left his family and fled with Gala to Paris, where he became an enthusiastic member of the surrealist movement. Some of his most famous paintings—*The Great Masturbator, Lugubrious Game,* and *Portrait*

office is open Monday through Friday from 8:30am to 3pm and 4:30 to 8pm, Saturday 9:30am to 1:30pm and 3:30pm to 6:30pm. From July to August, it's open Monday to Friday 8:30am to 9pm, Saturday 9am to 9pm, and Sunday 9am to 3pm. In September, it's open Monday to Friday 8:30am to 8pm and Saturday 9am to 8pm.

VISITING DALI

Casa-Museu Castell Gala Dalí 🐨🐨 *Finds*   For additional insights into the often bizarre aesthetic sensibilities of Spain's most famous surrealist, consider a 40km (25-mile) trek from Figueres eastward along highway C-252, following the signs to Parlava. In the village of Púbol, whose permanent population almost never exceeds 200, you'll find the Castell de Púbol. Dating from A.D. 1000, the rustic stone castle was partially in ruin when bought by Dalí as a residence for his estranged wife, Gala, in 1970, on the condition that he'd come only when she invited him. (She almost never did.) After her death in 1982, Dalí moved in for 2 years, heading for other residences in 1984 after his bedroom mysteriously caught fire one night. Quieter, more *of Paul Eluard*—date from his life at Port Lligat, the small Costa Brava town where he lived and worked off and on during the 1930s.

Following Dalí's break with the tenets of the surrealist movement, his work underwent a radical change, with a return to classicism and what he called his mystical and nuclear phase. He became one of the most fashionable painters in the United States and seemed so intent on self-promotion that the surrealist poet André Breton baptized him with the anagram "Avida Dollars." Dalí wrote a partly fictitious autobiography titled *The Secret Life of Salvador Dalí* and *Hidden Faces,* a novel containing autobiographical elements. These two short literary digressions earned him still greater prestige and wealth, as did his collaborations in the world of cinema (such as the dream set for Alfred Hitchcock's *Spellbound,* 1945) and in those of theater, opera, and ballet.

On August 8, 1958, Dalí and Gala were married according to the rites of the Catholic Church in a ceremony performed in the strictest secrecy at the shrine of Els Angels, just a few miles from Girona.

During the 1960s, Dalí painted some very large works, such as *The Battle of Tetuán.* Another important work painted at this period is *Perpignan Railway Station,* a veritable revelation of his paranoid-critical method that relates this center of Dalí's mythological universe to his obsession with painter Jean-François Millet's *The Angelus.*

In 1979 Dalí's health began to decline, and he retired to Port Lligat in a state of depression. When Gala died, he moved to Púbol, where, obsessed by the theory of catastrophes, he painted his last works, until he suffered severe burns in a fire that nearly cost him his life. Upon recovery, he moved to the Torre Galatea, a building he had bought as an extension to the museum in Figueres. Here he lived for 5 more years, hardly ever leaving his room, until his death in 1989.

serious, and much less surrealistically flamboyant than the other Dalí buildings in Port Lligat and Figueres, the castle is noteworthy for its severe Gothic and Romanesque dignity and for furniture and decor that follow the tastes of the surrealist master. Don't expect a lot of paintings—that's the specialty of the museum at Figueres—but do expect a fascinating insight into one of the most famous muses of the 20th century.

Carrer Gala Salvador Dalí s/n. ☏ 9/-248-86-55. Admission 6€ ($7.50) adults, 4€ ($5) students, free for children under 9. June 15–Sept 15 Tues–Sun 10:30am–8pm; Mar 13–June 14 and Sept 16–Nov 1 Tues–Sun 10:30am–6pm; Nov 2–Dec 31 10am–4:30pm.

Teatre-Museu Dalí ⊛⊛⊛   The internationally known artist Dalí was as famous for his surrealist and often erotic imagery as he was for his flamboyance and exhibitionism. At the Figueres museum, in the center of town beside the Rambla, you'll find his paintings, watercolors, gouaches, charcoals, and pastels, along with graphics and sculptures, many rendered with seductive and meticulously detailed imagery. His wide-ranging subject matter encompassed such repulsive issues as putrefaction and castration. You'll see, for instance, **The Happy Horse,** a grotesque and lurid purple beast the artist painted during one of his long exiles at Port Lligat. A tour of the museum is an experience. When a catalog was prepared, Dalí said with a perfectly straight face, "It is necessary that all of the people who come out of the museum have false information."

Plaça de Gala Dalí 5. 🕐 97-267-75-00. www.salvador-dali.org/museus/Figueres. Admission 10€ ($13) adults, 7€ ($8.75) students and seniors, free for children under 9. Call or see website for hours, which vary by the season. Closed Jan 1 and Dec 25 and Mon from Oct to May.

10 Cadaqués ⭑⭑

196km (122 miles) N of Barcelona, 31km (19 miles) E of Figueres

Cadaqués is still unspoiled and remote, despite the publicity it received when Salvador Dalí lived in the neighboring village of Port Lligat in a split-level house surmounted by a giant egg. The last resort on the Costa Brava before the French border, Cadaqués is reached by a small winding road, twisting over the mountains from Rosas, the nearest major center. When you get to Cadaqués, you really feel as if you're off the beaten path and miles from anywhere. The village winds around half a dozen small coves, with a narrow street running along the water's edge.

Scenically, Cadaqués is a knockout: crystal-blue water, fishing boats on the sandy beaches, old whitewashed houses, narrow twisting streets, and a 16th-century parish up on a hill.

ESSENTIALS
GETTING THERE   There are three **buses** per day that run from Figueres to Cadaqués (11am, 1pm, and 7:15pm). Trip time is 1¼ hours. The service is operated by SARFA (🕐 **97-225-87-13**).

VISITOR INFORMATION   The **tourist office,** Cotxe 2 (🕐 **97-225-83-15**), is open Monday through Saturday from 10:30am to 1pm and 4:30 to 7:30pm.

SEEING THE SIGHTS
Casa-Museu Port Lligat ⭑⭑ *Moments*   This fascinating private home turned museum completes (along with the Teatre-Museu Dalí and the Casa-Museu Castell Gala Dalí) the touted "Dalían Triangle" of northern Catalonia. The structure, home to the Dalís for over 40 years, lies in tiny Port Lligat and is surrounded by the eerie rock and coastal formations that feature heavily in his work. If walking from the town center, 15 minutes away, your first glimpse of the museum will be of the oversize white eggs that adorn the roof. Inside, the home has been pretty much left as it was when it was inhabited, with the expected eclectic collections of Dalían objects, art, and icons thrown together in surrealist fashion. The swimming pool and terrace, where Dalí threw many of his legendary parties in the '70s, are the highlights. The museum doesn't have a proper address, but you can't miss it. *Note:* Reservations are mandatory—call ahead to book.

🕐 97-225-10-15. Admission 8€ ($10) adults, 6€ ($7.50) students and seniors, free for children under 9. Tues–Sun 10:30am–9pm; Tues–Sun 10:30am–6pm rest of year.

WHERE TO STAY
Hotel Playa Sol ⭑   In a relatively quiet section of the port along the bay, this 1950s hotel offers a great view of the stone church that has become the town's symbol; it's located at the distant edge of the harbor and overlooks the bay of Cadaqués. Many of

The Most Famous Chef in the World

Ferran Adrià has been hailed not just as the most exciting chef in Spain but in the entire world. The press has dubbed him the "Salvador Dalí of the kitchen" because of his creative, wholly high-tech approach to cooking that challenges the concept of food as we know it. He operates his luxe **El Bulli,** Cala Montjoi (© **97-215-04-57;** fax 97-215-07-17; www.elbulli.com), out of an old farmhouse in the little hamlet of Roses near Cadaqués, but that doesn't stop hoards of discerning international palates from seeking him out, having waited perhaps a year for the privilege. Michelin grants it three stars, an accolade most often reserved for the top restaurants of Paris.

Your only option is to order the 30-course set menu, which changes each season. You never know what's going to appear, but anticipate the most delightful surprises, based on what's the finest produce in any given month. Adrià is an alchemist in the kitchen. Originally hailed for his array of savory "foams," an idea that has now been pirated by top restaurants from Miami to Melbourne, he is constantly experimenting with the composition of food; thus, a pea soup is made into tiny, solid droplets through a process using calcium chloride and basil, pulped into an edible "paper," and served with calamari "seeds" and a mandarin concentrate. You anticipate you're in for a delightful evening at the beginning when you're given addictive little dishes of polenta chips and caramelized sunflower seeds. Your *amuse-bouche* might be a "cappuccino" of guacamole. One dish alone should give Adrià culinary immortality: his lasagna of calamari.

Reservations for next season are by fax or e-mail (bulli@elbulli.com) on a first-come, first-served basis. The *menú de degustación* is 150€ ($188) per person. American Express, MasterCard, and Visa are accepted. The restaurant is open from Easter to the end of September. To get there from Girona, take N-1 north to Figueres, then Route 260 east to Roses, for a total of 56km (35 miles).

the rooms have balconies looking right onto the bay (specify when booking), and the smallish rooms are comfortably furnished. Most of the bathrooms have tub/shower combos. The hotel doesn't have an official restaurant, but it does offer lunch from June 15 to September 15 and breakfast all year-round. The swimming pool is a definite plus.

Platja Planch 3, 17488 Cadaqués. © **97-225-81-00.** Fax 97-225-80-54. www.playasol com. 50 units. 95€ 150€ ($119 $188) double. AE, DC, MC, V. Parking 8€ ($10). Closed Jan–Feb. **Amenities:** Bar; outdoor pool; outdoor tennis court; bike rental; limited room service. *In room:* A/C, TV.

Llane Petit *Value*   This is a little inn of considerable charm lying below the better known Hotel Rocamar opening right onto the beach. A hospitable place, it offers decent-size and well-maintained bathrooms with both tubs and showers. All accommodations open onto a little terrace. The owners keep the hotel under constant renovation during the slow months, so it's always fresh again when the summer hordes descend. Try to patronize the hotel's little dinner-only restaurant, as the cuisine is well prepared and affordable.

Platja Llane Petit s/n, 17488 Cadaqués. ℂ **97-225-10-20.** Fax 97-225-87-78. 37 units. 75€–120€ ($94–$150). AE, DC, MC, V. Rates include breakfast in off season. Free parking. Closed Jan 9–Feb 21. **Amenities:** Restaurant; bar; limited room service; laundry; dry cleaning. *In room:* A/C, TV, safe.

Rocamar ⊀⊀   On the beach, this government-rated three-star hotel is one of the better choices in town, attracting a fun-loving crowd of young northern Europeans in the summer. All the accommodations are well furnished, with rustic yet comfortable pieces, along with small and neatly kept bathrooms with both tubs and showers. The rooms in front have balconies opening onto the sea; those in back have balconies, with views of the mountains and beyond. The hotel is known for its good food served at affordable prices.

Doctor Bartomeus s/n, 17488 Cadaqués. ℂ **97-225-81-50.** Fax 97-225-86-50. www.rocamar.com. 71 units. 90€–175€ ($113–$219) double; 180€–260€ ($225–$325) suite. Rates include breakfast. DC, MC, V. Free parking. **Amenities:** Restaurant; bar; indoor pool; outdoor pool; tennis court; sauna; morning room service; massage; babysitting; laundry; dry cleaning. *In room:* A/C, TV, safe.

WHERE TO DINE

Es Trull *Value* SEAFOOD   On the harbor side street in the center of town, this cedar-shingled cafeteria is named for the ancient olive press dominating the interior. A filling fixed-price meal is served. According to the chef, if it comes from the sea and can be eaten, he'll prepare it with that special Catalan flair. You might try mussels in marinara sauce, grilled hake, or natural baby clams. Rice dishes are a specialty—not only paella but also black rice colored with squid ink and rice with calamari and shrimp.

Port Ditxos s/n. ℂ **97-225-81-96.** Reservations recommended in high season. Main courses 10€–30€ ($13–$36). AE, DC, MC, V. Daily 12:30–4pm and 7–11pm. Closed Nov–Easter.

La Galiota ⊀⊀ CATALAN/FRENCH   Dozens of surrealist paintings, including some by Dalí, adorn the walls of this award-winning restaurant, the finest in town. On a sloping street below the cathedral, the place has a downstairs sitting room and a dining room converted from what was a private house. Dalí himself was a patron (his favorite meal was cheese soufflé and chicken roasted with apples), and the chef's secret is in selecting only the freshest of ingredients and preparing them in a way that enhances their natural flavors. The roast leg of lamb, flavored with garlic, is a specialty. The marinated salmon is also excellent, as are the sea bass and the sole with orange sauce.

Carrer Narciso Monturiol 9. ℂ **97-225-81-87.** Reservations required. Main courses 18€–28€ ($23–$35). AE, DC, MC, V. Daily 1:30–3:30pm and 8:30–10:30pm. Closed Oct to mid-June.

12

A Side Trip to Majorca

"The Pearl of the Mediterranean," Majorca (pronounced "mah-*yohr*-kah") is Spain's most popular island and the largest of the Balearics, which include Menorca and Cabrera in the North, and Ibiza and Formentera in the South. Palma (the capital) has the busiest airport in the country, attracting millions of visitors each year, and yet, the island can be remarkably peaceful.

About 209km (130 miles) from Barcelona and 145km (90 miles) from Valencia, Majorca has a coastline 500km (311 miles) long. The exterior is an explorer's paradise of rugged cliffs and pine-shrouded sandy coves, although it's extremely overbuilt along certain coastal regions, especially the Bay of Palma, parts

of the Bay of Alcúdia, and the central block of the east coast. The mountainous northwest is beautifully unspoiled, a protected area, while the fertile central flatlands, with their occasional lime-washed windmills, offer a tranquil landscape of olive and almond groves (which burst into a sea of white blossom in February). The golden sands of Majorca are famous, with highly overbuilt pleasure beaches such as **El Arenal** and **Magaluf** spreading out in separate bays on either side of Palma. These tend to be chock-full of sun worshipers on package tours, while more isolated inlets, such as Cala Estellenchs on the rugged northwest coast and Cala Mesquida in the far northeast corner, offer almost total seclusion.

ISLAND ESSENTIALS

GETTING THERE At certain times of the year, the trip by boat or plane can be pleasant, but in August the air routes to Palma must surely qualify as the major bottleneck in Europe. Don't travel without advance reservations, and be sure you have a return plane ticket if you come in August—otherwise you may not get off the island until September! Package tours, which combine airfare, car rental, and accommodations, can save you a ton of money.

Iberia (✆ **90-240-05-00**) flies to Palma's Aeroport Son Sant Joan (✆ **97-178-90-00**) from Barcelona seven times daily and even more frequently in summer. **Spanair** (✆ **90-292-91-91**) flies into Palma from Barcelona up to seven times a day. **Air Europa** (✆ **90-240-15-01**) also has regular, daily flights to Palma. The budget airline Vueling (✆ **93-378-78-78;** www.vueling.com) only has one flight a day, but you can get there for as low as 20€ ($25) one-way.

Countless charter flights also make the run, especially from European cities of all shapes and sizes. Bookings are very tight in August, and delays of at least 24 hours, sometimes more, are common. If you're flying—say, Iberia—on a transatlantic flight from New York to Madrid or Barcelona, have Majorca written into your ticket before your departure if you plan to visit the Balearics as part of your Spanish itinerary.

From Palma de Majorca–Son Sant Joan airport, bus no. 1 takes you to the center of Palma, leaving every 15 to 20 minutes, from 6:10am to 2:10am daily. The trip takes

---

> **_Tips_** **Not an Island for All Seasons**
>
> July and August are high season for Majorca; don't even think of coming then
> without a reservation. It's possible to swim comfortably from June to October;
> after that it's too cold except for the hard-core.

---

about 30 minutes and costs 2.20€ ($2.75). A metered cab costs 20€ ($25) for the
25-minute drive into the city center.

Transmediterránea, Estació Marítim 2, Muelle de Pelaires in Palma (© **90-245-46-45** for schedules and reservations), operates one to three **ferries** a day from Barcelona
depending on the time of year, taking 8 hours and costing from 60€ ($75) for one-way
passage. Tickets can be booked at the Transmediterránea office in Barcelona, Moll Sant
Bertran 1–3 (© **93-295-91-00**), and in Valencia at the office at Terminal Transmediterránea Estación Marítima, Puerto de Valencia (© **96-376-10-62**). Any travel agent in
Spain can also book you a seat. Schedules and departure times are subject to change and
should always be checked and double-checked.

GETTING AROUND   At the tourist office in Palma, you can pick up a **bus** schedule that explains island routes. Or call **Emprese Municipal de Transportes** (© **97-121-44-44**). This company runs city buses from Estació Central D'Autobus, Plaça
Espanya, the main terminal. The standard one-way fare is 1.10€ ($1.35) within
Palma; at the station you can buy a booklet good for 10 rides, costing 8€ ($10).

The most popular destination routes on the island (Valldemossa, Deià, Sóller, and
Port de Sóller) are offered by **Darbus,** Carrer Estada s/n (© **97-175-06-22**), in Palma.

Ferrocarril de Sóller, Carrer Eusebio Estada 1 (© **97-175-20-51**), off Plaça
Espanya, is a **train** service operating between Palma and Sóller that makes for an
unforgettable journey passing through majestic mountain scenery. Trains run from
8am to 7:30pm, and a one-way ticket costs 5.50€ ($6.85). A "tourist train," so-
named because it makes a 10-minute stop at the Mirador del Pujol d'en Banya for
photos, leaves daily at 10:50am and costs 9€ ($11). In itself, it is a worthy sightseeing trip. Privately owned, this cute choo-choo was constructed by orange growers in
the early 1900s and still uses carriages from the Belle Epoque days. From Soller town
a vintage _tranvía_ (tram), built in 1913, runs every half-hour from 7am to 8:30pm
through the orange groves to Soller port. A one-way ticket costs 3€ ($3.75).

Another train runs to Inca; it's often called "the leather express" because most passengers are on board to buy inexpensive leather goods in the Inca shops and to visit
the Camper Factory Shop. This line is the **Servicios Ferroviarios de Majorca,** and it,
too, leaves from Plaça Espanya (© **97-175-22-45** for more information and schedules). The train ride is only 40 minutes, with 40 departures per day Monday through
Saturday and 32 per day on Sunday. A one-way fare costs 2€ ($2.50). For a radio taxi,
call © **97-176-45-45** or 97-140-14-14.

If you plan to stay in Palma, you don't need a car. The city is extremely traffic-clogged,
and parking is scarce. If you'd like to take a driving tour, rent a car at the Spanish-owned
Atesa at Passeig Marítim (© **97-145-66-02**), where rentals range from 50€ ($63) to
90€ ($113) per day. **Avis** at Passeig Marítim 16 (© **97-173-07-20**) is well stocked with
cars, too; its rates range from 60€ ($75) to 180€ ($225) per day. Both Atesa and Avis
maintain offices at the airport. Reservations should always be made in advance.

Majorca

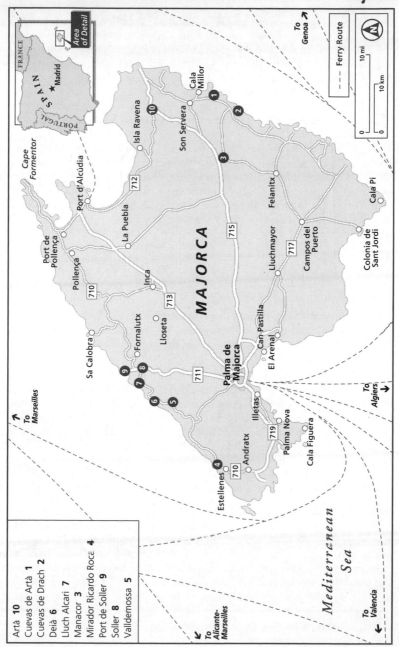

Artà **10**
Cuevas de Artà **1**
Cuevas de Drach **2**
Deià **6**
Lluch Alcari **7**
Manacor **3**
Mirador Ricardo Roca **4**
Port de Soller **9**
Soller **8**
Valldemossa **5**

1 Palma de Majorca *★*★

Palma, on the southern tip of the island, is the seat of the autonomous government of the Balearic Islands, as well as the center for most of Majorca's hotels, restaurants, and nightclubs. Founded by the Romans in 123 B.C., Palma was later reconstructed by the Moors in the style of a casbah, or walled city. Its roots are still visible, if obscured a bit by the high-rise hotels that have cropped up.

Old Palma has a wonderfully bohemian flavor with winding alleys and narrow cobblestone streets echoing back to the time when Palma was one of the chief ports in the Mediterranean.

Today Palma is a bustling city whose massive tourist industry has more than made up for its decline as a major seaport. It's estimated that nearly half the population of the island lives in Palma. The islanders call Palma simply "Ciutat" (City), and, as the largest of the Balearic ports, its bay is often clogged with yachts. The most impressive way to arrive here is by sea, with the skyline dominated by the turrets of Bellver Castle and Gothic bulk of the cathedral, known locally as La Seu (Catalan for "cathedral" or "headquarters").

ESSENTIALS

VISITOR INFORMATION   The **National Tourist Office** is in Palma at Plaça Reina 2 (© **97-171-22-16**). It's open Monday through Friday from 9am to 8pm, and Saturday from 10am to 2pm.

GETTING AROUND   Palma is the perfect strolling city and it is easy to get around on foot. Several bus routes skirt the bay itself, and taxis are reasonably priced. But if you want to get out and about elsewhere on the island, buses or rental cars are your only option.

FAST FACTS   The **U.S. Consulate,** Calle Puerto Pi 8 (© **97-140-37-07**), is open from 10:30am to 1:30pm, Monday through Friday. The **British Consulate,** Plaça Mayor 3 (© **97-171-24-45**), is open from 9am to 3pm, Monday through Friday.

In case of an **emergency,** dial © **112.** If you fall ill, head to the **Centro Médico,** Av. Juan March Ordinas 8, Palma de Majorca (© **97-121-22-00**), a private facility.

Majorca observes the same **holidays** as the rest of Spain but also celebrates June 29, the Feast of St. Peter, the patron saint of fishermen.

The central **post office** is at Carrer Paseo Bornet 10 (© **90-219-71-97**). Hours are Monday through Friday from 8:30am to 8:30pm, and Saturday from 9:30am to 2pm.

FUN ON & OFF THE BEACH

With so many good beaches within a stone's throw of the city center it would be madness to bathe on the beach in front of the cathedral. Head instead for the quiet fishing neighborhoods turned hip hang-outs of **Portixol** *★*★ and **Ciutat Jardí,** where there are a handful of tiny shingle beaches as well as the main sand strand, and numerous trendy bars and eateries. The closest public beaches are **Magaluf** and **Playa Nova**

Tips **Where to Get Those Phone Cards**

Local newsstands and tobacco shops sell phone cards valued between 3€ ($3.75) and 15€ ($19). They can be used in any public telephone booth, and allow you to make both domestic and international calls.

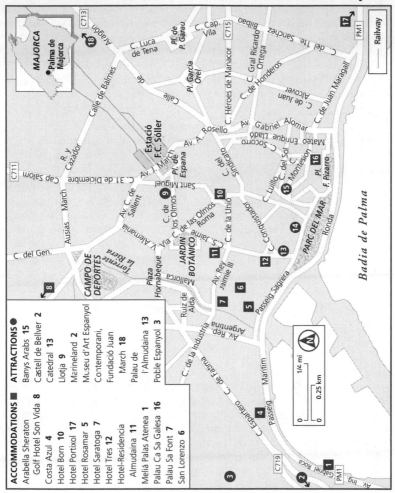

ACCOMMODATIONS ■

Arabella Sheraton
Golf Hotel Son Vida **8**
Costa Azul **4**
Hotel Born **10**
Hotel Portixol **17**
Hotel Rosamar **5**
Hotel Saratoga **7**
Hotel Tres **12**
Hotel-Residencia
Almudaina **11**
Meliá Palas Atenea **1**
Palau Ca Sa Galesa **16**
Palau Sa Font **7**
San Lorenzo **6**

ATTRACTIONS ●

Banys Arabs **15**
Castell de Bellver **2**
Catedral **13**
Llotja **9**
Marineland **2**
MLseu d'Art Espanyol
Contemporani,
Fundació Juan
March **18**
Palau de
l'Almudaina **13**
Poble Espanyol **3**

to the west (en route visit the upmarket marina resort of Portals Nous—good for ogling the jet set), and **Ca'n Pastilla** and **El Arenal** to the east. All can easily be reached by bus from downtown Palma within 20 to 30 minutes and are well equipped with bars, cafes, and tourist facilities. Swimming is excellent and summer beach parties abound. If it's peace and quiet you're after, though, head farther east to the diminutive **Cala Pi** and walk along the cliff tops until you find a space to call your own, or west beyond Palma Nova to **Cap de Cala Figuera** for nude bathing and grilled fish lunches.

You can swim from June to October; Majorcan winters are an ideal time to escape the masses and discover the delights of the city (though be sure to bring warm clothes). Majorcan weather in the spring and fall can be ideal, and in summer the coastal areas are pleasantly cooled by sea breezes.

BIKING   The best places for biking on the island are Ca'n Picafort, Alcúdia, and Port de Pollença, all along the north coast, and across the central plains. These can get choked with Tour de France wannabes in training, because they are relatively flat. Most city roads have special bike lanes on the island, but be on guard for fast-moving cars once you're out in the country. For rentals, go to **Belori Bike,** Edificio Pilari, Marbella 22, Playa de Palma (© **97-149-03-58**). Depending on their model, and how many gears they have, pedal bikes rent for around 10€ ($13) per day.

GOLF   Majorca is a golfer's dream. The best course is the Son Vida Club de Golf, Urbanización son Vida, about 13km (8 miles) east of Palma along the Andrade highway. This 18-hole course is shared by guests of the island's two best hotels, the Arabella Golf Hotel and the Son Vida. However, the course is open to all players who call for reservations (© **97-178-71-00**). Greens fees are 70€ ($88) for 18 holes.

HIKING   Because of the hilly terrain in Majorca, this sport is better pursued here than on Ibiza or Minorca. The mountains of the northwest, the Serra de Tramuntana, are best for exploring or there are plenty of rugged cliff-top walks for those who prefer to stop for swims. The tourist office (see "Visitor Information," above) will provide you with a free booklet called *20 Hiking Excursions on the Island of Majorca.*

HORSEBACK RIDING   The best stables on the island are at **The Riding School of Majorca,** on the Palma-Sóller road. Call © **97-161-31-57** to make arrangements and get directions from wherever you are on the island.

WATERSPORTS   Most beaches have outfitters who will rent you windsurfers and dinghies. The best diving operation is **Planet Escuba,** Pont Adriano (© **97-123-43-06** or 97-752-68-81). Divers here are highly skilled and will take you to the most intriguing sights underwater if you are a qualified diver.

SHOPPING

Stores in Palma offer handicrafts, elegant leather goods, Majorcan pearls, colorful linens, and fine needlework. The best shopping is on the following streets: San Miguel, Carrer Sindicato, Jaume II, Jaume III, Carrer Plateria, Vía Roman, and Passeig des Borne, plus the streets radiating from the Borne all the way to Plaça Cort, where the city hall stands. There are also crafts markets in the evenings from May through October on the Plaça de les Meraviles. Most shops close on Saturday afternoon and Sunday.

The famous **Casa Bonet,** Plaça Federico Chopin 2 (© **97-172-21-17**), founded in 1860, sells finely textured needlework. All the sheets, tablecloths, napkins, and pillowcases are made in Majorca from fine linen or cotton (and less expensively, from acrylic). Many are hand-embroidered, using ancient designs and floral motifs popularized by this establishment. For beautiful olive-wood salad bowls, salt-and-pepper grinders, and the like, try **El Olivo,** Calle Pescateria Vella 4 (© **97-172-70-25**).

Loewe, Av. Jaume III no. 1 (© **97-171-52-75**), offers fine leather, elegant accessories for men and women, luggage, and chic apparel for women. For funkier leather items, head for **Pink,** Av. Jaume III no. 3 (© **97-172-23-33**). **Passy,** Av. Jaume III no. 6 (© **97-171-33-38**), offers high-quality, locally made shoes, handbags, and accessories for men and women. There's another branch, not as well stocked, at Carrer Tous y Ferrer 8 (© **97-171-73-38**).

Fashionistas need look no further than the Passeig d'es Borne for sumptuous designer togs by **Carolina Herrera** or high street basics and accessories from Spanish mega-stores **Zara, Mango,** and **Massimo Dutti.**

Perlas Majorica, Av. Jaume III no. 11 (© **97-172-52-68**), is the authorized agency for authentic Majorcan pearls, offering a 10-year guarantee for their products. The pearls come in varied sizes and settings, and you can pick up some good deals here. Better still, go see how they are made at the factory in Manacor, Calle Pere Riche s/n (© **97-155-09-00**).

SEEING THE SIGHTS

It may not have the cultural richness of Seville or Barcelona, but Palma is well worth dedicating some time to getting lost in.

Viajes Sidetours, Passeig Marítim 19 (© **97-128-39-00**), offers numerous full- and half-day excursions throughout Palma and the surrounding countryside. The full-day excursion to Valldemossa and Sóller takes visitors through the monastery, where former island residents Chopin and his lover, George Sand, spent their winter and scandalized locals by residing together out of wedlock. After leaving the monastery, the tour explores the peaks of the Sierra Mallorquina, then makes its way to the seaside town of Sóller. A visit to the Arabian gardens of Raixa or Alfàbia is included in the 35€ ($44) cost of the tour, on Wednesday only.

Another full-day tour of the mountainous western side of the island is conducted by train and boat, including a ride on one of Europe's oldest railways to the town of Sóller and the Monasterio de Lluch, as well as a boat ride between the port of Sóller and La Calobra. Daily tours cost 50€ ($63). The eastern coast of Majorca is explored in the Caves of Drach and Hams tour. A concert on the world's largest underground lake (Lake Martel), tours through the caves, a stop at an olive-wood works, and a visit to the Majorica Pearl Factory are all covered daily in the 35€ ($44) cost. Times of departure may vary.

Banys Arabs   These authentic Moorish baths are located in pleasant gardens and date from the 10th century. They represent the only complete Moorish building in Palma. The main room has striking archways and columns supporting a dome that is pierced with skylights to represent the stars.

Can Serra 7. © **97-172-15-49.** Admission 1.60€ ($2) adults, free for children under 10. Apr–Nov daily 9am–8pm; Dec–Mar daily 9am–7pm. Bus: 15.

Castell de Bellver ⋦   Erected in 1309, this hilltop round castle was once the summer palace of the kings of Majorca—during the short period when there were kings of Majorca. By the 18th century it had become a military prison, and today it is fun to wander around. The castle, which was a fortress with a double moat, is well preserved and now houses the Museu Municipal which is devoted to archaeological objects, old coins, and a small collection of sculpture. It's really the panorama you get from here that's the chief attraction. In fact, the name Bellver means beautiful view.

Camilo José Cela s/n. © **97-173-06-57.** Admission 1.90€ ($2.35) adults; 1€ ($1.25) children, students, and seniors. Apr–Sept Mon–Fri 8am–9pm, closed Sun and bank holidays; Oct–Mar Mon–Fri 8am–8pm, Sun and bank holidays 10am–5pm. Bus: 3, 4, 20, 21, or 22 to Joan Miró (Gomila), then 20-min. walk.

Catedral ⋦⋦   This Catalonian Gothic cathedral, called La Seu, stands in the Old Town overlooking the seaside. It was begun during the reign of Jaume II (1276–1311) and completed in 1601. Its central vault is 43m (141 ft.) high, and its columns rise 20m (66 ft.). There is a wrought-iron *baldachin* (canopy) by Gaudí over the main altar. The treasury contains supposed pieces of the True Cross and relics of San Sebastián, patron saint of Palma. Museum and cathedral hours often change; call ahead to make sure they're accepting visitors.

Plaça Almoina 1, Almoyna. ✆ 97-172-31-30. Free admission to cathedral; museum and treasury 3.75€ ($4.70). Apr 1–May 31 and Oct Mon–Fri 10am–5:15pm; June–Sept Mon–Fri 10am–6:15pm; Nov 2–Mar Mon–Fri 10am–3:15pm; year-round Sat 10am–2:15pm. Bus: 15.

Llotja 🌟 This 15th-century Gothic structure is a leftover from the wealthy mercantile days of Majorca. La Lonja (its Spanish name) was, roughly, an exchange or guild. Exhibitions here are announced in local newspapers.

Passeig Sagrera. ✆ 97-171-17-05. Free admission. Tues–Sat 11am–2pm and 5–8pm; Sun 11am–2pm. Bus: 15.

Marineland 🄺🄸🄳🅂 Eighteen kilometers (11 miles) west of Palma, just off the coast road en route to Palma Nova, Marineland is a great one for the kids with dolphin and sea lion shows, as well as a Polynesian pearl-diving demonstration and a small zoo. You'll find a cafeteria, picnic area, and children's playground, as well as beach facilities.

Costa d'en Blanes s/n, Calviá. ✆ 97-167-51-25. Admission 20€ ($25) adults, 18€ ($23) seniors, 14€ ($18) children 3–12, free for children under 3. July–Aug daily 9:30am–6:45pm; Sept–June daily 9:30am–5:15pm. Closed Dec 16–Jan 31. Bus: Direct, marked MARINELAND, from Palma rail station.

Museu d'Art Espanyol Contemporani, Fundació Juan March 🌟 The Juan March Foundation's Museum of Spanish Contemporary Art reopened in 1997, with a series of newly acquired modern paintings. The works represent one of the most fertile periods of 20th-century art, with canvases by Picasso, Miró, Dalí, and Juan Gris, as well as by Antoni Tàpies, Carlos Saura, Miquel Barceló, Lluis Gordillo, Susana Solano, and Jordi Teixidor. A room devoted to temporary exhibits was added to the restored museum. One series, for example, featured 100 Picasso engravings from the 1930s. The oldest and best-known work in the museum is Picasso's *Head of a Woman,* from his cycle of paintings known as Les Demoiselles d'Avignon. These works form part of the collection that the Juan March Foundation began to amass in 1973.

Sant Miquel 11. ✆ 97-171-35-15. www.march.es. Free admission. Mon–Fri 10am–6:30pm; Sat 10:30am–2pm. Closed Sun and bank holidays. Bus: 1.

Palau de l'Almudaina Long ago, Muslim rulers erected this splendid fortress surrounded by Moorish-style gardens and fountains opposite the cathedral. During the short-lived reign of the kings of Majorca, it was converted into a royal residence evocative of the alcázar at Málaga. Now it houses a museum displaying antiques, arts, suits of armor, and Gobelin tapestries. Panoramic views of the harbor of Palma can be seen from here.

Palau Reial s/n. ✆ 97-121-41-34. Admission 3.40€ ($4.25) adults, 2.40€ ($3) children, free for all Wed. Apr–Sept Mon–Fri 10am–5:45pm; Oct–Mar Mon–Fri 10am–1:15pm and 4–5:15pm. Closed Sun and Jan 1, Jan 6, Jan 20, Apr 12, May 1, Dec 24–25, and Dec 31. Bus: 15.

Poble Espanyol Spain in miniature, this toy town–like curiosity represents buildings from all over the country (rather like the Poble Espanyol in Barcelona). Included is the Alhambra in Granada, the Torre de Oro in Seville, and El Greco's House in Toledo. As part of the "authentic" experience, bullfights are held in its *corrida* on summer Sundays.

Poble Espanyol 39. ✆ 97-173-70-70. Admission 5.50€ ($6.90) adults, 4.50€ ($5.60) children. Apr–Nov daily 9am–6pm; Dec–Mar daily 9am–5pm. Bus: 4 or 5.

WHERE TO STAY

Majorca has a staggering number of hotels, but it's still not enough to hold the crowds in August. If you go in high season, reserve well in advance. Some of our hotel recommendations in Palma are in the El Terreno section, the heart of "*la vida loca*" (the local nightlife); don't book into one of these hotels unless you like plenty of action, continuing until late at night. More conservative readers may find it unsavory. If you want peace and quiet, check our other suggestions. The Old Quarter is particularly good for smart, high-quality boutique hotels.

Palma's suburbs, notably Cala Mayor, about 4km (2½ miles) from the center, and San Agustín, about 5km (3 miles) from town, continue to sprawl. In El Arenal, part of Playas de Palma, there is a huge concentration of hotels. The beaches at El Arenal are quite good but have a Coney Island–type atmosphere. I've included a number of hotel recommendations in these suburbs for those who don't mind staying outside the city center.

VERY EXPENSIVE

Arabella Sheraton Golf Hotel Son Vida 🌟🌟 The natural environment surrounding this hotel has been fiercely protected, despite its close proximity 5km (3 miles) northwest of the center of Palma. Don't come here expecting raucous good times on the beach; the resort is elegant but rather staid and is better suited to an older, golf-playing crowd. There's no health club and no shuttle to the beach; many visitors drive to one of several nearby beaches. But it does boast one of the only hotel bullrings in Spain!

The complex is low-rise, intensely landscaped, and offers views over the lush green grounds (not of the sea) from many of its good-size rooms. Bedrooms and suites are fresh and white with dark-wood furniture, wall-to-wall carpeting, bathrooms with tub/shower combos, and in all but the least expensive accommodations, a balcony or veranda.

De la Vinagrella s/n, E-07013 Palma de Majorca. ☏ **97-178-71-00.** Fax 97-178-72-00. www.arabellasheraton.com. 93 units. 350€–400€ ($438–$500) double; 480€–580€ ($600–$725) suite. Rates include breakfast. AE, DC, MC, V. Parking free outside or 16€ ($20) in garage. Bus: 7. **Amenities:** 2 restaurants; bar; outdoor pool; 18-hole golf course; tennis courts; fitness center; sauna; business center; salon; 24-hr. room service; babysitting; laundry service; dry cleaning. *In room:* A/C, TV, minibar, hair dryer, iron, safe.

Palacio Ca Sa Galesa 🌟🌟🌟 *(Moments* This five-star boutique hotel is a delight and far more personal than the bigger chains. For generations this 15th-century town house languished as a decaying apartment building facing the side of the cathedral. But in 1993, an entrepreneurial couple from Cardiff, Wales, restored the place, salvaging the original marble floors and stained-glass windows, sheathing the walls of the public areas with silk, and adding modern amenities. Today, the setting is the most alluring in all of Palma, a labyrinthine space loaded with English and Spanish antiques and paintings. It also has a grand dining room available for private dinner parties, a cozy lounge with open fireplace adjoining a parlor where English teas are served in the afternoons, and a sunny roof terrace from which you can almost touch the cathedral. Honor bars are conveniently dotted about the place. The rooms themselves are sumptuous with antiques and Persian rugs, comfortable beds, and high-quality linens. All have neat bathrooms with tub/shower combos. There's no restaurant, but a hearty Majorcan buffet is served each morning (for an extra charge).

Miramar 8, 07001 Palma de Majorca. ☏ **97-171-54-00.** Fax 97-172-15-79. www.palaciocasagalesa.com. 12 units. 315€ ($394) double; 400€–435€ ($500–$544) suite. AE, DC, MC, V. Parking 12€ ($15). 7km (4 miles) from airport. Call in advance for directions. **Amenities:** Lounge; sauna; plunge pool; limited room service (noon–10pm) w/free tea/coffee; massage; babysitting; laundry service; dry cleaning. *In room:* A/C, TV, minibar, hair dryer, safe.

EXPENSIVE

Hotel Portixol 🏵🏵🏵 *Finds* Locations don't get much better than this achingly hip portside hotel. It has buckets of Scandinavian trim—big white airy bedrooms, most with fabulous sea views contrasted cleverly with cute features like zebra print rugs and the odd splash of Mediterranean color. But it's the added extras that make the difference: binoculars in all the rooms for, say, bird-watching; bicycles to hire; spa treatments; top-notch food; cocktails to rival any in New York; and the best swimming pool in town. The only danger at the Portixol is that you might never want to leave.

Sirena 27, 07006 Palma de Majorca. ℰ 97-127-18-00. Fax 97-127-50-25. www.portixol.com. 24 units. 200€–290€ ($250–$362) double; 390€ ($487) atico (penthouse). Rates include breakfast. AE, MC, V. Bus: 15. **Amenities:** Restaurant; outdoor pool; business center; salon; limited room service; massage; laundry service; dry cleaning. *In room:* A/C, TV, minibar, hair dryer, safe.

Hotel Tres 🏵🏵 A spectacular newcomer to Palma's burgeoning boutique hotel scene, the Hotel Tres is situated in two palaces dating back to 1576, and many of the original features have been preserved. Two roof terraces (connected by a bridge) offer an unusual space where guests can enjoy an infinity splash pool, sauna, and superb panoramic views of the city. Combining contemporary design with rustic charm, all 41 rooms and one suite are extremely comfortable with a tub or shower, fresh cotton sheets, and splashes of color in the form of plush sofas, throw cushions, and drapes. The suite has its own terrace and Jacuzzi. The handsome patio, shaded by a magnificent palm, serves as a breakfast area and is open to the public for snacks, wine, and cocktails in the evening.

Apuntadores 3, 07012 Palma de Majorca. ℰ 97-171-73-33. Fax 97-171-73-72. www.hoteltres.com. 42 units. 170€–200€ ($212–$250) double; 230€–350€ ($287–$437) suite. Rates include breakfast. AE, DC, MC, V. 8km (5 miles) from airport. **Amenities:** Wine and cocktail bar; splash pool; sauna. *In room:* A/C, TV/DVD, minibar, dataport, hair dryer, safe, CD player.

Meliá Palas Atenea 🏵 A member of the Sol Meliá chain, this modern hotel offers extensive leisure facilities for vacationers, while still catering to business travelers. It overlooks the Bay of Palma, within walking distance of the town's major restaurants and shops. Spacious guest rooms have terraces, many overlooking the harbor or Bellver Castle. Furnishings are standardized and somewhat characterless but the rooms are comfortable, ranging from medium-size to spacious. All are fitted with gleaming tile bathrooms equipped with tub/shower combos. An entire floor has been designed with business travelers' needs in mind.

Passeig Ingeniero Gabriel Roca 29, 07014 Palma de Majorca. ℰ 97-128-14-00. Fax 97-145-19-89. www.solmelia.com. 361 units. 220€ ($275) double; from 240€ ($300) suite. AE, DC, MC, V. Parking 12€ ($15). Bus: 1.8km (5 miles) from airport. **Amenities:** 2 restaurants; cafe; bar; nightclub; indoor pool; outdoor pool; Jacuzzi; sauna; business center; salon; 24-hr. room service; massage; laundry service; dry cleaning. *In room:* A/C, TV, minibar, hair dryer, coffeemaker, safe.

Palau Sa Font 🏵 Housed in a former 16th-century palace, this funky boutique hotel is popular among a younger crowd—especially hip weekenders from London. Jelly-bean colors update the distressed iron and island stone features, giving them a pleasantly old-meets-new feel. The bedrooms have been fully modernized and have plump comforters, linen curtains, rustic iron furnishings, and plain, soothing walls. Bathrooms are shiny and new, with either a tub or shower. Breakfast is a good enough reason to stay; the hotel offers a bounteous feast of smoked salmon, serrano ham, tortillas, and fresh fruits.

Apuntadores 38, 07017 Palma de Majorca. ℰ 97-171-22-77. Fax 97-171-26-18. www.palausafont.com. 19 units. 150€–210€ ($187–$262) double; 225€ ($281) junior suite. Rates include buffet breakfast. AE, MC, V. Closed Jan.

8km (5 miles) from airport. **Amenities:** Breakfast lounge; bar; outdoor pool; babysitting; laundry service. *In room:* A/C, TV, minibar, hair dryer.

MODERATE

Hotel Saratoga 🕸   Under the arches of an arcade beside the Old City's medieval moat stands the entrance to the Hotel Saratoga. Constructed in 1962 and renovated in 1992, the hotel features bright, well-furnished guest rooms, many with balconies or terraces with views of the bay and city of Palma. The typically midsize rooms have well-maintained, tiled bathrooms, most with tub/shower combos.

Passeig Majorca 6, 07012 Palma de Majorca. © **97-172-72-40.** Fax 97-172-73-12. www.hotelsaratoga.es. 187 units. 145€–160€ ($181–$200) double; 225€ ($281) suite. Rates include breakfast. AE, DC, MC, V. Parking 10€ ($13). Bus: 1, 3, 7, or 15. **Amenities:** Restaurant; bar; 2 pools (1 rooftop); spa; sauna; limited room service; babysitting; laundry service; dry cleaning. *In room:* A/C, TV, minibar, hair dryer, safe.

San Lorenzo 🕸🕸 *(Finds*   This pint-size antique hotel has just six rooms and is set in the middle of the maze of winding streets that form the Old City of Palma. The building is 17th century and the decor is a pleasant mixture of traditional Majorcan and modern. The rooms are airy, painted white, and have bathrooms that include tub/shower combos. All rooms have beamed ceilings and while some have only balconies, the more luxurious offer fireplaces and a private terrace. This hotel is perfect for relaxing after a day of sightseeing or shopping.

San Lorenzo 14, 07012 Palma de Majorca. © **97-172-82-00.** Fax 97-171-19-01. www.hotelsanlorenzo.com. 6 units. 130€–180€ ($162–$225) double; 220€ ($275) suite. AE, DC, MC, V. 8km (5 miles) from airport. **Amenities:** Bar; outdoor pool; limited room service; babysitting; laundry service; dry cleaning. *In room:* A/C, TV, minibar, hair dryer, iron, safe.

INEXPENSIVE

Costa Azul *(Value*   Head here for a bargain—despite the reasonable rates, you'll get views of the yachts in the harbor. This place isn't glamorous, but it is a good value. A short taxi ride will deposit you at night on the Plaça Gomila in El Terreno with its after-dark diversions. Barren, well-worn rooms are clean but modestly furnished, each with an en-suite bathroom equipped with a tub/shower combo.

Passeig Marítim 7, 07014 Palma de Majorca. © **97-173-19-40.** Fax 97-173-19-71. www.fehm.es/pmi/costa. 126 units. 90€ ($113) double. AE, DC, MC, V. Bus: 1 or 3. **Amenities:** Restaurant; bar; indoor pool; sauna; limited room service; babysitting; laundry service; dry cleaning. *In room:* A/C, TV, safe.

Hotel Born 🕸 *(Value*   If you want to be in the heart of the Old City and don't want to pay through the nose, there is no better bargain than this government-rated two-star hotel. A 16th-century palace, it once belonged to the Marquis of Ferrandell. It was vastly altered and extended during the 18th century with the addition of a Majorcan courtyard shaded by a giant palm tree (this is where breakfast is served in the summer). It still retains much of its original architecture, such as Romanesque arches, though amenities have been modernized. Bedrooms are generally spacious and well equipped, with neatly tiled bathrooms with a shower. Located off Plaça Rei Juan Carlos, the hotel opens onto a tranquil side street.

Sant Jaume 3, 07012 Palma de Majorca. © **97-171-29-42.** Fax 97-171-86-18. www.mallorcaonline.com/hotel/bornu. htm. 30 units. 100€ ($125) double; 125€ ($156) suite. Rates include breakfast. AE, DC, MC, V. **Amenities:** Bar; bike rentals. *In room:* A/C, TV.

AT ILLETAS

This suburb of Palma lies immediately west of the center.

Hotel Bonsol 🏖 *(Kids)*   Set across from the beach, about 6.5km (4 miles) west of Palma, this government-rated four-star hotel was built in 1953 and has been well maintained ever since. It charges less than hotels with similar amenities, and the nearby beach makes it quite popular with vacationing families, who eat in the airy, if spartan, dining room. The core is a four-story, white-sided masonry tower, with some of the suites clustered into a simple collection of outlying villas. The hotel overlooks a garden adjacent to the sea. The midsize rooms are larger than you might expect, efficient but comfortable, and well suited to beachside vacations.

Paseo de Illetas 30, 07181 Illetas. (C) **97-140-21-11.** Fax 97-140-25-59. www.mallorcaonline.com/hotel/bonsolu.htm. 147 units. From 110€ ($138) double. Rates include breakfast. AE, DC, MC, V. Free parking. Closed Nov 20–Jan 2. Bus: 108, 109, or 3. **Amenities:** 2 restaurants; lounge; outdoor pool; 2 tennis courts; fitness center; sauna; limited room service; babysitting; laundry service; dry cleaning. *In room:* A/C, TV, minibar, hair dryer, safe.

Hotel Meliá de Mar 🏖   Originally built in 1964, and still in excellent shape, the Meliá de Mar is one of the most comfortable (albeit expensive) hotels in Palma. This seven-story hotel is close to the beach and has a large, shady garden. The marble-floored lobby and light, summery furniture offer a cool refuge from the hot sun and a calm, deliberately uneventful setting that's evocative of some of the spa hotels of central Europe. Rooms, mainly midsize, have many fine features, including original art, terra-cotta-tiled balconies, marble or wrought-iron furnishings, excellent beds, and marble-clad bathrooms with deluxe toiletries, tub/shower combos, and dual basins.

Paseo Illetas 7, 07015 Palma de Majorca. (C) **97-140-25-11.** Fax 97-140-58-52. www.solmelia.com. 144 units. 275€ ($344) double; from 695€ ($869) suite. AE, DC, MC, V. Free parking. Closed Nov 1–Apr 15. Bus: 108, 109, or 3. **Amenities:** Restaurant; bar; heated outdoor pool; health spa; limited room service; massage; babysitting; laundry service; dry cleaning. *In room:* A/C, TV, minibar, hair dryer, safe.

AT PALMANOVA

On the western coast, and west of Palma, this hotel enjoys a privileged position in Costa d'en Blanes. Count on a 10-minute drive from the center of Palma.

Hotel Punta Negra 🏖🏖   Situated in an exclusive area just 1.5km (1 mile) away from the chic yachting port of Puerto Portals, this two-story hotel is flanked by two golden-sand beaches and numerous golf courses. Elegant and refined, it is classically Majorcan with traditional white walls, antique furnishings, carpeted floors, and panoramic views of either the sea or pine forests. The spacious and beautifully furnished rooms are equipped with elegant bathrooms containing tub/shower combos.

Carretera Andaitx Km 12, Costa d'en Blanes, 07181 Majorca. (C) **97-168-07-62.** Fax 97-168-39-19. www.h10.es. 137 units. 115€ ($144) double; 135€ ($169) suite. Rates include continental breakfast. AE, DC, MC, V. Free parking. Take Exit 4 off direct road to Palma Nova/Portals Nous. **Amenities:** 2 restaurants; bar; 2 outdoor pools; indoor pool; 7 clay tennis courts; sauna; salon; limited room service; babysitting; laundry service; dry cleaning. *In room:* A/C, TV, minibar, hair dryer, safe.

WHERE TO DINE

The most typical main dish of Majorca is pork, and it appears in myriad styles: cured, roasted, and made into sausages and meatballs, steaks, chops, and loins. The specialty in any restaurant offering typical Majorcan cuisine, *lomo con col,* is a typical dish where pork loin is wrapped in cabbage leaves, cooked in its own juices, and served with a sauce of tomatoes, grapes, pine nuts, and bay leaves.

The local sausage, *sobrasada,* is a soft, spreadable pork pâté mixed with paprika, giving it its characteristic bright red color. *Sopas mallorquinas* can mean almost anything, but usually involves mixed greens in a soup flavored with olive oil and thickened with bread. When *garbanzos* (chickpeas) and meat are added, it becomes a hearty meal in itself.

The best-known vegetable dish is *el tumbet*, a kind of cake with a layer of potato and another of lightly sautéed eggplant. Everything is covered with a tomato sauce and peppers, then boiled for a while. Eggplant, often served stuffed with meat or fish, is one of the island's vegetable mainstays. *Frito mallorquín* is essentially a peasant dish of fried onions and potatoes, mixed with red peppers, diced lamb liver, "lights" ("lungs"), and fennel. It's still hugely popular on the island and, like Scottish haggis, can be delicious when prepared right.

Majorcan wine is slowly gaining the recognition it deserves, and the region produces better-quality wines each year. The red wine bottled around Binissalem tends to be the best, and Macià Batle has won several awards for its rich, spicy reds. Most of the restaurants' wine, however, comes from mainland Spain. *Café carajillo*—coffee with cognac—is another Spanish drink particularly enjoyed by Majorcans.

EXPENSIVE

Koldo Royo &&& BASQUE   This Michelin one-star restaurant is a top spot to enjoy world-class New Basque Cuisine, which has recently enjoyed the spotlight in the international food pages. Staff are attentive and helpful in deciphering the sometimes unusual dishes on the menu, including baked hake cheeks, tripe, and lamprey eel. This big-windowed establishment lies about a half-kilometer (¾ mile) south of Palma's cathedral, adjacent to a marina and one of the island's most popular beaches.

Av. Ingeniero Gabriel Roca 3, Paseo Marítimo. © 97-173-24-35. Reservations required. Main courses 18€–32€ ($23–$40); tasting menu 58€ ($72). AE, DC, MC, V. Tues–Sat 1:30–3:30pm and 8:30–11:15pm. Closed 2 weeks in Nov. Bus: 1.

Porto Pí & MODERN MEDITERRANEAN   This favorite of King Juan Carlos and other royals occupies an elegant 19th-century mansion above the yacht harbor at the west end of Palma. Contemporary paintings complement the decor, and there is an outdoor terrace. The food has a creative Mediterranean influence. Specialties change with the season but might include house-style fish *en papillote*, angelfish with shellfish sauce, and quail stuffed with foie gras cooked in a wine sauce. Game is a specialty in winter.

Joan Miró 174. © 97-140-00-87. Reservations required. Main courses 14€–28€ ($18–$35); fixed-price menu 55€–60€ ($69–$75); tasting menu 65€ ($81). AE, DC, MC, V. Mon–Fri 1–3:30pm; daily 7:30–11:30pm. Bus: Palma-Illetas.

Tristán && NOUVELLE CUISINE   Several miles southwest of Palma, Tristán overlooks the marina of Port Portals and is one of the best restaurants in the Balearics, boasting a coveted two Michelin stars. This is very much a place to see and be seen,

---

(*Finds* A Special Treat

Dating from 1700, **Can Juan de S'aigo**, Carrer Sans 10 (© 97-171-07-59), is the oldest ice-cream parlor on the island. Correspondingly elegant and old-world, it serves its homemade ice creams (try the almond), pastries, cakes, *ensaimadas* (light-textured and airy specialty cakes of Palma), fine coffee, and several kinds of hot chocolate amid marble-top tables, beautiful tile floors, and an indoor garden with a fountain.

attracting well-heeled yachties and British B-list celebrities. Expect a refined, elegant menu of market-fresh produce with dishes such as juicy pigeon in rice paper; Mediterranean vegetables, or the catch of the day, are usually prepared in Majorcan style.

Port Portals, Portals Nous. ℂ **97-167-55-47.** Reservations required. Main courses 32€–45€ ($40–$56); fixed-price menu 95€ ($119); tasting menu 120€ ($150). AE, DC, MC, V. Daily 1–3:30pm and 8–11pm. Closed Oct 31–Mar 1. Bus: 22.

MODERATE

Arroseria Sa Cranca SEAFOOD   This sophisticated eatery specializes in rice dishes offering a huge diversity of flavors and styles from traditional Valencian paella (with rabbit and snails) to the Majorcan favorite of *arroz a banda* (a particularly succulent version with spider crabs, clams, and mussels) or *arroz negre* (black rice cooked in squid ink and served with a hearty dollop of aioli—garlic mayonnaise). Kick off with a platter of finger-lickin' grilled baby sardines or a well-seasoned version of *buñuelos de bacalau* (minced and herb-laden cod formed into rounded patties). Either of these might be followed with a *parrillada*—an array of grilled fish and shellfish— or any of the above-mentioned rice casseroles. Other variations include vegetables, roasted goat, or hake with tomatoes and garlic.

Passeig Marítim 13. ℂ **97-173-74-47.** Reservations recommended. Main courses 10€–22€ ($13–$28); fixed-price menu 20€ ($25). AE, DC, MC, V. Tues–Sun 1–4pm; Tues–Sat 8pm–midnight. Closed Sept 1–20. Bus: 1.

INEXPENSIVE

Ca'an Carlos *Value* MAJORCAN   Something of a Palma institution, this old-school restaurant is set in two dining rooms of a much-renovated stone-sided house that's at least a century old. Owner and cook Carlos turns out wonderfully authentic dishes with buckets of charm. The well-executed menu includes plenty of traditional fare including Majorca *sabrosada,* a soft pork sausage flavored with pepper and paprika; chicken or fish croquettes; stuffed squid; eggplant stuffed with pulverized shellfish; and a version of the Majorcan national dish, *cocida mallorquina,* a succulent stew.

De S'Aigua 5. ℂ **97-171-38-69.** Reservations recommended. Main courses 12€–24€ ($15–$30). AE, MC, V. Mon–Sat 1–4pm and 8–11pm. Closed 3 weeks in Aug. Bus: 3, 7, or 15.

La Bóveda *&* SPANISH   Located in the oldest part of Palma, just a few steps from the cathedral, this lively little bar is widely agreed to serve the best tapas in town. With just 14 tables set near the bar and a tiny basement, it gets crowded and raucous, but the food is well worth the jostling. Choose from juicy roasted veal, pork, chicken, and fish, lip-smacking seafood, maple-sweet *jamón,* fava beans with strips of ham, spinach tortillas, grilled or deep-fried calamari, and shrimp with garlic sauce. Wash it all down with bottles of full-bodied red or more-delicate white wines. Finally, finish it off with a refreshing, freshly made sorbet, garnished with a shot of vodka or bourbon.

Boteria 3. ℂ **97-171-48-63.** Reservations required for a table, not for the tapas bar. Main courses 8€–24€ ($10–$30); tapas selection 12€ ($15). AE, DC, MC, V. Mon–Sat 1–4pm and 8:30pm–12:30am. Closed Feb. Bus: 7 or 13.

Sa Caseta *&* *Finds* MAJORCAN   Those inclined toward something a little more gourmet will find tasty regional cooking in this old-style hacienda with its warren of smartly decorated dining rooms. But it's the salt cod dishes that made it famous. If you're traveling with friends, you might want to order some of the best suckling pig or roast baby lamb in Majorca. Perhaps it's not quite as tantalizing as the versions served in Old Castile, but it's a rewarding dish, especially when the weather is cool. On hotter days, you may prefer one of the local fish dishes, including monkfish in a shellfish sauce. Paella served with meaty salt cod and plump vegetables makes an unusual variation on this classic dish. *Sopas mallorquinas* (the island's famed vegetable soup) begin many a meal here. A series of homemade desserts, including ice cream, is a special feature.

Alférez Martínez Vaquer 1, Gènova. ℭ **97-140-42-81**. Reservations recommended. Main courses 16€–32€ ($20–$40); tasting menu 38€ ($47). AE, DC, MC, V. Daily 1pm–midnight. Bus: 4.

PALMA AFTER DARK

Majorca is packed with bars and dance clubs. Sure, there are some fun hangouts along the island's northern tier, but for a rocking, laser- and strobe-lit club, you'll have to hit Palma.

Set directly on the beach, close to a dense concentration of hotels, **Tito's,** Passeig Marítim (ℭ **97-173-00-17**), charges a cover of 16€ ($20), including the first drink. If you only visit one nightclub during your time on the island, this living legend—which has been going since 1923—should be it. A truly international crowd gathers here to mingle on a terrace overlooking the Mediterranean. Between June and September, it's open every night of the week from 11pm to at least 6am. The rest of the year, it's open only Thursday through Sunday, from 11pm to 6am.

Bar Barcelona, Carrer Apuntadores 5 (ℭ **97-171-35-57**), is a popular jazz club attracting a more grown-up crowd that can enjoy live jazz, blues, and occasionally flamenco with a body of local aficionados. It's open every night from 11pm to 3am, and there is no cover charge; drinks are reasonably priced, making this one of Palma's best value nights out.

B.C.M., Av. Olivera s/n, Magaluf (ℭ **97-113-15-46**), is the busiest, most lighthearted, and most cosmopolitan disco in Majorca. Boasting high-tech strobe lights and lasers, this sprawling, three-story venue offers a different sound system on each floor, giving you a wide variety of musical styles from which to choose. If you're young, eager to mingle, and like to dance, this place is for you. The cover charge of 14€ ($18) includes your first drink and entitles you to party until 4am.

Come and enjoy a Caribbean cocktail with one of Palma's more charismatic bar owners, Pasqual, who just might invite you to dance a bit of salsa at **Bodeguida del Medio,** Paseo el Mar, Cala Ratjada (no phone). The music is Latin-inspired and the crowd is a mix of locals and visitors from almost everywhere. Try their delicious mojito cocktail, more potent than it tastes. The inside is rustic, the outside more intimate and romantic, with Chinese lanterns illuminating a garden that overlooks the sea.

ABACO 🎇🎇, Carrer Sant Joan 1 (ℭ **97-171-59-11**), just might be the most opulently decorated nightclub in Spain—a cross between a harem and a czarist Russian church. The bar is decorated with a trove of European decorative arts. The place is always packed, with many customers congregating in a beautiful courtyard, which has exotic caged birds, fountains, more sculptures than the eye can absorb, extravagant bouquets, and hundreds of flickering candles. All this exoticism is enhanced by the lushly romantic music piped in through the sound system. Whether you view this as a bar, a museum, or a sociological survey, be sure to go. The bar is open daily from 9pm to 2:30am, from February to December only. Wandering around is free; however, drinks cost a whopping 10€ ($13) to 15€ ($19).

At the end of the Andratx motorway, adjacent to the Cala Figuera turnoff, the **Casino de Majorca,** Urbanización Sol de Majorca s/n, Costa del Calviá (ℭ **97-113-00-00**), is the place to go in search of lady luck. The cover charge is 5€ ($6.25); dinner with no drinks is 60€ ($75); the floor show without dinner but with two drinks is 45€ ($56).

Children under 12 get discounts of 50%. If you bring your passport, you can indulge in American or French roulette, blackjack, or dice, or simply pull the lever on one of the many slot machines. A glittery cabaret show, styled in Monte Carlo fashion, is accessible through a separate entrance from the section of the casino devoted to gambling. It's presented every Tuesday through Saturday at 10:30pm. You might want to precede it with dinner, which is served from 8pm. The casino's gambling facilities are open Monday through Thursday from 6pm to 4am (Sun until 3am), and Friday and Saturday from 8pm to 5am.

Although Majorca is generally a permissive place, it doesn't have the gay scene that Ibiza does. Still, one of Palma's most noteworthy gay bars is **Baccus,** Carrer Lluis Fábregas 1 (✆ **97-145-77-89**), catering to both gays and lesbians. It is open nightly from 9pm to at least 3am, and often later. There is no cover, and beers begin at 4€ ($5). If you feel like dancing, go to the largest and most popular disco in Palma, the **Black Cat,** Av. Joan Miró 75 (no phone), which attracts a mixed crowd of young locals as well as visitors from Spain and the rest of the world. There are nightly shows at 3:30am. It is open daily from midnight to 6am but doesn't begin to get crowded until 2am. It is closed on Mondays during the winter. Admission is 8€ ($10).

2 Valldemossa & Deià (Deyá)

Valldemossa is the site of the **Cartoixa Reial** ✦, Plaça de las Cartujas s/n (✆ **97-161-21-06**), where George Sand (alias Lucile Aurore Dupin or Baronne Dudevant) and the tubercular Frédéric Chopin wintered in 1838 and 1839. The monastery was founded in the 14th century, but the present buildings are from the 17th and 18th centuries. After monks abandoned the dwelling, their cells were rented to guests, which accounts for the appearance of Sand and Chopin, who managed to shock the conservative locals with their unorthodox (unmarried) living arrangements. (To add fuel to the fire, Sand wore trousers and smoked cigars.) They occupied cells two and four, but the only traces of their visit that remain there today are a small painting and a French piano. The peasants burned most of it after the couple returned to the mainland, fearing they'd catch Chopin's tuberculosis. Cartoixa Reial may be visited Monday through Saturday from 9:30am to 6pm, Sunday from 10am to 1pm for 7€ ($8.75) adults, free for children under 10. Out of season, it shuts down an hour earlier.

It is also possible to visit the **Palau del Rei Sancho,** next door to the monastery, on the same ticket. This is a Moorish retreat built by one of the island kings. Tours are given by guides in traditional dress.

From Valldemossa, continue through the mountains following the signposts for 11km (6½ miles) to Deià. But before you approach the village, consider a stopover at **Son Marroig** (✆ **97-163-91-58**), at Km 26. Now a museum, this was once the estate of Archduke Lluis Salvador. Born in 1847, he tired of court life in his early 20s and found refuge here with his young bride in 1870. Many of his personal furnishings and mementos, such as photographs and his ceramic collection, are still here, as is a turret that dates back to the 1500s. The estate is surrounded by lovely gardens leading to the cliffs' edge and offering endless views of the blue horizon. Here, you can also glimpse Sa Foradada, a monolithic rock noted for its keyhole gap through the middle, rising from a nearby sea bed. The museum is open from April to October, Monday through Saturday from 9:30am to 2pm and 3 to 8pm (closing at 6pm in winter). Admission is 3.50€ ($4.35).

Moments **Just Ask a Painter Where the Sun Sets Best**

After walking through the old streets, stand on a rock overlooking the sea and watch the sun set over a field of silvery olive trees and orange and lemon groves. It won't take long to figure out why painters and artists were so enamored of the place.

Set against a backdrop of olive-green mountains, **Deià (Deyá)** is peaceful and serene, with its sandstone houses and creeping bougainvillea. It has long had a special meaning for artists. Robert Graves, the English poet and novelist (*I, Claudius* and *Claudius the God*), lived in Deià, and died here in 1985. He is buried in the local cemetery. These days the mountainside cluster of exclusive residences, pricey restaurants, and luxury hotels is very much a haunt of the rich and/or famous. The tiniest and most beautiful village on the island is Lluc Alcari, perched on the cliffs halfway between Deià and Soller; it has superb Mediterranean views.

WHERE TO STAY

Deià offers some of the most tranquil and stunning retreats on Majorca—La Residencia and Es Molí—but it is possible to find somewhere cheaper if you head a bit out of town.

EXPENSIVE

Hotel Es Molí 🌟🌟 One of the most spectacular hotels on Majorca originated in the 1880s as a severely dignified manor house in the rocky highlands above Deià, home of the landowners who controlled access to the town's freshwater springs. Indeed, the hotel still has a private spring that now feeds the swimming pool. In 1966 two annexes were added, turning it into a fabulous four-star hotel. Rooms are beautifully furnished and impeccably maintained, often with access to a private veranda overlooking the gardens or the faraway village. All units have neatly kept bathrooms with tub/shower combos. Hardy souls make it a point to hike for 30 minutes to the public beach at Deià Bay; but there is a shuttle bus that delivers the less energetic to the hotel's private beach, 6km (4 miles) away.

Carretera Valldemossa s/n, 07179 Deià. ✆ **97-163-90-00.** Fax 97-163-93-33. www.esmoli.com. 87 units. 222€–242€ ($277–$302) double; 375€–420€ ($469–$525) suite. Rates include breakfast; half-board 20€ ($25) extra per person per day. AE, DC, MC, V. Free parking. Closed early Nov to early Apr. Take exit to Deià off direct road .5km (¾ mile) after going through Valldemossa. **Amenities:** Restaurant; bar; outdoor pool; outdoor tennis court; limited room service; babysitting; laundry service; dry cleaning. *In room:* A/C, TV, minibar, hair dryer, safe.

La Residencia 🌟🌟🌟 This, the most stylish, hip, elegant hotel on Majorca, really came into its own during the early 1990s when it was acquired by British businessman and founder of Virgin Airlines Richard Branson. Since Branson took over, the hilltop property, affectionately dubbed "La Res," quickly became a celebrity haven, proclaiming itself "your revenge on everyday life." Guests have included everyone from Queen Sofía and the emperor of Japan to America's sweethearts and rock-'n'-roll elite. It was taken over by Orient Express in 2002 but has retained its air of laid-back glamour. Surrounded by 5.3 hectares (13 acres) of rocky Mediterranean gardens, the hotel's two sprawling stone 16th-century mansions offer guests every conceivable luxury. Spacious rooms are outfitted with rustic antiques, terra-cotta floors, romantic four-poster beds, and in some cases, beamed ceilings, all with luxurious appointments, including bathrooms with tub/shower combos. Open hearths, deep leather sofas, wrought-iron candelabra, and a supremely accommodating staff have made this hotel internationally famous. Several newly opened luxury suites even have private swimming pools. Although it's technically defined as a four-star resort and a member of Relais & Châteaux, only Spanish technicalities prevent it from reaching deserved government-rated five-star status.

San Canals s/n, 07179 Deià. ℂ **97-163-90-11.** Fax 97-163-93-70. www.hotel-laresidencia.com. 63 units. 450€–600€ ($562–$750) double; from 750€ ($938) suite. Rates include breakfast. AE, DC, MC, V. Free parking. Take direct road to Deià turning off after Valldemossa. **Amenities:** 3 restaurants; 3 bars; 2 indoor pools; 1 outdoor pool; 2 lit composition tennis courts; fitness center; sauna; spa; limited room service; babysitting; laundry service; dry cleaning. *In room:* A/C, TV, hair dryer, safe.

INEXPENSIVE

Hotel Costa d'Or 🅡 🅥alue   This good-value former villa, 1.5km (1 mile) north of Deià on the road to Sóller, offers beautiful views of the vine-covered hills and the rugged coast beyond. Surrounded by lush gardens filled with fig trees, date palms, and orange groves, the hotel is quaintly furnished with odds-and-ends furniture. Although rooms by the pool can get a little noisy, all rooms are clean and comfortable. Most are simple but have decent views, and all come with good beds and neat bathrooms, most of which are equipped with tub/shower combos.

Lluch Alcari s/n, 07179 Deià. ℂ **97-163-90-25.** Fax 97-163-93-47. 41 units. 185€ ($231) double; 275€ ($344) suite. Rates include breakfast. DC, MC, V. Closed Nov–Mar 21. Take direct road to Deià turning off after Valldemossa. **Amenities:** Restaurant; health club; tennis court; outdoor pool; limited room service; laundry service; dry cleaning. *In room:* A/C, TV, hair dryer, minibar, safe.

WHERE TO DINE

Ca'n Quet 🅡 INTERNATIONAL   If you fancy something a little more gourmet, this restaurant is part of the Hotel Es Molí (see above), and is one of the most sought-after dining spots on the island. Set on a series of terraces above a winding road leading out of town, and festooned with pink geraniums, this is a delightful spot for a romantic lunch or dinner. Wander along the sloping pathways, and you'll find scented groves of citrus trees, roses, and a swimming pool ringed with neoclassical balustrades. In summer, you can sit at the sunny bar or shady terrace and, in winter, relax by the blazing fire in the elegant dining room. The food is meticulously prepared and makes good use of local produce: spanking fresh marinated fish *ceviches,* flavorful vegetable terrines, sumptuous seafood stews, tender duck with sherry sauce, and an ever-changing catch-of-the-day.

Carretera Valldemossa–Sóller. ℂ **97-163-91-96.** Reservations required. Main courses 18€–25€ ($23–$31); tasting menu 45€ ($56). AE, DC, MC, V. Tues–Sun 1–4pm and 8–11pm. Closed Nov–Mar. Bus: Sóller line from Palma de Majorca.

El Olivo 🅡🅡 🅜oments INTERNATIONAL/MEDITERRANEAN   La Residencia's upscale restaurant regularly counts kings, queens, and A-listers among the diners who come to enjoy its superlative Mediterranean cooking, candlelit decor, and occasional live classical music. If you're not staying at the hotel, the 30- to 40-minute drive north of Palma is well worth it for a really special evening. Offering regularly changing seasonal dishes to surprise and delight the senses, El Olivo is a must for traveling gourmands. Expect subtle, creative cuisine that excites the palette but goes easy on the stomach. The tasting menu is well worth the money to sample such joy-inducing dishes as foie gras soup infused with calvados, lightly roasted red mullet with baby spring vegetables, and tender pink rack of lamb delicately scented with herbs and tomato sauce.

In La Residencia Hotel, San Canals. ☎ **97-163-93-92.** Reservations recommended. Main courses 32€–59€ ($40–$74). Fixed-price menu 80€ ($100). AE, DC, MC, V. Daily 1–3pm and 8–11pm.

3 Port de Pollença & Formentor

Sixty-five kilometers (40 miles) north of Palma, and just a short drive from the peaceful inland market town of **Pollença,** lies the charming **Port de Pollença.** It borders a wide sheltered bay encompassed by Cape Formentor to the north and Cape del Pinar to the south and is flanked by two hills, **Puig** and **Calvario.** The latter's chapel provides the best views of both the resort and the clear-watered Mediterranean. The bay is a haven for watersports, particularly windsurfing, water-skiing, scuba diving, and sailing.

A series of low-rise hotels, private homes, restaurants, and snack bars lines the attractive beach, which is somewhat narrow at its northwestern end but has some of the island's finest, whitest sand and warmest, clearest water. The sand at the southeastern end of Pollença Bay was imported to create a broad ribbon of sunbathing space that stretches for several miles along the bay. Wrapping around its entirety is a pleasant pedestrian promenade as well as a hiking trail inland along the **Vall de Boquer** (6km/3¾ miles). There is only one luxury hotel in the area, the Hotel Formentor (see below), out on the Formentor Peninsula.

Cabo de Formentor 🏵, "Devil's Tail," can be reached from Port de Pollença via a spectacular road twisting along to the lighthouse at the cape's end. Formentor is Majorca's fjord country—a dramatic landscape of mountains, pine trees, rock, and sea, plus some of the best beaches in Majorca—studded with *miradores,* convenient clifftop terraces providing panoramic views of the area.

ESSENTIALS

GETTING THERE   Autocares Mallorca, based in Alcudia but with offices in Palma at Villalonga (☎ **97-153-00-57;** www.autocaresmallorca.com), has five daily **buses** leaving the Plaça Espanya in Palma, passing through Inca, and continuing on to Port de Pollença. Fares are 5€ ($6.25) one-way. You can continue on from Deià (see above) along C-710, or from Inca on C-713, all the way to Pollença.

VISITOR INFORMATION   The tourist information office (☎ **97-189-26-15**), on Carretera de Artá, is open from May to October, Monday through Saturday from 9am to 7pm. It's closed in the off season. From November to March, another office can answer telephone queries (☎ **97 154 72 57**). Hours are Monday through Saturday from 9:30am to 8pm.

WHERE TO STAY

Hotel Formentor 🏵🏵   This historic property dates back to 1231, but it didn't become a hotel until 1929. Since its inception, it's hosted a string of high-powered politicos and spiritual leaders, including Winston Churchill and the Dalai Lama, as well as various literary luminaries and screen goddesses like Liz Taylor. There is virtually nothing this hotel, an old-school five-star, doesn't have, from plush rooms filled with every imaginable comfort, antiques, and heavily brocaded fabrics, to amenities like a cinema, hairdresser, and boutique shopping. Marble bathrooms come with a shower and/or tub and abundant toiletries, and the sprawling grounds run right down to the beach.

Platja de Formentor s/n, 07470 Port de Pollença. (C) **97-189-91-00.** Fax 97-186-51-55. www.hotelformentor.net. 285€–450€ ($356–$562) double; 465€–725€ ($581–$906) suite. AE, DC, MC, V. **Amenities:** 2 restaurants; outdoor pool; minigolf nearby; 5 tennis courts (2 lit); sauna; car-rental desk. *In room:* A/C, TV/DVD, minibar, hair dryer, safe.

Hotel Illa d'Or ✿ Originally built in 1929, and enlarged and improved several times since then, this handsome four-star hotel sits at the relatively isolated northwestern edge of Pollença Bay—far from the heavily congested, touristy region around the port. Decorated in a mixture of colonial Spanish and English reproductions, it has a seafront terrace that juts out over the gently lapping waves with a view of the mountains behind. Rooms are midsize to spacious, each with comfortable furnishings, including good beds and bathrooms with tub/shower combos. The beach is just a few steps away.

Passeig Colón 265, 07470 Port de Pollença. (C) **97-186-51-00.** Fax 97-186-42-13. www.hoposa.es. 119 units. 160€–210€ ($200–$262) double; 325€–455€ ($406–$568) suite. Rates include breakfast. AE, DC, MC, V. Free parking. Closed Nov–Feb. Take direct road to Inca/Pollença. **Amenities:** Restaurant; 2 bars; 2 outdoor pools; tennis court; fitness center; Jacuzzi; sauna; bike rental; business center; limited room service; massage service; laundry service; dry cleaning. *In room:* A/C, TV, minibar, hair dryer, safe.

WHERE TO DINE

Restaurant Clivia ✿ MAJORCAN/SPANISH This is one of the most appealing restaurants in Pollença, attracting clientele from all over the island. It comprises two antique-filled dining rooms built around an outdoor patio in a century-old house in the heart of town. The menu is short, sharp, and well executed and offers mouthwatering veal, chicken, and pork dishes along with a more wide-ranging roster of seafood. The salt cod, monkfish, dorado, eel, squid, and whitefish, either baked in a salt crust or prepared as part of a succulent *parrillada* (platter) of shellfish, are all unbeatable. The restaurant, incidentally, takes its name from the bright red flowers *(las clivias)* that are planted profusely beside the patio and that bloom throughout the summer.

Av. Pollentia 4760. (C) **97-153-46-16.** Reservations recommended. Main courses 12€–25€ ($15–$32). AE, DC, MC, V. May–Oct Tues and Thurs–Sun 1–3pm and 7–11pm, Mon and Wed 7–11pm; Nov 1–14 and Dec 21–Apr Thurs–Tues 1–3pm and 7–11pm. Closed Nov 15–Dec 20.

Appendix A:
Barcelona Past & Present

Once called Spain's "second city," Barcelona no longer deserves that appellation. Long suppressed by the dominance of Madrid, Barcelona has truly found its own personality. Barcelona, like Milan, is both industrious and pleasure-seeking, serious but playful, and image conscious without losing its inherent grittiness. Warlords, kings, and dictators have all tried to mold the city to suit their interests, but Barcelona is nothing if not resilient, re-inventing itself time and time again and refusing to renounce its culture, language, and identity. Today, with a booming economy and arts scene, plus a citizen-friendly local government, Barcelona seems to epitomize modern Europe and continues to seduce with its special charms.

1 Barcelona Today

As Catalonia moves on its journey into the millennium, tourism continues to boom and to dominate the economy—it remains a hot, hot industry with yearly arrivals in Barcelona bypassing the 4.5-million mark and the Old City, at least in the summer, bustling with tour groups and buses.

Visitors from pre-1992, that pivotal year when Barcelona presented a new-and-improved city to the rest of the world at the Summer Olympics, sometimes barely recognize the place. After the gray years—during which the Franco-dominated central government withheld much-needed funds for public infrastructure and let rows of characterless high-rise hotels blight the coastline—Catalonia is no longer interested in the "lager lout" image. Although it's still possible to find bargains in rural areas and the coast, tourism of the $5-a-day variety is now a distant memory as prices have skyrocketed, especially since the introduction of the euro in 2002. The media have baptized Barcelona the coolest city in Europe with the city's restaurants, bars, shops, and hotels among the most cutting-edge on the Continent. But despite its chic image, Barcelona remains steeped in tradition, where history plays an important part in its *fiestas* (celebrations) as well as in everyday life.

If there is one fact you should have perfectly clear before arriving, it's that for an overwhelming majority of Catalans, their homeland is *not* Spain (in high season you may even be handed a leaflet or two telling you as much). Most locals consider themselves Catalan first and Spanish second, so bemoaning the lack of sangria and bullfights will only be met with the coldest of receptions. Historically robbed of its status as an independent nation, autonomy was returned to Catalonia via the 1978 Spanish constitution, and politicians have pretty much been at the negotiating table ever since, pushing for even greater self-rule. After more than 20 years as head of the **Generalitat (Catalan Regional Government),** the conservative Jordi Pujol lost to the socialist Pasqual Maragall (who served as mayor of Barcelona during the Olympic years) in 2003. In coalition with the left-wing ERC party (whose aim is *total* independence for Catalonia), Maragall has been accused of placing more emotive issues of a nationalist nature before policy-making. In 2006, José Montilla replaced Maragall as president of Catalonia. In that same year Catalonia, which contributes more to the central government's coffers than any other region, was rewarded when an *estatut* (statute)—approved by Spain's governing PSOE socialist party—gave it greater autonomous powers than ever before.

Immigration is now the region's biggest challenge. Apart from Spanish and Latin communities, Catalonia remained a monocultural society for centuries before the current wave of immigration. Immigrants now make up 5% of the total population of just over six million, reaching 50% in some inner-Barcelona pockets. Providing a good education, emphasizing religious tolerance, regulating the foreign workforce, and the immersion of Catalan language and culture are all now high on the agenda, amid a backdrop of hysterical cries from the right that the latter will be lost if Catalonia is to absorb any more foreigners.

Immigrants are essential, however, for Catalonia's primary industry. South Americans and North Africans are now employed in the vast acres of vineyards, olive groves, and other agrarian pursuits. Secondary industry sectors include chemical, car, and textile manufacturing, with a mushrooming technology sector attracting foreign investment and start-ups. Tourism employs a huge number of temporary workers during the summer, but unemployment still hovers, as it does in the rest of the country, at around 10%.

2 History 101

ORIGINS, INVASIONS & THE BIRTH OF A NATION

Before the arrival of the Romans, the plains surrounding what is now defined as Barcelona were populated by peaceful, agrarian people known as the Laetani, while other parts of the Catalonia were settled by the Iberians. The Greeks were the region's first immigrants, setting up a sizable trading colony on the northern coast at Empúries, the remains of which can still be seen today. Empúries was also the entry point for the Romans, who were at war with Carthage, a northern African power, for dominance over the western Mediterranean. Their base on the peninsula was New Carthage (Cartagena), a city rich in silver and bronze mines that the Romans saw as prime booty. In response to an attack on Rome led by Hannibal, the Romans started their subjugation of the Peninsula using

Dateline

- **550 B.C.** Greeks settle at Empúries in northern Catalonia.
- **218 B.C.** The Romans, using Empúries as an entry point, subjugate Spain. Barcino, principally a trading port, is founded.
- **A.D. 415** Barcelona occupied by the Visigoths.
- **719** The Muslim invasion of the Peninsula reaches Barcelona.
- **801** Barcelona taken by the Franks.
- **878** Guifré el Pilós (Wilfred the Hairy) defeats the Moors and becomes Count of Barcelona, the first in the line of a 5-century-long autonomous rule.
- **1064** The Usatges, the first Catalan Bill of Rights, is drafted.
- **1137** A royal marriage unites Catalonia and neighboring region of Aragon.
- **1213–35** Jaume I conquers Majorca, Ibiza, and Valencia.
- **1265** Barcelona forms the Consell de Cent, its own municipal government.
- **1282–1325** Catalonia conquers Corsica and Sicily.
- **1347–59** The Black Plague halves the city's population. The Generalitat (autonomous government) is founded.

Tarraco (Tarragona) as a base. Barcino (Barcelona), with its lack of a harbor, served merely as port of call between Tarraco and Narbonne in France—but out of that, a town grew. It mushroomed out from Mons Taber, the highest point of the city, where the cathedral now stands. Traces of Roman civilization can still be seen in Barcelona and to a much greater extent in Tarragona.

When Rome fell in the 5th century, the Visigoths pounced, taking a broad swath stretching from the eastern Pyrénées to Barcelona. The chaotic rule of the Visigoth kings, who imposed their sophisticated set of laws on existing Roman ones, lasted about 300 years. The Visigoths were prolific church builders, and Visigothic fragments still survive in Barcelona and, more vividly, in Tarragona's cathedral.

In A.D. 711, Moorish warriors led by Tarik crossed over into Spain and conquered the country. By 714, they controlled most of it, except for a few mountain regions around Asturias. Their occupation of Barcelona was short-lived, which accounts for why the city has virtually no vestiges of Moorish architecture compared with al-Andalús, or Andalusia, where their culture flourished.

In the Pyrénées, Catalonia's heartland, the Moors clashed head on with the Franks, who, led by Charlemagne, drove them back south. In 801, Louis the Pious, son of Charlemagne, took Barcelona and set up a buffer state, marking the territorial boundaries (known as the Marcha Hispánica) of what was to become medieval Catalonia and endowing the local language with elements of his own (Provençal). Counts were awarded various territories. Guifré el Pilós (Wilfred the Hairy; 878–97) acquired several (including Barcelona) and managed to unite the area through a bloody battle that history has deemed the birth of the Catalonia. In the 9th century, mortally wounded from a battle against the Moors, the Frankish emperor dipped the fingers of the hairy warrior in his own blood and traced them down the count's shield, creating the Quatre Barres, the future flag of Catalonia. What followed was a 500-year-long dynasty of Catalan count-kings with the freedom to forge a nation.

THE GOLDEN AGE & DECLINE

Catalonia entered the next millennium as a series of counties operating under the feudal system. It was gathering political strength, and artistic and artisan disciplines were beginning to flourish. Under Ramón Berenguer III (1096–1131) and his son, the region annexed the southern Tarragonese territories and neighboring Aragon as well. Further expansion came

- **1479** Fernando II, monarch of the crown of Catalonia Aragon, marries Isabel, queen of Castile, uniting all of Spain. Catalonia falls under Castilian rule.
- **1492** Columbus discovers America. The "Catholic Kings" expel all remaining Jews and Muslims.
- **1522** Under the rule of Charles V, Catalans are refused permission to trade in the New World.

- **1640–50** Catalan revolt known as the Guerra dels Segadors (Harvesters' War).
- **1702** The War of Succession begins.
- **1759** Barcelona falls to Franco-Spanish army. Catalan language banned.
- **1808–14** French occupy Catalonia.
- **1832** The Industrial Revolution begins in Barcelona with the first steam-driven factory.

- **1833–39** The Carlist wars begin. Trade unions and collectives form in Barcelona.
- **1859** Work begins on the "new city," L'Eixample.
- **1873** First Spanish Republic established.
- **1888** First International Exhibition in Barcelona held at the Ciutadella Park.

continues

under Jaume I (1213–76), who conquered Sicily and the Balearic Islands and set up Catalonia as the principal maritime power of the Mediterranean. Under his long reign, the second city walls (more extensive than the old Roman ones) and the massive *drassanes* (shipyards) were built, and a code of sea trade and a local parliament were established. Mercantile wealth led to the construction of such great Gothic edifices as the church of Santa María del Mar and its surrounding mansions, the Saló del Tinell at the Royal Palace, and the Saló del Cent. Catalan literature and language also greatly benefited from the city's continuing prosperity.

In 1479 this was interrupted, however, by the most far-reaching of all royal unions, that of Fernando II of Catalonia-Aragon (1452–1516) to Isabel of Castile (1451–1504). Spain was at last united, and Catalonia lost its autonomy in the shift. The pious "Catholic Kings" embarked on a bloody process of expelling all Muslims and Jews from Spain, including those remaining in Barcelona's El Call. Even though Columbus was received upon his return from the discovery of America in Barcelona, Catalans were prohibited from trading with the New World. In the early 17th century, under the rule of Felipe IV (1605–55), anti-centralist feeling was further agitated by Spain's "Thirty Year War" with France, Catalonia's neighbor,

with which Catalonia soon allied. The most emotive of all uprisings, the so-called Guerra dels Segadors (Harvesters' War), was squashed by Spanish troops and, as a final blow, in 1650 the king ceded Catalan lands north of the Pyrénées to France.

In 1700 a Bourbon prince, Philip V (1683–1746), became king, and the country fell under the influence of France. Philip V's right to the throne was challenged by a Habsburg archduke of Austria, thus giving rise to the War of Spanish Succession. Catalonia backed the wrong horse and Philip V, after taking the city on September 11, 1714 (still celebrated as the Diada, the Catalan national day), outlawed the language, closed all universities, and built a citadel (on the site of the Ciutadella Park) to keep an eye of the rowdy population.

THE *RENAIXENÇA* & MODERNISM

Backed by a hard-working populace, Barcelona was the first Spanish city to embrace the Industrial Revolution. Textiles, with raw materials being brought in from the New World, became big business, and Barcelona gained the reputation as the "Manchester of the South." This newfound wealth led to the 19th-century *renaixença* (renaissance), a heady time of artistic and economic growth not known since the prosperous 14th century.

- **1892–93** Collectives demand Catalan autonomy. Anarchist throws bombs in the Liceu Opera House.
- **1909** Setmana Tràgica; anarchists go on anticlerical rampage in Barcelona.
- **1923** Dictatorship led by General Primo de Rivera starts in Spain.
- **1929** Second International Exhibition, this time on Montjuïc.

- **1931** Francesc Macià negotiates autonomy for Catalonia during the Second Republic and declares himself president.
- **1939** Anarchist-occupied Barcelona is taken by Franco's army.
- **1953** Defense treaty between Spain and the U.S. signed.

- **1960s** The package tourism boom takes off on Catalonia's Costa Brava.
- **1975** Franco dies. Barcelonese drink the city dry in celebration.
- **1978** King Juan Carlos grants Catalonia autonomous rule.
- **1981** Coup attempt by right-wing officers fails. Democracy prevails.

In cultural terms it was symbolized by the revived Jocs Florals, a poetry competition that celebrated the Catalan language; the demolition of the city walls; construction of L'Eixample (*extension,* or "new city"); and, of course, the *modernista* movement, where Gaudí and his contemporaries held sway. The international exhibition of 1888, a showcase of the glories of the new, cashed-up Catalonia, drew over two million visitors. Politically speaking, the Lliga de Catalunya, Catalonia's first pro-independence party, was founded. Anarchist and communist groups were mushrooming underground and acting above; in 1893 bombs were thrown into the audience at the Liceu Opera House by an anarchist, to the horror of the rest of Europe. As in most periods of rapid growth, the gap between rich and poor was becoming increasingly more evident, and a subculture grew, planting the seeds of the city's reputation for excess, seediness, and political action.

In 1876 Spain became a constitutional monarchy. But labor unrest, disputes with the Catholic Church, and war in Morocco combined to create political chaos in the entire country. The political polarization of Barcelona and Madrid erupted in 1909. Furious that the national government had lost the colonies in America (and therefore valuable trade) and was conscripting Catalans for an unwanted war in Morocco, rabble-rousers set fire to dozens of religious institutions in the city. Known as the Setmana Tràgica (Tragic Week), over 100 people died and many more were injured. All suspected culprits, even some who had not been in Barcelona at the time, were executed.

THE 20TH CENTURY

On April 14, 1931, a revolution occurred, the second Spanish Republic was proclaimed, and King Alfonso XIII (1886–1941) and his family were forced to flee. Initially, the liberal constitutionalists ruled, but soon they were pushed aside by the socialists and anarchists. These adopted a constitution separating church and state, secularizing education, and containing several other radical provisions, including autonomous rule for Catalonia. In 1931 Francesc Macià (1859–1933) declared himself president of the Catalan republic.

But the extreme nature of these reforms fostered the growth of the conservative Falange party (*Falange española,* or "Spanish Phalanx"), modeled after Italy's and Germany's fascist parties. By the 1936 elections, the country was divided equally between left and right, with Catalonia firmly to the left. In Barcelona, attacks on bourgeois symbols (and people) and the occupation of

- **1982** Socialists gain power after 43 years of right-wing rule.
- **1986** Spain joins the European Community (now the European Union).
- **1992** Barcelona hosts the Summer Olympics.
- **1998** The Generalitat introduces controversial "linguistic normalization" laws in an effort to strengthen Catalan as the region's primary language.
- **2001** Spain moves forward as an economic powerhouse in Latin America.
- **2004** Spanish Prime Minister José Luis Zapatero officially requests that Catalan, along with Basque and Galician, be recognized as working languages of the E.U.
- **2006** A new estatut (statute) granting Catalonia more autonomous powers is passed by the Spanish Socialist government.

public buildings by collectives were common. On July 18, 1936, the army, supported by Mussolini and Hitler, tried to seize power, igniting the Spanish Civil War. General Francisco Franco, coming from Morocco to Spain, led the Nationalist (rightist) forces in fighting that ravaged the country. By October 1, Franco was clearly in charge of the leadership of nationalist Spain, abolishing popular suffrage and regional autonomy—in effect, establishing totalitarian rule. Over the next 3 years, Barcelona and the Catalan coast were bombed by German and Italian fighter planes, untold numbers of citizens were executed, and thousands fled across the Pyrénées into France. Then Franco's forces marched into Barcelona under the banner "Spain is here." The Catalan language and culture were once again forced underground, and Francesc Macià was sentenced to 30 years in prison.

Spurred on by even worse conditions in the south, where hunger and poverty were an everyday threat, millions of immigrants arrived in Barcelona in the middle of the century. The 1960s saw another economic boom, this time led by tourism, which grew into an important industry on the Costa Brava and Costa Daurada. Communists formed militant trade unions, and a working class was embittered by decades of repression. Before his death, General Franco selected as his successor Juan Carlos de Borbón y Borbón (b. 1938), son of the pretender to the Spanish throne. A new constitution was approved by the electorate and the king; it guaranteed human and civil rights, as well as free enterprise, and ended the status of the Roman Catholic Church as the church of Spain. It also granted limited autonomy to several regions, including Catalonia and the Basque provinces. The election of the conservative Convergència i Unio party, with Jordi Pujol (b. 1930) at the helm, came in 1980, spurring on decades of negotiations for even greater self-rule, a battle that still continues.

In 1981 a group of right-wing military officers seized the Cortés (parliament) in Madrid and called upon King Juan Carlos to establish a Francoist state. The king, however, refused, and the conspirators were arrested. The fledgling democracy overcame its first test, and Catalonia's morale and optimism were boosted even further when the socialists won the national elections a year later. Catalanista liberals, such as the Gauche Divine (Divine Left) party, dominated the city's counterculture for the rest of the decade, as engineers and town planners at the socialist-led city hall prepared Barcelona for the 1992 Olympic Games and its new, modern era. In 1998 Catalan became the official language of education and the judiciary, with quotas imposed on the media as well. The following year more than 43,000 adults enrolled for the free Catalan language courses supplied by the Generalitat. In 2004 the Spanish Socialist government in Madrid, led by the pragmatic José Luis Zapatero, gave the official approval for Catalan to be a written and spoken language within the European Union, and in 2006 helped pass a new *estatut*—or statute—granting the province more autonomy. These two measures were both strongly opposed by the conservative Partido Popular led by Mariano Rajoy.

Appendix B:
The Catalan Culture

Barcelona has always thrived on contact and commerce with countries beyond Spain's borders. From its earliest days, the city has been linked more closely to France and the rest of Europe than to Iberia. Each military and financial empire that swept through Catalonia left its cultural imprint.

1 The Language of Catalonia

Catalonia lies midway between France and Castilian Spain. The region is united by a common language, **Catalan.** Most people wrongly assume that Catalan is a dialect of Castilian Spanish. Like Spanish and all other Romance languages, it has its roots in Latin, but Spanish and Catalan developed independently of each other.

Today Catalan, alongside Spanish, is the official language of the *Països Catalans,* which include Catalonia, Andorra, the Balearic Islands, and Valencia (although the debate still rages as to whether the language of the Valencianos is a derivative of Catalan or a separate language). "Unofficial" Catalan-speaking pockets include parts of the region of Aragon, parts of the French Pyrénées, and the town of Alghero on the Italian island of Sardinia (as a result of an invasion by Catalan colonists in 1372). All told, Catalan is spoken by nearly 11 million people, making it the seventh most widely spoken language in Europe, more than both Swedish and Greek.

The restriction and outright prohibition of the language, first at the hands of the conquering Spanish-French forces in the 1714 War of Succession, and later under the iron fist of General Franco, means that language and politics have been inseparable in Catalonia. During the 13th to 15th centuries, Catalan was the lingua franca of the western Mediterranean; after the 18th

century it enjoyed a golden period known as the *renaixença* (renaissance), when all aspects of Catalan culture, but particularly language, literature, and architecture (see below), flourished in a fervor of nationalism. Following the dictatorship, the Catalan language was reinstated as the language of education, bureaucracy, trade, and the media, with an impetus from the autonomous government to impose it as a social language as well—a plan that didn't go down well with the thousands of Spanish-speaking people residing in Catalonia.

The reality for the visitor today is that both Catalan and Spanish are freely spoken in the city with the vocabulary of the two often mixed together to form a sort of Barcelonese vernacular. The languages are extremely territorial; in El Raval, the neighborhood with the biggest immigrant population, you are more likely to hear Spanish (or Urdu, English, or Arabic), while in L'Eixample you will be greeted with a *¡Bon dia!* (as opposed to the Castilian *¡Buenos días!*) when you walk into a bar. The Catalan language is also dominant in rural areas. While all Barcelona street names are signposted in Catalan, most people use a mixture of the two languages when actually *referring* to them, which is the same approach I have used in this book. In museums and galleries, descriptions are in Catalan, with a translation either in Spanish, English, or both. People who understand some Spanish (or French) should not have trouble deciphering them, and those that don't will return home with a few Catalan phrases up their sleeves.

As for the media, English-language newspapers are available in most of the news kiosks along La Rambla. The Spanish edition of the *International Herald Tribune* contains a section with highlights from *El País,* the country's major daily newspaper, translated into English. Also be on the lookout for *Catalonia Today,* a free newspaper covering local and international news. The Catalan-language television stations (TV3 and 33) transmit in a *dual,* which means that the original language of the show can be heard at the flick of a switch. Oddly, very few hotel TVs are equipped for it.

2 Barcelona's Architecture

Like many other cities in Spain, Barcelona claims its share of neolithic dolmens and ruins from the Roman periods. Relics of the Roman colony of Barcino can be seen (and more are being found all the time), as can monuments surviving from the Middle Ages, when the Romanesque solidity of no-nonsense barrel vaults, narrow windows, and fortified design were widely used.

In the 11th and 12th centuries, religious fervor swept through Europe, and pilgrims began to flock to Barcelona on their way west to Santiago de Compostela, bringing with them French building styles and the need for new and larger churches. The style that emerged, called Catalan Gothic, had harsher lines and more austere ornamentation than traditional Gothic. Appropriate for both civic and religious buildings, it used massive ogival (pointed) vaults, heavy columns, gigantic sheets of sheer stone, clifflike walls, and vast rose windows set with colored glass. One of Barcelona's purest and most-loved examples of this style is the **Basilica of Santa María del Mar,** northeast of the city's harbor. Built over a period of only 54 years, it is the purest example of Catalan Gothic in the city. Other examples include the Church of Santa María del Pi, the Saló del Tinell (part of the Museu de la Ciutat), and, of course, the mesmerizing Barri Gòtic itself.

It is the *modernisme* movement, however, that seems to most enthrall visitors to Barcelona. Barcelona boasts the highest concentration of *modernista* architecture in the world. *Modernisme* is a confusing term, as "modernism" generally denotes 20th-century functionality. It is best translated as Art Nouveau, a movement that took hold of Europe in the latter 1800s in the arts. In Barcelona, it shone in architecture with its star being **Antoni Gaudí** (see below), the eccentric and highly devout architect responsible for Barcelona's symbol: the Temple of the Sagrada Família.

The *modernistas* were obsessed with detail. They hailed the past in their architectural forms (from Arabic to Catalan Gothic) and then sublimely sprinkled them with nature-inspired features employing iron, glass, and florid ceramic motif, all of which are seen in dazzling abundance in the city. Other *modernista* architects include **Domènech i Montaner** and **Puig i Cadafalch,** whose elegant mansions and concert halls seemed perfectly suited to the enlightened, sophisticated prosperity of the 19th-century Catalonian bourgeoisie. A 19th-century economic boom coincided with the profusion of geniuses that emerged in the building business. Entrepreneurs who had made their fortunes in the fields and mines of the New World commissioned some of the beautiful and elaborate villas in Barcelona and nearby Sitges.

In 1858 the expansion of Barcelona into the northern **L'Eixample** district provided a blank canvas for *modernista* architects. The gridlike pattern of streets was intersected with broad diagonals. Although it was never endowed with the more radical details of its original design, it provided a carefully planned, elegant path in which a growing city could showcase its finest buildings.

Consistent with the general artistic stagnation in Spain during the Franco era (1939–75), the 1950s and 1960s saw a tremendous increase in the number of anonymous housing projects around the periphery of Barcelona and, in the inner city, eyesore-ridden decay. But as the last tears were being shed over the death of General Franco elsewhere in the country, Barcelona's intelligentsia were envisioning how to regenerate their city after decades of physical degradation under the dictator.

When Barcelona won its Olympic bid to host the Summer Games in 1992, work on their vision of "New Barcelona" accelerated. City planners made possible the creation of smart new urban beaches, a glitzy port and marina, city traffic–reducing ring roads, daring public sculptures and parks, and promenades and squares weaving through the Old City. The objective was to rejuvenate the *barri,* the distinct village-neighborhoods of Barcelona that often denote one's income or political stance (sometimes even the language or football team) and make up the city's peculiar territoriality. This radical and ingenious approach did not go unnoticed by the rest of the world. In 1999 the Royal Institute of British Architects presented Barcelona's City Council with their Gold Medal, the first time a city (as opposed to an architect, such as previous winners Le Corbusier and Frank Lloyd Wright) had received the accolade. Barcelona is now used as a model across Europe for town planners wishing to overhaul their own downtrodden cities.

Nearly 15 years after the city's Olympic Year, the physical face of Barcelona is still changing by leaps and bounds. With an engaged local government still at the helm, broad swaths of industrial wasteland have been reclaimed north of the city for parkland, a new marina, and ritzy residential neighborhoods. A new city nucleus in the north is being created around the terminal for the AVE high-speed train, which will link Madrid and Barcelona and will go from there to the French border. Still a city that's not afraid to take risks with its architecture, Barcelona's skyline has been enhanced by French architect Jean Nouvel's daring and controversial **Torre Agbar** (in the outer suburb of Glòries), which has become the towering symbol of a city embracing the future with bravado.

3 Art & Artists

From the cave paintings discovered at Lleida to several true giants of the 20th century—**Picasso, Dalí,** and Miró—Catalonia has had a long and significant artistic tradition. Today it is the Spanish center of the plastic arts and design culture.

The first art movement to attract attention in Barcelona was **Catalan Gothic sculpture,** which held sway from the 13th to the 15th centuries and produced such renowned masters as Mestre Bartomeu and Pere Johan. Sculptors working with Italian masters brought the Renaissance to Barcelona, but few great Catalonian legacies remain from this period. The rise of baroque art in the 17th and 18th centuries saw Catalonia filled with several impressive examples but nothing worth a special pilgrimage; the old masters such as El Greco and Velázquez worked in other parts of Spain (Toledo and Madrid, respectively).

In the neoclassical period of the 18th century, Catalonia—and, particularly,

Gaudí: The Saintly Architect

June 7, 1926, started as normally as any other day in the life of the architect **Antoni Gaudí i Cornet.** Leaving his humble studio at his work-in-progress, the Temple of the Sagrada Família, the old man shuffled through L'Eixample district with the help of his cane on his way to evening vespers. He did not hear the bells of the no. 30 tram as it came careering down the Gran Vía. While waiting for an ambulance, people searched the pockets of his threadbare suit for some clue as to his identity but none was to be found. Mistaking the great architect for a vagrant, he was taken to the nearby public hospital of Santa Creu.

For the next 3 days, Gaudí lay in agony. Apart from occasionally opening his mouth to utter the words, "Jesus, my God!" his only other communication was to protest a suggestion that he be moved to a private clinic. "My place is here, with the poor," he is reported to have said.

Gaudí was born in 1852 in the rural township of Reus. The son of a metalworker, he spent many hours studying the forms of flora, fauna, and topography of the typically Mediterranean agrarian terrain. "Nature is a great book, always open, that we should make ourselves read," he once said. As well as using organic forms for his lavish decorations (over 30 species of plant are seen on the famous Nativity Facade of the Sagrada Família), he was captivated by the structure of plants and trees. As far as he was concerned, there was no shape or form that could be devised on an architect's drawing table that did not already exist in nature. "All styles are organisms related to nature," he claimed.

Apart from Mother Nature, Gaudí's two other guiding lights were religion and Catalan nationalism. When the *modernista* movement was in full

---

Barcelona—arose from an artistic slumber. Art schools opened and foreign painters arrived, exerting considerable influence. The 19th century produced many Catalan artists who followed the general European trends of the time without forging any major creative breakthroughs.

The 20th century brought renewed artistic ferment to Barcelona, as reflected by the arrival of Málaga-born **Pablo Picasso.** (The Catalan capital today is the site of a major Picasso museum.) The great surrealist painters of the Spanish school, **Joan Miró** (who also has an eponymous museum in Barcelona) and **Salvador Dalí** (whose fantastical museum is along the Costa Brava, north of Barcelona), also came to the Catalan capital.

Many Catalan sculptors achieved acclaim in this century, including Casanovas, Llimon, and Blay. The Spanish Civil War brought cultural stagnation, yet against all odds many Catalan artists continued to make bold statements. **Antoni Tàpies** was one of the principal artists of this period (the Fundació Tàpies in Barcelona is devoted to his work). Among the various schools formed in Spain at the time was the **neofigurative band,** which included such artists as Vásquez Díaz and Pancho Cossio. The Museum of Contemporary Art in the neighborhood of El Raval (p. 172) illustrates the various 20th-century Catalan artistic movements, including the Dau al Set, the surrealist movement started in the 1940s by the "visual poet" swing, architects such as Luis Domènech i Montaner and Josep Puig i Cadafalch were designing buildings taking florid decoration and detail to the point of delirium. Gaudí, in the latter half of his life, disapproved of their excess and their capricious, outward-reaching (that is, European) notions. He even formed a counterculture, the Artistic Circle of Saint Luke, a collective of pious creatives with a love of God and the fatherland equal to his own.

He never married and when he was close to 50, moved into a house in the Parc Güell, the planned "garden city" above Barcelona, with his ailing niece and housekeeper. After they both died, his dietary habits, always seen as somewhat eccentric by the carnivorous Catalans (Gaudí was a strict vegetarian), became so erratic that a group of Carmelite nuns who lived in the park took it upon themselves to make sure that he was properly nourished. His appearance was also starting to take on a bizarre twist. He would let his beard and hair grow for months, forget to put on underwear, and wear old slippers both indoors and out.

What became apparent by the end of his life, and long after, was that Gaudí was one of the greatest architects the world has known, whose revolutionary techniques are still the subject of theory and investigation and whose vision was an inspiration for some of today's top architects, including Spain's own Santiago Calatrava. In 2003 **Año Gaudí**, the celebration of the 150th anniversary of his birth, saw an equal number of tourists flock to Barcelona as Paris for the first time ever. Expect even greater crowds if the Temple of the Sagrada Família is finished, as predicted, for the centenary of his death in 2026.

Joan Brossa. His art and many other works by leading sculptors dot the streets of Barcelona, making it a vibrant outdoor museum. Watch out for Roy Lichtenstein's *Barcelona Head* opposite the main post office in the Plaça d' Antoni López, Joan Miró's phallic *Dona i Cell* in the park of the same name, and Fernando Botero's giant cat on the Rambla del Raval.

Today many Barcelona artists are making major names for themselves, and their works are sold in the most prestigious galleries of the Western world. Outstanding among these is sculptor **Susana Solano,** who ranks among the most renowned names in Spanish contemporary art, and

the neoexpressionist Miguel Barceló. Design and the graphic arts have thrived in Barcelona since the heady days of *modernisme*. It seems that nothing in Barcelona, from a park bench to a mailbox, escapes the "designer touch." Leading names include the architect and interior and object designer Oscar Tusquets, and the quirky graphic artist Javier Mariscal, whose work can be seen in many of the city's designer housewares stores. The most important plastic-arts schools in Spain are located in Barcelona, and the city acts as a magnet for young, European creatives who flock here to set up shop.

Fun Fact Picasso & *Les Demoiselles*

Biographers of the 20th century's greatest artist, Spanish-born Pablo Picasso, claim that the artist was inspired to paint one of his masterpieces, *Les Demoiselles d'Avignon,* after a "glorious night" spent in a notorious bordello on Barcelona's Carrer D'Avinyó.

---

4 A Taste of Catalonia

Meals are an extremely important social activity in Catalonia; eating out remains a major pastime, whether in the evening with friends, at lunch in a local bar with workmates, or with the traditional Sunday family feast. Although Barcelona is a fast-paced city, mealtimes, especially lunchtime, are still respected, with the whole city shifting into first gear between the hours of 2 and 4pm. Many people either head home or crowd into a local eatery for a three-course *menú del día* (lunch of the day).

The food in Catalonia is quite different from that of the rest of the Spain. In Barcelona, the mainstay diet is typically Mediterranean, with an abundance of fish, legumes, and vegetables, the latter often served simply boiled with a drizzle of olive oil. Pork, in all its forms, is widely eaten whether as grilled filets, the famous Serrano ham, or delicious *embutidos* (cold cuts) from inland Catalonia. In more contemporary restaurants, portions tend to be smaller than in the U.S. Another local characteristic is the lack of tapas bars. Very good ones do exist but not in the same abundance as in the rest of Spain. Instead, Catalans tend to go for *raciones* (plates of cheese, pâtés, and cured meats) if they want something to pick at.

Many restaurants in Spain close on Sunday and Monday, so check ahead of time before heading out. Hotel dining rooms are generally open 7 days a week, and there's always something open in the touristy areas. If you really want to get a true taste of Catalan cuisine, stay away from places in Les Ramblas, ask your hotel concierge for recommendations, or check chapter 6 of this book. Dining in Barcelona can range from memorable to miserable (or memorable for all the wrong reasons!), so it pays to do a bit of research. If possible, always book ahead for reputable restaurants, especially on the weekends.

MEALS

BREAKFAST In Catalonia, as in the rest of Spain, the day starts with a light continental breakfast, usually in a bar. Most Spaniards have coffee, usually strong, served with hot milk—either a *café con leche* (half coffee, half milk) or a *cortado* (a shot of espresso "cut" with a dash of milk). If you find these too strong or bitter for your taste, you might ask for a more diluted *café americano.* Properly made tea is hard to find, but herbal infusions such as *poleo menta* (mint) or *manzanilla* (chamomile) are common. Along with these, most people just have a croissant *(cruasan),* doughnut, or *ensaimada* (a light, sugar-sprinkled pastry). If you want something more substantial, you can always ask for a *bocadillo* (roll) with cheese or grilled meat or cold cuts, or ask to see the list of *platos combinados* (combination plates). These consist of a fried egg, french fries, bacon, and a steak or a hamburger. A *bikini* is an old-fashioned, toasted ham-and-cheese sandwich.

LUNCH The most important meal of the day everywhere in Spain, lunch is comparable to the farm-style midday "dinner" in the United States. It usually includes three or four courses, although some smarter eateries in the Old Town now offer just one course with dessert for lighter eaters. It begins with a choice of soup, salad, or vegetables. Then comes the meat, chicken, or fish dish, simply grilled or in a rich stew or casserole. At some point, meat eaters should definitely try *botifarras,* the locally made sausages. Desserts are (thankfully) light: fruit, yogurt, or a *crema catalana* (crème brûlée). Wine and bread are always part of the meal. Lunch is served from 1:30 to 4pm, with "rush hour" at 2pm.

DINNER   Depending on what you have consumed at lunchtime, at dinner you choose either another extravaganza or a light meal.

Naturally, if you had a heavy or late lunch, you may want to simply go for a tapa or two or a few *raciones* in a wine bar. Dinner is the perfect time to try the quintessential Catalan snack, *pa amb tomàquet* (rustic bread rubbed with olive oil and tomato pulp and served with cheese, pâté, or cold cuts). This simple yet ingenious invention goes down extremely well with a bottle of wine.

If you choose to have dinner in a restaurant, expect a slightly finer version of what you had at lunch but with a larger bill, as the set-menu deal is a lunchtime-only thing.

The chic dining hour is 10 or 10:30pm. (In well-touristed regions and hardworking Catalonia, you can usually dine at 8pm, but you still may find yourself alone in the restaurant.) In most middle-class establishments, people dine around 9:30pm.

THE CUISINE
SOUPS & APPETIZERS   Soups are thick and hearty. They are divided into two categories: *sopa* (thick soup) and *potage* (a very thick, meal-in-itself soup). A *crema* is a cream soup, such as *crema de*

aspárrago. A classic soup that, according to the folk singer-songwriter Lluís Llach, "reflects all the wisdom of Catalan people" is the *escudella i carn d'olla* (a meat-and-vegetable hot pot similar to the French *pot au feu*). Traditionally a fisherman's breakfast, a *suquet* is a hearty fish-and-potato soup. Chilled *gazpacho* is particularly refreshing during the hot months.

EGGS   These are served in countless ways. A Spanish omelet, a *tortilla española,* is made with potatoes and usually onions. Local Catalan varieties include tortillas with white beans, asparagus, and garlic shoots, often served at the bar with some *pa amb tomàquet*. A simple omelet is called a *tortilla francesa.*

FISH   As in the rest of the Peninsula, the Catalans are avid fish eaters. The consumption of fish, and particularly shellfish, holds an almost cultlike status; it is eaten at all major celebrations. Although an enormous amount is imported, there are 35 fishing ports along the Catalan coastline. Some local varieties include *dorada* (a type of bream), *mero* (grouper), and *salmonette* (red mullet). Sardines (when in season) are cheap and delicious when pan-grilled with a bit of garlic and parsley. Prawns are often served in the same way (watch for prawns from Denia, which are supposedly the best), and mussels come either steamed or in a marinara sauce. Squid, octopus, and *sepia* (cuttlefish) feature heavily, from *calamari a la romana* (deep-fried squid) to *chipirones* (bite-size baby octopus, also fried) to squid cooked in its own ink. Although not native, salted cod *(bacallà)* is particularly revered by the Catalans and before you dismiss it as a poor man's fish, try the delicious *bacallà a la llauna* (baked) or *brandada de bacallà* (a creamy purée eaten with bread). Cod is a good choice in cheaper restaurants, where the fish on your *menú del día* may be frozen or of inferior quality. Premium fish and seafood in Catalonia does not come cheap, but that does not stop it being eaten in huge quantities.

PAELLA   The most internationally known Spanish dish is paella. Flavored with saffron, paella is an aromatic rice dish usually topped with shellfish and/or chicken, sausage, peppers, and local spices. Although it is widely available in Catalonia, it actually hails from Valencia. Similarly, you might like to try a *fideuà* (a local dish that replaces the rice with fine, angel-hair noodles) or an *arroz negre* (rice cooked in black squid ink). A true Catalan paella is made with rabbit and *botifarra,* a rich sausage. (Incidentally, what is known in the U.S. as Spanish rice isn't Spanish at all. If you ask an English-speaking waiter for Spanish rice, you'll be served paella.)

MEATS   Don't expect a steak of American proportions, but do try the spit-roasted suckling pig, so sweet and tender it can often be cut with a fork. The veal is also good, and the *lomo de cerdo* (loin of pork) is unmatched anywhere. Chicken is tender and tasty, whether a simply grilled chicken breast or spit-roasted until it turns a delectable golden brown. Catalan dishes tend to mix meat in unexpected combinations such as with seafood, fruit, or snails.

VEGETABLES & SALADS   Through more sophisticated agricultural methods and huge expanses of agrarian landscape, Spain now grows more (and, many would argue, tastier) fruit and vegetables than any other European region does. On their own, they are often served simply: boiled with a drizzle of olive oil. Main dishes often don't come with vegetables, except as a simple garnish on the side. You may want to consider ordering a vegetable entree to get in your vitamin quota. A popular one is *escalivada* (strips of char-grilled sweet peppers and eggplant served cold). In traditional restaurants, salads are normally a basic combination of lettuce, tomato, onions, and olives. An *ensalada catalana* adds local cold cuts. Vegetarians and vegans should always check that no meat is included in what appears to be a vegetable dish or salad on the menu.

LEGUMES   The Catalans are big on legumes; chickpeas, lentils, white and black-eyed beans regularly pop up in all sorts of delicious ways. Chickpeas are often served with baby squid; lentils with ham, chorizo, and blood sausage; *habas a la catalana* mixed broad beans with Serrano ham and mint. A traditional way to eat a *botifarra* (sausage) is with *mongetes* (white beans).

DESSERTS   The Catalans do not emphasize dessert, which could explain why, in view of how much is eaten, most manage to keep their weight down. Many opt for fresh fruit, a *macedonia* (fruit salad), or even a tub of yogurt. Flan, a home-cooked egg custard, appears on all menus, as does a *crema catalana* or crème brûlée. If you really need a carb hit, you can usually find a cheesecake (baked, not the creamy kind), a *puddin,* chocolate mousse, or some other kind of traditional dessert on the menu, but in the cheaper places they tend to be of pedestrian quality. As a dining oddity—although it's not odd at all to Spaniards—many restaurants serve fresh orange juice for dessert.

OLIVE OIL & GARLIC   Olive oil is used lavishly all over Spain, the largest olive-producing country on the planet. It is used in all cooked dishes and even as a butter replacement on bread. Garlic is also an integral part of the Spanish diet, but you can ask them to hold it on grilled and fried dishes.

WHAT TO DRINK

WATER   Although it is safe to drink, many find the taste of Barcelona's tap water unpleasant. Mineral water, in bottles of .5 to 5 liters, is available everywhere. Bubbly water is *agua con gas;*

noncarbonated is *agua sin gas*. Vichy Catalan, rather salty carbonated water that many people believe acts as a digestive aid, is very popular. Note that bottled water in some areas, bars, and cafes may cost as much as a beer.

SOFT DRINKS Schweppes, Fanta, and, naturally, Coca-Cola are all widely available. *Bitter Kas* is a carbonated drink with a Campari-like flavor. Your cheapest bet is a liter bottle of *gaseosa*, a sort of less-sugary lemonade. In summer you should also try an *horchata*. Not to be confused with the Mexican beverage of the same name, the Spanish *horchata* is a sweet, soy milk–like beverage made of tubers called *chufas*.

COFFEE Coffee is drunk at breakfast (see above) and post-meal. After lunch or dinner, you may like to try a *carajillo*, a short coffee with a dash of brandy, cognac, rum, or Baileys.

MILK Unfortunately, long-life milk sold in square boxes is the norm. Fresh milk can be found in larger supermarkets and *granjas*, bars that sell dairy products and drinks such as hot chocolate and (sometimes) milkshakes. *Leche merengada* is a delicious cinnamon-flavored milk that appears in the summer.

BEER Although not native to Spain, beer *(cerveza)* is now drunk (and sold) everywhere. Local brands include San Miguel and Estrella. All beer tends to be lighter, more like the U.S. version than the British. A *clara* is a glass of beer mixed with lemon soda. A small bottle of beer is called a *mediana*, and a glass is a *caña*.

WINE Until fairly recently, Spain was not taken particularly seriously as a wine-making region. Overshadowed by France and Italy, it was mainly associated with cheap red wine and sangria—yet thanks to the innovative practices of a handful of winemakers, and particularly of those in Catalonia, Spanish wine is currently undergoing a renaissance, offering some of the best wines (both in terms of price and quality) in the world.

The undisputed king of Catalan wines is Miguel Torres, whose family has been making wines in the Penedès wine region, just 45 minutes south of Barcelona, for over 100 years. Pioneering and enigmatic, Torres turned Catalan winemaking on its head, proving that the region was capable of excellent wines and making people sit up and pay attention. Today the Penedès, known for its undulating hills, balmy Mediterranean climate, and a varied terrain, produces soft fruity reds, refreshing whites, and—the region's *pièce de résistance*—cava (sparkling wine).

Made by the same method as French champagne, most of the high-end producers will swear that *cava* is as good as, if not better than, champagne, a point that Dom Pierre Pérignon—the Benedictine monk who invented champagne in the 17th century—would no doubt have disagreed with. Regardless, in 1872 Josep Raventós Fatjó (of the bodegas Can Cordoníu) popped his first bottle of fizz and this liquid gold was soon circulating in high society, including at the royal palace.

Penedès accounts for about 75% of all the *cava* made in Spain and there are infinite different varieties, from small "garage" bodega wines (which amount to no more than somebody producing a limited number of bottles in their garden shed) to heavyweight international brands like Freixenet and Cordoníu (which account for most of the world exports). The latter two are both in Sant Sadurni d'Anoia, the capital of *cava*-making, and Cordoníu is particularly interesting to visit. Housed in a spectacular *modernista* building that is part of the Spanish heritage trust, there are 15km (9 miles) of underground tunnels to explore while learning about the *cava*-making process.

For serious wine lovers, Catalan wine-making regions have far more to offer than *cava* alone, and it can make for a fascinating tour. The Romans were the first people to make wine in Penedès, and their ancient roads still crisscross the land. Recently pre-phylloxera vines have been discovered that some experts say show the way of the future. These wines are important because they use varieties of grapes that haven't been used before in modern winemaking. The Penedès winemakers feel that, rather than building an industry on known varieties, such as chardonnay and merlot, they will conquer the market with these new and, until now, undiscovered varieties that are unique to the area. For now, innovative winemakers, such as Josep Maria Noya of Albet i Noya (Spain's first organic winery) and Miguel Torres, continue to experiment with their crops, but it probably won't be long before unheard-of varieties start hitting the shelves.

Jean León—one of the region's most modern bodegas and now owned by Torres—was also responsible for shaking up a region that had hitherto made decent enough wines, though none that were particularly exciting. In the 1960s León returned to his beloved Spain from Hollywood in search of a vineyard where he could make wines suitable to serve at his restaurant, La Scala in Beverly Hills. It wasn't long before he and Miguel Torres became friends, sharing knowledge of the region, modern winemaking methods from the New World, and, most notably, new grape varieties. León introduced both chardonnay and cabernet sauvignon to the region.

The jewel in Catalonia's winemaking crown, however, is the Priorat. Wine has been produced here for at least 1,000 years, made mainly by monasteries, and for centuries it was widely acclaimed. But after phylloxera destroyed most of the crops in Europe it never really recovered—until recently, that is. In the early 1980s a troop of young winemakers began taking their craft seriously once again. The most notable of these was Carles Pastrana of Clos L'Obac, who set about establishing a set of D.O. *(denominación de origen)* standard rules and regulations. When you see the region with its impossibly rocky, vertical mountainsides and rough black soil, and couple that with the fact that many don't even water the land for fear of upsetting the delicate water-table balance, it seems impossible that anything good could ever come of it. And yet in the last 2 decades, the lush, dense reds of the Priorat have become renowned as some of the best and most exciting wines in the world.

SPIRITS   Vodkas, gins, rums, whiskeys, and brandies are available at any bar. If you don't recognize the label, it is probably local and, with the exception of brandies and cognacs, normally of an inferior quality. Measures here are about double those of anywhere else, which is just as well: In some bars and nightclubs you can pay as much as 12€ ($15) for a mixed drink *(cubata)*. One of the most popular is a *cuba libre* (rum and Coca-Cola).

Appendix C:
Useful Terms & Phrases

Most Catalans are very patient with foreigners who try to speak their languages. For English speakers, Catalan pronunciation is a lot easier than Spanish pronunciation, so give it a go. If you know a little French or Italian, you will probably find it quite easy. If not, most good restaurants and hotels have English speakers on hand.

1 Useful Words & Phrases

English	Spanish/Catalan	Pronunciation
Good day	**Buenos días/**	bweh-nohs dee-ahs/
	Bon dia	bohn *dee*-ah
How are you?	**¿Cómo está?/**	*koh*-moh es-*tah*/
	Com està?	com chs-*tah*
Very well	**Muy bien/Molt bé**	mwee byehn/mohl beh
Thank you	**Gracias/Gràcies**	*grah*-syahs/*grah*-syahs
You're welcome	**De nada/De res**	deh *nah*-dah/duh ress
Goodbye	**Adiós/Adéu**	ah-*dyos*/ah-*deh*-yoo
Please	**Por favor/Si us plau**	por fah-*vohr*/see yoos plow
Yes	**Sí/Sí**	see
No	**No/No**	noh
Excuse me	**Perdóneme/**	pehr-*doh*-neh-meh/
	Perdoni'm	per-*don*-eem
Where is . . . ?	**¿Dónde está . . . ?/**	*dohn*-deh es-*tah*/
	On és . . . ?	ohn ehs
the station	**la estación/la estació**	lah es-tah-*syohn*/la esta-*cyo*
a hotel	**un hotel/l'hotel**	oon oh-*tehl*/ehl ho-*tehl*
the market	**el mercado/el mercat**	ehl mehr-*kah*-doh/ehl mehr-*kah*
a restaurant	**un restaurante/**	oon rehs-tow-*rahn*-teh/
	un restaurant	oon rehs-tow-*rahn*
the toilet	**el baño/el lavabo**	ehl *bah*-nyoh/ehl lah-*vah*-boh
a doctor	**un médico/un metge**	oon *meh*-dee-koh/oon meht-*jah*
the road to . . .	**el camino a/**	ehl kah-*mee*-noh ah/
	al cami per	ahl kah-*mee* pehr
To the right	**A la derecha/**	ah lah deh-*reh*-chah/
	A la dreta	ah lah *dreh*-tah

English	Spanish/Catalan	Pronunciation
To the left	**A la izquierda/**	ah lah ees-*kyehr*-dah/
	A l'esquerra	ahl ehs-kee-*ra*
I would like . . .	**Quisiera/Voldría**	kee-*syeh*-rah/vohl-*dree*-ah
I want . . .	**Quiero/Vull**	*kyeh*-roh/*boo*-wee
to eat.	**Comer/Menjar**	ko-*mehr*/mehn-*jahr*
a room.	**una habitación/**	*oo*-nah ah-bee-tah-*syohn*/
	un habitacion	oon ah-bee-tah-*syohn*
Do you have . . . ?	**¿Tiene usted?/Té**	tyeh-neh oo-*sted*/teh
a book	**un libro/un llibre**	oon *lee*-broh/oon *yee*-breh
a dictionary	**un diccionario/**	oon deek-syoh-*nah*-ryoh/
	un diccionari	oon deek-syoh-*nah*-ree
How much is it?	**¿Cuánto cuesta?/**	*kwahn*-toh *kwehs*-tah/
	Quant es?	kwahnt ehs?
When?	**¿Cuándo?/Quan?**	*kwahn*-doh/kwahn
What?	**¿Qué?/Com?**	Keh/Cohm
There is	**(¿)Hay (. . . ?)/**	aye/ee ah/
(Is there . . . ?)	**Hi ha? *or* Hi han?**	ee ahn
What is there?	**¿Qué hay?/**	keh aye/
	Que hi ha?	keh ee ah
Yesterday	**Ayer/Ahir**	ah-*yehr*/ah-*yeer*
Today	**Hoy/Avui**	oy/ah-*wee*
Tomorrow	**Mañana/Demá**	mah-*nyah*-nah/deh-*mah*
Good	**Bueno/Bon**	*bweh*-noh/bohn
Bad	**Malo/Mal**	*mah*-loh/mahl
Better (Best)	**(Lo) Mejor/Millor**	(loh) meh-*hohr*/mee-*yohr*
More	**Más/Mes**	mahs/mehss
Less	**Menos/Menys**	*meh*-nohs/*meh*-nyus
Do you speak	**¿Habla inglés?/**	*ah*-blah een-*glehs*/
English?	**Parla anglès?**	*pahr*-lah ahn-*glehs*
I speak a little	**Hablo un poco**	*ah*-bloh oon *poh*-koh deh es-pah-
Spanish/Catalan.	**de español/**	*nyol*/*pahr*-loh *oo*-nah *mee*-kah *deh*
	Parlo una mica	kah-tah-
	de Catalan	
I don't understand.	**No entiendo/**	noh ehn-*tyehn*-doh/
	No comprenc	noh cohm-*prehnk*
What time is it?	**¿Qué hora es?/**	keh *oh*-rah ehss/
	Quina hora és?	*kee*-nah oh-rah *ehss*
The check, please.	**La cuenta, por**	lah *kwehn*-tah pohr fah-*vohr*/
	favor/El compte,	ehl *cohmp*-tah see yoos plow
	si us plau	

2 Numbers

NUMBER	SPANISH	CATALAN
1	uno (*oo*-noh)	un (oon)
2	dos (dohs)	dos (dohs)
3	tres (trehs)	tres (trehs)
4	cuatro(*kwah*-troh)	quatre (*kwah*-trah)
5	cinco (*seen*-koh)	cinc (sink)
6	seis (says)	sis (sees)
7	siete (*syeh*-teh)	set (seht)
8	ocho (*oh*-choh)	vuit (vweet)
9	nueve (*nweh*-beh)	nou (noo)
10	diez (dyehs)	deu (*deh*-yoo)
11	once (*ohn*-seh)	onze (*ohn*-zah)
12	doce (*doh*-seh)	dotze (*doh*-tzah)
13	trece (*treh*-seh)	tretze (*treh*-tzah)
14	catorce (kah-*tohr*-seh)	catorza (kah-*tohr*-zah)
15	quince (*keen*-seh)	quinza (*keen*-zah)
16	dieciséis (dyeh-see-*says*)	setze (*seh*-tzah)
17	diecisiete (dych-see-*syeh*-teh)	disset (dee-*seht*)
18	dieciocho (dyeh-*syoh*-choh)	divuit (dee-*vweet*)
19	diecinueve (dyeh-see-*nweh*-beh)	dinou (dee-*noo*)
20	veinte (*bayn*-teh)	vint (vehnt)
30	treinta (*trayn*-tah)	trenta (*trehn*-tah)
40	cuarenta (kwah-*rehn*-tah)	quaranta (kwah-*rahn*-tah)
50	cincuenta (seen-*kwehn*-tah)	cinquanta (theen-*kwahn*-tah)
60	sesenta (seh-*sehn*-tah)	seixanta (see-*shahn*-tah)
70	setenta (seh-*tehn*-tah)	setanta (seh-*tahn*-tah)
80	ochenta (oh-*chehn*-tah)	vuitanta (vwee-*tahn*-tah)
90	noventa (noh-*behn*-tah)	noranta (noh-*rahn*-tah)
100	cien (*syehn*)	cent (sent)

Index

See also Accommodations and Restaurant indexes, below.

GENERAL INDEX

A
AA, 19
ABACO (Palma de Majorca),
 301
Abercrombie & Kent
 International, 47
Above and Beyond Tours, 30
Access-Able Travel Source, 29
Access America, 23
Accessible Journeys, 29
Accommodations, 82–118. *See
 also* Accommodations Index
 all-inclusive resorts and
  hotels, 83
 Barceloneta, Vila Olímpica
  and Poble Nou, 112–115
 Barri Gòtic (Gothic
  Quarter), 84
 Barrio Alto and Gràcia,
  111–112
 best, 5–6, 85–86
 Cadaqués, 284–286
 Ciutat Vella (Old City), 87–97
 efficiency, 83
 Eixample, 84, 97–108
 family-friendly, 101
 Girona, 270–271
 Gràcia, 84
 Lloret de Mar, 273–274
 locations, 84
 Majorca
  Deià, 303–304
  Palma de Majorca,
   294–298
  Port de Pollença and
   Formentor, 305–306
 Montserrat, 253–254
 on the outskirts, 115–118
 with pools, 115
 price categories, 82
 Sant Feliu de Guíxols, 279
 Sants, Paral.lel and Montjuïc,
  108–111
 saving on, 82–83

 self-catering, 106–107
 Sitges, 263–264
 surfing for, 33
 Tarragona, 257–258
 tipping, 81
 Tossa de Mar, 276–277
 what's new in, 1–2
Acosta, 222
Addresses, finding, 66–67
Adolfo Domínguez, 217
Adrià, Ferran, 285
Aerobús, 38, 72
African American Association of
 Innkeepers International, 32
African-American travelers, 32
Aiguadolç (Sitges), 261
AirAmbulanceCard.com, 29
Aire-Sala Diana, 248
Air Europa, 37
Airfares, 33
 tips for getting the best,
  39–41
Air France, 38
Airlines and air travel, 36–42
 bankrupt airlines, 23
 film and video, 42
 long-haul flights, 41–42
 Majorca, 287–288
 from North America, 36–37
 from the United Kingdom,
  37–38
Airports, 1, 72
 getting into town from,
  38–39
 Majorca, 287
Airport security, 39, 40
Air Tickets Direct, 40
Alcanar, 259
Alfa, 245
Alitalia, 38
All-inclusive resorts and
 hotels, 83
All Saints' Day, 22
Almirall, 237
Alonso, 227

Alquimia, 113
Altafulla, 259
Altaïr, 214
American Airlines Vacations, 46
American Express
 currency exchange, 17
 offices, 75
 traveler's checks, 18–19
American Foundation for the
 Blind (AFB), 29
Amfiteatre Romà (Tarragona),
 254, 256
Amposta, 259
Angel Batlle, 213
Angel Jobal, 227
Antic Hospital de
 Santa Cruz, 204
Antic Merçat del Born, 203
Antiga Casa Sala, 227
Antiga Pasamaneria
 J. Soler, 216
Antilla Latin Club, 244
Antiques, 8, 213
Antonio Miró, 217
Apartments and aparthotels,
 84, 118
Apolo, 241
Apse of Santa Marìa
 de Taüll, 184
Aquarium de Barcelona, 8, 187
Aqua Urban Spa, 113
Archdeacon's House (Casa de
 L'Ardiaca), 196, 198
Archetours, 48
Architecture, 2, 314–315
Area code, 75
Art and artists, 315–318
Artesana i Coses, 226
Art Escudellers, 226
Art galleries, 221
Art Picasso, 221
Arxiu de la Corona
 d'Aragó, 198
ATMs (automated teller
 machines), 18

Australia
  consulate, 76
  customs regulations, 15
  health-related travel advice, 26
  passports, 79
  traveling to Spain from, 38
Auto Europe, 44
Automobile travel, 42–45
  Figueres, 281
  Girona, 267
  Lloret de Mar, 273
  Montserrat, 252
  Sant Feliu de Guíxols, 278
  Sitges, 260
  Tarragona, 254
Avis Rent a Car, 44
  accessibility program, 30

Baccus (Palma de Majorca), 302
Backroads, 32
Bagur, 281
Baja Beach Club, 242–243
Balcó del Mediterráni (Balcony of the Mediterranean; Tarragona), 254
B & B Italia, 2
Banys Arabs
  Girona, 268
  Palma de Majorca, 293
Baraka, 226
Bar Barcelona (Palma de Majorca), 301
Bar Boira (Girona), 272
Barcelona Card, 66
Barcelona Chair, 185
Barcelona Head (Lichtenstein), 7
Barcelona Information Office, 48
Barcelona Rouge, 237
Barceloneta, 56, 70
  accommodations, 112–115
  restaurants, 151–157
Bar de Tapes (Girona), 272
Bar Marsella, 58, 240
Bar Pastis, 242
Bar Pinotxo, 246
Barri Gòtic (Gothic Quarter), 4, 54, 67–68
  accommodations, 84, 87–97
  restaurants, 123–131
    snacks, tapas and drinks, 129–131
  shopping, 227
  sights and attractions, 160–166
  walking tour, 196–200

Barrio Alto
  accommodations, 111–112
  bars and pubs, 246–247
  restaurants, 157–158
Barri Xinès (Barrio Chino), 68–69
Bars and pubs, 237–249
  Barrio Alto, 246–247
  beach bars, 242–244
  best, 232
  champagne *(xampanyerias)*, 247–248
  gay and lesbian, 248–249
  L'Eixample, 244–245
  outer Barcelona, 247
B.C.M. (Palma de Majorca), 301
BCN Books, 214
BD Ediciones de Diseño, 207, 215
Beach clubs, port clubs and beach bars, 242–244
Beaches, 4, 70
  Costa Daurada, 259
  hazards, 25–26
  Majorca, 290–291
  Palafrugell area, 279–281
  Sitges, 261–262
  surfing and windsurfing, 195
Beach of the Boats (Sitges), 261
Bed-and-breakfast accommodations, 84
Beer, 321
Benedictine Monastery (Sant Feliu de Guíxols), 279
Biciclot, 74
Bicycling, 2, 74
  Majorca, 292
Bikini, 246
Biomedical Research Park, 2
Black Cat (Palma de Majorca), 302
The Black Horse, 237
Black Travel Online, 32
Blogs and travelogues, 34
Boadas, 232
Boat tours, 195
  Sant Feliu de Guíxols, 278
Bocata, 127
Bodegas (wineries), 265
Bodeguida del Medio (Palma de Majorca), 301
Boingo, 34
Books, recommended, 48–49
Bookstores, 214
Boqueria, 4, 220
Borneo, 237

Botanical Garden (Jardì Botànic), 186
Botero, Fernando, 7
Breakfast, 318
Bucket shops, 39–40
Budget, 44
Buffet y Ambigú, 214
Business hours, 75–76
Bus tours, 75
Bus travel, 72, 74
  Cadaqués, 284
  Lloret de Mar, 273
  Montserrat, 251–252
  Palfrugell, 280
  Sant Feliu de Guíxols, 278
  Tarragona, 254
Bus Turístic, 75

Cabo de Formentor, 305
Cacao Sampaka, 215
Cadaqués, 284–286
Caelum, 219
Café Bar Padam, 237
Café del Sol, 245
Café Dietrich, 248–249
Café Royale, 241
Café Zurich, 238
CaixaForum, 7, 181–182
Cala Pi (Majorca), 291
Calella de Palfrugell, 280
Calendar of events, 20–23
Caligula, 249
Calling cards, 80
Cambrils, 259
Cameras, digital, 42
Camper, 226
Canada
  consulate, 76
  customs regulations, 14
  health-related travel advice, 26
  passports, 79
  Tourist Office of Spain, 10
Can Juan de S'aigo (Majorca), 299
"Can Llopis" (Museu Romàntic; Sitges), 263
Can Paixano, 248
Ca'n Pastilla (Majorca), 291
Cap de Cala Figuera (Majorca), 291
Capella d'en Marcus, 202
Capella de Sant Jordi (Chapel of St. George), 7, 165
Capital for Foreign Exchange, 17

Cap Roig, 280
Car breakdowns, 45
Carnaval
  Barcelona, 20
  Sitges, 260
Carpe Diem Lounge Club, 243
Car rentals, 43–44
  insurance, 24
  surfing for, 34
Carrer d'en Robador, 204
Carrer Montcada, 202
Cartoixa Reial (Valldemossa), 302
Car travel, 42–45
  Figueres, 281
  Girona, 267
  Lloret de Mar, 273
  Montserrat, 252
  Sant Feliu de Guìxols, 278
  Sitges, 260
  Tarragona, 254
Casa Amatller, 60, 177, 178, 208
Casa Asia, 208
Casa Batlló, 177, 208
Casa Beethoven, 224
Casablanca, 233
Casa Bonet (Palma de Majorca), 292
Casa Colmina, 227
Casa Comalat, 208
Casa de la Ciutat/Ayuntamiento, 165–166, 200
Casa de L'Ardiaca (Archdeacon's House), 196, 198
Casa del Canonge (House of the Canon), 200
Casa de les Punxes (Casa Terrados), 207–208
Casa del Llibre, 214
Casa Lleó Morera, 177, 208
Casals, Pablo, Casa Pau Casals, 256
Casa Milà (La Pedrera), 60, 208, 210
Casa Morelli, 227
Casa-Museu Castell Gala Dalì (Figueres), 282–283
Casa-Museu Gaudì, 180
Casa-Museu Port Lligat (Cadaqués), 284
Casa Pau Casals, 256
Casas, 226
Casa Terrados (Casa de les Punxes), 207–208
Casa Vicens, 179
Cases Tomàs Roger, 207
Casino de Majorca (Palma de Majorca), 301–302
Casino Lloret de Mar, 275

Castell de Bellver (Palma de Majorca), 293
Castell de Tres Dragons (Castle of the Three Dragons), 168
Catalan language, 313–314
  useful words and phrases, 323–325
Catedral
  Barcelona, 7, 54, 160–161
  Girona, 268
  Palma de Majorca, 293–294
  Tarragona, 256
CCCB (Centre de Cultura Contemporània de Barcelona), 206
CEEFAX, 38
Cellphones, 35–36
Centers for Disease Control and Prevention, 25
Centre Bonastruc Ca Porta (Girona), 269
Centre Comercial Glòries, 228
Centre de Cultura Contemporània de Barcelona (CCCB), 171, 206
Centre del Modernisme (Casa Amatller), 178
Centre d'Urgències Perecamps, 77
Centre Municipal de Tennis, 194
Centro Médico (Palma de Majorca), 290
Ceramics and pottery, 7–8, 226
Cereria Subira, 227
Champagne bars (xampanyerias), 247–248
Chapel of Sant Elm (Sant Feliu de Guìxols), 279
Chapel of St. Christopher, 199
Chapel of St. George (Capella de Sant Jordi), 165
Children, families with
  best activities for, 8–9
  hotels, 101
  information and resources, 31
  restaurants, 145
Chocolate Museum (Museu de la Xocolata), 8, 169
Christmas (Nadal), 22–23
Churros, 246
Cibeles, 245
Cinemas, 233–234
City Hall, 245
Ciutat Jardì, 290
Ciutat Vella (Old City), 67–69
  accommodations, 87–97
  restaurants, 123–138
  sights and attractions, 160–173

Classical music, 49–50, 232–233
Clickair, 1
Climate, 19
Closed Chapel, 180
Club 13, 241
Club de Golf Vallromanes, 194
Cocktail Bar Boadas, 238
Codorniu (Sant Sadorni d'Anoia), 265
Collegi d'Architects, 196
Collserola Park, 61, 193
Colònia Güell, 188–189
Columbus Monument (Mirador de Colom), 51, 164
Comarruga, 259
Comité, 217
Comme-Bio, 222
Commercial Woman, 217
Conjunt Monumental de la Plaça del Rei (Museu d'Història de la Ciutat and Palau Reial Major), 161, 164
Connection kit, 35
Consolidators, 39–40
Consulates, 76
Continental Airlines Vacations, 46
Contribución y Moda, 224–225
Cooperativa d'Arquitectes Jordi Capell, 214
Corpus Christi, 21
Coses de Casa, 216
Cosmetics, 225
CosmoCaixa (Museu de la Ciència), 189
Costa Breve, 245
Courtyard of Orange Trees (Pati de Tarongers), 165
Credit cards, 18
Crime, 28
Cuisine, 49, 318–320
Cuisine, Catalan, 119–120
Cultural Center (Sant Feliu de Guìxols), 279
Currency and currency exchange, 16–18
Custo-Barcelona, 217
Customs regulations, 11, 14–15
Czar, 227

Dalì, Salvador, 49, 316
  Casa-Museu Castell Gala Dalì (Figueres), 282–283
  life of, 282–283
  Teatre-Museu Dalì (Figueres), 283–284
Dance clubs, 241–242

Danzatoria, 247
Dau al Set, 172
David i Goliat (Llena), 7
Decathlon, 229
Deep vein thrombosis, 25
Deià (Deyá; Majorca), 302
Dels Capellans (near Tarragona), 259
Delta, 37
Delta Vacations, 46
Department store, 215
Deputy's Palace (Palau del Lloctinent), 198
Diada de Catalunya, 22
Diada de St. Jordi, 21
Dia de la Hispanitat, 22
Dìa de los Reyes (Three Kings Day), 20
Diagonal Mar, 228
Digital cameras, 42
Dining, 119–159. *See also* Restaurant Index
    alfresco, 150
    Barceloneta and Vila Olìmpica, 151–157
    Barrio Alto, 157–158
    best, 6, 121–123
    Cadaqués, 286
    Ciutat Vella, 123–138
        El Raval, 135–138
        La Ribera, 131–135
    Eixample, 139–147
    family-friendly, 145
    Girona, 271
    Gràcia, 147–151
    Lloret de Mar, 274–275
    Majorca, Deià, 304–305
    meals, 120–121
    out of town, 158–159
    Palafrugell, 281
    Palma de Majorca, 298–301
    Poble Sec and Montjuïc, 138–139
    Sant Feliu de Guíxols, 279
    Sitges, 264, 266
    takeout, 127
    Tarragona, 258–260
    tipping, 80–81
    Tossa de Mar, 277–278
    vegetarian, 120, 121, 123, 128, 137
    what's new in, 2
Dinner, 319
Directory assistance, 80
Disabilities, travelers with, 29–30
Discos Castelló, 224
Discotheque, 244

Discover Spain Vacations, 47
Discrimination, 28–29
Dom, 215–216
Dona i Ocell (Miró), 7
Dot, 241
Drinks, 320–322
Driving rules, 44
Drugstores, 76

E & A Gispert, 219
EasyJet, 37
Eat, Drink, Life, 238
Economy class syndrome, 25
Eco-tourism, 33
Eixample, 70–71
    accommodations, 84, 97–108
    bars and clubs, 244–245
    restaurants, 139–147
    sights and attractions, 174–179
    walking tour, 207–210
El Arenal (Majorca), 291
El Born (bar), 238
El Born area, 4
    walking tour, 200–203
El Bosc de las Fades, 238
El Bulevard des Antiquaris, 213
El Café Que Pone Muebles Narvarro, 238–239
El Call (Jewish Quarter)
    Barcelona, 167
    Girona, 269
El Corte Inglés, 215
Electricity, 76
El Encants flea market, 223
El Grec, 21, 231
El Indio, 223
El Mercadillo, 217
El Milagre (Tarragona), 259
El Olivo (Palma de Majorca), 292
El Palau de la Música Catalana, 4, 166–168
El Prat de Llobregat Airport, 1, 72
    getting into town from, 38–39
El Raval, 58, 68
    accommodations, 87–97
    restaurants, 135–138
    sights and attractions, 171–173
    walking tour, 203–206
El Recó beach, 259
El Reloj, 246
Els Balomins (Sitges), 261

El Tablao de Carmen, 235–236
ELTExpress, 40
El Xampanyet, 232, 248
Ely Club (Tossa de Mar), 278
Embassies and consulates, 76
Emergencies, Palma de Majorca, 290
Entry requirements, 11
Escola Municipa d'Hípica, 195
Escolanìa, 252
Escorted tours, 47–48
Escribà, 215
Església dels Sants Just i Pastor, 199
Església de Santa Marìa del Mar, 7, 56, 202–203
Església de Sant Feliu (Girona), 268
Església de Sant Pau de Camp, 173, 204
Espai Barroc, 236
Espai Gaudì (Gaudì Space), 210
ETA (Euskadi Ta Askatasuna), 27
Etiquette, 76–77
Euro (€), 15
Eurolines Limited, 45
EuroPass, 38
Eurostar, 43
Expedia, 33, 44

FAD (Foment de les Arts Decoratives i del Disseny), 7, 171, 206
Families with children
    best activities for, 8–9
    hotels, 101
    information and resources, 31
    restaurants, 145
Familyhostel, 31
Family Travel Files, 31
Family Travel Forum, 31
Family Travel Network, 31
Farmacia Nordbeck, 207
Fashions (clothing), 217–219
    Palma de Majorca, 292
The Fastnet Bar, 232, 243
Ferries, Majorca, 288
Festa Major de Gràcia, 21–22
Festivals and special events, 20–23
Figueres, 281–284
Film, flying with, 42
Filmoteca, 233
Finca Güell, 190
Fira d'Santa Lucia, 21, 22
Fira of Barcelona, 2

Flamenco, 235–236
The Flooded Forest, 189
Flora Albaicìn, 227
FlyCheap, 40
Flying Wheels Travel, 29
FNAC, 214, 224
Foment de les Arts Decoratives i del Disseny (FAD), 7, 171, 206
Fonfone, 239
Font del Gat, 181
Font Màgica (Magic Fountain), 185
Food stores, 219–221
    shopping, 222
Formentor, 305–306
Forsyth Travel Library, 46
Forvm Ferlandina, 222
Foundation Tapestry, 182
Fragata Beach (Sitges), 261
Free or almost free activities, 7
Freixenet (Sant Sadorni d'Anoia), 265
Frommers.com, 34
Fundació Antoni Tàpies, 178
Fundació Francisco Godia, 178–179
Fundació Fran Daural, 186
Fundació Joan Miró, 9, 182
Funicular
    Montjuïc, 75
    Montserrat, 252

Galeria Olìmpica, 182–183
Galleries, 221
Ganiveteria Roca, 227
Gastón y Daniella, 216
Gat (Botero), 7
Gaudì i Cornet, Antoni, 8, 49, 314, 316–317
    Casa-Museu Gaudì, 180
    Colònia Güell, 188–189
    Finca Güell, 190
    Güell and, 181
    La Pedrera (Casa Milà), 174–175
    La Sagrada Família, 5, 55, 175–177
Gaudì Space (Espai Gaudì), 210
Gay and lesbian travelers
    information and resources, 30–31
    nightlife, 248–249
    Palma de Majorca, 302
    Sitges, 262, 266
Gay.com Travel, 31
Gehry, Frank, 7
Giménez & Zuazo, 217

Gimlet, 246
Ginger, 4, 239
Girona, 266–272
Girona airport, 72
Golden Triangle (Quadrat d'Or), 174
Golf, 194
    Majorca, 292
Gotham, 216
Gothic Quarter (Barri Gòtic), 4, 54, 67–68
    accommodations, 84, 87–97
    restaurants, 123–131
        snacks, tapas and drinks, 129–131
    shopping, 227
    sights and attractions, 160–166
    walking tour, 196–200
Gothic sculpture, 315
Gràcia, 60, 71
    accommodations, 84, 111–112
    bars and pubs, 245–246
    restaurants, 147–151
    sights and attractions, 179–180
Gran Hotel La Florida, spa at, 113
Gran Teatre del Liceu, 171–172, 204, 232–233
Great Britain
    consulate, 76
        Palma de Majorca, 290
    currency exchange, 17
    customs regulations, 14
    health-related travel advice, 26
    passports, 79
    Spanish National Tourist Office, 10
    travelers with disabilities, 30
    traveling to Spain from, 37–38
Grup del Treball, 172
Güell i Bacigalupi, Eusebi, 181
Guia del Ocio, 231

Happy Park, 8, 195
Harlem Jazz Club, 236
Hats, 8, 221
Health concerns, 24–26
Health insurance, 23–24
Hemingway, Ernest, 48–49
Henderson Travel & Tours, 32
Herbolistarias (herb shops), 77
Herbolisteria del Rei, 227
Hertz, 44

Hibernian Books, 214
High Tech, 2
Hiking, Majorca, 292
History Museum (Sant Feliu de Guixols), 279
History of Barcelona, 307–312
Hivernacle, 239
Holiday Care, 30
Holidays, 19–20
Hollywood (Lloret de Mar), 275
Holy Grotto (Santa Cova; Montserrat), 252
Holy Week (Semana Santa), 20
HomeExchange.org, 14
HomeLink International, 14
Horseback riding, 195
    Majorca, 292
Hospitals, 77
Hotel Arts, spa at, 113
Hotel Omm, spa at, 113
Hotels, 82–118. *See also* Accommodations Index
    all-inclusive resorts and hotels, 83
    Barceloneta, Vila Olìmpica and Poble Nou, 112–115
    Barri Gòtic (Gothic Quarter), 84
    Barrio Alto and Gràcia, 111–112
    best, 5–6, 85–86
    Cadaqués, 284–286
    Ciutat Vella (Old City), 87–97
    efficiency, 83
    Eixample, 84, 97–108
    family-friendly, 101
    Girona, 270–271
    Gràcia, 84
    Lloret de Mar, 273–274
    locations, 84
    Majorca
        Deià, 303–304
        Palma de Majorca, 294–298
        Port de Pollença and Formentor, 305–306
    Montserrat, 253–254
    on the outskirts, 115–118
    with pools, 115
    price categories, 82
    Sant Feliu de Guixols, 279
    Sants, Paral.lel and Montjuïc, 108–111
    saving on, 82–83
    self-catering, 106–107
    Sitges, 263–264
    surfing for, 33
    Tarragona, 257–258
    tipping, 81

Tossa de Mar, 276–277
what's new in, 1–2
Hot lines, 77
House-swapping, 14
Housewares, 215–216
Hoverspeed, 43

IAMAT (International Association for Medical Assistance to Travelers), 25
Iberia Airlines, 37, 46
ICan, 30
Icária Yelmo Cineplex, 233–234
Ici Et Là, 216
Iguapop, 221
Illes Formigues, 280
Information sources, 10, 62–63
    Cadaqués, 284
    Figueres, 281–282
    Girona, 267
    Lloret de Mar, 273
    Majorca, 305
    Montserrat, 252
    Palafrugell, 280
    Sant Feliu de Guíxols, 279
    Sitges, 260
    Tarragona, 254
    Tossa de Mar, 276
Inside Flyer, 41
Insight Vacations, 47–48
Institut del Teatre, 234
Insurance, 23–24
InsureMyTrip.com, 23
International Association for Medical Assistance to Travelers (IAMAT), 25
International Gay and Lesbian Travel Association (IGLTA), 30
International Society of Travel Medicine, 25
International Student Identity Card (ISIC), 32
International Youth Travel Card (IYTC), 32
Internet access, 34–35
InterVac.com, 14
InTouch USA, 35
IPass network, 35
Ireland
    consulate, 76
    passports, 79
Irish Winds, 243
Itaca, 226
Itineraries, suggested, 51–61
    Barcelona in 1 day, 51, 54–55
    Barcelona in 2 days, 55–58
    Barcelona in 3 days, 58–61

i2roam, 35
IYTC (International Youth Travel Card), 32

Jamboree, 237
Jardí Botànic, 186
Jardí Botànic Marimurtra (Blanes), 272
Jazz clubs, 236–237
Jean-Pierre Bua, 217
Jet lag, 41
Jewelry, 222
Jewish Quarter (El Call), 167
Josep Font, 218
Journeywoman, 31
JuliaTours, 39

Kastoria, 225–226
Kemwel Holiday Auto, 44
KGB, 246
Kids
    best activities for, 8–9
    hotels, 101
    information and resources, 31
    restaurants, 145

La Baguetina Catalana, 127
La Barceloneta, 56, 70
    accommodations, 112–115
    restaurants, 151–157
La Bauma (Tossa de Mar), 275
La Boqueria, 4, 220
La Botifarreria de Santa Maria, 219
La Boutique del Hotel, 218
La Casa dels Músics, 233
La Concha, 239
La Diada de Catalunya, 22
La Fianna, 239
La Galeria de Santa Maria Novella, 225
LAIE, 214
La Luz de Luna, 241–242
La Manual Alpargatera, 227–228
La Manzana de la Discordia, 60, 177, 208
La Mercè church, 7, 164
La Mercè festival, 22, 231
Languages, 77, 313–314
L'Antic Teatre, 234
La Oveja Negra, 239
La Paloma, 241
La Pedrera (Casa Milà), 174–175, 208, 210

La Piñeda beach, 259
La Punta (Sitges), 261
L'Aquarium de Barcelona, 8, 187
La Rambla, 4, 51
L'Arca de l'Aviva, 213
La Ribera, 55, 69–70
    accommodations, 87–97
    restaurants, 131–135
    sights and attractions, 166–171
    walking tour, 200–203
La Roca Village, 225
L'Arrabassade (near Tarragona), 259
La Sagrada Família, 5, 55, 175–177
L'Ascensor, 239
Las Golondrinas (Swallow Boats), 8, 195
La Terrazza, 244
L'Auditori, 233
Laundromats, 77
Lavamax, 77
Lavinia, 221
Layout of main squares, streets & arteries, 63, 66
Leather goods, 7, 222–223
Le Boudoir, 224
Le Cool magazine, 231
L'Eixample, 70–71
    accommodations, 84, 97–108
    bars and clubs, 244–245
    restaurants, 139–147
    sights and attractions, 174–179
    walking tour, 207–210
Le Kashba, 243–244
Les Cases d'Alcanar, 259
L'Hospital de la Santa Creu i San Pau, 174
Lichtenstein, Roy, 7
L'Illa Diagonal, 228
Lingerie, 224
Liquor laws, 78
Llafranch, 280
Llarga (near Tarragona), 259–260
Llena, Antoni, 7
Llibreria Quera, 224
Lloret de Mar, 272–275
Llotja (Palma de Majorca), 294
Loewe, 222
    Palma de Majorca, 292
Loft Avignon, 218–219
Lost and found, 77–78
Los Tarantos, 236
Lost-luggage insurance, 24

Lotusse, 228
L'ou com balla, 161
Lufthansa, 38
Luggage Express, 37
Lunch, 318–319
Lupo, 223
Luz de Gas, 237

MACBA (Museu d'Art Contemporani de Barcelona), 5, 9, 172, 206
Magaluf (Majorca), 290
Magic, 242
Magic Fountain (Font Màgica), 185
Mail, 78
Majorca, 287–306. See also Palma de Majorca
    transportation, 288
    traveling to, 287–288
Malls and shopping centers, 228
Mango, 219
Mantantial de Salud, 222
Manzana de la Discordia, 60, 177, 208
Maoz, 127
Maps, 44–45, 224
Maremagnum, 243
Margarita Blue, 239–240
Mar Gran (Tossa de Mar), 275
Marina Port Vell, 56, 58
Marineland (Palma de Majorca), 294
Maritime Museum, 8
Markets, 200, 204, 206, 223
    Palafrugell, 280
MasterCard, traveler's checks, 19
May Day, 21
MEDEX Assistance, 23
Medical insurance, 23–24
Mediterráneo (Sitges), 266
Medusa, 249
Méliès Cinemes, 234
Mercat de Boqueria, 204, 206
Mercat del Born, 168
Mercat de Los Flors, 234–235
Mercat de Santa Caterina, 2, 200
Mercury Fountain, 182
Metro (gay disco), 249
Metro (subway), 72, 74
Mies van der Rohe, Pavelló, 185
Mirablau, 232, 247
Mirador de Colón (Columbus Monument), 51, 164, 203

Miró, Joan, 7, 316
    Fundació Joan Miró, 9, 182
    Parc de Joan Miró, 193
MNAC (Museu Nacional d'Art de Catalunya), 9, 184–185
MNG Outlet, 225
Mobility International USA, 29
Modernisme (Art Nouveau), 4, 178, 184
    architecture, 314–315
    walking tour, 207–210
Modernisme movement, 260
Mojito, 243
Molly's Fair City, 240
Monasteri de Santes Creuses, 253
The Mond Bar, 245
The Mond Club, 245
Monestir de Pedralbes, 61, 190–191
Montblanc, 253
Montjuïc, 4, 7, 54, 71
    accommodations near, 108–111
    restaurants, 138–139
    sights and attractions, 181–186
Montjuïc funicular, 75
Montserrat, 8–9, 250–254
Moog, 242
Moss-Rehab, 29
Mostra d' Art, 223
Movies, 233–234
Multicultural travelers, 31–32
Museu Arqueològic (Girona), 268–269
Museu Barbier-Mueller Art Precolombì, 168, 202
Museu Cau Ferrat (Sitges), 262
Museu d'Arqueologia de Catalunya, 183
Museu d'Art (Girona), 269
Museu d'Art Contemporani de Barcelona (MACBA), 5, 9, 172, 206
Museu d'Art Espanyol Contemporani, Fundació Juan March (Palma de Majorca), 294
Museu de Calçat, 192
Museu de Carrosses Fúnebres (Museum of Funeral Carriages), 192
Museu de Carruatges, 192
Museu de Ciències Naturals de la Ciutadella, 168–169
Museu de Cinema (Girona), 269–270
Museu de la Cera (Wax Museum), 8, 165

Museu de la Ciència (Cosmo-Caixa), 189
Museu de la Xocolata (Chocolate Museum), 8, 169
Museu de les Arts Decoratives/Museu de Ceràmica, 190
Museu de L'Esport Dr. Melcior Colet, 192
Museu del Perfum, 192
Museu del Vi (Vilafranca del Penedés), 265
Museu de Montserrat, 252
Museu de Zoologia, 168
Museu d'Història de Catalunya, 187–188
Museu d'Història de la Ciutat and Palau Reial Major (Conjunt Monumental de la Plaça del Rei), 161, 164, 198
Museu Diocesà (Tarragona), 256
Museu d'Textil i d'Indumentària, 169
Museu Egipci de Barcelona, 179
Museu Etnogràfic Andino-Amazónic, 192
Museu Etnológic, 192
Museu FC Barcelona, 191
Museu Frederic Marès, 9, 165, 198
Museu i Necròpolis Paleocristians (Tarragona), 256–257
Museu Maricel (Sitges), 262–263
Museu Maritim, 58, 188
Museu Militar de Montjuïc, 183
Museum of Funeral Carriages (Museu de Carrosses Fúnebres), 192
Museums, best, 9
Museu Nacional Arqueològic (Tarragona), 256
Museu Nacional d'Art de Catalunya (MNAC), 9, 184–185
Museu Picasso, 56, 169–170, 202
Museu Romàntic ("Can Llopis"; Sitges), 263
Museu Tauri, 192
Museu Têxtil i d'Indumentària, 202
Music
    classical, 49–50, 232–233
    flamenco, 235–236
    live-music clubs, 236–237
Music stores, 224

Muxart, 228
My Favorite Things, 48
MyTravelite, 37

Nadal (Christmas), 22–23
Nao Colón, 240
Neighborhoods, 67–71
New Chaps, 249
Newspapers and magazines, 78
New York, 242
New Zealand
consulate, 76
customs regulations, 15
passports, 79
Nick Havanna, 245
Nightlife, 230–249
bars and pubs, 237–249
Barrio Alto, 246–247
beach bars, 242–244
best, 232
champagne (xampanye-
rias), 247–248
gay and lesbian, 248–249
L'Eixample, 244–245
outer Barcelona, 247
gay and lesbian, 248–249
Lloret de Mar, 275
Palma de Majorca, 301–302
performing arts, 232–237
Sitges, 266
Now, Voyager, 30

Olivia Cruises & Resorts, 30
On Land, 219
Operator assistance, 80
Orbitz, 33
Origins 99.9%, 221
Otto Zutz, 246–247
Outdoor and sporting pursuits,
194–195

Package tours, 46–47
Palafrugell, 279–281
Palatine Chapel of Santa
Agata, 198
Palau de Baró de Cuadras, 208
Palau de la Generalitat,
165, 199
Palau de l'Almudaina (Palma de
Majorca), 294
Palau de la Música Catalana,
4, 166–168, 207, 233
Palau de la Virreina, 173, 206
Palau del Lloctinent (Deputy's
Palace), 198

Palau del Rei Sancho
(Majorca), 302
Palau Güell, 172–173, 203–204
Palau Moixó, 199
Palau Reial, 198
Palau Sant Jordi, 231
Palma de Majorca, 290–302
accommodations, 294–298
restaurants, 298–301
transportation, 290
traveling to, 290
P & O Ferries, 43
Pans & Company, 127
Paraguas Rambla de
Las Flores, 227
Paral.lel accommodations,
108–111
Parc d'Atraccions Tibidabo,
8, 192–193
Parc de Joan Miró, 193
Parc de la Ciutadella, 7, 55,
170, 203
Parc de la Crueta del Coll, 7, 193
Parc de la Pau (Park of Peace), 2
Parc del Castell de l'Oreneta, 8
Parc de L' Estació del Nord, 193
Parc del Laberint d'Horta,
8, 194
Parc d'en Castell de l'Oreneta, 7
Parc Güell, 7, 55, 180
Parc Zoològic, 8, 170–171
Parks and gardens, 2, 7,
193–194
Parque Ciutadella, 8
Parque Güell, 8
Passeig Arqueològic
(Tarragona), 257
Passeig de Gràcia, 60
Passeig del Born, 203
Passports, 11, 78–79
Passy (Palma de Majorca), 292
Pati de Llimona, 199
Pati de Tarongers (Courtyard of
Orange Trees), 165
Pavelló Mies van der Rohe, 185
Pedralbes Centre, 228
Pedralbes Wellness Center, 113
Peix (Gehry), 1
Performing arts, 232–237
Perfume and cosmetics, 225
Perlas Majorica (Majorcan
pearls), 293
Petit Palace, 2
Petrabax Tours, 48
Picasso, Pablo, 9, 49, 316, 318
Museu Picasso, 9, 56,
169–170, 202
reproductions, 221

Pink (Palma de Majorca), 292
Piscina Bernardo Picornell, 194
Pitin Bar, 240
Plaça de Catalunya (Plaza de
Cataluña), 51, 63
Plaça de l'Angel, 200
Plaça de la Seu, 198
Plaça del Rei, 198
Plaça de Ramón Berenguer el
Gran, 200
Plaça de Sant Felip Neri, 196
Plaça de Sant Jaume, 199
Plaça de Sant Just, 199
Plaça Nova, 196
Plaça Reial, 54
Plaça Sant Jaume, 165–166
Platamundi, 222
Playa de la Ribera (Sitges), 261
Playa Nova (Majorca), 290–291
Playa San Sebastián
(Sitges), 261
Playas del Muerto (Sitges), 262
Poble Espanyol
Barcelona, 186, 244
Palma de Majorca, 294
Poble Nou, 84
accommodations, 112–115
Poble Sec, restaurants,
138–139
Police, 63, 79
Politours, 39
Pools, hotel, 115
Porcelain, 8, 225–226
Porta Ferrada (Sant Feliu de
Guìxols), 279
Port Aventura Amusement
Park, 257
Port de Pollença, 305–306
Portixol, 290
Port Olimpic, 70
Port Vell (Old Port), 69–70
Post offices, 78
Palma de Majorca, 290
Prescription medications, 26
Punto BCN, 249

Qantas, 38
Quadrat d'Or (Golden Triangle),
174
Queviures Murrià, 207

RADAR (Royal Association for
Disability and Rehabilita-
tion), 30
Rafa Teja Atelier, 226
Ràfols, 223

Rail travel, 72
  Figueres, 281
  Girona, 267
  Lloret de Mar, 273
  Majorca, 288
  Montserrat, 251
  Sitges, 260
  Tarragona, 254
  wine country, 265
Rainfall, average, 19
Rambla de Raval, 127, 204
Rambla Nova (Tarragona), 254
Rambla Vella (Tarragona), 254
Razzmatazz, 247
Real Automóvil Club de España
  (RACE), 45
Regia, 225
Reial Club de Golf El Prat, 194
Rei de la Magia, 227
RENFE (Spanish State Railways),
  45–46
Renoir-Floridablanca, 234
Respiratory illnesses, 26
Restaurants, 119–159. See also
  Restaurant Index
  alfresco, 150
  Barceloneta and Vila
    Olímpica, 151–157
  Barrio Alto, 157–158
  best, 6, 121–123
  Cadaqués, 286
  Ciutat Vella, 123–138
    El Raval, 135–138
    La Ribera, 131–135
  Eixample, 139–147
  family-friendly, 145
  Girona, 271
  Gràcia, 147–151
  Lloret de Mar, 274–275
  Majorca, Deià, 304–305
  meals, 120–121
  out of town, 158–159
  Palafrugell, 281
  Palma de Majorca, 298–301
  Poble Sec and Montjuïc,
    138–139
  Sant Feliu de Guíxols, 279
  Sitges, 264, 266
  takeout, 127
  Tarragona, 258–260
  tipping, 80–81
  Tossa de Mar, 277–278
  vegetarian, 120, 121, 123,
    128, 137
  what's new in, 2
Restrooms, 79
Reus airport, 72
The Riding School of Majorca,
  292

RoadPost, 35
Rodgers Travel, 32
Royal Association for Disability
  and Rehabilitation (RADAR),
  30
Royal Fitness Center, 113
Ruesch International, 17–18
Ryanair, 37

Saboroso, 48
Safety, 26–28
Sagrada Família, 5, 55,
  175–177
Saint George (St. Jordi in
  Catalan), 21
Sala d'Art Artur Ramón, 213
Sala de Ball (Girona), 272
Sala del Cel (Girona), 272
Sala Hipóstila, 180
Sala Parés, 221
Salou, 259
Salvation, 249
Santa Cova (Holy Grotto;
  Montserrat), 252
Santa Maria del Mar, Església
  de, 7, 56, 202, 314
Santa Maria del Pi, 7, 166
Santa Maria de Poblet, 253
Sant Carles de la Ràpita, 259
Sant Feliu, Església de (Girona),
  268
Sant Feliu de Guíxols, 278–279
Sant Pau del Camp, 173, 204
Sant Pere walking tour,
  200–203
Sant Salvador, 259
Sants Just i Pastor, Església
  dels, 199
Sants Railway Station, 1
  accommodations near,
    108–111
SATH (Society for Accessible
  Travel & Hospitality), 29
Savinosa (near Tarragona), 259
Science Museum, 8
Sea hazards, 25–26
Seasons, 19
Segovia, Andrés, 49
Self-catering apartments,
  106–107
Semana Santa (Holy Week), 20
Sephora, 225
Servicaixa, 232
Servicios Ferroviarios de
  Majorca, 288
Shipping your luggage, 37
Shoes, 226–228
Shoko, 244

Shopping, 211–229
  antiques, 213
  areas for, 211–212
  Barri Gòtic, 227
  best buys, 212–213
  best stuff to bring home, 7–8
  books, 214
  ceramics and pottery, 7–8, 226
  chocolates and cakes, 215
  department store, 215
  fabrics, textiles and
    trimmings, 216
  fashion, 217–219
  fine food and wine, 219–221
  galleries, 221
  hats, 221
  herbs and health foods, 222
  housewares, 215–216
  jewelry, 222
  leather goods, 222–223
  linen and towels, 223
  lingerie, 224
  maps, 224
  music, 224
  outlets and seconds,
    224–225
  Palma de Majorca, 292–293
  perfume and cosmetics, 225
  porcelain, 225–226
  scarves, shawls and acces-
    sories, 226
  shoes, 226–228
  shopping centers and malls,
    228
  sporting goods, 229
  what's new in, 2
Shopping centers and malls,
  228
Sidecar, 242
Side trips in Catalonia,
  250–286
  Montserrat, 250–254
  Sitges, 260–266
  Tarragona, 254–260
Sights and attractions,
  160–194
  Barri Gòtic, 160–166
  Ciutat Vella (Old City),
    160–173
  Eixample, 174–179
  El Raval, 171–173
  Gràcia, 179–180
  harborfront, 187–188
  La Ribera, 166–171
  Montjuïc, 181–186
  outer Barcelona, 188–193
  parks and gardens, 193–194
  Sitges, 262–263
Singapore Airlines, 38

The Single Gourmet Club, 32
Singles Travel International, 32
Single travelers, 32–33
Sitges, 260–266
SkyCap, 37
Smoking, 2, 79
Society for Accessible Travel & Hospitality, 29
So_Da, 240
Solano, Susana, 317
Solar Tours, 47
Solplan, 39
Sombreria Obach, 221
Sonar, 21, 171, 235
Son Marroig (Majorca), 302
Son Vida Club de Golf (Majorca), 292
Soul of America, 32
Spanish Heritage Tours, 47
Spanish State Railways (RENFE), 45–46
Spas, 113
Special events and festivals, 20–23
Special-interest trips, 48
Sporting goods, 229
Sports Express, 37
STA Travel, 32, 40
Student travel, 32
Sun exposure, 25
Surfing, 195
Swallow boats, 195
Swimming, 194

Tablao Flamenco Cordobés, 236
Tamariu, 280
Tapa't (Girona), 272
Tàpies, Antoni, 316
Tarragona, 254–260
Tascas (taverns), 230
Taxes, 79, 212
Taxis, 72, 74
Teatre-Museu Dalì (Figueres), 283–284
Teatre Nacional de Catalunya, 235
Teatre Victoria, 235
Tel-entrada, 232
Telephones, 79–80
Temperatures, average daytime, 19
Temple d'Augustus, 198
Temple de Sagrat Cor, 193
Tennis, 194
Terrorism, 26–28
Tèxtil Cafè, 56

Textil i d'Indumentaria, 219
Thai Airways, 38
Theater, 234–235
Thomas Cook, currency exchange, 17
Thomas Cook Timetable of European Passenger Railroads, 46
Three Kings Day (Dìa de los Reyes), 20
Tibibus, 75
Tibidabo, 4, 61, 71
Tigre laundromats, 77
Time zone, 80
Tipping, 80–81
Tirititran, 236
Tito's (Palma de Majorca), 301
T-Mobile Hotspot, 34
Toll-free numbers, 80
Torredembarra, 259
Toscano Anticuo, 245
Tossa de Mar, 275–278
Tourist information, 10, 62–63
    Cadaqués, 284
    Figueres, 281–282
    Girona, 267
    Lloret de Mar, 273
    Majorca, 305
    Montserrat, 252
    Palafrugell, 280
    Sant Feliu de Guìxols, 279
    Sitges, 260
    Tarragona, 254
    Tossa de Mar, 276
Tours
    escorted, 47–48
    package, 46–47
    walking, 196–210
        Barri Gòtic, 196–200
        Eixample, 207–210
        El Raval, 203–206
        La Ribera (El Born and Sant Pere), 200–203
Tous, 222
Trafalgar Tours, 47
Trailfinders, 38
Train travel, 72
    Figueres, 281
    Girona, 267
    Lloret de Mar, 273
    Majorca, 288
    Montserrat, 251
    Sitges, 260
    Tarragona, 254
    wine country, 265
Tramvìa Blau (Blue Streetcar), 74–75
Transbordador Aeri, 186

Transportation, 1, 72–75
    from the airport, 38–39
Transportation Security Administration (TSA), 39
Travel Assistance International, 23
Travel Bar, 241
Travel blogs and travelogues, 34
Travel Buddies Singles Travel Club, 32
TravelChums, 32
Travel CUTS, 32
Traveler's checks, 18–19
Travelex Insurance Services, 23
Travel Guard International, 23
Traveling Internationally with Your Kids, 31
Traveling to Barcelona
    by bus, 45
    by car, 42–45
    by plane, 36–42
    pre-departure checklist, 11
    by train, 45–46
Travel insurance, 23–24
Travel Insured International, 23
Travelocity, 33, 44
Trip-cancellation insurance, 23
Turisme de Barcelona, 62

Un Coxte Menys, 74
United Airlines, 37
United Kingdom
    consulate, 76
        Palma de Majorca, 290
    currency exchange, 17
    customs regulations, 14
    health-related travel advice, 26
    passports, 79
    Spanish National Tourist Office, 10
    travelers with disabilities, 30
    traveling to Spain from, 37–38
United States
    consulate, 76
        Palma de Majorca, 290
    currency exchange, 17
    customs regulations, 14
    health-related travel advice, 26
    passports, 78
    tourist offices in, 10
    traveling to Spain from, 36–37
United Vacations, 46

Universal, 247
Up and Down, 247
Urbana, 213
USIT, 32

Vallbona de les Monges, 253
Vall de Boquer (Majorca), 305
Valldemossa (Majorca), 302–305
Vegetarian restaurants, 120, 121, 123, 128, 137
Verbena de Sant Juan, 21
Verdi, 234
Viajes Iberia, 39
ViajesMarsans, 39
Viajes Sidetours (Palma de Majorca), 293
Video, flying with, 42
Vilafranca del Penedés, 265
Vila Olímpica
    accommodations, 112–115
    restaurants, 151–157
Vina Viniteca, 221
Vinçón, 216
Virtual Bellhop, 37
Visa, traveler's checks, 19
Visas, 11
Visitor information, 10, 62–63
    Cadaqués, 284
    Figueres, 281–282
    Girona, 267
    Lloret de Mar, 273
    Majorca, 305
    Montserrat, 252
    Palafrugell, 280
    Sant Feliu de Guíxols, 279
    Sitges, 260
    Tarragona, 254
    Tossa de Mar, 276
Vitra, 216
Vueling, 40

Walking tours, 196–210
    Barri Gòtic, 196–200
    Eixample, 207–210
    El Raval, 203–206
    La Ribera (El Born and Sant Pere), 200–203
Water, drinking, 81, 320–321
Watersports, Majorca, 292
Wax Museum (Museu de la Cera), 165
Wayport, 34–35
Websites, 10
    traveler's toolbox, 36

Western Union, 16, 78
Wheelchair accessibility, 29–30
Wi-Fi access, 34–35
Wind 220°, 195
Windsurfing, 195
Wine country, 265
Wineries (bodegas), 265
Wines, 321–322
Women'Secret, 224
Women travelers, 31

Xampanyeria Casablanca, 248
Xampanyerias (champagne bars), 247–248
Xampú Xampany, 248
Xancó Camiseria, 227
Xocoa, 215

Zanpanzar (Girona), 272
Zara, 218

ACCOMMODATIONS

Abat Cisneros, 253–254
Abba Garden Hotel, 117
AC Diplomatic, 85, 102
Acropolis Guest House, 112
Aparthotel Silver, 118
Arabella Sheraton Golf Hotel Son Vida (Palma de Majorca), 295
Avenida Palace, 101–102
Banys Orientals, 86
Barceló Hotel Sants, 111
Barcelona Catedral Hotel, 2
Barcelona Hilton, 115–116
Barcelona Universal Hotel, 111
Bellmirall (Girona), 270
Best Western Mar Menuda (Tossa de Mar), 276
B. Hotel Barcelona, 110–111
Calderón, 102
Canaima (Tossa de Mar), 276
Catalonia Albioni, 88
Catalonia Barcelona Plaza, 109
Citadines, 101, 118
Constanza, 102
Costa Azul (Palma de Majorca), 297
Curhotel Hipócrates (Sant Feliu de Guíxols), 279
Drolma, 85
Duques de Bergara, 90

Duquesa de Cardona, 87
El Far de Sant Sebastià (near Palfrugell), 280
Eurostars Gaudí, 103
Fashion House B&B, 105
Gallery Hotel, 103
Gat Raval, 86, 94
Gat Xino, 94
Grand Hotel Reymar (Tossa de Mar), 276
Gran Hotel La Florida, 85, 116
Gran Hotel Monterrey (Lloret de Mar), 273
Gran Hotel Torre Catalunya, 110
H10 Raco Del Pi, 92
Hesperia Sarrià, 117
Hispanos Siete Suiza, 118
Hostal de la Gavina (Sant Feliu de Guíxols), 279
Hostal d'Uxelles, 6, 86, 105–106
Hostal Girona, 106
Hostal Goya, 107
Hostal Opera, 94
Hostal Orleans, 95
Hostal Putxet, 112
Hostal Residencia Oliva, 108
Hostal Roger de Flor (Lloret de Mar), 273
Hostal Roma Reial, 95
Hotel Actual, 103
Hotel Apsis Atrium Palace, 103–104
Hotel Arts, 5, 85, 112, 114
Hotel Astari (Tarragona), 258
Hotel Astoria, 108
Hotel Axel, 104
Hotel Balmes, 108
Hotel Banys Orientals, 95
Hotel Barcelona Catedral, 95–96
Hotel Barcino, 90
Hotel Bonsol (Majorca), 298
Hotel Born (Palma de Majorca), 297
Hotel Cap d'Or (Tossa de Mar), 277
Hotel Carlemany (Girona), 270
Hotel Casa Fuster, 5, 85, 97
Hotel Ciutat de Girona, 270
Hotel Claris, 85, 98
Hotel Colón, 86, 87–88, 101
Hotel Condes de Barcelona, 98
Hotel Costa d'Or (Deià, Majorca), 304
Hotel Diana (Tossa de Mar), 277

Hotel El Cid (Sitges), 264
Hotel Es Molì (Deià, Majorca), 303
Hotel España, 5, 86, 96
Hotel Excelsior (Lloret de Mar), 274
Hotel Fira Palace, 101, 110
Hotel Formentor (Majorca), 305–306
Hotel Front Marìtim, 114
Hotel Grand Marina, 86, 114
Hotel Gravina, 90
Hotel Illa d'Or (Port de Pollença), 306
Hotel Imperial Tarraco (Tarragona), 257
Hotel Inglaterra, 104
Hotel Jazz, 104
Hotel Lauria (Tarragona), 258
Hotel Majestic, 98
Hotel Meliá Barcelona Sarrià, 111–112
Hotel Meliá de Mar (Majorca), 298
Hotel Miramar, 110
Hotel Neptuno (Tossa de Mar), 277
Hotel Neri, 90–91
Hotel NH Calderón, 88
Hotel Noucentista (Sitges), 264
Hotel Nouvel, 91
Hotel Omm, 85–86, 100
Hotel Onix, 105
Hotel Peninsular, 6, 86, 96
Hotel Peninsular (Girona), 270–271
Hotel Playa Sol (Cadaqués), 284–285
Hotel Portixol (Palma de Majorca), 296
Hotel Punta Negra (Majorca), 298
Hotel Regencia Colón, 91
Hotel Ritz, 5, 85, 100
Hotel Romàntic de Sitges, 263
Hotel Royal, 91
Hotel San Agustì, 92
Hotel Santa Marta (Lloret de Mar), 273
Hotel Saratoga (Palma de Majorca), 297
Hotel Tonet (Tossa de Mar), 277
Hotel Tres (Palma de Majorca), 296
Hotel Ultonia (Girona), 270
Hotel Vila del Mar (Lloret de Mar), 274

HUSA Oriente, 92
Jardì, 96
La Casa de les Lletres, 106
La Ciudadela Hotel, 96–97
La Residencia (Deià, Majorca), 303–304
Le Meridien Barcelona, 87
Llane Petit (Cadaqués), 285–286
Majestic, 85
Marina Folch, 6, 86, 115
Marina View B&B, 115
Mas de Torrent (near Palfrugell), 280
Meliá Gran Sitges, 263
Meliá Palas Atenea (Palma de Majorca), 296
Mesón Castilla, 92–93
Montecarlo, 93
NH Duc de la Victoria, 93
Palacio Ca Sa Galesa (Palma de Majorca), 295
Palau Sa Font (Palma de Majorca), 296–297
Parador de Alguablava, 281
Park Hotel, 86, 93
Petit Palace Opera Garden Ramblas, 93–94
Prestige, 85, 100–101
Pulitzer, 101
Relais d'Orsa, 116–117
Rey Juan Carlos I, 116
Rivoli Ramblas, 88
Rocamar (Cadaqués), 286
Sagrada Familìa B&B, 108
San Lorenzo (Palma de Majorca), 297
7 Balconies, 97
Silken Diagonal, 105
Silken Gran Hotel Havana, 101
Terramar (Sitges), 263–264
Tryp Barcelona Aeropuerto, 117–118
Vincci Marìtimo Hotel, 114

RESTAURANTS

Abac, 131
Agua, 154
Agut, 124
Agut d'Avignon, 123–124
Alkimia, 140
Anfiteatro, 150, 151
Anima, 135–136
Arola, 154–155
Arroseria Sa Cranca (Palma de Majorca), 300

The Bagel Shop, 130
Bahìa (Tossa de Mar), 277
Bar Celta, 138
Bar Daguiri, 156
Bar del Pi, 129
Bar Turò, 146
Beltxenea, 139
Bestial, 155
Bodega la Plata, 129
Botafumeiro, 147
Bronsoms (Girona), 271
Ca'an Carlos (Palma de Majorca), 300
Café Baume, 207
Café de L'Academia, 122–124, 150
Cafe de la Opera, 129–130
Café de l'Opera, 54
Ca l'Estevet, 136–137
Cal Pep, 123, 132, 138
Cal Ros (Girona), 271
Can Costa, 56, 151–152
Can Culleretes, 54, 124, 126
Can L'Isidre, 135
Can Majó, 6, 122, 155
Ca'n Quet (Majorca), 304
Can Solé, 152
Cantina Machito, 151
Can Travi Nou, 150
Casa Alfonso, 60, 146
Casa Buxó (Sant Feliu de Guixols), 279
Casa Calvet, 61, 142
Casa Leopoldo, 135
Casa Tejada, 146–147
CDLC (Carpe Diem), 122, 155
Cerveceria Catalana, 138
Cinc Sentits, 122, 142
Ciudad Condal, 138
Comerç 24, 6, 121, 132
Drolma, 139–140
Dulcinea, 145
El Bulli (near Figueres), 285
El Caballito Blanco, 146
El Cellar de Can Roca (Girona), 271
El Fresco (Sitges), 264
El Glop, 149
El Mató de Pedralbes, 158
El Olivo (Majorca), 304–305
El Racó de Can Fabes (Sant Celoni), 158–159
El Robust, 151
El Salón, 126
Els Pescadors, 6, 152–153
Els Quatre Gats, 4–5, 126
Els Tres Tombs, 137

El Trull (Lloret de Mar), 274
El Vaso de Oro, 156–157
El Velero (Sitges), 264
Epicurì (Tarragona), 258
Espai Sucre, 123, 132–133, 138
Es Trull (Cadaqués), 286
Flash-Flash Tortilleria, 149
Folquer, 149
Foodball, 123, 130
Fragata (Sitges), 264, 266
Gaig, 142
Garduña, 126
Gente de Pasta, 133
Gorrìa, 142–143
Hisop, 122, 143
Il Giardinetto, 144
Iposa, 128
Jaume de Provença, 140
Jean Luc Figueras, 147–148
Juicy Jones, 128
Kasparo, 137
Koldo Royo (Palma de
   Majorca), 299
La Balsa, 157–158
La Bella Napoli, 138–139
La Bodegueta, 139, 147
La Bombeta, 157
La Bóveda (Palma de Majorca),
   300
La Casona (Palafrugell), 281
La Cuina de Can Simon (Tossa
   de Mar), 278
La Cuineta, 126–127
La Dama, 140
La Dentellière, 128
La Font del Gat, 150

La Galiota (Cadaqués), 286
La Gavina, 151
La Miranda del Museu, 150
La Paradeta, 122, 133–134, 145
La Rosca, 128
Las Campañas (Casa Marcos),
   130
La Vinya del Senyor, 122, 157
Les Coques (Tarragona), 258
Les Petxines (Lloret de Mar),
   274
Les Voltes (Tarragona),
   259–260
L'Olive, 144–145
L'Orangerie, 150
Los Caracoles, 127
Lupino, 136
Mama Cafe, 136
Mare Nostrum (Sitges), 266
Merbeyé, 61
Mesón David, 122, 137, 145
Mesón del Café, 199
Montjuïc Castle Café, 54
Moo, 143
Mosquito, 138
Murivecchi, 134, 145
Neichel, 144
Organic, 123, 137
Pla, 123, 127
Pla de la Garsa, 134
Poble Espanyol, 145
Porto Pì (Palma de Majorca),
   299
Puda Can Manel, 156
Quimet & Quimet, 139
Quo Vadis, 135

Ramonet, 156
Reno, 144
Re-Pla, 133
Restaurant Clivia
   (Majorca), 306
Restaurante Santa Marta
   (Lloret de Mar), 274–275
Restaurant Hoffmann, 131–132
Roig Robì, 148–149
Romesco, 129
Rosalert, 145
Sa Caseta (Palma de Majorca),
   300–301
Salsitas, 129
Sandwich & Friends, 134
Santa María, 138
Sant Pau (Sant. Pol de Mar),
   159
Schilling, 130
Senyor Parellada, 133
7 Portes, 6, 123, 153–154
Shojiro, 149
Talaia Mar, 156
Taller de Tapas, 122, 134–135,
   138
Tèxtil Cafè, 150, 202
Torre d'Alta Mar, 123, 154
Tragaluz, 122, 146
Tristán (Palma de Majorca),
   299–300
Umita, 136
Venus Delicatessen, 130–131
Via Veneto, 6, 122, 158
Vinissim, 123, 131
Xocoa, 123

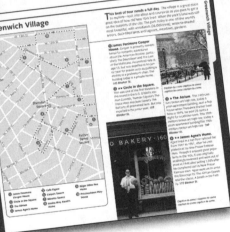

FROMMER'S® COMPLETE TRAVEL GUIDES

Alaska
Amalfi Coast
American Southwest
Amsterdam
Argentina & Chile
Arizona
Atlanta
Australia
Austria
Bahamas
Barcelona
Beijing
Belgium, Holland & Luxembourg
Belize
Bermuda
Boston
Brazil
British Columbia & the Canadian
    Rockies
Brussels & Bruges
Budapest & the Best of Hungary
Buenos Aires
Calgary
California
Canada
Cancún, Cozumel & the Yucatán
Cape Cod, Nantucket & Martha's
    Vineyard
Caribbean
Caribbean Ports of Call
Carolinas & Georgia
Chicago
China
Colorado
Costa Rica
Croatia
Cuba
Denmark
Denver, Boulder & Colorado Springs
Edinburgh & Glasgow
England
Europe
Europe by Rail
Florence, Tuscany & Umbria

Florida
France
Germany
Greece
Greek Islands
Hawaii
Hong Kong
Honolulu, Waikiki & Oahu
India
Ireland
Israel
Italy
Jamaica
Japan
Kauai
Las Vegas
London
Los Angeles
Los Cabos & Baja
Madrid
Maine Coast
Maryland & Delaware
Maui
Mexico
Montana & Wyoming
Montréal & Québec City
Moscow & St. Petersburg
Munich & the Bavarian Alps
Nashville & Memphis
New England
Newfoundland & Labrador
New Mexico
New Orleans
New York City
New York State
New Zealand
Northern Italy
Norway
Nova Scotia, New Brunswick &
    Prince Edward Island
Oregon
Paris
Peru
Philadelphia & the Amish Country

Portugal
Prague & the Best of the Czech
    Republic
Provence & the Riviera
Puerto Rico
Rome
San Antonio & Austin
San Diego
San Francisco
Santa Fe, Taos & Albuquerque
Scandinavia
Scotland
Seattle
Seville, Granada & the Best of
    Andalusia
Shanghai
Sicily
Singapore & Malaysia
South Africa
South America
South Florida
South Pacific
Southeast Asia
Spain
Sweden
Switzerland
Tahiti & French Polynesia
Texas
Thailand
Tokyo
Toronto
Turkey
USA
Utah
Vancouver & Victoria
Vermont, New Hampshire & Maine
Vienna & the Danube Valley
Vietnam
Virgin Islands
Virginia
Walt Disney World® & Orlando
Washington, D.C.
Washington State

FROMMER'S® DAY BY DAY GUIDES

Amsterdam
Chicago
Florence & Tuscany

London
New York City
Paris

Rome
San Francisco
Venice

PAULINE FROMMER'S GUIDES! SEE MORE. SPEND LESS.

Hawaii
Italy
New York City

FROMMER'S® PORTABLE GUIDES

Acapulco, Ixtapa & Zihuatanejo
Amsterdam
Aruba
Australia's Great Barrier Reef
Bahamas
Big Island of Hawaii
Boston
California Wine Country
Cancún
Cayman Islands
Charleston
Chicago
Dominican Republic

Dublin
Florence
Las Vegas
Las Vegas for Non-Gamblers
London
Maui
Nantucket & Martha's Vineyard
New Orleans
New York City
Paris
Portland
Puerto Rico
Puerto Vallarta, Manzanillo &
    Guadalajara

Rio de Janeiro
San Diego
San Francisco
Savannah
St. Martin, Sint Maarten, Anguila &
    St. Bart's
Turks & Caicos
Vancouver
Venice
Virgin Islands
Washington, D.C.
Whistler

FROMMER'S® CRUISE GUIDES
Alaska Cruises & Ports of Call
Cruises & Ports of Call
European Cruises & Ports of Call

FROMMER'S® NATIONAL PARK GUIDES
Algonquin Provincial Park
Banff & Jasper
Grand Canyon

National Parks of the American West
Rocky Mountain
Yellowstone & Grand Teton

Yosemite and Sequoia & Kings
Canyon
Zion & Bryce Canyon

FROMMER'S® MEMORABLE WALKS
London
New York

Paris
Rome

San Francisco

FROMMER'S® WITH KIDS GUIDES
Chicago
Hawaii
Las Vegas
London

National Parks
New York City
San Francisco

Toronto
Walt Disney World® & Orlando
Washington, D.C.

SUZY GERSHMAN'S BORN TO SHOP GUIDES
France
Hong Kong, Shanghai & Beijing
Italy

London
New York

Paris
San Francisco

FROMMER'S® IRREVERENT GUIDES
Amsterdam
Boston
Chicago
Las Vegas

London
Los Angeles
Manhattan
Paris

Rome
San Francisco
Walt Disney World®
Washington, D.C.

FROMMER'S® BEST-LOVED DRIVING TOURS
Austria
Britain
California
France

Germany
Ireland
Italy
New England

Northern Italy
Scotland
Spain
Tuscany & Umbria

THE UNOFFICIAL GUIDES®
Adventure Travel in Alaska
Beyond Disney
California with Kids
Central Italy
Chicago
Cruises
Disneyland®
England
Florida
Florida with Kids

Hawaii
Ireland
Las Vegas
London
Maui
Mexico's Best Beach Resorts
Mini Mickey
New Orleans
New York City

Paris
San Francisco
South Florida including Miami &
the Keys
Walt Disney World®
Walt Disney World® for
Grown-ups
Walt Disney World® with Kids
Washington, D.C.

SPECIAL-INTEREST TITLES
Athens Past & Present
Best Places to Raise Your Family
Cities Ranked & Rated
500 Places to Take Your Kids Before They Grow Up
Frommer's Best Day Trips from London
Frommer's Best RV & Tent Campgrounds
in the U.S.A.

Frommer's Exploring America by RV
Frommer's NYC Free & Dirt Cheap
Frommer's Road Atlas Europe
Frommer's Road Atlas Ireland
Great Escapes From NYC Without Wheels
Retirement Places Rated

FROMMER'S® PHRASEFINDER DICTIONARY GUIDES
French
Italian
Spanish

THE NEW TRAVELOCITY GUARANTEE

EVERYTHING YOU BOOK WILL BE RIGHT, OR WE'LL WORK WITH OUR TRAVEL PARTNERS TO MAKE IT RIGHT, RIGHT AWAY.

To drive home the point, we're going to use the word "right" in every single sentence.

Let's get right to it. Right to the meat! Only Travelocity guarantees everything about your booking will be right, or we'll work with our travel partners to make it right, right away. Right on!

Here's a picture taken smack dab right in the middle of Antigua, where the guarantee also covers you.

The guarantee covers all but one of the items pictured to the right.

For example, what if the ocean view you booked actually looks out at a downright ugly parking lot? You'd be right to call – we're there for you. And no one in their right mind would be pleased to learn the rental car place has closed and left them stranded. Call Travelocity and we'll help get you back on the right track.

Now, you may be thinking, "Yeah, right, I'm so sure." That's OK; you have the right to remain skeptical. That is until we mention help is always right around the corner. Call us right off the bat, knowing that our customer service reps are there for you 24/7. Righting wrongs. Left and right.

Now if you're guessing there are some things we can't control, like the weather, well you're right. But we can help you with most things   to get all the details in righting,* visit **travelocity.com/guarantee**.

*Sorry, spelling things right is one of the few things not covered under the guarantee.

I'd give my right arm for a guarantee like this, although I'm glad I don't have to.

travelocity
You'll never roam alone.

IF YOU BOOK IT, IT SHOULD BE THERE.

Only Travelocity guarantees it will be, or we'll work with our travel partners to make it right, right away. So if you're missing a balcony or anything else you booked, just call us 24/7. **1-888-TRAVELOCITY.**

travelocity
You'll never roam alone.